A MOTIF-INDEX OF
TRADITIONAL POLYNESIAN NARRATIVES

by

Bacil F. Kirtley

University of Hawaii Press

Honolulu 1971

Library of Congress Catalog Card Number 77-147157

ISBN 0-87022-416-6

Copyright © 1971 by University of Hawaii Press

INTRODUCTION

The present work analyzes and classifies traditional
Polynesian myths, tales, and legends according to a
system developed by Professor Stith Thompson in his
Motif-Index of Folk-Literature (1955-58). In matters of
form and style, consequently, Professor Thompson's work
has served, with a few modifications explained below,
as the pattern for this work. Since Professor Thompson
describes thoroughly the classification rationale of
a motif-index in his introduction, and since a general
synopsis of the overall scheme precedes the main body
of the present text, the plan of this study need not be
discussed.[1] Rather, the concept of a "motif," the unit
employed as a basis for the cataloguing should be
explained.

> A motif is the smallest element in a tale
> having the power to persist in tradition. In order
> to have this power it must have something unusual
> and striking about it. Most motifs fall into
> three classes. First are the actors in a tale--
> gods, or unusual animals, or marvelous creatures
> like witches, ogres, or fairies, or even
> conventionalized human characters like the
> favorite youngest child or the cruel stepmother.
> Second come certain items in the background of
> the action--magic objects, unusual customs,
> strange beliefs, and the like. In the third place
> there are single incidents--and these comprise the
> great majority of motifs. It is this last class
> that can have an independent existence and that
> may therefore serve as true tale-types. By far
> the largest number of traditional types consist
> of single motifs.[2]

The function of an index of motifs is to cite
bibliographical sources of narratives containing these
viable (often irreducible) story elements, and thus to

provide the investigator of specific story ideas with comparative information.

A motif-index, an impersonally and non-tendentiously selected catalogue of narrative details, documents systematically and objectively the emphases and the preoccupations of folk stories. Polynesian tales, if we may begin by elimination, show little interest in those themes which grew out of ethical contemplation. Narratives do not reward virtue nor punish wickedness for the mere reason that these traits fall within these particular moral provinces. Humility, modesty, and forbearance are not in themselves often shown to be ideals of conduct. That kind of incident, so prominent in Eurasian materials which celebrates wisdom or soundness and breadth of intellectual perspective is generally absent from Oceanic tales. Neither do Polynesian narratives embody general reflections about the nature of life and society. Hence, several chapters of Professor Thompson's Index, based to a large extent upon Eurasian texts, are represented feebly, two not at all, in this work. The motifs which would be categorized under these chapters seem to lie beyond the horizons of the Oceanic worldview.

If Oceanic narratives rarely treat ideas issuing from abstract ethical concepts, this neglect does not indicate that the stories deal with only immediate physical phenomena, for Polynesians created an extremely elaborate cosmogony and cosmology--at least as complex as that of ancient Greece--compiled in several island groups by priestly specialists bent, apparently, upon reducing to the metaphor of their culture much of the imminent universe. The large size of Chapter A attests to the thoroughness with which they worked. And Chapter I upon marvels and the marvelous, further indicates the rich vein of fantasy in Oceanic narratives.

iv

The equivalent in emphasis to Eurasian ethical
interests occurs in Oceania in material indexed under
Chapters G, K, Q, and S--chapters dominated by violence
to a greater degree than are narratives in many other
culture areas. The bloody tricks and retributions
documented here are not, as they first appear, lavished
entirely purposely and indiscriminately. True, ogres
are stabbed, burned, poisoned, and hanged for no reason
other than that they are ogres. Animals, or more
usually fishes, mutilate each other thoroughly, and for
no discernable cause or understandable motivation. Yet,
when a "whale-brother" of a Polynesian chief is killed,
the narrative evokes a frightful vengeance. The differ-
ence is that in the first two instances, the victims are
outside the laws which apply to the immediate ethnic or
allegiance group. The butts are disembodied marionettes
of fantasy. Pacific islanders stole shamelessly from the
early European navigators, while among themselves they
were reported to observe conscientiously possession rights.
Tribal obligations and ethics did not apply to strangers
(animals, ogres, and the like), but the murder of a
"whale-brother" demanded the formal vengeance urged by
tribal custom.

When magic (Chapter D), which permeates Oceanic
folklore, occurs, the narrative seldom emphasizes the
fact that something untoward is happening. Only infre-
quently does a narrative reveal that those who recounted
it were aware that magic forms an exceptional category
of experience. Characters simply perform feats, like
walking upon water, spontaneously and without explanation.
Only rarely do remarkable objects confer miraculous powers;
rather, the powers seem to reside in the very role of
the fictive characters.

Much of the subject matter of Oceanic narrative is

conditioned by the omnipresence of the sea. A vast number
of new motifs, appearing in several chapters, is concerned
with events of sea voyages, hurricanes, and fishing.
Thus geography, as well as culture, has shaped the myths
and tales of the South Seas to a marked extent.

As mentioned above, the manuscript style of this
volume is patterned after the <u>Motif-Index</u> <u>of</u> <u>Folk-Literat</u>
Motifs which correspond exactly with those in Professor
Thompson's work utilize his number and caption; motifs
which present essentially the same idea except for some
inconsequential detail bear his number and caption, but
are qualified in parentheses. New, unclassified motifs
have been assigned original numbers--extrapolated as
logically as possible--and entered under the most
appropriate existing categories. These motifs are
indicated in two ways: by an asterisk when the new motif
seemed a logical progression of Thompson's entry and a
final numerical designation seemed plausible; or by a
plus (+) sign when the position of the new entry in
Thompson's scheme appeared ambiguous.

The works cited and analyzed in this index are
intended to be representational of the narrative tradition
of the whole of Polynesia (the author, becoming familiar
with the immensity of relevant materials, abandoned his
original intention of analyzing all existent collections)
Some interesting texts from intensely collected groups
like New Zealand, Samoa, or Hawaii--areas abundantly
represented already--were passed over and weaker collectic
from culturally damaged and neglected groups like the
Australs, Chatham Islands, or some of the Outliers, were
included.

The Lau Islands and Rotuma, for cultural reasons,
and the Polynesian Outliers, for linguistic reasons, have
been included in this study of Polynesian narratives.

Motifs of obvious European derivation have been given, since one of the most patently useful functions of a motif-index is to further the investigation of intrusive alien themes into a body of tradition.

The bibliography following each motif is entered in a progression that goes from east to west, and, secondarily, from south to north.

One of the chief difficulties and one of the likeliest causes for error in preparing this work has been the necessity of interpreting events in Polynesian narratives into a scheme basically designed to cope with European folklore. For instance, the divisions of supernatural creatures into separate species (demons, trolls, fairies, succubi, et cetera), each having its position in the motif-index, is irrelevant when applied to Polynesia, where frequently all categories of the supernatural (ghost, god, demon) are lumped under a term denoting "spirit." The writer has generally followed the nomenclature of each text's translator, unless the analogy to European folklore was quite clear.

The author chose to compile a motif- rather than a type-index for the reason that only a small proportion of Polynesian narratives occurs in a plurality of island groups. Not a single whole tale, apparently, is distributed over the whole extent of Polynesia. As a result, a type-classification would touch upon only a small fragment of the area's oral traditions.

NOTES

1. Though this book itself does not include an alphabetical index, Volume VI of Thompson's work indexes his first five volumes. Motif numbers in this work are correlated with Thompson's, and his citations will apply here, if the item has been excerpted from Polynesian materials.

2. Stith Thompson, The Folktale (New York: Dryden Press, 1951), pp. 415-416.

ACKNOWLEDGMENTS

I wish to express my appreciation to the University
of Hawaii Graduate School for granting me financial aid,
and to the University of Hawaii Department of English
for assigning me reduced teaching loads--favors which
forwarded my project considerably.

ABBREVIATIONS FOR PERIODICALS

BPBM	Bernice Pauahi Bishop Museum
BSEO	Bulletin de la Société des Études Océaniennes
EN	Ethnologisches Notizblatt
FL	Folk-Lore
HHS	Hawaiian Historical Society
IAE	Internationales Archiv für Ethnographie
JAF	Journal of American Folklore
JRAI	Journal of the (Royal) Anthropological Institute of Great Britain and Ireland
JMG	Journal des Muséums Godeffroy
JPRSNSW	Journal and Proceedings of the Royal Society of New South Wales
JPS	Journal of the Polynesian Society
JTVI	Journal of the Transactions of the Victoria Institute
MC	Les Missions Catholiques
MSOS	Mitteilungen des Seminars für Orientalische Sprachen zu Berlin
RTP	Révue des Traditions Populaires
TNZI	Transactions of the New Zealand Institute
ZfE	Zeitschrift für Ethnologie

OTHER ABBREVIATIONS

Arch.	Archipelago
I.	Island
Is.	Islands
n.	note
nn.	notes
Strs.	Straits

BIBLIOGRAPHY

ABERCROMBY, JOHN, editor
1891   "Samoan Stories," FL, 2: 455-467.

AGOSTINI, J.
1900   "Folklore de Tahiti," RTP, 15: 157-165.

AITKEN, ROBERT THOMAS
1923   Mythology of Tubuai. Unpublished Master of
        Arts thesis, University of Hawaii, Honolulu.
1930.   Ethnology of Tubuai. BPBM Bulletin 70, Honolulu.

ANDERSEN, JOHANNES C.
1925   "Sina and Her Eel. The Origin of the Coconut
        in Samoa," JPS, 34: 142-145.

ARIKI-TARA-ARE, TE
1899   "History and Traditions of Rarotonga,"
        JPS, 8: 61-88, 171-178.
1920   Ibid., JPS, 29: 1-20, 45-69, 107-127, 165-188.
1921   Ibid., JPS, 30: 1-15, 53-70, 129-141, 201-226.

ARO, TE
1894   "The Slaying of Mokonui," JPS, 3: 166-167.

AUDRAN, HERVÉ
1917   "Moeava, ou le Grand Kaito Paumotu,"
        BSEO, 1, No. 2: 53-62.
1918   "Traditions of and Notes on the Paumotu (or
        Tuamotu Islands," JPS, 27: 26-35, 90-92,
        132-136.
1919a   Ibid., JPS, 28: 31-38, 161-167, 232-239.
1919b   "Un Glorieux Épisode de la Vie Moeava,"
        BSEO, 1, No. 5: 46-53.
1920   "Traditions of and Notes on the Paumoto (or
        Tuamotu) Islands," JPS, 29: 42-44.

BAESSLER, ARTHUR
1905   "Tahitische Legenden," ZfE, 37: 920-924.

BANAPA
1920   "An Old Tradition from Rakahanga Island,"
        JPS, 29: 88-90.

BEAGLEHOLE, ERNEST, and PEARL BEAGLEHOLE
1938   Ethnology of Pukapuka. BPBM Bulletin 150,
        Honolulu.

BEATTIE, J. HERRIES
1920   "Traditions and Legends Collected from the
        Natives of Murihiku (Southland, New Zealand),"
        JPS, 29: 98-112.

BECKWITH, MARTHA WARREN
1919   "The Hawaiian Romance of Laieikawai,"
        Thirty-Third Annual Report of the Bureau
        of American Ethnology 1911-12: 285-666.
        Washington.
1932   Kepelino's Traditions of Hawaii. BPBM
        Bulletin 95, Honolulu.
1940   Hawaiian Mythology. New Haven: Yale University

BEST, ELSON
1893   "Te Patunga O Ngarara-Huorau," JPS, 2: 211-219.
1897   "Te Rehu-O-Tanui: the Evolution of a Maori
        Atua," JPS, 6: 41-66.
1899   "Notes on Maori Mythology," JPS, 8: 93-121.
1905   "The Lore of the Whare-Kohanga," JPS, 14:
        205-216.
1906   Ibid., JPS, 15: 1-27, 147-163, 183-193.
1907   Ibid., JPS, 16: 1-13.
1924   The Maori. Polynesian Society Memoir No. 5,
        2 vols.; Wellington: Polynesian Society.
1925   Tuhoe, the Children of the Mist. Polynesian
        Society Memoir No. 6, 2 vols.; New Plymouth:
        T. Avery.
1927   "Hau and Wairaka," JPS, 36: 260-282.
1928a   "The Story of Rua and Tangaroa. An Origin
        Myth," JPS, 37: 257-259.
1928b   "The Story of Ngae and Tutunui," JPS, 37:
        261-270.
1929   "The Maui Myths as Narrated by Natives of
        Tolago Bay, North Island, New Zealand,"
        JPS, 38: 1-26.

BIRKET-SMITH, KAJ
1956   An Ethnological Sketch of Rennell Island. A
        Polynesian Outlier in Melanesia. Copenhagen:
        Munksgaard.

BRADLEY, DIANA
1956   "Notes and Observations from Rennell and
        Bellona Islands; British Solomon Islands,"
        JPS, 65: 332-341.

BROWN, GEORGE
1915   "Some Nature Myths from Samoa," FL, 26: 172-181.
1916   "Folk Tales from the Tongan Islands,: FL, 27:
        426-432.
1917   "Some Nature Myths from Samoa," FL, 28: 94-99.

BROWNE, ARTHUR
1897   "An Account of Some Early Ancestors of
        Rarotonga," JPS, 6: 1-10.

BÜLOW, W. von
1895   "Samoanische Sagen," Globus, 68: 139-141.
1898   "Eine samoanische Fluthsage," IAE, 11: 80-82.
1899   "Die samonaische Schöpfungssage," IAE, 12:
        58-66.

BURROWS, EDWIN G.
1936   Ethnology of Futuna. BPBM Bulletin 138,
        Honolulu.
1937   Ethnology of Uvea (Wallis Island). BPBM
        Bulletin 145, Honolulu.

BURROWS, WILLIAM
1923   "Some Notes and Legends of a South Sea Island.
        Fakaofo of the Tokelau or Union Group,"
        JPS, 32: 143-173.

CAILLOT, AUGUST CHARLES EUGÈNE
1914   Mythes, légendes et traditions des
        Polynésiens. Paris: E. Leroux.

CHRISTIAN, FREDERICK WILLIAM
1895   "Notes on the Marquesans," JPS, 4: 187-202.

CHURCHWARD, C. MAXWELL
1937-38 "Rotuman Legends," Oceania, 8: 104-116,
        247-260, 351-368, 482-497.
1938-39 Ibid., Oceania, 9: 109-126, 217-231, 326-339,
        462-473.

CLARK, KATE McCOSH
1896   Maori Tales and Legends. London: D. Nutt.

COLLOCOTT, E.E.V.
1919   "A Tongan Theogany," FL, 30: 234-238.
1921a   "Legends from Tonga," FL, 32: 45-58.
1921b   "Notes on Tongan Religion," JPS, 30:
        152-163, 227-240.
1922   "Tongan Astronomy and Calendar," BPBM
        Occasional Papers, Vol. 8, No. 4: 157-173.
        Honolulu.
1924   "Tongan Myths and Legends, III," FL, 35:
        275-283.
1928   Tales and Poems of Tonga. BPBM Bulletin 46,
        Honolulu.

COWAN, JAMES
1921   "The Patu-Paiarehe. Notes on Maori Folk-Tales

of the Fairy People," JPS, 30: 96-102, 142-151.

1925 Fairy Folk Tales of the Maori. Auckland: Whitcombe & Tombs.

1930 Legends of the Maori. Wellington: Harry H. Tombs, Ltd.

CUZENT, GILBERT
1923 "Histoire des Ainanu, Pipiri-Ma," BSEO, 1, No. 7: 37-40.

DANIELSSON, BENGT
1952 Raroia, Happy Island of the South Seas. Chicago: Rand McNally.

DAVID, MRS. EDGEWORTH
1899 Funafuti. London: J. Murray.

DICKEY, LYLE A.
1917 "Stories of Wailua, Kauai," HHS, Twenty-Fifth Annual Report: 14-36.

DIXON, ROLAND B.
1916 The Mythology of All Races. Ed. by Louis B. Gray. Vol. 9: Oceanic. Boston: M. Jones.

EILERS, ANNELIESE
1934 Inseln um Ponape: Kapingamarangi, Nukuor, Ngatik,Mokil, Ringelap. Hamburg: Friedrichsen de Gruyter.

ELBERT, SAMUEL H.
1948 Grammar and Comparative Study of the Language of Kapingamarangi; Texts and Word Lists. (Mimeographed.) [Washington:] National Research Council.

1949. "Uta-matua and Other Tales of Kapingamarangi," JAF, 62: 240-246.

ELBERT, SAMUEL H., and BACIL F. KIRTLEY
1966 "Seven Pileni Tales," JPS, 75: 348-372.

ELBERT, SAMUEL H. and TORBEN MONBERG
1964 MSS. Published in 1965 as Language and Culture of Rennell and Bellona Islands: Vol. 1, From the Two Canoes, Oral Traditions of Rennell and Bellona Islands. Honolulu-Copenhagen: University of Hawaii Press and Danish National Museum. (References are to story numbers, not to pages, for this entry).

EMERSON, NATHANIEL B.
1915   Pele and Hiiaka; a Myth from Hawaii.
        Honolulu: Honolulu Star Bulletin.

EMERSON, OLIVER P.
1921   "The Bad boy of Lahaina, the Goblin Killer
        of Lanai," HHS, Twenty-Ninth Annual Report:
        16-19.

EMORY, KENNETH P.
1924   The Island of Lanai, a Survey of Native Culture.
        BPBM Bulletin 12, Honolulu.
1949   "Myths and Tales from Kapingamarangi, A
        Polynesian Inhabited Island in Micronesia,"
        JAF, 62: 230-239.

ENGLERT, P. SEBASTIAN
1939   Tradiciones de la Isla de Pascua. Padre las
        Casas, Chile: Imprenta "San Francisco."

ESKRIDGE, ROBERT LEE
1931   Manga Reva. Indianapolis: Bobbs-Merrill.

FIRTH, RAYMOND
1930-31 "Totemism in Polynesia," Oceania, 1: 291-322,
        377-399.
1940   The Work of the Gods in Tikopia. 2 Vols.
        London: Percy Lund Humphries.
1961   History and Traditions of Tikopia.
        Wellington: Polynesian Society.

FISON, LORIMER
1904   Tales from Old Fiji. London: A. Moring.

FORBES, A.O.
1879   "Hawaiian Tradition of the Origin of Fire,"
        Hawaiian Annual for 1879: 59-60.
1881   "Legend of Maui Snaring the Sun," Hawaiian
        Annual for 1881: 59.
1882   "Legend of Kapeepeekauila, or the Rock of Kana,"
        Hawaiian Annual for 1882: 36-41.

FORNANDER, ABRAHAM
1916-20 Fornander Collection of Hawaiian Antiquities
        and Folk-Lore...with Translations. Revised and
        Illustrated with Notes by Thomas G. Thrum.
        BPBM, Memoirs Nos. 4, 5, 6. Honolulu.

FRASER, JOHN
1892   "The Samoan Story of Creation," JPS, I: 164-189.
1896   "Folk-Songs and Myths from Samoa," JPS, 5:
        171-183.

xv

1897   Ibid., JPS, 6: 19-37, 41-67, 107-123.
1900   Ibid., JPS, 9: 125-134.

GARDINER, J. STANLEY
1898   "The Natives of Rotuma," JRAI, 27: 457-524.

GIFFORD, EDWARD WINSLOW
1924   Tongan Myths and Tales. BPBM Bulletin 8,
           Honolulu.

GILL, WILLIAM WYATT
1876   Myths and Songs from the South Pacific.
           London: H.S. King.
1911   "Extracts from Papers of the Late Wm. Wyatt
           Gill, LL.D.," JPS, 20: 65-71.
1915   "Extracts from Dr. Wyatt Gill's Papers,"
           JPS, 24: 140-155.

GRACE, ARCHDEACON
1901   "Maori Traditions from D'Urville Island,
           New Zealand," JPS, 10: 65-71.
1907   Folk-tales of the Maori. Wellington:
           Gordon & Gotch.

GREEN, LAURA S.
1923   Hawaiian Stories and Wise Sayings. Ed. by
           Martha Warren Beckwith. Poughkeepsie,
           New York: Vassar College.
1926   Folk-tales from Hawaii. Ed. by Martha
           Warren Beckwith. Poughkeepsie, New York:
           Vassar College.
1929   The Legend of Kawelo. Poughkeepsie, New
           York: Vassar College.

GREY, SIR GEORGE EDWARD
1855   Polynesian Mythology, and Ancient Traditional
           History of the New Zealand Race. London:
           J. Murray.

GRIMBLE, SIR ARTHUR
1952   Pattern of Islands. London: Murray.

GUDGEON, W. E.
1905   "Maori Superstition," JPS, 14: 167-193.
1906   "The Tipua Kura, and Other Manifestations of
           the Spirit World," JPS, 15: 27-58.

GUPPY, H. B.
1890   "Coral Islands and Savage Myths," JTVI, 23:
           46-50.

HAMBRUCH, PAUL
1914-15 Nauru. 2 Vols. Hamburg: Friedrichsen de
           Gruyter.

1925   Faraulip. Liebeslegenden aus der Südsee.
     Hamburg: Asmus.

HAMES, INEZ
1960   Legends of Fiji and Rotuma. Auckland:
     Watterson & Roddick, Ltd.

HANDY, EDWARD S. C.
1930   Marquesan Legends. BPBM Bulletin 69,
     Honolulu.
1943   "Two Unique Petroglyphs in the Marquesas Which
     Point to Easter Island and Malaysia," in
     Studies in the Anthropology of Oceania and
     Asia. Ed. by C. S. Coon and J. M. Andrews.
     Harvard Univ., Cambridge, Mass.: Peabody
     Museum.

HAPAI, CHARLOTTE
1921   Legends of Wailuku. Honolulu.

HARE HONGI
1894   "The Contest between Fire and Water," JPS, 3:
     155-158.
1896   "Tama-Ahua," JPS, 5: 233-236.
1898   "Concerning Whare-Kura: Its Philosophies and
     Teachings," JPS, 7: 35-42.
1920   "The Gods of Maori Worship. Sons of Light,"
     JPS, 29: 24-28.

HEDLEY, CHARLES
1896   The Atoll of Funafuti, Ellice Group.
     Australian Museum, Sydney, Memoir No. 3.
     Part 1: "General Account of the Atoll of
     Funafuti," 1-72. Sydney.

HENRY, TEUIRA
1901   "Tahitian Folklore," JPS, 10: 51-52.
1928   Ancient Tahiti. BPBM Bulletin 48, Honolulu.

HENRY, TEUIRA, and M. AHNNE
1923   "Le grand lézard de Fautana," BSEO, 1, No. 7:
     35-36.

HIROA, TE RANGI   (SIR PETER H. BUCK)
1932   Ethnology of Tongareva. BPBM Bulletin 92,
     Honolulu.
1934   Mangaian Society. BPBM Bulletin 122, Honolulu.
1938   Ethnology of Mangareva. BPBM Bulletin 157,
     Honolulu.
1938a   Vikings of the Sunrise. New York: F. A. Stokes.

HOCART, A.M.
1929   Lau Islands, Fiji. BPBM Bulletin 62,
          Honolulu.

HONGI. See HARE HONGI.

HORNBOSTEL. See LAURA MAUD THOMPSON.

HUTCHIN, J. J. K.
1904   "Traditions and Some Words of the Language of
          Danger or Pukapuka Island," JPS, 13: 173-177

Ii, JOHN PAPA
1959   Fragments of Hawaiian History. Trans. by
          Mary Kawena Pukui. Ed. by Dorothy B. Barrère
          Honolulu: BPBM.

JOURDAIN, PIERRE
1934   "Légende des Trois Tortues," BSEO, 5:
          196-205.

KAMAKAU, SAMUEL M.
1961   Ruling Chiefs of Hawaii. Trans. by Mary
          Kawena Pukui. Honolulu: Kamehameha Schools.

KARAREHE, W. TE KAHUI
1898   "Te Tatau-O-Te-Po," JPS, 7: 59-63.

KAUIKA, WIREMU
1904   "Tutae-Poroporo," JPS, 13: 94-98.

KENNEDY, DONALD GILBERT
1931   "Field Notes on the Culture of Vaitupu,
          Ellice Islands," JPS, 39: Memoir No. 9,
          installment Nos. 6 & 7.

KIRTLEY, BACIL F.
1955   A Motif Index of Polynesian, Micronesian,
          and Melanesian Folktales. (Diss., 2 vols.
          Indiana Univ.). Pub. No. 14,600, University
          Microfilms, Ann Arbor, Michigan.
1963   "The Ear-Sleepers: Some Permutations of a
          Traveler's Tale," JAF, 76, No. 300: 119-130.
1967   "The Slain Eel-God and the Origin of the
          Coconut, with Satellite Themes,: in Folklore
          International: Essays in Traditional
          Literature, Belief, and Custom in Honor of
          Wayland Debs Hand. Hatboro, Pa.: Folklore
          Associates, Inc.

KNOCHE, WALTER
1920   "Ein Märchen und Zwei kleine Gesänge von der
        Osterinsel," ZfE, 44: 64-72.
1939   "Einige Beziehungen eines Märchens der
        Osterinsulaner zur Fischverehrung und zu
        Fischmenschen in Ozeanien," MAGW, 69:
        24-33.

KRÄMER, AUGUSTIN FRIEDRICH
1902-03 Die Samoa-Inseln. 2 Vols. Stuttgart:
        E. Schweitzerbart.

KUNIKE, H.
1928   "Rata's Boot. Eine Sage aus Aitutaki
        (Polynesien)," Der Erdball, 2: 29-33.

LAGARDE, G.
1933   "Le tiki lézard - Les Paepae," BSEO, 5:
        259-264.
1936   "Légende de Hinaraurea et de la Chenille de
        Papeiha," BSEO, 5: 697-700.

LARGE, J. T.
1903   "The Aitutaki Version of the Story of Iro,"
        JPS, 12: 133-144.

LAVAL, HONORÉ
1938   Mangareva. Braine-le-Comte (Belgique):
        Maisons des Pères des Sacrés-Coeurs.

LAVONDES, HENRI, and KEHUEINUI
1964   Récits Marquisiens. Papeete: Office de la
        Récherche Scientifique et Technique Outre-Mer.
1966   Récits Marquisiens. 2nd series. Papeete:
        Office de la Récherche Scientifique et
        Technique Outre-Mer.

LESSA, WILLIAM A.
1961   Tales from Ulithi Atoll. Berkeley and Los
        Angeles: Univ. of California Press.

LESSON, PIERRE ADOLPHE
1876   "Traditions des Îles Samoa," Revue
        d'Anthropologie, 5: 589-604.

LEVERD, ARMAND
1911   "The Paumotuan Version of Tafa'i, by Aipi
        of Ra'i-roa," JPS, 20: 172-184.
1912   "The Tahitian Version of Fafa'i (or Tawhaki),"
        JPS, 21: 1-12.

LISTER, J. J.
1892   "Notes on the Natives of Fakaofu (Bowditch

Island), Union Group," JRAI, 21: 43-63.

LOCKE, S.
1921   "The Visit of Pau to Hawaiki to Procure the
        Kumara," JPS, 30: 40-47.

LOEB, EDWIN M.
1926   History and Traditions of Niue. BPBM Bulletin
        32, Honolulu.

LOW, DRURY
1934   "Traditions of Aitutaki, Cook Islands," JPS,
        43: 17-24, 73-84, 171-186, 258-267.
1935   Ibid., JPS, 44: 26-31.

LUOMALA, KATHARINE
1949   Maui-of-a-Thousand-Tricks: His Oceanic and
        European Biographers. BPBM Bulletin 198,
        Honolulu.
1951   The Menehune of Polynesia and Other Mythical
        Little People of Oceania. BPBM Bulletin
        203, Honolulu.

McALLISTER, J. GILBERT
1933   Archaeology of Oahu. BPBM Bulletin 104,
        Honolulu.

MacGREGOR, GORDON
1937   Ethnology of Tokelau Islands. BPBM Bulletin
        146, Honolulu.

MALARDE, Y.
1933   "Légende des Tuamotu. L'Origine du
        Cocotier," BSEO, 5: 498-501, 671-674.

MASSAINOFF, A.
1933   "Moa et Mirou (Légende mangarévienne),"
        BSEO, 5: 55-59.

MEGEN, PIERRE VAN
1928   "Les Traditions des Habitants des Îles Cook,"
        Anthropos, 23: 1053-1054.

MÉTRAUX, ALFRED
1940   Ethnology of Easter Island. BPBM Bulletin
        160, Honolulu.

MORRIS, G. N.
1919   "Niue Folk-Lore," JPS, 28: 226-228.

NA TE WHETU
1894   "Ko Te Patunga O Te Kaiwhakaruaka," JPS, 3:
        16-19.

NELSON, O.F.
1925   "Legends of Samoa," JPS, 34: 24-42.

NEWELL, J. E.
1895   "The Legend of the Coming of Nareau from
        Samoa to Tarawa, and His Return to Samoa,"
        JPS, 4: 231-235.

O'FERRALL, W. C.
1904   "Native Stories from Santa Cruz and Reef
        Islands," JRAI, 34: 223-233.

ORSMOND, J. M.
1933a   "Le Déluge," BSEO, 5: 84-87.
1933b   "Légendes tahitiennes," BSEO, 5: 170-173.

PAKAUWERA, E. W.
1894   "The Story of Hine-Papo," JPS, 3: 98-104.

PAKOTI, JOHN
1895   "The First Inhabitants of Aitutaki; The
        History of Ru," JPS, 4: 65-70.

PARKINSON, RICHARD H. R.
1898   "Nachträge zur Ethnographie der Ontong-Java-
        Inseln," IAE, 11: 194-209.
1926   Dreissig Jahre in der Südsee. Stuttgart:
        Strecker & Schroder.

POTAE, HENARE
1928   "The Story of Tawhaki," JPS, 37: 359-366.

POWELL, T. A., and G. PRATT
1891   "Some Folksongs and Myths from Samoa.
        Introduction and Notes by John Fraser,"
        JPRSNSW, 22: 195-217.
1892   Ibid., 25: 70-85, 96-146, 241-286.
1893   Ibid., 26: 264-301.

PUKUI, MARY WIGGIN
1933   Hawaiian Folk Tales. Poughkeepsie, New York:
        Vassar College.
1943   "The Many-Harbored Sea of Pu'uloa," HHS,
        Fifty-Second Annual Report: 56-66.

PUKUI, MARY KAWENA, and CAROLINE CURTIS
n.d.   Legends of Hawaii. Honolulu: Kamehameha
        Schools Preparatory Department. (Mimeographed.)

REITER, F. X.
1907   "Traditions tonguiennes," Anthropos, 2:
        230-240, 438-448, 743-754.

1917-18   Ibid., 12-13: 1026-1046.
1919-20   Ibid., 14-15: 125-142.
1933   "Trois recits tonguiennes," Anthropos, 28:
           355-382.
1934   Ibid., 29: 497-514.

REMY, JULES
1868   Contributions of a Venerable Savage to the
           Ancient History of the Hawaiian Islands.
           Trans. by William T. Brigham. Boston:
           Privately printed.

RICE, WILLIAM HYDE
1923   Hawaiian Legends. BPBM Bulletin 3, Honolulu.

RIESENFELD, ALPHONSE
1950   The Megalithic Culture of Melanesia. Leiden:
           Brill. (Only Polynesian references excerpted

ROBERTS, R. G.
1957   "Four Folk Tales from the Ellice Islands,"
           JPS, 66: 365-373.
1958   "Te Atu Tuvalu: A Short History of the Ellice
           Islands," JPS, 67: 394-423.

ROCHEREAU, R. P.
1915   "Légendes Canaques. Une Page de Mythologie
           Fidjienne," MC, 47: 407-08, 419-20.

ROPITEAU, A.
1933   "Notes sur l'ile Maupiti," BSEO, 5: 113-130.

ROSE, RONALD
1959   South Seas Magic. London: Robert Hale.

RUSSELL, W. E.
1942   "Rotuma, Its History, Conditions, and Customs,"
           JPS,51: 229-255.

ST. JOHNSTON, THOMAS R.
1918   The Lau Islands (Fiji) and Their Fairy-Tales
           and Folk-lore. London: The Times Book Co.,
           Ltd.

SARFERT, ERNST, and HANS DAMM   (Cited as Sarfert.)
1931   Luangiua und Nukumanu, mit Anhäng uber Sikayan
           Nuguria, Tauu und Carteret-Inseln, 2 Halbband
           Soziale Verhaltnisse und Geisteskultur.
           Hamburg: Friedrichsen de Gruyter.

SAVAGE, STEPHEN
1910   "The Rarotongan Version of the Story of Rata,"
           JPS, 19: 142-168.

SEURAT, LÉON GASTON
1905   "Légendes de Paumotou," Révue de Traditions
          Populaires, 20: 433-440, 481-488.
1906   Ibid., 21: 125-131.

SHAND, ALEXANDER
1894   "The Moriori People of the Chatham Islands:
          Their Traditions and History," JPS, 3:
          76-92, 121-133.
1896   Ibid., 5: 195-211.
1898   Ibid., 7: 73-88.

SIERICH, O.
1900   "Samoanische Märchen," IAE, 13: 223-237.
1901   Ibid., 14: 15-23.
1902   Ibid., 15: 167-200.

SKINNER, W. H.
1897   "The Legend of Para-Hia," JPS, 6: 156-157.

SKINNER, H. D.
1923   The Morioris of Chatham Islands. Honolulu:
          Bishop Museum.

SKINNER, H. D., and WILLIAM BAUCKE
1928   The Morioris. Honolulu: Bishop Museum.

SMITH, CHARLOTTE HAPAI.
1966   Hilo Legends. Hilo, Hawaii: The Petroglyph
          Press.

SMITH, S. PERCY
1890   Tongarewa, or Penrhyn Island and its people.
          TNZI, 22: 85-103.
1892   "Uvea; Or, Wallis Island and Its People,"
          JPS, 1: 107-117.
1897   "The Peopling of the North," JPS, 6: supple-
          ment, 1-108.
1902   "Niue Island and Its People," JPS, 11:
          80-106, 163-178, 195-218.
1903   Ibid., JPS, 12: 1-21, 85-119.
1905   "The Story of Ngarara-Huarau," JPS, 14:
          202-204.
1909   "The Story of Kataore," JPS, 18: 210-216.
1910   "Aryan and Polynesian Points of Contact," JPS,
          19: 84-89.
1911a   Ibid., JPS, 20: 37-38, 170-172.
1911b   "The Story of Te Rapuwai and Kahui-Tipua, and
          Its Equivalent in the Union Group, Central
          Pacific," JPS, 20: 12-14.
1911c   "Ngati-Whatua Traditions," JPS, 20: 78-100.
1920   "Notes on the Ellice and Tokelau Groups," JPS,
          29: 144-148.

xxiii

1921   "The Polynesians in Indonesia," JPS, 30:
            19-27.

SMITH, WALTER J.
1955   Legends of Wailua. Lihue, Kauai, Hawaii:
            Garden Island Publishing Co.

STAIR, JOHN B.
1895a   "Samoa: Whence Peopled?" JPS, 4: 47-58.
1895b   "Flotsam and Jetsam from the Great Ocean:
            or, Summary of Early Samoan Voyages and
            Settlements," JPS, 4: 99-131.
1896   "Jottings on the Mythology and Spirit-Lore of
            Old Samoa," JPS, 5: 33-57.

STEINEN, KARL VON DEN
1933-34   "Marquesanische Mythen," ZfE, 65: 1-44,
            326-373.
1934-35   Ibid., ZfE, 66: 191-240.

STEVENSON, ROBERT LOUIS
1912   South Seas and Other Papers. Vol. 9.
            Vailima Edition. New York.

STIMSON, FRANK J.
n.d.   Ms. Collection of Tuamotuan Myths. Salem,
            Mass.: Peabody Museum archives.
1934   The Legends of Maui and Tahaki. BPBM
            Bulletin 127, Honolulu.
1937   Tuamotuan Legends (Islands of Anaa). BPBM
            Bulletin 148, Honolulu.

STUEBEL, O.
1896   "Samoanische Texte," Veröffentlichungen des
            königlichen Museum fur Volklerkunde, 4:
            x, 59-246.

TAHIAOTEAA
1933   "Légende Marquisienne," BSEO, 5: 490-498.

TAMA-RAU, and TUTAKA NGAHAU
1899   "The Story of Hape, the Wanderer," JPS, 8:
            51-57.

TARAKAWA, T., and PAORA RAPIHA
1899   "Mahu and Taewa-A-Rangi," JPS, 8: 127-134.

TEFAAFANA, TETUA A.
1917   "La Légende des 'Pierres Marchantes'
            (Ofaitere) de Papetoai, Racontée par un
            Ancien du Pays," BSEO, 1: 31.

TE RANGI HIROA (Sir Peter H. Buck). See HIROA, TE RANGI.

THOMPSON, STITH
1955-58   Motif-Index of Folk-Literature. Rev. and enl.
          ed.; 6 vols.; Bloomington: Indiana Univ.

THOMPSON, BASIL
1920   Savage Island. London: J. Murray.

THRUM, THOMAS G.
1895   "Stories of the Menehunes," Hawaiian Annual:
          112-117.
1906   "Kaala and Kaaialii, a Legend of Lanai,"
          Hawaiian Annual for 1906: 122-140.
1907   Hawaiian Folk Tales. Chicago: McClurg.
1920   "Story of the Race of People Called the
          Menehunes, of Kauai (a Hawaiian Tradition),"
          JPS, 29: 70-75.
1921   "The Hinas of Hawaiian Folklore," Hawaiian
          Annual for 1921: 102-114.
1923   More Hawaiian Folk Tales. Chicago: McClurg.

TRAVERS, T. L.
1887   "Notes of the Traditions and Manners and
          Customs of the Mori-oris," TNZI, 9: 15-27.

TREGEAR, EDWARD
1900   "The Creation Song of Hawaii," JPS, 9: 38-46.
1901   "The Fountain of Fish," JPS, 10: 185-190.
1903   "The Making and Un-making of Man," JPS, 12:
          182-183.

TU-WHAWHAKIA, KEREHOMA
1896   "The Story of Whaki-Tapui, and Tu-Taia-Roa,"
          JPS, 5: 155-170.

TURNER, GEORGE
1861   Nineteen Years in Polynesia. London: J. Snow.

WESTERVELT, WILLIAM DRAKE
1915   Legends of Gods and Ghosts. Boston: G. H. Ellis.
1915a   Legends of Old Honolulu. Boston: G. H. Ellis.
1943   Legend of the Ghosts of the Hilo Hills.
          Honolulu: privately printed.

WHETU, KARIPA TE
1897   "Kame-Tara and His Ogre Wife," JPS, 6: 97-106.

WHITE, JOHN
1887-90   The Ancient History of the Maori; His
          Mythology and Traditions. 6 vols.; Wellington:
          G. Disbury.

WILLIAMS, JOHN
  1895   "The Legend of Honoura," JPS, 4: 256-294.

WOHLERS, J. F. H.
  1875   "The Mythology and Traditions of the Maori
           of New Zealand," TNZI, 7: 3-53.
  1876   Ibid., 8: 108-123.

YOUNG, J. L.
  1898   "The Origin of the Name Tahiti: As Related
           by Marerenui, A Native of Faaiti Island,
           Paumotu Group," JPS, 7: 109-110.

GENERAL SYNOPSIS OF THE INDEX

A. MYTHOLOGICAL MOTIFS

A0   --A99.   Creator

A100 --A499.   Gods
    A100 --A199.   The gods in general
    A200 --A299.   Gods of the upper world
    A300 --A399.   Gods of the underworld
    A400 --A499.   Gods of the earth
A500 --A599.   Demigods and culture heroes

A600 --A899.   Cosmogony and cosmology
    A600 --A699.   The universe
    A700 --A799.   The heavens
    A800 --A899.   The earth
A900 --A999.   Topographical features of the earth
A1000--A1099.   World calamities
A1100--A1199.   Establishment of natural order

A1200--A1699.   Creation and ordering of human life
    A1200--A1299.   Creation of man
    A1300--A1399.   Ordering of human life
    A1400--A1499.   Acquisition of culture
    A1500--A1599.   Origin of customs
    A1600--A1699.   Distribution and differentiation of
                     peoples

A1700--A2199.   Creation of animal life
    A1700--A1799.   Creation of animal life--general
    A1800--A1899.   Creation of mammals
    A1900--A1999.   Creation of birds
    A2000--A2099.   Creation of insects
    A2100--A2199.   Creation of fish and other animals

A2200--A2599.   Animal characteristics
    A2200--A2299.   Various causes of animal characteristics
    A2300--A2399.   Causes of animal characteristics: body
    A2400--A2499.   Causes of animal characteristics:
                     appearance and habits
    A2500--A2599.   Animal characteristics--miscellaneous
A2600--A2699.   Origin of trees and plants
A2700--A2799.   Origin of plant characteristics
A2800--A2899.   Miscellaneous explanations

xxvii

B. ANIMALS

B0   --B99.   Mythical animals
B100 --B199.   Magic animals
B200 --B299.   Animals with human traits

B300 --B599.   Friendly animals
    B300 --B349.   Helpful animals--general
    B350 --B399.   Grateful animals
    B400 --B499.   Kinds of helpful animals
    B500 --B599.   Services of helpful animals
B600 --B699.   Marriage of person to animal
B700 --B799.   Fanciful traits of animals
B800 --B899.   Miscellaneous animal motifs

C. TABU

C0   --C99.   Tabu connected with supernatural beings
C100--C199.   Sex tabu
C200--C299.   Eating and drinking tabu
C300--C399.   Looking tabu
C400--C499.   Speaking tabu
C500--C549.   Tabu: touching
C550--C599.   Class tabu
C600--C699.   Unique prohibitions and compulsions
C700--C899.   Miscellaneous tabus
C900--C999.   Punishment for breaking tabu

D. MAGIC

D0   --D699.   Transformation
    D10   --D99.   Transformation: man to different man
    D100 --D199.   Transformation: man to animal
    D200 --D299.   Transformation: man to object
    D300 --D399.   Transformation: animal to person
    D400 --D499.   Other forms of transformation
    D500 --D599.   Means of transformation
    D600 --D699.   Miscellaneous transformation incidents
D700 --D799.   Disenchantment

D800 --D1699.   Magic objects
    D800 --D899.   Ownership of magic objects
    D900 --D1299.   Kinds of magic objects
    D1300--D1599.   Function of magic objects
    D1600--D1699.   Characteristics of magic objects

D1700--D2199.   Magic powers and manifestations
    D1710--D1799.   Possession and employment of magic
                     powers
    D1800--D2199.   Manifestations of magic power

E. THE DEAD

E0   --E199. Resuscitation

E200--E599. Ghosts and other revenants
    E200--E299. Malevolent return from the dead
    E300--E399. Friendly return from the dead
    E400--E499. Ghosts and revenants--miscellaneous
E500--E699. Reincarnation
E700--E799. The Soul

F. MARVELS

F0   --F199. Otherworld journeys

F200--F699. Marvelous creatures
    F200--F399. Fairies and elves
    F400--F499. Spirits and demons
    F500--F599. Remarkable persons
    F600--F699. Persons with extraordinary powers
F700--F899. Extraordinary places and things
F900--F1099. Extraordinary occurrences

G. OGRES

G10 --G399. Kinds of ogres
    G10 --G99. Cannibals and cannibalism
    G100--G199. Giant ogres
    G200--G299. Witches
    G300--G399. Other ogres
G400--G499. Falling into ogre's power
G500--G599. Ogre defeated
G600--G699. Other ogre motifs

H. TESTS

H0   --H199. Identity tests: recognition
H200 --H299. Tests of truth
H300 --H499. Marriage tests

H500 --H899. Tests of cleverness
    H500 --H529. Test of cleverness or ability
    H530 --H899. Riddles

H900 --H1199. Tests of prowess: tasks
    H900 --H999. Assignment and performance of tasks
    H1000--H1199. Nature of tasks

H1200--H1399. Tests of prowess: quests
    H1200--H1249. Attendant circumstances of quests
    H1250--H1399. Nature of quests

H1400--H1599. Other tests
    H1400--H1449. Tests of fear
    H1450--H1499. Tests of vigilance
    H1500--H1549. Tests of endurance and power of
                   survival
    H1550--H1569. Tests of character
    H1570--H1599. Miscellaneous tests

J. THE WISE AND THE FOOLISH

J0   --J199. Acquistion and possession of wisdom
               (knowledge)

J200 --J1099. Wise and unwise conduct
    J200 --J499. Choices
    J600 --J799. Forethought

J1100--J1699. Cleverness
    J1130--J1199. Cleverness in the law court
    J1650--J1699. Miscellaneous clever acts

J1700--J2749. Fools (and other unwise persons)
    J1700--J1749. Fools (general)
    J1750--J1849. Absurd misunderstandings
    J1850--J1999. Absurd disregard of facts
    J2000--J2049. Absurd absent-mindedness
    J2050--J2199. Absurd short-sightedness
    J2260--J2299. Absurd scientific theories
    J2300--J2349. Gullible fools
    J2350--J2369. Talkative fools
    J2400--J2449. Foolish imitation
    J2450--J2499. Literal fools

K. DECEPTIONS

K0   --K99.   Contests won by deception.
K100 --K299. Deceptive bargains
K300 --K499. Thefts and cheats
K500 --K699. Escape by deception
K700 --K799. Capture by deception
K800 --K999. Fatal deception
K1000--K1199. Deception into self-injury
K1200--K1299. Deception into humiliating position
K1300--K1399. Seduction or deceptive marriage
K1400--K1499. Dupe's property destroyed
K1500--K1599. Deceptions connected with adultery
K1600--K1699. Deceiver falls into own trap

Z. MISCELLANEOUS GROUPS OF MOTIFS

Z0 --Z99.   Formulas
Z100--Z199. Symbolism
Z200--Z299. Heroes
Z300--Z399. Unique exceptions

A. MYTHOLOGICAL MOTIFS

A0--A99. Creator.

A0. Creator. Polynesia: *Dixon, 1916, 21 n.47;
Easter I.: Métraux, 1940, 313; Englert, 1939,
17ff.; Mangareva: Caillot, 1914, 154; Hiroa,
1938, 420; Laval, 1938, 296f.; Tuamotus: Caillot,
1914, 8, 22; Societies: Henry, 1928, 335ff.;
Agostini, 1900, 81; Hawaii: Beckwith, 1940, 42;
Beckwith, 1932, 14f.; Fornander, 1918, VI, 268,
336; Westervelt, 1915, 71f.; Cooks: Gill, 1876,
17; Tonga: Hambruch, 1915, 281; Samoa: Stair,
1896, 34; Fraser, 1892, 175; Krämer, 1902, I,
392, 396ff.; Powell-Pratt, 1891, 208, 268ff.;
Stuebel, 1896, 59ff., 151; Niue: Thomson, 1902,
84; Chatham I.: Shand, 1894, 27, 128; Skinner,
1923, 58; N.Z.: Cowan, 1930, I, 8; Best, 1924,
86; Clark, 1896, 15; Hare Hongi,"A Maori
Cosmogony,"JPS XVI (1907), 113-118; White, 1887-90,
I, 18, 49f., 139f., 149, 155, 162; II, 2ff.;
Rotuma: Russell, 1942, 230; Reef Is.: O'Ferrall,
1904, 227; Rennell: Elbert-Monberg, 1964, No. 29;
Ontong Java: Parkinson, 1898, 194.

A2.+ Two creators. Niue: Guppy, 1890, 48.

A2.1. Three creators. Oceanic: *Dixon, 1916, 24;
Hawaii: Beckwith, 1940, 42; Beckwith, 1932, 8,
174; Fornander, 1918, VI, 268.

A5.1. Gods make earth to have place to rest their feet.
Hawaiian: Beckwith, 1940, 43.

A11. Invisible creator. N.Z.: Best, 1924, 87.

A12.1. Male and female creators. Hawaii: Henry,1928,
345.

A13.2. Bird as creator. Hawaii: Henry, 1928, 345;
Nukumanu: Sarfert, 1931, 313, 385.

A15.2.+ Twin creators. Rotuma: Churchward, 1937-38,
114.

A30. Creator's companions. Tahiti: Henry, 1928, 342;
Hawaii: Beckwith, 1940, 45.

A32. Creator's family. Societies: Agostini, 1900, 87.

1

A32.3. Creator's wife. Samoa: Stuebel, 1896, 59.

A32.3.2.+ Creator god marries his daughter. Mangareva: Laval, 1938, 299; Samoa: Nelson, 1925, 128.

A33.1.1. Creator's dog. The creator is accompanied by a dog. Hawaii: Beckwith, 1940, 347.

A33.2. Bird as creator's companion. Tonga, Samoa: Dixon, 1916, *164 n. 33, 34.

A38.1.+ Winds as creator's companions. Rarotonga: Ariki, 1899, 71.

A50. Conflict of good and evil creators. Niue: Loeb, 1926, 157.

A51. Creation of devil(s). Samoa: Krämer, 1902, 106.

A52. Creation of angels. Hawaii: Thrum, 1907, 18.

A60. Marplot at creation. Societies: Henry, 1928, 348, 353; Henry, 1901, 52; Hawaii: Beckwith, 1940, 45; Thrum, 1907, 18f.; Niue: Loeb, 1926, 157; N.Z.: Best, 1924, 107; Best, 1925, 767; White, 1887-90, I, 19; II, 87, 90.

A63.7. Rebel god is author of all poisonous things. Hawaii: Beckwith, 1940, 61.

A72.+ Creator gods complete work of primordial creator god. Samoa: Stair, 1896, 34.

A76. Creator's death. Tuamotus: Henry, 1928, 350.

A77. Creator's works survive him. Tuamotus: Henry, 1928, 351.

2

A100--A499. GODS

A100--A199. The gods in general

A100. Deity. *E. Tregear, "Asiatic Gods in the Pacific," 1893, 129-146; Societies: Henry, 1928, 394; Niue: Loeb, 1926, 157ff., 159-160, 165; Samoa: *Stair, 1896, 33ff.

A101. Supreme god. One god chief of all other gods. Mangareva: Hiroa, 1938, 419; Societies: Henry, 1928, 121, 128; Luomala, 1949, 141; Samoa: Fraser, 1897, 34; Tokelau: Lester, 1892, 50; N.Z.: Clark, 1896, 32; Hare Hongi, "A Maori Cosmogony," JPS XVI (1907), 113-118; *Te Haupapa-o-Tane "Io, the Supreme God, and Other Gods of the Maori," 1920, 139-143; Best, 1924, 66, 87, 234ff.; White, 1887-90, II, 1ff.; Best, 1925, 1027; Niue: Smith, 1902, 195; Nukumanu: Sarfert, 1931, 330; Ellice Is.: Grimble, 1952, 63; Ontong Java: Sarfert, 1931, 323.

A101.1. Supreme god as creator. Tahiti: Henry, 1928, 355; Henry, 1901, 51; Samoa: Fraser, 1892, 175: N.Z.: Hare Hongi, "A Maori Cosmogony," 1907, 113-118.

A104.1. Living person becomes god. *Hawaii: Beckwith, 1940, 2, ch. I passim; Beckwith, 1919, 337; Tokelau: Macgregor, 1937, 84.

A104.1.+ Men once gods and gods once men. Tikopia: Firth, 1930, 296.

A104.2. Dead body becomes god. Hawaii: Beckwith, 1940, 2.

A104.3. Miscellaneous objects become gods. Hawaii: Beckwith, 1940, 2.

A104.4. Spirits become gods. Hawaii: Beckwith, 1940, 45.

A106.1. Revolt of bad gods against the good. Hawaii: Thrum, 1907, 18.

A106.2.1. Revolting devil banished to hell (lower world). Tuamotus: Henry, 1928, 349.

A107. Gods of darkness and light. N.Z.: Best, 1924, 99ff.

*A107.1. Certain spirits doomed to live in darkness.
N.Z.: White, 1887-90, I, 40.

A108.1. God of the dead. Hawaii: Beckwith, 1940,
60; Nukumanu: Sarfert, 1931, 330.

A109.1. God as a triad. Hawaii: Beckwith, 1940, 44.

A109.2. Goddess as mother of Pacific Ocean. N.Z.:
Beckwith, 1940, 179.

A110. Origin of the gods. Tonga: Collocott, 1919,
234ff.; Collocott, 1924, 276f.

A111. Parents of the gods. Hawaii: Beckwith, 1940,
171.

A111.1. Mother of the gods. Oceanic: Beckwith, 1940,
294.

A111.2. Father of the gods. Tuamotus: Seurat, 1905,
486.

A111.3. Ancestor of the gods. Tahiti: Henry, 1928,
336.

A111.3.+ God of double sex. Tikopia: Firth, 1961,
62f.

A111.3.1. God dwells with his grandfathers. Marquesas:
Handy, 1930, 106.

A111.3.2. Sea creatures as ancestors of goddess.
Tuamotus: Stimson, n.d., T-G. 3/600.

A111.3.3. Great bird as ancestor of gods. Hawaii:
Beckwith, 1940, 92.

A112.1. God from incestuous union. Tonga: Caillot,
1914, 242ff.

A112.6. Gods as sons of supreme god. Tahiti: Henry,
1928, 147.

A112.7.1. God born from mother's ear. Mangareva: Hiroa
1938, 425; Laval, 1938, 303; Marquesas: Handy,
1930, 107.

A112.7.2. God born from mother's armpit. Marquesas:
Handy, 1930, 107.

A112.7.2.+ God born from boil on his mother's arm.
Cooks: Gill, 1876, 10.

4

A112.7.3. Goddess born from mother's eyes. Hawaii:
Beckwith, 1940, 186.

A112.7.4. God born after prematurely short pregnancy.
Marquesas: Handy, 1930, 107.

*A112.7.5. Deity born from mother's head. Hawaii:
Emerson, 1915, X; Tikopia: Firth, 1916, 29, 31.

A112.10. Divine child cast out at birth. Polynesia:
Beckwith, 1940, 257.

A112.11. Child born from union of god with hen.
Easter I.: Métraux, 1940, 130.

A112.11.+ Goddess born at bottom of the sea. Hawaii:
Thrum, 1923, 203.

A112.11.+ Gods originate as descent of coupling of
seaweed and slime, which gave birth to a stone,
which gave birth to twins: male and female.
Tonga: Caillot, 1914, 239-240.

A114.1.1.2. Origin of lesser gods from spittle of great
god. Hawaii: Beckwith, 1940, 169.

A114.2. God born from egg. Marquesas: Handy, 1930,
104; Tahiti: Henry, 1901, 51; Henry, 1928, 337;
Hawaii: Rice, 1923, 7.

A114.2.1. Deity born in shape of egg. Hawaii: Beckwith,
1940, 169.

A114.3. Deity born from skull. Easter I.: Métraux,
1940, 312.

A114.4. Deity born from tree. Hawaii: Beckwith, 1940,
279, 284.

*A114.5. God born of union of the sun and the night.
Samoa: *Krämer, 1902, I, 419, 419 n. 15.

*A114.6. Deity born from blood-clot. Mangareva:
Luomala, 1949, 156ff.

*A114.7. Messenger of god born of frozen, gilded cloud.
Tahiti: Henry, 1928, 370.

A115.2. God issues from earth. Tikopia: Firth, 1916,
55.

A115.3. Deity arises from mist. Hawaii: Beckwith,
1940, 71.

A115.4. Deity emerges from darkness of underworld. Cooks: Beckwith, 1940, 224; *Gill, 1876, 1ff.

A115.5. Emergence of gods from above and below. Marquesas: Handy, 1930, 138; Chatham I.: Shand, 1894, 122.

A115.6. Deity arises from shell of darkness where he ha been for million ages. Tahiti: Henry, 1928, 336.

*A115.8. Goddess falls from heaven. Lau Is: Hocart, 1929, 196.

*A115.8. God fished up with island. Ontong Java: Parkinson, 1898, 194.

A116. Twin gods. Tonga: Reiter, 1907, 236; Caillot, 1914, 240; Samoa: *Samuel Ella "O Le Tala Ia Taema Ma Na-Fanua" JPS VI, (1897), 152-155; Rotuma: Churchward, 1937-38, 114; Russell, 1942, 239; Tikopia: Firth, 1916, 42, 75.

A116.2. Twin goddesses (Siamese-twins). Samoa: Fraser, 1896, 171.

A117. Mortals become gods. N.Z.: Cowan, 1930, 100; Tikopia: Firth, 1916, 94, 96, 97; Ontong Java: Parkinson, 1898, 195.

A117.2. Mortal translated to heaven and deified. N.Z.: Clark, 1896, 167.

A117.3. In extreme old age spirits become gods. Hawaii: Beckwith, 1940, 67.

A117.4. Mortal transfigured to god on mountain top. N.Z.: Beckwith, 1940, 250.

A117.5. Gods are spirits of deified dead. Easter I.: Métraux, 1940, 316; Mangareva: Hiroa, 1938, 29, 424f.; Societies: Agostini, 1900, 90; Hawaii: Thrum, 1907, 222; N.Z.: White, 1887-90, IV, 59; Ellice Is.: Hedley, 1896, 46; Roberts, 1958, 401.

*A117.5.1. Aborted fetuses are deified. Mangareva: Hiroa, 1938, 119, 127, 365, 426f.; Laval, 1938, 191, 305.

A119.1. God made by magic. Tahiti: Henry, 1928, 341, 374-375.

A119.2. Goddess produced by heat of earth. Tahiti:

6

Beckwith, 1940, 178.

A119.3. Arrival of gods in particular country. Hawaii:
Beckwith, 1940, 2f., 11; Tonga: Gifford, 1924,
199.

A120.1. God as shape-shifter. Tahiti: Henry, 1928,
359; Hawaii: Fornander, 1916, IV, 516;
Westervelt, 1915, 30; Samoa: Stair, 1896, 37.

A120.1.+ God who is sometimes man, sometimes rock.
Tonga: Collocott, 1921b, 231.

A120.1.+ Goddess appears to young men as a beautiful
princess, to women as an ugly hag. Lau Is.:
St. Johnston, 1918, 113.

A120.2. Size-changing god. Hawaii: Beckwith, 1940, 127.

A120.3.+ Ghost gods. Hawaii: Emerson, 1915, 61.

A120.4. Formless gods. Tonga: Beckwith, 1940, 128.

A121.1. Moon as deity (cf. A240). Cooks: Large, 1903,
135; Hawaii: Fornander, 1916, IV, 84ff.; Ellice
Is.: Roberts, 1958, 401.

A121.2. Sun as deity (cf. A220). Cooks: Large, 1903,
135; Hawaii: Beckwith, 1940, 217; Ellice Is.:
Roberts, 1958, 401.

A122. God half mortal, half immortal. Hawaii:
Fornander, 1916, IV, 98.

A123. Monstrous gods. Tikopia: Firth, 1916, 103.

A123.1.2. God with two joined bodies. Tahiti: Henry,
1928, 344.

A123.1.3. God with good looking and ugly bodies.
Marquesas: Handy, 1930, 124.

A123.1.4. God with body of earthquake (whirlwind, etc.)
Hawaii: Beckwith, 1940, 30.

A123.1.5. God with body of caterpillars. Hawaii:
Beckwith, 1940, 30.

A123.1.6. God with body of stream of blood. Hawaii:
Beckwith, 1940, 30.

A123.1.7. Goddess with three supernatural bodies: fire,
cliff, sea. Hawaii: Beckwith, 1940, 496.

7

A123.2.1.1. God with two faces. Societies: Henry, 1901, 52; 1928, 402.

A123.2.2.1. Maggots squirm from mouth of man-eating god. Hawaii: Beckwith, 1940, 506.

A123.2.2.2. Goddess with eight mouths. Tonga: Gifford, 1924, 168.

A123.2.2.+ God whose mouth forms a gateway to his father's territory: it opens for desirable entrants closes for undesirable. Mangareva: Hiroa, 1938, 424.

A123.2.2.+ God with long tongue sucks in all edible things. Niue: Loeb, 1926, 161, 218.

G332. Sucking monster.

A123.3.1. God with many eyes. Tonga: Collocott, 1928, 24; Funafuti: David, 1899, 93.

A123.3.2. God with flashing eyes. Societies: Agostini, 1900, 89; Hawaii: Beckwith, 1940, 30.

*A123.3.3. God (Maui) with one eye like an eel, the other like greenstone. N.Z.: Best, 1924, 142.

A123.4.1.3. God with eight heads. Societies: Luomala, 1949, 153; Beckwith, 1940, 209; Henry, 1928, 408; *Luomala, 1949, 139ff.; Rarotonga: Luomala, 1949, 67, 72; Ariki, 1899, 71; Best, 1924, 142.

*A123.4.1.4. Two-headed god. N.Z.: Hongi, 1920, 24.

A123.4.2. God with head of stone. Hawaii: Beckwith, 1940, 88.

A123.4.2.+ God in form of a rolling head. Lau Is.: St. Johnston, 1918, 76.

A123.4.2.+ God who is a giant head. Lau Is.: Hocart, 1929, 192, 198.

A123.4.2.+ Son of god with eight ears. Ellice Is.: David, 1899, 93; Tonga: Collocott, 1928, 24.

A123.7.+ Purple goddess. Marquesas: Steinen, 1934-35, 217.

A123.7.+ Red and white god. Niue: Loeb, 1926, 159.

8

A123.7.+ God with striped body. Niue: Loeb, 1926, 161.

A123.7.+ Albino god (Tu). Niue: Loeb, 1926, 159;
Smith, 1902, 196.

A123.11. God with tail. Cooks: Clark, 1896, 140;
Tahiti: Beckwith, 1940, 113; Fijis: Beckwith,
1940, 76; Fison, 1904, 141.

A124. Luminous god. N.Z.: Henry, 1928, 467; Best,
1925, 907; Tikopia: Firth, 1916, 34, 88.

A124.5. God in form of comet. Hawaii: Beckwith,
1940, 113; Ii, 1959, 124; N.Z.: Best, 1925, 956;
White, 1887-90, I, 109; Bellona: Elbert-Monberg,
1964, Nos. 14, n., 16, 16 n.

A125. Deity in human form. (The human form is assumed
in most mythologies.) Hawaii: McAllister, 1933,
152; Pukui, 1933, 167; Westervelt, 1915, 34ff.;
Samoa: Henry, 1928, 346; N.Z.: White, 1887-90,
I, 108.

A125.4.+ God with sandy hair. Cooks: Gill, 1876, 13.

A128.1. Blind god. Marquesas: Steinen, 1933-34, 370.

A128.2. One-eyed god. Tahiti: Henry, 1928, 375.

A128.5. Lame god. Samoa: Powell-Pratt, 1892, 78.

*A128.6. One-armed god. Lau Is.: St. Johnston, 1918,
41, 72.

A131. Gods with animal features. Societies: Agostini,
1900, 90.

A131.1. God as part man, part fish. Tuamotus: Seurat,
1905, 487; Tahiti: Henry, 1928, 358; Cooks:
Gill, 1876, 3; Samoa: Beckwith, 1940, 76; Niue:
Loeb, 1926, 125.

A131.3.2. Goddess with pig's head. Tonga: Beckwith,
1940, 178.

*A131.9. God whose form is a snake, the lower part of
which is stone. Fijis: Tregear, 1903, 182.

A132. God in animal form. Hawaii: Westervelt, 1915,
204ff.

A132.0.1.2. God in three forms: gecko, shark, or
priest. Tonga: Beckwith, 1940, 128.

A132.1.   Snake-god.   Fijis (Lau Is.):   Beckwith, 1940,
138, 316;   Hocart, 1929, 201;   St. Johnston, 1918,
129ff.;   Rennell: Elbert-Monberg, 1964, No. 230.

A132.6.   Bird deity.   Pukapuka: Beaglehole, 1928, 376.

A132.6.1.   Bird-god.   Mangareva: Hiroa, 1938, 460;
Tahiti: Jourdain, 1934, 198;   Hawaii: Beckwith,
1940, 91ff., 370;   Fornander, 1916, IV, 516;   1918,
V, 314;   Emory, 1924, 12;   Niue: Loeb, 1926, 190;
Fijis: Beckwith, 1940, 131;   Lau Is.:   St. Johnston
1918, 126f.;   N.Z.:   Best, 1925, 956;   Cowan, 1930,
I, 21;   Tikopia: Firth, 1940, I, 113;   Rennell:
Elbert-Monberg, 1964, No. 8.

*A132.6.1.1.   Owl-god.   Hawaii: Fornander, 1918, V, 552;
Westervelt, 1915, 127ff.;   Thrum, 1907, 123.

A132.6.2.   Goddess in form of bird.   Hawaii: Westervelt,
1915, 100;   Samoa: Lesson, 1876, 590.

A132.6.3.   Cock-god.   Hawaii: Beckwith, 1940, 119.

A132.6.4.   Female deities as fly-catchers.   Hawaii:
Beckwith, 1940, 16.

A132.6.5.   Pigeon-god.   Tonga: Gifford, 1924, 62.

*A132.6.6.   Bat-god.   Tikopia: Firth, 1916, 72.

A132.7.   Swine-god.   Hawaii: McAllister, 1933, 160.

A132.8.   Dog-god.   N.Z.:   Best, 1925, 861.

A132.11.   Seal-god.   Easter I.:   Metraux, 1940, 310.

A132.12.   Eel-god.   Mangareva: Hiroa, 1938, 426;
Tahiti: Henry, 1928, 389;   Cooks: Gill, 1876,
77;   Hawaii: Thrum, 1907, 217;   Tonga: Collocott,
1928, 58;   Gifford, 1924, 57;   Samoa: Krämer,
1902, I, 450;   Stuebel, 1896, 151;   N.Z.:   *Best,
1924, 140-141;   Best, 1925, 954;   Clark, 1896,
163;   Lau Is.:   Beckwith, 1940, 131;   Hocart,
1929, 198;   Tikopia: Firth, 1916, 31, 51, 101,
113, 118, 135.

A132.13.   Fish-god.   Mangareva: Hiroa, 1938, 460;
Laval, 1938, 298, 306f.;   Marquesas: Handy, 1930,
137;   Tahiti: Henry, 1928, 612, 614;   Hawaii:
Beckwith, 1940, 128-129;   Rice, 1923, 37;   Fornander,
1918, V, 266, 272, 510;   Thrum, 1921, 106;   Thrum,
1923, 203;   Pukapuka: Beaglehole, 1938, 313;
Cooks: Gill, 1876, 29;   Tonga: Beckwith, 1940,

131; Gifford, 1924, 79; Collocott, 1921b, 160;
Lau Is.: Hocart, 1929, 211; Ontong Java:
Sarfert, 1931, 328.

*A132.13.1. Shark-god. Mangareva: Hiroa, 1938, 25;
Hawaii: Green, 1926, 102 n.2; McAllister, 1933,
123, 129; Thrum, 1907, 130, 188ff., 256ff.; Thrum,
1923, 149, 230, 300; Westervelt, 1915, 2, 49,
52ff., 55, 85, 193; Tonga: Collocott, 1928, 56ff.;
Chatham Is.: Skinner, 1923, 57; Lau Is.: St.
Johnston, 1918, 126.

*A132.13.2. Octopus-god. Tonga: Collocott, 1921b, 231;
Ellice Is.: Roberts, 1958, 413; Tikopia: Firth,
1916, 39.

*A132.13.3. Crab-god (goddess). Bellona: Elbert-Monberg,
1964, No. 150.

*A132.13.4. Whale-god. N.Z.: White, 1887-90, I, 108.

*A132.16. Lizard-god. Marquesas: Christian, 1895, 190;
Societies: Henry, 1928, 383; Cooks: Gill, 1876,
10, 291, 307; Hawaii: Beckwith, 1932, 18;
Fornander, 1918, V, 176, 520; Ii, 1959, 44; Thrum,
1923, 185, 188f., 192; N.Z.: Best, 1897, 43ff.;
White, 1887-90, I, 96; Lau Is.: Beckwith, 1940,
131; Hocart, 1929, 196; Tikopia: Firth, 1916,
103; Bellona: Elbert-Monberg, 1964, No. 150.

*A132.17. Insect-god. Tahiti: Henry, 1928, 598;
Hawaii: Green, 1923, 43; Rennell: Elbert-Monberg,
1964, No. 161, No. 172.

*A132.18. Flying-fox god. Tonga: Collocott, 1921b,
230.

*A132.19. Rat-god. Hawaii: Westervelt, 1915, 157ff.;
Lau Is.: St. Johnston, 1918, 113ff.

*A132.20. Dragon-god. Hawaii: Fornander, 1918, V,
410; Westervelt, 1915, 152.

A135. Man-eating god (goddess). Tokelau: Macgregor,
1937, 59; Hawaii: Beckwith, 1940, 29f.; N.Z.:
Beckwith, 1940, 243.

*A135.1. Blind cannibal god fishes from heaven for
human victims. Marquesas: Steinen, 1933-34, 370.

A136.1.4. God rides bird. Lau Is.: Hocart, 1929, 198.

A136.1.8.+ God flies. Tuamotus: Stimson, 1937, 54;

11

Hawaii: Thrum, 1923, 47; Lau Is.: St. Johnston, 1918, 80f.; Bellona: Elbert-Monberg, 1964, Nos. 14, 15, 16, 17.

*A136.4. Floating island is vessel of a god. Hawaii: Thrum, 1923, 115.

A137.4.1. God carries brothers and sisters on his back in basket. Marquesas: Handy, 1930, 116.

A137.16. God represented as meteor (cf. A124, A250). Mangareva: Hiroa, 1938, 459; Tahiti: Beckwith, 1940, 113; N.Z.: Best, 1925, 854; Ellice Is.: Roberts, 1958, 401.

A139.7.+ Perfumed odor emanates from god. N.Z.: Best, 1925, 907.

A139.8.1. God as a tree trunk. Hawaii: Beckwith, 1940, 284; Emerson, 1915, 163; Westervelt, 1915, 38; N.Z.: Best, 1925, 753.

A139.8.2. Goddess appears as coral reef. Mangareva: Hiroa, 1938, 460; Hawaii: Beckwith, 1940, 219.

A139.8.3. Smoldering fire of volcano as head of goddess. Hawaii: Beckwith, 1940, 188.

A139.8.4. God of the wind in shape of kite. Hawaii: Beckwith, 1940, 121.

A139.8.5. Goddess in form of tree. Hawaii: Beckwith, 1940, 17.

A139.8.6. God in shape of image. Hawaii: Beckwith, 1940, 2, Chap. I passim; Cooks: Gill, 1876, 15.

*A139.8.7. God in form of waterspout. Tokelau: Macgregor, 1937, 60; Niue: Smith, 1902, 196.

*A139.8.8. God in form of stone. Hawaii: Emerson, 1915, 211; Fornander, 1918, VI, 174; Pukui, 1943, 56; Thrum, 1907, 252; Samoa: Stuebel, 1896, 149; Tokelau: Lester, 1892, 50; Chatham Is.: Skinner, 1923, 55; N.Z.: Best, 1925, 863; Cowan, 1930, I, 189; Lau Is.: St. Johnston, 1918, 46; Tikopia: Firth, 1961, 72; Firth, 1916, 141; Rennell: Elbert-Monberg, 1964, Nos. 67, 235a, 235b, 236; Bellona: Elbert-Monberg, 1964, No. 66.

*A139.8.8.1. Gods assume forms of hills. Hawaii: Forander, 1916, IV, 518.

*A139.8.9. God in form of great mat. Tokelau: Macgregor, 1937, 61.

*A139.8.10. God in form of great canoe. Tokelau: Macgregor, 1937, 60.

*A139.8.11. God who is the ocean, foaming breakers are his jaws. Tahiti: Henry, 1928, 358.

*A139.8.12. God in form of feathers. Hawaii: Fornander, 1916, IV, 202.

*A139.8.13. God in form of will-0-the-wisp. Lau Is.: St. Johnston, 1918, 118.

A139.9.1. Goddess with red urine. Easter I.: Métraux, 1940, 315.

A139.9.3. Gods covered with red and yellow feathers. Tahiti: Henry, 1928, 338.

A139.10. God with myriad natures. Tahiti: Henry, 1928, 336.

A139.11. Gods recognized by natural phenomena associated with their worship -- color, scent, etc. Hawaii: Beckwith, 1940, 4.

*A139.16. Transformer god. Samoa: Fraser, 1891, 179.

*A139.17. Immovable god. Samoa: Fraser, 1891, 179.

*A139.18. Goddess is bound by cord to sky and to underworld, for visit from her would destroy the world. Tonga: Collocott, 1921b, 153.

A140. Gods as workmen. Tikopia: Firth, 1961, 96.

A141. God as craftsman. Tahiti: Henry, 1928, 342.

*A141.5. Gods build a fish pond (weir). Hawaii: McAllister, 1933, 185; Pukui, 1943, 65.

*A141.6. A god makes a bridge. Hawaii: Westervelt, 1915, 6.

A147. Gods as fishers (cf. A165.9). Hawaii: Beckwith, 1940, 24.

A151. Home of the gods. Elysium, Avalon, earthly paradise. Hawaii: Beckwith, 1940, 67; Rice,

13

1923, 116; Samoa: Stair, 1896, 34; Niue:
Loeb, 1926, 163, 220.

A151.1. Home of gods on high mountain. Hawaii:
Beckwith, 1940, 19.

A151.1.1. Home of gods inside of hill. Hawaii:
Beckwith, 1940, 39.

A151.1.2. Home of gods in cave. Marquesas: Handy,
1930, 104; Cooks: Gill, 1876, 5; Tonga:
Gifford, 1924, 81; Niue: Loeb, 1926, 157.

A151.1.3. Home of gods in volcano crater. Hawaii:
Beckwith, 1940, 167, 173; Fornander, 1916, IV,
104-106.

A151.1.4. Gods live in cloudland. Tahiti: Beckwith,
1940, 31; Hawaii: Beckwith, 1940, 64, 67, 346;
Niue: Loeb, 1926, 214.

A151.3. Home of gods under the sea. Cooks: Gill,
1876, 5; Hawaii: Green, 1926, 61; Thrum, 1921,
106; Rennell: Elbert-Monberg, 1964, No. 16;
Ontong Java: Parkinson, 1898, 194.

*A151.3.0.1. God lives on bottom of sea and builds
coral reefs. Ontong Java: Sarfert, 1931, 299.

A151.3.1. Gods live in spring. Tonga: Beckwith, 1940,
74.

A151.3.2. Home of gods on island. Tahiti: Beckwith,
1940, 178; Hawaii: Beckwith, 1940, 67f., 85;
Fornander, 1918, V, 364; Green, 1926, 115;
Fijis: Fison, 1904, 159.

*A151.3.3. God lives in reef. Tahiti: Henry, 1928,
448f.

A151.4.4. House of god with pillars made of dead
chief's bones. Samoa: Beckwith, 1940, 76.

A151.6.2. Sun and moon as habitations of gods.
Hawaii: Beckwith, 1940, 85.

A151.7. Deity lives in forest. Hawaii: Beckwith,
1940, 36f.

A151.7.1. Deity resides in tree. Hawaii: Ii, 1959,
44; Fijis: Fison, 1904, 12.

A151. 12. God's landing place: on island. Hawaii:

14

Beckwith, 1940, 11.

A151.13. God dwells alone in darkness. Hawaii:
Beckwith, 1940, 42.

A151.14. Various other dwelling places of gods.
Tahiti: Henry, 1940, 368ff.; Hawaii: Beckwith,
1940, 3, 11, 43, 67; Fornander, 1916, IV, 42ff.;
Westervelt, 1915, 224; Tonga: Caillot, 1914,
244f.; Collocott, 1919, 236; Collocott, 1924,
276f.; Lau Is.: St. Johnston, 1918, 113; Hocart,
1929, 119.

A153. Food of the gods. Ambrosia. Hawaii: Beckwith,
1940, 67.

A153.8. Cannibal gods (cf. G11.). N.Z.: White, 1887-90,
I, 108; Ellice Is.: Roberts, 1958, 372; Tikopia:
Firth, 1961, 113.

*A153.8.1. Tongue of god extends down from sky and
licks up human sacrifice. Hawaii: Fornander,
1916, IV, 218ff.; Kamakau, 1961, 14.

A153.9. Gods nourished by air. Marquesas: Handy,
1930, 105.

*A153.10. Gods eat raw food. N. Z.: White, 1887-90,
II, 9, 33.

A155.3. Birds of the gods. Hawaii: Beckwith, 1940,
36f., 115, 177; Rice, 1923, 38; Samoa: Lesson,
1876, 592; N.Z.: Locke, 1921, 42.

*A155.3.1. Cock who is awakener of god. Lau Is.:
Hocart, 1929, 223.

A157.1.1. Thunderbolt as gods' weapon. Hawaii:
Fornander, 1916, IV, 76.

A159.+ Canoe bailer of god. Tahiti: Henry, 1928, 356.

A159.+ Rainbow as sign of a god's presence. Hawaii:
Thrum, 1907, 191.

A159.+ Gods wreathe themselves in mists. Hawaii:
Thrum, 1923, 108.

A161.3. Queen of the gods. Hawaii: Beckwith, 1940,
13, Chap. II passim.

A161.4. God presides over all male spirits. Hawaii:
Beckwith, 1940, 13.

A161.5. Eldest god born in front, younger at back. (cf. A112.7.). Marquesas: Handy, 1930, 138.

A162. Conflicts of the gods. Tuamotus: Henry, 1928, 349; Hawaii: Emerson, 1915, XIV, 43ff., 52ff.; Ii, 1959, 44; Thrum, 1923, 192; Westervelt, 1915, 271f., 273ff.; N.Z.: Grey, 1855, 6, 8; Best, 1925, 755; White, 1887-90, I, 39, 94, V, 54f.; Rennell: Elbert-Monberg, 1964, 17a, 17b.

A162.1. Fight of the gods and giants. Samoa: Beckwith, 1940, 254.

*A162.3.3. Shooting stars used to kill spirit. Ontong Java: Parkinson, 1898, 197.

A162.7. Single combat between gods. Marquesas: Handy, 1930, 109; Societies: Henry, 1928, 458; Hawaii: Beckwith, 1940, 17, 206; Emerson, 1915, XIV.

A162.8. Rebellion of lesser gods against chief. Hawaii: Beckwith, 1940, 60, 118, 155.

A164.1. Brother-sister marriage of the gods. Marquesas: Handy, 1930, 122.

A165.1.3. Red sea-bird god's pet. Tahiti: Henry, 1928, 180.

*A165.1.3.1. Birds as companion to goddess. Hawaii: Beckwith, 1940, 37.

*A165.1.4. Black dove wakes god daily. Fijis: Fison, 1904, 28.

*A165.1.5. Shark of god. Societies: Henry, 1928, 403.

A165.2. Messenger of the gods. Tahiti: Beckwith, 1940, 31; Henry, 1928, 164; Hawaii: Westervelt, 1915, 118f.; N.Z.: Best, 1924, 88.

A165.2.2. Birds as messengers of the gods. Cooks: Gill, 1876, 291; Te Ariki, 1920, 168; Hawaii: Beckwith, 1940, 177; Samoa: Krämer, 1902, I, 392; Stuebel, 1896, 60f.; Niue: Loeb, 1926, 160; Fijis: Fison, 1904, 23.

*A165.2.5. Insects as messengers of the gods.

*A165.2.5.1. Butterfly as god's messenger. N.Z.: Best, 1924, 147.

*A165.2.5.2. Sandfly as god's messenger. N.Z.: Best,

1923, 147.

*A165.2.6. Fish as messengers of the gods.

*A165.2.6.1. Shark as god's messenger. Tahiti:
Henry, 1928, 351, 389.

*A165.2.6.2. Whale as god's messenger. Tahiti:
Beckwith, 1940, 360; Henry, 1928, 358.

*A165.2.6.3. Eel as god's messenger. Tahiti: Henry,
1928, 358.

*A165.3.0.1. Kava-mixer to gods. Rarotonga: Te Ariki,
1920,63.

A165.4. Watchman of the gods. Tahiti: Beckwith,
1940, 221.

A165.9. Fisherman of the gods. N.Z.: Clark, 1896,
56.

A168. Family of gods. Easter I.: Métraux, 1940, 311;
Tahiti: Henry, 1928, 231.

*A169.2. God who is prisoner of other gods. Niue:
Loeb, 1926, 161.

A171.0.2. God ascends to heaven. Societies: Henry,
1928, 411; Hawaii: Beckwith. 1940, 109; Samoa:
Fraser, 1897, 67; N.Z.: Beckwith, 1940, 83;
Ellice Is.: Roberts, 1958, 372.

*A171.0.2.1. Ascent of gods: they grow until their
heads pierce the sky, then their feet disappear
from the land. Hawaii: Rice, 1923, 127 f.

*A171.0.2.2. God of evil tries to scale the sides of
the heavens. N.Z.: Best, 1924, 101.

A171.0.3. God descends from heaven. Tokelau:
Macgregor, 1937, 81; Hawaii: Emerson, 1915, 152;
Tonga: *Caillot, 1914, 248, 248 n.2; N.Z.: Best,
1925, 869; White, 1887-90, II, 22f.

*A171.0.3.0.1. God must learn to eat food of mortals
after coming to live on earth. Tuamotus: Henry,
1928, 349.

A171.0.3.1. God descends on rainbow. Tahiti: Henry,
1928, 232; Hawaii: Beckwith, 1940, 37; Thrum,
1923, 110; Cooks: Cowan, 1930, I, 26; Tikopia:

17

Firth, 1961, 140.

A171.0.3.2. God descends in form of shooting star.
N.Z.: Beckwith, 1940, 113.

*A171.0.3.3. God descends in form of plover. Tonga:
Collocott, 1921b, 153.

*A171.1.1.1. God sails through sky in canoe. Societies:
Henry, 1928, 459.

*A171.1.3. God rides hawk as ship. Lau Is.: Hocart,
1929, 198.

A171.2. God flies in bird plumage. Tonga: Collocott,
1919, 236; Collocott, 1924, 276.

A171.3. God flies in pillar of floating clouds,
thunder, and lightning. Hawaii: Beckwith, 1940,
29.

*A171.3.1. Gods travel upon wind. Tahiti: Henry, 1928,
443.

*A171.4. God travels from invisible to visible world
by passing through the intestines of a tripang.
Tahiti: Orsmond, 1896, 170.

A173. Gods deposed for a time. Hawaii: Beckwith,
1940, 11, 17, 177.

*A173.3. God, chased from heaven, resides on earth.
Tuamotus: Henry, 1928, 349.

A175. God reduces elements to order. Societies:
Henry, 1928, 395ff.; Hawaii: Beckwith, 1940, 20ff.

A175.1. God supplies reproductive energy to all things.
Hawaii: Beckwith, 1940, 20, 32.

A176. God ordains ceremonies and regulations. Hawaii:
Beckwith, 1940, 40.

A177. God as thief. Societies: Tefaafana, 1917, 31;
N.Z.: Best, 1925, 776.

A179.2. God given dominion over floating island.
Hawaii: Beckwith, 1940, 71.

A179.3. God deliberately has enemies kill him.
Marquesas: Handy, 1930, 105.

A179.4. Head of god bitten off by shark. Marquesas:
Handy, 1930, 108.

18

A179.5. Deity reincarnated. Hawaii: Beckwith, 1940, 279.

A179.6. God has power to create men. Marquesas: Handy, 1930, 122.

A179.7. God divests self of earthly raiment and clothes self with lightning. N.Z.: Beckwith, 1940, 83.

A179.8. God hides from sun in shadow of a cloud. Tuamotus: Stimson, n.d., T-G. 3/191.

*A179.10. Lazy god. Niue: Loeb, 1926, 163.

*A179.11. Goddess frees land of lizard-like monsters. Hawaii: Emerson, 1915, 46.

A180. Gods in relation to mortals. Societies: Gill, 1876, 6.

A181.2. God as cultivator. Hawaii: Beckwith, 1940, 17.

A182. God reveals himself to mortals. Hawaii: Pukui, 1943, 64; Thrum, 1907, 251; N.Z.: White, 1887-90, II, 2; Rennell: Elbert-Monberg, 1964, No. 182.

A182.0.1. God does not reveal himself; men unable to endure his glory. N.Z.: Best, 1924, 87.

*A182.0.3. Gods when invited to feast come and eat every crumb of their offered food. Hawaii: Emerson, 1915, 28, 73, 155.

*A182.0.4. After prayers addressed to god (an image), the chicken feathers on its head flutter. Hawaii: Fornander, 1918, V, 28.

*A182.0.5. God speaks through a medium. N.Z.: White, 1887-90, III, 20.

A182.3.5. God advises mortal. Hawaii: Westervelt, 1915, 155.

*A182.3.7. God looks at earth from sky; when he sees that people are not working, he sends storms. Ontong Java: Sarfert, 1931, 323 ff.

A183. Deity invoked. Hawaii: Beckwith, 1940, 2, Chap. I passim.

A183.1. Male god invoked in east; female in west. Hawaii: Beckwith, 1940, 12.

A185. Deity cares for favorite individuals. Hawaii: Westervelt, 1915, 38.

A185.1. God helps mortal in battle. Hawaii: Westervelt, 1915, 219.

A185.2. Deity protects mortal. Hawaii: Dickey, 1917, 33; Fornander, 1918, V, 524; Westervelt, 1915, 194f.; Pukui-Curtis, n.d., 46; N.Z.: White, 1887-90, III, 246; Lau Is.: St. Johnston,1918, 72; Tikopia: Firth, 1961, 88, 113.

A185.3. Deity teaches mortal. Mangareva: Hiroa, 1938, 30; Hawaii: Green, 1929, 105.

*A185.7.1. Goddess has herself immured in an earth oven and when oven is opened, a vast quantity of food is there for her famine-stricken worshipers. Hawaii: Westervelt, 1943, 12ff.

*A185.7.2. Goddess takes form of pools of water in order to relieve her drought-stricken worshipers. Hawaii: Westervelt, 1943, 12f.

A185.10. Deity accompanies mortal on journey as guide. Tahiti: Beckwith, 1940, 221; Hawaii: Beckwith, 1940, 328; Fijis: Fison, 1904, 13f.; N.Z.: Best, 1925, 690, 954; White, 1887-90, III, 61.

A185.12.1. God resuscitates persons. Ontong Java: Parkinson, 1898, 206.

*A185.18. God is guardian of women. Pukapuka: Beaglehole, 1938, 309.

*A185.19. God aids woman in childbirth. Hawaii: Westervelt, 1915, 47f.

A188. Gods and goddesses in love with men. Tuamotus: Henry, 1928, 352; Societies: Henry, 1928, 231, 403; *Beckwith, 1940, 37f.; Cowan, 1930, I, 26; Hawaii: Beckwith, 1940, 23, 37; Dickey, 1917, 16; Emerson, 1915, 234, 239; Pukui, 1933, 127; Thrum, 1921, 107, 110, 186, 204; Cooks: Cowan, 1930, I, 26; Tonga: Gifford, 1924, 194; Collocott, 1924, 280; Brown, 1916, 430f.; Reiter, 1933, 356; Samoa: Stuebel, 1896, 64; Tokelau: Macgregor, 1937, 84; N.Z.: Best, 1924, 157; Best, 1925, 866, 907, 910; Cowan , 1930, I, 21, 22, 26; Clark, 1896, 148; White, 1887-90, I, 115, 125, 127; II, 22; Wohlers, 1875, 15; Lau Is.: St. Johnston, 1918, 118; Fison, 1904, 49; Nukumanu: Sarfert, 1931, 437f.; Tikopia: Firth, 1961, 22; Ontong Java: Sarfert, 1931, 325.

A188.1. Philandering god. Tonga: Gifford, 1924, 26.

A188.2. Gods as ancestors of mankind. Easter I.:
Métraux, 1940, 310; Tuamotus: Stimson, n.d.,
T-G. 3/1010; Tahiti: Beckwith, 1940, 37;
Hawaii: Beckwith, 1940, 2, 70, 294, 300.

*A189.14.1. God purposely lies through his medium.
N.Z.: White, 1887-90, III, 20.

*A189.14.2. Volcano goddess sends a flow of lava as
punishment for people's irreverence. Hawaii:
Green, 1923, 5f.

*A189.14.3. Two gods send famine to avenge man's
slaying. Mangareva: Hiroa, 1938, 34.

*A189.14.4. Goddess unjustly puts two faithful servants
to death. Hawaii: Emerson, 1915, 192.

*A189.14.5. Gods throw down hook from heavens. A man
puts it in his mouth; gods set hook; man aquires
painful disease. N.Z.: White, 1887-90, I, 67.

*A189.14.6. God causes stomach pains. N.Z.: White,
1887-90, I, 96.

A189.16. Gods give divinity to mortal. Tahiti:
Henry, 1928, 231.

A189.17. Night the period of gods, day the period of
mankind. Hawaii: Beckwith, 1940, 14.

*A191.0.1. Goddess changes from age to youth by rebirths.
Hawaii: Beckwith, 1940, 279.

A191.1. Great age of the gods. Nukumanu: Sarfert,
1931, 330.

A192.1. Death of the gods. Marquesas: Steinen,
1934-35, 228; Tahiti: Henry, 1928, 231; Hawaii:
Beckwith, 1940, 110.

A192.1.2. God killed and eaten. Easter I.: Métraux,
1940, 311.

*A192.1.4. God thrown to sky where his head is entangled
in stars; he perishes. Cooks: Gill, 1876, 59f.

A192.2. Departure of gods. Marquesas: Handy, 1930,
123; Hawaii: Westervelt, 1915, 110 f.; Tonga:
Gifford, 1924, 102; N.Z.: White, 1887-90, ı, 27,

38, 43f., 44f.; Rennell: Elbert-Monberg, 1964,
No. 17a.

A192.2.1. Deity departs for heaven (skies). Polynesia:
Beckwith, 1940, 38, 43, *241ff., 254; N.Z.:
Best, 1924, 158; Clark, 1896, 155; Tikopia:
Firth, 1930-31, 296; Fijis: Fison, 1904, 57, 160.

A192.2.1.1. Deity departs for moon. Tuamotus: Stimson,
n.d., T-G. 3/933; Hawaii: Beckwith, 1940, 220,
241.

A192.2.2. Divinity departs in boat over sea. Hawaii:
Beckwith, 1940, 29, 37.

A192.2.3. Divinity departs to submarine home. Hawaii:
Beckwith, 1940, 206.

A192.2.4. Divinity departs in column of flame.
Societies: Beckwith, 1940, 38.

A192.3. Expected return of deity. Fijis: Beckwith,
1940, 316.

A192.4. Divinity becomes mortal. Tonga: Beckwith,
1940, 75.

*A192.5. Divinity succeeded by his son. Tokelau:
Macgregor, 1937, 84.

A195.3. Bird as the shadow of a god. Societies:
**Henry, 1928, 121, 384ff.

*A195.4. Crabs as shadows of the gods. Societies:
Henry, 1928, 392.

*A195.5. Fish as shadows of the gods. Societies:
*Henry, 1928, 389ff.

*A195.6. Turtle as shadow of ocean gods. Societies:
Henry, 1928, 391f.

*A195.7. Insects as agents of gods or spirits. Societies:
Henry, 1928, 391f.

*A195.8. Trees as shadows of the gods. Societies:
Henry, 1928, 382.

*A195.9. Univalves as shadows of the gods. Societies:
Henry, 1928, 391.

A197. Deity controls elements. Tahiti: Henry, 1928,
337.

A199.7. Drums and flutes off-shore announce approach of gods. Hawaii: Beckwith, 1940, 16 n.3.

*A199.8. God of ocean who has two natures and two bodies. Tahiti: Henry, 1928, 359.

A200--A299. Gods of the upper world

A205. Witch-woman of upper world. Tuamotus: Stimson, n.d., Z-G. 13/249.

A210. Sky-god. Mangareva: Caillot, 1914, 153; Tuamotus: Danielsson, 1952, 122; Societies: Henry, 1928, 417; Cooks: Gill, 1876, 13, 27; Hawaii: Beckwith, 1940, 114, 294; Tonga: Caillot, 1914, 247f.; Collocott, 1922, 173; Reiter, 1907, 238; Reiter, 1933, 356; Samoa: Fraser, 1897, 34; Krämer, 1902, V, 392. Lesson, 1876, 592; Powell-Pratt, 1892, 270, 274; Stair, 1896, 34; Stuebel, 1896, 59f.; Niue: Loeb, 1926, 117, *158, 159; Tokelau: Macgregor, 1937, 59, 84; N.Z.: Best, 1924, 86, 105; Best, 1925, 916; Fijis: Fison, 1904, 20, 49; Rotuma: Russell, 1942, 243; Reef Is.: O'Ferrall, 1904, 230; Ontong Java: Sarfert, 1931, 323-325.

A210.1. Sky-goddess. Tonga: Gifford, 1924, 16; Reiter, 1907, 238; Fijis: Fison, 1904, 3.

A211. God of heaven. Marquesas: Handy, 1930, 133.

A220. Sun-god. Hawaii: Pukui, 1933, 137; Westervelt, 1915, 170; Pukapuka: Beaglehole, 1938, 311; Cooks: Gill, 1876, 51; Samoa: Kramer, 1902, I, 392; Chatham Is.: Skinner, 1923, 55; N.Z.: Best 1924, 275f.; White, 1887-90, II, 21; Ellice Is.: Grimble, 1952. 60.

A227.1. Man sun-god while ascending; female while setting. Hawaii: Beckwith, 1940, 12, Chap. II passim.

A240. Moon-god. Tuamotus: Malarde, 1933, 499; N.Z.: Best, 1924, 132ff.

A240.1. Moon-goddess. Hawaii: Westervelt, 1915, 117; Tonga: Gifford, 1924, 181; Collocott, 1921b, 238;

Samoa: Clark, 1896, 181; Tokelau: Macgregor, 1937, 79; N.Z.: Best, 1924, 131, 132ff.; Cowan, 1930, I, 26; Clark, 1896, 181; Hongi, 1920, 27.

A250. Star-god. Mangareva: Caillot, 1914, 154; Hiroa, 1938, 426; Laval, 1938, 302; Tahiti: Henry, 1928, 360; N.Z.: Best, 1925, 849ff.; Hongi, 1920, 26; Bellona: Elbert-Monberg, 1964, No. 62; Ontong Java: Sarfert, 1931, 323-324.

A121. Stars as deities. A137.16. God represented as meteor.

A251. God of morning star. Ontong Java: Sarfert, 1931, 324.

A252. God of evening star. Ontong Java: Sarfert, 1931, 324.

*A256. Deity who is the Milky Way. N.Z.: Best, 1925, 781.

A260. God of light. N.Z.: Clark, 1896, 14, 171 n.

*A260.2. God who eats the night. Marquesas: Steinen, 1933-34, 38.

*A260.3. All bright things come from the great happy waters of Tane. Chatham Is.: Shand, 1896, 133.

A270.1. Goddess of dawn. Tuamotus: Stimson, 1937, 56ff.; N.Z.: Best, 1924, 120.

*A271. Goddess of night. Samoa: Fraser, 1898, 19.

A280. Weather-god. N.Z.: Best, 1924, 105; Reef Is.: O'Ferrall, 1904, 225; Ontong Java: Sarfert, 1931, 324; Parkinson, 1898, 197f.

A281. Storm-god. Tokelau: Macgregor, 1937, 60; N.Z.: Best, 1925, 746; Hongi, 1920, 27; Tokelau: Lester, 1892, 51; Bellona: Elbert-Monberg, 1964, No. 62.

A282. Wind-god. Mangareva: Hiroa, 1938, 426; Societies Agostini, 1900, 88; *Henry, 1928, 392ff.; Caillot, 1914, 113; Pukapuka: Beaglehole, 1938, 311ff.;

24

Cooks: Gill, 1876, 5, 100, 319; *Ariki, 1899,
71; Hawaii: Beckwith, 1940, 86, 121; Rice, 1923,
69; Fornander, 1918, V, 160; Smith, 1966, 17ff.;
Westervelt, 1915, 31, 41; Niue: Loeb, 1926, 161;
Smith, 1902, 201; Chatham Is.: Shand, 1898, 79;
N.Z.: Best, 1899, 95; Best, 1925, 885ff.;
Dixon, 1916, 32; Cowan, 1930, I, 7f.; Grey, 1855,
2, 5; White, 1887-90, I, 24, 28; II, 89;
Bellona: Elbert-Monberg, 1964, No. 28.

*A282.0.2. Wind-children. N.Z.: Best, 1924, 101.

A282.1. God of whirlwind. Tonga: Collocott, 1922, 173;
Ontong Java: Sarfert, 1931, 323 f.

*A282.2. God of whirlwinds and waterspouts. Pukapuka:
Beaglehole, 1938, 408.

A284. God of thunder. Mangareva: Caillot, 1914, 154;
Hiroa, 1938, 424; Laval, 1938, 298; Marquesas:
Christian, 1895, 190; Societies: Agostini, 1900,
89; N.Z.: Beckwith, 1940, 250; Tikopia: Firth,
1961, 30; Rennell: Elbert-Monberg, 1964, No. 192.

A284.1. Goddess of thunder. N.Z.: Dixon, 1916, 57.

A285. God of lightning. Mangareva: Hiroa, 1938, 460;
Hawaii: Westervelt, 1915, 124; Chatham Is.:
Skinner, 1923, 57; N.Z.: Best, 1925, 792, 872;
Beckwith, 1920, 250; White, 1887-90, I, 55;
Ellice Is.: Kennedy, 1931, 194; Bellona:
Elbert-Monberg, 1964, No. 61.

A287. Rain-god. Easter I.: Métraux, 1940, 310;
Mangareva: Hiroa, 1938, 459; Laval, 1938, 305;
Hawaii: Beckwith, 1940, 97; Westervelt, 1943,
9ff.; Samoa: Beckwith, 1940, 19; N.Z.: Best,
192 , 864ff.; Ontong Java: Sarfert, 1931, 323.

A288. Rainbow-god (goddess). Mangareva: Henry, 1928,
371; Laval, 1938, 305; Hawaii: Westervelt, 1915,
128ff.; N.Z.: *Best, 1924, 156ff., 159; Best,
1899, 117; Best, 1925, 690, 858ff., 867, 1045;
White, 1887-90, I, 43, 143; III, 103; Niue: Loeb,
1926, 159; Ontong Java: Sarfert, 1931, 323.

*A288.1. God of rainbow uses his mother for a bridge.
N.Z.: Best, 1924, 160.

A300. God of the underworld.   Marquesas: Christian,
1895, 190; Handy, 1930, 122; Cooks: Gill, 1876,
13; Pukapuka: Beaglehole, 1938, 310; Hawaii:
Beckwith, 1940, 114; Tonga: Reiter, 1907, 238;
N.Z.: Kararehe, 1898, 59; Fijis: Beckwith, 1940,
138; Fison, 1904, 160.

*A300.0.1. Vocano-god(s) (cf. A300, *A300.0.2.).
Hawaii: Fornander, 1918, V, 576ff.; Samoa:
Bülow, 1895, 141; Krämer, 1902, I, 393;
Powell-Pratt, 1892, 78; N.Z.: Cowan, 1930, 7, 15.

*A300.0.2. Earthquake-god(s). Hawaii: Green, 1926,
111 n. 2; Samoa: Bülow, 1895, 141; Powell-Pratt,
1892, 77ff..; N.Z.: Best, 1925, 748, 778f.;
Cowan, 1930, I, 7; White, 1887-90, II, 4.

A300.1. Goddess of underworld. Oceania: *Beckwith,
1940, 294; Polynesia: *Beckwith, 1940, 114;
Tuamotus: Stimson, n.d., 3/1241; Marquesas:
Christian, 1895, 190; Handy, 1930, 121; Tonga:
Beckwith, 1940, 178; Pukapuka: Beaglehole, 1938,
328.

*A300.1.1. Volcano-goddess Hawaii: ***Beckwith, 1940,
Chaps. XI, XII, XIII and passim; ***Emerson, 1915,
IX-240 passim; Fornander, 1916, IV, 104ff.;
V, 332, 506ff., 576f.; Green, 1923, 5ff., 19ff.,
55; Pukui, 1933, 167; Pukui-Curtis, n.d., 42f.;
Thrum, 1907, 37ff.; Westervelt, 1915, 270ff.;
Westervelt, 1943, 8ff.

A305. Demigod of underworld. Tuamotus: Stimson, n.d.,
Z-G. 13/221, Z-G. 13/249, Z-G. 13/317; Cooks:
Best, 1924, 152; Hawaii: Beckwith, 1940, 155 n.3.

A308. Warrior chieftain of underworld. Tuamotus:
Stimson, n.d., Z-G. 13/203.

A310. God of the world of the dead. Tuamotus: Stimson,
n.d., Z-G. 13/39; Mangareva: Caillot, 1914, 153f.;
Laval, 1938, 303; Hawaii: Westervelt, 1915, 85,
94ff., 98ff.; Tokelau: Macgregor, 1937, 61, 69;
Chatham Is.: Shand, 1894, 125; Futuna: Burrows,
1936, 104; Fijis: Fison, 1904, 160; Nukumanu:
Sarfert, 1931, 330; Ellice Is.: Grimble, 1952,
62 f.

A310.1. Goddess of world of the dead. Cooks: Gill, 1876, 3, 20, 27, 174, 228-229; Mangareva: Caillot, 1914, 154; Chatham Is.: Shand, 1894, 125; N.Z.: Dixon, 1916, 74.

A310.4. God of suicide. Hawaii: Beckwith, 1940, 177; Emerson, 1915, 214.

A311. Conductor of the dead. Mangareva: Hiroa, 1938, 101; Tahiti: Henry, 1928, 378; Hawaii: *Beckwith, 1940, 156-158; Nukumanu: Sarfert, 1931, 331; Ontong Java: Sarfert, 1931, 323.

A317. Demon god lies in wait for spirits descending to underworld. Tuamotus: Stimson, n.d., T-G. 3/18, T-G. 3/1001.

*A319. Musician god of the underworld (Tulikalo). Pukapuka: Beaglehole, 1938, 313.

A400--A499. Gods of the earth

A400. God of earth. Tonga: Reiter, 1907, 238; N.Z.: Best, 1924, 105.

A400.1. Goddess of earth. Tonga: Reiter, 1907, 238; Ontong Java: Sarfert, 1931, 326.

A401. Mother Earth. The earth is conceived of as the mother of all things. Tonga: Caillot, 1914, 250; N.Z.: Best, 1924, 86; Grey, 1855, 108; Ontong Java: Sarfert, 1931, 325, 413, 414.

A405. Nature gods. Hawaii: Beckwith, 1940, 2, Chap. I passim.

A410. Local gods. Cooks: Gill, 1876, 5.

A418. Deity of particular mountain. Hawaii: Westervelt, 1915, 88.

A419.1. Deity of particular forest. Hawaii: Beckwith, 1940, 17.

A419.3. Gods of seat braces on canoe. Hawaii: Beckwith, 1940, 16.

A420. God of water. Hawaii: Beckwith, 1940, 541.

A420.1. Water-goddess. Hawaii: McAllister, 1933, 157.

A421. Sea-god(s). Mangareva: Hiroa, 1938, 419;
Laval, 1938, 141; Easter I.: Métraux, 1940, 311;
Tuamotus: Stimson, n.d., Z-G. 13/441; Danielsson,
1952, 121; Caillot, 1914, 95-109; Marquesas:
Christian, 1895, 189; Societies: Luomala, 1949,
141; Henry, 1928, 122, 358f., 450, 452-453;
Beckwith, 1940, 360; Dixon, 1916, 39; Cooks:
Dixon, 1916, 39; Hawaii: Beckwith, 1940, 19, 61,
97; Emerson, 1915, 202; Fornander, 1916, IV, 162;
Green, 1926, 122; Pukui, 1943, 65; Pukui-Curtis,
n.d., 71; Pukapuka: Beaglehole, 313, 315; Tonga:
Gifford, 1924, 87; Reiter, 1907, 239; Samoa:
Powell-Pratt, 1891-93, 274; Niue: Loeb, 1926, 159;
Tokelau: Macgregor, 1937, 61; N.Z.: Best, 1924,
105; Best, 1925, 746, 772ff.; Cowan, 1930, I, 7;
Grey, 1855, 6; *Grace, 1907, 186, 188 n.9; White,
1887-90, I, 24, 40; II, 162; V, 43; Tikopia:
Firth, 1961, 55.

A421.1. Sea-goddess. Tuamotus: Stimson, n.d.,
Z-G. 13/441.

A421.1.1. Sea-queen and hand maidens entice lovers.
Tuamotus: Stimson, n.d., Z-G. 13/441.

*A422. Gods of the tides. Hawaii: Fornander, 1916, IV,
510 n. 4; V, 160, 364 n.5.

*A424. God of blow-hole in reef. Niue: Loeb, 1926, 166.

A430.1. Goddess of vegetation. Hawaii; Beckwith,
1932, 188 n.

A431. God of fertility. Mangareva: Hiroa, 1938, 27,
422; Tuamotus: Stimson, 1937, 5; Hawaii:
Beckwith, 1940, 13, 93, Chap. II passim; N.Z.:
Best, 1924, 105.

A431.1. Goddess of fertility. Hawaii: Beckwith, 1940,
185; Ontong Java: Sarfert, 1931, 326.

A431.1.2. Goddess of fertility of wild forest plants.
Hawaii: Beckwith, 1940, 289; N.Z.: Best, 1925,
746; Cowan, 1930, I, 7.

A431.1.3. Goddess causes famine. Hawaii: Beckwith,
1940, 289.

A432. God of agriculture. Marquesas: Christian, 1895, 189; Societies: Agostini, 1900, 89; Hawaii: Beckwith, 1940, 15, 20, 61, Chap. II passim; N.Z.: Best, 1925, 746, 770ff.; Cowan, 1930, I, 7; Dixon, 1916, 32; Grey, 1855, 3; White, 1887-90, III, 103.

A433. Gods or goddesses of special crops. Mangareva: Hiroa, 1938, 422 (tumeric); Marquesas: Christian, 1895, 190 (yam); Cooks: Clark, 1896, 140; N.Z.: Best, 1899, 95 (sweet potato), 96 (gourd); White, 1887-90, I, 20; III, 170; V, 5ff. (fern-root); Tikopia: Firth, 1961, 98 (yams); Rennell: Elbert-Monberg, 1964, No. 193 (yams); Ontong Java: Parkinson, 1898, 195 (taro).

A435. God of trees and forests. Hawaii: Ii, 1959, 44; Westervelt, 1915, 98, 111; Chatham Is.: Skinner, 1923, 57; N.Z.: Best, 1899, 95; Best, 1925, 746; Cowan, 1930, I, 7, 9ff.; Dixon, 1916, 32; Grey, 1855, 2; White, 1887-90, I, 74; Tikopia: Firth, 1940, 133; Firth, 1961, 55, 60, 62; Rotuma: Russell, 1942, 239; Bellona: Elbert-Monberg, 1964, Nos. 19a, 19b, 20.

*A435.3. God of coconut palm. Marquesas: Christian, 1895, 190; Pukapuka: Beaglehole, 1938, 310.

*A435.4. God of pandanus. Marquesas: Christian, 1895, 190.

*A435.5. God of breadfruit tree. Mangareva: Caillot, 1914, 154; Laval, 1938, 305; Hiroa, 1938, 422; Marquesas: Christian, 1895, 190.

A440. God of animals. Niue: Loeb, 1926, 111.

*A441.1.3. God of swine. Societies: Henry, 1928, 391.

A441.2. God of domestic fowls. Hawaii: Beckwith, 1940, 120.

A443.2. God of wild fowls. N.Z.: Best, 1925, 755.

A443.2.1. God of owls. Hawaii: Beckwith, 1940, 123.

*A433.2.2. God of plover. Niue: Loeb, 1926, 117.

*A433.2.3. God of boatswain birds. Niue: Loeb, 1926, 107.

*A443.2.4. God of pigeons. Niue: Loeb, 1926, 107.

29

A445. God of fish. Mangareva: Hiroa, 1938, 422;
Tahiti: Henry, 1928, 358; Cooks: Gill, 1876,
5, 93; Hawaii: Beckwith, 1940, 11, 60, 90;
Rice, 1923, 122; Fornander, 1918, VI, 174;
Thrum, 1907, 215ff., 226ff., 269ff.; Thrum,
1923, 200ff.; Pukapuka: Beaglehole, 1938,
310; Chatham Is.: Skinner, 1923, 57; N.Z.:
Best, 1925, 755, 772ff.; Best, 1927, 261; Grey,
1855, 3, 7; Ontong Java: Sarfert, 1931, 328.

A445.1. God of the squid. Hawaii: Beckwith, 1940, 60.

A445.2. God of eels. Samoa: Clark, 1896, 70; N.Z.:
Clark, 1896, 163.

A446. God of reptiles. N.Z.: Grey, 1855, 7; Rennell:
Elbert-Monberg, 1964, No. 193.

A446.1. God of lizards. N.Z.: Clark, 1896, 91.

A446.1.1. God whose shadow on earth is a lizard.
Tahiti: Beckwith, 1940, 360.

A446.2. God of the cutworm. Hawaii: Beckwith, 1940,
135.

*A446.3. God of salamanders. Societies: Henry, 1928,
384, 391.

A451. Artisan-god. Tahiti: Henry, 1928, 438.

A451.2. God of carpenters. Marquesas: Christian, 1895,
190; Societies: Agostini, 1900, 90; Tonga:
Beckwith, 1940, 317.

A451.2.1. God as canoe builder. Hawaii: Beckwith, 1940,
15; Pukui, 1933, 147; Thrum, 1907, 216; Westervelt
1915, 37, 100, 233.

A454. God of healing. Societies: Agostini, 1900, 89;
Henry, 1928, 357, 391; Hawaii: Beckwith, 1940,
115; Westervelt, 1915, 94ff.; N.Z.: White,
1887-90, I, 126.

A455. God of fishing. Marquesas: Christian, 1895,
190; Societies: Agostini, 1900, 89; Hawaii:
Beckwith, 1940, 15; Fornander, 1918, VI, 172;
Luomala, 1951, 30; Ontong Java: Parkinson, 1898,
196.

A456. God of sailors. Societies: Agostini, 1900, 89;
Rarotonga: Te Ariki, 1920, 120.

A457. God of thieves. Easter I.: Métraux, 1940,
310; Marquesas: Christian, 1895, 189; Societies:
Agostini, 1900, 88; Henry, 1928, 391; Beckwith,
1940, 447; Cooks: Beckwith, 1940, 447; Gill,
1876, 126; N.Z.: Best, 1924, 107; Beckwith, 1940,
447.

*A459.2. Goddess of ovens and cooking. Rennell:
Elbert-Monberg, 1964, No. 181.

A461. God of wisdom. N.Z.: Best, 1924, 65.

A461.1. Goddess of wisdom. Tahiti: Henry, 1928, 85.

A462. God of beauty. Societies: Henry, 1928, 393.

A465.1. God of poetry. Marquesas: Christian, 1895,
190.

A465.2. God of music. Mangareva: Hiroa, 1938, 424.

A465.4. God(s) of the dance. Marquesas: Christian,
1895, 190; Societies: Agostini, 1900, 89;
Hawaii: Beckwith, 1940, 16; Westervelt, 1915, 29,
125.

A465.5.1. God of tattooing. Tahiti: Henry, 1928, 234.

*A467.0.1. God of pleasures. Mangareva: Caillot,
1914, 154.

A467.1. God (angel) of peace. Societies: Henry, 1928,
384; Niue: Loeb, 1926, 160; N.Z.: Cowan, 1930,
I, 7; White, 1887-90, IV, 164.

*A473.0.0.1. Hunger-god. Niue: Loeb, 1926, 163.

A475. God of love. Marquesas: Christian, 1895, 190;
Hawaii: Fornander, 1918, V, 338; Green, 1923,
34, 37ff.; N.Z.: Hongi, 1920, 27.

A475.0.2. Marriage-god. Marquesas: Christian, 1895,
190.

A475.1. Goddess of love. Hawaii: Beckwith, 1940,
185 f.

A477. God (goddess) of childbirth. Mangareva: Hiroa,
101, 426; Caillot, 1914, 150, 154; Marquesas:
Christian, 1895, 190; Hawaii: Beckwith, 1940,
285.

A478. God of disease. Chatham Is.: Skinner, 1923, 55; N.Z.: Best, 1924, 105.

*A478.7. God of invalids. N.Z.: White, 1887-90, I, 40.

A482.1. Goddess (god) of ill-luck. Niue: Loeb, 1926, 161.

*A482.1.0.1. Gods of misfortune. Mangareva: Hiroa, 1938, 34.

A485. God of war. Mangareva: Caillot, 1914, 154; Hiroa, 1938, 422; Marquesas: Christian, 1895, 190; Steinen, 1934-35, 209; Handy, 1930, 110; Tahiti: Henry, 1928, 120; Hawaii: Beckwith, 1932, 18; Beckwith, 1940, 15; Fornander, 1918, V, 78 n. 3; Green, 1926, 120; Samoa: Krämer, 1902, I, 451; *Stair, 1896, 37, 40-41; Powell-Pratt,1892, 106; Stuebel, 1896, 76;; Niue: Smith, 1902, 195; Loeb, 1926, 153, 160; Chatham Is.: Skinner, 1923, 57; N.Z.: Best, 1899, 95; Best, 1925, 746, 770, 854, 904, 1044ff., 1052; Clark, 1896, 14; Cowan, 1930, I, 7, 8, 89; Hongi, 1920, 26; White, 1887-90, I, 20, 41, 104, 130; III, 229; IV, 145, 164; Lau Is.: Hocart, 1929, 196.

*A485.1.1. Siamese-twin goddesses of war and tatooing. Samoa: Fraser, 1896, 171.

A486. The Furies. Goddesses of vengeance. Hawaii: Beckwith, 1940, 115.

A487. God of death. Tuamotus: Henry, 1928, 349; N.Z.: Clark, 1896, 8,135; Hongi, 1920, 26.

A487.1. Goddess of death. Cooks: Gill, 1876, 160 n. 1 173; N.Z.: Best, 1899, 96.

*A487.2. Poison-god. Hawaii: Beckwith, 1932, 18; Ii, 1959, 124; Westervelt, 1915, 98ff., 108ff.

*A489.5. God of feasts (and kava drinking). Marquesas: Christian, 1895, 190.

*A489.6. God of famines. Mangareva: Hiroa, 1938, 422.

A491. God of travelers. Tahiti: Beckwith, 1940, 221.

A493. God of fire. Marquesas: Steinen, 1934-35, 192; Tahiti: Henry, 1928, 130, 241; Cooks: Henry, 1928, 346; Gill, 1876, 51; Hawaii: Beckwith, 1940, 170; N.Z.: Clark, 1896, 41.

A493.1. Goddess of fire. Oceanic: *Beckwith, 1940, 167ff.; Tahiti: Henry, 1928, 359; Hawaii: Smith, 1966, 23; Westervelt, 1943, 8ff.; N.Z.: Best, 1899, 96; Best, 1925, 391.

A496. God of the seasons. N.Z.: Best, 1925, 778f.; Best, 1940, 105.

A497. Echo. Societies: Agostini, 1900, 89.

A499.3. God of stones. Hawaii: Beckwith, 1940, 88; Rotuma: *Churchward, 1938-39, 469.

A499.4. God of sorcery. Societies: Agostini, 1900, 89; Hawaii: Beckwith, 1940, 15, 29f., 108.

A499.4.1. Goddess of sorcery. Hawaii: Beckwith, 1940, 114.

A499.6. God of poison (cf. *A487.2.). Hawaii: Beckwith, 1940, 112.

*A499.8. God of harvest. N.Z.: *Hongi, 1920, 26.

*A499.10. Reef-god. Niue: Loeb, 1926, 161.

*A499.11. God of kite-flying. Cooks: Gill, 1876, 123.

A500--A599. Demigods and culture heroes

A500.Demigods and culture heroes. Hawaii: *Beckwith, 1940, 60; Tikopia: Firth, 1961, 95; Ontong Java: Parkinson, 1898, 194f.

A504. Male virgin demigod. Tuamotus: Stimson, n.d., Z-G. 3/1301.

A506. Half-spirit, half-man. Samoa: Beckwith, 1940, 368.

A510.2. Culture hero reborn. Marquesas: Steinen, 1933-34, 29, 31; 1934-35, 196; Handy, 1930, 104ff.

*A510.3. Culture hero comes from upperworld. N.Z.: White, 1887-90, II, 79.

A511.1. Birth of culture hero. Hawaii: Beckwith, 1940, 227.

A511.1.1. Culture hero snatched from mother's side. Tonga: Brown, 1916, 426.

*A511.1.1.0.1. Culture hero (Maui) born from mother's navel. Mangareva: Luomala, 1949, 151.

A511.1.2. Culture hero speaks before birth. Hawaii: Beckwith, 1940, 231.

*A511.1.2.3. Culture hero leaves womb before birth in order to play tricks. Hawaii: Beckwith, 1940, 230-231; Thrum, 1921, 104.

A511.1.3.3. Immaculate conception of culture hero. Hawaii: Beckwith, 1940, 227.

A511.1.4.1. Origin of culture hero from bursting stone. Tonga, Tokelau: Dixon, 1916, 111.

*A511.1.4.1.1. Culture hero born from clod. Tuamotus: Henry,1928, 520; Beckwith, 1940, 470; Tahiti: Henry, 1928, 580.

A511.1.4.2. Hero formed by god out of mother's apron. N.Z.: Beckwith, 1940, 231.

*A511.1.4.2.1. Magic birth: apron thrown in ocean becomes infant deity. N.Z.: Grey, 1855, 116.

*A511.1.4.5. Hero does not breathe during first months of his life. Hawaii: Thrum, 1907, 74.

A511.1.6. Culture hero posthumous child. Tonga: Gifford, 1924, 124.

*A511.1.7.1. Double birth of culture hero. Marquesas: Steinen, 1933-34, 29, 31.

A511.1.9. Culture hero born from egg. Tuamotus: Stimson, n.d., Z-G. 13/24; Marquesas: Steinen, 1934-35, 196; Beckwith, 1940, 470; Handy, 1930, 125; Handy, 1943, 24; Hawaii: Beckwith, 1940, 227ff., 423.

*A511.1.9.1. Double birth of culture hero: first as egg, then as child. Marquesas: Steinen, 1934-35, 196.

*A511.1.12. Hero born as eel is raised in a trough. Marquesas: Steinen, 1933-34, 29, 31.

34

A511.2.1. Abandonment of culture hero at birth.
Tuamotus: Henry, 1928, 520; Marquesas: Steinen,
1934-35, 196; Societies: Luomala, 1949, 144;
Henry, 1928, 408; Cooks: Ariki, 1899, 69-70;
Hawaii: Thrum, 1907, 75; N.Z. *Best, 1927, 15 n.,
16 n.; Best, 1924, 142; Clark, 1896, 29; Grey,
1855, 18; Luomala, 1949, 27, 30-32.

*A511.2.2.3. Culture hero raised by bird. N.Z.:
Luomala, 1949, 55; Rotuma: Russell, 1942, 243.

*A511.2.2.4. Hero nourished on air. Marquesas: Beckwith,
1940, 470.

*A511.2.2.5. Hero nourished on stones. Tuamotus:
Beckwith, 1940, 471; Henry, 1928, 520.

*A511.2.2.6. Foetus of hero formed and fashioned by
seaweed. N.Z.: Grey, 1855, 18.

*A511.2.3.1. Culture hero rescued from death at birth
by supernaturals and raised by them. N.Z.: White,
1887-90, II, 63, 71, 81.

*A511.2.4. Growing hero fed nothing except bananas.
Hawaii: Thrum, 1923, 209.

*A511.2.5. Hero raised in sacred temple. Hawaii: Thrum,
1923, 209.

*A511.2.6. Culture hero raised in deeps of the ocean.
N.Z.: Best, 1925, 936.

A511.3.1. Culture hero raised in seclusion. Tuamotus:
Stimson, n.d., Z-G. 13/24; Societies: Henry, 1928,
408; Hawaii: Beckwith, 1940, 507, 523, 526;
Thrum, 1907, 43; Pukapuka: Beaglehole, 1938, 406;
Nukumanu: Sarfert, 1931, 451.

A511.3.2. Culture hero reared (educated) by extraordinary
(supernatural) personages. Hawaii: Beckwith, 1940,
414; N.Z.: Best, 1924, 142; Rotuma: Churchward,
1937-38, 489-490.

*A511.3.3. Culture hero raises self. Tuamotus: Henry,
1928, 520; Beckwith, 1940, 471.

A511.4.1. Miraculous growth of culture hero. Societies:
Henry, 1928, 537; Williams, 1895, 263; Hawaii:
Beckwith, 1940, 480, 481; Dickey, 1917, 16f.;
Rice, 1923, 27; Tokelau: Macgregor, 1937, 87;
Ellice Is.:David, 1899, 108.

*A511.4.2. Culture hero speaks at birth. Marquesas:
Steinen, 1934-35, 196; Societies: Williams,
1895, 261.

A512.1. Culture hero's grandmother. N.Z.: Luomala,
1949, 54.

*A512.1.1. Culture hero's grandfather. Marquesas:
Handy, 1943, 24.

A512.3. Culture hero as son of god. Cooks: Luomala,
1949, 174; Hawaii: Beckwith, 1940, 13; Samoa:
Fraser, 1897, 34.

A512.4. Sun as father of culture hero. Ellice Is.:
Kennedy, 1931, 156.

A513.1. Demigods descend from heaven. N.Z.: Clark,
1896, 30.

A515.1. Culture hero brothers. Pukapuka: Beaglehole,
1938, 329; Nukumanu: Sarfert, 1931, 410.

A515.1.1. Twin culture heroes. Tonga: Gifford, 1924,
20.

A520.1. Gods as culture heroes. Hawaii: Beckwith,
1940, 16, Chap. 2 passim.

A521. Culture hero as dupe or trickster. Hawaii:
Beckwith, 1940, 20.

*A521.1. Deified ancestor (a corpse) as culture hero.
Mangareva: Hiroa, 1938, 28.

A522.2. Bird as culture hero. Tuamotus: Stimson, n.d.,
Z-G. 13/24; Samoa: Krämer, 1902, I, 405.

*A522.3.3. Culture hero born as lizard. Ellice Is.:
Kennedy, 1931, 190.

A523. Giant as culture hero. Marquesas: Handy, 1930,
104-107; Ellice Is.: David, 1899, 110.

*A523.2. Giant club of culture hero. Ellice Is.: David,
1899, 110.

A525. Good and bad culture heroes. Polynesia: Dixon,
1916, 122 n. 1.

A525.2. Culture hero (god) slays his grandfather.
Tuamotus: Henry, 1928, 350.

A526.5.1. Culture hero with different colored eyes, one brown, one green. N.Z.: Clark, 1896, 30.

A526.9. Lightning flashes from armpits of hero. N.Z.: Beckwith, 1940, 250; Best, 1925, 872, 880,917.

*A526.9.1. Body of deity glows like fire. Tikopia: Firth, 1930-31, I, 26.

*A526.10. Culture hero (demigod) has one eye like that of an eel and the other like a greenstone. N.Z.: White, 1887-90, II, 90.

*A526.11. Culture hero without body joints. Bellona: Elbert-Monberg, 1964, No. 32.

*A526.12. Demigods with hair like a rat. Hawaii: Dickey, 1917, 32.

*A526.13. Deformed (incomplete) culture hero. Rotuma: Russell, 1942, 240.

A527.1. Culture hero precocious. Hawaii: Thrum, 1923, 57ff.; Lau Is.: St. Johnston, 1918, 109.

*A527.3.2. Culture hero can fly. N.Z.: White, 1887-90, II, 80.

*A527.5. Hero given supernatural powers. Hawaii: Thrum, 1923, 171.

A530. Culture hero establishes law and order. Polynesia: *Luomala, 1949, 28-29; Mangareva: Caillot, 1914, 174.

A531. Culture hero overcomes monsters. Ellice Is.: David, 1899, 110.

A531.1.1. Culture hero banishes demons. Easter I.: Métraux, 1940, 370.

A531.4.1. Demigod conquers great octopus. Hawaii: Beckwith, 1940, 370.

*A537.1. Hero digs passage across island. Marquesas: Steinen, 1933-34, 29, 32.

A541. Culture hero teaches arts and crafts. Mangareva: Caillot, 1914, 174; Hawaii: Beckwith, 1940, 115; Dickey, 1917, 25; Samoa: Stuebel, 1896, 64ff.; N.Z.: *Best, 1899, 5, 15 n., 16 n.; Best, 1925, 775; Pukapuka: Beaglehole, 1938, 329; Fijis:

Fison, 1904, 17; Rotuma: Russell, 1942, 241;
Tikopia: Firth, 1961, 27, 96; Ontong Java:
Parkinson, 1898, 195.

A541.2. Culture hero as god of agriculture. Samoa:
Stuebel, 1896, 142, 143.

A545. Culture hero establishes customs. Tikopia:
Firth, 1961, 96.

A560. Culture hero's (demigod's) departure. Mangareva:
Caillot, 1914, 175f.; Hawaii: Beckwith, 1940,
421; Niue: Loeb, 1926, 150.

*A565.1. Culture hero dies attempting to win immortality
for mankind. Tuamotus: Stimson, 1934, 47; N.Z.:
Best, 1925, 946f.; Cowan, 1930, I, 17f.; White,
1887-90, II, 70, 78, 80, 91, 106f., 109, 112, 114f.
117.

     A1335. Origin of death.

*A565.2. Culture hero killed by sorcery. N.Z.: Best,
1925, 946.

*A565.3. Culture hero killed in fight with giant mussel.
Marquesas: Steinen, 1934-35, 200.

A566.2. Culture hero ascends to heaven (guided by
blind ancestress). N.Z.: Beckwith, 1940, 249;
Tikopia: Firth, 1961, 103; Rennell: Birket-Smith
1956, 23.

*A567.1. Hero departs to underworld. Tubuai: Aitken,
1930, 103.

A592.1. Demigod and witch woman of upper world have
son. Tuamotus: Stimson, n.d., Z-G. 13/249.

A600--A899. COSMOGONY AND COSMOLOGY

A600--A699. The universe

A600--A649. Creation of the universe

A600. Creation of the universe. Tuamotus: Seurat,
1905, 486; Tahiti: Henry, 1929, 336ff.; Hawaii:
Beckwith, 1940, 43ff.

A601. Universe created in specified time and order.
Hawaii: Beckwith, 1940, 45.

A601.1. Universe created in five periods of time.
Hawaii: Beckwith, 1940, 44.

A601.2. Universe created in six days. Hawaii: Beckwith,
1940, 45.

A605. Primeval chaos. Marquesas: *Dixon, 1916,
10 n. 13; Tahiti: Henry, 1928, 336, 340; Hawaii:
Beckwith, 1940, 42; N.Z.: Best, 1899, 94; Best,
1925, 742; Dixon, 1916, 6ff.

A605.1. Primeval darkness. Societies: Henry, 1928,
403; Hawaii: Beckwith, 1932, 8, 174; Beckwith,
1940, 312; Fornander, 1918, VI, 335; Thrum, 1907,
15; Chatham Is.: Shand, 1894, 121; Travers, 1877,
26; N.Z.: Best, 1924, 94; Cowan, 1930, I, 3;
White, 1887-90, I, 18, 151; Rennell: Birket-Smith,
1956, 22.

A610. Creation of universe by creator. The creator is
existing before all things. Societies: Dixon,
1916, 11, n. 18; 12, n. 19; Luomala, 1949, 141;
Marquesas: *Dixon, 1916, 11, n. 14; Hawaii:
Beckwith, 1940, 42; Samoa: Fraser, 1892, 175;
Chatham Is.: Shand, 1894, 127-128; N.Z.: Best,
1924, 86; Dixon, 1916, 11, n. 16, 17; 13 n. 20.

A610.2. Creation of heaven, earth, and hell. Hawaii:
Beckwith, 1940, 42.

A611. Fiat creation. Universe is created at command of
creator. Tahiti: Henry, 1928, 338; Hawaii:
Beckwith, 1932, 16; Samoa: Fraser, 1892, 175ff.;
Powell-Pratt, 1891, 209, 268.

*A611.0.2. God creates by chanting. N.Z.: White, 1887-90, I, 18f.

A612.1. World-soul. The universe a manifestation of th creator. Societies: Dixon, 1916, 12 n. 19.

A615. Universe as offspring of creator. Societies: Agostini, 1900, 82; N.Z.: Dixon, 1916, 8 n. 9.

A615.1. Universe from creator's masturbation with water with stone, and with earth. Easter I.: Métraux, 1940, 314.

A615.2. Universe from copulation of various objects to produce others. Easter I.: Metraux, 1940, 320f.; N.Z.: Best, 1899, 114; Best, 1905, 207.

A617. Creation of universe from clam-shell on primeval water by creator. Tahiti: Henry, 1928, 337.

*A617.0.1. Creator creates cosmos from rock upon which he stands. Samoa: Fraser, 1892, 175.

A617.2. Creation of earth from calabash. Hawaii: Beckwith, 1940, 304f.; Westervelt, 1915, 17, 70f.

*A617.3. Creator makes the universe from a large rock. Samoa: Powell-Pratt, 1892, 268.

*A617.4. Creation by god's stamping his feet. Niue: Guppy, 1890, 48; Thomson, 1902, 86.

A620. Spontaneous creation of universe. Marquesas: *Dixon, 1916, 10 n. 13; Tahiti: Henry, 1928, 343; N.Z.: *Dixon, 1916, 6ff.

A620.1. Spontaneous creation -- evolutionary type. From primeval chaos gradually arise worlds and life Hawaii: Beckwith, 1940, 3; *Dixon, 1916, 15 n. 25 26; N.Z.: White, 1887-90,I, 18f., 49f., 53f.

*A620.3. Creation occurs during sequence of battles between forces and objects (octopi, cliffs, fires and the like). Samoa: Bulow, 1899, 60ff.

A625. World parents: sky-father and earth-mother as parents of the universe. The sky-father descends upon the earth-mother and begets the world. Tuamotus: Danielsson, 1952, 121; Marquesas: Christian, 1895, 187; Societies: Agostini, 1900, 88; Henry, 1928, 337f.; Cooks: Dixon, 1916, 14 n. 21; Tongareva: Buck, 1932, 85; Niue:

Thomson, 1902, 84; Chatham Is.: Dixon, 1916,
10 n. 12; Shand, 1894, 121; Skinner, 1923, 57;
Travers, 1876, 26; N.Z. Best, 1924, 76, 86, 94;
Best, 1925, 673, 744ff.; Cowan, 1930, I, 3ff.;
Dixon, 1916, 7 n. 3, 8 n. 7, 9 n. 10, 31; Grey,
1855, 1; White, 1887-90, I, 47, 137f.; Wohlers,
1875, 5.

A625.2. Raising of the sky. Originally the sky is near
the earth (usually because of the conjunction of
the sky-father and earth-mother). It is raised to
its present place. Polynesia: ***Dixon, 1916,
31, 35, 50f., and notes; Mangareva: Luomala,
1949, 150; Hiroa, 1938, 422; Laval, 1938, 297;
Tuamotus: Buck, 1938a, 188; Danielsson, 1952,
121; Caillot, 1914, 8; Henry, 1928, 347; Luomala,
1949, 97; Tahiti: Henry, 1928, 410-411, 459;
Luomala, 1949, 144; Cooks: Beaglehole, 1938,
315, 375; Luomala, 1949, 155, 170, 175; Pakoti,
1895, 66; Gill, 1876, 59; Ariki, 1899, 64, 71;
Hawaii: Fornander, 1918, VI, 336; Tonga: Gifford,
1924, 18, 23; Caillot, 1914, 286f.; Collocott,
1921, 48f.; Reiter, 1917-18, 1041; Samoa: *Paul
Hambruch, Nauru, 2 vols. (Hamburg, 1914-15), 280;
Brown, 1915, 175; Powell-Pratt, 1891, 214ff.;
214 n. 26; Powell-Pratt, 1892, 269f.; Niue:
Loeb, 1926, 157, 204, 211; Smith, 1903, 98, 197;
Thomson, 1902, 85; Tokelaus: *Macgregor, 1937,
17, 166-167; Burrows, 1923, 153f.; Lister, 1892,
52; Chatham Is.: Shand, 1894, 121; Travers, 1877,
26; N.Z.: Best, 1899, 115; 1924, 96; 1925, 689,
745, 751; Cowan, 1930, I, 3f.; Clark, 1896, 13,
15, 171; Dixon, 1916, 31; Fornander, 1918, VI,
337; Grey, 1855, 2f.; White, 1887-90, I, 24, 25,
47f., 50, 52, 135, 138, 141, 152, 154f., 155, 161f.;
II, 64; Wohlers, 1875, 6f.; Uvea: Burrows,1937,
162; Ellice Is.: Roberts, 1958, 369; Tikopia:
Firth, 1961, 24; Bellona: Elbert-Monberg, 1964,
No. 10; Rennell: Elbert-Monberg, 1964, No. 11;
Ontong Java: Sarfert, 1931, 330; Nukumanu:
Sarfert, 1931, 437.

*A625.2.0.1. Heavens lifted by magic (chant). Tuamotus:
Henry, 1928, 351; Chatham Is.: Travers, 1877,
26.

A625.2.4. Deity clothes his father the sky after he has
separated him from earth. N.Z.: Clark, 1896, 16.

A625.2.5. After sky is lifted, plants and shrubs begin
to grow. N.Z.: Clark, 1896, 15.

*A625.2.6. Heavens once rested on leaves of plants. Cooks:

Pakoti, 1895, 66.

*A625.3. Sky stretched out. Tuamotus: Caillot, 1914, 8.

A631. Pre-existing world of gods above. Hawaii: Beckwith, 1940, 45; Samoa: Dixon, 1916, 18f.

A632. Succession of creations and cataclysms. Hawaii: Dixon, 1916, 15 n. 24.

A641. Cosmic egg. The universe brought forth from an egg. Societies: Dixon, 1916, 20; Henry, 1901, 51; Hawaii: Dixon, 1916, 20; Henry, 1928, 345; N.Z.: Dixon, 1916, 20.

A644. Universe from pre-existing rocks. Samoa: Dixon, 1916, 17.

A645. Creation of universe: genealogical type. A bege B, who begets C, etc. Finally the universe is brought forth in its present form. N.Z.: Best, 1899, 95.

A647. Universe from cosmic fowl. Hawaii: Beckwith, 1940, 217ff.

A650--A699. Nature of the universe

*A650.0.1. Succession of skies as now arranged was work of people. Tuamotus: Henry, 1928, 347; Tahiti: Henry, 1928, 417.

*A650.0.2. Universe like hollow of vast coconut shell. Cooks: *Gill, 1876, 1ff.

A651. Hierarchy of worlds. A series of worlds, one above the other. Cooks: *Gill, 1876, 1ff.; N.Z.: Dixon, 1916, 59; White, 1887-90, I, 20.

*A651.0.3. Three world systems. Tuamotus: Henry, 1928, 347; Rotuma: Chruchward, 1937-38, 489; Pukapuka: Beaglehole, 1938, 326.

A651.1. Series of upper worlds. N.Z.: Best, 1924, 88.

*A651.1.0.1. In lands in sky, day is eternal. Nukumanu: Sarfert, 1931, 331.

*A651.1.0.2.   Two heavens.   Niue: Loeb, 1926, 163;
Smith, 1903, 92.

A651.1.1.   Three heavens.   Tuamotus: *Paul Hambruch,
Nauru, 2 vols.   (Hamburg, 1914-15), 280;   Hawaii:
Beckwith, 1940, 42, 74;   Fornander, 1918, VI, 268;
Thrum, 1907, 15;   N.Z.:   Clark, 1896, 163ff.

A651.1.3.   Five heavens.   Mangareva: Laval, 1938, 304.

A651.1.4.   Seven heavens.   Societies: Agostini, 1900,
82.

A651.1.5.   Eight heavens.   Samoa: Beckwith, 1940, 210.

A651.1.6.   Nine heavens.   Societies: Henry, 1928, 458;
Samoa: *Fraser, 1892, 177;   Krämer, 1902, I, 123;
Powell-Pratt, 1892, 270;   Rose, 1959, 174;   Stair,
1896, 34.

*A651.1.6.2.   Nine lower heavens inhabited by albinos.
Nukumanu: Sarfert, 1931, 331.

A651.1.7.   Ten heavens.   Societies: Henry, 1928, 164,
343, 411;   Cooks: Gill, 1876, 18;   Tonga:
Gifford, 1924, 18;   Samoa: Stuebel, 1896, 143;
N.Z.:   Best, 1925, 806;   Clark, 1896, 186;   Cowan,
1930, I, 22;   Grey, 1855, 84;   White, 1887-90,
I, 83, 100f., 123, 135;   Wohlers, 1875, 8;   Paul
Hambruch, Nauru, 2 vols. (Hamburg, 1914-15), 280;
Nukumanu: Sarfert, 1931, 330 f.;   Tikopia: Firth,
1961, 46, 47;   Ontong Java: Sarfert, 193, 322 f.

*A651.1.7.1.   One of ten heavens is populated by albinos.
Ontong Java: Sarfert, 1931, 323, 325.

*A651.1.7.2.   The ten heavens are of azure stone.
Cooks: Gill, 1876, 21.

*A651.1.7.3.   Island paradise in tenth heaven: fruits,
tobacco, etc., grow abundantly without toil.
Nukumanu: Sarfert, 1931, 330.

*A651.1.7.4.   God measures distance between ten skies.
Societies: Henry, 1928, 417.

A651.1.8.   Series of upperworlds -- miscellaneous.
Tuamotus: Stimson, 1937, 24;   Tonga: Collocott,
1922, 157;   Chatham Is.:   Shand, 1898, 74, 76;
N.Z.:   Best, 1924, 66, 88;   Best, 1925, 916;   Grey,
1855, 83-84;   Nukumanu: Sarfert, 1931, 331.

*A651.1.8.2. Fourteen heavens. N.Z.: White, 1887-90, I, 65.

A652.1. Tree to heaven. Tonga: Beckwith, 1940, 482.

A655. World as egg. The two halves are heaven and eart Tuamotus: Henry, 1928, 347.

A661. Heaven. A blissful upper world. Cooks: Beckwith, 1940, 76.

A661.0.1. Gate of heaven. N.Z.: Best, 1924, 102.

*A664. Islands in upper world. Niue: Smith, 1904, 100; Nukumanu: Sarfert, 1931, 331.

*A664.1. Seas which surround islands in heavens are bounded by walls of clouds.

A665.0.1. God stabilizes the sky. Tahiti: Henry, 1928, 180, 413; Cooks: Pakoti, 1895, 66.

*A665.0.2. Gods who hold up heavens. Hawaii: Rice, 1923, 33.

A665.2.0.1. Pillars supporting sky. Tahiti: Henry, 1928, 342; Chatham Is.: Shand, 1894, 21.

A665.2.1. Four sky-columns. Four columns support the sky. N.Z.: Paul Hambruch, <u>Nauru</u>, 2 vols. (Hamburg 1914-15), 280.

A665.2.1.1. Four gods (beings) at world-quarters support the sky. Ontong Java: Sarfert, 1931, 322, 325, 413.

A665.2.1.3. Sky extended by means of pillars. Tahiti: Henry, 1928, 342.

A665.4. Tree supports sky. Tuamotus: Henry, 1928, 351; Societies: Luomala, 1949, 144, 400; Henry, 1928, 410; Cooks: Ariki, 1899, 64; Gill, 1876, 58; Nukumanu: Sarfert, 1931, 437.

A665.5. Sky held against earth by great octopus. Societies: Luomala, 1949, 143, 405; Henry, 1928, 338.

*A665.7. People along edge of earth support sky on their shoulders. Ellice Is.: Kennedy, 1931, 165.

*A665.8. Reeds prop up sky. Societies: Henry, 1928,

413; Samoa: Fraser, 1892, 176-177.

*A669.3. Inhabitants of upper world. Ontong Java: Sarfert, 1931, 437 f.

*A670.0.1. Island has a spiritual or essential counter-part in lower world. Cooks: Gill, 1876, 11.

*A670.0.3. Underworld is realm of harmony, light and peace. N.Z.: Best, 1924, 171.

A671. Hell. Lower world of torment. Cooks: Gill, 1876, 161; Futuna: Burrows, 1936, 104.

A671.1. Doorkeeper of hell. Tuamotus: Stimson, n.d., Z-G. 13/420; Marquesas: Christian, 1895, 190; Cooks: Gill, 1876, 51; N.Z.: Best, 1924, 97; Ellice Is.: Grimble, 1952, 60.

A671.2.4. The fires of hell. Cooks: Beckwith, 1940, 76.

A671.2.9. Scorpions in hell. Cooks: Gill, 1876, 173.

A675. Judges in the lower world. Tahiti: Henry, 1928, 378; Ellice Is.: Grimble, 1952, 60, 62 f.

A692. Islands of the blest. Hawaii: Beckwith, 1932, 46, 178; Samoa: Stair, 1896, 38.

A700--A799. The heavens

A700. Creation of the heavenly bodies. Tuamotus: *Henry, 1928, 348; Hawaii: Rice, 1923, 103.

A700.1. Heavely bodies from objects thrown into sky. Hawaii: Beckwith, 1940, 215.

*A700.3.1. Heavenly bodies born from mating of god and goddess. Tahiti: Henry, 1928, 359; N.Z.: Best, 1924, 97.

*A700.9. Heavenly bodies created when Po (night) and Ao (day) unite. Samoa: Fraser, 1892, 177 f.

A701. Creation of the sky. Hawaii: Beckwith, 1932, 174.

A701.1. Origin of sky from egg brought from primeval water. Tahiti: Henry, 1928, 339.

A702.7. Clouds as props of the sky. N.Z.: Clark, 1896, 18.

*A702.7.1. Four winds (or rays of the sun) as props of the sky. N.Z.: Best, 1924, 96.

*A702.7.2. A plant once held up the sky when all the large trees could not. Samoa: Brown, 1915, 175.

A702.8. Sky is black because once raised by means of dirty stick. Tonga: Gifford, 1924, 23.

*A702.10. God (Ru) supports heavens. Cooks: Gill, 1876, 51.

A705.1. Origin of clouds. N.Z.: Cowan, 1930, I, 7.

A705.1.1. Creator makes clouds from own vitals. Tahiti Henry, 1928, 339.

A705.1.2. Clouds as tapa beaten out by woman in moon. Cooks: Gill, 1876, 46; Samoa: Clark, 1896,120.

*A705.1.3. Clouds (children) spring from warmth and perspiration of Mother Earth. N.Z.: Best, 1924, 109.

*A705.1.4. Clouds are spirits of dead warriors. Cooks: Gill, 1876, 163.

A710--A739. The sun

A710. Creation of the sun. Societies: Luomala, 1949, 131; Hawaii: Beckwith, 1932, 28, 176; Thrum, 1907, 16; N.Z.: Best, 1925, 750; Luomala, 1949, 131.

A711. Sun as man who left earth. Man, usually of supernatural birth, ascends to sky and becomes the sun. Tuamotus: Stimson, n.d., T-G. 3/191.

A711.2. Sun as cannibal. Samoa: Krämer, 1902, I, 403f 410; Powell-Pratt, 1892, 123; N.Z.: Luomala, 194 132.

A153.8. Cannibal gods.

A714. Sun from object thrown into sky. Cooks: Dixon, 1916, 37.

A714.1. Sun and moon placed for eyes in the sky. Tuamotus: Seurat, 1905, 487; Cooks: Gill, 1876, 4; Societies, Cooks, Samoa, N.Z.: *Dixon, 1916, 37, and notes.

A714.7. Origin of sun: from right eye of god when he dies. N.Z., Ellice Is.: *Luomala, 1949, 131.

*A714.9. Origin of sun: from bisected child of a god. Cooks: Powell-Pratt, 1892, 76.

A715. Sun born of first couple. Samoa: Beckwith, 1940, 254; Stair, 1895, 48.

A715.1. Sun and moon born from a woman. N.Z.: White, 1887-90, II, 87.

*A715.7. Stars produced moon and sun. N.Z.: Best, 1924, 92.

*A715.8. Sun is child of night and day. Samoa: Powell-Pratt, 1892, 271.

*A715.9. Origin of the sun (begotten by a god). N.Z.: White, 1887-90, I, 50f.

*718.1.1. Sun and moon from halves of severed child. The half compressed into a ball and thrown into sky becomes sun; the other half, compressed and thrown into sky at night, becomes moon. Cooks: Gill, 1876, 44-45.

A718.2. Sun and moon as divine bodies of gods. Hawaii: Beckwith, 1940, 85.

A718.4. Sun from transformed maggots. N.Z.: Beckwith, 1940, 101.

*A718.5. Moon on stomach, sun on breast of sky-parent. N.Z.: Best, 1924, 111.

*A720.3. Sun and moon once joined together. N.Z.: Best, 1899, 104.

*A721.0.4. Sun hidden beneath the earth. Hawaii: Rice, 1923, 103.

A721.1. Theft of sun. N.Z.: Wohlers, 1875, 6.

*A721.1.1. Theft of rays of sun. Hawaii: Beckwith,

1940, 437.

*A721.6. Hero kills the sun. Marquesas: Steinen, 1934-35, 195.

*A721.7. Sun and moon put in calabash. Hawaii: Fornander, 1918, V, 268.

A722.3. Sun's night journey: in land of dead. Tonga: Collocott, 1922, 162.

*A722.3.1. Sun lights lower world during earth's night. Cooks: Gill, 1876, 155.

*A722.7.2. Place from which sun rises. Ontong Java: Sarfert, 1931, 440; Nukumanu: Sarfert, 1931, 439.

*A722.7.2.1. Sun emerges through hole in sky. Polynesia: Luomala, 1949, 132.

*A722.7.2.2. Sun rises from pit in east, departs through exit in west. Tuamotus: Stimson, 1937, 26; Luomala 1949, 132f.; Tahiti, Chatham Is.: Luomala, 1949, 132f.; N.Z.: Best, 1925, 798; White, 1887-90, II, 68, 77, 85; Wohlers, 1875, 14.

*A722.15. Sun is eaten every evening by a shark. Tokelaus: Burrows, 1923, 167.

*A726.4. Sun has ten rays. Societies: Henry, 1928, 430; Luomala, 1949, 132.

*A726.4.1. Sun's rays from wounds inflicted by culture hero. N.Z.: Grey, 1855, 56.

*A727.2. Sun god removed from sun and thrown to earth because he made earth excessively hot. Pukapuka: Beaglehole, 1938, 311.

A728. Sun caught in snare. General worldwide occurrences: ***Luomala, 1949, passim; Oceania: ***Luomala, 1949, passim; **Katharine Luomala, "Motif A728: Sun Caught in Snare and Certain Related Motifs," Fabula, VI (1964), 213-252; *Dixon, 1916, 44ff., n. 26; Mangareva: Caillot, 1914, 27, 155; Hiroa, 1938, 312; Laval, 1938, 297; *Luomala, 1949, 151, 154ff. ; Tuamotus: Danielsson, 1952, 122; Luomala, 1949, 97; Seurat, 1905, 438f.; Stimson, 1934, 9ff.; Stimson, 1937, 25, 26, 51; Marquesas: Steinen, 1934-34, 201; Societies: Agostini, 1900, 88; Baessler, 1905, 920f.; Dixon, 1916, 46; *Henry, 1928, 465 f. ; Luomala, 1949, 145; Cooks:

Cowan, 1930, I, 19; Hawaii: Forbes, 1881, 59;
Fornander, 1918, V, 538; VI, 272; Rice, 1923,
105; Smith, 1966, 6; Thrum, 1907, 31f.; Thrum,
1921, 104; Thrum, 1923, 200; Westervelt, 1915, 75;
Samoa: Dixon, 1916, 46; Krämer, 1902, I, 403, 404;
Sierich, 1902, 171; Chatham Is.: Shand, 1894, 122,
125; N.Z.: Best, 1925, 798; Cowan, 1930, I, 15;
Fornander, 1918, VI, 336; Grey, 1855, 36; White,
1887-90, II, 68, 69, 76, 77, 80, 85, 89, 90f.,
99f., 117; Wohlers, 1875, 13; Australs: Buck,
1938a, 167; Rennell: Elbert-Monberg, 1964, No. 40.

*A728.0.1. Hero braids ropes of sister's hair to snare
sun. Societies: Luomala, 1949, 145.

*A728.0.2. Ropes with which hero tied sun still seen at
dawn and dusk, when sun ascends or descends. Cooks:
Gill, 1876, 62.

A728.2. Sun-snarer: fast sun. The hero snares the sun's
legs with a rope as he is climbing up from the
underworld. He releases the sun upon the promise
to go more slowly. Tuamotus: Henry, 1928, 348;
Marquesas: Steinen, 1934-35, 195; Handy, 1930,
103; Hawaii: Beckwith, 1940, 10, 227, 230;
Cooks: Gill, 1876, 61; N.Z.: Best, 1899, 97;
Best, 1929, 13, 15 n., 16 n.

*A728.2.1. Hero fights with sun, breaks its leg (wings).
Marquesas: Steinen, 1934-35, 195, 201; Hawaii:
Henry, 1928, 468; N.Z.: Luomala, 1949, 132.

*A728.5. Hero snares sun: days made longer. Societies:
Henry, 1928, 430-431; N.Z.: Best, 1924, 143.

*A728.6. Sun refused to take correct position in universal
scheme. Tuamotus: Henry, 1928, 348.

A733.4. Beams of light are snares with which sun is
tied to earth (Cf. A728.). Societies: Henry, 1928,
432; N.Z.: Clark, 1896, 46.

*A734.2. Sun promises hero never to disappear again.
Hawaii: Rice, 1923, 104.

A735.1. Moon tied to sun so that when sun sinks, moon
is dragged up to light earth. N.Z.: Clark, 1896,
46.

A736. Sun as human being. Polynesia: Luomala, 1949,
132; Cooks: Gill, 1876, 61; Tokelaus: Burrows,
1923, 169; Nukumanu: Sarfert, 1931, 332.

A736.1.2. Sun-brother and moon-sister. Fijis: Fison, 1904, 36.

A736.1.4. Sun and moon married. Tahiti: Henry, 1928, 615, 618.

A736.2. Sun as a woman. Samoa: Sierich, 1902, 180.

A736.3. Sun and moon as brothers. N.Z.: Best, 1899, 104; 1924, 131; 1925, 804.

*A736.3.4. Moon and sun once accompanied each other. Reef Is.: O'Ferrall, 1904, 224.

A736.5. Children of the sun. Tonga: Gifford, 1924, 115; Samoa: Sierich, 1902, 180.

A736.7.1. Sun marries woman. N.Z.: Best, 1925, 787; Luomala, 1949, 132.

*A736.7.1.1. Sun has two wives. N.Z.: Best, 1899, 98.

A736.10. Human son of sun. Tonga: Gifford, 1924, 114.

*A736.12. Why the sun shines by day and the moon by night. Rennell: Elbert-Monberg, 1964, No. 27.

*A736.13. Why the sun is hot and the moon is cold. Rennell: Elbert-Monberg, 1964, No. 27.

A737.1. Eclipse caused by monster devouring sun or moon. Cooks: Gill, 1876, 47.

*A738.2.3. Sun is origin of all knowledge. N.Z.: Best, 1899, 100.

A740--A759. The moon

A740. Creation of the moon. Carl Hentze, Mythes et symboles lunaires (Antwerp, 1932). Hawaii: Beckwith, 1932, 28, 176; Thrum, 1907, 16; N.Z.: Best, 1925, 750; White, 1887-90, I, 50f.

A741. Moon from object (person) thrown into sky. Cooks: Dixon, 1916, 37; Hawaii: Beckwith, 1940, 215.

*A741.4. Origin of moon: from bisected child of a god. Rarotonga: Powell-Pratt, 1892, 76.

A743.1. Origin of moon from shell. N.Z.: Dixon, 1916, 250.

A745.1. Moon born from first couple. N.Z.: White, 1887-90, II, 87.

A751. Man in the moon. A man is said to be seen in the moon. Various explanations are given as to how he came to be there. N.Z.: *S. Percy Smith, 1896, 240-241; Dixon, 1916, 88; White, 1887-90, II, 22, 26; Wohlers, 1876, 118f.; Niue: Loeb, 1926, 178; Ellice Is.: Roberts, 1958, 369; Nukumanu: Sarfert, 1931, 323 n. 3, 332; Ontong Java: Parkinson, 1898, 197.

*A751.5.6. Origin of moon's spots: moon, tricked by sun, fell into marsh and was dirtied. Reef Is.: O'Ferrall, 1904, 224.

*A751.5.7. Origin of moon's spots: was held tightly by demigod. Hawaii: Fornander, 1916, IV, 86.

*A751.5.8. Why the moon is not as bright as the sun: it is clouded by the spirit of a dead god. Bellona: Elbert-Monberg, 1964, No. 25.

A751.8. Woman in the moon. (Hina). Tuamotus: Stimson, n.d., T-G. 3/1010; Seurat, 1905, 434, 487; Societies: Henry, 1928, 462-463; Hawaii: Beckwith, 1940, 242; Fornander, 1918, V, 658; Thrum, 1921, 106; Thrum, 1923, 71, 203; Samoa: Stuebel, 1896, 149; Cooks, Samoa, N.Z.: *Paul Hambruch Nauru, 2 vols. (Hamburg, 1914-15), 284-285; N.Z.: Best, 1899, 100; Best, 1924, 97, 108; Best, 1928b, 261; Ontong Java: Sarfert, 1931, 323.

A751.8.3. Goddess(es) in moon with calabash at side. Hawaii: Beckwith, 1940, 221; N.Z.: Best, 1924, 134; Best, 1925, 803; White, 1887-90, II, 21, 26.

A751.8.4. Woman in moon's oven seen on clear nights. Samoa: Clark, 1896, 120.

A751.8.5. Girl with tree carried to moon and is seen there. Samoa: Clark, 1896, 119.

A751.8.6. Goddess in moon beating tapa beneath tree. Societies: Henry, 1928, 408, 463; Tonga: Gifford, 1924, 181.

*A751.8.7. Goddess in moon watches over travelers at night. Societies: Henry, 1928, 408.

*A751.8.8. Woman (man) in moon takes mortal lover with her into moon. Cooks: Gill, 1876, 47.

*A751.8.9. Woman-in-the-moon's leg torn off as she ascends to the orb. Hawaii: Fornander, 1918, V, 658; Thrum, 1921, 106; Thrum, 1923, 71, 203.

*A751.8.10. Father and daughter dwell in moon. Tuamotus: Seurat, 1905, 435.

A751.9.2. Bag (shadow of basket) in the moon. Samoa: Clark, 1896, 89.

*A751.9.3. Markings on moon are ovens of god of meteors. N.Z.: Best, 1924, 133.

*A751.10.3. Hina as woman in moon. Polynesia: *Beckwith, 1940, 214ff.

A751.11. Other marks on the moon. Ontong Java: Sarfert, 1931, 324.

*A751.11.2. Woman throws a calabash in moon, where it remains. N.Z.: White, 1887-90, II, 22.

*A753.0.1. Moon is a female. N.Z.: White, 1887-90, II, 87, 90.

*A753.0.2. Moon is husband of all women. N.Z.: Best, 1905, 211.

A753.1.1. Moon abducts woman. Cooks: Gill, 1876, 45;N.Z *"Notes and Queries," JPS XI, 123; *Best, 1899, 100-101; Samoa: Clark, 1896, 118.

A753.1.2. Moon (as man) cohabits with woman. N.Z.: Beckwith,1940, 74.

A753.1.4. Moon married to mortal woman. N.Z.: Best, 1905, 211; Best, 1925, 774, 802ff.

*A753.2.1. Moon's halo is its house. Ontong Java: Sarfert, 1931, 323.

*A754.1.1. Moon emerges from a pit. N.Z.: White, 1887-90, IV, 32.

A755. Causes of moon's phases. Tahiti: Henry, 1901, 52; N.Z.: Best, 1924, 110; Dixon, 1916, 88.

A755.3. Moon's waning caused by her sickness. N.Z.: Clark, 1896, 182; White, 1887-90, I, 141, 142.

*A755.3.2. When moon dies, it bathes in water of life
and returns once more young and beautiful. N.Z.:
Best, 1899, 101; Best, 1924, 138; Best, 1925, 759,
804; Cowan, 1930, I, 7; White, 1887-90, II, 21,
26.

*A755.3.4. When moon disappears during each month, it
enters the sun. Best, 1899, 101; Best, 1925,
804f., 903.

*A755.4.3.1. Moon's phases caused by its being eaten.
Hawaii: Thrum, 1923, 204; N.Z.: White, 1887-90,
II, 21, 26; Wohlers, 1876, 119.

*A758.1. Hero (Maui) restores light to the moon. (Best's
interpretation). Cooks: Best, 1924, 146.

A759.3. Why the moon is pale. Cooks: Gill, 1876, 45.

A760--A789. The stars

A760. Creation and condition of the stars. Hawaii:
Beckwith, 1932, 176; Thrum, 1907, 16; N.Z.:
Editors, "The Origin of Stars," JPS XXX (1921)
259 ff.; Best, 1924, 92; Best, 1925, 750ff.;
Clark, 1896, 16; Cowan, 1930, I, 7; White,
1887-90, I, 25.

*A760.3. Origin of stars from shattered proto-star.
Cooks: Luomala, 1949, 135; Hiroa, 1938, 215;
Gill, 1876, 43.

A761. Ascent to stars. People or animals ascend to the
sky and become stars. Australs: Aitken, 1923,
293, 295; Mangareva, Tuamotus, Societies:
*Seurat, 1905, 487f.; Societies: Caillot, 1914,
114ff.; Hawaii: Henry, 1928, 345; Tonga:
Gifford, 1924, 20; Samoa: Stuebel, 1896, 62f.;
Tokelaus: Burrows, 1923, 172; N.Z.: Clark,
1896, 50; Rotuma: Russell, 1942, 244.

A761.6. Stars thought of as living beings. Marquesas:
Steinen, 1933-34, 373.

*A761.6.1. Government of stars (who act as men).
Kapingamarangi: Emory, 1949, 232.

*A761.6.2. Chief among stars. N.Z.: Best, 1899, 106;
Kapingamarangi: Emory, 1949, 232.

*A761.6.3. Stars once lived all together in house of
tapa. Marquesas: Steinen, 1933-34, 373.

*A761.6.4. Marriage between stars. N.Z.: Best, 1925,
813.

*A761.9. The stars are a goddess's fish. Hawaii:
Thrum, 1923, 204.

A762. Star descends as human being. Reef Is.:
O'Ferrall, 1904, 231.

*A762.1.1. Star-wife. Tuamotus: Stimson, n.d., T-G.
3/931.

A763. Stars from objects thrown into sky. Cooks:
Seurat, 1905, 487.

*A763.2.1. Stars and clouds placed aloft as adornment
of Sky Father. N.Z.: Cowan, 1930, I, 7; White,
1887-90, I, 25, 52, 138, 148f.; Wohlers, 1875, 7.

*A763.3. Stars once ornaments in house of goddess.
N.Z.: Best, 1899, 117.

*A763.4. Stars are ornaments on breast of Rangi, the
sky. N.Z.: Best, 1899, 117.

*A764.1.4. Stars are brothers of sun and moon. N.Z.:
Best, 1899, 104; 1925, 805.

*A764.5. Stars are a transformed eye. N.Z.: White,
1887-90, II, 88.

A766. Origin of constellations. Tongareva: Luomala,
1949, 135.

*A769.8. Stars twinkle because of curse. Tahiti:
Henry, 1901, 52.

A770. Origin of particular stars. Marquesas: Steinen,
1933-34, 194; Cooks: Gill, 1876, 40ff.; Hawaii:
Beckwith, 1932, 28; Tokelaus: Burrows, 1923,
171f.; Macgregor, 1937, 85.

A772. Origin of Orion. Tonga: Gifford, 1924, 100;
Rotuma: Churchward, 1937-38, 366, 482; Rennell:
Elbert-Monberg, 1964, Nos. 33, 34b; Bellona:
Elbert-Monberg, 1964, No. 34a.

A773. Origin of the Pleiades. Cooks: Gill, 1876, 43;
N.Z.: Clark, 1896, 106, 178; Rotuma: Churchward,

1937-38, 366.

*A774.1. Origin of Pole-star from person's eye. N.Z.:
White, 1887-90, II, 90.

A776.1. Origin of Vega (Alpha Lyrae). N.Z.: Beckwith,
1940, 101.

A777. Origin of constellation Scorpio. Societies:
Cuzent, 1923, 37ff.; Cooks: Clark, 1896, 81, 83;
Gill, 1876, 48, 74; Luomala, 1940, 135; Seurat,
1905, 487; N.Z.: Clark, 1896, 56.

A778. Origin of the Milky Way. Tuamotus: Seurat,
1905, 487f.; Societies: Henry, 1928, 404;
Hawaii: Beckwith, 1940, 74; Fornander, 1916, IV,
528; Cooks: *Luomala, 1949, 135; Ariki, 1899,
65 n.; N.Z.: Best, 1925, 751; *Luomala, 1949,
135; White, 1887-90, I, 138; Bellona : Elbert-
Monberg, 1964, No. 26; Nukumanu: Sarfert, 1931,
331.

A778.0.1. Origin of Magellanic Clouds. Tonga:
Gifford, 1924, 105, 109; N.Z.: White, 1887-90,
I, 52, 138, 149.

*A779.5. Origin of Canopus. N.Z.: Best, 1925, 751.

A780. The planets (comets, etc.). N.Z.: Best, 1925,
809ff.

*A781.0.1. Venus is right eye of sky-god. Societies:
Henry, 1928, 417.

A781.1. Origin of Morning Star. Samoa: Stuebel,
1896, 62f.; N.Z.: Clark, 1896, 50; White,
1887-90, II, 88.

A781.2. Origin of Evening Star. Tonga: Gifford,
1924, 110; N.Z.: Clark, 1896, 50; White, 1887-90,
II, 88.

*A788.0.1. Meteors are stars falling out of place
because they have been jostling one another. N.Z.:
Best, 1924, 110.

A788.4. Shooting stars are star-dung. Nukumanu:
Sarfert, 1931, 332.

*A790.2. Sun, moon, and Milky Way are guardians of
the stars. N.Z.: Best, 1924, 110.

A791. Origin of the rainbow. Hawaii: Beckwith, 1940, 234; Thrum, 1923, 260; N.Z.: Best, 1924, 159; Best, 1925, 871; Ontong Java: Parkinson, 1898, 197.

*A791.11. Rainbow is girdle of god. Cooks: Best, 1924, 161.

*A791.12. Rainbow appears as sign of god's approval. Pukapuka: Beaglehole, 1938, 310.

A797. Origin of colors at sunrise and sunset. Tuamotus: Stimson, n.d., T-G. 3/191; Stimson, 1937, 55; N.Z.: Best, 1925, 818; White, 1887-90, II, 126.

A800--A899. The earth

A810. Primeval water. In the beginning everything is covered with water. Polynesia (Societies, Tonga, Samoa, N.Z.): *Dixon, 1916, 8, n. 7, 18f., 20, 105, 157; Marquesas: Handy, 1930, 122; Hawaii: Thrum, 1907, 37; Tonga: Caillot, 1914, 248f.; Collocott, 1919, 236; Collocott, 1921b, 152; Collocott, 1924, 276; Reiter, 1907, 444; Samoa: Fraser, 1897, 21; Paul Hambruch Nauru, 2 vols. (Hamburg, 1914-15), 280; Krämer, 1902, I, 395f.; Lesson, 1876, 590; Nelson, 1925, 127; Powell-Pratt, 1891, 209; Stair, 1890, 35; N.Z.: Best, 1924, 86; Fijis: Fison, 1904, 139.

A811. Earth brought up from bottom of primeval water. Samoa: Fraser, 1897, 117.

A811.1. Earth originates from fish brought from bottom of ocean. Polynesia (Societies, Hawaii, Tonga, Samoa, N.Z.): *Dixon, 1916, 43f.

A955.8. Island fished up by demigod (hero).

A812.3. Creator sends crow, after creating her, to scout for earth-nucleus. Tonga: Reiter, 1907, 444 (god sends bird to discover land).

*A813.4. In beginning, only gods lived upon speck of land: all else was sea. Fijis: Fison, 1904, 139.

A814. Earth from object thrown on primeval water. Oceania: **Lessa, 1961, 275ff.

A814.1. Earth from stone thrown on primeval water.
Samoa, Tonga: *Dixon, 1916, 18, 163, n. 29-32;
Samoa: Stair, 1896, 35; Nelson, 1925, 127;
Tonga: Caillot, 1914, 250; Kapingamarangi:
Elbert, 1948, 122.

> A955.10. Islands from transformed object
> or person.

A814.2. Earth from sand strewn on primeval water.
Mangareva: Hiroa, 1938, 28; Rotuma: Churchward,
1937-38, 114; Burrows, 1923, 26; Ellice Is.:
Hedley, 1896, 43; Tikopia: Firth, 1961, 38, 39,
40; Nukumanu: Sarfert, 1931, 313, 382, 385.

A814.3. Earth from decayed matter on primeval water.
Tahiti: Henry, 1928, 439.

A814.4. Earth from tree grown in primeval water.
Fijis: Fison, 1904, 31.

A816. Earth rises from sea. Samoa: Fraser, 1897, 21.

A830. Creation of earth by creator. Marquesas: Handy,
1930, 122; Tahiti: Henry, 1928, 341; Samoa:
Fraser, 1892, 179-180.

A831.6. Earth from body of slain animal. Hawaii:
McAllister, 1833, 158.

*A833.1. God throws down refuse from body which
becomes island. Tonga: Reiter, 1907, 444.

A841. World-columns. Four (two, etc.) columns or
supports sustain the earth. Samoa: Stair, 1896,
56; N.Z.: Best, 1925, 743; Hongi, 1894, 156.

A844.1. Earth rests on turtle's back. Ellice Is.:
Grimble, 1952, 18.

A844.3. Earth supported by fish. Marquesas:
*Christian, 1895, 188, 199.

A849.1. Earth founded upon stone. Tuamotus: Henry,
1928, 351.

*A849.4. Ever-stationary spirits consitute the foundation
of the universe. Cooks: Gill, 1876, 3.

*A854. Flattening the land. Uvea: Burrows, 1937, 161;
Futuna: Burrows, 1936, 26; Fijis: Fison, 1904,
144-145.

A857.3.1. Roots created to hold land firm. Tahiti:
Henry, 1928, 342.

A900--A999. Topographical Features of the Earth

A901. Topographical features caused by experiences
of primitive hero (demigod, deity). Footprints
of the gods, thoroughfares of heroes, etc.
Cooks: Beaglehole, 1938, 377; Te Ariki, 1920, 2;
Hawaii: Beckwith, 1940, 18; N.Z.: Best, 1924,
165; Uvea: Burrows, 1937, 161; Futuna: Burrows,
1936, 26; Fijis: Fison, 1904, 144-145.

A901.2. Natural features because of combat of huge
rock columns with each other. Marquesas: Handy,
1930, 133.

A910--A949. Water features

A913. Origin of tides. N.Z.: White, 1887-90, I, 180.

*A913.0.1. God(s) responsible for tides. Niue: Loeb,
1926, 157; N.Z.: Best, 1924, 97.

A913.2. Tide caused by breathing of sea-monster.
N.Z.: *"Notes and Queries," JPS II (1893), 281
n. 47; Best, 1924, 156; Clark, 1896, 180;
Luomala, 1949, 116.

A913.3. Ebb-tide goes to great whirlpool. Tonga:
Gifford, 1924, 144.

*A913.5. Tides caused by god's curse of the sea. Tahiti:
Henry, 1901, 52.

*A913.6. When god paddles hands, ocean currents run.
Niue: Loeb, 1926, 125.

A920. Origin of the seas. Hawaii: Beckwith, 1932, 187;
Fornander, 1918, V, 368, 524; Thrum, 1907, 37;

Samoa: Stuebel, 1896, 59, 151; N.Z.: Best, 1899, 95; White, 1887-90, I,139f.

A920.1.0.1. Origin of particular lake. N.Z.: Best, 1925, 978ff.; Cowan, 1930, I, 42, 166; Rotuma: Hames, 1960, 31..

*A920.1.10.1. Pool of water made by water thrown there by angry god. Fijis: Hocart, 1929, 212.

*A920.1.17. Origin of blow-hole. Hawaii: Green, 1923, 11ff.; Rotuma: Churchward, 1937-38, 252.

A920.2. Origin of sea channels. Mangareva: Hiroa, 1938, 22; Societies: Henry, 1928, 452-453; Rarotonga: Te Ariki, 1920, 2; Tonga: Gifford, 1924, 87, 94; N.Z.: Best, 1925, 737-738; Nukumanu: Sarfert, 1931, 383.

*A920.3. Origin of bays, gulfs,and inlets: Ocean Maid constantly assailing Mother Earth. N.Z.: Best, 1924, 154.

A923. Ocean from creator's sweat. Societies, Tonga: *Paul Hambruch, 1914-15, 281.

A925.1. Origin of high sea waves. Tuamotus: Stimson, n.d., Z-G. 13/441.

A925.3. Origin of foul odor of sea. Tuamotus: Stimson, n.d., Z-G. 3/1110.

A925.4. Origin of fresh water welling up in sea. Hawaii: Beckwith,1940, 96.

A925.5. Origin of mournful sound of sea. Hawaii: Beckwith, 1940, 21.

A925.6. Origin of surf. Hawaii: Beckwith, 1940, 436.

A925.7. Origin of shining patches beneath sea. Tonga: Gifford, 1924, 200.

A928. Giant drinks up ocean. Hawaii: Beckwith, 1940, 437; Nukumanu: Sarfert, 1931, 380-381.

A930. Origin of streams. Mangareva: Hiroa, 1938, 22, 333; Hawaii: Dickey, 1917, 35.

A933. River from urine of goddess(man). Mangareva: Hiroa, 1938, 314; N.Z.: White, 1887-90, III, 96.

*A934.9.1. Origin of a river: supine giant backs up waters which break through a mountain. Hawaii: Dickey, 1917, 23.

*A939.1. Origin of river currents: two rivers race each other to see who can first reach their common ancestress, the ocean. N.Z.: Best, 1924, 210.

*A935.2. Origin of whirlpools: sacred sandstone thrown into sea at this place. Cooks: Gill, 1876, 165.

A941.0.1. Origin of particular spring (well). Hawaii: McAllister, 1933, 153; Thrum, 1907, 136f.; Westervelt, 1915, 26; Westervelt, 1943, 12f.; Tonga: Collocott, 1928, 7, 11; Samoa: Krämer, 1902, I, 354 n. 5; Rose, 1959, 45, 53; Ellice Is. Roberts, 1958, 407; Lau Is.: St. Johnston, 1918, 83.

A941.2. Springs originate from tears. Rotuma: Churchwa 1938-39, 124.

A941.3.2. Spring where god throws his staff or spear. Oceanic: *Beckwith, 1940, 64ff.

*A941.3.3. Spring where deity stamps. N.Z.: Grey, 1855 150.

A941.4.1. Spring breaks forth to commemorate place of death or burial. Hawaii: Beckwith, 1940, 188; Rice, 1923, 92.

A941.5. Spring breaks forth through power of saint.

A941.5.7. Origin of springs where deity dug. Hawaii: Beckwith, 1940, 212; Westervelt, 1915, 32.

*A941.5.9. Origin of springs: god steals water container and flies. His victims see him and throw a rock which hits the containers. The water which dripped out became springs. Fijis: Hocart, 1929, 213.

A941.7.2. Spring from roots of sacred tree when arrow is shot into it. Fijis: Beckwith, 1940, 317.

*A943. Origin of qualities of springs. Tokelaus: Burrows, 1923, 165.

*A943.1. Origin of spring water's bitter taste: sorcerer once slept there. Hawaii: Rice, 1923, 51.

*A945. Origin of a swamp (marsh). Hawaii: Emerson, 1915, 45; Fornander, 1918, V, 140; Samoa: Nelson, 1925, 132; Lau Is.: St. Johnston, 1918, 81.

*A946. Origin of lagoons. Rennell: Elbert-Monberg, 1964, No. 74.

A950--A999. Land features

A950. Origin of the land. Niue: Smith, 1903, 24; Ontong Java: Sarfert, 1931, 440.

*A951.1.1. Valley formed by movements of great reptile. N.Z.: Best, 1899, 114.

*A951.4. Contours of land (flattening) caused by deity. Cooks: Browne, 1897, 1; Samoa: Fraser, 1892, 179; Fraser, 1897, 71.

A952. Land rises out of sea. Tuamotus: Beckwith, 1940, 75; Societies: Henry, 1928, 399ff.; Hawaii: Fornander, 1916, IV, 6.

*A952.1. Island built up from bottom of the sea. Tokelaus: Macgregor, 1937, 80; Ontong Java: Parkinson, 1898, 194; Sarfert, 1931, 299.

A953. Land thrown down from heaven. Tonga: Gifford, 1924, 15; Reiter, 1933, 355.

A954. Land born from goddess. Hawaii: Beckwith, 1940, 302; Emory, 1924, 11; *Fornander, 1916, IV, 2ff.; Fornander, 1918, V, 540; Thrum, 1921, 102; Thrum, 1923, 198.

A955. Origin of islands. Samoa: Stuebel, 1896, 62.

A955.0.1. Islands created by order of deity. Marquesas: Handy, 1930, 122f.; Hawaii: Fornander, 1918, V, 518; Samoa: Nelson, 1925, 127; Powell-Pratt, 1892, 274; Stuebel, 1896, 151; Ontong Java: Parkinson, 1898, 194.

*A955.0.2. Island formed from scraps falling from god's workshop. Tonga: Collocott, 1919, 237; 1921b, 154; 1924, 277.

A955.2. Island created by shooting arrow. N.Z.: Best, 1927, 268.

*A955.2.1. Islet formed by hero's spear passing through mountain, breaking it off. Marquesas: Lagarde, 1933, 259.

A955.3. Origin of island's shape and position. Uvea: Burrows, 1937, 161; Futuna: Burrows, 1936, 26; Fijis: Fison, 1904, 144-145.

A955.3.2. Origin of island's position. Hawaii: Henry, 1928, 468.

A955.3.2.1. Hero moves islands into their present posit Societies: Henry, 1928, 559; Cooks: Browne, 1897 1; Samoa: Stuebel, 1896, 105; Chatham Is.: Te Ariki, 1920, 2; Uvea: Burrows, 1937, 162.

*A955.3.3. Waves spill over land first created; god the raises it a second time. Samoa: Stair, 1896, 35; Fraser, 1897, 23.

A955.8. Island fished-up by demigod (hero). Oceania: ***Beckwith, 1940, 226ff.; **Kirtley, 1955, s.v. Motif A955.8.; ***Lessa, 1961, 290ff.; ***Luōmala 1949, passim; Polynesia: *Smith, 1911a, 37 f.; Mangareva: Buck, 1938a, 167; Caillot, 1914, 155; Hiroa, 1938, 311; Luomala, 1949, 150; Tuamotus: Buck, 1938a, 204; Danielsson, 1952, 122; Caillot, 1914, 89; Stimson, n.d., Z-G. 13/52; Stimson, 1934, 23ff.; Stimson, 1937, 30ff.; Young, 1898, 109; Marquesas: Christian, 1895, 188 f.; Handy, 1930, 103; Lavondes, 1964, 46ff.; *Steinen, 1934-35, 194, 199 f.; Societies: Agostini, 1900, 88; Henry, 1928, 358, 466; Luomala, 1949, 136, 145; Cooks: Ariki, 1899, 72 f. Gill, 1876, 16, 48, 73; Guppy, 1890, 47; Seurat, 1905, 487; Hawaii: Beckwith, 1940, 61, 227, 308; Fornander, 1916, IV, 20ff.; Tonga: Beckwith, 1940, 369; Caillot, 1914, 253ff., 262; Collocott,1924, 279; Gifford, 1924, 15, 20; Guppy, 1890, 47; Reiter, 1933, 355; Samoa: Bülow, 1898, 81; Bülow, 1899, 59, 64; Nelson, 1925, 127; Stair, 1896, 35; Tokelau: Burrows, 1923, 153; *Macgrego 1937, 16, 166; Niue: Smith, 1902, 197; Thompson, 1902, 85f.; N.Z.: Best, 1924, 144; Best, 1925, 940f.; Best, 1929, 13, 15 n., 16 n.; Clark, 1896, 48ff.; Fornander, 1918, VI, 336; Grey, 1855, 43; Luomala, 1949, 45 f., 56; White, 1887-90, II, 70, 76, 80, 84, 88, 98, 100ff., 111f., 113, 114, 115, 117; White, 1887-90, III, 188; Wohlers, 1875, 13; Rotuma: Churchward, 1937-38, 492; Russell, 1942,

244; Futuna: Burrows, 1936, 26; Nukumanu: Sarfert, 1931, 386; Fijis: Fison, 1904, 143f.; Tikopia: Firth, 1961, 27, 33; Riesenfeld, 1950, 120f.; Reef Is.: *Elbert-Kirtley, 1966, 350ff.; Rennell: Birket-Smith, 1956, 22; Bradley, 1956, 334; Elbert-Monberg, 1964, Nos. 31a, 33, 36; Bellona: Elbert-Monberg, 1964, No. 39; Ontong Java: Parkinson, 1898, 194.

*A955.8.0.1. Islands fished up from underworld. Tahiti, Tokelau: Luomala, 1949, 119.

*A955.8.1. Bait used by hero to fish up islands. Mangareva: Hiroa, 1938, 311; *Luomala, 1949, 150; Cooks: Gill, 1876, 48; N.Z.: Best, 1924, 144; Grey, 1855, 42.

*A955.8.1.1. Hero fishes up island which is inhabited. N.Z.: White, 1887-90, II, 76, 88, 114f.; Wohlers, 1875, 13; Tikopia: Firth, 1961, 34.

*A955.8.2. Hero raises island by stamping upon it. Niue: Guppy, 1890, 48.

A955.9. Goddess gives birth to islands. Hawaii: Buck, 1938a, 241; Tonga: Gifford, 1924, 102.

A955.10. Islands from transformed object or person. Mangareva: Hiroa, 1938, 22; Marquesas: Handy, 1930, 44; Societies: Henry, 1928, 437, 442f., 558; Hawaii: Beckwith, 1940, 347; Fornander, 1916, IV, 8; Fornander, 1918, V, 534; Fornander, 1918, VI, 344;; Smith, 1966, 11; Tonga: Gifford, 1924, 24, 68, 179; Samoa: Krämer, 1902, I, 396ff.; Nelson, 1925, 127; N.Z.: Cowan, 1930, I, 14; Luomala, 1949, 136; Bellona: Elbert-Monberg, 1964, No. 10; Ontong Java: Parkinson, 1898, 194; Kapingamarangi: Elbert, 1949, 243.

A955.11. Islands originally form continent (larger island), later separated. Easter I.: Métraux, 1940, 389; Mangareva: Hiroa, 1938, 25; Laval, 1938, 12; Tuamotus: Seurat, 1905, 435; Stimson, 1934, 28; Marquesas: Handy, 1930, 112; Societies: Agostini, 1900, 88; Beckwith, 1940, 468; Cooks: Ariki, 1899, 74; Gill, 1876, 73f.; Guppy, 1890, 47; Hawaii: Beckwith, 1940, 216f., 230, 328; Fornander, 1916, IV, 20; Fornander, 1918, V, 520; Tonga: Gifford, 1924, 81; Lau Is.: St. Johnston, 1918, 120; Rotuma: Churchward, 1937-38, 115; Tikopia: Firth, 1961, 29; Reef Is.: O'Ferrall, 1904, 228.

A955.12. Old woman as guardian of floating islands of the gods. Hawaii: Beckwith, 1940, 68.

*A955.15. Origin of island from piece of coral. Hawaii: Buck, 1938a, 240; Emory, 1924, 11; Fornander, 1916, IV, 20ff.; Henry, 1928, 566.

*A955.17. Five islands from dismembered body of man-eating monster. Hawaii: Rice, 1923, 112.

*A955.18. Dirt which falls into ocean becomes an island. Samoa: Rose, 1959, 53f.; Rotuma: Russell, 1942, 230, 232, 239, 241; Ellice Is.: Hedley, 1896, 7, 43.

*A955.19. Origin of island from floating island which was fixed. Samoa: Krämer, 1902, I, 451.

A956. Origin of peninsulas. Societies: Baessler, 1905, 921; Tonga: Gifford, 1924, 68.

*A958. Origin of reefs. Marquesas: Handy, 1930, 106; Hawaii: Emerson, 1915, 45; Samoa: Nelson, 1925, 127; Powell-Pratt, 189, 247.

A960. Creation of mountains (hills). Societies: Tefaafana, 1917, 31; Hawaii: *Fornander, 1918, V, 544ff.; Luomala, 1951, 71; Thrum, 1923, 106f.; Tonga: Collocott, 1924, 280; N.Z.: Best, 1925, 983ff.; Cowan, 1930, I, 177f.; White, 1887-90, II, 70, 103.

*A960.0.1. Mountains are children of island. Societies: Ropiteau, 1933, 127.

*A961.1.1. Hill originates from excrement of great bird. Tonga: Collocott, 1921, 51

*A961.3.1. Hill from transformed lizard. Hawaii: Fornander, 1918, V, 514.

*A961.4.1. Mountain from water-monster. N.Z.: Best, 1925, 980.

A961.5. Mountains from bones (body) of slain giant. Hawaii: Fornander, 1918, V, 374, 508, 546, 548, 610; Tonga: Caillot, 1914, 296; Samoa: Krämer, 1902, I, 270 n. 1; N.Z.: Best, 1925, 986; Cowan, 1930, 44.

A962. Mountains (hills) from ancient activities of god (hero). Hawaii: Beckwith, 1940, 22; Tonga:

Collocott, 1928, 8.

A962.1. Mountain from part of deity's (hero's) body.
Societies: Henry, 1928, 339; Hawaii: Beckwith,
1940, 170, 188f.; Fornander, 1918, V, 580;
N.Z.: Beckwith, 1940, 379.

*A962.2.1. God makes hill. N.Z.: Best, 1929, 13.

A963.9. Clay soil dropped from sky to form hill.
Tonga: Gifford, 1924, 39; Reiter, 1933, 357.

A964. Mountains (hills) from ancient contest (fight).
Cooks: Guppy, 1890, 48.

A964.1. Holes in hills result of fight between gods.
Societies: Agostini, 1900, 75; Hawaii: Dickey,
1917, 23, 35; Fornander, 1918, V, 224; Smith,
1966, 11; Thrum, 1923, 161; Westervelt, 1915,
186, 266.

*A964.1.1. Holes made by spear of god preserved in
stone. Hawaii: Beckwith, 1940, 65.

*A964.2.2. Mountains could speak and move formerly.
Samoa: Brown, 1915, 180; N.Z.: Best, 1924,
204-205; Cowan, 1930, I, 177.

*A965.2. Marriage between mountains. N.Z.: Best,
1925, 881.

A966. Origin of volcanoes. Hawaii: Fornander, 1916,
IV, 104ff.; Fornander, 1918, V, 576f.; Green,
1923, 19ff.; McAllister, 1933, 71; Samoa:
Powell-Pratt, 1892, 79; N.Z.: Cowan, 1930, 15;
Clark, 1896, 43; Reef Is.: Elbert-Kirtley, 1966,
354f.; O'Ferrall, 1904, 228.

A967. Origin of mounds. Tonga: Gifford, 1924, 121.

A969.1. Mountain from buried giant. Hawaii: Rice,
1923, 115.

A969.6. Hill brought into country as adopted child.
Hawaii: Beckwith, 1940, 379.

A969.7. Origin of mountains as punishment. N.Z.:
White, 1887-90, II, 103.

A969.8. Origin of crevasse (gorge, ravine). N.Z.:
Cowan, 1930, 75; Hawaii: Thrum, 1907, 267.

*A969.10. Origin of hill: begotten by mountains. Hawaii
Fornander, 1918, V, 532.

*A969.11. Two mountains raised and lowered by two
turtles, upon which they rest. Hawaii: Fornander,
1918, V, 518.

*A969.12. Some mountains were once ships. N.Z.: White,
1887-90, II, 37.

*A969.13. Origin of archway in cliff. Tonga: Collocott,
1928, 8.

A970. Origin of rocks and stones. Cooks: Large,
1903, 134; Hawaii: Thrum, 1907, 73; N.Z.: Best,
1925, 782; White, 1887-90, V, 86; Bellona:
Elbert-Monberg, 1964, No. 39.

A972. Indentions on rocks from prints left by man (beast)
Tahiti: Henry, 1923, 36; Hawaii: Dickey, 1917,
20, 21; Tonga: Collocott, 1928, 10; N.Z.: White,
1887-90, V, 23; Tikopia: Firth, 1961, 107.

A972.1. Indentions on rocks from imprint of gods and
saints. Hawaii: Beckwith, 1940, 65, 142, 212f.;
Niue: Smith, 1903, 98; Tikopia: Firth, 1930-31,
296.

*A972.1.0.1. Peculiar markings on stone from tears of
goddess. N.Z.: Best, 1924, 165.

A974. Rocks from transformation of people to stone.
Marquesas: Handy, 1930, 106; Cooks: Gill, 1876,
59-60; Hawaii: Beckwith, 1940, 175; Emerson,
1915, 45; Smith, 1966, 19; Thrum, 1907, 219;
Tonga: Gifford, 1924, 99, 130; N.Z.: Best, 1925,
863; Rennell: Elbert-Monberg, 1964, No. 76.

A975. Why stones became hard. Oceanic: Beckwith,
1940, 80.

*A976.1. Origin of redness of rocks. Hawaii: Rice,
1923, 38; N.Z.: Best, 1927, 265.

A977. Origin of particular stones or groups of stones.
N.Z.: Best, 1925, 984.

A977.1. Giant responsible for certain stones. Hawaii:
Westervelt, 1915, 24-25.

*A977.5.5. Origin of three particular stones: swam to
places where they now rest. Hawaii: Rice, 1923, 32.

*A977.5.6. Great column of rock prone because of
defeat in combat with another column. Marquesas:
Handy, 1930, 132.

*A977.5.7. Rock in crouching form because it struggled
to rise and accompany goddess on journey. Hawaii:
Beckwith, 1940, 175.

*A977.5.8. Rain god dislocates giant stones. Hawaii:
Beckwith, 1940, 18.

A979. Other stories about stone origins. Marquesas:
Handy, 1930, 132; Societies: Henry, 1928, 341;
Hawaii: Beckwith, 1940, 18, 22.

*A979.0.1. Origin of coral. Tonga: Gifford, 1924, 130.

*A979.2. Origin of greenstone. N.Z.: Best, 1925, 841ff.;
White, 1887-90, II, 37, 128.

A983. Origin of valleys or hollows. Hawaii: Rice,
1923, 95; Tonga: Gifford, 1924, 89.

*A989.5. Red ochre in Earth Mother is blood of cut-off
arms of Sky Father. N.Z.: Best, 1924, 96.

*A999.1. Origin of caves. N.Z.: Best, 1924, 194.

A1000--A1099. World calamities and renewals

*A1002.2.5. Bird sent by god to warn people of
approaching catastrophe. Rarotonga: Te Ariki,
1920, 168.

A1003. Calamity as punishment for sin. Marquesas:
Tahiaoteaa, 1933, 496; Samoa: Fraser, 1897, 70;
N.Z.: Beckwith, 1940, 317.

A1005. Preservation of life during world calamity.
Tuamotus: Caillot, 1914, 24; Societies: Henry,
1940, 445.

A1006.1. New race from single pair (or several) after
world calamity. Marquesas: Handy, 1930, 110;
Tahiti: Henry, 1940, 446; Orsmond, 1933, 84, 86;
Hawaii: Beckwith, 1940, 315; Thrum, 1923, 234;
Samoa: Bülow, 1898, 81, 139; N.Z.: White,

67

1887-90, I, 109; Ellice Is.: Beckwith, 1940, 270.

*A1009.4. Stones and trees, carried to sky during deluge, rain down after flood waters recede. Tahiti: Henry, 1928; Orsmond, 1933, 85.

*A1009.5. Island turned upside down. Mangareva: Laval, 1938, 10; Marquesas: Tahiaoteaa, 1933, 496; N.Z.: White, 1887-90, I, 108f., 181; Rennell: Birket-Smith, 1956, 22.

A1010. Deluge. Inundation of whole world or section. Mangareva: Luomala, 1949, 157; Tuamotus: Caillot, 1914, 24; Marquesas: Christian, 1895, 188, 199; Tahiaoteaa, 1933, 496; Steinen, 1934-35, 225; Cooks: Te Ariki, 1920, 168; Gill, 1876, 78; Societies: Henry, 1928, 445, 450; Orsmond, 1933, 84f.; Hawaii: Beckwith, 1932, 34; Beckwith, 1940 307, 314; Fornander, 1918, V, 522f.; Fornander, 1918, VI, 276, 335; Luomala, 1951, 35; Rice, 1923, 34; Thrum, 1907, 20; Thrum, 1923, 234; Samoa: Bülow, 1898, 80f., 139; Fraser, 1897, 70; N.Z.: Beckwith, 1940, 316; Grey, 1855, 14, 61; White, 1887-90, I, 55, 166, 173f., 180; Best, 1925, 679f., 932; Fijis: Fison, 1904, 30f.; Hocart, 1929, 201; Ontong Java: Sarfert, 1931, 328.

A1010.2. Great flood lasts eight months. N.Z.: Beckwith, 1940, 316.

A1015. Flood caused by gods or other superior beings. Marquesas: Handy, 1930, 109f.

A1015.3. Flood caused by deity stamping on floor of heavens. N.Z.: Beckwith, 1940, 250; Clark, 1896, 162; White, 1887-90, I, 55.

A1016. Pseudo-scientific explanations of the flood. Tuamotus: Beckwith, 1940, 267.

A1017.2. Flood caused by prayer. N.Z.: Beckwith, 1940, 316.

A1018. Flood as punishment. Tuamotus: Caillot, 1914, 9, 23; Societies: Henry, 1928, 450; Cooks: Gill, 1876, 78; Beaglehole, 1938, 386; Hawaii: Beckwith, 1932, 34; Thrum, 1923, 228ff.; N.Z.: White, 1887-90, I, 173ff.; Fijis: Fison, 1904, 30f.

A1018.1. Flood as punishment for breaking tabu. Hawaii:

Beckwith, 1940, 23; Tahiti, N.Z., Fijis:
*Beckwith, 1940, 316-319; Fijis: Hocart, 1929,
218.

A1018.3. Flood brought as revenge for injury. Tuamotus:
Beckwith, 1940, 318.

A1019.1. Subsidence of earth beneath flood. Marquesas:
Christian, 1895, 118, 199; Samoa: Fraser,1897,
70.

A1021. Deluge: escape in boat. Tuamotus: Caillot,
1914, 9, 10, 23; Hawaii: Fornander, 1918, VI,
276, 335; Luomala, 1951, 38; Thrum, 1907, 20;
N.Z.: Beckwith, 1940, 316; White, 1887-90, I,
166, 174f.; Fijis: Fison, 1904, 30-31.

A1022. Escape from deluge on mountain. Hawaii:
Thrum, 1923, 232ff.

A1024. Escape from deluge in cave. Tahiti: Henry,
1928, 446-447; Orsmond, 1933, 85.

*A1029.7. Only mythical dwarfs survive the great flood.
Hawaii: Luomala, 1951, 35f.

A1030. World-fire. A conflagration destroys the earth.
Sometimes (as with the flood legends) the tradition
is somewhat local, and does not refer to an actual
destruction of the whole earth. Hawaii: Rice,
1923, 30; Thrum, 1907, 16; N.Z.: Best, 1925, 795;
Hongi, 1894, 155.

*A1031.7. Marplot sets fire to highest heaven.
Tuamotus: Henry, 1928, 348.

*A1031.8. Hero sets underworld on fire. Cooks: Gill,
1876, 56; N.Z.: Cowan, 1930, I, 16; White,
1887-90, II, 68, 83, 104f., 108f.

A1070. Fettered monster's escape at end of world.
Giant, or monster, is fettered in depths of earth.
His movement causes earthquakes. When he succeeds
in freeing himself from his fetters and escapes,
the world will end. Tonga: Caillot, 1914, 246;
Collocott, 1919, 236; 1921b, 153; 1924, 276.

*A1072.5. Fettered monster as god or goddess. Tahiti:
Henry, 1928, 359; Tonga: Collocott, 1921b, 153;
Reiter, 1907, 239.

A1100--A1199. Establishment of natural order

A1101.1. Golden age. A former age of perfection. Tuamotus: Stimson, n.d., Z-G. 13/50.

A1101.2.4. Formerly men could go safely beneath the sea. Tuamotus: Stimson, n.d., Z-G. 13/50.

*A1104. After creation of earth, created things floated upon sea. There was no fixedness. Samoa: Fraser, 1892, 176.

A1111. Impounded water. Water is kept by monster so that mankind cannot use it. A hero defeats the monster and releases the water. Fijis: Hocart, 1929, 224.

A1115. Why the sea is salt. Tahiti: Paul Hambruch, Nauru, (Hamburg, 1914-15), 281; Hawaii: Beckwith, 1940, 43, 437; Fornander, 1918, V, 368.

*A1116.2. Waves and surf much larger in beginning than today. They were torn apart. Hawaii: Fornander, 1916, IV, 522, 524.

*A1116.3. Why water is rough on one part of an island's coast. Tonga: Caillot, 1914, 295.

A1120. Establishment of present order: winds. Societie Caillot, 1914, 113; Hawaii: Fornander, 1918, VI, 336; Tonga: Gifford, 1924, 16; Chatham Is.: Shand, 1894, 122; Shand, 1898, 80; N.Z.: White, 1887-90, I, 28; II, 64.

A1121. Breathing of deity (spirit) causes winds. N.Z.: Clark, 1896, 19.

A1122, Cave of winds. Winds originally confined in caves. Niue: Loeb, 1926, 161, 204; Smith, 1902, 202; N.Z.: Dixon, 1916,55; White, 1887-90, II, 89; IV, 3.

*A1122.1.1. Origin of winds: taro leaf in cave where winds were held was broken and winds escaped. Niue: Loeb, 1926, 204.

A1122.4. Wind comes through holes in sky. Cooks: Ariki, 1899, 73; Gill, 1876, 7; Ontong Java: Sarfert, 1931, 325, 413.

*A1124. Winds kept in calabash. Hawaii: Rice, 1923, 69; Cooks: Gill, 1876, 5.

C322.1. Basket of winds.

*A1126.1. Winds are spear-shafts thrown by fighting wind gods. Pukapuka: Beaglehole, 1938, 312.

*A1127.0.1. Eight winds of heaven. Niue: Loeb, 1926, 225; Ontong Java: Sarfert, 1931, 325, 413.

A1127.2. Gentle west wind said to be exhausted from fleeing deity. N.Z.: Clark, 1896, 46.

*A1127.3. Northeast trade wind is king of all winds. Tahiti: Henry, 1928, 364.

*A1129.4. Winds come from the second and third heavens. N.Z.: Best, 1924, 152.

*A1129.5. From the winds all things acquire the breath of life. N.Z.: Best, 1924, 153.

*A1129.6. Winds destroy land (to punish people). Societies: Henry, 1928, 393.

A1131.1. Rain from tears. Chatham Is.: Shand, 1894, 121; N.Z.: Best, 1924, 97; Clark, 1896, 19; Wohlers, 1875, 8.

A1131.5. Rain from rain-god (rain spirit). See all references to A287. Ontong Java: Parkinson, 1898, 197.

*A1131.7. When it rains, god is watering sky-garden. N.Z.: Luomala, 1949, 119.

A1132. Origin of dew. N.Z.: White, 1887-90, I, 48.

*A1132.1. Dew drops are tears heaven sheds in mourning over his separation from earth. N.Z.: Grey, 1896, 15.

A1133. Origin of clouds. Hawaii: Westervelt, 1915, 69; N.Z.: Best, 1924, 109.

*A1133.1.1. Origin of clouds from god's intestines. Societies: Henry, 1928, 410.

*A1133.5. Clouds are god working in his sky-garden. N.Z.: Luomala, 1949, 119.

*A1133.6. Long horizontal streaks of cloud seen at dawn are Maui's rope. Chatham Is.: Shand, 1894, 123.

A1134. Origin of mist (fog). N.Z.: Best, 1924, 97; White, 1887-90, I, 48.

*A1134.1. Mists are the sighs of love Earth gives for Heaven. N.Z.: Grey, 1855, 15.

*A1135.1.2. Chill of winter months caused by dead warriors, to whom death's cold adheres, ascending to sky. Cooks: Gill, 1876, 163.

*A1135.5. Origin of ice. N.Z.: White, 1887-90, I, 48.

A1141. Origin of lightning. Societies: Agostini, 1900 89; Hawaii: Westervelt, 1915, 69; Rennell: Birket-Smith, 1956, 22.

A1141.6. Lightning produced by deity. N.Z.: Clark, 1896, 168; Grey, 1855, 80; Tokelaus: Macgregor, 1937, 59.

*A1141.8.1. Lightning is a person (goddess). N.Z.: Best, 1924, 161.

*A1141.8.2. Lightning is spirit-lover of girl. Kapingamarangi: Elbert , 1948, 94.

*A1141.8.3. Lightning is reflection of tapa cloth of maid in the moon (Ina). Cooks: Gill, 1876, 46.

*A1141.8.4. Why lightning comes before thunder rather than after it. Tokelau: Burrows, 1923, 163f.

A1142. Origin of thunder. Societies: Agostini, 1900, 89; Hawaii: Fornander, 1916, IV, 76; N.Z.: Best, 1925, 877; Tikopia: Firth, 1961, 95.

*A1142.3.1.1. Thunder is a cannibal. N.Z.: White, 1887-90, I, 87, 127.

A1142.5.1.1. Thunder from crashing of stones in moon as goddess beats tapa. Cooks: Gill, 1876, 46; Samoa: Clark, 1896, 121.

*A1142.10. Thunder is snapping stone thrown into sky by hero. Rotuma: Luomala, 1949, 135.

*A1142.12. Thunder from footsteps of demi-gods or thunder-people. N.Z.: Grey, 1855, 80.

A1145.1. Earthquakes from movements of subterranean monster. Tonga: Caillot, 1914, 246 n. 3; Samoa: Powell-Pratt, 1892, 79, 83 n.1; N.Z.: Best, 1925, 884; Fijis: Fison, 1904, 28.

*A1145.3. Earthquakes from movements of deity (who lives underground). Tonga: Collocott, 1922, 173; Samoa: Bülow, 1895, 141; N.Z.: *Best, 1899, 114; 1924, 100; Futuna: Burrows, 1936, 106, 225; Fijis: Fison, 1904, 160; Rennell: Elbert-Monberg, 1964, No. 44.

*A1145.4. Earthquakes from earth support being shaken by one-armed god. Samoa: Stair, 1896, 56.

A1147.1. Origin of red sky (blood). Tahiti: Henry, 1928, 339; N.Z.: Grey, 1855, 89.

A1150. Determination of seasons. Societies: Henry, 1928, 412; N.Z.: Best, 1899, 98.

*A1152.1. Seasons of hot and cold caused by turnings of an underground god. N.Z.: Best, 1925, 884.

A1157. Causes of seasons -- deities push sun back and forth at solstices. Hawaii: Beckwith, 1940, 119; N.Z.: Best, 1924, 112.

*A1157.1. When sun god lives with one wife, the world experiences summer, with another wife, winter. N.Z.: Best, 1925, 789.

*A1158. Why it is warm on a particular island. Societies: Baessler, 1905, 921.

*A1159. Summer and winter caused by god's turning in his subterranean abode. N.Z.: Best, 1899, 114.

A1160. Determination of the months. Chatham Is.: Shand, 1894, 112; 1898, 80; Ellice Is.: Roberts, 1958, 398.

A1170. Origin of night and day. N.Z.: Best, 1899, 95; Grey, 1855, 4; White, 1887-90, I, 130; II, 87, 90; Fijis: Fison, 1904, 139.

A1171. Origin of day. N.Z.: Best, 1924, 86.

*A1171.5. Day begins when sky lifted. Tahiti: Henry, 1928, 412.

A1172. Determination of night and day. Hawaii: Rice,

1923, 105; N.Z.: Best, 1924, 112; Clark, 1896, 43, 46.

*A1172.4. Goddess of night. The time she sleeps governs length of night. Samoa: Fraser, 1898, 19.

*A1173. Goddesses hold up the night. Hawaii: Rice, 192, 33.

A1174.4. Night caused by deity wrapping himself in dark mantle. N.Z.: Clark, 1896, 17, 21.

*A1188. Why all things can no longer talk. Samoa: Brown 1915, 175.

*A1191.1. Origin of names for thunder and lightning. Bellona: Elbert-Monberg, 1964, No. 30.

*A1191.2. How constellations got their names. Bellona: Elbert-Monberg, 1964, Nos. 34a, 57a n.; Rennell: ibid., 34b, 57b, 57c.

*A1191.3. Origin of names of the body parts. Samoa: Bülow, 1895, 139; Krämer, 1902, I, 405.

*A1191.4. Origin of names for the moon at different phases. (Cf. A1617.). Samoa: Stuebel, 1896, 149.

*A1197. Why coral is soft. Tonga: Brown, 1916, 430.

*A1198. Battle of earth and rocks: why earth covers rocks. Samoa: Brown, 1915, 180.

A1200--A1699. CREATION AND ORDERING OF HUMAN LIFE

A1200--A1299. Creation of man

A1200. Creation of man. (Cf. A1275.1. and ff.). Hawaii: Thrum, 1907, 16; N.Z.: White, 1887-90, I, 142; II, 64; Tikopia: Firth, 1961, 23, 61.

A1205. Unacceptable gods as first inhabitants of earth. Hawaii: Beckwith, 1940, 60.

A1210. Creation of man by creator. Easter I.:

Métraux, 1940, 312; Tuamotus: Henry, 1928, 347; Societies: Henry, 1928, 402; Tahiti, Hawaii: Dixon, 1916, 26.

A1211. Man made from creator's body. Cooks: Gill, 1876, 3.

A1211.1. Man from dirt mixed with creator's blood. N.Z.: White, 1887-90, I, 155.

A1211.3. Man from spittle of creator (mixed with earth). Oceanic: Dixon, 1916, 24; Hawaii: Fornander, 1918, VI, 275; Thrum, 1907, 16.

A1212. Man created in creator's image. Hawaii: Beckwith, 1940, 43.

A1216. Man as offspring of creator (deity). Samoa: Krämer, 1902, I, 409; N.Z.: Best, 1925, 748; Cowan, 1930, I, 8; White, 1887-90, I, 20f.; Tikopia: Firth, 1961, 28.

A1216.1. Mankind from masturbation of creator with earth. (Cf. A615.1.). Easter Is.: Englert, 1939, 18; Métraux, 1940, 314.

A1217. Devil's unsuccessful attempt to vivify his creations as God has done. Hawaii: Beckwith, 1940, 61; Thrum, 1907, 18f.

A1220. Creation of man through evolution. Hawaii: Dixon, 1916, 15f.; Samoa: ibid, 18, 28; N.Z.: ibid., 27.

*A1221.0.1. Wind impregnates earth, and daughter is born. Ontong Java: Sarfert, 1931, 325, 413-414.

A1221.2. Mankind from "Peace and Quiet fructified by Light." Hawaii: Dixon, 1916, 16.

A1221.4. Mankind from mating of tree and vine. Samoa: Bülow, 1899, 62; Dixon, 1916, 164, n. 37.

A1221.6. Mankind from human-animal mating. Rapa: Buck, 1938a, 173-174 (woman and clam); Niue: Loeb, 1926, 165 (woman and whale).

*A1221.7. Mankind begotten in union between plant and red clay. N.Z.: White, 1887-90, I, 154, 155.

A1222. Mankind originates from eggs. Oceanic: *Dixon, 1916, 109, 109 n. 17; Marquesas: Handy,

1930, 125; Fijis: Tregear, 1903, 182.

A1224.2. Mankind descended from worms or larvae.
Tonga: Caillot, 1914, 251f.; Collocott,
1919, 237; Collocott, 1921b, 154; Collocott,
1924, 277; Gifford, 1924, 15f.; Samoa: Bülow,
1895, 139; Fraser, 1892, 180; Fraser, 1897, 23;
Krämer, 1902, I, 392, 396f.; Lesson, 1876, 590;
Nelson, 1925, 127; Powell-Pratt, 1891, 209f.,
274; Stair, 1896, 35; Stuebel, 1896, 60, 61;
Uvea: Burrows, 1937, 162; Niue: Loeb, 1926,
211; Tokelau: *Macgregor, 1937, 17, 166;
Burrows, 1923, 152.

A1224.6. Mankind descended from fish. Mangareva:
Caillot, 1914, 144; Hawaii: Beckwith, 1940, 129;
Ellice Is.: Hedley, 1896, 42f.

A1225. First men undeveloped. Rudimentary and amorphou
gradually assume present shape. Tuamotus: Henry,
1928, 347; Societies: Dixon, 1916, 29, 164;
Hawaii: Luomala, 1949, 29; Samoa: Dixon, 1916,
164, n. 35 and n. 36.

A1231. First man descends from sky. Samoa: Krämer,
1902, I, 105; N.Z.: Best, 1925, 787; Rotuma:
Churchward, 1937-38, 251.

A1232. Mankind ascends from under the earth. Mangareva
Caillot, 1914, 144, 176; Marquesas: Christian,
1895, 187; Steinen, 1933-34, 341; Tonga:
Collocott, 1924, 279; Niue: Loeb, 1926, 157.

A1232.3. Mankind emerges from caves. Marquesas:
Christian, 1895, 187.

A1234. Mankind emerges from ground. Easter I.:
Métraux, 1940, 312; Tuamotus: Henry, 1928, 347;
Seurat, 1905, 487; Samoa: Krämer, 1902, I, 104.

A1236. Mankind emerges from tree. Ellice Is.:
Grimble, 1952, 46.

*A1236.3. Peopling vine from which men descend
(usually going through maggot stage). Tonga:
Reiter, 1907, 445; Samoa: Fraser, 1892, 180;
Fraser, 1897, 23.

*A1236.4. First humans grow from ti plant. Niue:
Guppy, 1890, 48; Thomson, 1902, 86.

*A1236.5. Primal pair is twins, born from a rock.
Tonga: Collocott, 1919, 234f.

A1241. Man made from clay (earth). Polynesia:
*Dixon, 1916, 24f.;   Mangareva: Hiroa, 1938,
307; Easter I.: Métraux, 1940, 315; Buck,
1938a, 226; Marquesas: Handy, 1930, 122f.;
Hawaii: Beckwith, 1932, 32, 176; Fornander,
1918, VI, 335; Luomala, 1951, 38; Westervelt,
1915, 71f.; Chatham Is.: Shand, 1894, 121;
Travers, 1876, 26; N.Z.: Best, 1899, 116;
Best, 1924, 115; White, 1887-90, I, 131, 134,
149f.; Tokelaus: Smith, 1920, 146.

*A1241.0.1. First woman created from sand.
Marquesas: Steinen, 1934-35, 232.

A1241.3. Man made from clay image and vivified.
Hawaii: *Beckwith, 1940, 43ff.; N.Z.: Cowan,
1930, I, 8; White, 1887-90, I, 155ff., 158f.,
159f., 162f.

A1245. Man created from stones. Pukapuka: Hutchin,
1904, 173; Tonga: Collocott, 1921b, 152;
Collocott, 1924, 275f.; *Dixon, 1916, 158;
Samoa: Dixon, 1916, 158; Paul Hambruch, Nauru,
(Hamburg, 1914-15), 280; Powell-Pratt, 1892,
268; Tokelaus: Burrows, 1923, 153; Lister,
1892, 52; Macgregor, 1937, 16, 18; Smith, 1920,
146.

A1245.2. Mankind from vivified stone image. Samoa:
Lesson, 1876, 593; Marquesas: Steinen, 1934-35,
228f.

A1251. Creation of man from tree. Niue: Dixon, 1916,
30.

A1252. Creation of man from wood. Marquesas: Steinen,
1934-35, 228f.

*A1255.3. Man born from ti root. Niue: Loeb, 1926, 164.

A1263.1.1. Man created from blood clot. Oceania(Samoa,
Chatham Is.): *Dixon, 1916. 30, 109 n. 17;
Chatham Is.: Shand, 1894, 78.

A1270. Primeval human pair. Tuamotus: Caillot, 1914,
8; Danielsson, 1952, 122; Pukapuka: Hutchin,
1904, 173; Hawaii: Beckwith, 1932, 32ff., 178ff.;
Fornander, 1918, V, 658; Samoa: Lesson, 1876, 593;
Stair, 1896, 36; N.Z.: Best, 1924, 116; Best,
1905, 206; Best, 1925, 743; Grey, 1855, 1, 4;

White, 1887-90, I, 150f., 162; Tikopia: Firth, 1961, 26f.

A1270.1. Primeval human pair live in innocence. Tonga: Gifford, 1924, 15.

A1273. Twin first parents. Cooks: Gill, 1876, 10; Tonga: Collocott, 1919, 234f.; 1921b, 152; 1924, 275f.

A1273.1. Incestuous first parents. Marquesas: Steinen, 1934-35, 232-233; Tonga: Reiter, 1907, 237; N.Z.: Best, 1899, 116.

A1275. Creation of first man's mate. (Cf. A1210. and ff.). Mangareva: Hiroa, 1938, 424; Laval, 1938, 298; Tuamotus: Danielsson, 1952, 122; Hawaii: Beckwith, 1932, 176ff.; Samoa: Stuebel, 1896, 59; N.Z.: Best, 1925, 766; Wohlers, 1875, 8.

A1275.1. Creation of first woman from man's rib (or other portion of body). Easter I.: Englert, 1939, 18; Hawaii: Beckwith, 1940, 43, 46; Dixon, 1916, 24; Fornander, 1918, VI, 335; Luomala, 1951, 38; Thrum, 1907, 16; Westervelt, 1915, 73.

*A1275.1.3. Creation of woman from dead male. Samoa: Stair, 1896, 36.

A1275.4. Creator makes woman and then begets man by her. Mangareva: Buck, 1938a, 204; Tuamotus: Buck, 1938a, 188; Marquesas, Societies, N.Z.: *Dixon, 1916, 24ff. and notes.

*A1275.11. Origin of women: first man digs hole, urinates in it, covers it up. Image reflected in pool develops and comes out as a living companion for him. N.Z.: Best, 1924, 479.

*A1275.12. Wives for first three men brought from underworld. Tonga: Collocott, 1921b, 154.

*A1276.1. First human pair both males. Samoa: Stair, 1896, 36.

A1280. First man (woman). (Cf. A1240. ff and A1275. ff Easter I.: Metraux, 1940, 315; Marquesas: Steinen, 1934-35, 232; Rapa: Buck, 1938a, 173; Societies: Henry, 1928, 402; Beckwith, 1940, 120; Hawaii: Beckwith, 1940, 276, 280f.; Chatham Is.: Travers, 1877, 26; N.Z.: Best, 1924, 115.

*A1281.2.2. People once shed skins (like snakes, crabs).
Marquesas: Steinen, 1933-34, 348.

*A1281.3.1. First man clothed in sand. Tahiti:
Henry, 1902, 32.

*A1281.7. Generations who crawled. Niue: Loeb, 1926,
164.

A1285.1. First man made chief over whole world. Hawaii:
Beckwith, 1940, 44.

A1300--A1399. Ordering of human life

A1301. Men at first as large as giants. N.Z.: Smith,
1911, 12.

*A1312.3. Origin of mankind's hollow backbone. N.Z.:
White, 1887-90, II, 66.

*A1313.2.2. Origin of female sex-organs: incision cut
by culture hero. Samoa: Abercromby, 1891, 456;
Kramer, 1902, I, 105; Bellona: Elbert-Monberg,
1964, No. 43.

A1315.2. Origin of bald heads. Tikopia: Firth, 1961,
24.

*A1315.7. Origin of eyebrows and hair under armpit.
Tikopia: Firth, 1961, 22.

*A1318. Origin of anal orifice: wound made by culture
hero. Hawaii: Luomala, 1949, 84.

A1319.1. Origin of Adam's apple. N.Z.: Best, 1924,
119.

*A1319.2.1. Origin of flat shape of human backs.
N.Z.: Best, 1929, 3.

*A1319.12.2. Why man can lo longer shed old skin.
Tahiti: Henry, 1901, 52; Niue: Loeb, 1926, 81;
Ontong Java: Sarfert, 1931, 337.

A1330. Beginnings of trouble for men. N.Z.: Best,
1925, 751, 756; White, 1887-90, I, 45.

A1331. Paradise lost. Original happy state forfeited because of one sin. Cooks: Gill, 1876, 282f.; Hawaii: Beckwith, 1940, 43ff., 61; Fornander, 1916, IV, 502; VI, 274; Luomala, 1951, 38; N.Z.: White, 1887-90, I, 40; II, 64.

A1331.1. Paradise lost because of forbidden fruit (drink) Hawaii: Beckwith, 1940, 45; Luomala, 1951, 38.

A1331.2.1. Paradise lost because first woman is seduced. Hawaii: Beckwith, 1940, 43, 61.

A1333. Confusion of tongues. Tuamotus: Henry, 1928, 352.

A1335. Origin of death. Andrew Lang "Myths of the Origin of Death" Princeton Review (July, 1884). Tuamotus: Henry, 1928, 348f.; Stimson, 1937, 10; Tahiti: Henry, 1901, 52; Cooks: Gill, 1876, 283, 286; Beckwith, 1940, 158; Hawaii: Beckwith, 1932, 32, 48; Beckwith, 1940, 43, 45; Fornander, 1918, VI, 274, 335; Thrum, 1907, 19; Chatham Is.: Shand, 1894, 125; N.Z.: Best, 1899, 166; Best, 1925, 757, 767; Cowan, 1930, I, 18; Dixon, 1916, 54; Fornander, 1918, VI, 336; Grey, 1855, 10; Luomala, 1949, 58; White, 1887-90, I, 45; II, 13, 18; Niue: Loeb, 1926, 81; Fijis: Fison, 1904, 152, 158; Tregear, 1903, 182f.; Tikopia: Firth, 1961, 32; Nukumanu, Ontong Java: Sarfert, 1931, 458.

A1335.1. Origin of death from falsified message. N.Z.: Best, 1899, 96.

*A1335.1.2. Origin of death because of the moon's statement that death is to be eternal. N.Z.: White, 1887-90, II, 87f., 90.

A1335.3. Origin of death from unsuccessful imitation of bad creator. The bad creator attempts in vain to endow his creations with life like the good creator. Fails and thus introduces death. Hawaii: Beckwith, 1940, 61.

A1335.3. Origin of death from unwise choice. Ellice Is.: Grimble, 1951, 65.

*A1335.3.1. Origin of death: man chooses to befriend the rat, not the lizard (which can shed its skin). Ontong Java: Parkinson, 1898, 206.

*A1335.4.1. Men once like crabs and could shed shells and become young again. (Cf. *A1335.17.). Hawaii:

Beckwith, 1832, 48.

*A1335.11.1. Men die because of wish of the Goddess of Death. N.Z.: Best, 1925, 945.

*A1335.16. Death as punishment for sexual intercourse. Niue: Loeb, 1926, 81f.

*A1335.16.1. Origin of death when goddess's vagina crushes hero attempting to enter her. N.Z.: Best, 1925, 947; White, 1887-90, II, 84f., 91, 112, 115; Wohlers, 1875, 14.

*A1335.17. Man can gain immortality by becoming like land-crabs and shedding skin. (Cf. *A1335.4.1.). Tuamotus: Stimson, 1937, 46.

*A1335.18. Hero attempts to gain immortality for man by exchanging his stomach for that of the sea-slug. Tuamotus: Buck, 1938a, 170; Stimson, 1934, 47f.; Stimson, 1937, 47.

*A1335.19. Death originates when companions of hero laugh while he is trying to pass through body of ogress (goddess of death). N.Z.: *Best, 1924, 148; Best, 1929, 14, 15 n., 16 n.; Grey, 1855, 58.

*A1335.20. Death of mankind punishment for violating laughter tabu. N.Z.: Cowan, 1930, I, 18.

*A1335.21. Accidental interference of his brothers prevents hero from obtaining immortality for mankind. Tuamotus: Stimson, 1934, 48.

*A1335.22. The dead once conversed with the living. Mangareva: HIroa, 1938, 26; Laval, 1938, 15, 22.

A1336. Origin of murder. N.Z.: White, 1887-90, I, 41.

A1337. Origin of disease. Hawaii: Beckwith, 1940, 113, 502; N.Z.: Best, 1925, 719; Ellice Is.: Roberts, 1958, 369; Tikopia: Firth, 1961, 32.

A1337.6. Origin of leprosy. N.Z.: White, 1887-90, II, 59.

*A1338.2. Why people break their bones when they fall from trees. Rennell: Elbert-Monberg, 1964, No. 77.

A1341.3. Origin of theft. N.Z.: Best, 1925, 958.

*A1346.2.5. Why people no longer catch fish in great
abundance. Samoa: Powell-Pratt, 1891, 201.

A1350. Origin of sex functions. N.Z.: Best, 1905,
206.

A1351. Origin of childbirth. *Gudmund Hatt,
Asiatic Influences in American Folklore, (København,
1949), 83ff. Oceania: *Dixon, 1916, 78ff. and
notes; Mangareva: Caillot, 1914, 149; Hiroa,
1938, 111; Laval, 1938, 299; Tuamotus: Caillot,
1914, 58; Marquesas: Beckwith, 1940, 502; Handy,
1930, 56, 58, 59, 122, 128; Lavondes, 1964, 62;
Steinen, 1933-34, 348, 361; Cooks: Gill, 1876,
266; Hawaii: Beckwith, 1940, 284; Niue: Smith,
1903, 5f., 102; *Beckwith, 1940, 503; N.Z.:
"Notes and Queries," 1905, 47; Beckwith, 1940,
502; Pakauwera, 1894, 104; White, 1887-90, II,
9f., 12f.; Wohlers, 1876, 123; Fijis: Beckwith,
1940, 504; Ellice Is.: Kennedy, 1931, 166f.;
Reef Is.: O'Ferrall, 1904, 231; Kapingamarangi:
Elbert, 1948, 93f.; Elbert, 1949, 244.

A1352. Origin of sexual intercourse. Marquesas:
Steinen, 1934-35, 230f.; Tonga: Gifford, 1924,
18; Niue: Loeb, 1926, 164; N.Z.: Best, 1924,
479; Best, 1925, 958.

*A1352.4. Bats once husbands of women. Tikopia:
Firth, 1930-31, 308.

*A1362. Why babies urinate on their fathers. Bellona:
Elbert-Monberg, 1964, No. 52a.

*A1370.1. Origin of criminality: from god's incest with
niece. Marquesas: Steinen, 1934-35, 227.

*A1370.2. Origin of love, pity, and sympathy: bequeathed
by the sun, moon, and stars who are constant in their
mutual affection. N.Z.: Best, 1899, 104.

A1400--A1499. Acquisition of culture

A1404. Gods teach people all they know. Marquesas:
Handy, 1930, 123.

A1412. Origin of light. Hawaii: Beckwith, 1932, 174;
Fornander, 1918, VI, 336; N.Z.: Best, 1925,
745-746; Cowan, 1930, I, 7; White, 1887-90, I,
47; II, 49ff.; Wohlers, 1875, 6.

A1412.3. Acquisition of daylight by culture hero.
N.Z.: Best, 1899, 115.

A1414. Origin of fire. *Sir James G. Frazer, Myths
of the Origin of Fire, (London, 1930); Edward
Tregear, "Origin of Fire in Relation to Polynesian
Folklore," Folklore Journal VI (1888) 147f.;
Polynesian Folklore I. "Hina's Voyage to the
Sacred Isle"; II. Origin of Fire, TNZI XIX,
486-504, XX, 369ff. -- Tuamotus: Danielsson, 1952,
122; Marquesas: *Steinen, 1934-35, 192, 196ff.;
Societies: Henry, 1928, 427; Hawaii: Thrum, 1921,
104; Niue: Smith, 1903, 98; N.Z.: Best, 1925,
789ff.; Pakauwera, 1894, 102f.; White, 1887-90,
I, 37; II, 18, 50; Wohlers, 1876, 109; Ellice Is.:
Kennedy, 1931, 166; Tikopia: Firth, 1961, 27;
Ontong Java: Parkinson, 1898, 194f.; Sarfert,
1931, 328, 410.

A1414.1. Origin of fire--rubbing sticks. Australs:
Buck, 1938a, 168; Marquesas: Handy, 1930, 13;
Societies: Henry, 1928, 427; Cooks: Gill, 1876,
57; Hawaii: Thrum, 1923, 199f.; Tokelau:
Burrows, 1923, 164; Ellice Is.: Kennedy, 1931,
168; Fijis: Tregear, 1903, 182.

A1414.2. Origin of fire--found in person's own body.
Marquesas: Christian, 1895, 189; *Steinen,
1934-35, 192, 196ff.; Handy, 1930, 13;
Chatham Is.: Shand, 1894, 123; N.Z.: Best, 1925,
791; Cowan, 1930, I, 16; Luomala, 1949, 56;
White, 1887-90, II, 68, 74, 83, 104, 108f., 112;
Wohlers, 1875, 12; Ontong Java: Sarfert, 1931,
410.

A1414.4. Origin of fire--gift from god (supernatural
person). Hawaii: Beckwith, 1940, 499; Samoa:
Luomala, 1949, 102; Stair, 1896, 57; N.Z.: Best,
1924, 151; Grey, 1855, 47; Clark, 1896, 42;
Fijis: Fison, 1904, 159.

A1414.7.1. Tree as repository of fire. Tonga:
Collocott, 1921, 48; Samoa: Krämer, 1902, I,
403 n. 1; Stuebel, 1896, 65; Niue: Loeb, 1926,
157; Chatham Is.: Shand, 1894, 123; N.Z.:
Best, 1899, 96; Hongi, 1894, 133; Wohlers, 1875,
12; Ellice Is.: Kennedy, 1931, 195; Fijis:
Fison, 1904, 159.

A1414.7.2. Rock as repository of fire. Chatham Is.:
Shand,1894, 123.

A1414.7.3. Cave as repository of fire. Marquesas:
Handy, 1930, 103.

A1415. Theft of fire. Mankind is without fire. A
culture hero steals it from the owner. Oceanic:
*Dixon, 1916, 47 n. 31, n. 34; 48 n. 35, n. 36; 49;
Polynesia: *Luomala, 1949, 154; Tuamotus:
Stimson, n.d., Z-G. 13/52; Stimson, 1937, 24;
Marquesas: Handy, 1930, 104; Lavondes, 1964, 50ff.;
*Steinen, 1934-35, 192, 196ff.; Tahiti: *Henry,
1928, 466; Cooks: Ariki, 1899, 73; Gill, 1876,
55f., 66ff.; Hawaii: Beckwith, 1940, 227; Dickey,
1917, 18f.; Forbes, 1879, 59f.; Smith, 1966, 15;
Tonga: Caillot, 1914, 271ff.; Collocott, 1919,
236; Collocott, 1921, 47f.; Gifford, 1924, 22;
Reiter, 1917-18, 1039f.; Samoa: Fraser, 1897,
108; Krämer, 1902, I, 393, 401f.; Lesson, 1876,
595ff.; Powell-Pratt, 1892, 81f.; Stuebel, 1896,
144; Niue: Loeb, 1926, 157, 213, 220; Smith,
1903, 98; Thomson, 1902, 86f.; Tokelaus: Burrows,
1923, 164; Lister, 1892, 51; Macgregor, 1937, 17;
Smith, 1920, 147; N.Z.: *Best, 1924, 144ff.;
Best, 1929, 9, 15n., 16n.; White, 1887-90, II,
68, 74, 83, 104, 108f., 109f.

A1415.0.2. Original fire property of one person (animal).
Tuamotus: Stimson, 1937, 24; Marquesas: Handy,
1930, 12, 103; Lavondes, 1964, 44; Cooks: Ariki,
1899, 73; Gill, 1876, 53, 66; Hawaii: Beckwith,
1940, 115, 121, 216; Forbes, 1879, 59; Fornander,
1918, V, 560ff.; Smith, 1966, 15f.; Thrum, 1907,
33ff.; Tonga: Caillot, 1914, 271f.; Samoa:
Powell-Pratt, 1892, 81; N.Z.: Best, 1929, 8, 15n.,
16n.; White, 1887-90, II, 68, 74, 83, 104, 108f.,
112; Wohlers, 1875, 12; Tokelaus: Smith, 1920,
147; Rotuma: Hames, 1960, 48.

A1415.2.1. Theft of fire by bird. N.Z., Tuamotus,
Mangaia: *Luomala, 1949, 154 (hero in form of
bird).

A1415.4. Vain attempts to circumvent theft of fire.
Polynesia: Dixon, 1916, 47.

A1420. Acquisition of food supply for human race.
Cooks: Gill, 1876, 14; Samoa: Powell-Pratt,
1892, 274; Fijis: Hocart, 1929, 211.

A1420.2. Gods teach how to seek and prepare food.

Marquesas: Handy, 1930, 114.

*A1420.7. Tree of food: tree once contained all food.
People needed only to pick it. Hawaii: Beckwith,
1940, 286f.

*A1420.8. Store house in world of the gods whence things
useful to humans come. Rennell: Elbert-Monberg,
1964, No. 8.

A1421. Hoarded game released. Animals kept imprisoned
by malevolent creature. Released by culture hero.
Hawaii: Beckwith, 1940, 434f.; Tonga: Gifford,
1924, 91.

A1423. Acquisition of vegetables and cereals.
Easter I.: Métraux, 1940, 364; Tuamotus: Audran,
1919, 225; Mangareva: Caillot, 1914, 174; Hawaii:
Beckwith, 1940, 61, 63; Fornander, 1916, IV, 572;
Tonga: Gifford, 1924, 194; Samoa: Beckwith,
1940, 439; Tikopia: Firth, 1940, 296.

A1423.0.1. Hoarded plants released. Cooks: Beckwith,
1940, 236; Hawaii: Beckwith, 1940, 290, 432;
Fornander, 1916, IV, 164, 570ff.; VI, 272; Green,
1926, 116.

A1423.1. Origin of yams (sweet potatoes, taro).
Easter I.: Métraux, 1940, 317; Samoa: Lesson,
1876, 594; Powell-Pratt, 1891-93, 274f.; Tonga:
Gifford, 1924, 163, 169; N.Z., Tonga, Samoa:
*Beckwith, 1940, 101; N.Z.: *Luomala, 1949, 118;
*Best, 1925, 703ff., 828f.; White, 1887-90, III,
128f.

A1423.3. Origin of coconut. Easter I., Mangareva,
Marquesas, Tuamotus, Societies, Cooks, Hawaii, Tonga,
Samoa, Niue, Tokelau, New Zealand, Rennell, Bellona:
**Kirtley, 1967, 89ff.; Cooks: Beckwith, 1940,
256; Tonga: Gifford, 1924, 182.

A2611.3. Coconut tree from head of slain
monster. A2681.5.1. Origin of coconut tree.

*A1423.3.1. Coconuts made edible and nourishing.
Bellona: Elbert-Monberg, 1964, Nos. 41a, 41b.

A1429.3. Acquisition of water. N.Z.: White, 1887-90,
I, 317.

A1429.3.2. Gods provide drinkable water. Hawaii:
Beckwith, 1940, 63f.

A1437. Acquisition of clothing. Hawaii: Rice, 1923,
126; Tikopia: Firth, 1961, 96.

*A1437.1. Origin of feathered cloaks. Hawaii: Thrum,
1907, 147ff.

A1438. Origin of medicine (healing). Hawaii:
Beckwith, 1940, 116f., 119; Thrum, 1907, 51ff.;
Westervelt, 1915, 95ff.

A1439.2. Origin of dyes. Easter I.: Métraux, 1940,
317.

A1440. Acquisition of crafts. N.Z.: Kararehe, 1898,
59.

A1441. Acquisition of agriculture. Marquesas: Handy,
1930, 128; Cooks: Gill, 1876, 11; N.Z.:
*Luomala, 1949, 118.

A1441.1. Origin of plowing. Hawaii: Beckwith, 1940,
69.

A1441.4. Origin of sowing and planting. Hawaii:
Beckwith, 1940, 367.

A1445.1. Origin of boat-building. Tuamotus: Seurat,
1905, 481; Marquesas: Handy, 1930, 128; Hawaii:
Beckwith, 1940, 15; Tonga: Steinen, 1933-34, 326;
Samoa: Beckwith, 1940, 271; Krämer, 1902, I, 400,
455ff.; Niue: Loeb, 1926, 221; Tikopia: Firth,
1916, 27, 95f.; Fijis: Fison, 1904, 27; Bellona:
Elbert-Monberg, 1964, No. 19b.

A1445.2. Origin of carpentry. Hawaii: Beckwith, 1940,
70; Ontong Java: Sarfert, 1931, 410.

A1445.2.1. Why carpenters are found everywhere:
flood scatters them on raft over world. Tonga:
Beckwith, 1940, 317; Gifford, 1924, 201.

A1446.2. Origin of the axe. Tonga: Caillot, 1914,
248; N.Z.: White, 1887-90, I, 86.

A1446.5.5. Origin of baskets. Tonga: Gifford, 1924,
140.

A1453.2. Origin of weaving. N.Z.: Best, 1939, 783.

A1453.5. Origin of bark-cloth (tapa). *Paul Hambruch,
Oceanische Rindenstoffe (Oldenburg, ca. 1931);
Hawaii: Westervelt, 1915, 59ff.

*A1453.8. Origin of hat-making. Pukapuka:
Beaglehole, 1938, 328.

*A1453.9. Origin of mats. Tonga: Caillot, 1914, 253;
Tokelau: Lister, 1892, 61.

*A1454.1. Origin of kind of sandals. Rarotonga:
Te Ariki, 1921, 6.

A1455. Origin of cooking. Australs: Buck, 1938a,
168; Marquesas: Handy, 1930, 104, 128; Hawaii:
Rice, 1923, 21f.; Tonga: Caillot, 1914, 284;
Samoa: Lesson, 1876, 593; Powell-Pratt, 1892,
79; N.Z.: Best, 1925, 829; White, 1887-90, I,
37; II, 9, 12, 33; Rotuma: Hames, 1960, 48;
Nukumanu: Sarfert, 1931, 381; Bellona:
Elbert-Monberg, 1964, No. 79; Ontong Java:
Parkinson, 1898, 195; Sarfert, 1931, 299.

A1455.1. Origin of the domestic hearth. Cooks: Gill,
1876, 130.

A1457. Origin of fishing. Mangareva: Caillot, 1914,
174; Hawaii: Thrum, 1907, 230ff.; Thrum, 1923,
195; Westervelt. 1915, 159f.; Samoa: Krämer,
1902, I, 392; Tikopia: Firth, 1961, 27; Bellona:
Elbert-Monberg, 1964, Nos. 35a, 35b.

A1457.1. Origin of the fish hook. Easter I.: Metraux,
1940, 317, 363; Samoa: Sierich, 1902, 170ff.;
Niue: Loeb, 1926, 97; N.Z.: White, 1887-90, I,
170; II, 109, 110f., 126.

*A1457.1.1. Origin of binding fishhook. Samoa: Krämer,
1902, I, 415; Bellona: Elbert-Monberg, 1964,
No. 49.

*A1457.1.2. Origin of rat-shaped octopus lure. Samoa
(Manono): Rose, 1959, 149.

*A1457.1.3. Origin of pearl fishhooks for bonitos.
Tokelau: Burrows, 1923, 169f.

*A1457.1.4. Origin of barbs on fishhooks. N.Z.: White,
1887-90, I, 119f.

A1457.3. Origin of the net for fishing. Cooks: Low,
1934, 179; Hawaii: Thrum, 1907, 230ff.; Tonga:
Gifford, 1924, 16; Niue: Loeb, 1926, 163; Smith,
1903, 95f.; N.Z.: *Best, 1929, 4, 15n., 16n.;
Clark, 1896, 27f.; Grey, 1855, 287ff.; White,
1887-90, II, 69; Nukumanu: Sarfert, 1931, 454.

A1457.4. Origin of fishing stations. Hawaii:
Beckwith, 1940, 19, 22f.

A1457.5. Origin of fish-traps. Hawaii: Beckwith,
1940, 194f.; N.Z.: Best, 1924, 146; White,
1887-90, II, 64, 91, 109, 110, 116, 117, 119.

A1457.6. Origin of fish ponds. Hawaii: Beckwith,
1940, 19.

*A1458.2. Origin of bird trap. N.Z.: White, 1887-90,
II, 64.

A1459.1. Acquisition of weapons. Cooks: Gill, 1876,
286.

A1459.1.2.1. Origin of obsidian-tipped spears.
Easter I.: Metraux, 1940, 376.

*A1459.1.2.2. Culture hero teaches people how to
barb spears. N.Z.: *Best, 1899, 5, 15n., 16n.;
White, 1887-90, II, 91, 109,110, 117, 119.

A1459.2. Acquisition of seamanship (sailing, etc.).
Hawaii: Beckwith, 1940, 86; Rice, 1923, 71;
Thrum, 1923, 58; Tikopia: Firth, 1961, 27.

A1459.3. Acquisition of sorcery. Hawaii: Beckwith,
1940, 115; N.Z.: Best, 1924, 107;
Cowan, 1930, I, 15, 28, 59, 65f.; II, 17, 19,73f.;
Te Ariki, 1921, 100.

*A1459.4. Origin of poisons. Hawaii: Westervelt, 1915,
110-115.

A1461.7. Origin of nose-flute. Hawaii: Beckwith,
1940, 538.

*A1461.10. Origin of slit gong. Pukapuka: Beaglehole,
1938, 330.

A1462. Origin of dancing. Cooks: Gill, 1876, 103;
Hawaii: Fornander, 1916, IV, 154.

A1464.2.1. Origin of particular song. N.Z.: Best,
1925, 937f.

A1465.1. Origin of tatooing. Easter I.: Métraux, 1940,
316f., 367; Hawaii: Fornander, 1916, IV, 156;
Cooks: Ariki, 1899, 74; Gill, 1876, 91; Samoa:
Abercromby, 1891, 461ff.; Krämer, 1902, I, 107,
120f.; Turner, 1861, 182; N.Z.: *S. Percy Smith,
"The Origin of Tatooing," JPS XX (1911), 167-169;

Best, 1924, 169; Clark, 1896, 139; Dixon, 1916,
73; White, 1887-90, II, 4ff.; Wohlers, 1876, 112f.;
Nukumanu: Sarfert, 1931, 384, 407ff., 443f.;
Bellona: Elbert-Monberg, 1964, 1a, n. 14;
Ontong Java: Parkinson, 1898, 195.

*A1465.1.1. Why men rather than women are tattooed.
Samoa: Abercromby, 1891, 461.

A1465.3.2. Origin of designs on cloth. Hawaii:
Beckwith, 1940, 100.

A1465.4. Origin of polishing stone. N.Z.: Clark,
1896, 103; White, 1887-90, I, 76.

*A1465.4.1. Origin of fashioning stone images. Marquesas:
Christian, 1895, 189.

A1465.5. Origin of wood carving. N.Z.: Best, 1928a,
258; Clark, 1896, 114; Cowan, 1930, I, 199.

*A1465.7. Origin of wearing nose plugs. Nukumanu:
Sarfert, 1931, 443f.

*A1469. Origin of games and amusements. Hawaii: Thrum,
1923, 112, 116; Green, 1923, 5; N.Z.: Best,
1925, 841; Cowan, 1930, I, 69f.

A1480. Acquisition of wisdom and learning. N.Z.:
Best, 1924, 103.

*A1486. Origin of counting. Cooks: Gill, 1876, 100;
Samoa: Sierich, 1902, 167f.; Tokelaus: Burrows,
1923, 162f.; Lister, 1892, 60ff.; Bellona:
Elbert-Monberg, 1964, No. 58.

A1491. Origin of art of walking on stilts. Marquesas:
Handy, 1930, 114.

A1495.1. Origin of ball game. Cooks: Beckwith, 1940,
336; Gill, 1876, 130.

*A1495.2. Origin of string figures. N.Z.: Luomala,
1949, 77.

*A1495.3. Origin of kite-flying. Cooks: Gill, 1876,
123.

A1500--A1599. Origin of customs

A1514.1. Origin of drinking ceremonies. Tonga:
Gifford, 1924, 35, 47, 72, 74.

A1516. Origin of cannibalism. Easter I.: Métraux,
1940, 377; Tuamotus: Henry, 1928, 350;
Chatham Is.: Shand, 1894, 189; N.Z.: Best,
1925, 756; Best, 1928b, 262; Clark, 1896, 15;
White, 1887-90, I, 41ff.; II, 127.

G10. Cannibalism.

A1517. Origin of eating tabus. Hawaii: Ii, 1959, 160;
Pukui, 1933, 176f.; Tonga: Collocott, 1921, 55ff.;
Collocott, 1928, 59; Gifford, 1924, 80; Reiter,
1919-20, 139f.; Samoa: Krämer, 1902, I, 214;
N.Z.: Best, 1925, 1048; White, 1887-90, II, 118,
120.

A1587. Origin of tabus. C220. Tabu:
eating certain things.

A1528. Why one presents stranger with first fish
caught. Hawaii: Beckwith, 1940, 22.

A1540. Origin of religious ceremonial. Samoa, Rennell:
Elbert-Monberg, 1964, No. 16, n.

A1541.4.0.1. Holy day established on seventh day.
Hawaii: Beckwith, 1940, 45.

A1542. Origin of religious dances. Hawaii: Beckwith,
1940, 359.

*A1542.3. Origin of fire-walking. *F. Arthur Jackson,
et al, "Fire-walking in Fiji, Japan, India and
Mauritius," JPS VIII (1899), 188-196; Fijis:
Jackson, JPS III (1894), 74.

A1544. Origin of religious images (idols). Easter I.:
Métraux, 1940, 261; Hawaii: Beckwith, 1940, 516;
Fornander, 1916, IV, 128, 540; Thrum, 1923, 47.

A1545. Origin of sacrifices. Hawaii: Westervelt,
1916, 277; N.Z.: White, 1887-90, I, 57.

90

A1545.5. Origin of human sacrifice. Hawaii: Beckwith, 1940, 370; Cooks: Gill, 1876, 289.

A1546.0.2. Origin of prayers. Easter I.: Métraux, 1940, 313; Hawaii: Beckwith, 1940, 19ff.

*A1546.0.4. Origin of religious structures (marae). Mangareva: Hiroa, 1938, 23.

*A1546.7.2.4. Shark as mythical ancestor. Hawaii: Beckwith, 1940, 132.

*A1546.8. Origin of caterpillar worship. Hawaii: Green, 1923, 43ff.

A1547. Origin of funeral customs. Mangareva: Hiroa, 1938, 27; Laval, 1938, 20f.

A1547.3. Origin of lamentations for the dead. Cooks: Gill, 1876, 130.

A1549.2. Origin of sundry religious ceremonials. N.Z.: White, 1887-90, I, 175.

A1552.2. Origin of royal marriages with close relatives. Tonga: Gifford, 1924, 187.

A1556. Origin of sexual restrictions. Hawaii: Fornander, 1916, IV, 158.

A1556.2. Origin of celibacy. Tonga: Collocott, 1928, 17.

A1567. Origin of circumcision. Hawaii: Thrum, 1907, 21.

A1579.1. Why children are not left alone in the house to sleep. Marquesas: Handy, 1930, 51.

A1585. Origin of laws: division of property in a family. Cooks: Gill, 1876, 7.

A1587. Origin of tabus. Hawaii: Fornander, 1916, IV, 158; Pukui, 1943, 57; Thrum, 1923, 52; N.Z.: Cowan, 1930, I, 245f.

A1517. Origin of eating tabus. C. Tabu.

91

A1599.16. Origin of allusive expression for the story of gods' incest and trickery. Marquesas: Handy, 1930, 123.

*A1599.17. Why people must be quiet at approach of royalty. Samoa: Krämer, 1902, I, 305.

*A1599.18. Origin of commoners stopping to work when a chief is near. Samoa: Powell-Pratt, 1892, 106.

A1600--A1699. Distribution and differentiation

of peoples

A1610. Origin of various tribes. Mangareva: Caillot, 1914, 198ff.; Societies: Agostini, 1900, 700; Cooks: Gill, 1876, 16; Low, 1934, 17ff.; Hawaii: Thrum, 1923, 1ff.; Samoa: Bülow, 1895, 139; Niue: Loeb, 1926, 157; Chatham Is.: Skinner-Baucke, 1928; N.Z.: Best, 1905, 209; Best, 1924, 93; Grace, 1907, 98; Gudgeon, 1905, 186; Tokelau: Burrows, 1923, 152; Fijis: Fison, 1904, 161; Ellice Is.: Roberts, 1958, 396ff.

*A1614.10. Origin of albinos. Niue: Smith, 1903, 102, 104.

A1616. Origin of particular languages. Tuamotus: Caillot, 1914, 11, 24f.

*A1616.3. Origin of language of chiefs. Hawaii: Beckwith, 1940, 378; Niue: Loeb, 1926, 56.

A1617. Origin of place name. Mangareva: Laval, 1938, 117; Societies: Baessler, 1905, 923f.; Cooks: Low, 1934, 21, 78, 178, 181, 182, 184, 264; Hawaii: Dickey, 1917, 14; Emory, 1924, 20, 24ff.; Green, 1929, 87; Smith, 1966, 2f.; Thrum, 1907, 56, 73; Westervelt, 1915, 1ff.; Samoa: Krämer, 1902, I, 306; Nelson, 1925, 131f., 136; Powell-Pratt, 1891, 202; 1892, 105; Stuebel, 1896, 103; N.Z.: Best, 1925, 721; White, 1887-90, III, 68; IV, 114; Ellice Is.: Roberts, 1958, 409.

A1630. Wandering of tribes. Migration legend. Hawaii:
Fornander, 1918, VI, 278; Luomala, 1951, 39;
Tokelau: Burrows, 1923, 152; N.Z.: *Best, 1925,
681ff., 770; White, 1887-90, II, 177ff.; Rotuma:
Russell, 1942, 230; Bellona: Elbert-Monberg, 1964,
Nos. 66, 124, 153; Rennell: Elbert-Monberg, 1964,
No. 67; Ontong Java: Parkinson, 1898, 194.

A1631.2. Tribe climbs down from sky to earth. Rotuma:
Russell, 1942, 233, 242.

*A1631.3. Mythical homeland where race originated.
Mangareva: Caillot, 1914, 145; Tuamotus: Audran,
1918, 132; Hawaii: Thrum, 1907, 17; Westervelt,
1915, 12ff.; Tonga: Caillot, 1914, 245; N.Z.:
Best, 1925, 673ff.; Cowan, 1930, I, 189, 198;
Grace, 1907, 91; White, 1887-90, V, 8.

A1640. Origin of tribal subdivisions. Easter I.:
Métraux, 1940, 83; N.Z.: Cowan, 1930, I, 133ff.;
Ellice Is.: Roberts, 1958, 398; Tikopia: Firth,
1961, 32.

A1641. Characteristics of tribal subdivisions. Samoa:
Bülow, 1895, 140.

A1650. Origin of different classes--social and
professional. Mangareva: Hiroa, 1938, 27f.;
Societies: Beckwith, 1940, 38; Hawaii: Thrum,
1923, 5f.; Niue: *Loeb, 1926, 57.

A1653. Origin of royalty. Tonga: Collocott, 1924,
282; Reiter, 1933, 36ff; Samoa: Stuebel,
1896, 92f.; Tikopia: Firth, 1961, 32.

A1653.1. Origin of kings (chiefs) from god(s). Societies:
Henry, 1928, 229, 232; Hawaii: Beckwith, 1940,
293, 367; Tonga: Gifford, 1924, 25, 28, 194;
Futuna: Burrows, 1936, 110.

A1657. Origin of slaves. Fijis: Fison, 1904, 161.

A1667.1. Why Europeans know more than natives.
Marquesas: Handy, 1930, 138.

A1700--A1799. Creation of animal life--general

A1702. Creation of animals by creator. Tahiti:
Henry, 1928, 339.

A1710. Creation of animals through transformation.
Hawaii: Beckwith, 1940, 465; N.Z.: Clark, 1896,
15.

A1714. Animals from various transformed objects.
Hawaii: Beckwith, 1940, 22, 465.

A1715. Animals from transformed man. Easter I.:
Knoche, 1939, 25; Tuamotus: Stimson, n.d.,
Z-G. 3/1100; Stimson, 1937, 41; Cooks: Beckwith,
1940, 101; Hawaii: Beckwith, 1940, 422; Samoa:
Powell-Pratt, 1892,107; N.Z.: Clark, 1896, 15;
Fornander, 1918, VI, 336; *Luomala, 1949, 50, 56;
White, 1887-90, II, 77, 80, 86, 109, 118, 119, 122.
124f.; Rotuma: Churchward, 1938-39, 466.

A1716. Animals from transformed ogre or giant. N.Z.:
Clark, 1896, 101; White, 1887-90, I, 80.

A1716.1. Animals from different parts of body of slain
giant (ogre). Hawaii: Rice, 1923, 110; Niue:
*Loeb, 1926, 186; N.Z.: Best, 1899, 99; Best,
1924, 108, 190; Ellice Is.: David, 1899, 99.

A1724. Animals from transformed parts of the body
(animal or human). Hawaii: Westervelt, 1915, 20,
144, 158; Tokelau: Burrows, 1923, 159; N.Z.:
White, 1887-90, III, 56; Tikopia: Firth, 1961,22.

A1724.1. Animals from body of slain person. Hawaii:
Luomala, 1951, 30.

A1727. Primordial animal mutilated to produce present
form. Hawaii: Beckwith, 1940, 135, 436, 500;
McAllister, 1933, 127; Tokelau: Burrows, 1923,
159; N.Z.: Clark, 1896, 50; White, 1887-90, II,
76, 84, 91, 116; Wohlers, 1875, 13.

A1730. Creation of animals as punishment. N.Z.:
Luomala, 1940, 50, 56.

*A1792.1. Animals issue from creator's mouth. Societies:
Henry, 1928, 381.

A1793. Animals emerge from tree. Hawaii: Beckwith,
1940, 287.

A1800--A1899. Creation of mammals

A1831. Creation of dog. Tuamotus: Buck, 1938a, 189;
Danielsson, 1952, 122; Hawaii: Beckwith, 1940,
436; Thrum, 1907, 16; N.Z.: Best, 1925, 939;
Clark, 1896, 50; Fornander, 1918, VI, 336;
Luomala, 1949, 50, 56; White, 1887-90, II, 77,
80, 86, 109, 118, 119, 122, 124f.

A1854. Creation of rat. N.Z.: Best, 1925, 831f.

A1871. Creation of hog (pig). Societies: Henry, 1928,
381; Cooks: Beckwith, 1940, 101; Hawaii: Thrum,
1907, 16; Samoa: Bulow, 1895, 140; Lesson, 1876,
597; Nelson, 1925, 141f.; Rotuma: Churchward,
1938-39, 466; Fijis: Fison, 1904, 46f.

*A1871.0.2. Origin of pigs from maggots in man's
putrefying body. Cooks: Gill, 1876, 137f.

A1900--A1999. Creation of birds

A1900. Creation of birds. N.Z.: Clark, 1896, 15;
White, 1887-90, I, 142f.; II, 64.

A1958. Origin of owl. Samoa: Powell-Pratt, 1892, 99.

*A1964. Creation of black heron. Samoa: Powell-Pratt,
1892, 107.

A1965. Creation of bittern. N.Z.: Clark, 1896, 101;
White, 1887-90, I, 80.

A1988. Creation of chicken. Societies: Henry, 1928,
381.

95

A2000--A2099. Creation of insects

A2001. Insects from body of slain monster. Hawaii:
Green, 1923, 43.

*A2007. Insects born of gods. N.Z.: Best, 1899, 99.

A2034. Origin of mosquitoes. Samoa: Krämer, 1902, I,
357.

A2091. Origin of spider. N.Z.: Best, 1899, 99.

A2100--A2199. Creation of fish and

other animals

A2100--A2139. Creation of fish

A2100. Creation of fish. Mangareva: Laval, 1938, 4;
Tuamotus: Stimson, n.d., Z-G. 3/1100; Hawaii:
Beckwith, 1932, 176; Beckwith, 1940, 287, 422;
Luomala, 1951, 30; Fornander, 1918, V, 154; VI,
336; Westervelt, 1915, 158; Tokelau: Burrows,
1923, 159; N.Z.: Clark, 1896, 15; White,
1887-90, I, 59; II, 64.

A2112. Creation of mullet. Hawaii: Beckwith, 1940,
63.

A2121. Creation of mackerel. Hawaii: Green, 1926, 99.

A2122. Origin of bonito. Tonga: Gifford, 1924, 57.

A2131. Origin of eel. Tuamotus: Stimson, 1937, 41;
Niue: Loeb, 1926, 186; N.Z.: Best, 108, 155,
479; Luomala, 1940, 120; White, 1887-90, II, 76,
84, 91, 116; Wohlers, 1875, 13; Tikopia: Firth,
22.

*A2135.3. Origin of sea monsters. N.Z.: White, 1887-90,

96

II, 84.

*A2137.1. Origin of shark: borne by goddess. Marquesas: Christian, 1895, 189.

*A2138. Origin of porpoise. Cooks: Gill, 1876, 98; Bellona: Elbert-Monberg, 1964, 57a n.

*A2139. Origin of fish --miscellaneous. Easter I.: Knoche, 1939, 25; Mangareva: Laval, 1938, 302; Hawaii: Pukui, 1933, 185; Westervelt, 1915, 145, 276; Samoa: Brown, 1915, 177; N.Z.: White, 1887-90, I, 59f.; III, 56, 116; Lau Is.: St. Johnston, 1918, 80; Bellona: Elbert-Monberg, 1964, No. 45.

*A2139.1. Creation of octopus (squid). Hawaii: Westervelt, 1915, 120; Best, 1927, 265.

A2145. Creation of snake (serpent). Samoa: Lesson, 1876, 598f.; N.Z.: Best, 1925, 774.

A2147. Creation of tortoise (turtle). Societies: Henry, 1928, 380-381; Hawaii: *Beckwith, 1940, 22, 465; Hawaii: Thrum, 1907, 239.

A2148. Creation of lizard. Hawaii: Fornander, 1918, VI, 336; Rice, 1923, 110; Thrum, 1907, 16; N.Z.: Best, 1924, 190; Te Aro, 1894, 166; White, 1887-90, II, 64; Bellona: Elbert-Monberg, 1964, No. 45.

*A2148.3. Coming of dragons to the islands. Hawaii: Westervelt, 1915, 148f.

A2160--A2199. Origin of amphibians and

other animal forms

A2171. Origin of crustaceans. N.Z. Best, 1924, 155; Tokelau: Burrows, 1923, 166.

A2171.3. Origin of lobster. Tahiti: Henry, 1928, 339.

A2171.4. Origin of shrimp. Tahiti: Henry, 1928, 339.

A2182.4. Origin of cutworm. Hawaii: Beckwith, 1940, 135.

97

A2200--A2299. Various causes of animal
characteristics

A2211.4. Why some whales die on land: first whale
did so. Tuamotus: Stimson, n.d., Z-G. 13/320.

A2211.14. Rat defecates on octopus's head: origin
of tubercles on head. Tonga: Gifford, 1924, 206.

A2211.15. Goddess scatters pubic hairs on fish: why
he has so many bones. Tuamotus: Stimson, n.d.
T-G. 2/44.

*A2211.16. Origin of fish's markings: from girl's
beatings. Cooks: Gill, 1876, 91.

*A2211.17. Origin of fish's markings: from goddess.
Niue: Smith, 1903, 98.

*A2211.18. Origin of black color of pekapeka birds:
from habit of hiding in caves. Niue: Loeb, 1926,
110.

A2213.2. Animal pressed: hence facial or bodily marks.
Rennell: Elbert-Monberg, 1964, No. 48; Bellona:
Elbert-Monberg, 1964, No. 39; Kapingamarangi:
Elbert, 1949, 245.

A2213.5.2. Fish struck by coconut: hence flat tail.
Tuamotus: Stimson, n.d., T-G. 3/600.

*A2213.5.3. Fish stamped on by girl: hence flat head.
Cooks: Gill, 1876, 92.

*A2213.6. Eel's elongated shape originated from fight
with flat fish. Ellice Is.: Kennedy, 1931, 170.

A2216. Animal characteristics: members bitten or cut
off. Tuamotus: Stimson, n.d., Z-G. 13/441;
Hawaii: Pukui-Curtis, n.d., 75.

A2217.1. Birds painted their present colors.
Kapingamarangi: Elbert, 1948, 128.

A2217.3. Marks on certain fish from fingerprints.
Tuamotus: Stimson, n.d., Z-G. 13/317, T-G. 3/600.

*A2217.3.4. Head of veka bird divided because it was
once scratched by enemy. Niue: Loeb, 1926, 192.

A2218. Animal characteristics from burning or singeing.
N.Z.: Best, 1927, 272.

A2218.3. Animal who steals fire scorched: cause of
his color. N.Z.: Best, 1924, 145f.

*A2218.3.1. Black marks over tern's eyes caused when
hero burned bird while stealing fire. Cooks:
Gill, 1876, 67f.

A2221.11. Deity rewards animal for bringing him water:
cause of present characteristics. N.Z.: Clark,
1896, 54.

A2231.1. Animal characteristics: punishment for
discourteous answer to god. N.Z.: Clark,
1896, 53.

*A2237.2. Sandpiper tells that hero has stolen: hero
punishes him by making his cry kivi. Ontong
Java: Sarfert, 1931, 434.

*A2241.2.1. Flying fox's wings borrowed from rat.
Samoa: Krämer, 1902, I, 359ff.; Niue: Smith,
28, 30; Fijis: Hocart, 1929, 218.

A2245. Animal characteristics: stolen from another
animal. Kapingamarangi: Elbert, 1948, 129.

*A2245.2. Bonito steals another fish's large tail;
leaves his own small one. Kapingamarangi: Elbert,
1948, 128.

*A2258.2. Fish get their shape, color and marking
from war with man tribe. N.Z.: Best,
1924, 184f.

A2261.6. Snipe messenger for warriors because he was
a messenger when a man. Tuamotus: Stimson,
n.d., Z-G. 13/10.

A2281. Enmity between animals from original quarrel.
Samoa: Paul Hambruch, Nauru (Hamburg, 1914-15),
287; Niue: Loeb, 1926, 194.

*A2286.3. Creator makes scales and shells of fishes
from his own fingernails and toenails. Tahiti:
Henry, 1928, 339.

A2300--A2399. Causes of animal
characteristics: body

*A2302.8. Dogs once much larger than today. They were
torn in bits in a fight. Hawaii: Fornander. 1916,
IV, 524.

A2305.1. Origin of fish's flat body. Ellice Is.:
Kennedy, 1931, 170.

A2305.1.2. Origin of flounder's flat body. Bellona:
Elbert-Monberg, 1964, No. 39; Rennell:
Elbert-Monberg, 1964, No. 48; Kapingamarangi:
Elbert, 1948, 126; Elbert, 1949, 245.

*A2305.1.4. Origin of sole's flat body. Cooks: Gill,
1876, 92.

A2312. Origin of fish's shells. Tahiti: Henry, 1928,
339.

A2312.3. Origin of dents in crab's shell. Tuamotus:
Stimson, n.d., T-G. 13/420; Bellona: Elbert-
Monberg, 1964, No. 47a; Rennell: Elbert-Monberg,
1964, No. 47b.

A2315. Origin of fish's scales. Tahiti: Henry, 1928,
339.

A2320.3.1. Origin of mudhen's red head. Hawaii:
Beckwith, 1940, 230; Forbes, 1879, 60; Thrum,
1907, 35; Bellona: Elbert-Monberg, 1964, No. 46a;
Rennell: Elbert-Monberg, 1964, 46b.

*A2320.8. Why shark has bump on its head. Cooks: Gill,
1876, 92.

A2335.4.3. Why dogs have black muzzle. N.Z.: White,
1887-90, II, 126.

*A2341.4. Why sea cucumber has two mouths. Samoa:
Kramer, 1902, I, 358.

*A2343.2.3. Why pigeon has red on bill: from helping
woman in childbirth. Chatham Is.: Shand, 1896,
133.

*A2345.10. Origin of shark's teeth. Oceania: **Lessa,
1961, 322ff.

*A2351.4.4. Origin of crane's long neck. Niue: Loeb,
1926, 191.

*A2351.8. Why turtle's neck is short. Tonga: Collocott,
1928, 22.

*A2365.2.2. Why turtle's penis is striped. Fijis:
Hocart, 1929, 218.

*A2371.2.13. Bird's long legs a reward for its kindness
to a demigod. N.Z.: White, 1887-90, II, 120.

*A2371.2.14. Why the crab has only two legs. Rennell:
Elbert-Monberg, 1964, No. 37; Bellona: ibid.,
No. 38.

*A2377.2. Origin of bat's wings. Fijis: Hocart, 1928,
218.

*A2378.1.3.1. Why lizards can shed their tails. N.Z.:
Best, 1924, 191.

*A2378.1.10. How rat got its tail. Fijis: Hocart,
1929, 218.

*A2378.1.11. Origin of bonito's tail: he stole it
from the box fish. Kapingamarangi: Elbert, 1949,
246.

*A2378.2.9. Why plovers are tailless. Hawaii: Forbes,
1882, 40; Thrum, 1907, 71f.

*A2378.4.8. Origin of bob-tailed dogs. Hawaii: Rice,
1923, 31.

*A2378.9.6. Origin of sting-ray's tail and barb. N.Z.:
Best, 1924, 184.

*A2381.2. Why fish upon particular island are poisonous.

Rennell: Elbert-Monberg, 1964, 195b, n.

*A2381.3. Why a kind of fish is oily. Tokelau: Burrows, 1923, 156.

A2400--A2499. Causes of animal characteristics: appearance and habits

A2411.2. Origin of color of bird. Cooks: Gill, 1876, 67-68; N.Z.: White, 1887-90, II, 120; Rennell: Elbert-Monberg, 1964, Nos. 53, 54.

A2411.2.1.16. Color of starling. Kapingamarangi: Elbert, 1948, 128; Elbert, 1949, 245.

A2411.2.6. Origin of color of other birds. Niue: Loeb, 1926, 110.

*A2411.2.6.12. Origin of color of hawk. N.Z.: Best, 1924, 145 f.

A2411.4. Origin of color of fish. Tuamotus: Stimson, 1937, 90.

A2411.4.2. Color of perch. N.Z.: Best, 1924, 184.

*A2411.4.4. Color of shark. Rennell: Elbert-Monberg, 1964, No. 37.

A2411.5.7. Color of shrimp. Hawaii: Beckwith, 1940, 234; Thrum, 1923, 260.

A2412.2. Markings on birds. N.Z.: White, 1887-90, II, 120.

A2412.3. Markings on insects. Mangareva: Hiroa, 1938, 322; N.Z.: Best, 1925, 994.

A2412.4. Markings on fish (See A2217.3, A2213.2.). Tokelau: Burrows, 1923, 154ff.; Niue: Smith, 1903, 98; N.Z.: Best, 1927, 265.

A2412.5.1. Markings on tortoise's back. Samoa: Krämer, 1902, I, 109.

*A2416.8. Why shark smells bad. Tokelau: Burrows, 1923, 155; Ellice Is.: Kennedy, 1931, 184; Bellona: Elbert-Monberg, 1964, Nos. 35a, 35b; Rennell: ibid., No. 37.

102

*A2421.9. Origin of the sandpiper's cry. Lau Is.:
St. Johnston,1918, 44f.

*A2433.1.1.1. Animal habitats determined by war of
fishes and birds. Samoa: Brown, 1915, 176.

A2433.2. Dog's characteristic haunt. Mangareva:
Massainoff, 1933, 57.

*A2433.4.7. Why chickens live upon land. Mangareva:
Massainoff, 1933, 57.

*A2433.5.8. Why caterpillars live in tree. Marquesas:
Handy, 1930, 115.

A2433.6.1.2. Why turtle lays eggs on beach. Hawaii:
*Beckwith, 1940, 22.

*A2434.3.4. Why plovers live on barren hill. Hawaii:
Beckwith, 1940, 467.

*A2434.3.5. Why one island has mosquitoes and other,
adjoining island, has none. Fijis: Hocart, 1929,
199; Fison, 1904, 96.

*A2434.3.6. Why certain fishes are found at specific
places. Hawaii: Fornander, 1918, V, 270f.; Thrum,
1907, 271f.; Samoa: Brown, 1915, 175; Fijis:
Hocart, 1929, 199; Fison, 1904, 96.

A2435.4. Food of birds. Samoa: Brown, 1915, 180;
Niue: Morris, 1919, 227.

*A2435.6.0.1. Food of sharks. Easter I.: Métraux, 1940,
319; Ontong Java: Sarfert, 1931, 328.

*A2442.1.1.1. Why some birds are flightless (rail,
cassowary). Uvea: Burrows, 1937, 168f.

*A2444.4. Why bonito is a deep-sea fish. Kapingamarangi:
Elbert, 1948, 129.

*A2444.5. Cause of flounder's erratic behavior. Bellona:
Elbert-Monberg, 1964, No. 39.

*A2455.0.1. Why some creatures are thievish. Niue:
Smith, 1903, 98.

*A2462.4. Why turtle draws its head beneath its shell.
Niue: Smith, 1903, 100.

*A2464.2. Why the sandfly attacks man by day, the
mosquito by night. N.Z.: Best, 1925, 993.

*A2468.4. Why dying dolphins change color. Tahiti:
Henry, 1928, 390.

A2479.6. Why caterpillars climb trees. Marquesas:
Handy, 1930, 115.

*A2479.10. Why bonito follow eel. Tonga: Gifford,
1924, 57.

*A2482.4. Why bonito appear at the same spot every
year. Tonga: Gifford, 1924, 60.

A2484.1. Why fish come in seasonally. Hawaii:
McAllister, 1933, 108; Samoa: Krämer, 1902, I,
355; Tonga: Gifford, 1924, 60.

*A2486.5. Why turtles lay eggs on beaches. Hawaii:
Thrum, 1907, 239.

*A2490.0.1. God (Tane) assigns birds, beasts, and fish
their habitat and season. Tahiti: Henry, 1928,
418ff.

A2491. Why certain animals avoid light. Niue: Loeb,
1926, 110.

*A2491.1.0.1. Origin of flying fox's nocturnal habits:
birds and beasts hate him for his hypocrisy.
Niue: Loeb, 1926, 195.

A2494.13.4. Enmity between owl and mice (rat). Hawaii:
Pukui-Curtis, n.d., 75; Samoa: Sierich, 1902,
185f.

A2494.16.7. Enmity between octopus and rat. Tonga:
Gifford, 1924, 206; Samoa: Paul Hambruch, Nauru
(Hamburg, 1914-15), 287; Krämer, 1902, I, 359;
Niue: Loeb, 1926, 194.

*A2494.16.8. Enmity between carnivorous fish and turtle.
Ellice Is.: Kennedy, 1931, 178.

A2500--A2599. Animal characteristics
--miscellaneous

*A2511.2. Origin of bad taste of fish's flesh: from
being urinated upon by god. Hawaii: Fornander,
1916, IV, 530; Niue: Loeb, 1926, 170.

*A2513.6. How fowl was domesticated. Societies:
Henry, 1928, 381.

*A2529. Why animal (coral rat) is weak. Tonga: Brown,
1916, 430.

A2584.1. Why certain district is free of mosquitoes.
Fijis: Hocart, 1929, 199; Fison, 1904, 94.

A2600--A2699. ORIGIN OF TREES AND PLANTS

A2600--A2649. Various origins of plants

A2600. Origin of plants. Hawaii: Beckwith, 1932,
174ff.; Niue: Guppy, 1890, 48; N.Z.: Clark,
1896, 15.

*A2603. Culture hero plants trees (which have legs)
feet down, but they do not prosper. He plants them
head down and they do well. N.Z.: White, 1887-90,
I, 27, 138, 143.

*A2604. A god draws plants from the ground as with a
rope. Tokelaus: Lister, 1892, 43f.

A2611. Plants from body of slain person or animal.
Marquesas: Steinen, 1934-35, 196, 227f.;
Societies: Henry, 1928, 420f.;   Cooks: Luomala,
1949, 169; Hawaii: Beckwith, 1940, 99; Tonga:
Beckwith, 1940, 101; Gifford, 1924, 72; Rotuma:
Churchward, 1938-39, 466.

A2611.0.1. Plants from grave of dead person or animal.
Hawaii: Thrum, 1923, 235; Westervelt, 1915,7, 63f.;
Samoa: Stuebel, 1896, 68ff.; N.Z.: Wohlers, 1875,
7.

A2611.0.2. Plants from foetus or body of stillborn
child. Hawaii: Beckwith, 1940, 98.

A2611.0.4. Parts of body of god transformed into plants. Hawaii: Beckwith, 1940, 188.

A2611.0.4.1. Women transformed into flowers. Marquesas. Handy, 1930, 135.

A2611.0.5. Parts of human or animal body transformed into plants. Societies: Henry, 1928, 373, 420f.; Hawaii: Beckwith, 1940, 99; Tonga: Beckwith, 1940, 101; Futuna: Burrows, 1936, 226.

*A2611.0.7. Woman (goddess) gives birth to plants. Marquesas: Christian, 1895, 189; N.Z.: Best, 1924, 155; Best, 1905, 209.

A2611.3. Coconut tree from head of slain monster (eel). Polynesia (general): **Kirtley, 1967, 89ff.; Luomala, 1949, 120; Mangareva: Hiroa, 1938, 312; Tuamotus: *Audran, 1918, 134, 134 n. 3; Beckwith, 1940, 103; Caillot, 1914, 27f.; Danielsson, 1952, 60f.; Luomala, 1949, 81; Malarde, 1933, 499, 672; Seurat, 1905, 438f.; Stimson, n.d., Z-G. 13/52; Stimson, 1934, 33ff.; Stimson, 1937, 41ff.; Societies: Agostini, 1900, 77; Baessler, 1905, 921f.; Tahiti: Henry, 1928, 617; Seurat, 1905, 437ff.; Cooks: Beckwith, 1940, 104; Gill, 1876, 78; Samoa: Andersen, 1925, 143; Lesson, 1876, 598; Nelson, 1925, 133; Stuebel, 1896, 68; Niue: Loeb, 1926, 105, 171; N.Z.: Best, 1924, 141; Bellona: Elbert-Monberg, 1964, Nos. 41a, 41b Rennell: Elbert-Monberg, 1964, No. 65.

*A2611.3.1. Coconut tree from head of human. (Cf. *D429.3.). Tuamotus: Danielsson, 1952, 60f.; Societies: *Henry, 1928, 420ff.

*A2611.3.2. Origin of coconut tree from transformed human. Hawaii: Dickey, 1917, 16.

*A2611.6.2. Origin of moss: from human hair. Societies Henry, 1928, 421.

*A2611.6.3. Fungus from transformed hair. Rennell: Elbert-Monberg, 1964, No. 20.

*A2611.8. Origin of kava: from person's planted body. Marquesas: Steinen, 1934-35, 196.

*A2614. Plants from dung. Tonga: Beckwith, 1940, 102; Collocott, 1928, 61; Ontong Java: Sarfert, 1931, 312, 384.

A2615.3. Canoe transformed into coconut tree. Hawaii:

Beckwith, 1940, 232.

A2617. Plants from transformed person (animal). Hawaii: Fornander, 1918, V, 676ff.; Pukui-Curtis, n.d., 39; Smith, 1955, 50; Thrum, 1923, 240.

A2617.1. Living boys and girls transformed into plants. Tahiti: Beckwith, 1940, 101.

A2625. Plants from clothing of deity. Tahiti: Henry, 1928, 338; Hawaii: Beckwith, 1940, 282.

*A2635. Plant brought (sent) from otherworld. Mangareva: Hiroa, 1938, 21; Tuamotus: Stimson, n.d., Z-G. 3/1332; Societies: Henry, 1928, 463; Hawaii: Beckwith, 1940, 242; Tonga: Caillot, 1914, 250f.; Reiter, 1934, 513; Gifford, 1924, 17; Samoa: Krämer, 1902, I, 392; Luomala, 1949, 119; Stair, 1896, 36; Rotuma: Churchward, 1937-38, 367f.; 1938-39, 125; N.Z.: Best, 1905, 209; Locke, 1921, 42; White, 1887-90, I, 145, 149; Futuna: Burrows, 1936, 226; Lau Is.: St. Johnston, 1918, 43f.; Rennell: Elbert-Monberg, 1964, Nos. 40, 194.

A2650--A2699. Origin of various plants and trees

A2650. Origin of flowers. N.Z.: Best, 1925, 916.

A2665. Origin of wild morning glory. Hawaii: Beckwith, 1940, 282.

A2681. Origin of trees. Mangareva: Hiroa, 1938, 23; N.Z.: Best, 1905, 207; Best, 1925, 765; White, 1887-90, I, 143, 145, 149; II, 64; Wohlers, 1875, 7.

A2681.5.1. Origin of coconut tree. (See A2611.3.). Polynesia (general): **Kirtley, 1967, 89ff.; Mangareva: Caillot, 1914, 174, 176; Tuamotus: Stimson, n.d., Z-G. 3/1332; Marquesas: Handy, 1930, 30; Societies: Beckwith, 1940, 101; Hawaii: Beckwith, 1940, 104, 232; Fornander, 1918, V, 590ff., 596ff.; Samoa: Stuebel, 1896, 145; Niue: Smith, 1903, 88; Lau Is.: St. Johnston,

1918, 43f.; Ontong Java: Parkinson, 1898, 195;
Sarfert, 1931, 412; Nukumanu: Sarfert, 1931, 412.

A2681.6. Origin of bamboo. Tuamotus: Stimson, n.d.,
Z-G. 3/1332; Tahiti: Henry, 1923, 36.

A2681.9. Origin of mulberry tree. Marquesas: Handy,
1930, 123; Hawaii: Westervelt, 1915, 7, 63f.

A2681.10. Origin of banyan tree. Marquesas: Handy,
1930, 123; Societies: Henry, 1928, 463.

A2681.11. Origin of breadfruit tree. Mangareva:
Caillot, 1914, 174; Societies: Henry, 1928, 420,
423ff.; Cooks: Ariki, 1899, 66; Luomala, 1949,
169; Hawaii: Beckwith, 1940, 68, 97, 98, 101;
Fornander, 1918, V, 676ff.; Pukui-Curtis, n.d.,
39; Thrum, 1923, 240; Samoa: Stuebel, 1896,
145; Kapingamarangi: Elbert, 1948, 114; Elbert,
1949, 245.

A1423. Acquisition of vegetables and
cereals.

*A2681.12. Origin of casuarina trees. Societies:
Henry, 1928, 420.

*A2681.13. Origin of Tahitian chestnuts. Societies:
Henry, 1929, 420.

*A2681.14. Origin of red-leaved dracaena plant. Rotuma:
Churchward, 1937-38, 367f.

*A2681.15. Origin of pandanus trees. Hawaii: Fornander
1918, V, 656.

*A2681.16. Origin of almond tree. Lau Is.: St. Johnsto
1918, 44.

*A2681.17. Origin of papaya. Tonga: Collocott,1928, 61

A2682. Origin of creepers. Hawaii: Westervelt, 1915,
48; Rennell: Elbert-Monberg, 1964, Nos. 76a, 78.

A2684. Origin of cultivated plants. Mangareva: Hiroa,
1938, 21; Hawaii: Thrum, 1923, 235ff.; Tonga:
Gifford, 1924, 17f.; Samoa: Luomala, 1949, 119;
Rennell: Elbert-Monberg, 1964, No. 191.

*A2684.4. Origin of sugar cane. Societies: Henry,
1928, 421; Tonga: Beckwith, 1940, 101; Samoa:

Stuebel, 1896, 68ff.

A2686.3.1. Origin of kava plant (piper methysticum).
Marquesas: Steinen, 1934-35, 196, 227f.;
Christian, 1895, 189; Tonga: Beckwith, 1940,
101; Gifford, 1924, 72, 75; Samoa: Krämer,
1902, I, 393, 416ff.; Powell-Pratt, 1892, 97, 104,
107f.; Stuebel, 1896, 68ff., 150; Futuna:
Burrows, 1936, 226; Rotuma: Churchward, 1938-39,
466.

A2686.4.1. Origin of sweet potato. Hawaii: Beckwith,
1940, 99, 242; N.Z.: Best, 1905, 209; Best, 1925,
920, 923f.; Locke, 1921, 42; Luomala, 1949, 117;
White, 1887-90, I, 142; III, 98, 102, 106, 107,
108ff., 111ff., 114ff., 116ff.; IV, 3ff.; V, 5ff.

A2686.4.2. Origin of taro. Societies: Henry, 1928,
421; Hawaii: Beckwith, 1932, 192; Beckwith, 1940,
98; Tonga: Reiter, 1934, 513;; Samoa: Kramer,
1902, I, 392; Stair, 1896, 36; Rotuma: Churchward,
1937-38, 367; Rennell: Elbert-Monberg, 1964,
Nos. 40, 194; Ontong Java: Parkinson, 1898, 195.

A2686.4.3. Origin of yams. Societies: Henry, 1928,
421; Tonga: Gifford, 1924, 17; Reiter, 1933,
357; Reiter, 1934, 513; Samoa: Kramer, 1902, I,
115f.

A2686.7. Origin of gourds. N.Z.: Best, 1925, 774, 782.

A2687.3. Origin of (kind of) berries. Hawaii:
Beckwith, 1940, 188, 282; Fornander, 1918, V,
576ff.

A2687.5. Origin of banana. Societies: Henry, 1928,
421; Tonga: Gifford, 1924, 17; Futuna: Burrows,
1936, 226.

*A2687.6. Origin of hutu fruit. Societies: Henry,
1928, 420.

*A2687.7. Origin of ora fig. Societies: Henry, 1928,
463.

A2688. Origin of weeds. Tonga: Gifford, 1924, 22.

*A2688.2. Origin of seaweed. N.Z.: Best, 1924, 155.

*A2689. Origin of kind of fern. N.Z.: Best, 1925, 782;
White, 1887-90, I, 39.

A2692. Origin of poisonous plants. Tonga: Gifford,
1924, 27.

A2700--A2749. Various origins of plant
characteristics

A2741.3. Sky rests on top of trees: hence flat leaves.
Hawaii: Beckwith, 1940, 495; Cooks: Gill, 1876,
58; Niue: Loeb, 1926, 211.

*A2744. Origin of eyes of coconut. Cooks: Gill, 1876,
58.

A2750--A2799. Origin of various plant
characteristics

A2751.1. Origin of bark on plants. Societies: Henry,
1928, 421.

A2751.4.6. Why kava plant is grey. Tonga: Gifford,
1924, 72.

*A2755.1.0.1. Why certain trees have reddish wood.
N.Z.: White, 1887-90, II, 91, 116, 117.

A2755.2. Origin of blood colored sap in trees. Tonga:
Collocott, 1928, 7; Bellona: Elbert-Monberg, 1964
No. 50a; Rennell: Elbert-Monberg, 1964, 50b.

*A2755.2.2. Why the fei tree has purple sap. Tahiti:
Henry, 1928, 579.

*A2755.3.3. Why bamboo is sharp on the inside and not
the outside. Hawaii: Fornander, 1918, V, 588.

*A2758. Why the stalks of certain plants are hollow.
Hawaii: Forbes, 1879, 60.

A2764.1. Why taro leaves are hollow. Hawaii; Beckwith
1940, 229.

A2768. Why leaves hang head downward. N.Z.: Clark,
1896, 96.

*A2769.2. Why banana leaves droop. Niue: Loeb, 1926,
213.

*A2771.8.0.1. All fruits once bitter. Mangareva:
Massainoff, 1933, 58.

*A2771.8.3. Why fruit of kanumea tree is sour. Niue:
Loeb, 1926, 213.

*A2771.8.4. Why some fruits are bitter, others sweet.
Mangareva: Massainoff, 1933, 58.

*A2771.8.5. Why a plant is bitter. Tonga: Reiter,
1933, 359.

*A2774.2. Why trees grow with their roots, instead of
their branches, in the earth. N.Z.: Cowan,
1930, I, 4; White, 1887-90, I, 27, 138, 143.

A2778.1. Why coconut tree is tall. Hawaii: Beckwith,
1940, 98.

A2782. Origin of combustible property of wood. Tonga:
Gifford, 1920, 23; Samoa: Powell-Pratt, 1892,
82, 85 n. 34; Niue: Thomson, 1902, 87; N.Z.:
Best, 1925, 795.

A2785.1. Origin of shape of wiliwili tree. Hawaii:
Beckwith, 1940, 495.

*A2785.2. Origin of shape of arrow-root tree. Cooks:
Gill, 1876, 58.

*A2785.3. Why some trees lift their foliage erect.
Samoa: Brown, 1915, 180.

*A2785.4. Why some trees bend down their tops.
Mangareva: Hiroa, 1938, 313; Samoa: Brown, 1915.
180; Niue: Loeb,1926, 213; N.Z.: White,
1887-90, I, 78.

*A2791.1.1. Why tree neither speaks nor bears fruit:
man did not plant it as instructed. Samoa:
Brown, 1917, 98f.

*A2791.14. Why some plants are not edible. Mangareva:
Hiroa, 1938, 21; Rennell: Elbert-Monberg, 1964,
No. 40.

*A2793.10. Why certain trees do not grow in certain
locations. Lau Is.: St. Johnston, 1918, 111;
Rennell: Elbert-Monberg, 1964, 74.

*A2793.11. Why a kind of grass is so viable: it was
used to cover the corpse of a culture hero. To
Tonga: Caillot, 1914, 277.

111

A2800--A2899. MISCELLANEOUS EXPLANATIONS

A2800--A2842. Miscellaneous explanations:
origins

*A2818. Origin of puff balls which grow on rotten
wood: from human ears. Societies: Henry, 1928,
421.

A2828. Origin of particular kinds of basket. Tonga:
Gifford, 1924, 140.

*A2836. Why wells are on one island, pandanus trees on
another. Tokelau: Macgregor,1937, 62f.

A2850--A2899. Miscellaneous explanations:
characteristics

A2775. Why babies have soft spots in head. Hawaii:
Beckwith, 1940, 507.

A2872. Why coral is soft. Tonga: Gifford, 1924,
136.

B. ANIMALS

B0--B99. Mythical animals

B11. Dragon. Hawaii: Westervelt, 1915, 41, 42, 53f., 102, 116ff.

B11.2.0.1. She dragon (dragon-woman). Hawaii: Westervelt, 1915, 152ff., 257.

B11.2.1.2. Dragon as modified lizard. (The giant lizard monsters of Polynesia and elsewhere are here equated with the Eurasian dragon concept. The terms most commonly used in Polynesia are as follows: New Zealand--taniwha, ngarora; Hawaii, Tahiti--mo'o; Pukapuka--ngolo.)
Tuamotus: Stimson, 1937, 147ff.; Tahiti: Henry, 1923, 35; Henry, 1928, 621f.; Hawaii: Beckwith, 1940, 125; Dickey, 1917, 28; Emerson, 1915, 35, 49, 83f.; Fornander, 1916, IV, 38ff.; 1918, V, 38f., 412; 1918, VI, 344; Luomala, 1951, 30; Rice, 1923, 91, 112; Westervelt, 1915, 42, 103; Cooks: Gill, 1911, 150; Pukapuka: Beaglehole, 1938, 328; Hutchin, 1904, 174; Tonga: Collocott, 1914, 291; Collocott, 1921, 50; Reiter, 1917-18, 1044; N.Z.: Best, 1893, 211ff., 219; *Best, 1924, 187ff., 193; Best, 1925, 715, 959ff.; Cowan, 1930, I, 78f., 235; Gudgeon, 1905, 182, 186; Skinner, 1897, 156 f.; Smith, 1909, 210, 212; *Steinen, 1933-34, 4f.; Te Aro, 1894, 166; Te Whetu, 1897, 18.

B11.2.1.3. Dragon as modified fish (sea monster). Tuamotus: Seurat, 1906, 127; Hawaii: Beckwith, 1919, 27; Emerson, 1915, xiv; N.Z.: Best, 1925, 80, 923, 959ff.; Cowan, 1930, I, 64; White, 1887-90, III, 180; V, 12; Bellona: Elbert-Monberg, 1964, Nos. 41a, 41b.

B11.2.1.4. Dragon as modified shell-fish. Cooks: Savage, 1910, 151.

*B11.2.11.0.1. Mythical dragon (ngarora)blows steam from nose. N.Z.: Best, 1893, 219.

*B11.2.11.0.2. Mythical dragon (taniwha) whose eyes cast flaming rays of light. N.Z.: Smith, 1905, 203.

B11.2.12. Dragon of enormous size. Hawaii: Emerson, 1915, 91.

*B11.2.15. Lizard monster with a detachable tongue. Hawaii: Luomala, 1951, 30.

B11.3.1.1. Dragon lives in lake. N.Z.: Best, 1925, 967; Cowan, 1930, I, 131ff.

*B11.3.1.3. Water monster inhabits a stream. N.Z.: Best, 1925, 966.

B11.3.5. Dragon lives under the ground. By his movements trees and buildings are dislodged. N.Z.: Best, 1899, 114; Best, 1925, 966f.; Gudgeon, 1905, 188; White, 1887-90, III, 180.

*B11.3.9. Dragon lives at bottom of pit. Hawaii: Fornander, 1916, IV, 38ff.

B11.4.1. Flying dragon. Hawaii: Westervelt, 1915, 165.

B11.5.1. Dragon's power of self-transformation. Able to take any shape. N.Z.: Grace, 1907, 94ff.; *Gudgeon, 1905, 181ff.

*B11.5.6. Lizard monsters which jump like grasshoppers. Hawaii: Emerson, 1915, 49.

*B11.6.1.3. Sea monsters led by hero save battle for latter's father. Tuamotus: Stimson, n.d., T-G. 3/615.

*B11.6.1.4. Water-monster avenges master's death. N.Z.: Kauika, 1904, 95.

*B11.6.1.5. Dragon rescues people from drowning. N.Z.: Gudgeon, 1906, 41.

B11.6.2. Dragon guards treasure. Hawaii: Dickey, 1917, 28.

*B11.6.2.0.1. Guardian dragon of a tribe. N.Z.: Cowan, 1930, I, 78ff.

*B11.6.11. Dragon guards path. Hawaii: Westervelt, 1915, 197f.

*B11.6.12. Dragons are watchmen of the shark-god. Hawaii: Westervelt, 1915, 51f.

*B11.6.13. Dragons make a bridge across a river.

Hawaii: Westervelt, 1915, 258.

*B11.7.1.1.1.   Lizard monster causes thunder and lightning.
N.Z.:   Skinner, 1897, 156.

*B11.7.1.1.2.   Reptile monster causes landslides.   N.Z.:
Gudgeon, 1905, 188.

B11.7.2.   Dragon guards lake.   Hawaii: Beckwith, 1940,
125.

*B11.10.0.2.   First fruits offered to lizard monster.
N.Z.:   Skinner, 1897, 157.

*B11.10.2.1.   Man-eating dragon.   N.Z.:   Cowan, 1930,
I, 85ff., 134ff.

*B11.19.4.   Mythical lizard kills all passersby.   Hawaii:
Rice, 1923, 112;   N.Z.:   Te Aro, 1921, 167;
Te Whetu, 1895, 18.

B11.11.   Fight with dragon.   Hawaii: Emerson, 1915, 35;
Westervelt, 1915, 198.

B11.12.7.   Human-dragon marriage.   N.Z.:   Best, 1925,
715.

B15.1.2.1.4.   Two-headed dog.   N.Z.:   Smith, 1911, 12;
White, 1887-90, III, 124, 190.

*B15.1.2.1.5.   Two-headed bird.   N.Z.:   Gudgeon, 1906, 45.

*B15.1.2.6.2.   Seven-headed eel.   Tuamotus: Seurat,
1905, 485.

*B15.1.2.7.1.   Snake with eight heads.   Tonga: Gifford,
1924, 178.

*B15.1.2.8.3.   Nine-headed dove.   Samoa: Stuebel, 1896,
149.

B15.4.1.4.   Eight-eyed bat.   Hawaii: Beckwith, 1940,
233;   Thrum, 1923, 252ff.

*B15.4.1.5.   Eight-eyed hog.   Hawaii: Thrum, 1921, 109;
Thrum, 1923, 207;   Westervelt, 1915, 258.

*B15.7.7.2.   Eel with eight tails.   N.Z.:   Best, 1925,
970.

*B15.7.18.   Bird whose feathers are armed with talons.
Hawaii: Fornander, 1916, IV, 64;   Westervelt,
1915, 68.

B16.1.2. Devastating dog. Hawaii: Beckwith, 1919, 335, 472; Fornander, 1918, V, 412; Tonga: Brown, 1916, 430; Caillot, 1914, 297ff.; Collocott, 1921a,51, 53; Collocott, 1921b, 153; Reiter, 1919-20, 125ff., 128; N.Z.: Cowan, 1930, I, 108ff.

B16.1.4. Devastating swine. Societies: Henry, 1928, 538, 562f.; Hawaii: Fornander, 1918, V, 362; Westervelt, 1915, 252ff., 258ff.; Reef Is.: O'Ferrall, 1904, 231f.

*B16.2.10. Man-eating rat. Tonga: Caillot, 1914, 288ff.; Collocott, 1921a, 49f.; Reiter, 1917-18, 1042f.

B16.3. Devastating birds. See B33.

*B16.4.2. Man-eating shark. Cooks: Gill, 1876, 225; Savage, 1910, 151; Hawaii: Green, 1926, 102ff.; Pukui, 1933, 155; Westervelt, 1915, 56f.; Tonga: Collocott, 1921a, 52; Tokelaus: Burrows, 1923, 156.

*B16.4.3. Monstrous man-eating swordfish. Cooks: Savage, 1910, 152.

*B16.4.4. Man-eating eel. Niue: Loeb, 1926, 158.

*B16.4.5. Man-eating crab. Uvea: Burrows, 1937, 169 n. 18.

B16.5. Devastating (man-eating) reptiles. Tuamotus: Stimson, 1937, 147f.; Tahiti: Henry, 1923, 35; Hawaii: Dickey, 1917, 29; Emerson, 1915, 83ff.; Fornander, 1916, IV, 38ff.; 1918, V, 412; Tonga: Caillot, 1914, 291; Collocott, 1921a, 50; Reiter, 1917-18, 1044; N.Z.: Cowan, 1930, I,188; White, 1887-90, V, 56f.

*B16.5.1.0.1. Man-eating lizard monsters. N.Z.: *Gudgeon, 1905, 181ff.

B16.5.1.2. Devastating (man-eating) sea-monster (serpent) Samoa: Lesson, 1876, 603; Niue: Loeb, 1926, 186.

B16.6.5. Devastating centipede. Cooks: Gill, 1876, 150.

*B16.6.5.1. Devastating caterpillar. Tahiti: Lagarde, 1933, 699.

*B17.2.1.2.1. Man-eating eel. Polynesia (general): **Kirtley, 1967, 89ff.; Marquesas: *Steinen,

1933-34, 1, 2; Samoa: Stuebel, 1896, 151, 153;
Hawaii: Smith, 1966, 8f.; Chatham Is.: Shand,
1896, 203.

*B17.2.5. Marauding and devastating seals. Tuamotus:
Caillot, 1914, 42.

*B19.14. Red pigs. N.Z.: Cowan, 1930, I, 69.

B25. Man-dog. Hawaii: Beckwith, 1940, 205.

B29.2. Echidna. Half woman, half serpent. N.Z.:
White, 1887-90, II, 28.

B29.2.1. Serpent with human head. N.Z.: Best,
1893, 219.

*B29.2.4. Lizard-woman. Hawaii: Fornander, 1916, IV,
54; Green, 1926, 113; Smith, 1966, 18; N.Z.:
Best, 1924, 190; Wohlers, 1876, 117.

B29.3. Man-hog. Hawaii: *Beckwith, 1940, Chap. XIV,
201ff.; Westervelt, 1915, 258.

*B29.3.1. Man-hog roots up growing crops while in hog
form. Hawaii: Beckwith, 1940, 204.

*B29.10. Rat-people. Hawaii: Fornander, 1916, IV,
54, 122ff., 162; Thrum, 1923, 150ff.

B30. Mythical birds. Tuamotus: Stimson, n.d.,
Z-G. 3/1276; Hawaii: Beckwith, 1940, 29; Fornander,
1916, IV, 64; 1918, V, 600; 1918, VI, 343;
Westervelt, 1915, 68ff.; Rennell: Elbert-Monberg,
1964, No. 8.

B30.1. Mythical white albatross. Hawaii: Beckwith,
1940, 92.

*B30.3. Mythical chicken. Hawaii: McAllister, 1933,
76.

B31.1. Roc. A giant bird which carries off men in its
claws. Tuamotus: Beckwith, 1940, 261, 267;
Hawaii: Beckwith, 1940, 45, 492; Fornander, 1916,
IV, 64; Westervelt, 1915, 68; N.Z.: Pakauwera,
1894, 102-103; White, 1887-90, II, 142; Fijis:
Fison, 1904, 82.

*B31.1.3. Giant bird picks up canoe, deposits it (and
occupants) in tree. Ellice Is.: Kennedy, 1931,
168.

117

*B31.1.4. Giant bird attempts to sink canoe. Tahiti: Henry,1928, 472; Hawaii: Beckwith, 1940, 92 (canoe sinks when bird vomits over it).

*B31.4.1. Giant white vampire-bat. Fijis: Fison, 1904, 125.

B31.6.1. Giant blackbird. Tahiti: Henry, 1928, 494, 503.

B31.6.2. Giant bird uproots trees. Societies: Henry, 1928, 384.

*B31.6.2.2. Giant bird overturns hill. Societies: Henry, 1928, 384.

B33. Man-eating birds. Hawaii: Emory, 1924, 12; Fornander, 1916, IV, 64; Tonga: Caillot,1914, 291ff.; Collocott, 1921a, 50; Reiter, 1917-18, 1044ff.; Samoa: Brown, 1917, 95; Stuebel, 1896, 145; Tokelaus: Burrows, 1923, 163f.; Chatham Is.: Shand, 1896, 203; N.Z.: White, 1887-90, II, 33; III, 194.

*B33.0.1. Man-eating bat. Hawaii: Beckwith, 1940, 227.

*B39.2. Demon bird. Tuamotus: Beckwith, 1940,261, 267.

*B39.3. Bird-in-the-sun. N.Z.: Smith, 1897, 22.

B50. Bird-men. Hawaii: Beckwith, 1940, 80; Emory, 1924, 12; Thrum, 1923, 166f., 181f., 184; Westervelt, 1915, 46.

D150. Transformation: man to bird.

B53.0.1. Siren in mermaid form. Hawaii: Beckwith, 1940, 495; Green, 1926, 97.

*B58. Chicken-people. Hawaii: Fornander, 1918, V, 266; McAllister, 1933, 154; Thrum, 1923, 165f.; Westervelt, 1915, 206ff.

B60. Mythical fish. Hawaii: Thrum, 1923, 155.

B60.1. Parent of all fishes. Hawaii: Beckwith, 1940, 24.

*B60.2. Mythical fish: back covered with stones and seaweed. Hawaii: Rice, 1923, 117.

B61. Leviathan. Giant fish (sea monster). Hawaii:
Remy, 1868, 42; Westervelt, 1915, 215; N.Z.:
Best, 1925, 966ff.; White, 1887-90, IV, 107,
132, 146; V, 12, 43.

B63. Mythical octopus. Societies: Henry, 1928,
410ff.; Marquesas: Handy, 1930, 74; Hawaii:
Beckwith, 1940, 22.

B64. Mythical eel. Marquesas: *Steinen, 1933-34,
1ff.; Tahiti, Hawaii, Tonga, Samoa: *Beckwith,
1940, 102ff.; Hawaii: Thrum, 1923, 68; N.Z.:
Best, 1925, 833ff.; Cowan, 1930, I, 69.

B65. Mythical shark. Tuamotus: Stimson, n.d.,
Z-G. 13/317; Hawaii: Beckwith, 1940, 128ff.;
Fornander,1918, V, 366ff.; Green, 1926, 102;
Thrum, 1923, 293.

*B69. Mythical fish: miscellaneous.

*B69.1. Mythical sting-ray. Tuamotus: Stimson, n.d.,
Z-G. 13/317.

*B69.2. Mythical sword-fish. Tuamotus: Stimson, n.d.,
Z-G. 13/441.

*B69.3. A fish with legs. Hawaii: Green, 1926, 111f.

B80.2. Monster: half-man, half-fish (usually shark).
Marquesas: Steinen, 1934-35, 238; Hawaii:
Beckwith, 1940, 141; Fornander, 1918, V, 140;
Green, 1926, 103; N.Z.: Cowan, 1930, 10, 89ff.;
White, 1887-90, II, 128.

*B80.3. Octopus-man: octopus body, human head. Rotuma:
Churchward, 1938-39, 467.

*B80.4. Eel-man. Tuamotus: Audran, 1918, 134; Tahiti:
Beckwith, 1940, 102; Samoa: Nelson, 1925, 132.

*B80.5. Fish-man with shark's mouth in his back. Hawaii:
Rice, 1923, 111.

B81. Mermaid. Woman with tail of fish. Lives in sea.
Hawaii: Beckwith, 1940, 541; Green, 1926, 111,
113; N.Z.: White, 1887-90, II, 127f.

B81.2. Mermaid marries man. Hawaii: Beckwith, 1940,
541.

B82. Merman. Tuamotus: Audran, 1918, 92; N.Z.:

Best, 1925, 959, 968.

B91. Mythical serpent. Fijis: Fison, 1904, 27.

B91.5. Sea-serpent. Tuamotus: Henry, 1928, 525;
Stimson, n.d., T-G. 3/615; Tahiti: Henry, 1928,
469, 471; Niue: *Loeb, 1926, 186; Chatham Is.:
Shand, 1896, 209; N.Z.: Best, 1893, 217; Best,
1924, 156; Kauika, 1904, 94ff.

*B91.5.0.1. Sea-serpent demands that people in canoe
sacrifice woman. Tahiti: Henry, 1928, 471.

B11.10. Sacrifice of human being to
dragon.

B92. Other mythical reptiles. Hawaii: Beckwith,
1940, 125.

*B92.2. Mythical turtle. Ellice Is.: Grimble, 1952,
18; Ontong Java: Sarfert, 1931, 329.

*B99.3. Mythical caterpillar. Tahiti: Lagarde, 1933,
699.

B100--B199. MAGIC ANIMALS

B120--B169. Animals with magic wisdom

B122. Bird with magic wisdom. Tuamotus: Stimson,
n.d., Z-G. 13/317.

B122.1. Bird as advisor. Tuamotus: Stimson, n.d.,
Z-G. 13/317.

*B122.1.3. Bird instructs prince how to kill sting-ray.
Tuamotus: Stimson, n.d., Z-G. 13/317.

*B124.2. Boy trained by mythical whale to become
great warrior. Tuamotus: Stimson, n.d., T-G.
3/615.

*B131.3.1. Two roosters inform king of projected flight
of princess. Tuamotus: Stimson, n.d., Z-G. 13/221.

*B137. Truth-telling fish tells of theft. N.Z.:

Gudgeon, 1906, 35.

B143. Prophetic bird. Tuamotus: Stimson, n.d.,
Z-G. 13/317; Marquesas: Handy, 1930, 117;
N.Z.: Clark, 1896, 95; Kapingamarangi: Elbert,
1948, 119.

*B143.1.7. Bird shows man where to fish. Marquesas:
Handy, 1930, 117.

B147.2. Birds furnish omens. Tuamotus: Stimson,
n.d., Z-G. 13/317.

B147.2.2.4. Owl as bird of ill-omen. Tahiti: Henry,
1928, 383.

*B151.2.0.4. Two birds signal where king is to be
buried. Rotuma: Churchward, 1937-38, 252.

*B152.4. Blue bottlefly leads people to murderer.
N.Z.: Grace, 1901, 66.

*B152.5. Pig indicates whether or not person (or bones
of dead) of chiefly rank. Hawaii: Fornander, 1916,
IV, 188.

B170--B189. Other magic animals

*B171.3. Supernatural fowl. Hawaii: Beckwith, 1940,
203.

B172. Magic bird. Niue: Loeb, 1926, 191; N.Z.:
Gudgeon, 1906, 44.

*B172.12. Magic bird has power of witchcraft. N.Z.:
Gudgeon, 1906, 44.

B175. Magic fish. Samoa: Fraser, 1897, 76.

*B176.2. Magic lizard. N.Z.: Best, 1897, 44.

*B179.3. Magic cricket. Societies: Henry, 1928, 393.

*B179.4. Magic dragonfly. Dragonfly loosed in thieves'
house; inhabitants are blinded and dazed.
Societies: Henry, 1928, 391.

121

*B179.6. Magic caterpillar. After being cut to pieces, body parts rejoin. Tahiti: Lagarde, 1933, 699.

B182.1. Magic dog. Hawaii: *Beckwith, 1940, 347-348 and notes 347-348.

B200--B299. ANIMALS WITH HUMAN TRAITS

B211.1.7. Speaking dog. Mangareva: Massainoff, 1933, Hawaii: Green, 1923, 48; Pukui, 1933, 178.

B211.2.7. Speaking sea-beast (whale). Tuamotus: Stimson, 1937, 126.

B211.2.8. Speaking mouse. Bellona: Elbert-Monberg, 1964, No. 50a; Rennell: ibid., 50b, 51.

B211.2.9. Speaking rat. Mangareva: Hiroa, 1938, 327; Samoa: Krämer, 1902, I, 415; Sierich, 1902, 173, 183; N.Z.: White, 1887-90, II, 28; Uvea: Burrows, 1937, 168; Rennell: Elbert-Monberg, 1964, Nos. 50c, 51a.

B211.3. Speaking bird. Easter I.: Métraux, 1940, 373; Mangareva: Hiroa, 1938, 326; Tuamotus: Stimson, n.d., Z-G. 3/1260; Stimson, 1937, 46; Cooks: Kunike, 1928, 29; Rarotonga: Te Ariki, 1920, 124; Hawaii: Fornander, 1916, IV, 12, 18, 52ff., 444, 458, 462, 534; V, 600; Kamakau, 1961, 38; Westervelt, 1915, 233; Samoa: Krämer, 1902, I, 125 Lesson, 1876, 592; Tonga: Collocott, 1928, 59; Tokelau: Burrows, 1923, 163; N.Z.: Best, 1925, 920; Grace, 1907, 86; White, 1887-90, II, 175; III, 122f.; Rennell: Elbert-Monberg, 1964, No. 40; Kapingamarangi: Elbert, 1949, 241.

B211.3.2. Speaking cock. Tuamotus: Seurat, 1906, 125.

B211.3.2.1. Speaking chicken. Societies: Henry, 1928, 381.

B211.3.5. Speaking dove. Reef Is.: Elbert-Kirtley, 1966, 358.

*B211.3.12. Speaking owl. Hawaii: Fornander, 1916, IV, 600; Pukui-Curtis, n.d., 74ff.; Thrum, 1907, 200; Westervelt, 1915, 133f.; Samoa: Stair, 1895, 101; N.Z.: White, 1887-90, II, 128, 134.

*B211.3.13. Speaking pigeon. Tuamotus: Audran, 1919, 34, 48; Tonga: Collocott, 1928, 23; N.Z.: White, 1887-90, I, 84; Ellice Is.: David, 1899, 94.

*B211.3.14. Speaking sea-swallow. Societies: Henry, 1928, 411.

*B211.3.15. Speaking plovers. Rotuma: Churchward, 1937-38, 493.

*B211.3.16. Speaking kula birds. Marquesas: Steinen, 1933-34, 12.

*B211.3.18. Speaking snipe. Uvea: Burrows, 1937, 165.

*B211.3.19. Speaking ducks. Tuamotus: Stimson, 1937, 101; Hawaii: Fornander, 1916, IV, 226.

*B211.3.20. Speaking mud-hens. Hawaii: Forbes, 1879, 60.

B211.4. Speaking insects. N.Z.: Best, 1925, 993.

*B211.4.4. Speaking fly. Chatham Is.: Shand, 1895, 211.

*B211.4.7. Speaking caterpillars. Hawaii: Green, 1923, 44.

B211.5. Speaking fish. Mangareva: Caillot, 1914, 195; Tuamotus: Stimson, 1937, 69f.; Marquesas: Lavondes, 1964, 64; Hawaii: Thrum, 1923, 224; Tonga: Collocott, 1928, 33; Tokelau: Burrows, 1923, 170; N.Z.: Best, 1925, 994; Grace, 1907, 154ff.

*B211.5.1. Speaking shark. Tuamotus: Leverd, 1911, 178; Hawaii: Green, 1926, 105; Pukui, 1943, 58; Thrum, 1923, 230, 295ff.; Rotuma: Churchward, 1938-39, 229; Russell, 1942, 248.

*B211.5.2. Speaking eel. Mangareva: Hiroa, 1938, 315; Tuamotus: Henry, 1928, 620; Stimson, 1934, 10ff.; Marquesas: Steinen, 1933-34, 29, 31; Handy, 1930, 79; Tahiti: Henry, 1928, 617; Cooks: Savage, 1910, 145; Hawaii: Westervelt, 1915, 213; Samoa: Andersen, 1925, 143; N.Z.: White, 1887-90, I, 124.

B211.6.1. Speaking serpent. Cooks: Kunike, 1928, 29; Fijis: Hocart, 1929, 223; Rennell: Elbert-Monberg, 1964, Nos. 51a, 51b.

*B211.6.2. Speaking lizard. Tuamotus: Stimson, 1937,
143, 147; Hawaii: Fornander, 1916, IV, 39ff.;
N.Z.: Best, 1925, 994; White, 1887-90, II, 28;
Tokelaus: Macgregor, 1937, 83; Fijis: Hocart,
1929, 196; Bellona: Elbert-Monberg, 1964, No. 49.

*B211.6.3. Speaking turtle. Easter I.: Métraux, 1940,
373; Tuamotus: Seurat, 1906, 125; Societies:
Henry, 1928, 381; Hawaii: Westervelt, 1915, 212;
Reef Is.: Elbert-Kirtley, 1966, 369.

*B211.6.4. Speaking crocodile. Samoa: Sierich, 1902,
167.

*B211.8.1. Speaking crab. Easter I.: Metraux, 1940,
365; Uvea: Burrows, 1937, 168-169.

B223.1. Kingdom of sharks. Hawaii: Beckwith, 1940,
140; Thrum, 1923, 295ff., 301, 307.

B232. Parliament of birds. N.Z.: H.T.,1901, 74.

*B242.2.13. King of rails. Uvea: Burrows, 1937, 168.

B243. King of fishes. N.Z.: Grace, 1907, 156.

B243.1.3. Shark as king of fishes. Societies:
Ropiteau, 1933, 128; Cooks: Gill, 1876, 92;
Hawaii: Beckwith, 1940, 140; Fornander, 1918, V,
294, 366ff.; Thrum, 1923, 295ff., 307;
Westervelt, 1915, 44, 60ff.

B244.3. King of lizards. Cooks: Gill, 1876, 225;
Hawaii: Fornander, 1916, IV, 534.

B261. War of birds and quadrupeds. Niue: Loeb,
1926, 194.

*B261.1.0.1. Flying-fox, during war of birds and beasts,
pretends to be bird when these are victorious, an
animal when animals are winning. Niue: Loeb, 1926
195.

*B261.1.0.2. Sea-cucumber fights with one side and then
another in the fight between fishes and birds.
Samoa: Brown, 1915, 174; Krämer, 1902, I, 358.

*B261.1.0.3. The palolo is rejected as combatant in
war of fish and birds. Samoa: Krämer, 1902, I,
356.

B263.5. War between groups of birds. Marquesas:
Steinen, 1934-35, 234; N.Z.: Best, 1924, 179, 181.

*B263.9. War between dogs and lizards. Dogs and lizards
have war; dogs win and eat lizards (it affects
dogs' fertility, and that is why there are fewer
dogs than in former days). N. Z.: Best, 1924, 185.

*B263.10. War of fishes. Nukumanu: Sarfert, 1931,
459f.

*B263.10.1. War between fish and men: whale commands
fish army. N.Z.: Best, 1924, 184.

*B263.10.2. War between birds and fishes. Samoa: Brown,
1915, 173f.; Krämer, 1902, I, 356, 358.

*B263.10.4. Battle of sharks. Hawaii: Green, 1926,
105ff.; Thrum, 1923, 308.

*B263.11. Battle between dragons and volcanoes. Hawaii:
Westervelt, 1915, 157f.

*B264.2.1. Fight between owl and eel. Samoa: Stair,
1895, 101.

*B264.6. Fight between serpent and bird. Cooks:
Beckwith, 1940, 269; Kunike, 1928, 29; Seurat,
1905, 485; Samoa: Elbert-Kirtley, 1966, 363;
Western Polynesia: Elbert-Kirtley, 1966, 362,
362 n. 20.

*B264.9. Fight between heron and lizard. N.Z.: Clark,
1896, 95.

*B268.5.2. Army of herons. Tahiti: Orsmond, 1933, 172.

*B271.4. Pigeon and flying-fox dispute about which
carries head best. Niue: Loeb, 1926, 203.

*B283.1.1. Wedding of shell and urchin. Easter I.:
Métraux, 1940, 373.

B291.1. Bird as messenger. Tuamotus: Audran, 1918,
30; Audran, 1919, 48, 59; Stimson, n.d.,
MB-DD-33, Z-G. 13/317; Marquesas: Beckwith, 1940,
91; Societies: Seurat, 1905, 438; Hawaii:
Beckwith, 1919, 335, 464, 472, 474, 476, 478;
*Beckwith, 1940, 90f.; Rice, 1923, 94; Fornander,
1916, IV, 52ff., 444, 534, 544; Thrum, 1907, 125;

Cooks: Clark, 1896, 142; Gill, 1876, 233; Tonga: Brown, 1916, 429; Samoa: Sierich, 1900, 231f.; N.Z.: Grace, 1907, 79; White, 1887-90, III, 59.

*B291.1.13. Plover as messenger. Hawaii: Rice, 1923, 99.

*B291.3.3. Rat serves as messenger. Mangareva: Hiroa, 1938, 327; Hawaii: Thrum, 1923, 152.

B291.4.3. Whale as messenger. Tahiti: Beckwith, 1940, 360.

*B291.4.4. Fish messengers. Mangareva: Caillot, 1914, 205.

*B291.4.5. Cuttlefish as messenger. Niue: Loeb, 1926, 193.

*B291.4.6. White vampire-bat as messenger. Fijis: Fison, 1904, 125.

B292.2.2. Bird as domestic servant. Hawaii: Beckwith, 1940, 526.

*B292.9.4. Owl that farms. Hawaii: Green, 1926, 67.

*B293.7. Dance of fish. Cooks: Gill, 1876, 102.

*B295.2. Animals build canoe. Samoa: Paul Hambruch, Nauru (Hamburg, 1914-15), 286; Krämer, 1902, I, 358; Sierich, 1902, 185; Niue: Loeb, 1926, 194; Uvea: Burrows, 1937, 167.

*B295.2.1. Animals make voyage in canoe. (Usually have shipwreck). Tonga: Collocott, 1928, 59; Gifford, 1924, 206; Samoa: Hambruch, 1914-15, 286 Kramer, 1902, I, 358; Sierich, 1902, 185; Tokelau: Burrows, 1923, 158; Ellice Is.: Kennedy, 1931, 16; David, 1899, 99.

*B296.2. Animal (which is a land-dweller) crosses water on back of another animal. Samoa: Krämer, 1902, I, 359; Sierich, 1902, 186.

*B296.3. A shark goes on a visiting tour. Hawaii: Thrum 1923, 294ff.

*B298.2. Snipe and sandpiper race. Uvea: Burrows, 1937, 166.

*B298.3. Animals (fishes) play hide-and-seek. Kapingamarangi: Elbert, 1949, 245.

126

*B298.4. Lizard and turtle have tug-of-war with conch
    shell. Fijis: Hocart, 1929, 218.

*B299.3.1. Fish which chews betel nut. Rennell:
    Elbert-Monberg, 1964, No. 47b.

*B299.14. Animals build house. Nukumanu: Sarfert,
    1931, 387.

*B299.15. Starling and bridle-tern decorate each other.
    Kapingamarangi: Elbert, 1948, 128.

            B300--B599. FRIENDLY ANIMALS

        B300--B349. Helpful animals--general

*B301.5.1. Ancestral shark resuscitates youth and his
    sweetheart. Tahiti: Henry, 1928, 631.

*B301.9. Pet fish. Tuamotus: Stimson, n.d., Z-G.
    13/499.

*B301.9.2. Whale fed and tamed. Tuamotus: Stimson,
    n.d., Z-G. 13/203.

*B301.10. Pet seals. Chatham I.: Shand, 1896, 206.

B336. Helpful animal killed (threatened) by
    ungrateful hero. Rotuma: Russell, 1942, 248.

        B350--B399. Grateful animals

B364.4. Bird grateful for being saved from attacking
    serpent. Cooks: Beckwith, 1940, 269; Reef Is.:
    Elbert-Kirtley, 1966, 358f.

            127

B400--B449. Helpful beasts

B421. Helpful dog. Hawaii: Beckwith, 1919, 472; Westervelt, 1915, 108ff.; N.Z.: Grace, 1907, 6ff.

B422. Helpful cat. Tonga: Gifford, 1924, 201.

B435.1. Helpful fox. Tonga: Gifford, 1924, 123.

B437.1. Helpful rat. Marquesas: Steinen, 1933-34, 26-27; Hawaii: Thrum, 1923, 26, 52; Reef Is.: O'Ferrall, 1904, 228; Rennell: Elbert-Monberg, 1964, Nos. 50c, 51a.

B437.2. Helpful mouse. Reef Is.: O'Ferrall, 1904, 228.

B450. Helpful birds (undifferentiated or species of no narrative significance). Australs: Aitken, 1930, 108; Mangareva: Hiroa, 1938, 326, 334; Tuamotus: Seurat, 1905, 434; Stimson, n.d., Z-G. 3/1276; Hawaii: Beckwith, 1919, 566; McAllister, 1933, 117; Thrum, 1907, 71; Westervelt, 1915, 43ff., 122; Samoa: Seirich, 1900, 237; Stuebel, 1896, 77; N.Z.: Clark, 1896, 54; Wohlers, 1875, 27; Rennell: Elbert-Monberg, 1964, No. 40.

B457.1. Helpful dove. Marquesas: Handy, 1930, 115; Samoa: Sierich, 1900, 231f.

B457.2. Helpful pigeon. Cooks: Gill, 1876, 53; Samoa: Krämer, 1902, I, 140-142; Tokelaus: Burrows, 1923, 155; Reef Is.: Elbert-Kirtley, 1966, 358.

B461.2. Helpful owl. Hawaii: Fornander, 1916, IV, 598ff.; V, 524, 540; Thrum, 1907, 201; Thrum, 1923, 201, 211; N.Z.: White, 1887-90, II, 128, 134; III, 5.

*B463.1.2. Helpful fairy terns. Kapingamarangi: Elbert, 1948, 85.

B463.2. Helpful heron. Cooks: Beckwith, 1940, 269.

B463.4. Helpful stork. Ellice Is.: Kennedy, 1931, 207.

*B469.11. Helpful swamp-hen. Bellona: Elbert-Monberg, 1964, No. 46a; Rennell: ibid., 46b.

B470. Helpful fish. Tuamotus: Stimson, n.d., Z-G. 3/1241, Z-G. 13/167; Stimson, 1937, 70f., 103ff.; Marquesas: Steinen, 1933-34, 342; Hawaii: Beckwith, 1940, 24; Green, 1926, 122; Thrum, 1923, 51, 225; Tokelau: Burrows, 1923, 158; N.Z.: Gudgeon, 1906, 35; Tikopia: Firth, 1961, 113.

B470.1. Small fish as helper. Marquesas: Handy, 1930, 99.

B471. Helpful shark. Societies: Dixon, 1916, 64; Henry, 1928, 389f.; Hawaii: Green, 1926, 105; McAllister, 1933, 164; Westervelt, 1915, 44f., 194; Tonga: Gifford, 1924, 76; Rotuma: Russell, 1942, 248.

B472. Helpful whale. Tuamotus: Stimson, n.d., T-G. 3/600; Stimson, 1937, 126f.; Marquesas: Handy, 1930, 60; N.Z.: Cowan, 1930, I, 69; Dixon, 1916, 83; White, 1887-90, II, 127, 129, 133, 136f., 145; Wohlers, 1875, 27.

> R245. Whale-boat. A man is carried across the water on a whale.

B473. Helpful dolphin. Tuamotus: Stimson, n.d., Z-G. 13/441; Marquesas: Steinen, 1933-34, 349, 361.

B476. Helpful eel. Tuamotus: Stimson, n.d., Z-G. 3/1295; Hawaii: Beckwith, 1940, 478, 511; Samoa: Krämer, 1902, I, 258-259; Kapingamarangi: Elbert, 1949, 245.

B477. Helpful octopus. Marquesas: Handy, 1930, 76; Samoa: Krämer, 1902, I, 258f.

B478. Helpful crab. Easter I.: Métraux, 1940, 365; Societies: Henry, 1928, 392.

*B479.1. Helpful shellfish. Tuamotus: Stimson, n.d., Z-G. 13/301; Tahiti: Beckwith, 1940, 260.

*B479.2. Helpful swordfish. Hawaii: Beckwith, 1940, 466.

B480. Helpful insects. N.Z.: Best, 1925, 946; Tikopia: Firth, 1961, 49.

B481.1. Helpful ant. Tokelau: Burrows, 1923, 162.

B481.3. Helpful bee. Tokelau: Burrows, 1923, 162.

B481.4. Helpful wasps. Tokelau: Lister, 1892, 61.

*B482.0.1. Insect helpers of god. Cooks: Clark, 1896, 146.

B483.1. Helpful fly. Easter I.: Métraux, 1940, 385; N.Z.: Grace, 1901, 66.

B489.1. Helpful spider. Tuamotus: Stimson, 1937, 89; Niue: Loeb, 1926, 218.

B491.2. Helpful lizard. Cooks: Gill, 1876, 229; Hawaii: Beckwith, 1919, 336; Fornander, 1916, IV, 40; Reef Is.: Elbert-Kirtley, 1966, 359.

B491.5. Helpful turtle (tortoise). Mangareva: Hiroa, 1938, 313; Hawaii: Beckwith, 1940, 514; Tonga: Gifford, 1924, 50; Samoa: Krämer, 1902, I, 130; Niue: Smith, 1903, 100; Tokelau: Burrows, 1923, 155f.

B500--B599. Services of helpful animals

B520. Animals save person's life. See also B540. Hawaii: Dickey, 1917, 35f.; Samoa: Powell-Pratt, 1892, 125.

B521. Animal warns of fatal danger. Hawaii: Westervelt, 1915, 176; Lau Is.: St. Johnston, 1918, 86.

*B521.3.3.2. Cricket tries to warn man of intended treachery. Cooks: Gill, 1876, 306.

*B521.3.6. Crab warns hero that evil spirits are about to poison him. Easter I.: Métraux, 1940, 365.

B521.5. Owl saves man from plunging over cliff. Flaps wings and arrests man's attention. Hawaii: Beckwith, 1940, 124.

B521.6. Birds warn of enemy's approach. Hawaii:
Beckwith, 1940, 390.

B522. Animal saves man from death sentence. Hawaii:
Fornander, 1916, IV, 560; Thrum, 1907, 201f.;
Westervelt, 1915, 135.

*B522.4.2. Infant thrown into sea is thrown back onto
the beach by tame whales. Pukapuka: Beaglehole,
1938, 382.

B523. Animal saves man from pursuer. N.Z.: Best,
1925, 737; Tikopia: Firth, 1961, 113.

B523.3. Great clam fights hero's pursuer. Tahiti:
Beckwith, 1940, 260.

B524. Animal overcomes man's adversary. Hawaii: Pukui,
1943, 57; Thrum, 1907, 71; Westervelt, 1915, 181.

*B524.1.14. Lizards aid hero in killing demons. Cooks:
Gill, 1876, 235.

*B524.2.2. Bird saves men who fight ogre by flying into
eyes of ogre. Fijis: Fison, 1904, 126.

B527.3. Owl saves man from drowning: flaps wings to
call attention to direction of land. Hawaii:
Beckwith, 1940, 125.

*B527.6. Sailfish swims to windward of canoe, protects
it from stormy seas. Pukapuka: Beaglehole, 1938,
393.

*B527.6.1. Helpful fish save canoe in storm at sea.
Hawaii: Green, 1926, 122.

*B529.3. Helpful owl resuscitates maiden. Hawaii:
Westervelt, 1915, 85.

*B529.4. Helpful owl puts out sorceror's fire and saves
victim. Hawaii: Ii, 1959, 8.

B531. Animals provide food for men. Hawaii: McAllister,
1933, 117; Westervelt, 1915, 44ff.; N.Z.: Grace,
1907, 8.

*B531.5.1. Swine gives himself to master to be slain and
eaten. Marquesas: Steinen, 1933-34, 26f.

*B531.6. Birds provide man (men) with food (water).
Marquesas: Steinen, 1933-34, 26 f.

*B531.7. Whale strands his comrade whales so that people
may feast. N.Z.: Gudgeon, 1906, 40.

*B531.8. Rat gnaws rope and releases food for humans.
Hawaii: Beckwith, 1932, 78; Beckwith, 1940, 356;
Green, 1926, 118; Thrum, 1923, 26.

*B531.9. Helpful fish aids his human friend to catch
other fish. Hawaii: Dickey, 1917, 19; Fornander,
1918, V, 162.

*B535.0.7.3. Two wingless birds raise culture-hero.
N.Z.: Luomala, 1949, 55.

*B538.3. Heroine hides from demon of the sea beneath
turtle. Kapingamarangi: Elbert, 1948, 76.

B541.1. Escape from sea on fish's back. (See also
B551.) Tuamotus: Leverd, 1911, 177 f.;
Stimson, n.d., T-G. 3/912; Societies: Henry,
1928, 389, 630; Hawaii: Beckwith, 1940,134;
Westervelt,1915, 115; N.Z.: Best, 1925, 960ff.;
Shand, 1896, 197, also note; Fijis: Beckwith,
1940, 131, 134.

*B541.1.0.1. Man walks ashore from boat over backs of
helpful fish. (Cf. B555.) Mangareva: Laval,
1938, 15.

B541.1.1. Fish swallows man to rescue him from sea.
Tahiti: Henry, 1928, 612; Hawaii: Rice, 1923,
126.

*B541.4.2. Fish carry person's raft upon the sea.
Tokelau: Macgregor, 1937, 81.

B541.5. Fish rescues ship. Hawaii: Beckwith, 1940,
133.

*B541.5.1. Shark god saves shipwrecked people. Hawaii:
Beckwith, 1940, 129.

*B543.1.1. Fly seeks missing boy. N.Z.: Hongi, 1898,
37.

*B543.1.3. Herons gather to attack great heron which
has stolen chief's wife. Tahiti: Orsmond, 1933,
172.

*B544.2. Fly unties boys' ropes so they may escape.
Easter I.: Métraux, 1940, 385.

132

*B544.3. Helpful owl frees captive's bonds. Hawaii:
Fornander, 1918, V, 540; Thrum, 1921, 105; Thrum,
1923, 201.

*B548.2.6. Whale raises sunken ship. Tuamotus:
Stimson, n.d., Z-G. 13/203.

*B548.8. Guardian sharks drag overturned canoes to beach.
Tonga: Gifford, 1924, 77.

*B549.6. Shark procures man his son from distant island.
Societies: Henry, 1928, 389-390.

B551.1. Fish carries man across water. See also
B541.1. and references in R246. Mangareva: Caillot,
1914, 195f.; Hiroa, 1938, 25; Laval, 1938, 308;
Tuamotus: Caillot, 1914, 76f., 83; Leverd, 1911,
175, 177, 178; Seurat, 1905, 435; Stimson, n.d.,
T-G. 2/44, T-G. 3/912; Stimson, 1937, 103f.;
Marquesas: Lavondes, 1964, 64, 68; Steinen,
1933-34, 342, 349, 361; Societies: *Dixon, 1916,
72, n. 56; Gill, 1976, 253; Henry, 1928, 389,
392; Cooks: Ariki, 1899, 172; Gill, 1876, 91f.;
Hawaii: Beckwith, 1940, 134; McAllister, 1933,
164; Pukui, 1933, 184; Rice, 1923, 131;
Westervelt, 1915, 194; Tonga: Gifford, 1924, 142;
Samoa: Brown, 1917, 95; N.Z.: Beattie, 1915, 136;
Best, 1925, 719, 773, 921, 923, 954; Best, 1927,
270; Best, 1928, 261, 264, 266; Cowan, 1930, I,
69, 97; Locke, 1921, 40; Shand, 1896, 197, 197 n.;
White, 1887-90, II, 127, 129, 133, 136f., 145; III,
116; Wohlers, 1875, 27; Uvea: Burrows, 1937,
169; Lau Is.: St. Johnston, 1918, 129; Fijis:
Beckwith, 1940, 131; Ellice Is.: Kennedy, 1931,
165, 184; Rotuma: Churchward, 1938-39, 228;
Russell, 1942, 248.

B551.5. Turtle (tortoise) carries person across river
(ocean). Easter I.: Métraux, 1940, 373;
Mangareva: Hiroa, 1938, 313; Tuamotus: Stimson,
n.d., T-G. 3/912; Hawaii: Fornander, 1916, IV,
604; Tonga: Collocott, 1928, 22; Gifford, 1924,
53; Samoa: Krämer, 1902, I, 130; Niue: Smith,
1903, 100; Tokelau: Burrows, 1923, 154f.; Fijis:
Fison, 1904, 20; Nukumanu: Sarfert, 1931, 443;
Bellona: Elbert-Monberg, 1964, No. 55a;
Kapingamarangi: Elbert, 1948, 75.

*B551.6. Great lizard transports person. Hawaii:
Beckwith, 1919, 336, 534, 540, 554, 570; Fornander,
1916, IV, 42.

B552. Man carried by bird. Easter I.: Métraux, 1940,
375; Australs: Aitken, 1923, 243; Tubuai:
Aitken, 1930, 108; Tuamotus: Seurat, 1905, 434;
Stimson, n.d., Z-G. 3/1241; Marquesas: Lavondes,
1964, 54; Steinen, 1934-35, 218; Hawaii: Beckwith,
1919, 566; Westervelt, 1915, 42, 121f.; Cooks:
Gill, 1876, 94, 233; Tonga: Beckwith, 1940, 504;
Samoa: Krämer, 1902, I, 142; Sierich, 1900, 237;
Stair, 1895, 102; Tokelau: Burrows, 1923, 157;
N.Z.: Best, 1924, 208; Best, 1925, 919ff., 924;
Best, 1938, 262; Locke, 1921, 42; White,
1887-90, I, 84; III, 117; Ellice Is.: Kennedy,
1931, 186, 207; Fijis: Hocart, 1929, 205;
Rennell: Bradley, 1956, 334; Elbert-Monberg,1964,
No. 13.

*B552.4. Birds carry beautiful maiden about on their
wings. Hawaii: Beckwith, 1919, 370, 434, 466,
532; Pukui, 1933, 159; Thrum, 1923, 135.

*B558.10. Helpful fish pull boat. Hawaii: Westervelt,
1915, 182.

*B560.2. Bluebottle fly leads man to corpse of his son.
N.Z.: Grace, 1901, 66.

*B560.3. Birds give sign to a mother that her son is
dead. Mangareva: Hiroa, 1938, 330.

*B561.1. Birds utter correct prophecy. Hawaii:
Pukui-Curtis, n.d., 83; Samoa: Stuebel, 1896,
150.

*B561.2. Bird tattles to adulter's wife of his fault.
Hawaii: Fornander, 1916, IV, 12, 18.

*B562.3. Clairvoyant bird gives news of distant events.
N.Z.: Grace, 1907, 88.

B563. Animals direct man on journey. Mangareva:
Caillot, 1914, 172; Hawaii: Pukui, 1933, 129;
N.Z.: Grace, 1907, 11ff.; White, 1887-90, IV,
108, 112; Ellice Is.: Kennedy, 1931, 157;
Reef Is.: Elbert-Kirtley, 1966, 358; Bellona:
Elbert-Monberg, 1964, No. 50a; Rennell: ibid. ,
50b, 50c.

B563.2. Birds point out road to hero (person).
Mangareva: Hiroa, 1938, 335; Tuamotus: Stimson,
n.d., Z-G. 1/96, Z-G. 3/1122; Stimson, 1937, 136;
Hawaii: Rice, 1923, 94; Thrum, 1923, 225.

*B563.2.1. Bird guides rescuers to shipwrecked travelers. N.Z.: Grace, 1907, 89f.

B563.6. Birds as scouts. Tuamotus: Stimson, n.d., Z-G. 3/1386, Z-G. 13/317, Z-G. 13/380; Hawaii: Beckwith, 1940, 466; Cooks: Clark, 1896, 142; N.Z.: White, 1887-90, II, 136; Wohlers, 1875, 27.

B563.7. Bird conducts navigators to landing place. Hawaii: Beckwith, 1940, 92; Rotuma: Churchward, 1937-38, 258-259; Fijis: Fison, 1904, 117.

*B563.8. Birds lead father to corpses of his sons. Niue: Loeb, 1926, 152.

B571. Animals perform tasks for men. Hawaii: Thrum, 1923, 211; Samoa: Stuebel, 1896, 87.

*B571.3.1. Helpful animal attacks man's enemies. Hawaii: Forbes, 1882, 40; Fornander, 1916, IV, 444; Green, 1926, 105.

B572.1. Animals build palace (house) for man. Hawaii: Westervelt, 1915, 122; Samoa: Beckwith, 1940, 536; Sierich, 1902, 183; Tokelau: Macgregor, 1937, 83.

*B572.1.1. Rat thatches house with feathers. Hawaii: Thrum, 1923, 154; Westervlet, 1915, 178f.

B572.2. Birds (or other animals or insects) build canoe for master (person). Mangareva: Hiroa, 1938, 326; Cooks: Beckwith, 1940, 269; Gill, 1876, 144; Kunike, 1928, 30; Seurat, 1905, 486; Hawaii: Dickey, 1917, 21; Tokelau: Burrows, 1923, 162; N.Z.: Clark, 1896, 98; Reef Is.: Elbert-Kirtley, 1966, 359.

*B572.2.1. Helpful bees weave person a sail. Tokelau: Burrows, 1923, 162; Lister, 1892, 61.

*B572.2.2. Crabs aid twins in building canoe. Cooks: Editors JPS VI (1897), 97 note.

*B572.3. Hero's rat-brother helps him build canoe. Hawaii: Beckwith, 1940, 408.

B574. Animals as domestic servants. Marquesas: Steinen, 1933-34, 26-27; Tuamotus: Stimson, n.d., T-G. 3/13.

*B574.1. Birds as servants. Hawaii: Beckwith, 1919, 334, 434, 442, 532; Fornander, 1916, IV, 544; Pukui, Curtis, n.d., 53; Westervelt, 1915, 39,

43ff., 122; Samoa: Sierich, 1902, 193.

B575. Animal as constant attendant of man. Tuamotus: Stimson, n.d., MB-FF/206, T-G. 3/900; Hawaii: Beckwith, 1940, 37, 526; N.Z.: Clark, 1896, 54.

B576. Animal as guard. Tuamotus: Stimson, n.d., MB-DD/33; Tonga: Gifford, 1924, 77, 84; N.Z.: Beckwith, 1940, 349, 524; Fijis: Beckwith, 1940, 131.

B576.1. Animal as guard of person or house. Mangareva: Hiroa, 1938, 334; Tuamotus: Stimson, n.d., T-G. 1/18, Z-G. 13/203; Stimson, 1937, 140, 143, 147; Societies: Caillot, 1914, 134f.; Hawaii: Beckwith, 1919, 468, 564; Beckwith, 1940, 24, 84, 129, 349; Fornander, 1916, IV, 54ff., 226, 446, 554; V, 378; Green, 1926, 102; McAllister, 1933, 153; Pukui, 1933, 159; Westervelt, 1915, 85, 212; Samoa: Stuebel, 1896, 77; N.Z.: White, 1887-90, II, 128, 134; III, 5.

*B576.1.0.1. Guardian fishes. Tuamotus: Stimson, n.d., Z-G. 3/1353; Hawaii: Beckwith, 1940, 443; Kapingamarangi: Elbert, 1948, 115.

*B576.3.2. Shark drives schools of fish to shore for his human friend. Hawaii: Beckwith, 1940, 133.

*B576.6. Fish guard island (surrounding waters). Societ: Henry, 1928, 389; Tonga: Gifford, 1924, 84.

*B576.7. Great bird guards banana plant. Rotuma: Churchward, 1937-38, 490.

*B579.8. Helpful crabs raise hero's sunken canoe. Tuamotus: Seurat, 1905, 483f.

*B581.1. Dog steals for his master. Hawaii: Fornander, 1916, IV, 558; Westervelt, 1915, 180ff.

B582.2.5. Dove helps deity draw his wife into a net. Marquesas: Handy, 1930, 115.

*B582.2.6. Bird pecks off woman's kilt that man may seduce her. Pukapuka: Beaglehole, 1938, 317.

*B587.4. Fish helps man win wager. Hawaii: Beckwith, 1940, 24.

B600--B699. MARRIAGE OF PERSON TO ANIMAL

*B600.1.2. Four lizards ask for maiden's hand: one refused. Tokelau: Macgregor, 1937, 83.

B602. Marriage to bird. Marquesas: Handy, 1930, 120; Tokelau: Burrows, 1923, 171; Macgregor, 1937, 85.

*B602.9. Marriage to rail. Uvea: Burrows, 1937, 168.

*B602.13. Bird-woman as wife. N.Z.: Beckwith, 1940, 249.

B603. Marriage to fish (whale). Mangareva: Hiroa, 1938, 25; Marquesas: Lavondes, 1964, 8; Hawaii: Westervelt, 1915, 60f.

B603.2. Marriage to eel. Cf. B612.1. Polynesia (general): **Kirtley, 1967, 89ff.; Beckwith, 1940, 103; Caillot, 1914, 104; Luomala, 1949, 81; Malarde, 1933, 671; Seurat, 1905, 438; Stimson, n.d., Z-G. 3/1295; Stimson, 1934, 28ff.; Niue: Loeb, 1926, 105.

B604.2.1. Marriage to turtle. Reef Is.: Elbert-Kirtley, 1966

B604.4. Marriage to lizard. N.Z.: Best, 1893, 218; Best, 1924, 188, 190.

*B606. Marriage to insect. Tahiti: Lagarde, 1933, 699.

*B611.9. Pig paramour. Marquesas: Handy, 1930, 138.

B612. Fish paramour. See B603. Oceania: *Knoche, 1939, 26ff.; Marquesas: Steinen, 1933-34, 342; Steinen, 1934-35, 238; Samoa: Powell-Pratt, 1892, 255.

B612.1. Eel paramour. Polynesia (general): **Kirtley, 1967, 89ff.; Tuamotus: Stimson, 1937, 10, 37ff.; Marquesas: Steinen, 1933-34, 29, 31; Handy, 1930, 79 f.; Cooks: Dixon, 1916, 55; Gill, 1876, 77; Beckwith, 1940, 103; Hawaii: Beckwith, 1940, 136; McAllister, 1933, 115ff.; Tonga: Gifford, 1924, 182 f.; Samoa: Andersen, 1925, 142; Beckwith, 1940, 103; Clark, 1896, 70; Krämer, 1902, I, 393, 438; Lesson, 1876, 598; Nelson, 1925, 132; Stuebel, 1896, 68; N.Z.: Best, 1924, 140; Best, 1925, 833f.; Dixon, 1916, 55; White, 1887-90, II, 76, 83, 115; Kapingamarangi: Elbert, 1948, 114.

*B612.4. Whale paramour. Niue: Loeb, 1926, 165.

B613.1. Snake paramour. Rennell: Elbert-Monberg, 1964, Nos. 51a, 51b.

B613.3. Lizard paramour. Tonga: Gifford, 1924, 194-195; Tikopia: Firth, 1961, 30.

*B613.4. Turtle paramour. Easter I.: Métraux, 1940, 373.

B614. Bird paramour. Marquesas: Handy, 1930, 120.

B631.3. Fish bears men-children. Mangareva: Hiroa, 1938, 335; Tokelau: Burrows, 1923, 165.

*B631.10. Human offspring from lizard. Tahiti: Henry, 1928, 622; Tonga: Gifford, 1924, 104.

*B631.11. Human offspring from turtle. Hawaii: Fornander, 1916, IV, 604.

*B631.12. Land crab gives birth to human daughter. Funafuti: David, 1899, 102.

*B631.14. Pig gives birth to human girl. Marquesas: Handy, 1930, 138.

*B631.16. Bird gives birth to human infant. Hawaii: Fornander, 1916, IV, 52ff.; Tonga: Collocott, 1928, 21; Samoa: Powell-Pratt, 1891, 198.

*B631.17. Crab gives birth to human. Tonga: Collocott, 1928, 33; Ellice Is.: Kennedy, 1931, 199; Kapingamarangi: Elbert, 1949, 244.

*B631.18. Clam gives birth to human. Tonga: Collocott, 1928, 33.

B632. Animal offspring from marriage to animal. Australs: Aitken, 1923, 250; Tuamotus: Seurat, 1905, 434; Hawaii: Fornander, 1918, V, 516; Samoa: Krämer, 1902, I, 139ff.

B633. Human and animal offspring from marriage to animal. Australs: Aitken, 1923, 241; Tuamotus: Caillot, 1914, 74; Seurat, 1905, 434; Marquesas: Steinen, 1933-34, 349, 361; Handy, 1930, 60; Cooks: Ariki, 1899, 172; Hawaii: Rice, 1923, 25; Thrum, 1923, 201; Samoa: Sierich, 1902, 183; Tokelau: Burrows, 1923, 154ff.; Macgregor, 1937, 83.

138

*B634.2. Monstrous offspring from animal marriage: boy covered with feathers. Tuamotus: Stimson, n.d., Z-G. 3/1146.

B640.1. Marriage to beast by day and man by night. Hawaii: Beckwith, 1940, 135.

*B654.1. Marriage to eel in human form. Tuamotus: Stimson, n.d., Z-G. 3/1295.

B700--B799. FANCIFUL TRAITS OF ANIMALS

*B739.2. Turtle smells like human urine. Ellice Is.: Kennedy, 1931, 178, 184.

B755. Animal (bird) calls the dawn. The sun rises as a result of the animal's call. Marquesas: Beckwith, 1940, 262; Hawaii: Fornander, 1918, V, 234.

*B762.2. Man-eating shark always kills eight persons. Hawaii: Beckwith, 1940, 141.

*B765.5.1. Snake (eel) living in person's body. Marquesas: Steinen, 1934-35, 226.

*B770.0.1. Shark guardian wages continual war against man-eating sharks. Hawaii: Beckwith, 1940, 139.

*B771.6. Swine hears master's call, swims to him. Marquesas: Steinen, 1933-34, 26.

*B773.4. Bird declines marriage with princess because he is not of her land. Tuamotus: Stimson, n.d., MB-FF/206.

B871.1.2. Giant boar (swine). Marquesas: Steinen,
1934-35, 194; Societies: Henry, 1928, 562;
Hawaii: Rice, 1923, 51.

B871.1.7. Giant dog (hound). Hawaii: Beckwith, 1919,
472; Fornander, 1916, IV, 446, 524; Rice, 1923,
38; Westervelt, 1915, 83ff., 93ff.; Tonga:
Collocott, 1921, 51; Reiter, 1919-20, 125ff..

*B871.2.10. Giant bat. Tuamotus: Stimson, 1937, 49ff.

*B871.2.11. Giant rat. N.Z.: Wohlers, 1875, 22.

B872. Giant birds. Tuamotus: Stimson, n.d., Z-G.
3/1229; Beckwith, 1940, 261; Hawaii: Thrum,
1923, 182; Westervelt, 1915, 66ff., 121f.; Samoa
Brown, 1917, 95; Tonga: Caillot, 1914, 292ff.;
Tokelau: Burrows, 1923, 163, 171; N.Z.: Best,
1925, 919, 924; White, 1887-90, II, 142; III, 11?
Wohlers, 1876, 110; Fijis: Fison, 1904, 4, 83;
Ellice Is.: Kennedy, 1931, 168; Rotuma: Russell,
1942, 244.

B30. Mythical birds.

*B872.5. Giant heron. Marquesas: Steinen, 1934-35, 194
Tahiti: Orsmond, 1933, 172.

*B872.6. Giant owl (large enough to carry off man).
Hawaii: Rice, 1923, 38.

*B872.7. Giant stork. Tahiti: Henry, 1928, 472.

*B872.8. Giant pigeon (dove). Samoa: Krämer, 1902, I,
141f.; Stuebel, 1896, 149.

B873. Giant insect. N.Z.: White, 1887-90, V, 54.

B873.3. Giant spider. Tuamotus: Stimson, 1937, 89;
Hawaii: Beckwith, 1919, 556.

B873.4. Giant ant. Rotuma: Churchward, 1937-38, 491;
Russell, 1942, 244.

*B873.5. Giant flies. Rotuma: Churchward, 1938-39, 22C

*B873.6. Giant caterpillar. Tahiti: Lagarde, 1933,
697; Hawaii: Westervelt, 1915, 166, 168; Tikopia

Firth, 1961, 49.

*B873.7. Giant worms. Marquesas: Steinen, 1933-34, 34.

B874. Giant fish. Tuamotus: Stimson, 1937, 138;
Marquesas: Lavondes, 1964, 100; Hawaii: Fornander,
1918, V, 12ff.; Funafuti: David, 1899, 98.

B874.2. Giant eel. Polynesia (general): **Kirtley,
1967, 89ff.; Tuamotus: Caillot, 1914, 39, 105;
Henry, 1928, 620; Malarde, 1933, 671; Seurat,
1905, 438, 481; Stimson, n.d., Z-G. 3/1295;
Stimson, 1934, 28ff.; Stimson, 1937, 128; Societies:
Baessler, 1905, 921; Tahiti: Henry, 1928, 438, 616;
Hawaii: Smith, 1966, 1, 8f.; Thrum, 1907, 217ff.;
Westervelt, 1915, 190, 212f.; Samoa: Andersen,
1925, 142ff.; Nelson, 1925, 132; Stuebel, 1896,
67f.; Uvea: Burrows, 1937, 164; N.Z.: Cowan,
1930, I, 190f.; White, 1887-90, II, 91;
Kapingamarangi: Elbert, 1949, 245.

B874.5. Giant shark. Tuamotus: Stimson, 1937, 136;
Marquesas: Handy, 1930, 110; Societies: Caillot,
1914, 137f.; Hawaii: Beckwith, 1940, 129;
Emerson, 1915, 160; Forbes, 1882, 39; Fornander,
1916, IV, 526; 1918, V, 294, 366ff.; Green, 1926,
106.

B874.6. Giant clam. Tahiti: Beckwith, 1940, 260, 266;
Cooks: Gill, 1876, 146; Kunike, 1928, 32.

*B874.6.2. Giant tridacna. Tuamotus: Henry, 1928, 503;
Seurat, 1905, 484; Tahiti: Henry, 1928, 472;
Rennell: Elbert-Monberg, 1964, Nos. 33, 34b;
Bellona: ibid., No. 34a.

*B874.9. Giant octopus. Cooks: Gill, 1876, 147;
Kunike, 1928, 32; Savage, 1910, 150; Hawaii:
Thrum, 1907, 234f.

*B874.11. Giant billfish. Tahiti: Henry, 1928, 496.

*B874.12. Giant cavalla fish. Tuamotus: Henry, 1928,
503.

*B874.13. Giant squid. Hawaii: Westervelt, 1915, 159.

*B874.14. Monster holothurian (trepang). Tuamotus:
Seurat, 1905, 484.

*B875.1.1. Giant sea snake. Rennell: Elbert-Monberg,
1964, No. 109.

141

B875.3. Giant turtle. Hawaii: Forbes, 1882, 39;
Westervelt, 1915, 212f.; Ontong Java: Sarfert,
1931, 329.

*B875.3.1. Giant turtle mistaken for island. Samoa:
Nelson, 1925, 134.

*B875.5. Giant lizard. Tahiti: Henry, 1923, 35;
Hawaii: Beckwith, 1919, 335, 466, 468, 534, 554,
556, 570; Pukui-Curtis, n.d., 103ff.; N.Z.:
Cowan, 1930, I, 187.

B876.2.1. Giant crab. Tuamotus: Caillot, 1914, 39.

*B876.2.2. Giant crayfish. Easter I.: Métraux, 1940,
88.

B877.1. Giant sea monster. Hawaii: Thrum, 1923, 165ff
N.Z.: Grace, 1907, 96f., 173, 190.

C. TABU

For discussion of tabu in general see Elsdon Best
The Maori Vol. I, pp. 233-262 (Wellington, 1924). See
also in C. R. H. Taylor A Pacific Bibliography
(Wellington, 1965) entries under the various island
groups pertaining to religion and folklore.

C0--C99. TABU CONNECTED WITH
SUPERNATURAL BEINGS

C0. Tabu: contact with supernatural. Niue: *Loeb,
1926, 172-173; Ellice Is.: Roberts, 1958, 368.

C21. Ogre's name uttered. He appears. Bellona:
Elbert-Monberg, 1964, Nos. 185a, 185b.

C31. Tabu: offending supernatural wife. Upon slight
offense the wife leaves for her old home. Hawaii:
Green, 1926, 114; N.Z.: Best, 1925, 911; Cowan,
1930, I, 22; Dixon, 1916, 58, 72; Grace, 1907,
137f.; White, 1887-90, II, 136; Wohlers, 1875,
16.

C31.2. Tabu: mentioning origin of supernatural wife.
N.Z.: Gudgeon, 1905, 187.

C31.5. Tabu: boasting of supernatural wife. N.Z.:
Best, 1925, 867, 870.

*C31.13. Tabu: hero warned not to take wife outside
before she bears child. N.Z.: Potae, 1928, 362.

*C31.14. Tabu: causing supernatural wife to bear children.
Australs: Aitken, 1923, 258.

*C36.3. Tabu: bearing child of animal husband. Hawaii:
Thrum, 1907, 257.

*C41.5. Tabu: using water of sacred spring. N.Z.:
Best, 1925, 978.

C43.2. Tabu: cutting certain trees lest tree-spirits
be offended. Cooks: Gill, 1876, 82.

*C43.2.1. Tabu: disturbing tree of demon. Societies:
Henry, 1928, 561-562.

C43.3. Felled tree restored for failure to make proper offerings to tree spirit. Marquesas: Lavondes, 1966, 152, 200; Tuamotus: Beckwith, 1940, 267; Cooks: Savage, 1910, 147; Tonga: Collocott, 1921, 46f.; N.Z.: Best, 1925, 740; White, 1887-90, V, 8f.

*C46.2. Tabu: looking at earth-spirit. Nukumanu: Sarfert, 1931, 332.

C50. Tabu: offending the gods. Mangareva: Laval, 1938, 85; Hawaii: Emerson, 1915, 3, 29; Rennell; Elbert-Monberg, 1964, No. 16 n.

C51. Tabu: touching possessions of a god. Hawaii: Westervelt, 1915, 50.

C51.1. Tabu: profaning shrine (putting sacred area to profane use). Hawaii: McAllister, 1933, 110; N.Z.: Best, 1925, 854.

*C51.1.3.1. Tabu: touching smoke from certain fires. Hawaii: Westervelt, 1915, 5f., 8; N.Z.: Pakauwera, 1894, 102ff.

*C51.1.3.2. Man who worships plover-god made ill when touched by smoke of fire upon which plover is cooked. Hawaii: Beckwith, 1940, 138.

C51.1.11. Visits of goddess cease when her sacred spring is disturbed. Tahiti: Henry, 1928, 85.

C51.1.12. Tabu: striking tree which belongs to deity. Hawaii: Beckwith, 1940, 111.

*C51.1.16. Tabu: removing stones from, or otherwise disturbing, sacred structure. Societies: Eric Ramsden, Strange Stories from the South Seas (Wellington: A.H. and A.W. Reed, 1944), 62; Hawaii: Dickey, 1917, 29; McAllister, 1933, 146, 177, 185; Thrum, 1923, 218.

*C51.1.17. Tabu: erecting any structure upon a sacred temple site. Hawaii: McAllister, 1933, 86, 141.

*C51.1.18. Tabu: going near sacred effigy. N.Z.: White, 1887-90, V, 52ff.

C51.2. Tabu: stealing from god. Hawaii: Westervelt, 1915, 15.

C51.2.2. Tabu: cutting sacred trees or groves.
Mangareva: Hiroa, 1938, 92; Hawaii: Westervelt,
1915, 28, 49; Tikopia: Firth, 1961, 47, 93.

C51.9. Tabu: pointing boat toward island of the gods.
Hawaii: Beckwith, 1940, 67.

*C51.10. Tabu: pointing at island. Samoa: Beckwith,
1940, 450.

C63. Tabu: attacking deity (sacred persons). Fijis:
Beckwith, 1940, 138.

C67. Tabu: neglect of sacred fires. Hawaii:
Beckwith, 1940, 111.

*C75.2. Tabu: offending the sun. Hawaii: Pukui, 1933,
139.

C92.1.6. Tabu: killing other sacred bird. Tuamotus:
Stimson, n.d., T-G. 2/44.

*C92.1.9. Tabu: killing sacred dog. N.Z.: White,
1887-90, IV, 109, 112.

*C92.1.10. Tabu: catching certain fish. Hawaii:
McAllister, 1933, 164.

C93. Tabu: trespassing sacred precinct. N.Z.: Best,
1924, 257.

C93.6. Tabu: cutting down tree wherein resides deity.
Hawaii: Beckwith, 1940, 281; Societies: Henry,
1928, 561-562.

> C43.2. Tabu: cutting certain trees lest
> tree-spirits be offended.

C93.8. Tabu: landing on floating island of the gods
without invitation. Hawaii: Beckwith, 1940, 68.

*C94.10. Tabu: to make oven near burial place.
Ellice Is.:David, 1899, 101.

*C110.2.   Tabu: noble woman having sexual relations with
a slave.   N.Z.:   White, 1887-90, IV, 30f., 36.

C112.   Tabu: sexual intercourse with unearthly beings.
Marquesas: Steinen, 1934-35, 207;   Lau Is.:
Hocart, 1929, 191-192;   St. Johnston, 1918, 42, 112.

C115.   Tabu: adultery.   N.Z.:   Best, 1893, 215.

C117.1.   Tabu: intercourse with resuscitated wife
for particular number of days.   Marquesas:
Handy, 1930, 113.

*C117.2.   Tabu: intercourse with wife outdoors.   N.Z.:
Smith, 1897, 22.

C119.1.4.   Tabu: sexual intercourse during religious
festival.   Marquesas: Handy, 1930, 113.

*C119.1.7.   Tabu: sexual embrace during journey.
Hawaii: Beckwith, 1940, 173.

C140.   Tabu connected with menses.   Hawaii: Beckwith,
1940, 530f.

*C141.5.   Tabu: menstruating woman to board canoe.
Mangareva: Hiroa, 1938, 29.

C142.   Tabu: sexual intercourse during menses.   Hawaii:
Beckwith, 1940, 531;   Niue: Loeb, 1926, 173.

C146.1.   Menstruating woman must wear amulet of leaves
when approaching certain valley.   Hawaii: Beckwith,
1940, 212.

C181.10.   Tabu: women riding in canoe.   Marquesas:
Handy, 1930,134;   Tonga: Brown, 1916, 426;   Niue:
Loeb, 1926, 100;   Pukapuka: Beaglehole, 1938, 309.

*C181.13.   Place where hero fell is forbidden to women
(and children).   Niue: Loeb, 1926, 150.

*C181.14.   Tabu: woman touching fishing lures.   Marquesas:
Lavondes, 1964, 10.

C182.2.   Tabu: man entering woman's quarters in her
absence.   Tonga: Gifford, 1924, 53.

*C182.4. Tabu: man using woman's waterhole. Tonga: Gifford, 1924, 53.

C200--C299. EATING AND DRINKING TABU

C200--C249. Eating tabus

C211. Tabu: eating in other world. Hawaii: Beckwith, 1940, 148, 493; Westervelt, 1915, 101, 103f.; N.Z.: Best, 1924, 192; Clark, 1896, 8; Dixon, 1916, 77; Grace, 1907, 254; White, 1887-90, II, 166; Fijis: Hocart, 1929, 211; Ontong Java: Sarfert, 1931, 327.

C211.2.1. Tabu: eating in land of ghosts. N.Z.: Clark, 1896, 8.

*C211.4. Tabu: eating in sacred house. N.Z.: Cowan, 1930, I, 260.

C220. Tabu: eating certain things. Hawaii: Fornander, 1916, IV, 66; Pukui, 1943, 59; Thrum, 1907, 270f.; Tonga: Collocott, 1921, 57; N.Z.: White, 1887-90, III, 200, 202.

C220.1. Tabu: eating food produced by a spell. Marquesas: Handy, 1930, 114.

C221. Tabu: eating meat. Hawaii: Thrum, 1907, 257; Westervelt, 1915, 61.

C221.1.1.4. Tabu: eating dog. Tuamotus: Audran, 1918, 92; N.Z.: White, 1887-90, IV, 109, 112.

C221.1.2. Tabu: eating bird. Marquesas: Handy, 1930, 64, 131.

C221.1.2.2. Tabu: eating pigeon. Marquesas: Handy, 1930, 67.

C221.1.3.1. Tabu: eating certain fish. Tuamotus: Caillot, 1914, 47; Marquesas: Lavondes, 1964, 66; Tonga: Collocott, 1921, 55ff.; Samoa: Powell-Pratt, 1892, 741; Lau Is.: St. Johnston, 1918, 129. N.Z.: Best, 1924, 217.

C221.1.3.2. Tabu: eating eel. Cooks: Beckwith, 1940,

262; Gill, 1876, 79.

C221.1.3.3. Tabu: eating crabs. Societies: Henry,
1928, 392; Uvea: Burrows, 1937, 85; Fijis:
Hocart, 1929, 208.

C221.1.3.4. Tabu: eating shark. Tonga: Gifford, 1924,
80; Fijis: Hocart, 1929, 208.

C221.2. Tabu: eating totem animal (or animal namesake).
Tokelau: Macgregor, 1937, 63.

C221.3.3. Tabu: eating bird's eggs at certain time of
year. Easter I.: Métraux, 1940, 312.

C221.4.2. Tabu: eating fish caught with fish-hook
made without proper incantations. N.Z.: Clark,
1896, 154.

C221.4.3. Tabu: eating animals recklessly killed.
Hawaii: Beckwith, 1940, 138.

C224.3. Tabu: eating breadfruit. Mangareva: Laval,
1938, 72.

C225. Tabu: eating certain fruit. Hawaii: Beckwith,
1932, 32; Fornander, 1918, V, 578; 1918, VI, 274.

C229.4. Tabu: eating firstlings (animals, fruit, etc.).
Niue: Loeb, 1926, 174.

*C229.5.1. Tabu: eating coconut with turtle flesh.
Pukapuka: Beaglehole, 1938, 310.

*C229.7. Tabu: women eating sacrificial fish. Niue:
Loeb, 1926, 174.

*C229.8. Tabu: women eating flesh of bonito. Niue:
Loeb, 1926, 170.

C231. Tabu: eating before certain time. N.Z.: White,
1887-90, IV, 51, 201f.

C241.2. Tabu: eating chief's food. Marquesas: Handy,
1930, 114; Samoa: Beckwith, 1940, 512.

*C241.2.1. Tabu: eating of chief's crop of kava. Hawaii:
Beckwith, 1940, 350.

*C264. Tabu: drinking water at sea. Fijis: Hocart,
1924, 212-213.

*C265. Tabu: to drink from certain brook. N.Z.: Cowan,
1930, I, 38, 188.

C300--C399. Looking tabu

C300. Looking tabu. Samoa: Krämer, 1902, I, 393;
Stuebel, 1896, 64; Tokelau: Burrows, 1923, 169.

C311.1. Tabu: seeing supernatural creatures. Samoa:
Stuebel, 1896, 64.

*C311.1.1.0.1. Tabu: watching ghostly procession.
Hawaii: Beckwith, 1932, 199.

*C311.1.8.0.1. Evil spirits kill those who perceive them
in their true forms. Easter I.: Métraux, 1940,
260.

C311.1.8.1. Gods flee at approach of dawn. Hawaii:
Luomala, 1951, 70ff.; Tonga: Collocott, 1928, 61;
Gifford, 1924, 140; Samoa: Brown, 1917, 98;
N.Z.: Best, 1925, 936.

C842. Tabu: exposure to sunlight.
E452. Ghost laid at cockcrow (dawn).

*C311.3. Tabu: seeing magic performed. Reef Is.:
Elbert-Kirtley, 1966, 350f.

C315.5. Tabu: looking at certain island. N.Z.:
Beckwith, 1940, 349.

*C315.7. Tabu: looking at a certain fishhook. Samoa:
Krämer, 1902, I, 413, 413 n. 5; Powell-Pratt,
1892, 244; Sierich, 1902, 171.

*C315.8. Tabu: looking at a present for a certain period
of time. Tokelau: Burrows, 1923, 169.

C322. Tabu: looking into bag. Tokelau: Beckwith, 1940,
25.

C322.1. Bag of winds. Wind is confined in a bag. Man breaks promise against looking into bag (calabash, basket) and releases winds. Cooks: Gill, 1876, 5; Hawaii: Rice, 1923, 69; Samoa, Chatham Is.: Dixon, 1916, 55; Chatham Is.: Shand, 1898, 79; N.Z.: Best, 1925, 899.

D1543.7. Magic calabash (gourd) controls winds.

C322.2. Tabu: opening bag (basket) too soon. Marquesas: Handy, 1930, 120.

C327. Tabu: looking into basket. Marquesas: Handy, 1930, 120, 122.

C331. Tabu: looking back. Tuamotus: Stimson, n.d., Z-G. 3/1241; Stimson, 1934, 23f.; Marquesas: Lavondes, 1964, 48; Societies: Henry, 1928, 559; Hawaii: Beckwith, 1940, 499; Dickey, 1917, 18; Fornander, 1916, IV, 520; Henry, 1928, 468; McAllister, 1933, 127; Rice, 1923, 26; Smith, 1966, 20; Thrum, 1923, 251; Tonga: Caillot, 1914, 270; Gifford, 1924, 22; Reiter, 1917-18, 1032; Samoa: Krämer, 1902, I, 413, 413 n. 5; Sierich, 1902, 184; N.Z.: Best, 1925, 975; Smith, 1911c, 91; Ontong Java: Sarfert, 1931, 442.

C331.3. Tabu: looking back during flight. Tuamotus: Stimson, n.d., Z-G. 3/1241.

*C331.3.1. Tabu: looking back and speaking in magic boat. Hawaii: Westervelt, 1915, 176.

*C331.3.2. Tabu: looking while being carried upon turtle's back. Fijis: Fison, 1904, 20.

C332. Tabu: looking around. Tonga: Collocott, 1921, 46f.

*C338. Tabu: looking down. N.Z.: Grey, 1855, 72; White, 1887-90, I, 117.

*C339. Looking tabu -- miscellaneous.

*C339.1. Tabu: man's looking shoreward when canoe near island. Ellice Is.: Kennedy, 1931, 166.

*C339.2. Tabu: to look out of house. Hawaii: Westervelt, 1915, 96; Thrum, 1907, 55.

C400--C499. Speaking tabu

C400. Speaking tabu. Societies: Henry, 1928, 559.

*C401.8. Tabu: talking during thunderstorm. Hawaii: Emerson, 1915, 233.

C420. Tabu: uttering secrets. Hawaii: Pukui-Curtis, n.d., 21ff.

C423.3. Tabu: revealing experiences in other world. Fijis: Hocart, 1929, 211.

C423.5. Tabu: revealing sacred mysteries. Hawaii: Beckwith, 1940, 144.

C430. Name tabu: prohibition against uttering the name of a person or thing. Bellona: Elbert-Monberg, 1964, Nos. 185a, 185b.

C431. Tabu: uttering name of god (or gods). Hawaii: Fornander, 1918, V, 18; Thrum, 1923, 157.

*C438. Tabu: calling a child a child. Must be called a rat (lest jealous gods take children). Fijis: Hocart, 1929, 192.

C460. Laughing tabu. N.Z.: Clark, 1896, 54; Cowan, 1930, I, 18; White, 1887-90, II, 106f., 112, 114f.

*C460.1. Laughing tabu: Maui enters body of goddess of death in form of grub. Companions laugh; he is discovered and killed. N.Z.: Best, 1924, 148.

*C463. Man leaves his mistress in Land of Women when she laughs at a white hair in his head. Marquesas: Lavondes, 1964, 62ff.

C480.1. Whistling tabu. Futuna: Burrows, 1936, 227.

C481.1. Tabu: birds not to sing around home of goddess. Hawaii: Beckwith, 1940, 166.

C482.1. Tabu: people weeping in land of gods. Hawaii: Beckwith, 1940, 69; Rice, 1923, 128.

C710. Tabus connected with other-world journeys.

C483.1. Tabu: whistling in other world. Tuamotus:
Stimson, n.d., Z-G. 3/1301.

C484.1. Tabu: coughing in other world. Tuamotus:
Stimson, n.d., Z-G. 3/1301.

*C499.4. Person who mocks albino himself becomes one.
Niue: Loeb, 1926, 187.

C500--C549. Tabu: touching

C501. Tabu: contact with things belonging to a king.
Hawaii: Beckwith, 1940, 95, 98; N.Z.: Grace,
1907, 209; White, 1887-90, II, 9f., 24, 30, 38,
48, 49f., 50, 269.

*C501.1. Tabu: touching shadow of a king. Hawaii:
Fornander, 1916, IV, 352; N.Z.: White, 1887-90,
III, 265.

C510. Tabu: touching tree (plant). Chatham Is.:
Beckwith, 1940, 19, nn. 10, 11, 12; N.Z.:
W. T. Morpeth "The Hunakeha Tree" JPS, XIV (1905),
216.

C515. Tabu: touching (plucking) flowers. Hawaii:
Beckwith, 1940, 17.

*C517.1. Tabu: toucing fruit. Tahiti: Henry, 1928,
582-583.

C518. Tabu: cutting down tree. (Cf. C43.3., C51.2.2.).
Tuamotus: Stimson, n.d., Z-G. 3/1174; Hawaii:
Westervelt, 1915, 49; N.Z.: Clark, 1896.

*C519.2. Tabu: trimming top of felled tree used for
canoe-building. If trimmed, tree will become
whole again. Marquesas: Steinen, 1933-34, 343.

*C519.3. Two women forbidden to cut particular
banana-stalks. Rotuma: Churchward, 1938-39, 117.

C520. Tabu: touching ground. Tahiti: Beckwith, 1940,
246.

*C526. Tabu: touching certain stone. Lau Is.:

St. Johnston, 1918, 92.

*C527. Tabu: landing boat on certain shore. Hawaii: Fornander, 1916, IV, 164.

C537.2. Tabu: touching hairless dog. Hawaii: Beckwith, 1940, 343.

C541. Tabu: contact with the dead. Chatham Is.: Travers, 1876, 25.

C544.1. Tabu: crushing lizard's eggs. Hawaii: Beckwith, 1940, 127.

C545.1. Tabu: touching old clothes. (Abandoned clothes should be thrown away.) Tahiti: Henry, 1928, 143.

C546. Tabu: striking certain rock. Samoa: Beckwith, 1940, 19, nn. 10-12; Fijis: Hocart, 1929, 209.

*C549.3. Tabu: crossing light of another man's torch. Niue: Loeb,1926, 100.

*C549.4. Tabu: touching sacred fishhooks. Mangareva: Laval, 1938, 181.

C550--C599. Class tabu

*C551.2. Tabu: touching person's hair. Hawaii: Forbes, 1882, 40.

*C551.3. Turtles tabu to all except king or chief(s). Futuna: Burrows, 1936, 103; Ellice Is.: Kennedy, 1931, 178.

*C551.4. Tabu: anyone but priests eating hearts of slain. N.Z.: Clark, 1896, 132.

C561.1. Tabu: slave going near fetish. N.Z.: Clark, 1896, 128.

*C561.2. Tabu: for other than chiefs to keep calendar. Cooks: Gill, 1876, 317.

C564.4. Cloth from certain bark tabu to all except chiefs. Hawaii: Beckwith, 1940, 144.

C564.5. Tabu: altar smoke from sacrifice touching young chief. Hawaii: Beckwith, 1940, 346.

*C564.5.1. Tabu: for priest-chiefs to make a fire. Bellona: Elbert-Monberg, 1964, No. 173.

C564.6. Tabu: teaching of genealogy of chiefs to commoners. Hawaii: Beckwith, 1940, 309.

C564.7. Tabu: touching head of chief. Hawaii, Marquesas, Fijis: Beckwith, 1940, 468

C564.8. Tabu: chieftainess preparing food. N.Z.: Clark, 1896, 2.

C564.9. Tabu: chief going outdoors in spite of provocations. Hawaii: Beckwith, 1940, 118.

*C564.10. Tabu: king looking at sky. Niue: Smith, 1903, 86.

*C564.11. Tabu: ruler's house (forbidden to children). Ellice Is.: Kennedy, 1931, 165.

*C564.12. Tabu: chiefs' carrying anything upon back. Ellice Is.: Kennedy, 1931, 199.

C573. Tabus of priests. N.Z.: Clark, 1896, 132, 149.

C600--C699. UNIQUE PROHIBITIONS

AND COMPULSIONS

C600--C649. The one forbidden thing

C610. The one forbidden place. Tuamotus: Stimson, n.d., Z-G. 13/317; Marquesas: Handy, 1930, 36; Lavondes, 1964, 64; Hawaii: Beckwith, 1940, 70, 166.

C611. Forbidden chamber. Person allowed to enter all chambers of house except one. Tonga: Gifford, 1924, 189.

C611.1. Forbidden door. All doors may be entered except one. Rotuma: Churchward, 1937-38, 367; 1938-39, 124, 219; Russell, 1942, 247.

C612. Forbidden forest. Hawaii: Beckwith, 1940, 142.

C615.1. Forbidden lake (pool). Tikopia: Firth, 1961, 47.

C615.5. Certain pool to be approached only when properly attired. Hawaii: Beckwith, 1940, 288.

*C615.6. Prohibition: going into the sea. Hawaii: Thrum, 1907, 131.

C617. Forbidden country (island). Kapingamarangi: Eilers, 1934, 127.

*C617.2. Forbidden valley. Tuamotus: Stimson, 1937, 121.

*C619.5. Tabu: untattooed woman to be on island. Ontong Java: Sarfert, 1931, 295.

*C619.6. Tabu: fishing in certain place. Tokelau: Burrows, 1923, 173; Rennell: Elbert-Monberg, 1964, No. 16.

*C619.7. Tabu: killing people who are in the place of refuge. N.Z.: White, 1887-90, V, 16ff.

C621.2.2. Tabu: touching banana. Hawaii: Beckwith, 1940, 146; Rotuma: Russell, 1942, 244.

*C621.2.3. Tabu: opening coconut. Niue: Smith, 1903, 100.

C631. Tabu: breaking the sabbath. Niue: Loeb, 1926, 36.

*C631.4.1. Tabu: lighting fires at night. Tokelau: Smith, 1920, 145, 147.

*C638. Tabu: going to sacred place during certain nights of the moon. Hawaii: Smith, 1955, 75.

*C645. Tabu: crossing running water. N.Z.: Cowan, 1930, I, 60.

*C646. Tabu: leaving well uncovered. Tonga: Collocott, 1928, 11.

C650--C699. The one compulsory thing

*C661.2. Turtle must be given a coconut and woven
mat (for transporting man). Fijis: Fison,
1904, 20.

*C688. Injunction: man to kiss no one before he kisses
his father. Hawaii: Green, 1926, 114.

C700--C899. Miscellaneous tabus

C710. Tabus connected with other-world journeys.
Marquesas: Beckwith, 1940, 149.

*C712.2. Tabu: taking anything away from underworld.
Tuamotus: Stimson, n.d., Z-G. 3/1386.

C721.1. Tabu: bathing during certain time. Tahiti:
Henry, 1928, 438.

C721.2. Tabu: bathing in certain place. Samoa:
Krämer, 1902, I, 439; Fijis: Hocart, 1929, 208.

*C722.2. Tabu: throwing cut hair in sea. Nukumanu:
Sarfert, 1931, 452.

C726.1. Tabu: throwing away nail trimmings (should be
buried or thrown into sea). Tahiti: Henry, 1928,
143.

C731. Tabu: resting on journey. Societies: Seurat,
1905, 437; Cooks: Gill, 1876, 81; Tokelau:
Burrows, 1923, 161.

*C731.1. Tabu: laying aside burden upon journey.
Societies: Seurat, 1905, 437f.

C735.1.2. Tabu: sleeping before task is finished.
Tuamotus: Stimson, n.d., Z-G. 3/1174.

C751.8. Tabu: carrying food at night. Hawaii:
Beckwith, 1940, 144.

C752.1.6. Tabu: using magic power after nightfall.
Tuamotus: Stimson, n.d., Z-G. 13/166.

C752.2.1. Tabu: supernatural creatures being
abroad after sunrise. Hawaii: Beckwith, 1940,
333; N.Z.: Best, 1924, 157.

> E452. Ghost laid at cock-crow.
> F383.4. Fairy must leave at cock-crow.

C755.1. Tabu: leaving house within certain time.
Samoa: Henry, 1928, 346.

C755.7. Tabu: landing on certain island during forbidden period. Hawaii: Beckwith, 1940, 508, 511.

*C770.2. Gods are offended when man boasts of his
country's superior beauty. They overwhelm country
with lava. Hawaii: *Beckwith, 1940, 191, 191 n. 5.

C830--C899. Unclassified tabus

*C841.3.1. Tabu: killing caterpillars. Hawaii:
Green, 1923, 45.

C841.9. Tabu: killing certain fish. Hawaii:
McAllister, 1933, 151.

*C841.12. Tabu: killing certain birds. Societies:
Henry, 1928, 540; N.Z.: Cowan, 1930, I, 241f.

*C841.13. Tabu: driving away cricket. Societies:
Henry, 1928, 391.

*C841.14. Tabu: molesting great octopus. Societies:
Henry, 1928, 396.

*C841.15. Tabu: catching crab. Rennell: Elbert-Monberg,
1964, No. 186.

*C841.16. Tabu: killing fireflies. Rennell: Elbert-
Monberg, 1964, No. 172.

*C841.17. Tabu: catching or killing albino fish or game.
N.Z.: Grace, 1907, 141, 197.

C842. Tabu: exposure to sunlight. Tuamotus: Stimson,

1937, 87; Hawaii: Luomala, 1951, 70ff.; N.Z.:
Best, 1925, 936; Lau Is.: St. Johnston, 1918,
37; Rennell: Elbert-Monberg, 1964, Nos. 173, 186,
187.

C311.1.8.1. Gods flee at approach of dawn.
E452. Ghost laid at cock-crow (dawn).

C843.1. Tabu: pointing at rainbow. Niue: Loeb,
1926, 159.

C868. Tabu: leaving land entirely unoccupied.
Tuamotus: Stimson, n.d., T-G. 3/711.

C895. Tabu: using stone fish-hooks. Easter I.:
Métraux, 1940, 363.

C900--C999. Punishment for breaking tabu

*C905.3. Fairies punish breach of tabu. N.Z.: Cowan,
1920, 144.

*C905.4. Spirits (ghosts) punish breach of tabu.
Rotuma: Churchward, 1938-39, 118.

*C905.5. Lizard monster (taniwha) punishes breach
of tabu. N.Z.: Best, 1924, 193.

C920. Death for breaking tabu. Mangareva: Hiroa,
1938, 377; Laval, 1938, 45; Tuamotus: Stimson,
n.d., T-G. 3/912, Z-G. 13/127, Z-G. 3/1174;
Stimson, 1937, 58ff.; Marquesas: Handy, 1930,
60, 67, 138; Stevenson, 1912, 37ff.; Societies:
Henry, 1928, 561ff.; Cooks: Gill, 1876, 82;
Hawaii: Dickey, 1917, 29; Fornander, 1916, IV,
66, 164; McAllister, 1933, 86, 146; Pukui, 1933,
139; Thrum, 1907, 55, 57; Thrum, 1923, 49, 97;
Westervelt, 1915, 28, 179; Niue: Loeb, 1926,
89, 170, 172; Tokelau: Burrows, 1923,169, 173;
Macgregor, 1937, 61; N.Z.: Cowan, 1930, I, 39,
188; Grace, 1907, 229; White, 1887-90, III, 200,
211; Rotuma: Russell, 1942, 245; Fijis (Lau):
Hocart, 1929, 211; St. Johnston, 1918, 46, 112;
Nukumanu: Sarfert, 1931, 332; Rennell: Elbert-
Monberg, 1964, No. 235a; Tikopia: Firth, 1961,
135.

C920.1. Death of children for breaking tabu. N.Z.:
Cowan, 1930, I, 260.

C920.2. Death of wife for breaking tabu. N.Z.: Cowan,
1930, I, 260.

*C920.3. Death of husband when wife breaks tabu. Cooks:
Gill, 1876, 81.

C921. Immediate death for breaking tabu. Mangareva:
Laval, 1938, 85; Hawaii: McAllister, 1933, 146;
Samoa: Powell-Pratt, 1892, 242; Rennell:
Elbert-Monberg, 1964, No. 158.

C922.1. Death by choking for breaking tabu. Hawaii:
Beckwith, 1940, 22, 146.

C923. Death by drowning for breaking tabu. Tuamotus:
Stimson, n.d., T-G. 2/44, Z-G. 13/441; Marquesas:
Handy, 1930, 134; Tahiti: Henry, 1928, 438;
Cooks: Savage, 1910, 146; Hawaii: Beckwith, 1940,
118; Pukapuka: Beaglehole, 1938, 310; Samoa:
Beckwith, 1940, 25, 512; Niue: Loeb, 1926. 100;
N.Z.: *Grace, 1901, 69, 70 n.; Smith, 1911, 91.

C927. Burning as punishment for breaking tabu. Hawaii:
Beckwith, 1940, 264.

C929.5. Death by being swallowed for breaking tabu.
Rarotonga: Beckwith, 1940, 262.

C929.6. Man sacrificed to the gods for breaking tabu.
Hawaii: Beckwith, 1940, 511.

*C929.7. Death from eating tabu foods. Rarotonga:
Te Ariki, 1920, 178.

*C929.8. Sharks eat person violating tabu. Mangareva:
Hiroa, 1938, 92; Laval, 1938, 194; Tokelau:
Burrows, 1923, 169; Fijis: Hocart, 1929, 209.

*C929.9. Ghosts kill and eat women who eat forbidden
bananas. Rotuma: Churchward, 1938-39, 118.

*C929.10. Sea monsters destroy person breaking tabu.
N.Z.: Best, 1925, 963.

C932. Loss of wife (husband) for breaking tabu. N.Z.:
Beckwith, 1940, 249; Smith, 1910, 86 ff.

C933.1. Luck in hunting lost for breaking tabu.
Marquesas: Handy, 1930, 64.

C933.2. Luck in fishing lost for breaking tabu. Easter
I.: Métraux, 1940, 363; Tuamotus: Stimson, n.d.,
T-G. 3/600; Marquesas: Lavondes, 1964, 10;
Hawaii: McAllister, 1933, 164; Pukui, 1943, 65;
Tonga: Gifford, 1924, 601.

*C933.2.1. Fish caught by person without divine protectio:
come back to life. Hawaii: Green, 1923, 46f.

C934. Food supply fails because of broken tabu. Hawaii:
Beckwith, 1940, 111; Samoa: Beckwith, 1940, 450.

C934.1. Loss of crops because of broken tabu. Hawaii:
McAllister, 1933, 177; N.Z.: White, 1887-90, IV,
8.

*C934.1.1. Loss to mankind of valuable food-giving
tree because person does not plant it as directed.
Samoa: Brown, 1917, 98f.

*C934.4. Droughth brought by violating tabu. Niue:
Loeb, 1926, 173.

C936. War lost because of breaking tabu. N.Z.: White,
1887-90, IV, 112.

*C936.1. Spy in a hostile fort goes to sleep because of
broken tabu. N.Z.: White, 1887-90, IV, 51, 202.

C937.1. Immortality lost because of breach of tabu.
Samoa: Powell-Pratt, 1892, 249; N.Z.: Best, 1924,
148.

*C939.1.1. Well's water turns bitter after prohibition
neglected. Tonga: Collocott, 1928, 11.

C939.3. Felled trees (cut weeds) return to their places
because of broken tabu. Polynesia(general):
**Elbert-Kirtley, 1966, 355ff.; Tonga: Gifford,
1924, 22; Reiter, 1917-18, 1032; N.Z.: Clark,
1896, 95.

*C939.3.1. Work spoiled when looking-behind tabu
violated. Tonga: *Caillot, 1914, 270, 270 n. 1.

*C939.7. Islands cannot be joined after men break tabu
and look behind. Hawaii: Henry, 1928, 468.

*C939.8. Shipwreck for breaking tabu. Mangareva: Laval,

1938, 121; Samoa: Krämer, 1902, I, 413, n. 5;
Tokelau: Burrows, 1923, 170.

*C939.9. Gift opened prematurely falls in the sea.
Samoa: Sierich, 1902, 172.

*C939.10. Hotel built upon site of pagan temple is not
successful. Hawaii: McAllister, 1933, 141.

*C939.11. Sacred enclosure used as cattle pen:
animals placed there die. Hawaii: McAllister,
1933,110.

*C939.12. Failure to reach island paradise because of
broken tabu. Hawaii: Pukui-Curtis, n.d., 23.

*C939.13. Great drum becomes soundless to punish
man's breaking his word. Lau Is.: St. Johnston,
1918, 74.

*C939.14. Woman breaking prohibition loses her husband's
love. Mangareva: Hiroa, 1938, 361.

C940. Sickness or weakness for breaking tabu. Tokelau:
Macgregor, 1937, 69; Futuna: Burrows, 1936, 109.

C941. Particular disease (yaws) caused by breaking tabu.
Societies: Eric Ramsden, Strange Stories from the
South Seas (Wellington, 1944), 62; Hawaii:
Dickey, 1917, 29; Tikopia: Firth, 1961, 133.

C941.2. Swelling of limbs from breaking tabu. Ellice
Is.: Roberts, 1958, 368f.

*C941.2.1. Swelling of glands from breaking tabu.
Societies: Henry, 1928, 392.

*C941.2.2. Swelling of stomach from breaking tabu.
Niue: Loeb, 1926, 179.

C941.3.1. Sore mouth as punishment for breaking tabu.
Hawaii: Beckwith, 1940, 133.

*C941.3.2. Sore under armpit for breaking tabu.
Pukapuka: Beaglehole, 1938, 309, 406.

*C942.5. Spirit gnaws fat from body of thieves poaching
on fishing reserve. Pukapuka: Beaglehole, 1938,
313.

*C942.6. Body of person shrivels if he points at

rainbow. Niue: Loeb, 1926, 159.

C943. Loss of sight for breaking tabu. Tahiti: Henry, 1928, 143; Cooks: Gill, 1876, 83; Tonga: Collocott, 1921, 57; Niue: Loeb, 1926, 167; N.Z.: Clark, 1896, 154; Wohlers, 1875, 16.

C946.3. Magic growth of members for breaking tabu. Ellice Is.: Kennedy, 1931, 166.

*C946.4. Lameness as punishment for breaking tabu. Niue: Loeb, 1926, 35.

C947. Magic power lost by breaking tabu. Reef Is.: Elbert-Kirtley, 1966, 350f.

C948.4. Man's liver snatched away because of broken tabu. Hawaii: Beckwith, 1940, 118; Westervelt, 1915, 96.

*C948.9. Boy who troubles turtle becomes marked like turtle on his back. Niue: Loeb, 1926, 171.

C949.2. Baldness for breaking tabu. Tahiti: Henry, 1928, 143, 391.

*C949.6. Men become pregnant for breaking tabu. Fijis: Hocart, 1929, 192.

*C950.1. Girl responsible for death of evil spirit carried away by the sea. Easter I.: Métraux, 1940, 369.

C953. Person must remain in other world because of broken tabu. Marquesas: Handy, 1930, 120, 122; Cooks: Gill, 1876, 132.

C954. Person carried off to other world for breaking tabu. N.Z.: Best, 1924, 193; Cowan, 1921, 144; Cowan, 1930, 50; Grace, 1907, 142, 199, 210; Gudgeon, 1906, 47; Potae, 1928, 362; Smith, 1897, 22; Rennell: Elbert-Monberg, 1964, No. 186.

C955. Banishment from heaven for breaking tabu. Hawaii: Beckwith, 1940, 44, 69, 71, 77; Rice, 1923, 131.

C960. Transformation for breaking tabu. N.Z.: White, 1887-90, III, 80.

C961.2. Transformation to stone for breaking tabu. Hawaii: Beckwith, 1940, 212; Emerson, 1915, 233; N.Z.: Beckwith, 1940, 349.

C961.3.1. Transformation to wooden image for breaking tabu. Marquesas: Handy, 1930, 113.

C961.4. Transformation to mountain ridge for breaking tabu. Hawaii: Beckwith, 1940, 189.

C966. Change of language for breaking tabu. N.Z.: White, 1887-90, IV, 109, 112.

C984.1. Great wind because of broken tabu. Societies: Henry, 1928, 540-541.

C984.3. Storm because of broken tabu. Mangareva: Hiroa, 1938, 67, 421; Cooks: Low, 1934, 67; Hawaii: Westervelt, 1915, 49, 192ff.; N.Z.: Cowan, 1930, I, 242f.; Grace, 1907, 211.

C984.3. Flood because of broken tabu. Marquesas: Handy, 1930, 114; Hawaii: Beckwith, 1940, 23; Emerson, 1915, 211, n. (d); Chatham Is.: Beckwith, 1940, 19, nn. 10-12; N.Z.: Best, 1925, 885, 898; Cowan, 1930, I, 61f.

C984.4. Tidal wave for breaking tabu. Fijis: Beckwith, 1940, 19; Hocart, 1929, 214, 218.

*C984.4.2. Monsters of deep rise up and overwhelm thousands of people when woman eats tabu fish. N.Z.: Best 1893, 217.

C984.8. Island split apart for broken tabu. Tahiti: Beckwith, 1940, 468.

*C984.8.1. Island breaks off or slips back into sea because of violated tabu. Tuamotus: Stimson, 1934, 28; Marquesas: Lavondes, 1964, 48; Hawaii: Dickey, 1917, 18; McAllister, 1933, 127; Smith, 1966, 20f.; Thrum, 1923, 251; N.Z.: Best, 1925, 941f.

*C984.10. A plague of fleas for broken tabu. Societies: Agostini, 1900, 74.

*C984.11. River runs red after tabu broken. Societies: Agostini, 1900, 73.

*C984.12. Lake disappears because of broken tabu. N.Z.:
Best, 1925, 974.

*C984.13. Violation of sex tabu causes earthquake.
Rennell: Elbert-Monberg, 1964, No. 21.

C986. Abduction by animal for breaking tabu. Hawaii:
Westervelt, 1915, 146f.

*C986.1.1. Sea-monsters abduct people who break tabu.
N.Z.: Best, 1925, 963.

*C986.2. Girl bathing in forbidden pool is raped by fish.
Samoa: Krämer, 1902, I, 439.

C993. Unborn child affected by mother's broken tabu.
Cooks: Beckwith, 1940, 262; Tonga: Collocott,
1921, 160.

*C999. Miscellaneous punishments for breaking tabu --
additional motifs.

*C999.1. Canoe voyage interrupted, boat damaged or
stopped as result of breaking tabu. Cooks:
Pakoti, 1895, 67; Pukapuka: Beaglehole, 1938,
309; N.Z.: Best, 1893, 215; White, 1887-90,
IV, 30f., 36; Fijis: Hocart, 1929, 213;
Nukumanu: Sarfert, 1931, 452.

*C999.3. Boy fed prohibited meat diet turns into
cannibal. Hawaii: Thrum, 1907, 259f.

*C999.4. Ritual removal of tabu. N.Z.: Best, 1924,
79ff.

D. MAGIC

D0--D99. Transformation

D10--D99. Transformation: man to different
man

D10. Transformation to person of different sex.
Tahiti: Henry, 1928, 372.

D11.1. Transformation: ogre to man. Tonga: Collocott,
1928, 17, 26.

D40. Transformation to likeness of another person.
Tuamotus: Stimson, 1937, 130; Tonga: Collocott,
1928, 26; Chatham Is.: Shand, 1894, 125.

D40.2. Transformation to likeness of another woman.
Mangareva: Laval, 1938, 302.

D42. God in guise of mortal. Marquesas: Handy, 1930,
109; Hawaii: Rice, 1923, 9.

*D42.3. Spirit assumes appearance of man's wife.
Manihiki: Editors, JPS VI (1897), 97, note;
Tonga: Collocott, 1928, 26; N.Z.: Beattie, 1915,
136; Ellice Is.: Roberts, 1958, 365; Kapingamarangi: Emory, 1949, 239.

D47.2. Transformation: normal men to ogres. N.Z.:
White, 1887-90, V, 82.

D52.1. Transformation: man (hero) becomes hideous.
Marquesas: Handy, 1930, 124; N.Z.: Grace, 1907,
143ff., 201; Ontong Java: Sarfert, 1931, 441.

D52.2. Ugly man becomes handsome. Marquesas: Handy,
1930, 124; Tonga: Collocott, 1928, 51; Samoa:
Beckwith, 1940, 473.

*D55.0.1. After extraordinarily filling meal a boy
becomes a filled-out, mature man. Hawaii:
Fornander, 1916, IV, 456.

165

D55.1.1. Man magically stretches self to overcome cliff.
Hawaii: Dixon, 1916, 91.

*D55.1.1.3. God can stretch hands to horizon. Niue:
Loeb, 1928, 209.

*D55.1.1.6. Telescopic powers of stetching. Tuamotus:
Beckwith, 1940, 470; Hawaii: Beckwith, 1940, 464;
Rice, 1923, 95.

*D55.1.1.7. Man stretches body so it may be used as
bridge between islands. Hawaii: Beckwith, 1940,
507.

D55.1.2. Transformation: person to giant. Hawaii:
Beckwith, 1940, 539; Cooks: Gill, 1876, 59.

D55.2. Person becomes magically smaller. Marquesas:
Lavondes, 1966, 88, 204; Handy, 1943, 24;
Steinen, 1934-35, 202; Hawaii: Westervelt, 1915,
238; Samoa: Sierich, 1901, 22; Tokelaus: Burrows
1923, 167; Tikopia: Firth, 1961, 29.

D55.2.5. Transformation: adult to child. Marquesas:
Lavondes, 1964, 88, 96, 204; Steinen, 1934-35,
223.

*D55.2.7. Person goes to sea inside a pumpkin. Cooks:
Kunike, 1928, 31.

*D55.2.8. Person magically shrinks himself; floats
down a stream wrapped in a taro leaf. Samoa:
Powell-Pratt, 1892, 98.

*D55.2.9. Person killed and put in shell of small limpet.
Hawaii: Fornander, 1916, IV, 530.

D56.1. Transformation to older person. Mangareva:
Hiroa, 1938, 323; Marquesas: Lavondes, 1966, 88ff.
Hawaii: Emerson, 1915, 82; Fornander, 1916, IV,
604; N.Z.: Grey, 1855, 73.

D100--D199. TRANSFORMATION:

MAN TO ANIMAL

D100. Transformation: man to animal. Hawaii: Beckwith, 1940, 141.

D110--D149. Transformation: man to mammal

D110. Transformation: man to wild beast (mammal). *Feuilletau de Bruyn, W.K.H., "Iets over de Lykanthropie of het weerwolfgeloof der Papoea's van de Schoulen-Eilenden," Nieuw Guinea V (1940) 106-116.

D117.3. Transformation: man to rat. Mangareva: Hiroa, 1938, 310, 381; Luomala, 1949, 150; Hawaii: Beckwith, 1940,17, 425f.; Fornander, 1916, IV, 164, 450; V, 370; Pukui, 1933, 147; Thrum, 1923, 26; Westervelt,1915, 174ff.; N.Z.: Best, 1924, 147; Ellice Is.: Kennedy, 1931, 164; Ontong Java: Sarfert, 1931, 296.

*D117.5. Transformation: man to bat. Tikopia: Firth, 1961, 73.

D127.3. Transformation: man to whale. Tuamotus: Stimson, n.d., Z-G. 13/10; Tikopia: Firth, 1961, 48.

D127.5. Transformation: man to dolphin. Samoa: Krämer, 1902, I, 354.

D127.6. Transformation: man to porpoise. Tuamotus: Stimson, 1934, 53; Marquesas: Handy, 1930, 92; Tonga: Gifford, 1924, 77; N.Z.: Grace, 1907, 156; Bellona: Elbert-Monberg, 1964, Nos. 57a, 57a n.; Rennell: ibid., No. 57c.

D136. Transformation: man to swine (were-hog). Tahiti: Beckwith, 1940, 37; Henry, 1928, 232; Hawaii: Dickey, 1917, 20; Fornander, 1918, V, 314, 362; McAllister, 1933, 160; Thrum, 1907, 197; Thrum, 1923, 207f.; Westervelt, 1915, 246ff.

167

D141. Transformation: man to dog. Tuamotus: Caillot, 1914, 107; Luomala, 1949, 81; Stimson, n.d., Z-G. 13/52; Stimson, 1934, 39; Stimson, 1937, 48, Hawaii: Beckwith, 1940, 349; Fornander, 1918, VI, 336; N.Z.: *Best, 1924, 135; Best, 1925, 939; Best, 1929, 10, 16 n.; Clark, 1896, 50; Grace, 1907, 102; Grey, 1855, 52; White, 1887-90, II, 77, 80, 86, 109, 111, 122, 124f., 125; Wohlers, 1875, 14.

D141.0.1. Kynanthropy. Hawaii: Fornander, 1918, V, 332, 364, 414.

D142. Transformation: man to cat. Tonga: Gifford, 1924, 20.

D142.2. God assumes form of a cat. Tonga: Gifford, 1924, 20.

D150. Transformation: man to bird. Oceania: **Lessa, 1961, 326ff.; Mangareva: Hiroa, 1938, 361, 370; Laval, 1938, 301; Tuamotus: Stimson, n.d., T-G. 3/619; Stimson, 1934, 18, 35; Stimson, 1937, 45, 134; Marquesas: Handy, 1930, 55, 108; Cooks: Gill, 1876, 59, 94; Hawaii: Beckwith, 1919, 470; Beckwith, 1932, 32; Beckwith, 1940, 115, 428; Fornander, 1918, V, 414; Thrum, 1923, 167ff., 184; Westervelt, 1915, 229ff.; N.Z.: Best, 1925, 817, 937; Dixon, 1916, 79; White, 1887-90, II, 115; Rotuma: Churchward, 1938-39, 337; Rennell: Bradley, 1956, 335; Elbert-Monberg, 1964, Nos.174, 175, 176.

D152.1. Transformation: man to hawk. N.Z.: Best, 1924, 145.

D152.2. Transformation: human to eagle. N.Z.: Wohlers 1875, 12.

D153.2. Transformation: man to owl. Samoa: Powell-Pratt, 1892, 99, 107.

D154.1.0.1. Transformation: god to dove (pigeon). N.Z.: Cowan, 1930, I, 21.

D154.2. Transformation: man to pigeon. Tuamotus: Stimson, n.d., Z-G. 13/52; Stimson, 1937, 16; Marquesas: Handy, 1930, 103; Tonga: Collocott, 1928, 24f.; N.Z.: Best, 1924, 136, 143; Best, 1929, 7, 15 n., 16 n.; Cowan, 1930, I, 15, 21; Clark, 1896, 36; Grey, 1855, 27ff., 86; Luomala, 1949, 56, 153; White, 1887-90, I, 83, 86; III, 67, 73, 96f.; Wohlers, 1875, 11; Ellis Is.: David,

1899, 94.

D162. Transformation: man to crane. N.Z.: Dixon, 1916, 79; Wohlers, 1876, 112; White, 1887-90, II, 39.

D166.1. Transformation: man to chicken. Hawaii: Fornander, 1918, V, 266; McAllister, 1933, 154.

D166.1.1. Transformation: man to cock. Mangareva: Massainoff, 1933, V, 57; Rotuma: Churchward, 1937-38, 493.

*D169.5. Transformation: woman to cormorant. N.Z.: Best, 1924, 202; Gudgeon, 1906, 46.

D170. Transformation: man to fish (were-fish). Easter I.: *Knoche, 1939, 25ff.; Métraux, 1940, 372; Mangareva: Buck, 1938, 204; Hiroa, 1938, 320, 370; Laval, 1938, 308; Tuamotus: Stimson, n.d., Z-G. 3/1100; Marquesas: Handy, 1930, 135; Steinen, 1934-35, 236; Societies: Dixon, 1916, 65; Hawaii: Beckwith, 1940, 204, 525; Fornander, 1918, V, 194, 266; 1918, VI, 172ff.; Green, 1929, 33; Pukui, 1933, 185; Thrum, 1907, 243, 273; Thrum, 1921, 108; Thrum, 1923, 193, 206; Westervelt, 1915, 144; Tonga: Gifford, 1924, 84; Samoa: Sierich, 1902,190; N.Z.: Beattie, 1920, 136; White, 1887-90, III, 52; Rotuma: Churchward, 1937-38, 494.

D173. Transformation: man to eel. Polynesia (general): **Kirtley, 1967, 89ff.; *Dixon, 1916, 55, 56, nn. 75, 76; Tuamotus: Stimson, n.d., Z-G. 13/10; Stimson, 1937, 41; Hawaii: Beckwith, 1940, 21; Fornander, 1918, V, 534; McAllister, 1933, 118f.; Samoa: Clark, 1896, 70; Krämer, 1902, I, 393.

D174. Transformation: person to cuttlefish (octopus). Rarotonga: Te Ariki, 1920, 4; Kapingamarangi: Elbert, 1948, 105; Elbert, 1949, 244.

D175. Transformation: man to crab. Easter I.: Knoche, 1920, 66; Manihiki: Editors, JPS VI (1897) 97, note.

D178. Transformation: man to shark. Hawaii: Beckwith, 1940, 140; Fornander, 1918, V, 142; Green, 1926, 102, n. 2; McAllister, 1933, 123; Pukui, 1943, 57; Thrum, 1907, 131, 258; Thrum,

1920, 71; Westervelt, 1915, 61, 259; Tonga: Beckwith, 1940, 130; Gifford, 1924, 76, 184; N.Z.: Grace, 1907, 149, 151; Fijis: Beckwith, 1940, 131; Ontong Java, Nukumanu: Sarfert, 1931, 435.

*D178.1. Were-shark. Hawaii: Dickey, 1917, 29, 33; Emerson, 1915, 160f.; Fornander, 1918, V, 140, 372; McAllister, 1933, 157, 164; Rice, 1923, 111; Smith, 1955, 65ff.; Thrum, 1907, 259ff.; Thrum, 1920, 71; Thrum, 1923, 217; Westervelt, 1915, 2, 52ff., 60f.

D179.5. Transformation: man to sword-fish. Cooks: Clark, 1896, 140.

*D179.6. Transformation: woman to clam. Tokelau: Burrows, 1923, 166.

*D179.7. Transformation: man to prawn. Tahiti: Orsmond, 1933a, 172.

D180. Transformation: man to insect. Cooks: Gill, 1876, 53.

D181. Transformation: man to spider. Rotuma: Churchward, 1937-38, 493.

D182.2. Transformation: man to ant. Ontong Java, Nukumanu: Sarfert, 1931, 429, 433.

D191. Transformation: man to serpent (snake). Rennell: Elbert-Monberg, 1964, Nos. 51a, 51b.

*D191.0.1. Snake transformed to man has patches of scale upon his forehead. Rennell: Elbert-Monberg, 1964, Nos. 51a, 51b.

D192. Transformation: man to worm. N.Z.: Best, 1924, 148; Ontong Java, Nukumanu: Sarfert, 1931, 434.

D192.1. Transformation: man to caterpillar. Hawaii: Green, 1923, 43ff.; N.Z.: Best, 1924, 148.

D193. Transformation: man to turtle (or tortoise). Tahiti: Jourdain, 1937, 203; Hawaii: Beckwith, 1940, 137; Smith, 1955, 37; Reef Is.: Elbert-Kirtley, 1966, 369.

D197. Transformation: man to lizard. Easter I.:
Henri Lavachery, "Homme-lézard de l'ile de Paques,"
Mus. Roy. d'Art et d'Histoire Brussels, Bul. 1-6,
71-76, 1946; Mangareva: Hiroa, 1938, 311;
Luomala, 1949, 150; Rarotonga: Te Ariki, 1920, 4;
Hawaii: Thrum, 1920, 71; Thrum, 1923, 217;
Westervelt, 1915, 52ff.; Ontong Java, Nukumanu:
Sarfert, 1931, 431; Bellona: Elbert-Monberg,
1964, No. 190.

*D199.2.2. Transformation: person to sea serpent.
Tonga: Reiter, 1907, 752.

*D199.2.3. Transformation: person into water-monster.
N.Z.: Best, 1925, 979.

*D199.4. Transformation: woman into mermaid. N.Z.:
White, 1887-90, II, 127f.

D200--D299. Transformation: man

to object

D210.1. Plants as transformed bodies of gods. Hawaii:
Beckwith, 1940, 93.

D212. Transformation: man (woman) into flower. Hawaii:
Beckwith, 1940, 93.

D213. Transformation: man (person) to plant. Hawaii:
Fornander, 1918, V, 270, 582; Green, 1923, 34.

D213.3. Transformation: man to turmeric plant.
Easter I.: Métraux, 1940, 365.

D213.4. Transformation: man to vine. Hawaii: Beckwith,
1940, 93, 99.

*D213.9. Transformation: man to kava plant. Marquesas:
Steinen, 1934-35, 228.

D215. Transformation: man (god) to tree. Hawaii:
Beckwith, 1940, 101, 254, 478, 495, 532; Dickey,
1917, 30; Fornander, 1918, V, 148, 514, 676;
Green, 1916, 39, 50, 99; Pukui, 1933, 149;
Pukui-Curtis, n.d., 68; Smith, 1955, 50;
Westervelt, 1915, 47; N.Z.: Cowan, 1930, I, 248;
Grey, 1855, 165; White, 1887-90, III, 215.

*D215.9. Transformation: man to breadfruit tree.
Tahiti: Beckwith, 1940, 101; Hawaii:
Westervelt, 1915, 7.

D216. Transformation: man to log. Hawaii: Beckwith,
1940, 100; Fornander, 1916, IV, 60; 1918, V, 272;
N.Z.: Cowan, 1930, I, 153.

D221. Transformation: man to gourd (calabash). Cooks:
Beckwith, 1940, 268.

D231. Transformation: man to stone. Mangareva: Hiroa,
1938, 333; Tuamotus: Stimson, n.d., T-G. 3/6;
Marquesas: Handy, 1930, 106; Societies: Jourdain,
1934, 202; Tefaafana, 1917, 31; Cooks: Savage,
1910, 155; Hawaii: Beckwith, 1940, 65, 191, 342,
422; Dickey, 1917, 30f., 33; Emerson, 1915, 91,
233; Forbes, 1881, 59; Fornander, 1916, IV, 60,
496; V, 538; Green, 1923, 5, 27; Green, 1926,
55, 121f.; Luomala, 1951, 16; McAllister, 1923,
132, 151, 152; Rice, 1923, 32; Thrum, 1907, 33,
146; Westervelt, 1915, 47, 252, 266; Tonga:
Collocott, 1922, 160; Gifford, 1924, 98f., 183;
Samoa: Krämer, 1902, I, 452; Powell-Pratt, 1891,
202, n. 2; Stair, 1896, 36; Stuebel, 1896, 67,
148, 149; Tokelaus: Burrows, 1923, 172;
Macgregor, 1937, 85; Niue: Loeb, 1926, 187, 202;
Chatham Is.: Skinner-Baucke, 1928, 379; N.Z.:
Best, 1899, 132; Best, 1925, 979; Best, 1926,
202; Best, 1927, 272; Cowan, 1930, 70, 74ff.;
Luomala, 1951, 72; White, 1887-90, III, 80, 95;
IV, 35, 110; V, 82; Futuna: Burrows, 1936,
109, 225, 227f.; Fijis: Hocart, 1929, 215;
Tikopia: Firth, 1961, 116; Rennell: Elbert-
Monberg, 1964, No. 76a.

D233. Transformation: man to shell. Tokelaus:
Burrows, 1923, 166; Macgregor, 1937, 85.

D237. Transformation: man to coral.' Mangareva:
Hiroa, 1938, 320; Marquesas: Handy, 1930, 106;
Lavondes, 1966, 134ff., 170; Hawaii: Fornander,
1916, IV, 60; Tonga: Gifford, 1924, 94, 100.

D244. Transformation: man to pumice. Hawaii:
Beckwith, 1940, 215.

D255.1. Transformation: man into canoe. Marquesas:
Steinen, 1934-35, 222; Hawaii: Beckwith, 1940,
231, 478; Dickey, 1917, 16; Rice, 1923, 16.

D258. Transformation: man to fishhook: Easter I.:
Métraux, 1940, 364.

*D267. Transformation: man to rope. Hawaii:
Beckwith, 1940, 436; Rice, 1923, 98.

D268.1. Transformation: man to housepost. Tuamotus:
Stimson, n.d., Z-G. 13/276.

D268.2. Transformation: man to figure on ridgepole of
house. N.Z.: Best, 1928a, 257; Clark, 1896, 110.

D281.1. Transformation: man to wind. Hawaii:
Westervelt, 1915, 41ff., 212.

D281.1.1. Transformation: man to whirlwind. Hawaii:
Green, 1923, 13.

D281.2. Transformation: man to lightning. Hawaii:
Green, 1926, 99.

D283.1. Transformation: man (person) to pool of water.
Hawaii: Beckwith, 1940, 532; Fornander, 1918, V,
270; McAllister, 1933, 108; Westervelt, 1915, 260.

D283.2. Transformation to spring of water. Hawaii:
Beckwith, 1940, 17; Pukui, 1933, 147.

D283.4. Transformation: man to seafoam. Tuamotus:
Stimson, n.d., Z-D. 13/203.

D283.5. Transformation: man to ocean wave. Tuamotus:
Stimson, n.d., Z-G. 13/249; N.Z.: Beckwith, 1940,
318.

*D283.7. Transformation: sorceress becomes a whole
ocean. Hawaii: Fornander,1916, IV, 70.

*D283.8. Transformation: woman to rainbow. Hawaii:
Westervelt, 1915, 119.

D284. Transformation: man (person) to island. Hawaii:
Fornander, 1918, V, 534; Tonga: Gifford, 1924, 24.

D285. Transformation: man to fire. Hawaii: Fornander,
1916, IV, 70.

D291. Transformation: man to mountain (hill,cliff).
Hawaii: Fornander, 1916, IV, 70; V, 146, 534, 548,
610; Rice, 1923, 109; Thrum, 1907, 131; N.Z.:
White, 1887-90, II, 37; III, 80.

*D291.1. Transformation: man to volcano. Reef Is.:
O'Ferrall, 1904, 228.

D293. Transformation: man to star. Tubuai: Aitken,
1930, 113; Tuamotus: Stimson, n.d., T-G. 3/1005;
Tokelaus: Macgregor, 1937, 85; Rotuma: Russell,
1942, 244; Rennell: Elbert-Monberg, 1964, No. 33;
Bellona: ibid., No. 34a.

D294. Transformation: man to puff of dust. Tuamotus:
Stimson, n.d., Z-G. 13/203.

D300--D399. TRANSFORMATION: ANIMAL TO

PERSON

D310--D349. Transformation: mammal to

person

D336. Transformation: swine to person. Hawaii:
Rice, 1923, 51.

D336.1. Transformation: pig to person. Mangareva:
Hiroa, 1938, 328; Hawaii: Westervelt, 1915, 249ff.

D341. Transformation: dog to person. Hawaii:
Westervelt, 1915, 83ff.

D350. Transformation: bird to person. Easter I.:
Métraux, 1940, 373; Mangareva: Hiroa, 1938, 361;
Hawaii: Fornander, 1916, IV, 534; Thrum, 1923,
167ff.; Westervelt, 1915, 224; N.Z.: Grey, 1855,
249; White, 1887-90, II, 40.

D354.1. Transformation: dove to person. Nukumanu:
Sarfert, 1931, 445f.

D361.1. Swan Maiden. Polynesia: *Dixon, 1916, 64,
138, nn. 13-18 ; **Lessa, 1961, 38f., 120ff.

*D363. Transformation: chicken to human. Hawaii:
Fornander, 1918, V, 234; Westervelt, 1915, 207.

*D367. Transformation: pigeon to man. Tuamotus:
Stimson, 1934, 18; Samoa: Powell-Pratt, 1891,
198; N.Z.: White, 1887-90, II, 67, 73, 82, 97.

D370. Transformation: fish to man. Tuamotus: Stimson, n.d., Z-G. 13/194; Hawaii: Fornander, 1918, V, 194ff.; Pukui, 1933, 176, n. 3; Thrum, 1907, 244; Thrum, 1923, 206; Westervelt, 1915, 142.

D373. Transformation: eel to person. Tuamotus: Stimson, n.d., Z-G. 3/1295; Cooks: Gill, 1876, 77; Hawaii: McAllister, 1933, 118f.; Pukui, 1933, 171; Westervelt, 1915, 214; Tonga: Gifford, 1924, 182.

*D374. Transformation: clam to human. Tokelaus: Burrows, 1923, 165f.

*D374.1. Clam shell broken open and a beautiful girl is revealed. Tonga: Collocott, 1928, 33.

*D377. Bird transformed into water spirit. Samoa: Krämer, 1902, I, 432.

*D379.1. Transformation: shark to man. Hawaii: McAllister, 1933, 123; Thrum, 1907, 189, 236ff., 256ff.; Westervelt, 1915, 60ff.; Fijis: Hocart, 1929, 211.

*D379.2. Transformation: sea-cucumber to man. Hawaii: Pukui, 1933, 171.

D391. Transformation: serpent (snake) to person. Rennell: Elbert-Monberg, 1964, Nos. 51a, 51b.

D392. Transformation: worm to person. Tonga: Gifford, 1924, 25.

D397. Transformation: lizard to person. Hawaii: Green, 1926, 113; Thrum, 1920, 71; Ellice Is.: Kennedy, 1931, 190; Tikopia: Firth, 1961, 30, 34.

D399.1. Transformation: water-dragon to person. Hawaii: Westervelt, 1915, 155, 169, 174f.; N.Z.: Grace, 1907, 174.

*D399.2. Transformation: lizard-monster to beautiful woman. Tahiti: Henry, 1928, 622.

*D411.2.3. Transformation: rat to fish. Hawaii:
Thrum, 1923, 156; Westervelt, 1915, 181.

D412.3.2. Transformation: pig to fish. Tahiti:
Henry, 1928, 232; Hawaii: Westervelt, 1915, 261,
267.

*D412.5.8. Transformation: dog to shark. Hawaii:
Thrum, 1923, 307.

*D415.2. Transformation: caterpillars into sea-cucumbers.
Hawaii: Green, 1923, 45.

*D419.1.3. Transformation: scales of taniwha
(lizard-monster) to lizards. N.Z.: Te Aro, 1894,
166.

*D419.1.4. Transformation: dragon to a swarm of
caterpillars. Hawaii: Westervelt, 1915, 166, 168.

*D419.3. Transformation: giant fish into many small
fish. Ellice Is.: David, 1899, 99.

*D419.4. Transformation: fish to lizards. Hawaii:
Thrum, 1907, 240.

*D419.5. Transformation: fish to eels. Hawaii:
McAllister, 1933, 152.

*D419.6. Transformation: fish to turtle. Societies:
Caillot, 1914, 139.

*D419.7. Transformation: fish to rooster. Hawaii:
Fornander, 1918, V, 234.

*D422.2.4. Transformation: dog to stone. N.Z.: Best,
1924, 202; Hawaii: Westervelt, 1915, 89.

*D422.3.2. Transformation: pig to stone. Hawaii:
Green, 1923, 7; Rotuma: Russell, 1942, 242.

*D423.5. Transformation: fowl to rock. Tonga:
Collocott, 1928, 11.

*D425.2.1. Transformation: lizard to stone. N.Z.:
Best, 1924, 202.

*D425.2.1.1. Transformation: lizard to hill. Hawaii:

Fornander, 1918, V, 514.

*D425.2.2. Transformation: lizard to bamboo clump.
Tahiti: Henry, 1928, 622.

D426.1.1. Transformation: eel to stone. Hawaii:
Beckwith, 1940, 21.

D426.1.2. Transformation: eel to dry land. Tuamotus:
Stimson, n.d., Z-G. 13/221.

D426.2. Transformation: octopus to stone. Hawaii:
Beckwith, 1940, 22; Thrum, 1907, 235.

*D426.3. Transformation: fish into island. Societies:
Henry,1928, 558.

*D426.4. Transformation: shark to stone. Mangareva:
Hiroa, 1938, 25; Laval, 1938, 10; Marquesas:
Lavondes, 1964, 66; Hawaii: Dickey, 1917, 29;
Green, 1926, 107; McAllister, 1933, 164; Thrum,
1907, 219; Westervelt, 1915, 41; N.Z.: *Best,
1925, 842.

*D426.5. Transformation: fish to sea foam. Societies:
Caillot, 1914, 137.

*D426.6. Shark transformed into Milky Way. Hawaii:
Fornander, 1916, IV, 528.

D429.1. Transformation: water monster to Milky Way.
Rarotonga: BEckwith, 1940, 439.

D429.2.2. Transformation: dragon to stone. Hawaii:
Dickey, 1917, 29; Westervelt, 1915, 257; N.Z.:
Skinner, 1897, 156.

*D429.2.3. Transformation: dragon into stream of blood.
Hawaii: Westervelt, 1915, 168, 174.

*D429.2.4. Transformation: dragon into whirlwind.
Hawaii: Westervelt, 1915, 167.

*D429.3. Transformation: eel's head into coconut.
Cf. *A2611.3.1. Societies: Seurat, 1905, 438.

D431.2. Transformation: tree to person. Hawaii:
Pukui, 1933, 181; Pukui-Curtis, n.d., 29.

*D431.2.1. Transformation: log of wood into man.
Hawaii: Fornander, 1918, V, 272.

D431.3. Transformation: leaf (of tree) to person. Marquesas: Lavondes, 1964, 48.

D431.6. Transformation: plant to person. Hawaii: Beckwith, 1940, 515; N.Z.: Whetu, 1897, 99.

D432.1. Transformation: stone to person. Hawaii: Fornander, 1916, IV, 60.

D434.2. Transformation: rope to person. Hawaii: Beckwith, 1940, 465; Rice, 1923, 93.

D434.3. Transformation: canoe-builder to person. Hawaii: Beckwith, 1940, 233; Dickey, 1917, 18

*D437.6. Transformation: blood into person. Hawaii: Fornander, 1918, V, 546.

*D437.7. Transformation: a human chest into a woman. Mangareva: Hiroa, 1938, 421.

*D437.8. Transformation: woman's head into a woman. Mangareva: Hiroa, 1938, 32.

D439.5.1. Transformation: moon to person. Samoa: Clark, 1896, 118.

*D439.5.3. Transformation: sun to person. Ontong Java: Sarfert, 1931, 440.

*D439.7. Transformation: lightning to person. N.Z.: White, 1887-90, I, 51.

*D439.8. Transformation: rainbow to person. Hawaii: Westervelt, 1915, 118; N.Z.: White, 1887-90, III, 113.

D441.1. Transformation: tree to animal. Hawaii: Beckwith, 1940, 478; Bellona: Elbert-Monberg, 1964, No. 45.

D442.1. Transformation: stone to animal. Hawaii: Beckwith, 1940, 22; Thrum, 1907, 239.

*D442.4. Transformation: island to fish. Tahiti: Henry, 1928, 437ff.

*D444.12. Transformation: canoe to shark. Hawaii: Dickey, 1917, 30.

*D444.13. Transformation: spear to fish. Hawaii: Thrum, 1923, 179.

178

*D447.3.3. Transformation: blood-clot into parrot.
Samoa: Stuebel, 1896, 145.

D447.4. Transformation: fishtail to shark. Hawaii:
Beckwith, 1940, 134.

*D447.11. Transformation: human heart to shark.
Societies: Ropiteau, 1933, 128.

*D449.5. Goddess turns the stars (moon) into fish (food).
Hawaii: Thrum, 1921, 106.

D450--D499. Transformation: object to
object

*D451.1.0.2. Transformation: log into canoe. Hawaii:
Pukui-Curtis, n.d., 19.

*D451.3.5. Transformation: fruits into island.
Mangareva: Laval, 1938, 5.

D451.4.2. Transformation: blossom to canoe. Societies:
Henry, 1928, 561.

D451.8. Transformation: leaf to another object.
Hawaii: Beckwith, 1940, 478.

*D451.9.2. Transformation: breadfruit to canoe.
Reef Is.: *Elbert-Kirtley, 1966, 353, 354 n. 13.

*D451.9.3. Transformation: coconut shell to boat.
Tuamotus: Stimson, 1937, 56.

D452.1.8. Transformation: stone to island. Tonga:
Gifford, 1924, 191.

D454.3.4.1. Transformation: cloak to mountain.
Tuamotus: Stimson, n.d., Z-G. 13/420.

D454.10.1. Transformation: ship to mountains. N.Z.:
Beckwith, 1940, 467.

D454.10.2. Transformation: canoe to rock. Cooks:
Savage, 1910, 154; Hawaii: Smith, 1966, 1;
Westervelt, 1915, 104, 249, 255; Tonga: Collocott,
1928, 7; Gifford, 1924, 76; Samoa: Lesson, 1876,
603; Stuebel, 1896, 148; N.Z.: Cowan, 1930, I,
14, 154; White, 1887-90, II, 37; IV, 8, 31, 58;

Tikopia: Firth, 1961, 40, 116.

D471.3.   Transformation: ship to stone.

*D454.10.3.   Transformation: canoe to log.   N.Z.:
Beattie, 1920, 137.

*D454.10.5.   Transformation: canoe to star constellation.
Tonga: Collocott, 1922, 160.

*D454.17.   Transformation: seine to barrier reef.   Uvea:
Burrows, 1937, 161.

*D457.1.5.   Transformation: blood into man.   Reef Is.:
O'Ferrall, 1904, 229.

D457.14.1.   Transformation: ogress's tongue to surfboard.
Hawaii: Beckwith, 1940, 194.

*D458.   Transformation: stars of evening to stars of
morning.   N.Z.:   Grey, 1855, 140.

D471.3.   Transformation: ship to stone.   Oceanic:
*Smith, 1921, 23.   See D454.10.2.   Transformation:
canoe to rock (stone).

*D471.12.   Transformation: stream of water to girdle.
Tuamotus: Stimson, 1937, 127.

*D471.13.   Transformation: kite to stone.   Hawaii:
Smith, 1966, 19.

*D474.7.1.   Transformation: spittle to milk.   Niue:
Smith, 1903, 92.

D476.2.   Edible substance changed to inedible.   (All
food man tries to eat turns into trash).   N.Z.:
Grace, 1907, 142.

D482.1.   Transformation: stretching tree.   A tree
magically shoots upward.   Polynesia   (Marquesas,
Tuamotus, Rarotonga, Mangaia, Samoa, Tonga):
*Beckwith, 1940, 478-488;   Rotuma: Churchward,
1938-39, 329.

D482.4.   Transformation: stretching cliff.   A cliff
magically shoots up into the air.   Hawaii:
Dixon, 1916, 90.

*D484.   Moon stretches itself at maiden's request.
Marquesas: Steinen, 1934-35, 232.

*D487.4. Shark becomes monstrous. N.Z.: Kauika,
1904, 94.

*D489.4. One rock enlarged to build temple. Tubuai:
Aitken, 1930, 103.

D491.1. Compressible magic animals (pig). Hawaii:
Dickey, 1917, 20.

*D491.2.3. Compressible container made to hold great
amount. Samoa: Fraser, 1896, 175.

D491.3. Magic dog shrinks in size. Hawaii: Westervelt,
1915, 83ff.

D491.7. Ship becomes small boat. Tuamotus: Stimson,
n.d., T-G. 3/900.

*D491.8. Large body of water (lake, well) stolen in
container (like coconut shell). Tokelaus:
Macgregor, 1937, 62.

*D491.9. Boats made very small and owners hide them in
their clothes. Hawaii: Westervelt, 1915, 145.

*D492.4. Rooster magically changes color. Hawaii:
Westervelt, 1915, 239f.

D493. Spirit changes to animal. Tuamotus: Stimson,
n.d., T-G. 3/1001, Z-G. 3/1353.

D500--D599. MEANS OF TRANSFORMATION

D510. Transformation by breaking tabu. Tahiti:
Beckwith, 1940, 468.

D522. Transformation through magic word (charm). Cf.
D1760ff. Means of producing magic power. Tuamotus:
Stimson, n.d., Z-G. 13/203; N.Z.: White, 1887-90,
II, 37.

D531. Transformation by putting on skin. By putting on
skin, feathers, etc. of an animal, a person is
transformed to that animal. Rotuma: Churchward,
1938-39, 338; Reef Is.: Elbert-Kirtley, 1966, 369.

*D555.3. Transformation by drinking sea water. Ellice Is.: Kennedy, 1931, 175.

D562. Transformation by bathing (in sea). Tonga: Collocott, 1928, 17; Rennell: Elbert-Monberg, 1964, Nos. 51a, 51b.

*D562.0.1. A boy, whose father was a shark, himself becomes a shark when he enters water. Hawaii: Westervelt, 1915, 61.

D565.6. Transformation by touching water. Niue: Loeb, 1926, 187, 202.

*D566.5. Transformation by hitting with a club. Rennell: Bradley, 1956, 335.

*D566.6. Transformation by slicing in pieces. Rennell: Elbert-Monberg, 1964, Nos. 51a, 51b.

D572.1. Transformation by magic stick. Hawaii: Beckwith, 1940, 276, 280.

D583. Transformation by lousing. N.Z.: Dixon, 1916, 55.

*D586.1. Transformation to shark (fish) by entering sea, transformation to human form whenever on land. Cf.*D562.0.1. Tonga: Reiter, 1907, 750; Fijis: Hocart, 1929, 211.

*D591.1. Transformation by immersing in calabash of water. Hawaii: Rice, 1923, 93.

*D599.1. Transformation by wrapping convolvulus vine around person. Marquesas: Steinen, 1934-35, 202, 207.

*D599.5. Transformation at the sound of a cock. Societies: Tefaafana, 1917, 3.

D600--D699. MISCELLANEOUS TRANSFORMATION

INCIDENTS

D610. Repeated transformation. Transformation into
one form after another. Hawaii: Rice, 1923,
101; Ellice Is.: Roberts, 1958, 365.

*D610.2. Person who appears sometimes as a giant,
sometimes as a pygmy, and sometimes as a lizard.
Hawaii: Dickey, 1917, 27.

*D610.3. Person transforms himself into several
different shapes and repeatedly meets people who
are looking for him. Marquesas: Lavondes, 1966,
88ff., 156ff., 204.

D615. Transformation combat. Fight between contestants
who strive to outdo each other in successive
transformations. Tuamotus: Stimson, n.d.,
T-G. 3/1001; Societies: Caillot, 1914, 139f.;
Hawaii: Beckwith, 1940, 429; Dixon, 1916, 90f.;
Emerson, 1915, 37; Westervelt, 1915, 239ff.

D621.1. Animal by day, man by night. Societies,
Cooks, Samoa, Tokelau: *Dixon, 1916, 55f.;
Hawaii: Beckwith, 1940, 135; Rice, 1923, 110.

D621.1.1. Man by day, animal (fish, insect) by night.
Hawaii: Green, 1923, 43; Pukui, 1933, 171.

D621.3. Ugly by day; fair by night. Mangareva:
Hiroa, 1938, 334.

D630. Transformation and disenchantment at will.
Tuamotus: Stimson, n.d., Z-G. 13/52; Easter I.:
Métraux, 1940, 363; Hawaii: Beckwith, 1940,
401ff.; Fornander, 1918, V, 140; McAllister,
1933, 173; Thrum, 1923, 150ff.; N.Z.: Grace,
1907, 147ff.; White, 1887-90, III, 124, 189, 190;
Ontong Java, Nukumanu: Sarfert, 1931, 431f.

D630.4. Deity has power of self-transformation. Hawaii:
Beckwith, 1940, 93, 117ff., 172ff., 186, 276 ff.,
512.

D631. Size changed at will. Samoa: Sierich, 1901, 22;
Tikopia: Firth, 1961, 29.

D631.1. Person changes size at will. Marquesas: Handy, 1930, 106.

D631.4.4. Creature born from egg changes size at will. Marquesas: Handy, 1930, 124.

D641. Transformation to reach difficult place. Hawaii: Beckwith, 1940, 540; Fornander, 1916, IV, 164; N.Z.: Dixon, 1916, 79.

*D641.1.3. Chief transforms self to stone for love of his wife, who had been transformed to stone. Tonga: Gifford, 1924, 95.

*D641.1.4. Girl transforms self to reef to be near her beloved shark. Tonga: Gifford, 1924, 100.

D641.3. Transformation in order to enter rival's stomach. Tonga: Gifford, 1924, 76.

D641.4. Transformation to travel to otherworld. N.Z.: Best, 1925, 817, 937; Grey, 1855, 27; White, 1887-90, II, 67, 73, 82, 96f.

D642. Transformation to escape difficult situation. Hawaii: Beckwith, 1940, 514; Rice, 1923, 30.

D642.2. Transformation to escape death. Easter I.: Knoche, 1920, 66; Societies: Caillot, 1914, 139; Cooks: Gill, 1876, 59; Hawaii: Dickey, 1917, 28; Fornander, 1918, V, 414; Thrum, 1907, 262; Tonga: Gifford, 1924, 76; Ontong Java: Sarfert, 1931, 32 429.

*D642.2.1. Transformation to escape drowning. Mangareva: Hiroa, 1938, 370; N.Z.: White, 1887-90, III, 52.

D642.5. Transformation to escape notice. Tuamotus: Stimson, n.d., T-G. 3/1010, Z-G. 13/1241; Marquesas: Handy, 1930, 124; Hawaii: Beckwith, 1940, 450; Dickey, 1917, 20; Cooks: Beckwith, 1940, 268; Tonga: Gifford, 1924, 156f.

*D642.5.0.1. Transformation out of shame of encountering someone. Hawaii: Fornander, 1916, IV, 60; Tonga: Reiter, 1934, 499; Tokelaus: Burrows, 1923, 167; Tikopia: Firth, 1961, 29, 60.

D642.5.1. Transformation to hide from ogress. Hawaii: Beckwith, 1940, 194.

*D642.5.2. Transformation in order to stow away in canoe.
Mangareva: Hiroa, 1938, 310.

D642.6. Transformation to escape ogress. Samoa:
Sierich, 1901, 22; Ellice Is.: Kennedy, 1931, 202.

D642.7. Transformation to elude persuers. Hawaii:
Thrum, 1923, 193; Tonga: Gifford, 1924, 183;
Niue: Loeb, 1926, 187.

*D642.8. Transformation as a disguise. Mangareva:
Hiroa, 1938, 323, 338, 351; Hawaii: Emerson,
1915, 82f.

*D643.3. Person transforms self into a giant hog and
makes a bridge of his body so that his followers
may escape. Hawaii: McAllister, 1933, 160.

*D643.4. Rats transform themselves to fish to aid hero
in fight against giant fish. Hawaii: Thrum,
1923, 156.

D644. Transformation to travel fast. Hawaii:
Fornander, 1918, V, 232, 244.

D646.1. Transformation to fish to be caught. Ellice
Is.: Kennedy, 1931, 192.

D647. Transformation to seek lost (or unknown) person.
Mangareva: Hiroa, 1938, 361.

D651. Transformation to defeat enemies. Mangareva:
Buck, 1938a, 204; Hiroa, 1938, 320; Hawaii:
Emerson, 1915, 45; Fornander, 1918, V, 362;
Green, 1926, 107.

D651.1. Transformation to kill enemy. Tuamotus:
Beckwith, 1940, 503f.; Hawaii: Green, 1926, 99;
Ellice Is.:David, 1899, 95.

*D651.1.4. Ogress transforms herself to a bird in
order to pursue a canoe. Mangareva: Hiroa, 1938,
421; Laval, 1938, 301.

D651.3. Transformation to destroy enemy's property.
Rotuma: Churchward, 1937-38, 494f.

*D651.7. Transformation to discover identity of father.
Tuamotus: Henry, 1928, 352.

*D651.8. Transformation to spider to discover names of
rivals. Rotuma: Churchward, 1937-38, 493.

*D651.10. Transformation to abduct enemy. Mangareva: Hiroa, 1938, 381; Samoa: Stuebel, 1896, 66, 144; Kapingamarangi: Elbert, 1949, 244.

*D655.3. Man transforms self to shark in order to eat people (fish). Hawaii: Dickey, 1917, 29, 33; McAllister, 1933, 156; Westervelt, 1915, 62; Thrum, 1907, 258ff.

*D655.4. Person transforms himself into pigeon in order to kill other pigeons. N.Z.: Wohlers, 1875, 11.

D657. Transformation to steal. Hawaii: Beckwith, 1940, 21, 203, 349; Thrum, 1907, 197; Ontong Java, Nukumanu: Sarfert, 1931, 435.

D658. Transformation to seduce. Ellice Is.: Roberts, 1958, 365.

*D658.1.1. Transformation of god to eel to seduce bathing girl. Samoa: Krämer, 1902, I, 393.

D658.3.1. Transformation to seduce man. Cf. D42.3. Ellice Is.: Roberts, 1958, 365.

*D658.3.4. Transformation to woo girl. Hawaii: Thrum, 1907, 256.

*D658.3.5. Man without woman is transformed to cock, flies to Tahiti and finds hens without limit. Mangareva: Massainoff, 1933, 57.

D659.3. Transformation to show displeasure. Tonga: Gifford, 1924, 19.

D661. Transformation as punishment. Tubuai: Aitken, 1930, 114; Mangareva: Hiroa, 1938, 370; Tuamotus: Caillot, 1914, 107, 108; Stimson, n.d., T-G. 2/27; Z-G. 13/10; Stimson, 1934, 39, 44; Stimson, 1937, 48; Buck, 1938b, 189; Marquesas: Tahiaoteaa, 1933, 494; Societies: Dixon, 1916, 65; Tahiti: Beckwith, 1940, 251; Hawaii: Beckwith, 1940, 232, 495; Dickey, 1917, 18; Fornander, 1918, V, 534; VI, 337; Green, 1923, 5, 27, 55, 99; *Luomala, 1951, 16f.; Rice, 1923, 36; Smith, 1955, 50; Thrum, 1907, 146; Westervelt, 1915, 252; Samoa: Powell-Pratt, 1892, 99, 107; N.Z.: Best, 1925, 939, 979; Best, 1929, 10, 16 n.; Cowan, 1930, I, 248; White, 1887-90, II, 111, 118, 119, 122, 124f., 125; Wholers, 1875, 14; Rotuma: Luomala, 1949, 135; Russell, 1942, 244; Pukapuka: Luomala, 1949, 135.

D666. Transformation to save a person. Hawaii:
Pukui-Curtis, n.d., 72; Thrum, 1923, 206;
Westervelt, 1915, 7.

D672. Obstacle flight. Fugitives throw objects
behind them which magically become obstacles in
pursuer's path. Marquesas: Handy, 1930, 117;
Samoa: Nelson, 1925, 132; Niue: Loeb, 1926,
202; Ellice Is.: Kennedy, 1931, 204.

D673. Reversed obstacle flight. Magic obstacles
raised in front of fugitive. Tuamotus:
Stimson, n.d., Z-G. 13/221; Tonga: Collocott,
1928, 60; Samoa: Sierich, 1901, 22.

D698. Gods have power to transform themselves.
Hawaii: Beckwith, 1940, 2 and Ch. I passim.

D700--D799. DISENCHANTMENT

D712.1.2. Disenchantment by cutting in two. N.Z.:
Whetu, 1897, 100.

*D712.1.3. Disenchantment by cutting in pieces.
Marquesas: Steinen, 1933-34, 29, 31.

D712.2.1. Disenchantment by throwing in fire.
Tuamotus: Caillot, 1914, 64.

D721. Disenchantment by removing skin or covering. See
all references to D361.1., Swan Maiden. Tuamotus:
Stimson, n.d., Z-G. 13/346.

D762.2. Disenchantment by being wakened from magic
sleep by proper agent. Hawaii: Fornander, 1916,
IV, 170.

D785. Disenchantment by magic contest. Marquesas:
Handy, 1930, 107.

D799. Disenchantment by other means. Reef Is.:
O'Ferrall, 1904, 227.

187

D906. Magic wind. Hawaii: Rice, 1923, 104; Fijis: Fison, 1904, 109.

*D909. Magic weather phenomena -- miscellaneous.

*D909.1. Magic thunder (communicates message). N.Z.: White, 1887-90, II, 18.

*D909.2. Magic lightning. Funafuti: David, 1899, 97.

*D911.2. Magic water spouts. Kapingamarangi: Elbert, 1948, 121.

D921. Magic lake (pond). Funafuti: David, 1899, 97; Kennedy, 1931, 174.

D925. Magic fountain. Hawaii: Thrum, 1923, 171.

*D929. Magic body of water -- miscellaneous.

*D929.1. Magic fishpond. Hawaii: Dickey, 1917, 27.

D931. Magic rock (stone). Societies: Henry, 1928, 328; Hawaii: Beckwith, 1940, 22; Thrum, 1907, 222; Tonga: Beckwith, 1940, 467; Collocott, 1928, 27f.; N.Z.: Best, 1897, 7f.; Best, 1924, 67, 103; Cowan, 1930, 76; White, 1887-90, IV, 110; Fijis: Hocart, 1929, 218; Bellona: Elbert-Monberg, 1964, No. 66.

D932.0.1. Mountain (ridge) created by magic. Hawaii: Forbes, 1882, 37.

*D935.5. Magic gravel. N.Z.: White, 1887-90, III, 60ff.

*D935.6. Magic coral. Hawaii: Fornander, 1916, IV, 20ff.

D941. Magic forest. Marquesas: Lavondes, 1964, 12.

*D941.2. Magic grove (of coconuts). Tuamotus: Stimson, n.d., T-G. 3/600.

D950. Magic tree. Polynesia(general): **Elbert-Kirtley, 1966, 355ff.; Mangareva: Hiroa, 1938, 326; Tuamotus: Seurat, 1905, 483; Cooks: Gill, 1876, 66; Seurat, 1905, 485; Hawaii: Luomala, 1951, 15; Thrum, 1907, 112; Westervelt, 1915, 122f.; Tonga: Beckwith, 1940, 486; Collocott, 1928, 12, 15; Samoa: Brown, 1917, 97; Stuebel, 1896, 148; N.Z.: Best, 1906, 5ff.; Best, 1925, 714f.; Gudgeon, 1906, 29, 32f.; Whetu, 1897, 99; White, 1887-90, I, 69f., 74, 75; III, 2; V, 8f.; Fijis: Fison, 1904, 82; Reef Is.: O'Ferrall, 1904, 231; Kapingamarangi: Emory, 1949, 233.

> C939.3. Felled trees return to their places because of broken tabu. D1602.2. Felled tree raises itself again.

*D950.0.1.2. A thief can not steal the fruit of a magic tree. Hawaii: Pukui-Curtis, n.d., 40.

D954. Magic bough. Tonga: Collocott, 1928, 55.

D961.1. Garden produced by magic. Cooks: Ariki, 1899, 172.

D965. Magic plant. Tonga: Reiter, 1917-18, 1036f.; Samoa: Krämer, 1902, I, 257.

D965.2. Magic gourd. Cooks: Savage, 1910, 150ff.; Hawaii: Beckwith, 1919, 337, 610ff.

D983.2. Magic yam (sweet potato). N.Z.: White, 1887-90, III, 116.

D985. Magic nut. Mangareva: Hiroa, 1938, 328.

D990--D1029. Magic bodily members

D996. Magic hand(s). Hawaii: Fornander, 1918, V, 370.

*D996.1.1. Magic fingernail (toenail). N.Z.: Grey, 1855, 47f.

D997.1. Magic heart--human. Societies: Henry, 1928, 554.

D1001. Magic spittle. Marquesas: Steinen, 1933-34, 369; Pukapuka: Beaglehole, 1938, 330; Hawaii: Beckwith, 1940, 176; Rice, 1923, 30; Thrum, 190? 53; Westervelt, 1915, 95; N.Z.: Dixon, 1916, 59; White, 1887-90, I, 57; Ellice Is.: David, 1899, 106; Kennedy, 1931, 192; Ontong Java: Sarfert, 1931, 407.

D1007. Magic bone--human. Chatham Is.: Shand, 1896, 203; N.Z.: Grey, 1855, 35.

*D1009.2.1. Teeth magically removed and restored. Rennell: Elbert-Monberg, 1964, No. 184.

D1021. Magic feathers. Hawaii: Fornander, 1916, IV, 54; Westervelt, 1915, 71.

D1022. Magic wings. Fijis: Fison, 1904, 23.

D1030. Magic food. Marquesas: Steinen, 1934-35, 218; Hawaii: Fornander, 1916, IV, 456.

D1030.1. Food supplied by magic. Tokelau: Macgregor, 1937, 86.

D1050. Magic clothes. Tuamotus: Stimson, n.d., Z-G. 13/346; Hawaii: Rice, 1923, 24.

D1050.1. Clothes produced by magic. N.Z.: White, 1887-90, II, 135; Wohlers, 1875, 25.

D1051. Magic cloth. Hawaii: Rice, 1923, 125.

D1052. Magic garment (robe, tunic). Hawaii: *Beckwith, 1940, 491; Rice, 1923, 125.

D1053. Magic mantle (cloak). Easter I.: Métraux, 1940, 367; Hawaii: Beckwith, 1919, 488.

D1056. Magic shirt. Hawaii: Emerson, 1915, 85.

D1057. Magic belt. Tuamotus: Audran, 1919, 36, 51; N.Z.: White, 1887-90, IV, 83f.

D1057.1. Magic girdle. Tuamotus: Stimson, n.d., T-G. 3/109, Z-G. 13/152, Z-G. 13/221, Z-G. 3/1146, Z-G. 3/1301; Stimson, 1937, 61; Hawaii: Thrum, 1923, 175f.; N.Z.: Grey, 1855, 54.

D1058.1. Magic shift. Hawaii: Emerson, 1915, 84f.

D1067. Magic head-wear. N.Z.: Gudgeon, 1897, 36; Ellice Is.: Kennedy, 1931, 166.

D1077. Magic fan. Tonga: Collocott, 1928, 18.

D1084. Magic spear. Hawaii: Beckwith, 1940, 492; Dickey, 1917, 34; Rice, 1923, 101; Smith, 1966, 11; Thrum, 1923, 176ff.; Westervelt, 1915, 221; N.Z.: Best, 1925, 940; Cowan, 1930, 68f.

D1092. Magic arrow. Hawaii: Dixon, 1916, 75; Pukui-Curtis, n.d., 26; Thrum, 1907, 44.

D1093. Magic missile. N.Z.: Hongi, 1896, 234, 236.

D1094. Magic cudgel (club). Hawaii: Fornander, 1916, IV, 501; V, 374; Westervelt, 1915, 44, 174; Samoa: Powell-Pratt, 1891, 205; Tonga: Gifford, 1924, 178.

D1118. Magic airships. Marquesas: Handy, 1930, 53; Hawaii: Thrum, 1923, 256ff.; Kapingamarangi: Elbert, 1949, 243.

D1532. Magic object bears person aloft.

D1118.1. Magic air-riding basket. Cooks: Gill, 1876, 114.

*D1118.2. Magic wooden bird. Kapingamarangi: Elbert, 1948, 77.

D1121. Magic boat. Hawaii: Westervelt, 1915, 176ff.

D1121.0.1. Boat made by magic. Marquesas: Steinen, 1933-34, 343.

D1122. Magic canoe. Mangareva: Hiroa, 1938, 325; Marquesas: Handy, 1930, 46; Hawaii: Rice, 1923, 7.

D1122.1. Canoe made by magic. Hawaii: Forbes, 1882, 38; Bellona: Elbert-Monberg, 1964, No. 196.

D1124.1. Magic paddle. Hawaii: Westervelt, 1915, 151.

D1133. Magic house. Samoa: Powell-Pratt, 1892, 243.

D1133.1. House created by magic. Cooks: Ariki, 1899, 172; Hawaii: Beckwith, 1919, 438.

D1136. Magic fort. N.Z.: Grey, 1855, 69.

*D1147.1. Magic oven. N.Z.: Grey, 1855, 275.

*D1149.4. Stone walls created by magic. Tikopia: Firth, 1961, 40.

D1171.11. Magic basket. Tonga: Gifford, 1924, 113.

D1172.2. Magic bowl. Tonga: Reiter, 1934, 514 n. 52.

D1196. Magic net. N.Z.: Westervelt, 1915, 243.

*D1203.1. Magic snare. Hawaii: Green, 1929, 93.

D1206. Magic axe. Tuamotus: Henry, 1928, 529; Tahiti: Beckwith, 1940, 468; Henry, 1928, 484; Samoa: Lesson, 1876, 602.

D1209.5. Magic fishhook. Mangareva: Luomala, 1949, 151; Tuamotus: Henry, 1928, 509; Hawaii: *Beckwith, 1940, 24f.; N.Z.: Dixon, 1916, 43; Grace, 1907, 214; Ontong Java: Sarfert, 1931, 440.

  D1653.2. Infallible fish-hook.

*D1209.5.1. Magic squid-catching shell. Hawaii: Westervelt, 1915, 149f.

D1223.1. Magic flute. Hawaii: Beckwith, 1919, 492, 526ff.; Dickey, 1917, 26.

D1224. Magic pipes (musical). Hawaii: Green, 1923, 50ff.

D1232. Magic lute. Hawaii: Thrum, 1923, 128ff.

D1240. Magic waters and medicines. N.Z.: Best, 1924, 138.

D1242.1. Magic water. Hawaii: Westervelt, 1915, 33, 212; Samoa: Krämer, 1902, I, 126-127.

D1254. Magic staff. Mangareva: Luomala, 1949, 151; Marquesas: Handy, 1930, 134; Cooks: Brown, 1897, 1; Hawaii: Dixon, 1916, 90; Rice, 1923, 119; Niue: Smith, 1903, 9, 112; N.Z.: White, 1887-90, I, 176; IV, 84.

D1254.2. Magic rod. Hawaii: *Beckwith, 1940, 466; Thrum, 1907, 68ff.

D1257. Magic fishhook. See D1209.5. Hawaii: Beckwith, 1940, 420; N.Z.: Clark, 1896, 153.

D1258.1. Bridge made by magic. N.Z.: Westervelt, 1915, 242.

D1268. Magic statue (idol). Hawaii: Westervelt, 1915, 214.

D1271. Magic fire. Tuamotus: Stimson, n.d., Z-G. 13/52; Hawaii: Emory, 1924, 18; Rice, 1923, 104.

D1273. Magic formula (charm). Tuamotus: Henry, 1928, 498; Hawaii: Beckwith, 1940, 376; Niue: *Loeb, 1926, 180ff.; N.Z.: Grey, 1855, 279.

D1275. Magic song. Reef Is.: O'Ferral, 1904, 227.

*D1299.6. Magic kite. N.Z.: White,1887-90, III, 119.

D1300--D1599. FUNCTION OF MAGIC OBJECTS

D1300--D1379. Magic objects effect changes in
persons

*D1310.13. Feather gives supernatural information. Hawaii: Fornander, 1916, IV, 66; Westervelt, 1915, 71.

*D1310.14. Magic thunder communicates message. N.Z.: White, 1887-90, II, 18.

*D1311.3.1.2. By looking in bathing pool, demon magically sees picture of fleeing lovers. (Cf. D1323.12.). Tuamotus: Stimson, n.d., Z-G. 13/420.

D1311.4. Oracular tree. Marquesas: Lavondes, 1966, 42, 110ff.

D1311.8. Divination by head (skull). Tuamotus: Henry, 1928, 512; Societies: Henry, 1928, 391.

D1311.16. Oracular stone. Tuamotus: Stimson, n.d., Z-G. 3/1386; Hawaii: Beckwith, 1940, 89.

D1311.17. Divination by magic weapon. Hawaii: Westervelt, 1915, 223; N.Z.: White, 1887-90, V, 49f.

*D1312.1.2. Pulsations of man's extracted heart as advisor. Societies: Henry, 1928, 554.

D1312.2. Magic bone gives advice. Chatham Is.: Shand, 1896, 203.

*D1312.5. Magic arrow gives advice. Hawaii: Thrum, 1907, 44.

*D1312.6. Magic spear gives advice. Hawaii: Thrum, 1923, 176ff.

D1313. Magic object points out road. N.Z.: Best, 1924, 183; Hongi, 1896, 234, 236.

D1313.1.1. Magic ball of thread indicates road. Cooks: Gill, 1876, 287.

*D1313.18. Magic arrow guides person. Hawaii: Pukui, 1933, 181; Pukui-Curtis, n.d., 26 , 29f.; Thrum, 1907, 86.

*D1313.19. Magic spear guides person. Hawaii: Thrum, 1923, 179ff.; Westervelt, 1915, 221.

*D1313.20. Magic dart guides man. N.Z.: Westervelt, 1915, 244.

*D1313.21. Colored cloud guides person. Hawaii: Fornander, 1916, IV, 536.

*D1313.22. Meteor guides men. Hawaii: Thrum, 1907, 253.

D1314.1.3. Magic arrow shot to determine where to seek bride. Hawaii: Dixon, 1916, 75f., n. 65.

*D1314.16. Stones lead migrants to place of settlement. Rennell: Elbert-Monberg, 1964, No. 67.

D1323.12. Clairvoyance by looking at object filled with water. Tuamotus: Stimson, n.d., Z-G. 13/420; Marquesas: Handy, 1930, 109, 118; Hawaii: Beckwith, 1919, 610ff.; Beckwith, 1940, 528; Westervelt, 1915, 43f.

*D1331.1.6. Eye-shades (mataili) give magic sight. Ellice Is.: Kennedy, 1931, 166.

D1335.2.2. Water as magic strengthening drink. Hawaii: Westervelt, 1915, 212.

D1335.14. Magic strengthening staff. Cooks: Browne, 1897,1.

D1337.1.2. Water gives magic beauty. Hawaii: Westervelt, 1915, 212.

D1338.1.1. Fountain of youth. Water from certain fountain rejuvenates. Cooks: Te Ariki, 1920, 108; Futuna: Burrows, 1936, 104.

D1338.1.2. Water of youth. Hawaii: Rice, 1923, 106.

D1342. Magic object gives health. Samoa: Nelson, 1925, 136.

D1344.9. Magic garment renders invulnerable. Hawaii: Rice, 1923, 22.

*D1347.7. Chant causes fecundity. N.Z.: White, 1887-90, IV, 110.

*D1349.2.4. Wings of sky-king's bird brush boy, give immunity from old age. Fijis: Fison, 1904, 23.

D1355.1. Love-producing music. Hawaii: Beckwith, 1919, 526ff.

D1361.12. Magic cloak of invisibility. Hawaii: Rice, 1923, 125.

D1380.2. Tree protects. Hawaii: Pukui-Curtis, n.d., 68.

D1381.3. Magic garment protects against attack. Hawaii: Fornander, 1916, IV, 42, 76.

D1381.5. Magic shirt protects from attack. Hawaii: Beckwith, 1940, 499.

D1382.6. Magic shirt protects from cold and burning.
Hawaii: Beckwith, 1940, 491.

*D1392.2. Magic coconut saves boy's life. Hawaii:
Pukui-Curtis, n.d., 33.

D1400--D1439. Magic object gives power over
other persons

*D1400.1.1.1. Magic belt conquers enemies. N.Z.:
White, 1887-90, IV, 83f.

D1400.1.4.4. Magic spear conquers enemy. Hawaii:
Rice, 1923, 101.

D1400.1.4.6. Magic stone axe conquers enemy. Hawaii:
Beckwith, 1940, 395; Samoa: Lesson, 1876, 602.

D1400.1.7. Magic staff defeats enemies. Niue:
Smith, 1903, 10, 112.

D1400.1.19. Magic feather defeats enemy. Hawaii:
Fornander, 1916, IV, 42.

*D1400.1.24. Magic sweet potato brings victory in battle.
N.Z.: White, 1887-90, III,116.

D1402.0.1. Magic object burns up person. Hawaii:
Fornander, 1916, IV, 42.

D1402.1. Magic plant kills. N.Z.: White, 1887-90,
III, 116.

D1402.7.2.2. Magic all-killing spear head. Hawaii:
Beckwith, 1940, 418.

D1402.19. Magic statue kills. N.Z.: Grey, 1855, 284.

*D1402.33. Magic, self-returning shell kills.
Tokelaus: Macgregor, 1937, 81.

*D1431.1.1. Rock abducts girl for chief. Tonga:
Beckwith, 1940, 467.

196

D1444.1. Magic object catches fish. Hawaii: Beckwith, 1940, 19, 22; Fornander, 1918, V, 148; Lau Is.: St. Johnston, 1918, 125f.

D1444.1.3. Magic branch catches fish. Hawaii: Beckwith, 1940, 276.

D1444.1.4. Magic charm allows person to hook mythical eel. Cooks: Beckwith, 1940, 104.

D1470.1.1. Magic wishing-stone. N.Z.: Best, 1924, 103.

*D1470.1.2. Magic wishing-tree. Tonga: Collocott, 1928, 12.

*D1470.1.50. Magic wishing-image. Samoa: Sierich, 1900, 233.

D1470.2.1. Provisions received from magic tree. Cooks: Gill, 1876, 66; Hawaii: Luomala, 1951, 51; Westervelt, 1915, 122f.; Samoa: Brown, 1917, 97; Fijis: Fison, 1904, 82.

D1472.1.2.4. Magic rock supplies water. Hawaii: McAllister, 1933, 152; Samoa: Krämer, 1902, I, 400, 402.

D1472.1.3. Magic tree supplies food. Hawaii: Beckwith, 1940, 287.

D1472.1.3.2. Food-providing leaf. Hawaii: Beckwith, 1940, 491; Fornander, 1916, IV, 42.

D1472.1.9. Magic pot (bowl) supplies food and drink. Samoa: Stuebel, 1896, 146f.

D1472.1.23. Magic basket supplies food. Tonga: Gifford, 1924, 113.

*D1472.1.24.5. Body of fish supplies food, renews itself. Hawaii: Green, 1923, 46f.; Samoa: Krämer, 1902, I, 387.

*D1472.1.37. Food-producing club. Hawaii: Fornander, 1916, IV, 50.

D1472.2.4. Charm prepares feast. Marquesas: Handy, 1930, 114.

*D1489. Magic fishpond, though far inland, provides sea-fish. Hawaii: Dickey, 1917, 27.

D1500.1.4.2. Magic healing leaves. Tonga: Gifford, 1924, 28; Reiter, 1933, 360.

D1501.7. Leaves assist in childbearing. Marquesas: Handy, 1930, 58.

D1503.15. Wound healed with own blood. Hawaii: Beckwith, 1940, 118.

D1503.16. Wound healed by water from place wounded man's heel dragged. Marquesas: Handy, 1930, 117.

D1505.2. Spittle restores sight. N.Z.: Dixon, 1916, 59.

D1505.5.5. Magic coconut water restores sight. Marquesas: Beckwith, 1940, 485.

D1505.18.1. Coconut shoot restores sight. Hawaii: Beckwith, 1940, 492.

D1520. Magic object affords miraculous transportation. Cooks: Gill, 1876, 114.

D1520.1.1. Transportation by stretching and swaying tree. The tree stretches and bends over so as to land hero in a distant country. Marquesas, Hawaii, N.Z., Tonga: *Beckwith, 1940, Ch. XXXIV passim; Societies: Dixon, 1916, 66; Samoa: Sierich, 1901, 17; Rotuma: Churchward, 1938-39, 329; Fijis: Beckwith, 1940, 483.

D1520.2. Magic transportation by cloud. Tikopia: Firth, 1961, 50.

D1520.27.1. Magic transportation by club. Hawaii: Fornander, 1918, V, 146, 148, 374.

D1520.30. Magic transportation on rock (stone). Tikopia: Firth, 1961, 101.

*D1520.38. Transportation upon magic spear. Hawaii: Thrum, 1923, 179ff.; Westervelt, 1915, 221.

D1523.2 Self-propelling ship (boat). Marquesas: Handy, 1930, 46; Hawaii: Westervelt, 1915, 142, 176ff.

*D1523.2.1.1. Magic paddle sends canoe many miles at each stroke. Hawaii: Westervelt, 1915, 151.

*D1523.2.9. Fishhook thrown into sea magically pulls canoe and occupants to land. Tuamotus: Henry, 1928,

509.

*D1524.8.2. Magic canoe made of a flower blossom.
Hawaii: Green, 1929, 7, 15.

*D1524.8.3. Magic canoe made of a seed-pod. N.Z.:
White, 1887-90, II, 174.

D1524.10. Magic staff comes to one over water.
Marquesas: Handy, 1930, 134.

*D1524.13. Sea voyage within a calabash. Societies:
Caillot, 1914, 112; Cooks: Savage, 1910, 150.

*D1524.14. Sea voyage within a log. Cf. *D1556.0.1.
N.Z.: White, 1887-90, II, 24; Wohlers,1876,
118, 120.

*D1524.15. Sea voyage within a pumpkin. Cooks:
Kunike, 1928, 31.

*D1524.16. Sea voyage in a canoe-bailer. N.Z.: White,
1887-90, II, 18; III, 11, 140.

*D1524.17. Sea voyage within a sea-shell. N.Z.: White,
1887-90, II, 158.

*D1524.18. Sea voyage in a wooden bowl. N.Z.: White,
1887-90, I, 171; II, 24.

*D1524.19. Sea voyage on a duck's feather. N.Z.:
White, 1887-90, III, 116.

D1532. Magic object bears person aloft. Kapingamarangi:
Elbert, 1948, 77.

D1541.1.4. Shirt laid upon altar raises storm. Hawaii:
Beckwith, 1940, 531.

D1541.1.7. Magic calabash holding bones raises storm.
(Cf. C322.1. and D1543.7.). Hawaii: Beckwith,
1940, 449.

D1543.7. Magic calabash (gourd) controls winds.
Hawaii: Beckwith, 1940, 86, 405; Dickey, 1917, 24;
Fornander, 1916, IV, 518; 1918, V, 72, 76, 106ff.,
114, 116, 122, 124; Green, 1929, 7; Thrum, 1923,
63; Samoa: Stuebel, 1896, 66.

C322.1. Bag of winds. D965.2. Magic
gourd. D1541.1.7. Magic calabash holding
bones raises storm.

199

D1551. Waters magically divide and close. Marquesas:
Handy, 1930, 101.

D1552. Mountains or rocks open and close. Hawaii:
Fornander, 1918, V, 166; N.Z.: Grey, 1855, 188;
Beckwith, 1940, 195.

D1552.2. Mountain opens to magic formula (Open Sesame).
Oceania: **Lessa, 1961, 334ff.; Polynesia:
*Dixon, 1916, 48, nn. 37-31; 63; Tuamotus:
Leverd, 1911, 173; Societies: Dixon, 1916, 63;
Henry, 1928, 553; Gill, 1876, 251; Cooks:
Dixon, 1916, 48, nn. 37-31; Gill, 1876, 52;
Hawaii: Beckwith, 1940, 339; Fornander, 1918, V,
164, 166; Tonga: Caillot, 1914, 301ff.; Collocot
1921, 52; Samoa: Bülow, 1895, 141; Dixon, 1916,
48, nn. 37ff.; Lesson, 1876, 595; Powell-Pratt,
1892, 80f.; Sierich, 1902, 182; Stair, 1896, 56;
Stuebel, 1896, 65, 143; Niue: Smith, 1903, 106;
Chatham Is.: Shand, 1896, 209; N.Z.: Best, 1927,
272; Clark, 1896, 36; Cowan, 1930, 123; Dixon,
1916, 48 nn. 37-41; Kapingamarangi: Elbert,
1948, 108.

D1552.5. Cave opens and hides fugitives. Tahiti:
Beckwith, 1940, 244; Niue: Smith, 1903, 106;
N.Z.: *Beckwith, 1940, 196, 196 n. 16.

*D1552.13. Magically closing stone wall. Hawaii:
Westervelt, 1915, 106.

D1553. Symplegades. Rocks that clash together at
intervals. Marquesas: Lavondes, 1964, 18;
Cooks: Gill, 1876, 52; N.Z.: Clark, 1896,
36ff.; Rotuma: Luomala, 1949, 135.

E750.2.4. Road to abode of dead blocked
by two bars continually clashing together.

*D1553.1. Islands which clash together at intervals.
Tuamotus: Stimson, n.d., Z-G. 3/1122.

D1555. Underground passage magically opens. Cooks:
Gill, 1876, 224.

D1556. Self-opening tree-trunk. Hawaii: Westervelt,
1915, 161.

*D1556.0.1. Log magically opens to serve as unsinkable
boat for person. Cf. *D1524.14. N.Z.: White,
1887-90, II, 24; Wohlers, 1876, 118, 120.

D1556.1. Magic formula causes tree to open. Cooks: Banapa, 1920, 89.

D1556.2. Tree opens to give shelter to abandoned girls (refugees). Hawaii: Westervelt, 1915, 27.

*D1556.3. Tree (bamboo) magically hides fugitives. Hawaii: Beckwith, 1940, 279.

*D1556.4. Goddess magically enters breadfruit tree. Hawaii: Thrum, 1923, 185.

D1557. Magic charm causes door to open. N.Z.: Best, 1925, 954.

*D1558. Magic opening house gable. N.Z.: Beckwith, 1940, 195; Fijis: Hocart, 1929, 191.

*D1559. Other magical openings.

*D1559.1. Harbor entrance opened and closed by spell. N.Z.: White, 1887-90, V, 12.

*D1561.2.6. Magic staff enables man to lift great burden without feeling its weight. Hawaii: Rice, 1923, 119.

D1562.1. Magic staff destroys obstacles. Hawaii: Dixon, 1916, 90.

*D1564.10. Magic wind fells and strips trees. Fijis: Fison, 1904, 109.

D1566.2.7. Magic girdle produces stream of water to quench fire. Tuamotus: Stimson, n.d., Z-G. 13/221.

*D1599.7. Magic tree has power of causing children to be conceived. If woman wishes male child, she clasps eastern side; if female, the western side. N.Z.: Best, 1896, 5ff.; Gudgeon, 1906, 29, 32f.

*D1599.8. Coconut tree shifts constantly, attempting to expose to people's sight thief hidden in its branches. Kapingamarangi: Emory, 1949, 234.

*D1599.9. Magic object guards property. Hawaii: Westervelt, 1915, 105; Tonga: Collocott, 1928, 18; N.Z.: Best, 1925, 973.

D1600--D1699. CHARACTERISTICS OF MAGIC OBJECTS

D1600--D1649. Automatic magic objects

D1601. Object labors automatically. Reef Is.:
Elbert-Kirtley, 1966, 350.

D1601.14. Self-chopping axe. Samoa: Lesson, 1876,
602.

D1601.14.2. Magic adze cuts down tree. Marquesas:
Handy, 1930, 70; Samoa: Elbert-Kirtley, 1966,
361.

*D1601.14.4. Magic adze shapes canoe. Ellice Is.:
Kennedy, 1931, 214.

*D1601.18.4. Self-sounding shell. Hawaii: Westervelt,
1915, 106ff.

D1601.35. Magic water bottle brings water. Tonga:
Gifford, 1924, 178.

*D1601.38. Magic shell dipper fetches water. Tonga:
Collocott, 1928, 55.

D1602.2. Felled tree raises itself again. Polynesia:
**Beckwith, 1940, 263ff.; **Elbert-Kirtley,
1966, 355ff.; Mangareva: Hiroa, 1938, 326;
Tuamotus: Henry, 1928, 499; Seurat, 1905, 483;
Stimson, 1937, 121ff.; Marquesas: *Beckwith,
1940, 269; *Steinen, 1933-34, 39, 326ff., 343,
346; Societies:Henry, 1928, 483f.; Cooks:
Beaglehole, 1938, 330f.; Beckwith, 1940, 252,
269; Elbert-Kirtley, 1966, 362; Gill, 1876, 82f.,
143; Kunike, 1928, 29; Seurat, 1905, 485; Hawaii:
Beckwith, 1940, 263ff.; Rice, 1923, 96f.; Thrum,
1907, 112; Westervelt, 1915, 34f.; Tonga:
Collocott, 1908, 15; Samoa:Stair, 1895, 100;
Elbert-Kirtley, 1966, 361, 363; Stuebel, 1896, 148;
N.Z.: Beckwith, 1940, 265; Best, 1925, 714f.;
Clark, 1896, 95; Grey, 1855, 114; Whetu, 1897,
99; White, 1887-90, I, 69f., 74, 75; III, 2;
V, 8f.; Tikopia: Firth, 1961, 98; Reef Is.:
Elbert-Kirtley, 1966, 358f.; Riesenfeld, 1950,
128; Ellice Is.: Kennedy, 1931, 206, 214;
Beckwith, 1940, 270.

C939.3. Felled trees return to their places
because of broken tabu. D950. Magic tree.

202

*D1602.2.3. Chopped up canoe magically restored whole.
Reef Is.: Elbert-Kirtley, 1966, 362.

*D1602.16.1. Magic arrow strikes person after person.
Hawaii: Westervelt, 1915, 171.

*D1602.20. Stolen object magically returns itself to
owner. Hawaii: Fornander, 1918, V, 532; N.Z.:
Cowan, 1930, I, 215f.; White, 1887-90, III, 187.

*D1609.4. Convolvulus vine magically harvests crop.
Hawaii: Rice, 1923, 119.

*D1609.5. Tree moves upstream against current. N.Z.:
Gudgeon, 1906, 30.

*D1609.6. Coconut tree magically moves self to other
side of island when thief comes. Kapingamarangi:
Emory, 1949, 233.

D1610.2. Speaking tree. Marquesas: Steinen, 1934-35,
211; Samoa: Brown, 1917, 94, 96f.; Fijis:
Fison, 1904, 140; Santa Cruz: Riesenfeld, 1950,
129; Reef Is.: O'Ferrall, 1904, 231; Nukumanu:
Sarfert, 1931, 453; Ontong Java: Sarfert, 1931,
324, 438.

*D1610.2.0.2. Two trees contend which is better. Niue:
Loeb, 1926, 202.

*D1610.2.0.3. Tree pleads when its branches broken.
Hawaii: Fornander, 1918, V, 602; Green, 1923, 34.

D1610.2.2. Speaking bush. Hawaii: Fornander, 1916,
IV, 596.

*D1610.2.3. Speaking leaves. Samoa: Sierich, 1902,
168.

*D1610.2.4. Speaking forest. Marquesas: Lavondes,
1964, 14ff.; N.Z.: Cowan, 1930, 49.

D1610.3. Speaking plant. Marquesas: Steinen, 1934-35,
211, 212; Hawaii: Green, 1923, 39.

*D1610.3.5. Speaking sweet potato (yam). N.Z.: White,
1887-90, III, 116.

*D1610.3.5.1. Yams offer to grow upon person's land.
Samoa: Krämer, 1902, I, 420.

*D1610.3.6. Talking breadfruit. Mangareva: Laval,
1938, 18.

D1610.5. Speaking head. Tahiti: Henry, 1928, 494; Hawaii: Fornander, 1916, IV, 564ff.

D1610.6.1. Speaking vulva. N.Z.: Best, 1925, 947.

*D1610.6.5. Speaking breast. Marquesas: Steinen, 1933-3 33.

*D1610.6.6. Speaking hands. Hawaii: Fornander, 1918, V, 370.

*D1610.6.7. Severed knee speaks. Rotuma: Churchward, 1938-39, 120.

D1610.9.2. Speaking arrow. Hawaii: Dixon, 1916, 75; Fornander, 1918, V, 182; Thrum, 1907, 44.

D1610.9.3. Speaking spear. Marquesas: Lagarde, 1933, 260; Hawaii: Westervelt, 1915, 222ff.

D1610.10.2. Speaking bananas. Easter I.: Métraux, 1940, 375.

*D1610.10.4. Speaking berries. N.Z.: Best, 1906, 6; Gudgeon, 1906, 33.

*D1610.11.2. Talking toy boat (made of leaves). Aitutaki: Pakoti, 1905, 68.

D1610.18. Speaking rock (stone). Easter I.: Englert, 1939, 29f.; Marquesas: Lavondes, 1964, 18; Steinen, 1934-35, 210; Tonga: Collocott, 1928, 28; Lau Is.: St. Johnston, 1918, 46; Ontong Java: Sarfert, 1931, 440.

*D1610.18.1. Speaking coral. Hawaii: Westervelt, 1915, 170.

D1610.19. Earth speaks. Hawaii: Fornander, 1916, IV, 522, 532.

*D1610.21.3. Echo-producing images. Samoa: Powell-Pratt 1892, 124.

D1610.22. Speaking nut (shell). Cooks: Beaglehole, 1938, 330.

D1610.30.1. Speaking house post. Tuamotus: Stimson, n.d., Z-G. 13/276; N.Z.: *Best, 1928b, 257, 259.

*D1610.30.2. Speaking house. Marquesas: Steinen, 1934-35, 211.

D1610.33. Speaking cliff. Marquesas: Lavondes, 1964, 16; Hawaii: Fornander, 1916, IV, 596.

*D1610.36.1. Speaking waves. Easter I.: Englert, 1939, 30; Tahiti: Henry, 1928, 472.

*D1610.36.2. Speaking surf. Hawaii: Fornander, 1916, IV, 522.

*D1610.37. Speaking heavenly bodies. Marquesas: Steinen, 1933-34, 373; 1934-35, 232; Tongareva: Hiroa, 1938, 215; Reef Is.: O'Ferrall, 1904, 231.

*D1610.38. Speaking wind. Marquesas: Steinen, 1933-34, 371.

*D1610.39. Smoke speaks. Hawaii: Fornander, 1916, IV, 568.

*D1610.40. Speaking shells. Hawaii: Fornander, 1916, IV, 170.

*D1610.41. Speaking mat. Samoa: Sierich,1901, 21.

D1611. Magic object answers for fugitive. Left behind to impersonate fugitive and delay pursuit. Easter I.: Métraux, 1940, 59, 375; N.Z.: Dixon, 1916, 85 n. 91; Ellice Is.: David, 1899, 101; Kennedy, 1931, 207.

D1611.5. Magic spittle impersonates fugitives. Hawaii: Beckwith, 1940, 176.

D1612.1.2. Banana tree tells who cut its branches. Easter I.: Métraux, 1940, 364.

*D1615.10. Singing log. N.Z.: Best, 1924, 202.

*D1615.11. Singing lute. Hawaii: Thrum, 1923, 128ff.

*D1615.12. Singing shells. Hawaii: Westervelt, 1915, 40, 45.

D1619.2.1. Eaten magic dog howls from eater's belly. N.Z.: Dixon, 1916, 86; Grey, 1924, 124.

*D1619.2.3. Eaten rooster crows from mouth of person who ate it. Marquesas: Steinen, 1934-35, 234.

D1639.6. Carved image jumps at maker's command. Easter I.: Métraux, 1940, 262.

*D1639.7. Red-pine log, like a living thing, cruises around lakes. N.Z.: Cowan, 1930, 131.

*D1641.2.0.1. Self-moving and animate stones. Hawaii: Green, 1926, 65; Tonga: Collocott, 1928, 27; Tokelaus: Burrows, 1923, 151; N.Z.: Best, 1925, 952; Cowan, 1930, 73ff.; Rennell: Elbert-Monberg, 1964, 67; Bellona: Elbert-Monberg, 1964, No. 125b.

*D1641.2.6. Large stone, when offended, comes, takes stones from ovens. Fijis: Hocart, 1929, 198.

D1641.7.1. Self-rolling head. Hawaii: Thrum, 1923, 243-247; Lau Is.: St. Johnston, 1918, 76.

D1641.16. Bananas run and hide when stone is thrown at them. Easter I.: Métraux, 1940, 375.

D1643.2. Rock travels. Tonga: Beckwith, 1940, 467; N.Z.: Gudgeon, 1906, 34.

D1643.3. Magic island moves about as owner wishes. Cooks: Beckwith, 1940, 467.

D1643.4. Magic pipe travels about. Hawaii: Beckwith, 1940, 540.

D1645.6. Self-luminous feathers. Mangareva: Hiroa, 1938, 37; Laval, 1938, 54.

*D1645.12. Self-luminous turtle shell. Samoa: Nelson, 1925, 136.

*D1645.13. Self-luminous sea-shell. Hawaii: Thrum, 1907, 234.

*D1651.7.4. Musical instrument plays only at night, never by day. Hawaii: Beckwith, 1919, 436.

D1651.14. Magic cock flies only at owner's command. Easter I.: Métraux, 1940, 367.

D1652. Inexhaustible object. Oceania: **Lessa, 1961, 356ff.

D1652.1.6. Inexhaustible coconut. Samoa: Krämer, 1902, I, 144; Fijis: Fison, 1904, 81.

D1652.1.7.2. Magic banana skin always full of fruit.
Hawaii: Beckwith, 1940, 493; Westervelt, 1915,
67ff.

D1652.1.10. Inexhaustible fish. Hawaii: Beckwith,
1940, 20.

D1652.5.1. Magic goblet (bowl) cannot be filled.
Tonga: Reiter, 1934, 514, n. 52.

*D1652.21. Whale's teeth magically multiply. Samoa:
Sierich, 1902, 184.

D1653.2. Infallible fish-hook. (Cf. D1209.5.)

*D1653.2.1. Magic squid-catching shell. Hawaii:
Westervelt, 1915, 149f.

D1658. Grateful objects. Marquesas: Steinen, 1934-35,
211f.; Hawaii: Beckwith, 1940, 465f.; Santa
Cruz (Reef Is.): Riesenfeld, 1950, 128f.

D1687. Object magically becomes heavy. (Cf. D2035).
Mangareva: Hiroa, 1938, 368; Hawaii: Westervelt,
1915, 252; N.Z.: White, 1887-90, II, 24; Wohlers,
1876, 119.

*D1687.1. Tiny rock effectively anchors large canoe.
Hawaii: Fornander, 1916, IV, 294.

D1700--D1799. Possession and means of employment
of magic powers

D1711. Magician. Tonga: Collocott, 1928, 55; N.Z.:
Cowan, 1930, 91ff., 110ff.; Grey, 1855, 273.

*D1711.9.1. Man who is hairless possessor of magic power.
Hawaii: Rice, 1923, 113.

D1719.1. Contest in magic. Mangareva: Hiroa, 1938,
369f.; Hawaii: Green, 1923, 11f.; Tonga: Collocott,
1928, 55; Lau Is.: St. Johnston, 1918, 49; N.Z.:
White, 1887-90, II, 73, 81; V, 59ff.;
Kapingamarangi: Elbert, 1948, 121; Elbert, 1949,
241f.

*D1726.3. God transfers his magic power by spitting in man's mouth. Hawaii: Westervelt, 1915, 95.

D1735. Magic powers from swallowing. Tahiti: Beckwith, 1940, 246.

*D1735.5. Kava leaves chewed as a curse. Niue: Loeb, 1926, 171.

*D1735.6. Biting removes magic power from bitten object to biter. N.Z.: Gudgeon, 1906, 30.

*D1735.6.1. Person acquires supernatural powers by biting the ear of a corpse. N.Z.: Best, 1925, 954.

*D1737.2. Father places son's foot on own head, thus transfers his mana. Niue: Loeb, 1926, 185.

*D1741.10. Magician deprived of his power by a foe's magic. N.Z.: White, 1887-90, V, 59.

*D1741.11. Magician loses his power after marriage. N.Z.: Cowan, 1930, 22.

*D1745.3. Magic efficacy spoiled when seen by onlooker. Rennell: Elbert-Monberg, 1964, Nos. 31a, 33, 80a.

*D1749.3. After chips removed, felled tree cannot be magically righted. Bellona: Elbert-Monberg, 1964, No. 19a.

*D1749.4. Sacred image magically deprived of hateful power. N.Z.: White, 1887-90, V, 54.

D1766.1. Magic result produced by prayer (incantation). Hawaii: Westervelt, 1915, 71f.

*D1774.1. Magic from incantation. Tuamotus: Stimson, 1937, 30f., 34ff., 39, 44f.; Cooks: Low, 1934, 20; Hawaii: Fornander, 1918, V, 276; Westervelt, 1915, 71f., 94; N.Z.: Cowan, 1930, I, 67, 163; Grace, 1907, 189; White, 1887-90, I, 127; II, 36, 40, 135, 144; III, 99; IV, 51f., 110f., 114, 202, 244; V, 43, 86; Bellona: Elbert-Monberg, 1964, Nos. 185a, 185b.

D1781. Magic results from singing. Reef Is.: O'Ferrall, 1904, 227.

*D1781.1. Chant produces magic result. Tuamotus:
Stimson, 1937, 5; Hawaii: McAllister, 1933, 140;
Thrum, 1923, 294; Samoa: Krämer, 1902, I, 408;
Tokelaus: Burrows, 1923, 153f.; Tikopia: Firth,
1961, 45.

D1782. Sympathetic magic. Magic results obtained by
imitating desired action. Fijis: Fison, 1904,
31f.

D1787. Magic results from burning (from fire). Hawaii:
Green, 1926, 57.

D1788.1. Magic results from contact with water. Hawaii:
Green, 1926, 57.

D1792. Magic results from curse. Samoa: Stair,
1896, 44.

*D1799.7. Whistling produces magic power. Niue:
Loeb, 1926, 180.

*D1799.8. Magic effected by pointing index finger.
Samoa: Krämer, 1902, I, 428.

*D1799.10. Magic power produced by striking, kicking or
stamping foot. Fijis: Hocart, 1929, 208.

*D1799.11. Look produces magic power. Cooks:
Beaglehole, 1938, 381.

*D1799.13. Magic power produced by urination. Ellice Is.:
Kennedy, 1931, 206.

D1800--D2199. MANIFESTATIONS OF MAGIC POWER

D1800--D1949. Lasting magic qualities

D1810. Magic knowledge. Mangareva: Laval, 1938, 141;
Tuamotus: Audran, 1917, 61; Stimson, n.d., Z-G.
3/1386; Cooks: Te Ariki, 1921, 3; Hawaii:
Fornander, 1916, IV, 50; V, 124, 156, 412; Remy,
1868, 36ff.; Westervelt, 1915, 55f., 177; Samoa:
Krämer, 1902, I, 129.

D1810.0.2. Magic knowledge of magician. Mangareva:
Laval, 1938, 196; Hawaii: Fornander, 1916, IV,
82ff., 498; Green, 1929, 45; Thrum, 1923, 26;
Westervelt, 1915, 37, 127; Tonga: Collocott,
1928, 52ff.; Niue: Loeb, 1926, 34; N.Z.:

209

White, 1887-90, III, 58f.

D1810.8. Magic knowledge from dream. Marquesas:
Lavondes, 1966, 54, 144; Hawaii: Beckwith, 1919,
356, 364, 366, 404, 412; Fornander, 1918, V, 74ff.;
Thrum, 1907, 220; Thrum, 1923, 293, 305;
Westervelt, 1915, 130, 205ff.; N.Z.: Cowan,
1930, I, 206; White, 1887-90, II, 11; III, 186;
Wohlers, 1876, 123; Bellona: Elbert-Monberg, 1964,
No. 66.

D1810.8.1. Truth given in vision. Fijis: Fison,
1904, 114.

D1810.8.2. Information received through dream. Societies
Baessler, 1905, 921; Hawaii: Green, 1929, 7;
Pukui-Curtis, n.d., 25.

*D1810.9.1. Magic knowledge from tutelary deity. Hawaii:
Fornander, 1916, IV, 54.

*D1810.14. Magic gourd gives omniscience. Hawaii:
Beckwith, 1919, 337.

*D1810.15. Person's ornament glows when he is a victor
in a battle. Tuamotus: Caillot, 1914, 55f.

*D1810.16. Leaves give girl knowledge of her lover.
Samoa: Krämer, 1902, I, 133.

*D1810.17. Magic knowledge from natural phenomena.
Hawaii: Fornander, 1918, V, 230; N.Z.: White,
1887-90, II, 18.

*D1810.18. Knowledge magically conveyed through
beating drum. Hawaii: Fornander, 1916, IV, 128.

*D1810.19. Performing a human sacrifice enables a
younger brother to discover his elder. Hawaii:
Fornander, 1916, IV, 126ff.

*D1810.20. Magic knowledge obtained by watching betel-nut
bag. Reef Is.: Elbert-Kirtley, 1966, 358f.

*D1810.21. Magic knowledge from sea waves. Easter I.:
Englert, 1939, 30; Samoa: Krämer, 1902, I, 269;
Bellona: Elbert-Monberg, 1964, No. 50 a; Rennell:
ibid., 50b.

210

*D1810.22. Information obtained from actions of stick
thrown on sea. Hawaii: Emerson, 1915, 48.

*D1810.23. Magic kites give information. N.Z.:
White, 1887-90, III, 119.

*D1818.24. Dancing of tree-leaves gives magic information.
Hawaii: Westervelt, 1915, 124f.

*D1810.25. The position of the stars gives magic
knowledge. N.Z.: Best, 1925, 812.

*D1810.26. Casting darts gives magic knowledge. N.Z.:
Best, 1925, 843.

*D1810.27. Fluttering of the eyelid gives magic
knowledge. Marquesas: Lavondes, 1966, 52.

*D1811.3. Magic knowledge from child's behavior:
child each morning sticks his tongue out in the
direction food source lies. N.Z.: Best, 1925,
923.

*D1811.4. Magic knowledge from instinct: person given
own son's heart to eat cannot swallow it.
Mangareva: Laval, 1938, 118.

D1812. Magic power of prophecy. Mangareva: Hiroa,
1938, 321; Laval, 1938, 197ff.; Hawaii: Beckwith,
1919, 336, 572; Fornander, 1916, IV, 164, 264ff.;
Green, 1926, 71; Pukui, 1943, 61f.; Thrum, 1907,
265; Westervelt, 1915, 163f.; Tonga: Collocott,
1928, 53; N.Z.: White, 1887-90, IV, 93; V, 53.

D1812.0.1. Foreknowledge of hour of death. Hawaii:
Pukui, 1933, 129ff.; Thrum, 1907, 207; Lau Is.:
St. Johnston, 1918, 117.

*D1812.0.1.3. Rainbow appears over a priest's house on
day he is to die. Hawaii: Thrum, 1907, 208f.

*D1812.0.6. Foreknowledge of storm at sea. Hawaii:
Fornander, 1918, V, 88.

*D1812.0.7. Coming of new religion prophesied correctly.
Mangareva: Hiroa, 1938, 93; Laval, 1938, 197f.

*D1812.0.8. Coming of strange race correctly prophesied.
Hawaii: Thrum, 1907, 206.

*D1812.2.5. Prophetic piece of coral. Hawaii:
Fornander, 1916, IV, 20.

*D1812.2.6. Severed head possesses prophetic power. Samoa: Krämer, 1902, 122ff.

D1812.3.3. Future revealed in dream. Easter I.: Metraux, 1940, 56, 85; Mangareva: Hiroa, 1938, 343; Laval, 1938, 88; Tuamotus: Stimson, n.d., Z-G. 13/317; Henry, 1928, 501; Marquesas: Steinen, 1933-34, 29, 31, 346; Tahiti: Henry, 1928, 625; Hawaii: Beckwith, 1919, 502, 522; Fornander, 1916, IV, 444f., 498; McAllister, 1933, 146; Rice, 1923, 99; Thrum, 1907, 23; Tonga: Collocott, 1928, 57; Chatham Is.: Shand, 1895, 211f.; Shand, 1896, 132; N.Z.: Beattie, 1920, 190; Cowan, 1930, I, 169f.; White, 1887-90, III, 186; Rennell: Elbert-Monberg, 1964, No. 199; Fijis: Fison, 1904, 113.

D1812.5. Future learned through omens. Mangareva: Laval, 1938, 58; Tuamotus: Caillot, 1914, 51f.; Marquesas: Christian, 1895, 188; Tahiti: *Henry, 1928, 226-228; Hawaii: Kamakau, 1961, 9; Niue: *Loeb, 1926, 179f.; N.Z.: Best, 1907, 1; Best, 1925, 1001 ff.; Nukumanu: Sarfert, 1931, 332.

*D1812.5.0.2.1. Behavior of birds gives knowledge of a man's fate. Easter I.: Englert, 1939, 47.

D1812.5.0.4.1. Divination from rising smoke. Hawaii: Beckwith, 1940, 21; Fornander, 1918, V, 326, 516; VI, 172; Rice, 1923, 28; Thrum, 1923, 176, 178; Westervelt, 1915, 219.

D1812.5.0.6. Divination by throwing objects into water. Hawaii: Emerson, 1915, 48.

*D1812.5.0.8.2. Divination from behavior of black pig. Hawaii: Westervelt, 1915, 205f.

D1812.5.0.10. Divination from clouds. Hawaii: Beckwith, 1919, 472ff.; Pukui, 1933, 137; Smith, 1966, 8; Westervelt, 1915, 56f.

*D1812.5.0.14.1. Headdress changes colors during battle (enables priests to foretell outcome). N.Z.: Gudgeon, 1906, 36.

*D1812.5.0.15.1. Magic knowledge of weather gained from sound of wind in a tree. N.Z.: Cowan, 1930, I, 252.
*D1812.5.0.15.2. Appearance of fog gives magic knowledge of future. Hawaii: Fornander, 1918, V, 262, 414.

*D1812.5.0.15.3. Omens revealed through thunder and
  lightning. Hawaii: Fornander, 1918, V, 230;
  Thrum, 1923, 82; Samoa: Stuebel, 1896, 76;
  N.Z.: Best, 1925, 874ff.; Rennell: Elbert-Monberg,
  1964, Nos. 196, 200.

*D1812.5.0.15.4. Weather phenomena to indicate fate of
  hero. Hawaii: Westerelt, 1915, 211.

*D1812.5.0.15.5. Prophetic visions seen in mists of
  sacred mountain. N.Z.: Cowan, 1930, I, 227.

*D1812.5.0.15.6. Magic knowledge through earthquakes.
  Samoa: Powell-Pratt, 1892, 82.

*D1812.5.0.18. Divination from feathers. N.Z.:
  White, 1887-90, IV, 88, 98.

*D1812.5.0.21. Future read from vomit. Hawaii:
  Fornander, 1916, IV, 40.

*D1812.5.0.22. Future foretold from chief's evasion of
  spear thrown at him. Hawaii: Fornander, 1916,
  IV, 206 ff.

*D1812.5.0.23. Parents foretell child's future by feeling
  its limbs. Hawaii: Fornander, 1918, V, 2.

*D1812.5.0.24. Future foretold by casting lots. Hawaii:
  Thrum, 1907, 205.

*D1812.5.0.25. Future determined from inspection of a
  polished bone. Rennell: Elbert-Monberg, 1964,
  No. 220.

*D1812.5.0.26. Future learned from behavior of flown
  kites. Hawaii: Fornander, 1918, V, 4.

*D1812.5.0.27. Divination by spinning coconut. Tonga,
  Ellice Is.: Hedley, 1896, 48.

*D1812.5.0.28. Divination from movement of kava bubbles.
  Hawaii: Westervelt, 1915, 199, 210.

*D1812.5.0.29. Future divined from degree of success in
  cooking pigs for a celebration feast. Hawaii: Ii,
  1959, 10.

*D1812.5.0.30. Color of breaking surf foretells future.
  Samoa: Krämer, 1902, I, 269.

*D1812.5.0.31. Woman's gesture indicates she will bear
  a girl rather than boy. Hawaii: Beckwith, 1919, 346.

213

*D1812.5.0.32. Body-twitchings are omens of the future. N.Z.: White, 1887-90, II, 2ff.; V, 36.

D1812.5.1. Bad omens. N.Z.: Gudgeon, 1906, 45; Grey, 1855, 222f.; Rotuma: Churchward, 1938-39, 219; Ellice Is.: Kennedy, 1931, 184; Kapinga-marangi: Elbert, 1948, 77.

*D1812.5.1.1.4.1. Breakers crashing blood-red as a bad omen. Samoa: Krämer, 1902, I, 125, 269.

*D1812.5.1.1.6.1. Blood of a man's dead wife floats to sea and surrounds his canoe. Hawaii: Pukui, 1933, 165.

*D1812.5.1.1.6.2. Stream runs blood as token of person's murder. Tonga: Collocott, 1928, 31.

*D1812.5.1.1.7. When man's son dies, spot of blood appears on man's chest. Marquesas: Lavondes, 1966, 96.

*D1812.5.1.1.7.1. Person dies and blood appears on the bosom of his mother. Marquesas: Lavondes, 1966, 132, 166.

*D1812.5.1.1.8. Ghost's appearance omen of death. Mangareva: Eskridge, 1931, 223.

*D1812.5.1.1.9. Ghost-dog's appearance is harbinger of volcanic eruption. Jack Bryan, "Pele's Phantom Dog Returns," Honolulu Star-Bulletin , Vol. 53, No. 315 (Nov. 10, 1964), 1.

*D1812.5.1.6.2. Comet's appearance is a sign of person's death. N.Z.: Best, 1925, 853.

*D1812.5.1.6.3. Ghost marchers appear when chief is dying or newly dead. Hawaii: Beckwith, 1932, 198.

*D1812.5.1.6.4. Ancestral spirit appears before the death of one of its descendants or before some other disaster. N.Z.: Best, 1925, 975f.

D1812.5.1.10. Sight of phantom ship (canoe) bad omen. Tuamotus: Caillot, 1914, 62ff.; N.Z.: Cowan, 1930, I, 10, 165, n.

D1812.5.1.12.2. Bird calls as evil omen. N.Z.: White, 1887-90, II, 88.

D1812.5.1.12.3. Spider dropping on person's back as evil omen. Samoa: Clark, 1896, 117.

D1812.5.1.17.1. Spirit host fighting in air as evil omen. N.Z.: Cowan, 1921, 147.

*D1812.5.1.32. Breaking fish line a bad omen. Tuamotus: Stimson, 1937, 99.

*D1812.5.1.33. Landslides anticipate misfortunes. N.Z.: Best, 1925, 876f.

*D1812.5.1.34. To see a certain rock in a lake is an omen of death. N.Z.: Cowan, 1930, 125f.

D1812.5.2.11. Spider dropping on one's front a good omen. Samoa: Clark, 1896, 117.

*D1812.5.2.12. Large number of fish jump ashore as omen of birth of chief's son. Mangareva: Laval, 1938, 8.

D1813. Magic knowledge of events in distant place. Tuamotus: Caillot, 1914, 55f.; Marquesas: Lavondes, 1964, 90ff.; Hawaii: Fornander, 1918, V, 230, 414; Westervelt, 1915, 124f., 180.

D1814.1. Advice from magician (fortune-teller). Tuamotus: Stimson, n.d., T-G. 3/45, Z/G. 3/1323; Hawaii: Rice, 1923, 54.

D1817.0.3. Magic detection of murder. N.Z.: White, 1887-90, III, 119.

D1821.3.7. Magic sight by looking at shining object. N.Z.: Beattie, 1920, 135.

D1821.3.7.1. Magic sight by looking into glass (calabash, gourd) of water. Hawaii: Rice, 1923, 100; Thrum, 1907, 129; N.Z.: Gudgeon, 1906, 37.

*D1821.12. Magic sight by looking at stone which reflects all occurrences in all realms. N.Z.: Best, 1924, 89.

D1825.1. Second sight. Power to see future happenings. N.Z.: *S. Percy Smith, "Clairvoyance Among the Maoris," JPS XXIX, (1920), 149-162.

D1825.2. Magic power to see distant objects. Hawaii: Rice, 1923, 11.

D1831. Magic strength resides in hair. Hawaii: Beckwith, 1940, 466; Rice, 1923, 101.

D1832. Magic strength by bathing. Hawaii: Thrum, 1923, 171; Westervelt, 1915, 212.

*D1835.7. Magic strength from incantation (prayer). Tuamotus: Leverd, 1911, 175; Hawaii: Fornander, 1916, IV, 412; V, 324.

*D1835.8. Material object strengthened by magic. N.Z.: Grace, 1907, 177f.; Tikopia: Firth, 1961, 111.

*D1835.9. Person goes between thighs of dying man and receives thus his priestly power. N.Z.: White, 1887-90, IV, 94.

*D1835.10. Person breathes in the ear of a dying man and receives his power. N.Z.: White, 1887-90, IV, 94.

D1840. Magic invulnerability. Tuamotus: Leverd, 1911, 174.

D1841.3. Burning magically evaded. Mangareva: Laval, 1938, 308; Hawaii: Fornander, 1918, V, 516; Rennell: Elbert-Monberg, 1964, 2c.

D1841.3.1. Magic animal proof against burning. Ontong Java: Sarfert, 1931, 441.

*D1841.3.4. Bird of god is killed, but slayers cannot cook it. Rarotonga: Te Ariki, 1920, 121; Luomala, 1949, 165; Hawaii: Beckwith, 1940, 96; N.Z.: Best, 1897, 44; Ellice Is.: Kennedy, 1931, 160.

D1841.5. Invulnerability from weapons. N.Z.: Grey, 1855, 86.

D1841.5.1. Man proof against weapons. Hawaii: Ii, 1959, 10f.; Rice, 1923, 56, 58; Fijis: Hocart, 1929, 201.

D1841.5.1.1. Invulnerability from thrown stones. Marquesas: Steinen, 1933-34, 372; Hawaii: Green, 1929, 99ff.

D1841.5.2. Magic animal proof against weapons. N.Z.: Whetu, 1897, 98.

*D1841.5.4. Arrow caused to halt flight in mid-air --
target unscathed. Bellona: Elbert-Monberg, 1964,
No. 142.

*D1841.6. Immunity from drowning. Hawaii: Westervelt,
1915, 151.

D1841.9. Invulnerability from demons. N.Z.: Cowan,
1921, 142.

*D1845.3. Invulnerability while at fountain which
reflect's person's face. N.Z.: Grey, 1855, 110.

*D1846.7. Magic invulnerability gained by drinking
blood. Hawaii: Green, 1929, 45.

D1860. Magic beautification. Mangareva: Hiroa, 1938,
375; Hawaii: Fornander, 1916, IV, 552;
Westervelt, 1915, 212; Samoa: Krämer, 1902, I,
416; Tonga: Collocott, 1928, 17; Chatham Is.:
Shand, 1896, 133.

D1866.1. Beautification by bathing. Easter I.:
Métraux, 1940, 388; Mangareva: Hiroa, 1938, 343;
Tonga: Gifford, 1924, 186; Funafuti: David,
1899, 97.

*D1866.4. Beautification by burial under leaves for
eight days. Cooks: Gill, 1876, 227.

*D1866.6. Flash of lightning shines on ugly girl, makes
her beautiful. Ellice Is.: David, 1899, 97.

D1880. Magic rejuvenation. N.Z.: Best, 1925, 760.

D1881. Magic self-rejuvenation. Samoa: Powell-Pratt,
1892, 249.

D1882. Rejuvenation of supernatural person. Rennell:
Elbert-Monberg, 1964, No. 97.

D1883. Eternal youth. (See D1338. and D1349.2.)
N.Z.: White, 1887-90, I, 169.

D1887. Rejuvenation by bathing. Marquesas: Steinen,
1934-35, 217; Hawaii: Westervelt, 1915, 33.

D1889.6. Rejuvenation by changing skin. Marquesas:
Steinen, 1933-34, 348.

D1889.7. Rejuvenation by being reborn. Mangareva:
Caillot, 1914, 166.

D1889.8. Rejuvenation by riding surf. Marquesas: Beckwith, 1940, 502; Handy, 1930, 60.

D1890. Magic aging. Mangareva: Hiroa, 1938, 338, 351; Hawaii: Fornander, 1916, IV, 456.

D1891. Transformation to old man to escape recognition. Maori: Dixon, 1916, 60.

*D1891.1. A child (a transformed pig) repeatedly appears in the water near a voyaging caone and asks to be taken aboard. At each appearance it looks much older than previously. Mangareva: Hiroa, 1938, 328.

D1900. Love induced by magic. Hawaii: Green, 1923, 35; Samoa: Krämer, 1902, I, 143; N.Z.: Gudgeon, 1906, 51ff.

D1903. Power of inducing love given by animals. N.Z.: Gudgeon, 1906, 53.

*D1905.4. Love induced by magic flute. Hawaii: Dickey, 1917, 26.

D1925. Fecundity magically induced. Tuamotus: Stimson, 1937, 5.

*D1935.1. Work done by magic. Rennell: Elbert-Monberg, 1964, No. 80a; Bellona: ibid., No. 80b.

D1950--D2049. Temporary Magic Characteristics

D1960. Magic sleep. Easter I.: Englert, 1939, 57f.; Tuamotus: Henry, 1928, 511; Stimson, 1934, 44, 67; Marquesas: Steinen, 1933-34, 29, 32; Cooks: Ariki, 1899, 172; Large, 1903, 134; Hawaii: Rice, 1923, 25; Tonga: Collocott, 1928, 16, 18; Niue: Loeb, 1926, 186; N.Z.: Beattie, 1920, 134; Best, 1925, 776; Best, 1928a, 261, 265; Cowan, 1930, I, 67, 70; Grey, 1855, 95; Tarakawa, 1899, 131; White, 1887-90, II, 43, 130, 139, 146; Wohlers, 1875, 29.

D1962.2. Magic sleep by lousing. Easter I.: Knoche, 1920, 66; Mangareva: Hiroa, 1938, 375; Tuamotus: Buck, 1938a, 189; Seurat, 1905, 435f.; Stimson, 1934, 38f.; Stimson, 1937, 48; Marquesas: Handy, 1930, 24; Tonga: Collocott, 1928, 14; N.Z.: White, 1887-90, II, 77, 86, 424; Wohlers, 1875, 14; Ellice Is.: Roberts, 1958, 400; Rotuma: Churchward, 1938-39, 219; Ontong Java: Sarfert, 1931, 456.

*D1964.7. Fairies cast person in magic sleep. N.Z.: Cowan, 1930, 59.

D1980. Magic invisibility. Marquesas: Handy, 1930, 118; Hawaii: Fornander, 1918, VI, 336; Rice, 1923, 52; Thrum, 1907, 224; Westervelt, 1915, 264; N.Z.: Best, 1925, 915; Grey, 1855, 63.

D1981.1. Magic invisibility of gods. Hawaii: Rice, 1923, 9.

*D1982.2.1. Canoe magically appears. Rarotonga: Te Ariki, 1920, 119.

*D1982.6. Two gods make invisible island. Fijis: Fison, 1904, 16f.

*D1982.7. Water holes made invisible. Hawaii: Westervelt, 1915, 265.

*D1982.8. Drum played by invisible hands. Hawaii: Westervelt, 1915, 171.

*D1985.3. Incantation makes man escape detection by his enemies. N.Z.: White, 1887-90, IV, 51f., 202.

D2031.18. Person appears to be in several places at once. Marquesas: Lavondes, 1966, 86.

*D2031.20. Two men magcially caused to embrace stones, which they believe to be females. Hawaii: Emerson, 1915, 28.

D2035. Magic heaviness. N.Z.: Grey, 1855, 145.

*D2037. Magic lightness (of weight). Fijis: Fison, 1904, 109.

*D2039. Boy causes woman to be magically impregnated from eating fish. Samoa: Krämer, 1902, I, 130.

D2060. Death or bodily injury by magic. Hawaii: Beckwith, 1940, 176; Fornander, 1918, V, 14; N.Z.: H.T., 1901, 73; Smith, 1909, 211; Lau Is.: St. Johnston, 1918, 52, 56f.

D2061. Magic murder. Easter I.: Englert, 1939, 48; Mangareva: Caillot, 1914, 182; Hiroa, 1938, 52; Tuamotus: Stimson, 1937, 9; Marquesas: Lavondes, 1966, 94, 162; Hawaii: Beckwith, 1940, 115, 120; Fornander, 1916, IV, 230, 472; V, 502; Ii, 1959, 124f.; Pukui, 1933, 156f.; Westervelt, 1915, 71f., 110; Samoa: Krämer, 1902, I, 122f., 132, 137; Niue: Loeb, 1926, 183; Chatham Is.: Skinner-Baucke, 1928, 380; N.Z.: Best, 1925, 834; Cowan, 1930, I, 97ff., 111, 156ff.; Grace, 1907, 182f., 184; Gudgeon, 1906, 54; White, 1887-90, II, 124, 128; III, 129, 140, 144; IV, 83, 89; V, 56, 59ff.; Lau Is.: St. Johnston, 1918, 52, 88; Tikopia: Firth, 1961, 79.

*D2061.0.1. Tribe wiped out by magic. N.Z.: Cowan, 1930, I, 103ff.

D2061.1.1. Person magically reduced to ashes. Hawaii: Beckwith, 1940, 176; Fornander, 1916, IV, 54, 60; Thrum, 1907, 224f.

D2061.1.5. Plague magically invoked. Hawaii: Beckwith, 1940, 116; Samoa: Sierich, 1902, 197f.

*D2061.1.6. Magic drowning. Hawaii: Beckwith, 1940, 87; Samoa: Krämer, 1902, I, 387.

*D2061.1.7. Person magically caused to fall; he dies from fall. Cooks: Beaglehole, 1938, 328.

*D2061.1.8. Person magically possessed by god dies. Bellona: Elbert-Monberg, 1964, No. 150.

*D2061.1.9. Incantation causes spider web, upon which hero climbs, to break. N.Z.: White, 1887-90, I, 57.

*D2061.1.10. In sorcery contest both participants kill each other. Lau Is.: St. Johnston, 1918, 54.

*D2061.1.11. Worm magically caused to enter a person's body and destroy him. N.Z.: Best, 1925, 861.

D2061.2.1. Death-giving glance. Cooks: Beaglehole, 1938, 381; Niue: Smith, 1902, 86; N.Z.: Grey, 1855, 273.

D2061.2.2. Murder by sympathetic magic. Hawaii: Emory, 1924, 18; Ii, 1959, 8; N.Z.: Best, 1925, 946; White, 1887-90, III, 260; Lau Is.: St. Johnston, 1918, 50ff.; Reef Is.: O'Ferrall, 1904, 225.

D2061.2.3. Murder by pointing. Mangareva: Hiroa, 1938, 340.

D2061.2.4. Death by cursing. Samoa: Krämer, 1902, I, 430.

*D2061.2.10. Shooting stars magically caused to kill. Ontong Java: Sarfert, 1931, 324.

*D2061.2.11. Persons killed by magically summoned tidal wave. Hawaii: Dickey, 1917, 31.

*D2061.2.12. Perfume placed in gourd enables people to kill man by magic. Marquesas: Lavondes, 1966, 94, 162, 204.

*D2061.2.13. Person struck and cut in half with stem of coconut leaf. Samoa: Powell -Pratt, 1892, 98, 105.

*D2061.2.14. Fleet magically destroyed by storm at sea. N.Z.: Cowan, 1930, I, 198f.

*D2061.2.15. Incantation turns man's axe stroke against himself and he cuts off his own head. Hawaii: Fornander, 1918, V, 276.

D2062. Maiming by magic. Tuamotus: Stimson, n.d., Z-G. 3/1340; N.Z.: Beattie, 1920, 132.

D2062.1. Heart removed by magic. Rennell: Elbert-Monberg, 1964, No. 97.

D2062.2. Blinding by magic. N.Z.: Grey, 1855, 69.

D2062.2.1. Blinding by curse. N.Z.: Wohlers,1876, 114.

*D2062.2.1.2. Sandflies made by magic to fill person's eyes. Hawaii: Forbes, 1882, 40.

*D2062.6. Magic deafness. N.Z.: Best, 1925, 794f.

*D2062.7. Teeth magically removed. Hawaii: Elbert-Monberg, 1964, No. 184.

*D2062.8. Magician causes runner to become lame. Hawaii: Thrum, 1923, 81.

*D2062.9. Person magically caused to pierce himself with fishhook. Tuamotus: Stimson, 1937, 62.

D2064. Magic sickness. Mangareva: Hiroa, 1938, 425; Hawaii: Westervelt, 1915, 95f.; N.Z.: Cowan, 1930, I, 155ff.; Fijis: Fison, 1904, xxi.

*D2064.9. Person possessed by god swells in size. Bellona: Elbert-Monberg, 1964, No. 152.

D2065. Magic insanity. Hawaii: Fornander, 1918, V, 312; N.Z.: White, 1887-90, III, 260.

*D2069.3. Person magically made weak. Hawaii: Fornander, 1918, V, 322.

*D2069.3.1. Magic spell causes girl dancer to tire. Tuamotus: Stimson, 1934, 6.

D2070. Bewitching. Niue: Smith, 1902, 197f.; N.Z.: Best, 1927, 270; *S. Percy Smith, "The Evils of Makutu, or Witchcraft," JPS XXX (1921), 172-184; White, 1887-90, V, 52ff.

*D2020.2. Person blinds his enemies with a magic storm of feathers. Mangareva: Hiroa, 1938, 328.

D2071.2.1. Person kills animals with glance of evil eye. N.Z.: Cowan, 1930, 111; White, 1887-90, IV, 93.

D2072. Magic paralysis. N.Z.: Cowan, 1930, 111; Ontong Java, Nukumanu: Sarfert, 1931, 427f.

D2072.0.3. Ship (canoe) held back by magic. Samoa: Stuebel, 1896, 69, 145; Tokelaus: Burrows, 1923, 162; Lister, 1892, 61; N.Z.: Best, 1925, 736f.; Tikopia: Firth, 1961, 116.

D2072.0.5. Person paralyzed. Ontong Java, Nukumanu: Sarfert, 1931, 428.

D2074.1.2. Fish or sea animals magically called. Mangareva: Hiroa, 1938, 36; Marquesas, Tuamotus: Beckwith, 1940, 269, 289; Hawaii: McAllister, 1933, 7; Thrum, 1923, 250, 252, 294; N.Z.: Best, 1927, 270; Cowan, 1930, 97; White, 1887-90, II, 129, 133, 140; III, 60ff.; IV, 110f., 114, 184

D2081. Land made magically sterile. N.Z.: Grey, 1855, 33; *Luomala, 1949, 118; Tikopia: Firth, 1961, 100.

D2082.0.2. Tree magically withers. N.Z.: Cowan, 1930, 111, 114f.; Grey, 1855, 273, 277.

*D2084.4. Birds magically spoil canoe being manufactured. Hawaii: Pukui-Curtis, n.d., 84.

D2085. Game animals magically made overwary. N.Z.: White, 1887-90, IV, 117.

*D2085.2. Charm causes nets of fishermen to be filled with only inedible fish. Marquesas: Handy, 1930, 118.

*D2086.4. Axe magically dulled. Hawaii: Fornander, 1918, V, 310.

D2089.6. House destroyed by magic. Marquesas: Handy, 1930, 81; Fornander, 1916, IV, 608.

*D2089.9.2. Magic spell enchants a road so that travelers are bewildered and die. N.Z.: White, 1887-90, IV, 91.

*D2089.13. Chant causes woman's loincloth to loosen. N.Z.: White, 1887-90, II, 144.

*D2089.14. Stones and wood of earthen oven magically caused to scatter. Ellice Is.: Roberts, 1958, 371.

D2091. Magic attack against enemy. N.Z.: White, 1887-90, V, 97.

D2091.15. Magic earth-slip overcomes enemies. Rennell: Elbert-Monberg, 1964, No. 90.

D2096. Magic putrefaction. Hawaii: Kamakau, 1961, 38.

D2098. Ship (canoe) magically sunk. Marquesas: Lavondes, 1966, 156; Hawaii: Emerson, 1915, 63; Emory, 1924, 12; Samoa: Krämer, 1902, I, 123; N.Z.: Best, 1925, 908.

D2099.4. Calabashes broken by magic. Easter I.: Métraux, 1940, 367.

*D2099.5. Journey magically lengthened. Tuamotus:
Stimson, n.d., T-G. 3/45; Cooks: Beaglehole, 1938,
407; Hawaii: Westervelt, 1915, 40f.; N.Z.:
Best, 1929, 9; Grey, 1855, 40; Tu-whawhakia,
1896, 156; White, 1887-90, II, 124.

D2121.4. Magic journey by making
distance vanish.

*D2099.6. Island turned upside down (sunk) by magic.
Marquesas: Steinen, 1934-35, 225; Samoa: Fraser,
1897, 70.

*D2099.7. Woman spits, spittle starts conflagration
which burns everything on island. Hawaii: Rice,
1923, 30.

*D2099.8. Food which has spell upon it will not cook.
N.Z.: Cowan, 1930, I, 192.

D2100--D2149. Other manifestations of magic power

D2105. Provisions magically furnished. Hawaii:
Beckwith, 1919, 442; Green, 1928, 37; Tonga:
Collocott, 1928, 60; Samoa: Krämer, 1902, I, 408;
N.Z.: White, 1887-90, I, 88f., 127; II, 135;
Wohlers, 1875, 25; Reef Is.: O'Ferrall, 1904, 228.

D2105.7. Fruit obtained from tree by magic. Marquesas:
Lavondes, 1964, 104.

*D2105.8. Person, when hungry, shakes his hair and birds
fall out. N.Z.: Best, 1925, 817.

*D2105.9. Fish magically caused to rain down from sky.
N.Z.: Wohlers, 1875, 30.

*D2105.10. Person is cooked in oven, emerges unhurt,
and oven is left filled with food. Hawaii: Green,
1926, 59; Smith, 1966, 23ff.; Samoa: Sierich,
1901, 21.

*D2105.11. Crops of food plants produced by magic.
Samoa: Krämer, 1902, I, 421; N.Z.: White,
1887-90, III, 99; Bellona: Elbert-Monberg, 1964,
No. 80b.

D2106.1.5. Multiplication of food by saint (priest).

Hawaii: McAllister, 1933, 140.

*D2106.4. Stones magically multiply. Samoa: Stuebel, 1896, 59, 60.

*D2106.5. Eight large fields of potatoes planted from one load of tops. Hawaii: Fornander, 1918, V, 176.

D2120. Magic transportation. (See also D1520.ff. Transportation on magic objects). Cooks: Beaglehole, 1938, 384.

D2121. Magic journey. N.Z.: Cowan, 1930, I, 163; Futuna: Burrows, 1936, 226.

D2121.7. Magic journey in cloud. Hawaii: Westervelt, 1915, 43ff.; Ellice Is.: Kennedy, 1931, 175; Tikopia: Firth, 1961, 50.

D2121.7.3. Magic transportation on smoke. Easter I.: Métraux, 1940, 368.

D2122. Journey with magic speed. Marquesas: Steinen, 1933-34, 29, 32; Hawaii: Westervelt, 1915, 95, 251; N.Z.: Best, 1925, 738, 800; Cowan, 1930, I, 233; White, 1887-90, IV, 84.

*D2122.5. Man magically clears obstructions from his path. N.Z.: White, 1887-90, II, 42, 79; Wohlers, 1876, 113.

D2125. Magic journey over water. Tikopia: Firth, 1961, 55.

D2125.1. Magic power to walk on water. Rarotonga: Te Ariki,1920, 120; Hawaii: Dickey, 1917, 20; Fornander, 1918, V, 164; McAllister, 1933, 185; Thrum, 1907, 83; N.Z.: Beckwith, 1940, 250; Best, 1925, 989f.; Rotuma: Russell, 1942, 250.

D2125.1.1. Magic transportation by waves. Tuamotus: Stimson, n.d., Z-G. 13/249.

*D2125.4. Person swims with magic speed. N.Z.: White, 1887-90, II, 56; Wohlers, 1876, 120.

D2126. Magic underwater journey. Oceania: *William A. Lessa, "Myth and Blackmail in the Western Carolines," 1956, 66ff.

D2135. Magic air journey. Hawaii: Green, 1923, 25;

N.Z.: Best, 1925, 896, 955.

D2135.0.1. Levitation. Person able to raise self in the air. Tubuai: Aitken, 1930, 112; Cooks: Gill, 1876, 68; Beaglehole, 1938, 379; Te Ariki, 1920, 175; Hawaii: Beckwith, 1940, 350; N.Z.: Tama-Rau, 1899, 54f.; Rotuma: Churchward, 1937-38, 114; Ellice Is.: Smith, 1920, 145.

D2135.0.3. Magic ability to fly. Australs: Aitken, 1923, 289; Hawaii: Fornander, 1916, IV, 72, 82ff.; V, 364, 366, 370; Thrum, 1907, 92ff., 174; Westervelt, 1915, 106ff., 123f., 215; Samoa: Stuebel, 1896, 144; N.Z.: Cowan, 1930, 21; White, 1887-90, I, 58; II, 80; Lau Is.: St. Johnston, 1918, 83; Tikopia: Firth, 1961, 31, 72.

*D2135.6. Flying taro plants. Hawaii: Westervelt, 1915, 27f.

D2136.1. Rocks moved by magic. Hawaii: Thrum, 1907, 238f.; Niue: Loeb, 1926, 183; N.Z.: White, 1887-90, V, 86; Tikopia: Firth, 1961, 101; Kapingamarangi: Elbert, 1948, 121.

D2136.3. Mountains magically transported. N.Z.: Best, 1925, 931.

D2136.6. Island magically transported. Tuamotus: Stimson, n.d., Z-G. 3/1122, Z-G. 3/1146, T-G. 3/912, Z-G. 13/499; Seurat, 1905, 436; Cooks: Gill, 1876, 102.

D2136.9. Magic house removed. Marquesas: Steinen, 1934-35, 224; N.Z.: *Best, 1929, 261f., 265.

*D2136.10.1. Palm fronds collected by magic. Tikopia: Firth, 1961, 98f.

*D2136.11. Canoe magically transported (launched). Mangareva: Hiroa, 1938, 30, 329; Tahiti: Leverd, 1912, 1; Hawaii: Fornander, 1916, IV, 442; Thrum, 1907, 114; N.Z.: White, 1887-90, I, 76, 77, 78, 79; II, 160; Reef Is.: O'Ferrall, 1904, 227; Riesenfeld, 1950, 128; Elbert-Kirtley, 1966, 362; Bellona: Elbert-Monberg, 1964, No. 66.

*D2136.12. Sleeping man magically transported to distant island. Samoa: Steinen, 1933-34, 356f.; Tokelaus: Burrows, 1923, 161; N.Z.: Best, 1929, 261f., 265; Cowan, 1930, 51, 58f.; White, 1887-90, II, 130, 133, 139, 146; Wohlers, 1875, 29.

226

*D2136.13. Sand magically transported. Marquesas:
Steinen, 1934-35, 226.

D2140. Magic control of the elements. Hawaii:
Fornander, 1918, V, 232f.

D2141. Storm (at sea) produced by magic. Cooks:
Te Ariki, 1920, 122; 1921, 205; Hawaii: Beckwith,
1919, 354; Beckwith, 1940, 448, 507; Fornander,
1916, IV, 516ff.; Rice, 1923, 80; Smith, 1966,
12; Thrum, 1923, 155; Westervelt, 1915, 177, 178,
180, 193; Samoa: Stuebel, 1896, 148; N.Z.:
Grace, 1907, 120; White, 1887-90, III, 64, 98,
166, 177, 203, 213; Kapingamarangi: Elbert,
1949, 242.

D2141.0.7. Storm raised by incantation. N.Z.:
Pakauwera,, 1894, 102.

D2141.0.10. Woman hoists skirt to raise thunderstorm.
Hawaii: Beckwith, 1940, 113.

D2141.1. Storm magically stilled. Tonga: Gifford,
1924, 117.

D2142.0.1. Magician (witch) controls winds. Tuamotus:
Stimson, n.d., T-G. 3/45; Societies: Henry, 1928,
393; Niue: Loeb, 1926, 204; Samoa: Stair, 1896,
57.

D2142.0.4. Leper controls winds. Tuamotus: Stimson,
n.d., T-G. 3/45.

D2142.0.5. Wind controlled by girl's spirit. Marquesas:
Handy, 1930, 29.

D2142.1. Wind produced by magic. Tuamotus: Stimson,
n.d., T-G. 3/109, Z-G. 1/96, Z-G. 3/1323;
Marquesas: Handy, 1930, 119; Lavondes, 1966, 78;
Societies: Caillot, 1914, 113; Hawaii:
Fornander, 1918, V, 92, 104, 232; Green, 1929, 7;
Tokelaus: Burrows, 1923, 154; N.Z.: Best 1925,
886ff.; Grace, 1907, 120; White, 1887-90, II, 53;
Rotuma: Hames, 1960, 23.

D2142.1.6. Wind raised by whistling. Niue: Loeb,
1926, 180.

D2142.2. Wind stilled by magic. Tuamotus: Stimson,
n.d., Z-G. 13/555; Beckwith, 1940, 289.

D2143.1. Rain produced by magic. Hawaii: Dickey, 1917, 26f.; Fornander, 1918, V, 342; Pukui, 1933, 137; Rice, 1923, 107; Thrum, 1923, 128, 131f.; Westervelt, 1915, 169, 271; Tonga: Caillot, 1914, 284; Collocott, 1921, 48; Reiter, 1917-18, 1040; Samoa: Powell-Pratt, 1891-93, 280; Tokelaus: Burrows, 1923, 163; Chatham Is.: Shand, 1896, 209; Skinner, 1923, 62ff.; N.Z.: Best, 1925, 795; Cowan, 1930, I, 16, 76; White, 1887-90, II, 68, 79, 81, 136; Rennell: Elbert-Monberg, 1964, No. 21; Bellona: Elbert-Monberg, 1964, No. 58.

*D2143.1.0.3. Rain stopped by magic. N.Z.: Best, 1925, 883ff.

D2143.2. Drought produced by magic. Mangareva: Hiroa, 1938, 24; Hawaii: Fornander, 1918, V, 602.

D2143.3. Fog (mist) produced by magic. Hawaii: Beckwith, 1919, 498, 504, 514, 532, 534; Fornander, 1918, V, 556; Thrum, 1923, 129; Westervelt, 1915, 230; N.Z.: White, 1887-90, III, 9, 22f.; Tikopia: Firth, 1961, 140.

*D2143.3.2. Fog magically dispersed. N.Z.: Best, 1925, 902.

D2143.5. Frost produced by magic. N.Z.: White, 1887-9C II, 72, 79, 81.

D2143.6. Magic control of snow. Chatham Is.: Shand, 1896, 209.

*D2143.7. Winds contained in a calabash. Hawaii: Westervelt, 1915, 59f.

D2144. Magic control of cold and heat. Tuamotus: Henry, 1928, 528; Hawaii: Beckwith, 1919, 335.

D2144.1. Cold produced by magic. Hawaii: Beckwith, 1919, 484ff.; Westervelt, 1915, 240.

D2144.3. Heat produced by magic. Hawaii: Beckwith, 1919, 486, 488.

D2145.1. Winter magically produced. Tuamotus: Henry, 1928, 528.

D2146.1.1. Day magically lengthened (or sun caused to stand still). Cooks: Gill, 1876, 184; Te Ariki,

1920, 64; Hawaii: Emerson, 1915, 137;
Fornander, 1918, VI, 344; Thrum, 1907, 24; N.Z.:
Best, 1899, 97; White, 1887-90, I, 96.

D2146.2.1. Night produced by magic. Cooks: Gill,
1876, 89; N.Z.: White, 1887-90, II, 148.

D2146.2.2. Night magically lengthened. Hawaii:
Fornander, 1918, V, 540; Thrum, 1921, 105; Thrum,
1923, 201, 257; N.Z.: White, 1887-90, II, 50.

D2146.2.3. Night magically shortened. Marquesas:
Beckwith, 1940, 262; Handy, 1930, 109.

*D2146.2.4. Darkness of night made blacker by sorcery.
Hawaii: Thrum, 1923, 172; Westervelt, 1915, 212.

D2147.2. Cloud magically appears. Tuamotus: Stimson,
n.d., Z-G. 13/499.

D2148. Earth magically caused to quake. Niue:
Smith, 1903, 100.

*D2148.3.1. Lava flow halted by magic. Hawaii:
Westervelt, 1915, 271.

*D2148.4. Magic control of volcanoes. Hawaii:
Beckwith, 1940, 500; Westervelt, 1915, 20, 174;
N.Z.: Cowan, 1930, 18f., 148ff.

D2149.1. Thunderbolt (thunder or lightning) magically
produced. Marquesas: Handy, 1930, 65; Hawaii:
Westervelt, 1915, 182; Chatham Is.: Shand, 1896,
209; N.Z.: Best, 1925, 879f.; Rennell: Elbert-
Monberg, 1964, No. 21, No. 192; Bellona: Elbert-
Monberg, 1964, No. 30.

*D2149.1.1.1. Chieftainess has lightning at her
command. Societies: Henry, 1928, 464.

D2150--D2199. Miscellaneous magical

manifestations

D2151. Magic control of waters. Hawaii: Fornander,
1918, V, 202; Reef Is.: O'Ferrall, 1904, 228.

D2151.0.2. Waters made to dry up. N.Z.: White, 1887-90, I, 92; II, 22, 24, 55, 159, 170f.; Wohlers, 1876, 119.

D2151.0.3. Wall of water magically warded off. Hawaii: Beckwith, 1940, 466.

*D2151.0.4. Sea caused magically to part. Hawaii: Luomala, 1951, 38.

D2151.1. Magic control of seas. Tuamotus: Stimson, n.d., T-G. 3/403; Societies: Henry, 1928, 393; N.Z.: Grey, 1855, 298.

D2151.1.2. Tide held back. Tuamotus: Stimson, n.d., T-G. 3/730.

D2151.1.3. Sea calmed by prayer(magic). Mangareva: Hiroa, 1938, 335; Tuamotus: Stimson, n.d., T-G. 3/109; Hawaii: Rice, 1923, 55; N.Z.: Beattie, 1920, 134; Ellice Is.: Roberts, 1958, 402.

*D2151.1.7. Magic waterspout. Kapingamarangi: Elbert, 1949, 241.

D2151.3. Magic control of waves. Mangareva: Hiroa, 1938, 329; Societies: Jourdain, 1933, 204; Tuamotus: Stimson, 1937, 39, 104; N.Z.: White, 1887-90, II, 40.

D2151.3.1. Magic tidal wave. Mangareva: Hiroa, 1938, 333; Tuamotus: Stimson, n.d., T-G. 3/109; Stimson, 1934, 32; Marquesas: Handy, 1930, 65, 119; Hawaii: Dickey, 1917, 31; Green, 1926, 106; Thrum, 1907, 130; N.Z.: Beckwith, 1940, 318; Best, 1925, 680; Grace, 1907, 158f.; White, 1887-90, III, 40f., 49, 51, 53, 55; Fijis: Hocart, 1929, 218; Bellona: Elbert-Monberg, 1964, No. 66.

*D2151.3.3. Surf magically raised. Hawaii: Fornander, 1918, V, 126ff., 232, 710.

D2151.5.2. Pond magically dried up. Tuamotus: Stimson, n.d., Z-G. 13/499.

D2151.6. Magic control of wells (springs). Hawaii: Fornander, 1918, VI, 272; Pukui-Curtis, n.d., 102; Westervelt, 1915, 26, 35ff.

*D2151.6.0.1. Well magically dried up. Tuamotus: Caillot, 1914, 85.

D2151.6.1. Saint causes wells to fail. Tuamotus: Stimson, n.d., T-G. 3/403.

*D2151.6.3. Spring (well) produced by magic. Oceania: *S. Percy Smith, "The Polynesians in Indonesia," JPS LXV (1906), 24; Mangareva: Hiroa, 1938, 340f.; Marquesas: Steinen, 1934-35, 225; Hawaii: Beckwith, 1940, 64; Samoa: Powell-Pratt, 1892, 80; Niue: Smith, 1903, 100; N.Z.: Best, 1925, 970; Cowan, 1930, I, 247; *Smith, 1921, 24.

D2151.8. Magic flood. Mangareva: Hiroa, 1938, 370; Marquesas: Lavondes, 1964, 106; Steinen, 1934-35, 231; Handy, 1928, 109; Tuamotus: Stimson, n.d., Z-G. 13/167; Cooks: Beckwith, 1940, 103; Savage, 1910, 146; Te Ariki, 1920, 165; Hawaii: Thrum, 1907, 243; Westervelt, 1915, 57; Samoa: Clark, 1896, 74; Niue: Loeb, 1926, 147; N.Z.: *Beckwith, 1940, 249, 249 n.; Best, 1925, 962; White, 1887-90, I, 76, 77, 174; V, 58; Fijis: Fison, 1904, 30; Banks Is.: Riesenfeld, 1950, 128; Reef Is.: Elbert-Kirtley, 1966, 359.

*D2153.4. Woman's kicks magically cause land to recede before approaching canoe. Fijis: Hocart, 1904, 208.

*D2154. Sand-bank magically arises. Ellice Is.: Kennedy, 1931, 178.

*D2156.12. Fish magically summoned. Hawaii: Thrum, 1907, 227f., 247; Samoa: Stuebel, 1896, 69; Rennell: Elbert-Monberg, 1964, No. 228a.

*D2156.13. Priest's incantation causes oysters to release boat to which they cling. N.Z.: White, 1887-90, V, 12.

D2157.1. Land made magically fertile. Bellona: Elbert-Monberg, 1964, No. 75.

D2157.2. Magic quick growth of crops. Mangareva: Hiroa, 1938, 27, 329; Hawaii: Beckwith, 1940, 120; N.Z.: White, 1887-90, IV, 244; V, 88; Reef Is.: Elbert-Kirtley, 1966, 350.

D2157.3. Withered tree magically made green. N.Z.: Cowan, 1930, 115.

*D2157.3.1.1. Trees magically caused to bear fruit. Nukumanu: Sarfert, 1931, 456.

D2157.4. Miraculous speedy growth of a tree. Societies: Henry, 1928, 538; Hawaii: Pukui, 1933, 180;

Rice, 1923, 118f.

*D2157.4.1. Branches struck from sacred tree grow fast again immediately. Societies: Henry, 1928, 538; Rennell: Elbert-Monberg, 1964, No. 88.

*D2157.7. Vines magically cover an object. Hawaii: Fornander, 1916, IV, 568; V, 182.

*D2157.8. Fruit magically ripened. Samoa: Krämer, 1902, I, 421.

D2158. Magic control of fires. Mangareva: Hiroa, 1938, 369; Hawaii: Thrum, 1907, 224f.

D2158.1. Magic kindling of fire. Marquesas: Lavondes, 1964, 104; Reef Is.: Elbert-Kirtley, 1966, 350.

D2158.1.5.2. Cooking and baking done without fire. Hawaii: Rice, 1923, 14.

D2158.2. Magic extinguishing of fires. Hawaii: Beckwith, 1940, 176.

D2161. Magic healing power. Marquesas: Handy, 1943, 24; Societies: Henry, 1928, 373; Cooks: Beaglehole, 1938, 381; Hawaii: Beckwith, 1940, 118; Westervelt, 1915, 72, 244; Tonga: Collocott 1928, 46; Samoa: Stuebel, 1896, 64, 69; N.Z.: White, 1887-90, II, 36; Tikopia: Firth, 1961, 76; Rennell: Elbert-Monberg, 1964, Nos. 138, 235a.

*D2161.1.4. Magic cure of yaws. Ellice Is.: David, 1899, 96, 174.

D2161.2. Magic cure of wound. Chatham Is.: Shand, 1894, 189; Tikopia: Firth, 1961, 113.

*D2161.2.4. Person magically restores his skin, pulled off by enemies. Mangareva: Hiroa, 1938, 322.

D2161.3.1. Blindness magically cured. Mangareva: Hiroa, 1938, 323; Tuamotus: Leverd, 1911, 177; Stimson, 1937, 82; Marquesas: Steinen, 1933-34, 372; Societies: Henry, 1928, 560; Cooks: Banapa, 1920, 90; Gill, 1876, 66, 113; Te Ariki, 1920, 117, 207f.; Hawaii: Beckwith, 1940, 264; Fornander, 1916, IV, 92; Samoa: Sierich, 1902, 178; Niue: Smith, 1903, 94; Tokelaus: Burrows, 1923, 168; Chatham Is.: Shand, 1898, 73; N.Z.: Best, 1925, 912; Cowan, 1930, I, 22; Grey, 1855,

71; *Potae, 1928, 361, 366; White, 1887-90,
I, 57, 58, 90, 102, 110f., 116, 122, 128; Wohlers,
1875, 18; Rotuma: Churchward, 1938-39, 330;
Ontong Java, Nukumanu: Sarfert, 1931, 424;
Bellona: Elbert-Monberg, 1964, Nos. 1a, 1b;
Rennell: ibid., 1c; Kapingamarangi: Elbert,
1949, 243.

D261.3.1.1. Eyes torn out magically replaced. Tuamotus:
Stimson, 1937, 87, 146.

D2161.3.7. Lameness magically cured. Hawaii: Beckwith,
1940, 175.

*D2161.3.7.2. Hero joins people who have only one leg,
arm and eye and makes whole person of each pair.
Marquesas: Steinen, 1934-35, 216.

*D2161.3.12. Cannibalism magically cured. Chatham Is.:
Shand, 1896, 203.

*D2161.3.13. Teeth magically restored. Rennell:
Elbert-Monberg, 1964, No. 184.

D2161.4.14. Magic cure by bathing. Ellice Is.: David,
1899, 96, 174.

*D2161.4.20. Sick person made well by drinking the water-
of-life. Hawaii: Westervelt, 1915, 39f.

D2161.5.1. Cure by holy man. Societies: Henry, 1928,
373.

D2163.2. Magic reinforcements. N.Z.: Dixon, 1916, 61.

D2165. Escapes by magic. Tuamotus: Seurat, 1906, 127;
Hawaii: Fornander, 1918, V, 324.

D2165.4. Opening in house made by magic so as to escape.
Hawaii: Beckwith, 1919, 548.

D2166. Magic help from falling. Hawaii: Dickey, 1917,
34.

D2167. Corpse magically saved from corruption. Easter I.:
Métraux, 1940, 311.

D2171. Magic adesion. Marquesas: Handy, 1930, 95;
Steinen, 1934-35, 224; Tahiaoteaa, 1933, 495f.

D2171.1. Object magically attaches itself to a person. Marquesas: Lavondes, 1964, 106; N.Z.: Gudgeon, 1906, 52.

D2171.1.3. Person magically sticks to floor (ground). Hawaii: Fornander, 1916, IV, 532.

*D2171.4.4. Hero drags sago palm and other palms trail behind. Tikopia: Firth, 1961, 99.

D2176. Exorcising by magic. Tuamotus: Caillot, 1914, 62ff.; N.Z.: Grace, 1907, 145.

*D2177.5. Imprisonment within tree. Tuamotus: Stimson, n.d., T-G. 3/59; Ellice Is.: Roberts, 1958, 400.

D2178. Objects produced by magic. Hawaii: Thrum, 1923, 173.

D2188. Magic disappearance. Mangareva: Hiroa, 1938, 20; Tuamotus: Stimson, 1937, 62; Hawaii: Westervelt, 1915, 164; N.Z.: Cowan, 1930, 47.

D2188.2. Person vanishes. Tuamotus: Stimson, n.d., Z-G. 3/1241; Hawaii: McAllister, 1933, 150; Green, 1923, 5; Pukui-Curtis, n.d., 39; Westervelt 1915, 260; Tikopia: Firth, 1961, 41.

D2188.1. Ability to disappear or appear at will. Tikopia: Firth, 1961, 72.

D2188.2. Person vanishes. Tuamotus: Stimson, n.d., Z-G. 3/1241.

*D2188.4. During a prayer to the gods, the portion of a feast assigned them disappears. Hawaii: Emerson, 1915, 28, 73, 155.

*D2188.5. Tree magically appears and disappears. Rennell: Elbert-Monberg, 1964, No. 138.

D2192. Work of day magically overthrown at night. Tuamotus, Marquesas, Tahiti, N.Z.: *Beckwith, 1940, 265-269; Hawaii: Beckwith, 1940, 465; Ellice Is.: Beckwith, 1940, 270.

D2197. Magic dominance over animals. Fijis: Hocart, 1928, 213.

*D2199.3. Axe buried in the sand overnight is found sharpened the following morning. Cooks: Savage, 1910, 146f.

*D2199.4. Entrance to harbor shut by magic. N.Z.:
Cowan, 1930, I, 44.

*D2199.5. Sky lowered by magic. Ellice Is.: Roberts,
1958, 371.

*D2199.6. Person commanded to come to magician by
incantation does so. N.Z.: White, 1887-90,
II, 36.

*D2199.7. Cord magically suspended in air. Hawaii:
Fornander, 1916, IV, 552.

*D2199.8. Canoe chopped into pieces is restored
whole by magic. Reef Is.: O'Ferrall, 1904,
227.

E0--E199. Resuscitation

E0. Resuscitation. Polynesia: *Beckwith, 1940,
     Chap. X passim; Marquesas: Handy, 1930, 83;
     Tuamotus: Stimson, n.d., 3/912, Z-G. 13/127;
     Societies: Henry, 1928, 562-563, 614f.; Cooks:
     Te Ariki, 1920, 121; Te Ariki, 1921, 4; Hawaii:
     Beckwith, 1940, 479; Dickey, 1917, 24;
     *Fornander, 1916, IV, 530; V, 186f., 186, n. 8,
     192, 312; Thrum, 1923, 107; Westervelt, 1915,
     129ff., 187f.; Niue: Smith, 1903, 90; N.Z.:
     White, 1887-90, I, 130; Tikopia: Firth, 1961,
     55, 60; Rennell: Elbert-Monberg, 1964, No. 21.

E1. Person comes to life. Hawaii: Fornander, 1918,
     V, 230, 242, 714; Tonga: Gifford, 1924, 130;
     N.Z.: Cowan, 1930, I, 51; Wohlers, 1876, 115;
     Bellona: Elbert-Monberg, 1964, No. 149.

E3. Dead animal comes to life. Hawaii: Pukui,
     1933, 175.

E15. Resuscitation by burning. Easter I.: Métraux,
      1940, 68.

*E29.4.2. Resuscitation of woman when fruit of tree in
     which she is incarnated is eaten. Marquesas: Handy
     1930, 39; Steinen, 1933-34, 369.

*E29.6.1. People resuscitated when urine poured in their
     mouths. N.Z.: White, 1887-90, III, 95.

E29.7. Resuscitation by striking with lightning.
     Hawaii: Beckwith, 1940, 410.

*E29.9. People restored to life when devil who ate
     their souls is killed. Tokelaus: Burrows,
     1923, 172.

E30. Resuscitation by arrangement of members. Parts
     of a dismembered corpse are brought together and
     resuscitation follows. (Sometimes combined with
     other methods). -- Tuamotus: Seurat, 1905, 485;
     Stimson, n.d., Z-G. 3/1117; Marquesas: Handy,
     1930, 104; Cooks: Gill, 1876, 69; Hawaii:

Emerson, 1915, 237; Fornander, 1916, IV, 568;
Tonga: Collocott, 1928, 51; Samoa: Powell-Pratt,
1892, 98, 105; Rennell: Elbert-Monberg, 1964,
No. 31a, 33.

E30.1. Felled tree restored by assembling all cut parts.
Polynesia: Dixon, 1916, *68, n. 38.

E31. Limbs of dead voluntarily reassemble and revive.
Tahiti: Lagarde, 1933, 699; N.Z.: Gudgeon, 1906,
43-44; Kapingamarangi: Elbert, 1948, 119.

E32. Resuscitated eaten animal. An animal is eaten.
When his bones are reassembled, he revives.
Australs: Aitken, 1923, 250; Societies: Caillot,
1914, 134-136; Hawaii: Thrum, 1923, 253; Rotuma:
Churchward, 1938-39, 229.

E32.0.1. Eaten person resuscitated. Tuamotus:
Caillot, 1914, 79; Marquesas: Lavondes, 1964, 36ff.;
Tonga: Beckwith, 1940, 483; Caillot, 1914, 259,
n. 2, 281; Ellice Is.: Roberts, 1958, 373.

E35. Resuscitation from fragments of body. Tuamotus:
Stimson, n.d., Z-G. 3/1233; Stimson, 1934, 52;
Cooks: Beckwith, 1940, 253; Hawaii: Beckwith,
1940, 123, 139; Green, 1926, 103; Thrum, 1923,
307; Samoa: Krämer, 1902, I, 412; Rennell:
Elbert-Monberg, 1964, No. 1c.

E38. Resuscitation by replacement of soul. Mangareva:
Hiroa, 1938, 335; Easter I.: Métraux, 1940, 375;
Societies: Henry, 1928, 564; Hawaii: Beckwith,
1940, 124, 145, 152, 174; Tonga: Collocott, 1928,
20; Samoa: Krämer, 1902, I, 124, 133, 139;
Tokelaus: Burrows, 1923, 160, 172; N.Z.: Best,
1925, 945; Dixon, 1916, 78; White, 1887-90, II,
167; Ellice Is.: Kennedy, 1931, 198; Rennell:
Elbert-Monberg, 1964, Nos. 110, 113, 194; Bellona:
ibid., Nos. 1a, 1b.

E38.1. Resuscitation by returning dead person's soul
to body. Hawaii: Emerson, 1915, 73; Samoa:
*Beckwith, 1940, 150.

*E38.2. Soul of person resuscitated is forced into his
body through the toe or foot. Hawaii: Emerson,
1915, 73, 138ff.; Fornander, 1918, V, 186; Thrum,
1907, 47, 61, 151f.; Westervelt, 1915, 107, 218,
239.

E41. Resuscitation from excrement of one who has eaten
person (animal). Tonga: Gifford, 1924, 140;

Beckwith, 1940, 483, 504; Samoa: Brown, 1917, 96.

E50. Resuscitation by magic. Tuamotus: Stimson, n.d., 3/49, z-G. 3/1353, z-G. 13/1241; Hawaii: Beckwith 1940, 154 and Chap. X passim; Luomala, 1951, 29.

E52. Resuscitation by magic charm. Tuamotus: Stimson, 1937, 9; Hawaii: Fornander, 1918, V, 244; Westervelt, 1915, 86, 200, 240; N.Z.: Best, 1925, 911; Grey, 1855, 116, 185; Westervelt, 1915, 244; Rennell: Elbert-Monberg, 1964, Nos. 235a, 235.

E63. Resuscitation by prayer. N.Z.: Dixon, 1916, 82.

E63.1. Body palced in building and worshipped until it comes to life. Hawaii: Beckwith, 1940, 420.

E63.2. Resuscitation by nine-day dance and prayers. Hawaii: Beckwith, 1940, 184.

E64.18. Resuscitation by leaf. Mangareva: Hiroa, 1938, 341; Tonga: Caillot, 1914, 278; Caillot, 1921, 47f., 281f.; Reiter, 1917-18, 1037; Reiter, 1933, 360.

*E64.23. Resuscitation with "life-affecting fan." Tonga: *Beckwith, 1940, 150.

E66. Resuscitation by breathing on corpse. Hawaii: Thrum, 1907, 123.

E73. Resuscitation by incantation. (See E52.).

*E79.4. Resuscitation by warming corpse with fire. N.Z.: White, 1887-90, II, 123.

*E79.5. Resuscitation by touching corpse with a fish. N.Z.: White, 1887-90, III, 7.

E80. Water of life. Resuscitation by water. Cooks: Te Ariki, 1921, 210; Hawaii: *Beckwith, 1940, 74, 121, 145, 153, 264, 507; Fornander, 1916, IV, 82, 98; V, 678; Rice, 1923, 106; Thrum, 1907, 23; Westervelt, 1915, 33, 38ff., 44, 66, 72; Tonga: Collocott, 1928, 12; Samoa: Krämer, 1902, I, 126f. Sierich, 1902, 179f.; N.Z.: Best, 1925, 751; White, 1887-90, I, 141, 142; II, 21; Fijis: Beckwith, 1940, 76; Fison, 1904, 140; Rennell: Elbert-Monberg, 1964, No. 1c.

E80.1. Resuscitation by bathing. N.Z.: Grace, 1907, 257.

*E80.5. Tongue of dead shark becomes a whole living shark when touched with sea water. Hawaii: Thrum, 1923, 307.

E100. Resuscitation by medicines. Hawaii: Thrum, 1907, 56; Tokelau: Macgregor, 1937, 86.

E105. Resuscitation by herbs (leaves). Cf. E64.18. Marquesas: Handy, 1930, 34; Hawaii: Rice, 1923, 66; Tonga: Reiter, 1917-18, 1037.

E113. Resuscitation from blood. Tuamotus: Stimson, n.d., T-G. 3/912; Hawaii: Thrum, 1907, 56; Tonga: Collocott, 1928, 31; Gifford, 1924, 185.

E114. Resuscitation by spittle. Tonga: Gifford, 1924, 185.

E121. Resuscitation by supernatural person. Hawaii: Pukui, 1933,182; Thrum, 1907, 126; Westervelt, 1915, 87ff., 101.

E121.1. Resuscitation by a god. Cooks: Te Ariki, 1920, 121; Gill, 1876, 174; N.Z.: Hongi, 1896, 235; Rennell: Elbert-Monberg, 1964, No. 105.

*E122.3. Resuscitation by spirit in form of blowfly. N.Z.: Beckwith, 1940, 375.

*E122.4. Resuscitation by whale. Tuamotus: Stimson, n.d., T-G. 3/615.

E125.2. Resuscitation by sister(s). Societies: Henry, 1928, 614-615; Hawaii: Beckwith, 1940, 152.

*E125.4. Resuscitation by cousin. Societies: Henry, 1928, 562-563.

E151. Repeated resuscitation. A person dies and is resuscitated repeatedly. Cooks: Te Ariki, 1920, 116; Hawaii: Beckwith, 1940, 153; Thrum, 1907, 123ff.; Westervelt, 1915, 85; Tikopia: Firth, 1961, 55, 61f.

E152. Body still warm restored to life. Hawaii: Beckwith, 1940, 152.

*E155.7. A child washes ashore and it dies; drawn
back in the sea by waves, it lives. Easter I.:
Knoche, 1939, 25.

*E156.1. Boy, resuscitated in rat-like body, hears
knocking during night. Different parts of his
body (human) appear; he dons them. Hawaii:
Beckwith, 1940, 480.

*E156.2. Resuscitation and rebirth of body carried to
sea. (Five days after disposal, the head floats
to shore. Later other parts of body wash to beach
where they assemble together, and the person
becomes like a new born infant.) Mangareva:
Caillot, 1914, 166.

E162.1. Resuscitation after three days. Marquesas:
Handy, 1930, 34; Hawaii: Fornander, 1916, IV,
484.

E168. Cooked animal comes to life. Hawaii: Beckwith,
1940, 137; Green, 1923, 48f.; Green, 1926, 106;
Samoa: Krämer, 1902, I, 387; N.Z.: Best, 1924,
189; Futuna: Burrows, 1936, 226.

*E172. Fish resuscitated after being cleaned and salted.
Hawaii: Beckwith, 1940, 137.

*E173. Animal resuscitates people. Hawaii: Beckwith,
1940, 124.

E182. Dead body incorruptible. Hawaii: Thrum, 1907,
212.

E186. Failure at resuscitation. Hawaii: Fornander,
1916, IV, 80ff.

*E186.1. Spirit returns to body and finds it partially
corrupted. Tahiti: Stevenson, 1912, 141.

*E187. Male resuscitated as female. Samoa: Stair,
1896, 36.

E200--E299. Malevolent return from the dead

E200. Malevolent return from the dead. Easter I.:
Métraux, 1940, 316; Tuamotus: Stevenson, 1912,
128; Marquesas: Stevenson, 1912, 30f.; Hawaii:
Fornander, 1918, V, 364, 418, 422ff., 428;
*Westervelt, 1915, 245.

E221. Dead spouse's malevolent return. Usually to
protest with survivor because of evil ways.
Hawaii: Green, 1926, 93; Chatham Is.: Shand,
1894, 125; Rennell: Elbert-Monberg, 1964,
No. 195a, No. 198.

*E223. Girl's dead father attempts to kill her.
Marquesas: Lavondes, 1964, 80.

E225. Ghost of murdered child. Niue: Loeb, 1926, 176.

E225.1. Ghost of abortion. N.Z.: Best, 1897, 42.

*E225.2. Evil spirits originate from souls of still-born
babies. N.Z.: Best, 1925, 1044.

E231. Return from dead to reveal murder. Hawaii:
Beckwith, 1940, 152, 480; Rennell: Elbert-Monberg,
1964, No. 199.

E232. Return from dead to slay wicked person. Futuna:
Burrows, 1936, 229.

E232.1. Return from dead to slay own murderer. Chatham
Is.: Shand, 1894, 125; Rennell: Elbert-Monberg,
1964, Nos. 195a, 198.

*E232.1.1. Ghostly vengeance by proxy: a chief kills a
man and hangs his corpse upon tree. A dog eats fat
dripping from the corpse and then kills the chief.
Hawaii: Westervelt, 1915, 161f.

*E232.2. Ghosts of birds cause their slayer to fall in
his own oven and perish. Hawaii: Green, 1926,
109.

E234.0.1. Ghost returns to demand vengeance. Rotuma:
Churchward, 1937-38, 253 f.

E234.3. Return from dead to avenge death. Cooks:

241

Large, 1903, 135-136.

E235.2. Ghost returns to demand proper burial. Hawaii: Beckwith, 1940, 199.

E235.2.2. Ghost returns because corpse was not properly buried. Hawaii: Beckwith, 1940, 346; Fijis: Hocart, 1929, 210.

E235.6. Return from dead to punish disturber of grave. Hawaii: Beckwith, 1940, 99.

*E236.0.1. Two brothers deny their sister a share of the common inheritance. Their father returns from the dead, hurls the boys into an abyss. Futuna: Burrows, 1936, 229.

E250. Bloodthirsty revenants. Easter I.: Englert, 1939, 66ff.

E253. Ghost tries to kill person for food. Tuamotus: Stevenson, 1912, 128; Marquesas: Stevenson, 1912, 31; Hawaii: Fornander, 1916, IV, 42; V, 368, 428; Rotuma: Churchward, 1937-38, 365.

G11.10. Cannibalistic spirits.

E256. Ghosts eat corpse. Samoa: Stair, 1896, 53.

E261. Wandering ghost makes attack. Unprovoked and usually unmotivated. Hawaii: Westervelt, 1915, 19f.; Fijis: Hocart, 1929, 210.

E261.4. Ghost pursues man. Marquesas: Lavondes, 1964, 82; Hawaii: Fornander, 1916, IV, 482.

*E261.6. Ghosts tear out eyes of living. Marquesas: Stevenson, 1912, 133.

E262. Ghost rides on man's back. Hawaii: Westervelt, 1915, 251.

E265.1. Meeting ghost causes sickness. Cooks: Beaglehole, 1938, 333; N.Z.: Best, 1925, 1052; Santa Cruz: O'Ferral, 1904, 223.

*E265.1.4. Ghost gives son disease with which to afflict his cousin. Samoa: Hambruch, 1925, 112.

E265.2. Meeting ghost causes person to go mad. N.Z.: Best, 1925, 1052.

E265.3. Meeting ghost causes death. Samoa: Stevenson, 1912, 129; Hawaii: Fornander, 1918, V, 542; Niue: Loeb, 1926, 171; Chatham Is.: Travers, 1876, 26; Tikopia: Firth, 1961, 135.

E266. Dead carry off living. Marquesas: Steinen, 1934-35, 240; Samoa: Stair, 1896, 48; Stevenson, 1912, 140.

*E266.3. Ghost-women lure man away from his wedding feast. Marquesas: Handy, 1930, 48.

*E267.1. Spirits of dead cause sharks to eat offending relatives. Ontong Java: Parkinson, 1898, 197.

E271. Sea-ghosts. Ghosts which haunt the sea. Mangareva: Eskridge, 1931, 218; Societies: Henry, 1928, 496; Hawaii: Pukui-Curtis, n.d., 34f.; Kapingamarangi: Elbert, 1949, 243; Nukumanu: Sarfert, 1931, 337.

*E271.3. Ghosts (spirits) ride in spectral canoe. N.Z.: Gudgeon, 1906, 190.

E272. Road-ghosts. Ghosts which haunt roads. Hawaii: Fornander, 1918, V, 506.

*E279.2.1. Ghost carries sleepers outdoors, where they find themselves in the morning. Hawaii: Fornander, 1916, IV, 474ff.

E279.3. Ghost pulls bedclothing from sleeper. N.Z.: Grace, 1907, 135.

*E279.9. Ghost-possessed rock (or coral). Tuamotus: Beckwith, 1940, 268.

*E286. Ghosts kill people who sleep in haunted precinct. Niue: Loeb, 1926, 170.

E300--E399. Friendly return from the dead

E300. Friendly return from the dead. Tuamotus: Stimson, n.d., Z-G. 3/1353.

E320. Dead relative's friendly return. N.Z.: Best, 1924, 314.

E322. Dead wife's friendly return. Marquesas: Handy, 1930, 34.

E323. Dead mother's friendly return. Fijis: Fison, 1904, 110f.

E323.2. Dead mother returns to aid persecuted children. Oceanic: **Dixon, 1916, 89, nn. 97-100.

E323.4. Advice from dead mother. Samoa: Hambruch, 1925, 112.

E324. Dead child's friendly return to parents. Frequently to stop weeping. Tuamotus: Stimson, n.d., Z-G. 3/1353; Niue: Smith, 1903, 90.

E327. Dead father's friendly return. Hawaii: Thrum, 1907, 247; Rotuma: Churchward, 1937-38, 365; N.Z.: Cowan, 1930, I, 55; Ontong Java: Sarfert, 1931, 409.

*E329. Dead relatives interact amiably with their living kin -- miscellaneous.

*E329.1. Ancestral spirits protect and aid their living kin. Hawaii: Emerson, 1921, 16; Fornander, 1916, IV, 54ff.; 76; V, 126ff.; Green, 1929, 11; *Westervelt, 1915, 119f., 173, 248ff.; Samoa: Sierich, 1902, 119; Chatham Is.: Skinner, 1923, 60f.; N.Z.: Best, 1925, 769; Cowan, 1930, 66; White, 1887-90, I, 33; Lau Is.: St. Johnston, 1918, 86; Ontong Java: Parkinson, 1898, 196.

*E329.2. Spirits of dead consecreated and become guardians of the living. Hawaii: Luomala, 1951, 31.

*E329.3. Floating island is home of ancestral ghosts. Hawaii: Westervelt, 1915, 103.

*E329.4. Bones of dead person rattle in the presence of relative. N.Z.: White, 1887-90, II, 133, 148.

*E337.1.5. Hula resounds at sacred spring on special night of moon. Hawaii: McAllister, 1933, 177.

*E339. Miscellaneous haunted places.

*E399.1. Haunted grove. N.Z.: Cowan, 1930, I, 89.

*E339.2. Haunted hill. Hawaii: Fornander, 1918, V, 542.

*E339.3. Haunted road. Hawaii: Fornander, 1918, V, 506.

*E339.4. Haunted waterfall. Hawaii: Dickey, 1917, 34.

*E339.5. Haunted pagan religious structure. Hawaii:
Dickey, 1917, 15; McAllister, 1933, 123; Thrum,
1923, 119f.; Westervelt, 1915, 9, 248.

*E339.6. Haunted island. Tuamotus: Audran, 1917, 61;
Hawaii: Emory, 1924, 12, 13, 14; Fornander, 1916,
IV, 476, 486; 1918, V, 298, 428, 542; Ellice Is.:
Roberts, 1958, 368.

*E339.7. Haunted beach. N.Z.: Cowan, 1930, I, 51.

E341.2. Dead grateful for food. Samoa: Stuebel,
1896, 147.

E361. Return from the dead to stop weeping. Niue:
Smith, 1903, 90.

E363.2. Ghost returns to protect the living. Samoa:
Sierich, 1900, 235; Rennell: Elbert-Monberg,
1964, No. 206.

*E363.2.1. Dead avenge injuries done friends on earth.
N.Z.: Clark, 1896, 102.

E363.3. Ghost warns the living. Tuamotus: Stevenson,
1912, 134f.; Hawaii: Westervelt, 1915, 10f.

E363.5. Dead provide material aid to living. Mangareva:
Caillot, 1914, 203; Hiroa, 1938, 377; Tuamotus:
Stevenson, 1912, 135f.; Hawaii: Fornander, 1916,
IV, 474; Thrum, 1907, 149; Chatham Is.: Travers,
1876, 25.

E363.6. Ghost aids living otherwise. Ontong Java:
Sarfert, 1931, 410.

*E363.6.2. Spirit of dead man cures youth, makes him
handsome. Samoa: Hambruch, 1925, 116.

*E363.7. Wraith of dead man guides his living friend.
Hawaii: Emerson, 1915, 216.

E366. Return from dead to give counsel. Hawaii: Green,
1926, 95.

*E379.6. Bones of dead person rattle a greeting in presence of living relative. N.Z.: Cowan, 1930, I, 34; White, 1887-90, I, 76, 124; II, 133; IV, 81, 113; Wohlers, 1875, 24.

*E379.7. Corpse washes ashore three successive days as a sign that revenge for its death must be exacted. Mangareva: Hiroa, 1938, 34.

E387.1. Ghost summoned in order to talk to it. N.Z.: Beattie, 1920, 134.

E387.3. Ghost summoned for purposes of necromancy. Societies: Henry, 1928, 380.

E400--E599. Ghost and revenants--miscellaneous

E400. Ghosts and revenants -- miscellaneous. Niue: *Loeb, 1926, 158f.; Rennell: Elbert-Monberg, 1964, No. 183.

*E401.0.2. Ghosts of dead wander along beach. Cooks: Gill, 1876, 156; Samoa: Hambruch, 1925, 115; Fijis: Fison, 1904, 104.

E402.1.1.4. Ghost sings. Hawaii: Fornander, 1918, V, 418.

*E402.1.1.7. Ghosts whistle. Tuamotus: Stevenson, 1912, 122, 134; Stimson, n.d., T-G. 3/1007; Hawaii: Dickey, 1917, 27; Fornander, 1918, V, 530; Niue: Loeb,1926, 180.

*E402.1.1.8. Ghost wails in waterfall in which she was killed. Hawaii: Dickey, 1917, 34.

E402.1.3. Invisible ghost plays musical instrument. Hawaii: Dickey, 1917, 15.

E402.1.3.1. Ghost sounds conch shell. Hawaii: Beckwith, 1940, 349.

*E402.5. Ghost makes sound like a large tree crashing. Tuamotus: Stevenson, 1912, 132f.

*E402.6. Noises on haunted hill sound as if the hill were tumbling down. Hawaii: Fornander, 1918, V, 542.

*E402.7. Ghost glides a few inches above the ground. Tahiti: Stevenson, 1912, 140.

E410. The unquiet grave. Dead unable to rest in peace. (Cf. D2151.1.2.3.) (See also E200-E399 passim). Hawaii: Emerson, 1915, 236ff.; Fornander, 1918, V, 574ff.; Pukui, 1943, 60.

*E410.3. Multisectioned body of dead woman seen whole again and sitting upon her grave. N.Z.: White, 1887-90, II, 36.

*E412.2.3. Ghost fishes at night at a place he fished when alive. Societies: Agostini, 1900, 73.

E412.3. Dead without proper funeral rites cannot rest. Hawaii: Beckwith, 1940, 123, 199; Fornander, 1916, IV, 472; McAllister, 1933, 102; Thrum, 1907, 126; Westervelt, 1915, 9f.; Samoa: Stevenson, 1912, 137; Ellice Is.: Roberts, 1958, 413.

E413. Murdered person cannot rest in grave. Hawaii: Westervelt, 1915, 86f.

*E413.1. Spirits of murdered children follow their father's canoe. Tuamotus: Audran, 1918, 34.

E417. Dead person speaks from grave. Samoa: Hambruch, 1925, 112.

*E419.13. Corpse put out to sea on raft repeatedly found on shore at same place. Mangareva: Laval, 1938, 22, 45.

*E421.1.3.1. Dog faints at sign of ghost. Hawaii: Pukui, 1943, 61.

*E421.2.2. A quivering muscle or eyelid betrays the presence of a ghost. Hawaii: Westervelt, 1915, 251.

*E421.2.3. Ghost leaves black footprints on sand. Mangareva: Eskridge, 1931, 218.

E421.3. Luminous (blazing) ghost. Tuamotus: Stimson,

n.d., Z-G. 3/1353; Hawaii: Fornander, 1916, IV, 472, 530; Samoa: Stuebel, 1896, 151.

E421.3.2. Ghost as firebrand. Rarotonga: Te Ariki, 1920, 63.

*E421.6. Ghost as white mist. Hawaii: McAllister, 1933, 92.

E422. The living corpse. Revenant is not a specter but has the attributes of a living person. He wanders about till his "second death," complete disintegration in the grave. -- Tuamotus: Stimson, n.d., Z-G. 3/1353; Hawaii: Beckwith, 1940, 144; Samoa: Stair, 1896, 39; Rennell: Elbert-Monberg, 1964, No. 194.

*E422.0.2. Corpse of man who vowed to return to his native island will not sink (presumably it will drift there). Rennell: Elbert-Monberg, 1964, No. 224.

*E422.1.7.1. Revenant with long teeth. Societies: Henry, 1928, 380.

E422.1.8. Revenant with peculiar nails. N.Z.: Clark, 1896 , 161.

E422.1.11.4. Revenant as skeleton. N.Z.: Hongi, 1898, 39.

*E422.1.11.4.1. Revenant as skull. Societies: Henry, 1928, 380.

E422.1.11.5. Revenant as blood. Hawaii: Pukui, 1933, 165.

*E422.1.11.5.2. Revenants of the violently slain smell of blood. Ontong Java: Sarfert, 1931, 335.

*E422.1.11.6. Ghostly footsteps. Mangareva: Eskridge, 1931, 203.

*E422.1.12. Ghost as decayed corpse. Tuamotus: Stevenson, 1912, 132f.

*E422.1.13. Ghost accompanied by fragrant odor. Tahiti: Stevenson, 1912, 139f.

*E422.1.14. Ghost with four eyes. Santa Cruz: O'Ferral: 1904, 224.

1904, 224.

E422.2.4. Revenant black. Niue: Loeb, 1926, 87.

*E422.4.8. Spirits clothed in weeds, vines, and heliotrope.
Cooks: Gill, 1876, 156.

*E422.5. Bald-headed ghost. Hawaii: Fornander, 1918,
V, 422.

E423. Revenant in animal form. Hawaii: Luomala,
1951, 30ff.; Samoa: Stevenson, 1912, 129.

E423.1.1. Revenant as dog. See E521.2. Mangareva:
Eskridge, 1931, 202, 283f.; Hawaii: Jack Bryan,
"Pele's Phantom Dog Returns," Honolulu Star-Bulletin,
Vol. 38, No. 315 (Nov. 10, 1964), 1; Westervelt,
1915, 84, 96.

E423.2.8. Revenant as rat. Easter I.: Englert, 1939,
59.

*E423.2.8.1. Rat is "shadow" of ghosts. Societies:
Henry, 1928, 383.

E423.3. Revenant as bird. Tuamotus: Stevenson, 1912,
132; Rennell: Elbert-Monberg, 1964, No. 195a.

*E423.3.5.1. Owl is "shadow" of ghosts. Societies:
Henry, 1928, 384.

E423.3.6. Revenant as chicken. Tuamotus: Stevenson,
1912, 134f.

E423.7. Revenant as fly. N.Z.: Wohlers, 1876, 115.

*E423.10. Revenant as insect. Niue: Loeb, 1926, 171.

E425.1.3. Revenant as seductive woman. Marquesas:
Handy, 1930, 48.

*E425.4. Ghost appears in dream. Hawaii: Fornander,
1916, IV, 80; Westervelt, 1915, 9f.

*E431.21. Ghosts of the newly dead are ritually killed
by the community. Chatham Is.: Travers, 1876,
26.

*E431.22. Corpse whose ghost wanders is dug up, reinterred
face down. Cooks: Stevenson, 1912, 137.

*E434.1.1. Man saved from pursuing ghost when he arrives
   at sacred shrine. Hawaii: Beckwith, 1940, 199.

*E434.12. Green leaf tied to food carried at night
   prevents spirits attacking. Hawaii: Beckwith,
   1940, 144.

*E436.4. Test of whether being is ghost or not: a
   ghost casts no reflection in basin of water as do
   the living. Hawaii: *Beckwith, 1940, 145.

*E436.5. Test of whether being is ghost or not: leaves
   of ape plant put down. Living who tread plant
   tear it, dead do not. Hawaii: Beckwith,
   1940, 145, 445.

*E423.6. Test of whether being is ghost or not: some-
   thing done to startle it. If ghost, it disappears.
   Hawaii: Beckwith, 1940, 145.

*E439.11. Malignant spirit frightened away when woman
   exposes herself. Hawaii: Beckwith, 1940, 151;
   Fornander, 1916, IV, 482.

*E439.12. Storehouse built facing north and south in
   order that dead, going westward, will not pass throu
   N.Z.: *Clark, 1896, 2, 170 n.

*E439.13. Branch from a certain shrub protects against
   ghosts. Tonga: Collocott, 1928, 13.

E443.2.4. Ghost laid by priest. Samoa: Stair, 1896,
   49.

E443.3. Ghosts exorcized by name. Hawaii: Beckwith,
   1940, 442.

E446.2. Ghost laid by burning body. Hawaii: Fornander,
   1918, V, 530ff.

E452. Ghost laid at cock-crow (dawn). See also
   C311.1.8.1., and C842. Oceania: *Dixon, 1916, 141,
   n. 24; Hawaii: Beckwith, 1940, 480; N.Z.: Best,
   1924, 302.

*E459.8. Gost requited when shrine is built for his bones
   Hawaii: Beckwith, 1940, 123.

E461. Fight of revenant with living person. Lau Is.:
   St. Johnston, 1918, 89f.

E474. Cohabitation of living person and ghost. Easter I.: Métraux, 1940, 369; Marquesas: Handy, 1930, 35.

E474.1. Offspring of living and dead person. Mangareva: Laval, 1938, 25.

E480. Abode of the dead. Tokelaus: *Macgregor, 1937, 69.

E480.2. Three worlds of dead. Hawaii: Beckwith, 1932, 48; Beckwith, 1940, 124, 155, 160; Fornander, 1918, V, 572; Rice, 1923, 125.

*E480.2.1. Two spirit worlds. N.Z.: Best, 1924, 104, 314-315; Chatham Is.: Best, 1924, 314-315.

E481. Land of the dead. Oceania: **Rosalind Moss, The Life After Death in Oceania and the Malay Archipelago (Oxford, 1925); Mangareva: Laval, 1938, 302; Hawaii: Fornander, 1918, VI, 337; Westervelt, 1915, 99, 107; Tonga: Caillot, 1914, 245; N.Z.: White, 1887-90, IV, 129; Wohlers, 1876, 111; Reef Is.: O'Ferrall, 1904, 229; Rennell: Elbert-Monberg, 1964, No. 178.

E481.1. Land of the dead in lower world. Oceania: *A. Carrol, "Location of Bulutu, Burutu, or Pulotu," 1895, 153-154; Marquesas: Lavondes, 1964, 2, n. 2, 20; Cooks: *Beaglehole, 1938, 326ff.; Societies: Henry, 1928, 378; Hawaii: Beckwith, 1940, 146f.; Westervelt, 1915, 243; Samoa: Stuebel, 1896, 150; Tonga: Gifford, 1924, 183; Chatham Is.: Shand, 1894, 125; N.Z.: Cowan, 1930, I, 8, 17ff.; Grace, 1907, 56f., 251.

E481.1.1. Old woman ruler of dead in lower world. Mangareva: Caillot, 1914, 154; Cooks: Gill, 1876, 130, 228f.; Hawaii: Westervelt, 1915, 106; Tonga: Collocott, 1928, 17; Samoa: Stuebel, 1896, 150; N.Z.: Best, 1925, 768, 944ff.; Cowan, 1930, I, 52f.; Grace, 1907, 251; Karaeke, 1898, 59.

E481.1.2. Houses in lower world of dead. Tuamotus: Stimson, n.d., Z-G. 3/1174; N.Z.: Best, 1924, 104.

E481.2. Land of dead across water. Samoa: Stair, 1896, 39; N.Z.: Grace, 1907, 250f.

E481.2.0.1. Island of the dead. Hawaii: Beckwith, 1940, 72; Emory, 1924, 12, 13, 14; Fornander, 1916, IV, 476, 486; Ellice Is.: Roberts, 1958, 368.

E481.2.2. Boat to land of dead. N.Z.: Grace, 1907, 251.

E481.3.2. Abode of the dead in stones. Easter I.: Englert, 1939, 59.

E481.4. Beautiful land of dead. Mangareva: Caillot, 1914, 154; Societies: Agostini, 1900, 83f.; Hawaii: Pukui-Curtis, n.d., 18; Thrum, 1907, 49f.; Niue: Smith, 1902, 197; Fijis: *Fison, 1904, 163.

*E481.4.1.1. A god's mouth forms the portal to land of the happy dead. Mangareva: Laval, 1938, 302.

E481.6.2. Land of dead in west. Cooks: Gill, 1876, 159f.; Samoa: Gill, 1876, 159-160; Stair, 1896, 39; N.Z.: Cowan, 1930, I, 48.

E481.8. Land of dead in sky. Cooks: Beckwith, 1940, 76; Ontong Java: Sarfert, 1931, 323.

E481.8.2. Moon as land of dead. Samoa: Clark, 1896, 181; Lester, 1892, 51; Tokelaus: Macgregor, 1937, 69; Smith, 1920, 147.

E481.9. King (ruler) of world of dead. Hawaii: Beckwith, 1932, 48; Fornander, 1918, VI, 268; Green, 1926, 81; Thrum, 1907, 18, 49; Westervelt, 1915, 104, 179, 215ff.; Tonga: Collocott, 1928, 16, 17.

*E481.10. Land of dead beneath the sea. Hawaii: Fornander, 1918, V, 186; Samoa: Sierich, 1902, 179; N.Z.: Cowan, 1930, I, 48, 50.

*E481.10.1. Dead souls enter sea at a blow hole. Chatham Is.: Skinner, 1923, 60.

*E481.11. Guide of souls in land of dead. Mangareva: Hiroa, 1938, 426; Laval, 1938, 304; Hawaii: Beckwith, 1932, 50.

*E489.3.1. Dead buried with objects to propiate god of shades. Cooks: *Gill, 1876, 170.

E489.5. Dancing in afterworld. Cooks: Gill, 1876, 164.

*E489.5.1. Spirits in land of dead dance around newly

departed dead for ten days. Reef Is.: O'Ferrall, 1904, 229.

*E489.12. Souls of dead return to the mythical homeland of the race. N.Z.: Best, 1925, 681.

E490. Meetings of the dead. Hawaii: Westervelt, 1915, 4, 248; N.Z.: Best, 1925, 996.

E491. Procession of the dead (Marchers of the Night). Hawaii: Beckwith, 1932, 198ff., 200; *Beckwith, 1940, 164, 164 n. 59, 343; Thrum, 1907, 48; Westervelt, 1915, 131, 251.

*E491.1. Natural distrubances accompany ghost marchers. Hawaii: Beckwith, 1932, 199.

E493. Dead men dance. Marquesas: Stevenson, 1912, 31; Societies: Henry, 1928, 225.

E499.1. Gay banquet of the dead. Hawaii: Beckwith, 1932, 200; Westervelt, 1915, 247.

*E499.6. Souls of eight priests run a race. Owner of winning soul may pick island for himself. Ontong Java: Sarfert, 1931, 297.

*E502.1. Places of men who fall in battle at once filled by warriors from shades. Cooks: Gill, 1876, 287.

*E503. Phantom armies. Cooks: Gill, 1876, 224; Hawaii: Beckwith, 1940, 391; N.Z.: Cowan, 1921, 147.

*E510.1. Drowned seamen, covered with sea-weed,man boat. Tuamotus: Stimson, n.d., Z-G. 13/441.

E521.2. Ghost of dog. Mangareva: Eskridge, 1931, 202, 283f.; Hawaii: Jack Bryan, "Pele's Phantom Dog Returns," Honolulu Star Bulletin, Vol. 38, No. 315 (Nov. 10, 1964), 1; Beckwith, 1940,137, 346; Westervelt, 1915, 96; N.Z.: Best, 1925, 895; Gudgeon, 1905, 190.

E523. Ghost of fish. Tuamotus: Stimson, n.d., T-G. 3;912; Hawaii: Pukui, 1933, 177.

E524. Ghost of bird. Hawaii: Green, 1926, 109.

*E525. Spirit of louse. Easter I.: Métraux, 1940, 375.

*E526. Ghost of snake. Rennell: Elbert-Monberg, 1964, No. 56b.

E535.3. Ghost ship. Societies: Henry, 1928, 512.

E535.3.1. Phantom canoe. N.Z.: Cowan, 1930, 10, 148f.

E535.3.2. Phantom boat. Societies: Henry, 1928, 91.

*E540.1. Dead carry on as if alive. Hawaii: Fornander, 1916, IV, 490; 1918, V, 574.

E541. Revenants eat. Marquesas: Handy, 1930, 42; Fornander, 1916, IV, 490.

E541.1. Food placed out for returning souls of dead. Hawaii: Rice, 1923, 97.

E541.2. Ghost eats living human beings. Rotuma: Churchward, 1938-39, 118; Kapingamarangi: Emory, 1949, 237.

*E541.6. Ghosts feed on butterflies (moths). Hawaii: Beckwith, 1919, 337, 612; Westervelt, 1915, 103, 247 .

    E752.7.1. Abandoned souls feed on spiders and night moths.

E545. The dead speak. Cooks: Te Ariki, 1920, 63.

E545.3. Dead announce own death. Mangareva: Caillot, 1914, 202; Cooks: Beaglehole, 1938, 385, 409; Large, 1903, 135; Hawaii: Fornander, 1916, IV, 472; 1918, V, 190ff.; McAllister, 1933, 102; Pukui, 1933, 165; Thrum, 1907, 126, 131, 143; Westervelt, 1915, 87; Tonga: Collocott, 1928, 19, 38; N.Z.: Cowan, 1930, I, 166f.; Grace, 1907, 171; White, 1887-90, IV, 59; Rennell: Elbert-Monberg, 1964, Nos. 56b, 199.

*E545.3.1. Corpse placed in canoe drifts to spot where are his brothers. Bellona: Elbert-Monberg, 1964, No. 141.

E575. Ghost as omen of calamity. N.Z.: Cowan, 1930, 10, 148f.

254

E587.3. Ghosts walk from curfew to cockcrow. Hawaii: Fornander, 1916, IV, 548.

E587.6. Ghosts walk at full moon. Hawaii: Beckwith, 1940, 198.

*E587.7. Ghost appear on certain sacred nights. Hawaii: *Beckwith, 1940, 164 n. 59.

*E587.8. Spirits follow the sun. Cooks: Gill, 1876, 156, 158.

*E589. Ghost moves through tops of trees. Tuamotus: Stevenson 1912, 132.

E593.5. Ghost steals food and treasure. Hawaii: Beckwith, 1940, 123.

*E599.14. Ghosts cause dreams. Niue: Loeb, 1926, 165.

*E599.14.1. Dead eel communicates with woman in dream. Tahiti: Beckwith, 1940, 103.

E600--E699. Reincarnation

E605. Reincarnation in another human form. Hawaii: Pukui, 1933, 155; N.Z.: Cowan, 1930, I, 160f., 162f.

E605.2. Reincarnation: god reborn as man. Marquesas: Handy, 1930, 109; Hawaii: Beckwith, 1940, 119.

E605.4. Reincarnation: man becomes spirit. Hawaii: Beckwith, 1940, 109.

E607.2.1. Person is swallowed and then reborn. Marquesas: Steinen, 1933-34, 29, 31.

E607.2.2. Rebirth by crawling into woman's womb. (Idea present in Maui story, though hero fails at accomplishment.) N.Z.: Best, 1924, 148.

*E607.2.3. Rebirth by passing through intestines of goddess of death and her followers. Cooks: Gill, 1876, 162.

*E607.2.4. Rebirth in stages: head of god impregnates his mother three times. Each time, a section of his body is reborn. Marquesas: Handy, 1930, 109.

E607.3. Hauling canoe over dead man's body causes return from dead in new form. N.Z.: Dixon, 1916, 55.

E610. Reincarnation as animal. Societies: Henry, 1928, 390; N.Z.: Best, 1925, 1042ff.

E610.1. Reincarnation: man to animal to man. Hawaii: Beckwith, 1940, 480.

E612.13. Reincarnation as rat. Hawaii: Beckwith, 1940, 480.

E613. Reincarnation as bird. Societies: Caillot, 1914, 121f.; Hawaii: Thrum, 1923, 148, 181f.; Westervelt, 1915, 206f., 223f.; Niue: Loeb, 1926, 110; N.Z.: Best, 1925, 960; Cowan, 1930, I, 241f.; Grace, 1907, 86: Rennell: Elbert-Monberg 1964, Nos. 2a, 2b; Ontong Java: Parkinson, 1898, 197.

E613.1. Reincarnation as duck. Hawaii: Westervelt, 1915, 252.

E613.2. Reincarnation as owl. Hawaii: Beckwith, 1940, 123; Fornander, 1916, IV, 598; V, 574; Thrum, 1921, 112; Westervelt, 1915, 115, 252.

E613.12. Reincarnation as parrot. Niue: Loeb, 1926, 152.

*E613.13. Reincarnation as stork. Tahiti: Henry, 1928, 222.

*E613.14. Spirit of dead woman incarnated in a cormorant. N.Z.: Best, 1925, 975f.

E614.1. Reincarnation as snake. Tonga: Gifford, 1924, 19 (sea-snake).

E614.2. Reincarnation as lizard. Tonga: Gifford, 1924, 108.

E614.4. Reincarnation as tortoise (turtle). Easter I.: Métraux, 1940, 372; Hawaii: Smith, 1955, 37; Tonga: Collocott, 1928, 9.

*E614.6. Reincarnation as a dragon-like monster. Hawaii: *Westervelt, 1915, 252, 255ff.; N.Z.: Best, 1925, 960ff.

256

E616. Reincarnation as insect. N.Z.: Best, 1925, 1042ff.; Wohlers, 1876, 111f.

*E616.6. Reincarnation as fly. Chatham Is.: Shand, 1895, 211.

E617. Reincarnation as fish. Societies: Henry, 1928, 389, 438; Cooks: Gill, 1876, 29; Hawaii: Beckwith, 1940, 479; N.Z.: Grace, 1907, 153ff.

E617.3. Reincarnation as shark. Easter I.: Métraux, 1940, 319; Societies: Caillot, 1914, 133; Henry, 1928, 389, 624; Hawaii: Beckwith, 1940, 128; Emerson, 1915, 160; Fornander, 1918, V, 574; Green, 1926, 75; Thrum, 1923, 149; Westervelt, 1915, 115, 252; Tonga: Collocott,1928, 56; Rennell: Elbert-Monberg, 1964, No. 125a.

E617.4. Reincarnation as whale. N.Z.: Best, 1928b, 262.

*E617.5. Reincarnation as dolphin. Societies: Henry, 1928, 390.

*E617.6. Reincarnation as eel. Tuamotus: Stimson, n.d., Z-G. 3/1295, Z-G. 13/10; Hawaii: Beckwith, 1940, 511; Fornander, 1918, V, 574; Pukui, 1933, 182.

E629.2. Reincarnation as crab. Tuamotus: Seurat, 1905, 483.

*E629.3. Reincarnation as merman. N.Z.: Best, 1925, 960, 968.

E630. Reincarnation in object. N.Z.: Best, 1925, 1042ff.

E631. Reincarnation in plant (tree) growing from grave. Easter I.: Métraux, 1940, 376; Marquesas: Steinen, 1933-34, 368; Handy, 1930, 39; Hawaii: Beckwith, 1940, 478, 523; Fornander, 1918, V, 582; Green, 1923, 34; Pukui, 1933, 141ff., 180; Westervelt, 1915, 63f.

E631.0.1. Twining branches grow from graves of lovers. Rotuma: Churchward, 1937-38, 365.

E631.1. Flower from grave. Marquesas: Lavondes, 1964, 80.

*E631.5.4. Reincarnation of deformed child as taro plant. Hawaii: Beckwith, 1940, 298.

*E631.5.5. Reincarnation as gourd vine. Hawaii: Beckwith, 1940, 99.

*E631.5.6. Reincarnation as kava plant. Rotuma: Churchward, 1938-39, 465; Tonga: Gifford, 1924, 75.

*E631.5.7. Reincarnation as banana plants. Rotuma: Churchward, 1938-39, 116; Russell, 1942, 245.

E631.6. Reincarnation in tree from grave. Easter I.: Metraux, 1940, 376; Hawaii: Beckwith, 1940, 108; Tokelaus: Macgregor, 1937, 81.

*E632.2. Speaking bones. N.Z.: Grey, 1855, 101.

*E636.0.1. Reincarnation as clouds. Cooks: Gill, 1876, 163.

E642. Reincarnation as stone. N.Z.: Gudgeon, 1906, 34.

*E647. Reincarnation as stars. Tokelaus: Smith, 1920, 147.

E649.1. Reincarnation as hill. Hawaii: Beckwith, 1940, 188.

E670. Repeated reincarnation. Marquesas: Handy, 1930, 106; Hawaii: Beckwith, 1940, 279.

*E690.0.1. Breath of dying person inhaled by spiritual heir. Polynesia: *Smith, 1921, 26.

258

E700. The Soul (life principle). Bellona: Elbert-Monberg, 1964, Nos. 1a, 1b.

E710. External soul. A person (often a giant or ogre) keeps his soul or life separate from the rest of his body. Tuamotus: Stimson, n.d., Z-G. 13/174; Hawaii: Westervelt, 1915, 92f.

E711. Soul kept in object. Easter I.: Englert, 1939, 17; Tuamotus: Stimson, 1934, 19; Hawaii: Thrum, 1923, 176; Tokelaus: Burrows, 1923, 160.

E711.2. Soul in plant. Hawaii: Fornander, 1918, V, 140.

E711.2.1. Soul in calabash (gourd). Hawaii: Beckwith, 1940, 145.

*E711.16. Soul in belt (loincloth). N.Z.: Best, 1925, 954; Rennell: Elbert-Monberg, 1964, No. 110; Tikopia: Firth, 1961, 136.

E712.6. Soul hidden in fish basket. Samoa: Beckwith, 1940, 200.

E712.7. Soul hidden in water bottle. Tuamotus: Stimson, n.d., z-G. 13/174.

*E712.8. Soul hidden in hat. Tuamotus: Stimson, n.d., Z-G. 3/1174.

E714.1. Soul (life) in the blood. Cooks: Beckwith, 1940, 131; Tonga: Gifford, 1924, 185.

E714.3. Soul in head. Cooks: Large, 1903, 135.

*E714.7.2. Demon's supernatural power resides in his fingernails. Tuamotus: Stimson, n.d., Z-G. 13/301.

*E714.7.3. Soul of winged monster in claws. N.Z.: Pakauwera, 1894, 103.

E714.12. Soul in hair. Hawaii: Beckwith, 1919, 560; Fornander, 1916, IV, 446.

*E714.14. Soul in tail. Hawaii: Beckwith, 1940, 491.

*E714.15. Soul in tongue, which lives after rest of
body dies. Hawaii: Green, 1926, 103.

E715.1. Separable soul in bird. Hawaii: Beckwith,
1940, 442.

E720.1. Souls of human beings seen in dreams. Rennell:
Elbert-Monberg, 1964, No. 199.

E721. Soul journeys from the body. Hawaii: Beckwith,
1919, 366; Fornander, 1916, IV, 532; Thrum, 1906,
136f.; Thrum, 1907, 59; Westervelt, 1915, 204;
Tonga: Gifford, 1924, 154; Tokelaus: Burrows,
1923,160; N.Z.: White, 1887-90, II, 155;
Bellona: Elbert-Monberg, 1964, No. 149.

*E721.0.2. Spirit leaves body during sneezing. (Customar
saying by bystander: "A, kua oki mai kow" -- Ha!
You have come back.) Cooks: Gill, 1876, 177.

E721.1. Soul wanders from body in sleep. Dreams
explained as experiences of the soul on these
wanderings. Easter I.: Englert, 1939, 23f.;
Metraux, 1940, 56, 363; Marquesas: Handy, 1930,
81; Hawaii: Beckwith, 1940, 144, 173f., 177,
*Chap. XI passim, 517; Emerson, 1915, 3; Rice,
1923, 129; Cooks: Beaglehole, 1938, 325; N.Z."
Best, 1925, 716; Fijis: Hocart, 1929, 185.

E721.1.2. Soul of sleeper prevented from returning to
his body. Cooks: Beaglehole, 1938, 326;
Hawaii: Beckwith, 1940, 174; Samoa: Stuebel,
1896, 147; Tokelaus: Macgregor, 1937, 59.

*E721.1.2.6. Hero instructs that his body is not to be
touched while he sojourns to land of dead. He
returns to find it buried. Tonga: Gifford, 1924,
154.

*E721.1.2.7. Spirit of sorcerer peering into calabash
of water caught and destroyed. Hawaii: Thrum,
1907, 129; Westervelt, 1915, 92f.

E721.2. Body in trance while soul is absent. Societies:
Henry, 1928, 220.

*E721.2.1. Spirit ordered to return to body of person in
trance. Societies: Henry, 1928, 221.

*E721.4.1. Wandering souls of sleepers netted and killed
by spirits. Samoa: Stuebel, 1896, 147.

*E721.6.1. Soul balances upon oscillating stone in underworld: if it trips, soul cannot return to earth. Cooks: Beaglehole, 1938, 328-329.

E721.7. Soul leaves body to visit hell (heaven). Hawaii: Thrum, 1907, 59ff., 76; Westervelt, 1915, 195; Tonga: Gifford, 1924, 154.

E721.10. Soul takes voyage. Cooks: Beckwith, 1940, 157.

*E721.11. Souls of sleepers fight. When soul killed, sleeper sickens and dies. Cooks: Beaglehole, 1938, 325.

*E721.12. While a man's soul is in other world, a bird pecks out one of his eyes. Lau Is.: St. Johnston, 1918, 44.

E722.2.11. Soul leaves body through eye. Hawaii: Beckwith, 1940, 144; Westervelt, 1915, 100, 232.

*E722.2.13. Spirit returns to body through incision in great toe. Hawaii: Rice, 1923, 15.

*E722.2.14. Heron as fetcher of souls. Societies: Beckwith, 1940, 110.

*E722.3.0.1. Soul purged of earthly associations after death. Fijis: Beckwith, 1940, 157.

E722.3.1.1. Soul remains about dead body. Futuna: Burrows, 1936, 104.

E722.3.2. Soul wanders until corpse decays. Societies: Henry, 1928, 222.

*E723.7.9. Wraith of man copulates with woman. Mangareva: Hiroa, 1938, 325; Hawaii: Fornander, 1916, IV, 546.

*E723.9. Wraith takes long voyage and secures forgotten item. Mangareva: Hiroa, 1938, 26; Laval, 1938, 13.

E725.1. Soul leaves man's body and enters animal's. Marquesas: Handy, 1930, 103; Societies: Henry, 1928, 222; Cooks: Beckwith, 1940, 131.

*E725.2.2. Twins possessed by devils. Tonga: Gifford, 1924, 192.

E726. Soul enters body and animates it. Tuamotus: Stimson, n.d., Z-G. 13/420; Marquesas: Handy, 1930, 103; Samoa: *Beckwith, 1940, 150.

E726.3. Soul reunited with body. Societies: Henry, 1928, 222; Cooks: Gill, 1876, 160; Samoa: *Beckwith, 1940, 150.

*E728.0.1. People possessed by ghosts die. Societies: Henry, 1928, 380.

E732. Soul in form of bird. Easter I.: Metraux, 1940, 375; Marquesas: Handy, 1930, 36, 103; Societies: Henry, 1928, 222.

E733.1. Soul in form of serpent. Oceanic: *Dixon, 1916, 119.

E734. Soul in form of insect. Hawaii: Westervelt, 1915, 100.

E734.1. Soul in form of butterfly. Hawaii: Beckwith, 1940, 148; Dixon, 1916, 76; N.Z.: Best, 1924, 299.

E734.5. Soul in form of cricket. Cooks: Gill, 1876, 162.

E741.1. Soul in form of star. Tokelaus: Smith, 1920, 147.

*E741.2. Spirit of pet shark of gods placed in the Milky Way. Hawaii: Beckwith, 1940, 436.

E742.2. Soul as will-o-the-wisp. N.Z.: Best, 1925, 877.

*E744.4. Soul as drop of rain. Easter I.: Métraux, 1940, 375.

E745.4. Soul as flower. Hawaii: Beckwith, 1940, 17.

*E745.7. Soul as tree. Hawaii: Beckwith, 1940, 478.

E750. Perils of the soul. Cooks: Beaglehole, 1938, 328; Fijis: Beckwith, 1940, 158.

E750.1. Souls wander after death. Hawaii: Beckwith, 1940, 124, 157; Reef Is.: O'Ferrall, 1904, 229;

Nukumanu: Sarfert, 1931, 337.

*E750.1.0.1. Souls of dead must wander through nine
lower heavens until they arrive at the tenth
heaven. Nukumanu: Sarfert, 1931, 331.

*E750.1.2. Desolate spirits must wander until some
guardian (aumakua) takes pity on them. Hawaii:
*Beckwith, 1940, 154.

E750.2.3. Branching tree as roadway for souls. Cooks:
Te Ariki, 1920, 109; Gill, 1876, 160 f., 170;
Hawaii: Beckwith, 1932, 50ff.; *Beckwith, 1940,
154, 155, 156, 156 n. 35, 36, 37, 157 n. 38, 40,
158; Westervelt, 1915, 18, 245f.

*E750.2.3.1. Souls of children cling to tree on
roadway of souls. Fijis: Beckwith, 1940, 158.

*E750.2.4. Souls in peril from big fish. Reef Is.:
O'Ferrall, 1904, 229.

*E750.2.5. Dragon is obstacle to souls going to land of
the dead. Hawaii: Westervelt, 1915, 247.

*E750.2.6. Great caterpillar is obstacle to souls
going to land of the dead. Hawaii: Westervelt,
1915, 247.

*E750.2.7. Souls who do not know proper incantations
are thrown into dark spirit world. Hawaii:
Westervelt, 1915, 105.

*E750.2.8. Souls must pass between two spirits which
destroy the clumsy. N.Z.: Wohlers, 1876, 111.

*E750.5. Leaping-off place whence souls enter underworld.
Marquesas: Handy, 1930, n. 19, 120; Societies:
Henry, 1928, 563-564; Cooks: Gill, 1876, 159;
Hawaii: *Beckwith, 1940, 156 f.; Emerson,
1915, 100; Fornander, 1918, V, 544; McAllister,
1933, 125f.; Pukui, 1943, 60; Thrum, 1907, 50;
Westervelt, 1915, 101, 246; Hawaii, Fijis, N.Z.,
Chatham Is.: *Editor (S. Percy Smith) "Notes and
Queries," JPS XII (1903), 131; Tonga: Collocott,
1928, 12; Samoa: Stair, 1896, 39; N.Z.: Cowan,
1930, I, 48; Westervelt, 1915, 243; *Taylor White,
"Te Reinga," JPS VII (1898), 178ff.; Lau Is.:
St. Johnston, 1918, 29.

*E750.6. Spirits depart in bands for lower world upon
day of solstice. Cooks: Gill, 1876, 158.

*E750.7. Souls of those newly dead can move only in the
direction they are guided. Hawaii: Westervelt,
1915, 102f.

*E751.8. Souls who wander to land without protection
of guide are repulsed with thunder and lightning.
Ontong Java: Sarfert, 1931, 323.

E752. Lost souls. Tokelaus: Macgregor, 1937, 69.

E752.1. Soul in jeopardy after leaving body. Tuamotus:
Caillot, 1914, 63; Tuamotus, Societies: Stevenson,
1912, 134f.; Hawaii: Westervelt, 1943, 15.

*E752.1.3.1. Albinos who inhabit lower nine of ten
sky-worlds seek to destroy souls which ascend to
tenth heaven. Nukumanu: Sarfert, 1931, 331.

E752.2. Soul carried off by demon (devil). Easter I.:
Métraux, 1930, 375; Mangareva: Hiroa, 1938, 371,
373; Hawaii: Emerson, 1915, 75, 237; Tokelaus:
Burrows, 1923, 160, 172; Macgregor, 1937, 62, 69,
80; Lau Is.: St. Johnston, 1918, 115; Rennell:
Elbert-Monberg, 1964, Nos. 110,113, 177; Bellona:
ibid., Nos. 1a, 1b.

*E752.2.1. Soul fisher: god lets down fishhook on
string (from heaven) and hooks a man's soul.
Marquesas: Handy, 1930, 133 f.

*E752.2.2. Souls of dead captured in net,(usually
destined for underworld) or captured by god. Cooks:
Beaglehole, 1938, 328-329, 331; Gill, 1876, 161,
166, 169; Hawaii: Beckwith, 1940, 480;
Pukui-Curtis, n.d., 37; Westervelt, 1915, 243;
Tokelaus: Macgregor, 1937, 61; Chatham Is.:
Shand, 1894, 125; N.Z.: Best, 1925, 944; Cowan,
1930, I, 55; Lau Is.: St. Johnston, 1918, 62.

*E752.2.3. God of wind entangles souls of enemies of
chief. Hawaii: Beckwith, 1940, 121.

*E752.2.4. Spirit of ogress becomes like a cobweb
in shaman's hands. Tuamotus: Stimson, n.d., Z-G.
3/1386.

E752.7.1. Abandoned souls feed on spiders and night moths
Hawaii: Beckwith, 1940, 154; McAllister, 1933, 126
Thrum, 1907, 49; Pukui, 1943, 61; Chatham Is.:
Skinner, 1923, 57.

    E541.6. Ghosts feed on spiders, moths and
    other insects.

*E752.7.2. Dead given bowl of centipedes to eat.
Cooks: Gill, 1876, 173.

*E752.7.3. Rats gnaw heads of bad men who have not
died in battle. Niue: Loeb, 1926, 144.

E752.9. Souls of wicked eaten by deity. Easter I.:
Métraux, 1940; Cooks: Gill, 1876, 170.

*E752.9.1. Souls of dead eaten by gods (sometimes cooked
and eaten). Tuamotus, Societies: Stevenson,
1912, 134f.; Rarotonga: Te Ariki, 1920, 63;
Cooks: Gill, 1876, 160 n. 1; Hawaii: Beckwith,
1940, 110; Thrum, 1907, 49.

*E752.10.0.1. Soul defiled when corpse defiled.
Niue: Loeb, 1926, 144.

*E752.11. Souls become houseposts or fence palings of god
of otherworld. Tonga: Reiter, 1907, 239; Samoa:
Stair, 1896, 36.

*E752.12. Dead with torn bodies drift around upon the
sea. Nukumanu: Sarfert, 1931, 337.

*E752.14. Souls impaled upon stakes if living kin do
not perform necessary rites. Ellice Is.:
Grimble, 1952, 62.

*E752.15. Souls imprisoned in baskets. Samoa: Krämer,
1902, I, 123f.; Tokelaus: Burrows, 1923, 160.

*E752.16. Soul captured and confined in a calabash.
Hawaii: Emerson, 1915, 237.

*E752.17. Soul captured and confined in loin-cloth.
Hawaii: Emerson, 1915, 72.

*E754.2.0.2. Elysium of warriors. Cooks: *Gill, 1876,
162ff.

*E754.8. Souls of dead warriors ascend mountain on path
of spears and clubs by which warriors were slain.
Cooks: Gill, 1876, 163.

*E754.9. Dead warriors leap from mountain into sky
(where they become clouds). Cooks: Gill, 1876, 163.

*E754.10. Souls of dead become guardians of the living.
Hawaii: Fornander, 1918, V, 574.

*E755.0.4. Souls go to an enchanted island. Lau Is.:
St. Johnston, 1918, 42.

*E755.0.5. Guardian of gate leading to world of dead
siezes spirits having to pass through and takes
them before ruler. Tuamotus: Stimson, n.d.,
T-G. 3/1001.

E755.1.1. Heavenly hierarchy. N.Z.: Clark, 1896, 182.

*E755.1.1.1. Afterworld to which man goes determined by
status of his family's guardian spirit. Hawaii:
Beckwith, 1940, 161.

*E755.1.5. Springs in otherworld which wash away souls'
memories of life on earth. Cooks: Beaglehole,
1938, 329.

E755.2. Souls in hell (Hades). Mangareva: Caillot,
1914, 154; Laval, 1938, 303, 304; Marquesas:
Thrum, 1907, 18, 50; Societies: Stevenson, 1912,
141; Hawaii: Beckwith, 1932, 48; McAllister, 1933
126; Thrum, 1907, 18, 50; Westervelt, 1915, 89;
N.Z.: Thrum, 1907, 18, 50; Futuna: Burrows,
1936, 104; Rennell: Elbert-Monberg, 1964, No. 171.

*E755.2.4.2. Ever-glowing oven of goddess of death in
which souls are cooked. Cooks: Gill, 1876, 161.

*E755.2.10. Spirits use man's eyes as lamps in
otherworld. (Cf. F163.3.2.). Societies: Beckwith,
1940, 251.

*E755.2.11. Dead submerged in lake of fresh water where
they wriggle like fish. Cooks: Gill, 1876, 161.

*E759.3. Person steals another's soul. Samoa, Tokelau:
Beckwith, 1940, 150, 200.

E761.3. Life token: tree (flower) fades. Polynesia:
*Dixon, 1916, 234, n. 46.; Hawaii: Fornander, 1918
V, 278.

*E761.1.14. Life token: blood spurts on hero's breast
when his rooster is killed. Marquesas: Steinen,
1934-35, 234.

*E761.1.15. Life token: after brother's death, girl stick
reed into ground -- blood gushes forth. Tonga: Gifl
1924, 185.

266

E765.3.3. Life bound up with tree. Chatham Is.: Travers, 1877, 22; N.Z.: Best, 1906, 25; Clark, 1896, 186.

E765.3.5. Man's magic contains his life essence. Hawaii: Beckwith, 1940, 541.

E765.4.7. Man dies when tortoise shell is dug up. Tonga: Gifford, 1924, 52.

*E773. Vital feathers. Hawaii: Westervelt, 1915, 71.

E780. Vital bodily members. They possess life independent of the rest of the body. Rotuma: Churchward, 1938-39, 120.

*E780.1.1. Vital body: person's body reassembles itself and he cannot be killed. Tuamotus: Audran, 1919, 237; Hawaii: Fornander, 1916, IV, 70; Kapingamarangi: Elbert, 1949, 240f.

E781. Eyes successfully replaced. Tuamotus: Stimson, 1934, 68; Hawaii: Beckwith, 1940, 200.

*E782.0.1. Man has himself killed and cut in two so that his legs and buttocks may be affixed to body of murdered king which lacks these members. Tonga: Gifford, 1924, 31.

*E782.0.2. Two men exchange the calves of their legs. Marquesas: Lavondes, 1964, 4ff.

*E782.1.2. Vital hands exist without body. N.Z.: Cowan, 1930, 52.

*E782.5.1. Vital tongue. Hawaii: Beckwith, 1940, 139.

E783. Vital head. Retains life after being cut off. (See D1641.7.1. Self-rolling head.). Mangareva: Hiroa, 1938, 32; Hawaii: Westervelt, 1915, 105; Fijis: Hocart, 1929, 215; N.Z.: Cowan, 1930, 52.

E783.1. Head cut off and successfully replaced. Tonga: Gifford, 1924, 205.

E783.2. Severed head grows. Tuamotus: Henry, 1928, 620; Seurat, 1905, 485; Hawaii: McAllister, 1933, 119; N.Z.: White, 1887-90, II, 47.

E783.5. Vital head speaks. Mangareva: Hiroa, 1938, 358 Marquesas: Handy, 1930, 106; Cooks: Te Ariki, 1920, 126; Large, 1903, 135; Tahiti: Beckwith, 1940, 266; Hawaii: Fornander, 1916, IV, 70, 564ff Samoa: Beckwith, 1940, 473; Krämer, 1902, 122ff.

*E783.5.2. Vital heads serve as guards. Hawaii: Westervelt, 1915, 105.

E783.6. Headless body vital. Tonga: Gifford, 1924, 205; N.Z.: Best, 1925, 998; Rennell: Elbert-Monberg, 1964, No. 82.

*E784.1. A whole shark grows from its vital tongue. Hawaii: Pukui, 1943, 58.

*E786.1. Vital heart. Tokelaus: Macgregor, 1937, 88; Societies: Henry, 1928, 554-555.

*E789.3. Vital knee. Rotuma: Churchward, 1938-39, 119.

*E789.5. A lizard-woman is burned. Her scales come individually to life and attempt to escape the flames. N.Z.: Wohlers, 1876, 117.

*E795. Priests worship soul until it is strong enough to take on human form. Hawaii: Beckwith, 1940, 480.

F. MARVELS

F0--F199. OTHER WORLD JOURNEYS

F0. Journey to other world. Tonga: Collocott, 1928, 37.

F1. Journey to otherworld as dream or vision. Futuna: Burrows, 1936, 226.

F10--F79. The upper world

F10. Journey to upper world. Marquesas: Steinen, 1934-35, 217; Tuamotus: Stimson, 1937, 50ff.; Hawaii: Beckwith, 1919, 336, 554, 580; Samoa: Hambruch, 1914-15, 286; Krämer, 1902, I, 385, 416; Stuebel, 1896, 145; Tokelaus: Burrows, 1923, 166; Chatham Is.: Shand, 1898, 74; N.Z., Hawaii: *Smith, JPS supplement to VI (1897), 23; 1921, 26; N.Z.: White, 1887-90, I, 56f., 58, 59, 63ff., 100ff., 112ff., 116f., 125; III, 107; Wohlers, 1875, 8; Rotuma: Churchward, 1937-38, 251; Tikopia: Firth, 1961, 55.

F12. Journey to see deity. Usually to the upper world. Tuamotus: Stimson, n.d., T-G. 3/79.

F15. Visit to star-world. Reef Is.: O'Ferrall, 1904, 231; Riesenfeld, 1950, 129.

F16. Visit to land of moon. Tuamotus: Seurat, 1905, 434; N.Z.: White, 1887-90, II, 22; Ellice Is.: Roberts, 1958, 368; Nukumanu: Sarfert, 1931, 331f.

F17. Visit to land of the sun. Hawaii: Beckwith, 1919, 566; Samoa: Krämer, 1902, I, 133; N.Z.: White, 1887-90, II, 22.

F32. God visits earth. Hawaii: Beckwith, 1940, 3.

F32.1. God descends to found royal dynasty. Tonga: Gifford, 1924, 28.

269

F51. Sky-rope. Access to upper world by means of a rope. Oceania: *Beckwith, 1940, 255; *Dixon, 1916 66, 156f., 160; Tonga: Gifford, 1924, 20; Tokelaus: Burrows, 1923, 167; N.Z.: White, 1887-90, I, 123; Wohlers, 1875, 18f.

F51.1.1. Spider-web sky-rope. Spider makes web on which ascent or descent is accomplished. Oceania: Dixon, 1916, 59, 66; Hawaii: Beckwith, 1919, 556; Beckwith, 1940, 254f., 530; Smith JPS supplement to VI (1897), 24; Chatham Is.: Shand, 1898, 74; N.Z.: Best, 1924, 212; Best, 1925, 912ff.; Clark, 1896, 163f.; Cowan, 1930, I, 25; White, 1887-90, I, 57, 59; II, 90.

> *F77.3. Spider transports people from upper world.

F51.1.2. Vine as sky-rope. N.Z.: Cowan, 1930, I, 22; Grey, 1855, 71.

F51.2. Sky-basket. Ascent to or descent from upper world in basket. N.Z.: Best, 1924, 212; Rotuma: Russell, 1942, 247.

*F51.3. Ascent to upper world on platform. Rotuma: Chruchward, 1937-38, 367; 1938-39, 124f.; Nukumanu Sarfert, 1931, 449; Reef Is.: Riesenfeld, 1950, 129.

F54. Tree to upper world. Tuamotus: Stimson, 1934, 68; Marquesas: Steinen, 1933-34, 373; Cooks: *Te Ariki, 1921, 4f.; Hawaii: Beckwith, 1940, 232; Tonga: Beckwith, 1940, 482; Caillot, 1914, 259, n. 2; Collocott, 1924, 279; Gifford, 1924, 25, 39; Reiter, 1933, 356; Samoa: Beckwith, 1940, 486; Hambruch, 1914-15, 284; Powell-Pratt, 1891-93, 278; Tokelaus: Burrows, 1923, 168f.; Cooks, N.Z., Banks Is.: Hambruch, 1914-15, 284; Ellice Is.: Kennedy, 1931, 157; Roberts, 1958, 370; Rotuma: Churchward 1938-39, 329; Russell, 1942, 243; Fijis: Fison, 1904, 51; Ontong Java: Sarfert, 1931, 324; Nukumanu: Sarfert, 1931, 437f.; Rennell: Elbert-Monberg, 1964, No. 27.

F54.1. Tree stretches to sky. Tuamotus: Stimson, 1937, 81; Marquesas: Lavondes, 1966, 78, 150; Steinen, 1933-34, 373; Hawaii: Dickey, 1917, 16; Fornander 1916, IV, 598; V, 596; Pukui, 1933, 180; Pukui-Curtis, n.d., 28; Rice, 1923, 22; Westervelt, 1915 173; Tonga: Beckwith, 1940, 486; Reiter, 1933, 356; Samoa: Krämer, 1902, I, 144; Sierich, 1901,

17, 21.

F56. Sky-window. An opening into the sky gives access
to upper world. Hawaii: Rice, 1923, 104; Tonga:
Gifford, 1924, 149; Rotuma: Churchward, 1937-38,
367; 1938-39, 124; Russell, 1942, 247.

F56.3. Sky-window at horizon. Tonga: Gifford, 1924,
149; Rennell: Elbert-Monberg, 1964, No. 23.

F57. Road to heaven. Tonga: Collocott, 1928, 42.

F57.2. Person's tongue as path to sky. Marquesas:
Beckwith, 1940, 499; Hawaii: Rice, 1923, 24.

F57.3. Path to heaven on beard. Marquesas: Steinen,
1933-34, 371; Hawaii: Beckwith, 1940, 256.

F57.4. Wall as path to upper world. Polynesia:
*Beckwith, 1940, 255.

F59.1. Man stretches self till he reaches other world.
Hawaii: Beckwith, 1940, 476; Rice, 1923, 103.

F61.1. Ascent to sky on cloud. N.Z.: White, 1887-90,
I, 56, 88, 127, 129; Tikopia: Firth, 1961, 50.

F61.3. Transportation from heaven in mist(rain). N.Z.:
Best, 1925, 866, 871; Tokelau: Burrows, 1923, 160.

F61.3.1. Ascent to upper world in smoke. Oceania:
**Lessa, 1961, 369ff.; Hawaii: Thrum, 1907, 224;
Ellice Is.: Kennedy, 1931, 194; Kapingamarangi:
Elbert, 1948, 95.

D2121.7.3. Magic transportation on smoke.

*F61.4. Ascent to upper world on whirlwind. Tokelaus:
Macgregor, 1937, 84; N.Z.: Best, 1924, 101.

*F61.5. Person ascends to heavens by clinging to a kite.
N.Z.: Cowan, 1930, I, 25; White, 1887-90, I, 129f.

F62.1. Birds carry person to upper world. Tuamotus:
Seurat, 1905, 434; Marquesas: Lavondes, 1964, 54;
Hawaii: Beckwith, 1919, 566; Ellice Is.: Roberts,
1958, 373.

*F63.4.1. Stars take man to sky. Reef Is.: O'Ferrall,
1904, 231; Riesenfeld, 1950, 129.

F68. Ascent to upper world by magic. Societies:
Ropiteau, 1933, 126; Hawaii: Fornander, 1916, IV,
76, 526; N.Z.: Beckwith, 1940, 250; Best, 1925,
828; White, 1887-90, II, 80; Tikopia: Firth,
1961, 45.

*F68.1. Ascent to heavens by leaping to magically
lowered sky. Ellice Is.: Roberts, 1958, 371.

*F69. Journey from upper world inside magic coconut
which is thrown. Australs: Buck, 1938a, 169.

*F70. Ascent to heavens upon great lizard. Hawaii:
Beckwith, 1919, 554.

*F71. Descent from upper-world in raft. Reef Is.:
O'Ferrall, 1904, 231.

*F72. Person jumps into heavens. Samoa: Krämer, 1902,
I, 456.

*F73. Person chops hole to pass through the horizon.
Bellona: Elbert-Monberg, 1964, No. 55a.

*F77.2. Hero ascends to upper world by kite-string.
N.Z.: Hambruch, 1914-15, 283.

*F77.6. Transportation from sky to earth on turtle.
Fijis: Fison, 1904, 21.

F80--F109. The Lower World

F80. Journey to lower world. Oceania: **Lessa, 1961,
372ff.; Tuamotus: Stimson, 1937, 126; Hawaii:
*Beckwith, 1940, 160, 160 n. 52, 161, 161 n. 53, 54;
Thrum, 1907, 48; Tonga: Caillot, 1914, 260f.;
Collocott, 1928, 12f., 14; Niue: Loeb, 1926, 212;
N.Z.: White, 1887-90, II, 67, 73, 82, 97; III, 129;
Reef Is.: Elbert-Kirtley, 1966, 350f.; Bellona:
Elbert-Monberg, 1964, No. 50a; Rennell: ibid., 50b.

*F80.1.1.1. Eight-walled building in underworld. Cooks:
Beaglehole, 1938, 310.

F80.1.2. Darkness of lower world. Tuamotus: Caillot,
1914, 29.

F81. Descent to lower world of dead (Hell, Hades).
Hawaii: Beckwith, 1940, 464.

F81.1. Orpheus. Journey to land of dead to bring back
person from the dead. Polynesia: *Dixon, 1916,
72ff.; Mangareva: Hiroa, 1938, 335; Laval, 1938,
300; Tuamotus: Henry, 1928, 527; Leverd, 1911,
176; Marquesas: Steinen, 1933-34, 38; 1934-35,
212; Christian, 1895, 188; Cooks: Beckwith, 1940,
150; Te Ariki, 1921, 6; Hawaii: Fornander, 1918,
V, 186; Thrum, 1907, 45ff.; Westervelt, 1915, 18ff.,
217, 233ff.; Tonga: Collocott, 1928, 14, 37;
Samoa: Beckwith, 1940, 150; Krämer, 1902, I,
125ff., 133; Sierich, 1902, 179; Stuebel, 1896,
150f.; N.Z.: Cowan, 1930, I, 22; Clark, 1896, 111;
Grace, 1907, 250ff., 256; Tregear, 1901, 185;
Westervelt, 1915, 243f.; White, 1887-90, I, 131f.,
136f., 145ff.; II, 4ff., 166; Wohlers, 1875, 9;
Bellona: Elbert-Monberg, 1964, No. 50; Rennell:
ibid., 50b, 50c.

*F81.7. Journey to lower world to get father's bones.
Tahiti: Gill, 1876, 255.

F87. Journey to otherworld to secure bride. Tuamotus:
Stimson, n.d., Z-G. 13/221.

*F88. Princess carried off to underworld. Tuamotus:
Stimson, n.d., Z-G. 13/420.

F90. Access to lower world. Cooks: Gill, 1876, 70;
Hawaii: *Beckwith, 1940, 161 n. 53; McAllister,
1933, 94, 98; Westervelt, 1915, 18; Samoa:
*Stair, 1896, 38.

F91. Door (gate) entrance to lower world. Marquesas:
Steinen, 1934-35, 193.

F92. Pit entrance to lower world. Entrance through pit,
hole, spring, or cavern. Marquesas: Handy, 1930,
110; Cooks: Best, 1924, 317; Hawaii: Westervelt,
1915, 233; Tonga: Collocott, 1928, 12; N.Z.:
Clark, 1896, 100; Gudgeon, 1905, 191; Luomala,
1949, 55; Rotuma: Churchward, 1937-38, 490.

F92.1. Visit to lower world through hole made by
lifting clumps of grass (reed). Polynesia: *Dixon,
1916, 47f.; Tonga: Caillot, 1914, 267; Collocott,
1921, 46; Collocott, 1928, 12, 18; Samoa:
Fraser, 1897, 108; Powell-Pratt, 1892, 81; Stuebel,
1896, 65; Niue: Dixon, 1916, 47f.; N.Z.: Best,
1929, 6; Grey, 1855, 24; Luomala, 1949, 118;
White, 1887-90, II, 66, 95; Rennell: Elbert-Monberg,
1964, Nos. 31a, 31b, 33.

*F92.1.1. Stone covers entrance to underworld. Rotuma:
Churchward, 1937-38, 490.

F92.2.1. Girl gathering flowers swallowed up by earth
and taken to lower world. Cooks: Dixon, 1916, 74.

*F92.2.2. Woman falls from tree, cleaves earth, lands in
Spirit world. Cooks: Gill, 1876, 222.

F92.3. Visit to lower world through opening rocks.
Rocks that open with a charm. Cooks: Gill,
1876, 52; Cooks, Samoa, N.Z.: Dixon, 1916, 48.

F92.4. Entrance to lower world through mountain.
Hawaii: *Beckwith, 1940, 155, 156, 156 nn.34-36,
157 n. 38.

F92.5. Entrance to lower world by making hole in ground.
Hawaii: Westervelt, 1915, 215.

*F92.5.1. A god opens a path to the underworld with a
spear. Rennell: Elbert-Monberg, 1964, No. 186.

*F92.8. Volcano (crater) entrance to other world.
Societies: Henry, 1901, 51; 1928, 378, 584;
Tonga: Collocott, 1928, 13.

*F92.9. Entrance to underworld beneath ashes in an oven.
Bellona: Elbert-Monberg, 1964, No. 50a; Rennell:
ibid., 50b.

*F92.10. Entrance to underworld covered by mat.
Rennell: Elbert-Monberg, 1964, No. 21.

*F92.11. Entrance to underworld concealed by housepost.
N.Z.: White, 1887-90, II, 82; Wohlers, 1875, 11.

*F92.12. A tree covers the path to the lower world.
Tonga: Reiter, 1917-18, 1030.

F93. Water entrance to lower world. Mangareva: Hiroa,
1938, 20, 374; Tuamotus: Stimson, n.d., Z-G.
3/1241; Stimson, 1937, 112; Marquesas:
Lavondes, 1964, 22; Cooks: Beaglehole, 1938, 327;
Hawaii: Thrum, 1907, 45f.; Westervelt, 1915, 178f.;
Tonga: Collocott, 1928, 12f.; Samoa: Sierich,
1902, 174ff.; *Stair, 1895b, 123; N.Z.:
Westervelt, 1915, 243; Ellice Is.: Kennedy, 1931,
164.

*F93.3. Reef as entrance to lower world. Tuamotus:
Stimson, n.d., Z-G. 13/420.

*F93.4. Whirlpool as entrance to lower world. Cooks: Gill, 1876, 165; Fijis: Fison, 1904, 75.

F95. Path to lower world. Cooks: Gill, 1876, 155.

F95.4. Path to underworld marked by knots tied in grass by spirits. N.Z.: Clark, 1896, 48.

F95.5. Tree as roadway to underworld. Mangareva: Hiroa, 1938, 324; Cooks: Banapa, 1920, 89; Beckwith, 1940, 158; Rotuma: Churchward, 1937-38, 490; Reef Is.: Elbert-Kirtley, 1966, 351.

F96. Rope (vine) to lower world. Hawaii: Beckwith, 1940, 147; Fornander, 1918, V, 186; N.Z.: Kararehe, 1898, 59.

*F99.1. Descent to lower world on current of wind. Cooks: Gill, 1876, 8.

F101. Return from lower world. Hawaii: Fornander, 1918, V, 268.

F101.1. Return from lower world up steep slope. N.Z.: Dixon, 1916, 73.

F101.2. Return from lower world by being slung by bent tree. N.Z.: Beckwith, 1940, 148; Dixon, 1916, 78.

*F101.9. Hero escapes from underworld by swinging upwards on a vine. Hawaii: Westervelt, 1915, 237f.; N.Z.: Westervelt, 1915, 243.

*F101.10. Escape from underworld upon swing. Hawaii: Thrum, 1907, 46-47.

*F101.11. Soul carried from underworld in a cane. Hawaii: Westervelt, 1915, 20.

*F102.5. Bird guides person to otherworld. Tuamotus: Stimson, n.d., Z-G. 3/1241.

*F102.6. Guiding thread of sennit along path to underworld. Cooks: Beaglehole, 1938, 327.

F109.1. Visit to lower world made head first. Hawaii: Beckwith, 1940, 148.

*F109.3. Road to lower world filled in so that it is no longer usable. Samoa: Powell-Pratt, 1892, 79.

F111. Journey to earthly paradise. Land of happiness. Hawaii: Pukui, 1933,159; Pukui-Curtis, n.d., 19; Rice, 1923, 106; Thrum, 1923, 204; Lau Is.: St. Johnston, 1918, 29ff.; Nukumanu: Sarfert, 1931, 331.

F112. Journey to Land of Women. Polynesia: *Beckwith, 1940, 498ff.; Tuamotus: Caillot, 1914, 70; Seurat, 1905, 434; Marquesas: Beckwith, 1940, 472; Handy, 1930, 56; Lavondes, 1964, 60; Steinen, 1933-34, 348, 360; Cooks: Banapa, 1920, 88; "Notes and Queries," JPS XIII (1904), 265; Beaglehole, 1938, 401; Hawaii: Beckwith, 1940, 36; Fijis: Hocart, 1929, 165; Tikopia: Firth, 1961, 30.

F112.1. Man on Island of Fair Women overcome by loving women. Oceanic: Dixon, 1916, 66, 140, 141 n. 22.

*F112.1.1. Woman in Land of Women keeps castaway hidden for herself. Tuamotus: Caillot, 1914, 71.

F113. Land of men. Marquesas: Steinen, 1934-35, 229.

*F127.5. Journey to Land of Sting-ray. Tuamotus: Stimson, n.d., Z-G. 13/317.

F129.4.5. Voyage to Island of Darkness. Hawaii: Beckwith, 1940, 500.

F129.4.6. Voyage to Island of Silence. Hawaii: Beckwith, 1940, 500.

*F129.8. Journey to Land of Albinos. Samoa: Sierich, 1900, 237.

F130. Location of otherworld. Mangareva: Caillot, 1914, 176; Hiroa, 1938, 321; Hawaii: Fornander, 1916, IV, 76, 168, 522; Westervelt, 1915, 128ff., 169; Tonga: Collocott, 1921, 45; 1928, 12ff., 41; Reiter, 1917-18, 1026; Samoa: Abercromby, 1891, 459; Stuebel, 1896, 65, 143, 145; Tokelaus: Burrows, 1923, 160, 166; N.Z.: White, 1887-90, I,

119; Wohlers, 1875, 15; Ontong Java:
Parkinson, 1898, 197.

F10. Journey to upper world. F80. Journey
to lower world.

*F131.2. Subterranean elysium beneath volcano. Tahiti:
Henry, 1928, 144.

F132.1.1. Earthly paradise in air over mountain. Tahiti:
Beckwith, 1940, 76.

F133. Submarine otherworld. Tuamotus: Stimson, n.d.,
Z-G. 13/317; Societies: Henry, 1928, 407;
Hawaii: Beckwith, 1940, 69; N.Z.: Clark, 1896,
111; Steinen, 1933-34, 333; White, 1887-90, II,
162; Rotuma: Russell, 1942, 250; Rennell:
Elbert-Monberg, 1964, No. 16.

F134. Otherworld on island. Oceania: *Beckwith,
1940, Ch. XXXVI passim; Hawaii: Beckwith, 1932,
46; 1940, 72, 79; Fornander, 1918, V, 384,
410ff.; Green, 1926, 97; Rice, 1923, 116;
Samoa, Fijis: Beckwith, 1940, 76; N.Z.:
"Notes and Queries," JPS XIV (1905), 47;
Ellice Is.: Grimble, 1952, 46.

F136.2. Otherworld in west. Hawaii: Beckwith, 1940,
79.

F140.1. Guardian of spirit-land boundary. N.Z.:
Clark, 1896, 135.

F150.2. Entrance to other world guarded by monsters
(animals). Tuamotus: Stimson, 1937, 113; Cooks:
Gill, 1876, 53; Hawaii: Rice, 1923, 23;
Ellice Is.: Kennedy, 1931, 194.

F150.2.2. Entrance to otherworld guarded by spirits.
N.Z.: Clark, 1896, 37.

F150.2.3. Entrance to otherworld guarded by north and
south winds. Tonga: Gifford, 1924, 171.

F151.1. Perilous path to otherworld. Mangareva:
Hiroa, 1938, 374.

F151.1.5. Place in underworld beyond which hero cannot
pass without being tattooed. N.Z.: Clark, 1896,
136.

F152.1.1. Rainbow bridge to otherworld. Societies:
Henry, 1928, 618; Cooks: Cowan, 1930, I, 26;
Gill, 1876, 47; Hawaii: Beckwith, 1919, 336,
580ff., 584, 590, 612, 614; 1940, 37f., 321, 434,
492; Dixon, 1916, 67; Fornander, 1916, IV, 66;
1918, VI, 272; Thrum, 1907, 21; 1923, 110;
Tikopia: Firth, 1961, 140.

F153. Underworld reached by diving into water (or
particular wave). Tuamotus: Stimson, n.d.,
Z-G. 3/1301; Marquesas: Lavondes, 1966, 100,
168ff.; Niue: Smith, 1903, 22; N.Z.: Locke,
1921, 40f.; Lau Is.: Hocart, 1929, 210;
St. Johnston, 1918, 42.

*F153.2. Water poured in tao leaf. Woman jumps into
this, arrives in other world. Marquesas:
Steinen, 1934-35, 204.

F154. Path to sun on sun's rays. N.Z.: Smith,
JPS supplement to VI (1897), 23.

F155. Journey to otherworld by clinging magically
to an object. Marquesas: Lavondes, 1964, 20.

F156. Door to otherworld. Tuamotus: Stimson, 1934,
18.

*F157.2. Journey to otherworld on whale. Hawaii:
Rice, 1923, 127; N.Z.: Locke, 1921, 40f.

F158. Pit entrance to other world. Rotuma: Russell,
1942, 243.

*F159.5. Magic spell transports one to otherworld.
Marquesas: Lavondes, 1964, 22.

F160. Nature of the otherworld. N.Z.: White, 1887-90,
II, 4.

F162.3. Tree in otherworld. Hawaii: Beckwith, 1940,
286; Tonga: Gifford, 1924, 149, 162.

F162.6.2. Lake with water of life in otherworld.
Hawaii: Beckwith, 1940, 492; N.Z.: Clark,
1896, 182.

F162.9. Mountains in otherworld. Marquesas: Handy,
1930, 119.

F163.3.2.1. House in underworld lined with human eyes
(used as lamps). Tuamotus: Stimson, n.d.,
MB-DD-33, T-G. 1/18, Z-G. 13/276; Societies:
Beckwith, 1940, 246; Tonga: Gifford, 1924, 168.

F163.3.2.2. House in otherworld made of bones of dead.
Tonga: Gifford, 1924, 171.

F167.1.4.1. Giant clams in otherworld. Tonga:
Gifford, 1924, 169.

F167.8. Otherworld people unacquainted with fire.
Polynesia: Dixon, 1916, 72, 78; Cooks: Gill,
1876, 265ff.; Hawaii: *Beckwith, 1940, 498 ff.;
Samoa: Luomala, 1949, 102; N.Z.: Beckwith,
1940, 502; Pakauwera, 1894, 102f.; Ellice Is.:
Kennedy, 1931, 168.

F167.15. Great tattooer in otherworld. N.Z.:
Clark, 1896, 136.

*F171.10. In otherworld hero meets blind ancestress who
ceaselessly counts items of food. Tuamotus:
*Beckwith, 1940, 252f.; Leverd, 1911, 176; Stimson,
1934, 63; 1937, 81; Marquesas: Steinen, 1933-34,
372; Societies: Gill, 1876, 251; Henry, 1928,
560; Cooks: Banapa, 1920, 90; Beckwith, 1940, 253;
Gill, 1876, 65f., 109; Te Ariki, 1921, 207;
Hawaii: Beckwith, 1940, 257; Fornander, 1916, IV,
90, 162; Thrum, 1923, 24; Tonga: Collocott, 1928,
37; Samoa: *Beckwith, 1940, 254; Niue: Smith,
1902, 92; Tokelaus: Burrows, 1923, 168;
Chatham Is.: Shand, 1898, 73ff.; N.Z.: *Beckwith,
1940, 249f.; Best, 1925, 912; *Potae, 1928, 361,
366; White, 1887-90, I, 56, 89, 100f., 116;
Wohlers, 1875, 17; Ellice Is.: Kennedy, 1931, 164;
Rotuma: Churchward, 1938-39, 329; Tikopia:
Firth, 1961, 48; Rennell: Elbert-Monberg, 1964,
No. 1c; Bellona: ibid., Nos. 1a, 1b; Ontong Java,
Nukumanu: Sarfert, 1931, 424; Kapingamarangi:
Elbert, 1949, 243.

K333. Theft from blind person.

F200--F699. MARVELOUS CREATURES

F200--F399. Fairies and elves

F200. Fairies (elves et cetera. Human like creatures,
whatever their names, depicted by tradition as
tinged with supernatural traits and dwelling on the

279

periphery of human experience.) Oceania:
***Luomala, 1951, passim; Martha Warren Beckwith,
"Polynesian Analogues to the Celtic Otherworld
and Fairy Mistress Themes," Vassar Mediaval Studies
C. F. Fiske, ed., 1923, pp. 29-55; *Edward Tregear,
"The Fairies and Giants of Polynesia," Longmans
Magazine XVII (1891), 440-452. Societies:
Henry, 1928, 383; Cooks: *Gill, 1876, Ch. XI,
256ff.; Hawaii: Beckwith, 1940, 326, 328;
McAllister, 1933, 89; *Thrum, 1907, 107ff.; 1920,
70ff.; N.Z.: *Cowan, 1921, 96ff., 142ff.; 1930,
2ff., 63ff., 188, 190; Tregear, 1901, 185; White,
1887-90, III, 189.

F205. Little people from the sky. Hawaii: Beckwith,
1940, 326ff.

F210. Fairyland (otherworld depicted with traditional
fairyland aspects). N.Z.: Cowan, 1930, 27f.

F211.3. Fairies live under earth. Rennell: Elbert-
Monberg, 1964, Nos. 81, 89; Bellona: ibid.,
Nos. 87, 91.

F212. Fairyland under water. Cooks: Gill, 1876, 265.

F213. Fairyland on an island. Hawaii: Luomala, 1951,
9, 23.

F214. Fairies live in hills (mountains). Hawaii:
Luomala, 1951, 25, 71; Thrum, 1920, 70; N.Z.:
Best, 1925, 994; Cowan, 1921, 147; 1930, 3, 34,
191, 226.

F215.1. Fairyland in sky. Cooks: Gill, 1876, 264.

F216. Fairies live in forest. Hawaii: Luomala, 1951,
33, 71; N.Z.: Best, 1924, 167, 224.

*F217.4. Fairies hide in mist. N.Z.: Best, 1924, 219;
Cowan, 1921, 150.

F219.3. Fairies dwell in land to the east. N.Z.:
Clark, 1896, 98.

F220. Dwelling of fairies. Hawaii: Emerson, 1915, 186;
Luomala, 1951, 18.

F221. House of fairy. Hawaii: Thrum, 1920, 70.

F232.5. Fairies have hairy bodies. Hawaii: Luomala, 1951, 10; Thrum, 1920, 70; 1923, 214; Rennell and Bellona: *Elbert-Monberg, 1964, Chap. IX, passim.

F232.6. Fairies as giants. N.Z.: Cowan, 1930, I, 60.

*F233.3.2. Fairies have red hair and skins (or fair skins). N.Z.: Cowan, 1930, 3, 34; 1930a, 2; Grace, 1907, 38.

F233.5. Fairies have yellow (golden) hair (clothing). Societies: Beckwith, 1940, 335; N.Z.: Best, 1924, 219; 1925, 995; Clark, 1896, 24; Cowan, 1921, 148, 151; 1930, 51; Grey, 1855, 295; Gudgeon, 1896, 42.

F233.6. Fairies fair (fine, white). N.Z.: Grey, 1855, 289, 295.

F234.0.2. Fairy as shape-shifter. Hawaii: Emerson, 1915, 85; Pukui, 1933, 161.

F235.2. Fairies visible only at certain times. N.Z.: Best, 1925, 996; Cowan, 1930, I, 60; Rennell: Elbert-Monberg, 1964, Nos. 85, 86; Bellona: ibid., No. 91.

*F235.2.3. Fairies become visible or invisible at will. Tahiti: Henry, 1928, 490.

*F235.3.1. Fairies invisible to all except their descendants. Hawaii: Thrum, 1895, 114; 1907, 110; Luomala, 1951, 14.

F236.1.1. Fairies in red clothes. Hawaii: Luomala, 1951, 72; N.Z.: Cowan, 1930a, 35.

F239.4.3. Fairy is tiny. Tuamotus: Stimson, 1937, 137; Hawaii: Luomala, 1951, 10; Thrum, 1907, 116; 1920, 70; 1923, 214; Samoa: Stair, 1895, 104; Rennell and Bellona: *Elbert-Monberg, Chap. IX, passim.

F242.2. Fairy boat. N.Z.: Clark, 1896, 24.

*F243.6. Fairies eat only bananas. Hawaii: Luomala, 1951, 27.

*F243.7. Fairies eat only berries. Hawaii: Luomala, 1951, 18.

*F243.8. Fairies eat food raw. Hawaii: Luomala, 1951, 18, 25.

F251. Origin of fairies. Hawaii: Thrum, 1895, 114; 1907, 22; Westervelt, 1915, 6; N.Z.: Best, 1925, 1000; White, 1887-90, V, 6f.; Bellona: *Elbert-Monberg, 1964, No. 66; Rennell: ibid., No. 67, Chap. IX.

*F252.0.1. Fairy society parallels human society. Hawaii: Luomala, 1951, 23.

F255.5. Fairies do not bend grass as they walk. Cooks: Gill,1876, 257; N.Z.: Beckwith, 1940, 335.

*F255.6. Fairies must finish any task of work in one night, or else leave it forever unfinished. Hawaii: Luomala, 1951, 17, 19, 22, 23; Thrum, 1895, 113; 1907, 109; N.Z.: Cowan, 1930a, 9.

F260. Behavior of fairies. Tahiti: Henry, 1928, 489.

F261.2.1. Fairies dance on leaves without disturbing them. Cooks: Beckwith, 1940, 336; Gill, 1876, 257.

F262. Fairies make music. N.Z.: Cowan, 1921, 151; 1930a, 42; 1930, I, 67.

*F262.1.1. Song learned from fairies. N.Z.: Cowan, 1930a, 39ff., 63f.; 1930, I, 190.

F265. Fairy bathes. Marquesas: Handy, 1930, 119; Cooks: Gill, 1876, 256f.

F267. Fairies attend (play) games. Hawaii: Luomala, 1951, 15.

F271.0.1. Fairies as craftsmen. Hawaii: Beckwith, 1940, 329; Bellona: Elbert-Monberg, 1964, No. 73.

F271.0.2. Fairies lacking axes work with their teeth. Hawaii: Beckwith, 1940, 333.

F271.2.0.1. Fairies build great structures in one night. Cf. *F255.6. Hawaii: Beckwith, 1940, 333; Luomala 1951, 15; Thrum, 1920, 71; Bellona: Elbert-Monberg 1964, No. 75.

*F271.2.0.1.1. Fairies build temples and religious structures. Hawaii: Dickey, 1917, 25, 30; *Luomala, 1951, 4, 10, 15f., 19ff., 30, 34, 36, 47; McAllister, 1933, 79, 82, 121, 140, 186; Thrum, 1895, 114, 117; 1907, 110f., 115, 116f.; 1920, 70f.; 1923, 215f.; Westervelt, 1915, 6, 90ff., 131.

F271.2.1. Fairies excavate passage. Hawaii: Thrum, 1920, 70.

*F271.2.1.1. Fairies build (excavate) watercourse (ditch). Hawaii: *Luomala, 1951, 14, 19, 21, 22, 23, 33, 36.

F271.2.3. Fairies build canoe. Tuamotus: Beckwith, 1940, 267; Henry, 1928, 500f.; Tahiti: Henry, 1928, 489; Hawaii: Beckwith, 1940, 332; Luomala, 1951, 19; McAllister, 1933, 86; Rice, 1923, 26; Thrum, 1895, 116; Westervelt, 1915, 35, 141f.; Samoa: Stair, 1895, 101; N.Z.: Grey, 1855, 114.

*F343.21. Fairies (supernaturals) build person a canoe.

*F271.2.4. Fairies build fishponds (dam). Hawaii: Luomala, 1951, 14, 17, 22, 23; McAllister, 1933, 69, 165, 168; Pukui, 1943, 56; Thrum, 1920, 71; Westervelt, 1915, 6, 90.

*F271.2.5. The menehune convey a spring of water in one night to a distant spot. Hawaii: Westervelt, 1933, 141.

*F271.2.6. Fairies make lagoons. Rennell: Elbert-Monberg, 1964, No. 74.

*F271.2.7. Fairies build roads. Hawaii: Luomala, 1951, 4, 36.

*F271.2.8. Fairies trasport large stone to its present location. Hawaii: McAllister, 1933, 86.

*F271.2.9. Fairies cut petroglyphs. Hawaii: Luomala, 1951, 47.

*F271.2.10. Fairies build house of feathers in one night. Hawaii: Westervelt, 1915, 184.

*F271.2.11. Fairies make huge number of bowls and platters in one night. Hawaii: Green, 1926, 75.

*F271.2.12. Mythical little people make tapa. Hawaii: Green, 1929, 9.

*F271.11. Fairies fish. N.Z.: Grey, 1855, 288.

F273.2. Fairy shows remarkable skill as runner. Hawaii: Beckwith, 1951, 33.

F277.0.1. War between fairy settlements. N.Z.: Cowan, 1930, 67f.

*F277.0.4. Battle of fairies and owls. Hawaii: Luomala, 1951, 16; Westervelt, 1915, 131f.

F278.2. Fairies create magic concealing mist. N.Z.: Best, 1925, 996f.; Cowan, 1930, I, 67; 1930a, 3, 7, 42, 58.

*F278.2.1. Fairies cause rain. Hawaii: Luomala, 1951, 17.

F282. Fairies travel through air. Rotuma: Hames, 1960, 31.

*F286. Fairies make so much noise that they startle wildlife many miles away. Hawaii: *Luomala, 1951, 14, 22.

*F287. Fairies leave island to preserve their own racial purity. Hawaii: Luomala, 1951, 12, 29, 36.

F300--F399. Fairies and Mortals

F300. Marriage or liaison with fairy. Cooks: Beckwith, 1940, 503; Gill, 1876, 265; Hawaii: Luomala, 1951 11; N.Z.: Clark, 1896, 27; Cowan, 1930, I, 190.

F301. Fairy lover. Kapingamarangi: Elbert, 1948, 93.

*F301.9. Fairy lover comes to girl at night, leaves her before dawn. N.Z.: Cowan, 1921, 98, 142; 1930a, 24f., 59f.; Smith, 1910, 86; Ellice Is.: Kennedy, 1931, 171.

F302. Fairy mistress. Mortal man marries or lives with fairy woman. Hawaii: Beckwith, 1940, 500; N.Z.: Smith, 1910, 86.

284

F305.2. Offspring of fairy and mortal extraordinarily beautiful. Cooks: Gill, 1876, 266.

*F305.4. Albino offspring of women and fairy-lovers. N.Z.: Cowan, 1921, 149; 1930, I, 190.

F311. Fairies adopt human child. Hawaii: Green, 1929, 13.

F320. Fairies carry people away to fairyland. N.Z.: Best, 1924, 222; Cowan, 1921, 144.

F322. Fairies steal man's wife. N.Z.: Cowan, 1930a, 58, 66.

F340. Gifts from fairies. Hawaii: Luomala, 1951, 8.

*F343.21. Fairies (supernaturals) build person a canoe. Cf. F271.2.3. Tuamotus: Stimson, 1937, 124; Hawaii: *Luomala, 1951, 16, 19, 30, 48f., 70; Thrum, 1907, 113f., 115; N.Z.: White, 1887-90, I, 70, 74, 76.

*F343.22. Fairies give food. Hawaii: Green, 1926, 75ff.; 1929, 21; Rennell: Elbert-Monberg, 1964, Nos. 88, 89, 91; Bellona: ibid., Nos. 87, 91.

F346. Fairy helps mortal with labor. Hawaii: Luomala, 1951, 36.

F363. Fairies cause death. Hawaii: Luomala, 1951, 16f.; N.Z.: Grace, 1907, 55.

*F363.7. Fairies suffocate people. Hawaii: Luomala, 1951, 71.

F365.7. Fairies steal cooking (food). Hawaii: Thrum, 1920, 72; 1923, 218f.

F369.5. Fairies destroy crops. Hawaii: Westervelt, 1915, 150.

*F369.9. Fairies snatch cover off sleepers. Hawaii: Luomala, 1951, 25.

F370. Visit to fairyland. Rennell: Elbert-Monberg, 1964, Nos. 88, 89, 90.

F380. Defeating or ridding oneself of fairies. N.Z.: Best, 1924, 222; Rennell: Elbert-Monberg, 1964, No. 86n.

F383.4. Fairy (and other supernaturals) must leave at cock-crow (dawn). Tuamotus: Stimson, n.d., Z-G. 3/1146; Societies: Henry, 1928, 589; Ropiteau, 1933, 127; Cooks: Beaglehole, 1938, 376; Te Ariki, 1920, 124; Hawaii: Beckwith, 1940, 333, 480; Luomala, 1951, 19; Rice, 1923, 35; Thrum, 1895, 115; 1907, 111, 116; 1920, 71; 1923, 217; Tonga: Gifford, 1924, 88, 90, 144; Niue: Smith, 1903, 96; N.Z.: Cowan, 1930, 9; Gudgeon, 1906, 42; Tregear, 1901, 185; White, 1887-90, I, 56, 101f.; Uvea: Burrows, 1937, 162; Fijis: Hocart, 1929, 194, 213; Nukumanu: Sarfert, 1931, 454.

E452. Ghost laid at cock-crow (dawn).

F383.4.2. Fairies leave at rise of morning star. Cooks: Beckwith, 1940, 336.

F383.4.3. Sunlight fatal to fairies. Cf. F383.4. Marquesas: Steinen, 1934-35, 206; N.Z.: Clark, 1896, 98; Grey, 1855, 66; Hongi, 1898, 40.

*F383.6. Fairies dislike fire. N.Z.: Cowan, 1930a, 10, 40f., 61f., 163; Grace, 1907, 38.

*F383.6.1. Fairies avoid steam from cooking ovens. N.Z.: Cowan, 1930a, 10, 35, 61ff.; Grace, 1930a, 4.

*F383.7. Fairies afraid of dogs and owls. Hawaii: Luomala, 1951, 15.

*F383.8. Fairy kept at distance with red-earth mixed with shark oil. N.Z.: Cowan, 1930, 61f.

F387. Fairy captured. Tuamotus: Stimson, n.d., Z-G. 13/441; Cooks: Gill, 1876, 265; Niue: Smith, 1903, 102; N.Z.: Clark, 1896, 27.

F400. Spirits and demons (general). Societies: Henry, 1928, 483f., 498f.; N.Z.: Best, 1925, 968ff.; Grey, 1855, 280ff.

F401.2. Luminous spirits. Samoa: Stuebel, 1896, 77; Kapingamarangi: Elbert, 1948, 94.

F401.3. Spirit in animal form. Hawaii: Thrum, 1923, 164ff.

*F401.3.3.2. Spirit as (white) dog. Hawaii: Pukui, 1933, 178; Tonga: Reiter, 1919-20, 125ff.; Samoa: Stuebel, 1896, 66; N.Z.: Best, 1925, 895, 973f., 1045; Fijis: Hocart, 1929, 215.

F401.3.7. Spirit in form of bird. Tuamotus: Stevenson, 1912, 135; Samoa: Stuebel, 1896, 150; N.Z.: Best, 1925, 974; Cowan, 1930, I, 154; Rennell: Elbert-Monberg, 1964, 2c; Ontong Java: Parkinson, 1898, 197.

*F401.3.9. Spirit in form of fish (eel). Mangareva: Hiroa, 1938, 370; Tuamotus: Henry, 1928, 619; Stimson, 1937, 116f.; Hawaii: Pukui, 1933, 154, n. 1, 155, 171; Westervelt, 1915, 159; Tonga: Collocott, 1928, 12; Samoa: Stuebel, 1896, 75f.; Tokelau: Lister, 1892, 51; N.Z.: Best, 1925, 838, 969ff.; Ontong Java: Sarfert, 1931, 329.

*F401.3.10. Spirit in form of boar. Cooks: Beckwith, 1940, 412.

*F401.3.11. Spirit in form sometimes human, sometimes demonic. Easter Is.: Englert, 1939, 70; Mangareva: Hiroa, 1938, 321, 376; Hawaii: Fornander, 1918, V, 136; Thrum, 1923, 209; Samoa: Krämer, 1902, I, 140, 303; Powell-Pratt, 1892, 247; Tokelaus: Burrows, 1923, 159, 160f., 172; Ellice Is.: Roberts, 1958, 365, 401; Ontong Java: Sarfert, 1931, 456.

*F401.3.12. Spirit in form of turtle. Easter Is.: Englert, 1939, 28.

*F401.3.13. Spirit in form of lizard. Hawaii: Pukui, 1933, 178; N.Z.: Best, 1925, 1049; Tikopia: Firth, 1961, 32.

*F401.3.14. Spirit in form of rat. Hawaii: Fornander, 1916, IV, 550.

*F401.4.2. Ten spirits with different numbers of heads: one has one head, another two heads, etc. Tonga: Collocott, 1928, 14; Rotuma: Churchward, 1938-39, 120.

*F401.5.2. Spirit who has teeth as long as his arms. Samoa: Stuebel, 1896, 81.

*F401.6.1. Spirits in skeletal form during day, covered with flesh at night. Easter Is.: Englert, 1939, 66ff.

*F401.6.2. Humpbacked spirits. Lau Is.: St. Johnston, 1918, 34.

*F401.12. Spirit with many eyes. Funafuti: David, 1899, 107.

*F401.13. Spirit with head of a snake, body of sea-snake. Fijis: Hocart, 1928, 223.

*F401.14. Spirit capable of taking a number of different forms. Hawaii: Emerson, 1915, 88f.

*F401.15. Demon in form of wooden log. N.Z.: Best, 1925, 971.

*F401.16. Female spirit who can appear either as a great beauty or as a terrifying crone. Samoa: Stuebel, 1896, 82f.

*F401.17. Invisible demon. N.Z.: Grace, 1907, 64.

*F401.18. Demon with extraordinarily long tongue which can simulate a bridge. Hawaii: Emerson, 1915, 85.

*F401.19. Spirit resembles a meteor. Tahiti: Stevenson, 1912, 135.

G11.8.1. Cannibal meteor.

F402. Evil spirits. Demons. Australs: Aitken, 1923, 272; Marquesas: E.S.C. Handy, The Native Culture in the Marquesas BPBM Bulletin 9 (Honolulu, 1923), 43; Samoa: Stair, 1896, 34.

288

F402.1.1. Spirit leads person astray. Ontong Java: Sarfert, 1931, 327.

*F402.1.1.1. Spirits steal children. Tokelaus: Macgregor, 1937, 62.

F402.1.4. Demons assume human forms in order to deceive. Marquesas: Lavondes, 1964, 26ff.; Cooks: Smith, 1897, 97, note; Samoa: Powell-Pratt, 1892, 247; Tokelaus: Burrows, 1923, 160f.; Rennell: Elbert-Monberg, 1964, Nos. 52a, 175, 176; Bellona: ibid., 52b; Kapingamarangi: Elbert, 1948, 81, 88f.; 1949, 244.

*F402.1.4.2. Spirits who appear beautiful to men they like, ugly and covered with rash to those they dislike. Fijis: Hocart, 1929, 198.

*F402.1.4.3. Spirits who appear to young men as beautiful girls, and to old men as old women. Fijis: Hocart, 1929, 215.

*F402.1.4.4. Spirit assumes the form of a mortal's spouse, whom it replaces. Marquesas: Lavondes, 1964, 26ff.; Rennell: Elbert-Monberg, 1964, Nos. 52a, 175, 176; Bellona: ibid., No. 52b; Kapingamarangi: Elbert, 1949, 244.

*F402.1.4.5. Spirit by day, man in form by night, makes love to a girl. Samoa: Stuebel, 1896, 152, 154.

F402.1.5. Demon causes disease. N.Z.: Best, 1925, 1045; Ontong Java: Parkinson, 1898, 207.

F402.1.11. Spirit causes death. Easter Is.: Knoche, 1939, 25; N.Z.: Best, 1925, 862, 995; Grace, 1907, 38.

F402.1.11.2. Evil spirit kills and eats person. Tonga: Collocott, 1928, 59f.; N.Z.: Wohlers, 1876, 112.

*F402.1.11.2.1. Spirit consumes man's body: man jumps from tree and never reaches earth. Cooks: Beaglehole, 1938, 405.

*F402.1.15.2. Spirit marries mortal woman. Mangareva: Hiroa, 1938, 372; Samoa: Powell-Pratt, 1892, 247; Tokelaus: Burrows, 1923, 160f.; Kapingamarangi: Elbert, 1949, 245.

*F402.1.15.3. Mortal takes spirit wife. N.Z.: Grace, 1907, 136ff.

*F402.1.15.4. Sky spirit descends and seduces girl. Kapingamarangi: Elbert, 1949, 244.

*F402.1.16. Spirit possesses human being. Tuamotus: Caillot, 1914, 61ff., 64; Marquesas: Lavondes, 1964, 60; Samoa: Stuebel, 1896, 78, 152, 153, 156; Rotuma: Russell, 1942, 249ff.; Bellona: Elbert-Monberg, 1964, No. 190.

*F402.1.17. Evil spirits abduct human. Easter Is.: Knoche, 1939, 24; N.Z.: Best, 1925, 1051.

*F402.1.17.1. Evil spirits take unborn infant from belly of pregnant woman. Tuamotus: Caillot, 1914, 62.

*F402.1.18. Spirits cut down trees with their teeth. Samoa: Stuebel, 1896, 64.

*F402.1.19. Spirit smashes mountain with his club. Samoa: Stuebel, 1896, 87.

F402.2.1. King (chief) of demons. Samoa: Stuebel, 1896, 151.

*F402.6.0.1. Island (land) where spirits live. Hawaii: Fornander, 1918, V, 196; Samoa: Powell-Pratt, 1891, 204; Lau Is.: St. Johnston, 1918, 29ff.

*F402.6.0.2. Spirits live in land beneath the sea. Samoa: Stuebel, 1896, 144.

*F402.6.0.3. Demons from nether world. N.Z.: Grace, 1907, 38, 56.

*F402.6.0.3.1. Spirits stay in underworld by day, wander the earth by night. Samoa: Stuebel, 1896, 151.

F402.6.1. Demon lives in tree. Marquesas: Steinen, 1934-35, 216; Cooks: Gill, 1876, 84; Samoa: Stair, 1896, 52; Fijis: Hocart, 1929, 207.

F402.6.1.1. Demon lives at root of tree. Cooks: Beckwith, 1940, 252.

F402.6.4.1. Spirits (demons) live in cave. Tonga: Collocott, 1928, 10, 12; Samoa: Powell-Pratt, 1892, 133.

*F402.6.5. Spirits who live underground. Mangareva: Massainoff, 1933, 56.

F403.2. Spirits help mortal. Familiar spirits.
Easter I.: Métraux, 1940, 319; Tuamotus:
Stimson, n.d., Z-G. 13/174; Hawaii:
Westervelt, 1915, 114; Tokelaus: Lister, 1892,
51; N.Z.: Grace, 1907, 93; Wohlers, 1875, 22;
Tikopia: Firth, 1961, 91.

F403.2.1. Acquisition of familiar spirit. N.Z.:
Grace, 1907, 189.

F403.2.2.1. Familiar spirit in animal form. N.Z.:
Gudgeon, 1906, 35.

*F403.2.2.1.1. Shark as familiar. Hawaii: Emory,
1924, 17; N.Z.: Grace, 1907, 189.

F403.2.2.5. Demon as familiar spirit. N.Z.: Grace,
1907, 61ff.

F403.2.3.7. Army of spirits and ghosts. Tuamotus:
Henry, 1928, 511; N.Z.: Grace, 1907, 67f.

*F403.2.3.8. Demon guards albino creatures. N.Z.:
Grace, 1907, 141, 142.

*F403.2.3.9. Spirit punishes thefts. Samoa: Stuebel,
1896, 150.

*F403.2.3.10. Spirits provide food, clothes, and shelter
for royal refugees. Hawaii: Fornander, 1918, V,
196.

*F403.2.3.11. Invisible demons exterminate hostile army.
N.Z.: Grace, 1907, 65f.

*F403.2.3.12. Spirits build canoe. Samoa: Stuebel,
1896, 64.

*F403.2.3.13. Spirit guards a man's garden. Samoa:
Stuebel, 1896, 77f.

*F403.2.3.14. Demons return stolen goods to their
masters. N.Z.: Best, 1925, 1051.

*F403.2.3.15. A friendly spirit enables man to cast
himself from a high tree without injury to himself.
N.Z.: Best, 1925, 1049.

F404.2. Conjuring spirits. Easter I.: Métraux, 1940,
317.

F405. Means of combatting spirits. Hawaii: Emerson,

1915, 71; Luomala, 1951, 32.

F405.12. Demons flee from fire. Australs: Aitken, 1923, 257.

*F405.15. Spirits living in hollow tree caught in snare. Fijis: Hocart, 1929, 207; Fison, 1904, 13.

*F405.18. Spirit decapitated. Samoa: Stuebel, 1896, 87.

*F405.19. Spirit (ghost) caught in net. Hawaii: Fornander, 1916, IV, 550.

*F405.20. Menacing spirits driven away by recitation of formula. Bellona: Elbert-Monberg, 1964, Nos. 1a, 1b; Rennell: ibid., 1c.

*F411.4. Spirits fly. Samoa: Krämer, 1902, I, 115; N.Z.: Best, 1925, 1051.

*F411.5. Spirit descends from the sky in the rain. Tokelaus: Burrows, 1923,160.

*F411.6. Demons make a canoe voyage. Tonga: Reiter, 1934, 497ff.; Samoa: Stuebel, 1896, 146f.

*F411.7. Road traveled by spirits is hot, that traveled by mortals, cold. Bellona: Elbert-Monberg 1964, Nos. 1a, n. 11.

*F412.3. Appearance of kind of a bird indicates presence of spirit. Samoa: Stuebel, 1896, 81f.

F413. Origin of spirits. Hawaii: Fornander, 1918, VI, 268; N.Z.: Best, 1905, 212; Fijis: Beckwith, 1940, 336.

F419.2. Thieving spirit. Samoa: Krämer, 1902, I, 115.

*F419.4. Spirits eat raw food. N.Z.: Grace, 1907, 201.

*F419.5. Food of demon is illusory. Rennell: Elbert-Monberg, 1964, Nos. 175, 176.

*F419.6. Demon feeds upon shells and snakes. Rennell: Elbert-Monberg, 1964, 52b; Bellona: ibid, 52a.

F420. Water-spirits. N.Z.: Gudgeon, 1905, 187; Hongi, 1898, 40; Tama-Rau, 1899, 52; Whetu, 1897, 98; Fijis: Hocart, 1929, 195, 201; Nuku-manu: Sarfert, 1931, 334.

F420.1.1. Water-spirit as man. N.Z.: Beckwith, 1940, 150.

F420.1.2. Water-spirit as woman. Tuamotus: Stimson, 1937, 98; Hawaii: Beckwith, 1940, 541; Dickey, 1917, 35.

F420.1.3.2. Water-spirit as fish. Tuamotus: Stimson, n.d., Z-G. 13/174.

*F420.1.3.2.2. Sea-spirit breaks fishhooks lowered into sea. Hawaii: Beckwith, 1940, 215.

*F420.1.4.11. Water-spirits in form of waterspouts. Nukumanu: Sarfert, 1931, 332.

F420.1.5.2. Mysterious voice - water-spirit - is calling from sea. Societies: Henry, 1928, 471; Nukumanu: Sarfert, 1931, 386.

F420.3.4.2. Water-spirits must be in water before dawn. Niue: Smith, 1903, 96; N.Z.: Tregear, 1901, 185.

*F420.5.1.11. Water-spirit who rides dolphin's back places drowned people on the beaches. Marquesas: Tahiaoteaa, 1933, 492.

*F420.5.1.12. Two water-spirits carry sunken canoe and occupant to ocean's surface, bale canoe, and leave. Societies: Henry, 1928, 542.

F420.5.2.1.1. Water-maiden enamors man and draws him under water. Hawaii: Dickey, 1917, 35.

F420.5.2.2.2. Water-spirits kidnap mortals and keep them under water. Hawaii: Green, 1926, 97; Nukumanu: Sarfert, 1931, 332.

F420.5.2.7.3. Water-spirit wrecks ship. N.Z.: Beattie, 1920, 192; Fijis: Hocart, 1929, 208.

F420.5.2.7.4. Water-spirit holds ship back. N.Z.: Beattie, 1920, 136.

*F420.5.3.8. Sea-spirit disturbs fishing net. Samoa: Bülow, 1895, 140.

F420.6.1. Marriage or liaison of mortals and water-spirits. Tuamotus: Stimson, 1937, 98; Hawaii: Dickey, 1917, 35; N.Z.: Gudgeon, 1905, 187.

*F420.7.0.1. Spirit of reef. Samoa: Krämer, 1902, I, 401; Ontong Java: Parkinson, 1898, 197.

*F420.7.2. Sea demon trapped and killed. N.Z.: White, 1887-90, V, 75f., 78, 79.

*F421.0.1. Demon in form of lake. N.Z.: Best, 1925, 974.

F423. Sea spirits. Australs: Aitken, 1923, 257; Tuamotus: Caillot, 1914, 61; Stimson, 1934, 50; 1937, 68ff.; Hawaii: Beckwith, 1940, 215; Tokelaus: Burrows, 1923, 172; Macgregor, 1937, 61; N.Z.: Best, 1925, 1045; White, 1887-90, V, 75f., 77, 78, 79; Rotuma: Russell, 1942, 249ff.; Nukumanu: Sarfert, 1931, 446 n. 3; Rennell: Elbert-Monberg, 1964, No. 78; Ontong Java: Parkinson, 1898, 196f.; Kapingamarangi: Elbert, 1948, 76.

*F423.0.1. Sea demons emerge by night and attack islanders. Rotuma: Russell, 1942, 233, 249ff.

*F423.2. Spirits which live in sea by day, on earth by night. Hawaii: Luomala, 1951, 70.

>D620. Periodic transformation.
>F252.3.1. Soldiers of fairy king are trees by day and men by night.

F424. River-spirit. Marquesas: Lavondes, 1964, 36.

F426. Spirit of water-fall. Hawaii: Westervelt, 1915, 47.

*F429.2. Spirits of water-well. Tonga: Collocott, 1928, 11.

F431. Cloud-spirit. Ellice Is.: Kennedy, 1931, 175.

F432. Wind-spirit. Nukumanu: Sarfert, 1931, 332.

F439.1. Rainbow spirit. (Cf. A288. Rainbow goddess.) Hawaii: Beckwith, 1940, 135, 152; Westervelt, 1915 84ff., 118ff.; Ontong Java: Parkinson, 1898, 207.

F439.1.2. Rainbow spirit as helper on journey. Hawaii: Beckwith, 1940, 515f.

F439.1.3. Rainbow spirit as messenger. Hawaii: Beckwith, 1940, 521.

*F439.1.4. Rain-spirits. Kapingamarangi: Elbert, 1948, 74.

*F439.1.5. Mist-maiden. N.Z.: Best, 1905, 209; 1924, 158.

*F440.2. Fern spirits. N.Z.: *Whetu, 1897, 100.

F441. Wood-spirit. Tuamotus: Beckwith, 1940, 267; Societies: Henry, 1928, 384; Hawaii: Luomala, 1951, 29, 48; Samoa: Krämer, 1902, I, 415; Powell-Pratt, 1891, 203, n. 8; Stuebel, 1896, 148; Tokelaus: Macgregor, 1937, 84; N.Z.: Best, 1925, 995, 999; Gudgeon, 1906, 42; White, 1887-90, I, 56; Rennell: Elbert-Monberg, 1964, No. 78.

F441.2. Tree-spirit. Societies: Henry, 1928, 561; Hawaii: Westervelt, 1915, 98f., 111ff.; Samoa: Krämer, 1902, I, 415; N.Z.: Best, 1925, 970f.; Santa Cruz: O'Ferrall, 1904, 224; Ontong Java: Sarfert, 1931, 326; Nukumanu: Sarfert, 1931, 453.

F441.2.1. Wood-nymph. Societies: Henry, 1928, 542.

*F441.4.7. Wood-spirit in form of tap-root. Cooks: Gill, 1876, 84.

*F441.6.5. Forest spirits restore chopped tree whole after person fails to show proper respect. See also C939.3., D950., D1602.2. Polynesia(general): *Elbert-Kirtley, 1966, 355ff.; Tuamotus: Stimson, 1937, 121ff.; Marquesas: Lavondes, 1966, 72ff.; 148ff., 194ff.; Cooks: Savage, 1910, 147; Hawaii: *Luomala,1951, 16, 69f.; Thrum, 1895, 116; Samoa: Stuebel, 1896, 148; N.Z.: Best, 1925, 999f.; White, 1887-90, I, 70, 74, 75, 76, 90f.; III, 2f.; Wohlers, 1875, 21f.; Bellona: Elbert-Monberg, 1964, Nos. 19a, 19b.

*F441.6.6. Wood-spirit abducts mortal woman. N.Z.: Best, 1925, 998.

F443. Echo as wood-spirit. Cooks: *Gill, 1876, 116f.

F445. Field-spirits. Ontong Java: Sarfert, 1931, 326; Nukumanu: *Sarfert, 1931, 333f.

F450. Underground spirits. Oceania: **Beckwith, 1940, 321-336; Cooks: Gill, 1876, 76, 258.

F451. Dwarf. (Underground spirit). Hawaii: Rice, 1923, 35; Westervelt, 1915, 117; 1915a, 102, 174.

F451.3.2. Dwarf rendered powerless. Societies: Tefaafana, 1917, 37.

C752.2.1. Tabu: supernatural creature being abroad after sunrise.

F451.4.1. Dwarfs live under the ground. Hawaii: Fornander, 1918, VI, 336.

F451.5.1. Helpful dwarfs. Hawaii: Rice, 1923, 35.

F451.5.4. Mortal goes to land of dwarfs. Tahiti: Henry, 1928, 580.

F451.9. Dwarfs emigrate. Hawaii: Beckwith, 1940, 332.

F451.9.1.14. Dwarfs forced to flee by deity. Hawaii: Beckwith, 1940, 328.

F460. Mountain-spirits. Tuamotus: Stimson, 1937, 69; N.Z.: Beckwith, 1940, 334; Best, 1925, 967, 973, 974, 980ff.; Grey, 1855, 150.

*F460.1.8. Mountain-men created imperfect, and are hidden within mountain. N.Z.: White, 1887-90, I, 47.

F471.1. Nightmare. Presses person in dream. Cooks: Beaglehole, 1938, 316.

F471.2. Incubus. A male demon who comes in sleep and has sexual intercourse with a woman. Nukumanu: Sarfert, 1931, 332.

F471.2.0.1. Demon lover. Tahiti: Henry, 1928, 221.

*F471.2.0.2. Albinos born from union of incubus and woman. Nukumanu: Sarfert, 1931, 332.

F471.2.1. Succubus: female incubus. Nukumanu: Sarfert, 1931, 332.

F473.1. Poltergeist throws objects. Tahiti: Henry, 1928, 224; Cooks: Gill, 1876, 159; Samoa: Stair, 1896, 50ff.

F473.5. Poltergeist makes noises. Tahiti: Henry, 1928, 224; Samoa: Stair, 1896, 50ff.

*F473.6.10. Poltergeist deals blows in the dark. Samoa: Stair, 1896, 48.

F480. House-spirits. Fijis: Fison, 1904, 43.

F491. Will-o'-the-Wisp. Light seen over marshy places. Cooks: Gill, 1876, 125; Samoa: Stair, 1896, 48; Chatham Is.: Skinner, 1923, 57; N.Z.: Best, 1925, 877.

F494.3. Earth spirit. Tokelaus: Macgregor, 1937, 61; Ontong Java: Sarfert, 1931, 326; Nukumanu: *Sarfert, 1931, 332f.

F495. Stone-spirit. Tahiti: Henry, 1928, 471; Hawaii: Emerson, 1915, 3f.; N.Z.: Best, 1925, 972; Futuna: Burrows, 1936, 225; Nukumanu: Sarfert, 1931, 333.

F499.1. Sky-spirit. Cooks: Gill, 1896, 235, 237, 264; N.Z.: Grey, 1855, 66; Rotuma: Churchward, 1938-39, 218; Kapingamarangi: Elbert, 1948, 93.

*F499.1.2. Stars are demons. N.Z.: Best, 1925, 848, 852.

G11.8.1. Stars as cannibals.

*F499.4. Comet as evil spirit. Tahiti: Henry, 1928, 227.

*F499.5. Reflection of the moon as spirit. Easter Is.: Métraux, 1940, 372.

*F499.6. Half-spirit, half-man. Hawaii: Beckwith, 1940, 414; Samoa: Stuebel, 1896, 147; Nukumanu: Sarfert, 1931, 334.

*F499.7. Spirits of the air. Hawaii: Beckwith, 1940, 54.

*F502. Person consisting only of one breast. Marquesas: Steinen, 1933-34, 33.

F511.0.1. Headless person. Hawaii: Beckwith, 1940, 93.

*F511.0.2.8. Ten-headed being. Rotuma: Russell, 1942, 246ff.

F511.0.3. Persons whose heads are stone-hammers. Lau Is.: St. Johnston, 1918, 109.

F511.0.4. Man carries his head under his arm. Tonga: Gifford, 1924, 31.

*F511.0.9.4. Person with pigeon's head. Tonga: Gifford 1924, 31; Reiter, 1933, 365

*F511.0.10. Person with head joined to another person's body. Rarotonga: Te Ariki, 1920, 179.

F511.1.1. Two-faced person. Easter I.: Métraux, 1940, 85; N.Z.: White, 1887-90, III, 114.

*F511.1.2.0.1. Monster with a hundred faces. N.Z.: White, 1887-90, IV, 107.

*F511.1.5. Monstrous person whose face is flat, "like a cliff." N.Z.: Best, 1925, 903.

F512.2.1. Persons with four eyes. Tuamotus: Caillot, 1914, 43; Kapingamarangi: Elbert, 1948, 80.

F512.2.1.2. Eight-eyed person. Tuamotus: Stimson, n.d T-G. 3/15; Hawaii: Beckwith, 1940, 233; Fornande 1918, VI, 335.

*F512.2.1.2.1. Nine-eyed person. Funafuti: David, 1890 109; Samoa: Powell-Pratt, 1891, 198.

*F512.6. Bald-headed monster with one hundred eyes. N.Z White, 1887-90, IV, 110, 112.

*F513.0.7. Person with human mouth in face, shark's mouth between shoulder blades. Hawaii: Thrum, 1907, 257ff.; Westervelt, 1915, 61.

*F513.0.8. People with dainty mouths (like bugs).
Hawaii: Green, 1926, 121; Luomala, 1951, 34f.

*F513.0.9. People with enormous mouths. Hawaii: Green,
1926, 121; Thrum, 1923, 174.

*F513.2.1. Person who has, in place of a tongue, a hollow
tube, for sucking in fish. N.Z.: Best, 1925, 968.

*F513.2.2. Extraordinarily long tongue can simulate
a bridge. Hawaii: Emerson, 1915, 85.

*F514.2.1. Man with nose like a coxcomb. Samoa:
Abercromby, 1891, 458; Stuebel, 1896, 152, 154.

*F516.1.0.1. Child without arms or legs. Samoa:
Sierich, 1902, 181.

*F516.1.2. People with one arm. Marquesas: Steinen,
1934-35, 216.

*F516.1.3. People with arms and legs so short that they
are scarcely visible. N.Z.: Wohlers,1876, 122f.

F516.4. Man with elastic reach. Hawaii: Beckwith,
1940, 263; Dickey, 1917, 21; Forbes, 1882, 38;
Luomala, 1951, 34, 39; Rice, 1923, 98; Thrum,
1907, 67f.

F517.0.1. Person with one leg. Marquesas: Steinen,
1934-35, 216.

F517.0.2.1. Man with legs so long he can steady boat
as he stands in ocean. Hawaii: Beckwith, 1940,
354; Fornander, 1916, IV, 98, 160.

*F517.0.2.2. Man with elastically extending legs.
Hawaii: Thrum, 1907, 72.

*F517.0.2.3. Person with eight legs. Hawaii:
Fornander, 1918, VI, 335.

F518. Persons with tails. Ellice Is.: Kennedy,
1931, 166.

*F519. Person (animal) with elastic body. Hawaii:
Forbes, 1882, 40; Fornander, 1916, IV, 438ff.,
1918, V, 320, 518; Thrum, 1907, 72f.; Westervelt,
1915a, 253f.

F521.1. Man covered with hair like animal. Tuamotus: Caillot, 1914, 57ff.; Samoa: Nelson, 1925, 140; N.Z.: Cowan, 1930, 168ff.; Luomala, 1951, 72.

F521.2. Feathered people. Tuamotus: Stimson, n.d., Z-G. 3/1353, Z-G. 13/380; Samoa: Krämer, 1902, I, 455.

*F521.4. Person of stone. Hawaii: Rice, 1923, 100.

*F521.5.1. Person covered with bark. N.Z.: Grace, 1907, 143ff., 201.

*F521.6. Person with body of hair. Rotuma: Churchward, 1937-38, 259.

*F521.6.1. Man with hair on his back. Societies: Ropiteau,1933, 125.

F522. Person with wings. Hawaii: Beckwith, 1919, 554; Emory, 1924, 12; Fornander, 1919, VI, 336; Samoa: Powell-Pratt, 1891, 203f.; N.Z.: Grey, 1855, 185.

F523. Two persons with bodies joined. Siamese twins. Tuamotus: Audran, 1918, 92; Tonga: Reiter, 1907, 752; Samoa: Abercromby, 1891, 457; Fraser, 1896, 171, 174; Stuebel, 1896, 152, 154; Krämer, 1902, I, 107; Rotuma: Churchward, 1938-39, 330.

*F523.1. Siamese twins frightened, run in different directions, and are thus separated. Samoa: Abercromby, 1891, 457; Stuebel, 1896, 154.

F524. Person with several bodies. Hawaii: Fornander, 1918, V, 314ff., 550ff.; Green, 1923,11.

F525.1.1. Man with one side of stone. Hawaii: Dixon, 1916, 89; Forbes, 1882, 37; Fornander, 1916, IV, 98; Green, 1923, 11; Thrum, 1907, 65; N.Z.: Best, 1924, 224.

F525.2. Man splits into two parts. Tonga: Gifford, 1924, 32; Reiter, 1907, 752; Samoa: Fraser, 1896, 172, 175; Rotuma: Churchward, 1938-39, 330.

*F525.7. Person who is dead and putrid on one side of body, but alive on the other. N.Z.: White, 1887-90, II, 75.

F527.1. Red person. Tuamotus: Stimson, 1937, 89; Hawaii: Fornander, 1916, IV, 78; Thrum, 1921, 107, 205; Westervelt, 1915, 132.

*F527.7. Albino men. Samoa: Sierich, 1900, 233ff.; Rotuma: Churchward, 1938-39, 466.

*F529.1.2. Men with recesses in their backs for storing plunder. Samoa: Powell-Pratt, 1891, 203f.

*F529.2.2. Woman with extraordinary anus. Marquesas: Steinen, 1933-34, 30, 32.

F529.7.1. Person without joints. Bellona: Elbert-Monberg, 1964, No. 32.

*F529.9. Remarkable man who is so fat that when he dies, his fat flows underground to the sea, which is oily for a number of days. Cooks: Beaglehole, 1938, 385f.

*F529.10. People who are all hands, elbows, and shoulders. N.Z.: White, 1887-90, II, 12.

*F529.11. Girl so weak she falls in rubbish heap and so thin that, since people do not see her, she is soon covered with rubbish. Tokelaus: Burrows, 1923, 166.

*F529.12. Being with eight livers on his exterior. Samoa: Powell-Pratt, 1891-93, 276, 279.

F531. Giants. A person of enormous size. Tuamotus: Audran, 1918, 90ff.; Stimson, n.d., Z-G. 3/1323 Societies: Ropiteau, 1933, 128; Hawaii: Dickey, 1917, 27; Fornander, 1916, IV, 166ff.; 1918, V, 52, 146; Remy, 1868, 38ff.; Thrum, 1923, 149; Tonga: Caillot, 1914, 243; Tokelaus: Macgregor, 1939, 88; N.Z.: Cowan, 1930, I, 238ff.; 1930a, 7; Grey, 1855, 149; Rotuma: Churchward, 1938-39, 219.

F531.1.1.5.1. Giant with eight eyes. Polynesia: Beckwith, 1940, 210.

F531.1.2.2.1. Two-headed giant. Rotuma: Churchward, 1938-39, 219.

*F531.1.2.2.4.1. Eight-headed giant. Cooks: Luomala, 1949, 169.

*F531.1.3.7. Giant with a foot seven-feet long. Rennell: Elbert-Monberg, 1964, No. 67.

F531.1.5. Breasts of giantess. Rarotonga: Te Ariki, 1921, 5.

F531.1.6.7.2. Giant with eight arms. Polynesia: Beckwith, 1940, 210.

F531.2.1. Extremely tall giant. Australs: Aitken, 1923, 277; Tuamotus: Stimson, 1937, 100; Marquesas: Lavondes, 1966, 98, 116; Cooks: Beaglehole, 382, 386; Hawaii: Fornander, 1916, IV, 436; V, 56, 374; Fijis: Beckwith, 1940, 210.

*F531.2.1.7. Person so tall that he feels no pain when his feet are cut off. Hawaii: Fornander, 1918, V, 518.

F531.2.4. Giant's large footprints. Hawaii: Rice, 1923, 99.

F531.2.5. Extremely fat giant. Samoa: Luomala, 1949, 67.

*F531.2.18. Giant so large he hides the sun. Hawaii: Rice, 1923, 64.

F531.3.1. Giant wades the ocean. Tuamotus: Audran, 1919, 32ff.; Societies: Agostini, 1900, 88; Williams, 1895, 275; Fijis: Fison, 1904, 121; Funafuti: David, 1899, 180f.

F531.3.4.2. Giant drinks up a river (lake, sea). N.Z.: Cowan, 1925, 170; White, 1887-90, III, 124f., 190.

F531.3.5. Giant steps prodigious distance. Hawaii: Beckwith, 1940, 474; Rice, 1923, 102; N.Z.: Smith, 1911,12.

*F531.3.5.4. Giant strides from island to island. Tuamotus: Audran, 1919, 32, 47, 51.

*F531.3.5.5. Giants stride from mountain range to mountai range. N.Z.: White, 1887-90, III, 124, 190.

*F531.3.11.1. Giant opens his mouth to resemble cave entrance: gobbles unwary entrants. Tonga: Gifford, 1924, 82.

*F531.4.4.1. Giant uses uprooted tree as club. Hawaii: Thrum, 1923, 160; Fijis: Fison, 1904, 126.

F531.4.5. Giant's enormous weapons. Hawaii: Fornander, 1916, IV, 446.

*F531.4.7.4. Giant wears loincloth a hundred fathoms
long. Samoa: Luomala, 1949, 67; Powell-Pratt,
1892, 80.

F535. Pygmy. Remarkably small man. Hawaii:
Fornander, 1918, V, 498, 500; N.Z.: Cowan,
1930, I, 33f.; Fijis: Fison, 1904, 77.

F535.1. Thumbling. Person the size of a thumb.
Hawaii: Green, 1929, 5.

F541.11. Removable eyes (used as fishbait). Hawaii:
*Beckwith, 1940, 199f.; McAllister, 1933, 94;
Samoa: Krämer, 1902, I, 139.

F542.2. Big ears. One used as a mattress and one as
a covering, and the like. Oceania: **Kirtley,
1963, 119ff.

*F542.3. Big ears--contain a banana in the hollow.
Mangareva: Laval, 1938, 15.

*F544.0.5. Extraordinarily large mouth: opened, the
upper lip touches the sky, the lower the ground.
Hawaii: Fornander, 1918, V, 410.

F544.1.4. Lips used as a spear. N.Z.: Beckwith,
1940, 200; Grey, 1855, 185.

F544.2.2. Long tongue. Lau Is.: St. Johnston,
1918, 116.

F544.2.2.1. Long tongue used to bridge a stream.
Hawaii: Beckwith, 1940, 175; Emerson, 1915, 85.

*F544.2.5. Detachable tongue used as a surfboard.
Hawaii: Luomala, 1951, 30.

*F544.3.2.2. Person with fiery red teeth. Rotuma:
Churchward, 1938-39, 223.

F545.1. Remarkable beard. Marquesas: Steinen,
1933-34, 371.

*F545.2.5. Person with eight foreheads. Hawaii:
Fornander, 1918, V, 328ff., 370.

*F545.2.6. Person with remarkably sharp forehead.
Hawaii: Fornander, 1916, IV, 530; V, 328ff.,
370.

*F545.2.7. Person with detachable forehead. Hawaii: Fornander, 1918, V, 328ff., 370.

*F545.2.8. Man with elastic forehead. Hawaii: Fornander, 1916, IV, 530.

F546. Remarkable breast. Kapingamarangi: Elbert, 1949, 243.

*F546.7. Woman with cold bosom (her cloak is covered with snow). Hawaii: Beckwith, 1919, 402.

F547.1.1. Vagina dentata. Woman kills her husbands with her toothed vagina. Marquesas: Steinen, 1934-35, 225, 226; Samoa: Abercromby, 1891, 456.

F547.2. Hermaphrodite. Hawaii: Beckwith, 1940, 407.

F547.3.1. Long penis. Fijis: Hocart, 1929, 191; N.Z.: White, 1887-90, IV, 183.

*F547.3.6.1. Penis that husks coconuts. Fijis: Hocart, 1929, 195.

*F547.3.7. Penis used as ladder. Hawaii: Beckwith, 1940, 212.

*F547.3.8. Detachable penis (moves independently). Tuamotus: Stimson, n.d., T-G. 3/109; Tikopia: Firth, 1961, 22.

*F547.3.9. Extraordinary penis so large it is used as fish trap. Ontong Java: Sarfert, 1931, 443.

F547.4. Extraordinary clitoris. Fijis: Hocart, 1929, 217.

F547.5.1. Removable vagina. Hawaii: Beckwith, 113, 186 213.

*F551.6. Remarkably big foot. Oceania: *Lessa, 1961; Hawaii: Rice, 1923, 102; Reef Is.: O'Ferral, 1904 232.

*F551.7. Girl with remarkably tender feet must be carried about. Tonga: Collocott, 1928, 41, 44f.

F552.1.3. Extraordinary fingernails (used as weapons). Australs: Aitken, 1923, 263; Tuamotus: Caillot, 1914, 57; Rurutu: Aitken, 1930, 109; N.Z.: Cowan, 1930, 121ff.; 1930a, 121f., 168; Gudgeon,

1906, 43; Tikopia: Firth, 1961, 87; Kapingamarangi: Elbert, 1949, 243.

*F552.1.3.1. Retractable fingernails. N.Z.: White, 1887-90, I, 90, 129.

F552.2. Remarkably strong hands. Tonga: Beckwith, 1940, 486.

F555.3. Very long hair. Samoa: Sierich, 1902, 191.

F557. Removable organs (limbs, etc.). Tuamotus: Stimson, 1934, 8; Marquesas: Lavondes, 1964, 2, 20; Nukumanu: Sarfert, 1931, 455; Ontong Java: Sarfert, 1931, 385.

*F557.2. Person gives her intestines for use as a mooring rope. Hawaii: Fornander, 1916, IV, 518.

*F557.4. Removable head. Tokelaus: Burrows, 1923, 160; Rennell: Elbert-Monberg, 1964, No. 65.

*F559.2.1. People with navals twisted around to their backs. Societies: Henry, 1928, 416.

F559.4. Remarkable skull. Tahiti: Orsmond, 1933b, 171.

*F559.6.2. Man with double stomach. Niue: Loeb, 1926, 165.

*F559.7.0.1. Man with double heart. Niue: Loeb, 1926, 165.

*F559.7.3. Man with eight hearts. Pukapuka: Beaglehole, 1938, 380.

*F559.9. Remarkable armpits: lightning flashes from them. N.Z.: White, 1887-90, I, 118; Wohlers, 1876, 121.

*F559.10. Man magically stretches self. Cf. D55.1.1. Hawaii: Forbes, 1882, 40; Fornander, 1918, V, 320.

*F559.10.1. Pig-man magically enlongates self and serves as bridge by which his companions may escape. Hawaii: Westervelt, 1915, 253, 254.

F561.1. People who prefer raw flesh. Tuamotus: Caillot, 1914, 59, 63; Marquesas: Lavondes, 1964, 44; N.Z.: Best, 1925, 998; Dixon, 1916, 78, n. 77;

White, 1887-90, II, 9, 12, 18, 32; Wohlers, 1876, 109, 122f.

*F561.9. People eat only mud. Rarotonga: Ariki, 1899, 65.

*F561.10. Person who eats coral. Hawaii: Fornander, 1916, IV, 518.

*F561.11. Hero eats shells of fish, not meat. Tuamotus: Henry, 1928, 529.

*F561.12. Person who lives upon king's urine and excrement. Hawaii: Fornander, 1916, IV, 512; V, 400.

*F561.13. Person has birds living in his hair: when hungry, he shakes his head. N.Z.: White, 1887-90, I, 83, 135, 145; Wohlers, 1875, 9.

F562.2. Residence in tree. Marquesas: Handy, 1930, 56; Hawaii: Beckwith, 1919, 430; Samoa: Krämer, 1902, I, 303, 408f.; N.Z.: White, 1887-90, II, 8f., 32.

F562.3. Residence in (under) water. Easter I.: Métraux, 1940, 372; Mangareva: Hiroa, 1938, 354; Marquesas: Lavondes, 1966, 98, 170; Steinen, 1934-35, 235f.; Samoa: Powell-Pratt, 1892, 98; N.Z.: Grey, 1855, 61f.; Ellice Is.: Kennedy, 1931, 197.

*F562.3.1. Fishermen pull child up in their net. Hawaii: Thrum, 1923, 226; Westervelt, 1915, 195; Samoa: Powell-Pratt, 1892, 71; Kapingamarangi: Elbert, 1949, 245.

*F562.3.2. Child wrapped in red mist and living upon surface of the sea. Hawaii: Westervelt, 1915, 38.

*F562.6. Person lives beneath the earth. Easter I.: Métraux, 1940, 368; Mangareva: Hiroa, 1938, 358; Tuamotus: Caillot, 1914, 46; Marquesas: Steinen, 1933-34, 38; Ontong Java: Sarfert, 1931, 296, 384.

*F562.6.1. Man digging in sand finds man beneath earth (pulls him up). Fijis: Jackson, 1894, 74; Ontong Java: Sarfert, 1931, 295, 299.

*F562.6.3. People who spend day on earth, night in lower world. Marquesas: Lavondes, 1964, 22.

*F562.7. People live in mountain top. Niue: Loeb, 1926, 149.

*F562.8. Girl lives in oyster-shell. Rotuma: Churchward, 1938-39, 333.

*F562.9. Person who lives on back of fish. Marquesas: Tahiaoteaa, 1933, 491f.; Tuamotus: Leverd, 1911, 175.

*F562.10. Man living in sun. Hawaii: Beckwith, 1919, 566.

*F562.11. Person lives borne upon wings of birds. Hawaii: Pukui-Curtis, n.d., 53; Samoa: Sierich, 1900, 237.

F564.3.1. Long sleep, long waking. Societies: Williams, 1895, 271; Rarotonga: Te Ariki, 1920, 122; Aitutaki: Large, 1903, 134; Hawaii: Beckwith, 1940, 416; Dickey, 1917, 19f.; Fornander, 1918, V, 158, 168; Green, 1923, 52; Thrum, 1907, 74ff.; Tikopia: Firth, 1961, 50.

*F564.3.7.1. Person whose sleep lasts for seven days. Marquesas: Lavondes, 1966, 52, 116, 150, 186; Steinen, 1933-34, 343.

*F564.5. Hero sinks in sea while asleep; he continues to sleep. Rarotonga: Te Ariki, 1920, 122.

*F564.6. Heavy sleeper: struck ten times with lash:at tenth stroke, he calmly awakens. Societies: Henry, 1928, 581.

*F564.6.1. Heavy sleeper: he is consumed with fire before he awakens. Hawaii: Fornander, 1918, V, 528.

*F564.6.2. Heavy sleeper: sleeps for months until a kukui nut takes root in his nose. Hawaii: Fornander, 1918, V, 544.

*F564.7. Person with four eyes: two sleep while two remain awaki. Tuamotus: Caillot, 1914, 46.

*F564.8. Albino women come to island each night to fetch food and leave before dawn. Niue: Smith, 1903, 102.

F566.2. Land where women live separate from men. Tikopia: Firth, 1930-31, 308.

F567. Wild man. Man lives alone in wood like a beast. Cooks: Large, 1903, 137; Low, 1935, 28; Hawaii: Beckwith, 1940, 393; N.Z.: Cowan, 1930, I, 60, 64, 114f.; 1930a, 7; Gudgeon, 1906, 43; White, 1887-90, II, 8f.

*F567.0.1. Wild man's body encrusted with shells. Cooks: Low, 1935, 29.

*F567.0.2. Wild man lives in a cave. Samoa: Nelson, 1925, 140.

*F567.0.3. Wild man captured. Hawaii: Luomala, 1951, 54.

F567.1. Wild woman. Marquesas: Tahiaoteaa, 1933, 497; Hawaii: Beckwith, 1940, 506.

F571. Extremely old person. Hawaii: Fornander, 1918, VI, 276.

F574. Luminous person. Mangareva: Hiroa, 1938, 369; Tahiti: Henry, 1928, 615; Hawaii: Fornander, 1916, IV, 172, 540; Thrum, 1923, 119, 168; Tonga: Collocott, 1928, 27; Samoa: Powell-Pratt, 1891, 204; N.Z.: Cowan, 1930, I, 25; Ellice Is.: Kennedy, 1931, 174.

F574.1. Resplendent beauty. Hawaii: Fornander, 1916, IV, 602.

F574.1.4. Man's (woman's) beauty eclipses splendor of the sun. Hawaii: Fornander, 1916, IV, 78.

F574.3.3. Hero luminous. Marquesas: Steinen, 1933-34, 31; 1934-35, 203f., 208; Cooks: Beckwith, 1940, 247; Te Ariki, 1921, 2; Gill, 1876, 227; N.Z.: Beckwith, 1940, 250.

*F574.3.3.1. Hero's birthmark, a centipede design, glows in the dark. Cooks: Te Ariki, 1920, 122.

*F574.3.4. Person's knee burns like fire. Ellice Is.: Kennedy, 1931, 159; Nukumanu: Sarfert, 1931, 334.

*F574.3.5. Two children carry light in their breasts. Nukumanu: Sarfert, 1931, 450.

F575.1. Remarkably beautiful woman. Hawaii: Thrum, 1907, 204.

*F584.2. Person remarkably heavy in weight. Societies: Henry, 1928, 557.

F591. Person who never laughs. Ellice Is.: Roberts, 1958, 407.

H1194. Task: making a person laugh.

F593. Person's extraordinary body temperature. (Cf. F686.).

*F593.2. Extraordinarily hot person (his heat burns objects). Mangareva: Laval, 1938, 8; Hawaii: Westervelt, 1915, 76ff.; Reef Is.: O'Ferrall, 1904, 228; Tikopia: Firth, 1961, 34, 36.

*F593.3. Extraordinarily cold man. Hawaii: Westervelt, 1915, 76ff.

F595. Man's body exudes sweet scent. Easter I.: Métraux, 1940, 369.

*F595.1. Sisters with remarkably sweet scent. Hawaii: Beckwith, 1940, 530; 1919, 412, 414, 416, 418.

F597. Woman without womb. Samoa: Abercromby, 1891, 455; Krämer, 1902, I, 104f.

*F599. Extraordinary persons - miscellaneous.

*F599.1. People who flee from sight of a fire. N.Z.: White, 1887-90, II, 9, 12, 18.

F600--F699. PERSONS WITH EXTRAORDINARY POWERS

F601. Extraordinary companions. Cooks: Beckwith, 1940, 270; Savage, 1910, 149; Hawaii: Beckwith, 1940, 356; Rice, 1923, 99ff.; Westervelt, 1915, 75ff.; 1915a, 76ff., 79ff.; Tonga: Beckwith, 1940, 271; Samoa: Stuebel, 1896, 142; Fijis: Fison, 1904, 80ff.

F601.0.1. Skillful companions. Cooks: Beckwith, 1940, 268.

F601.1. Extraordinary companions perform hero's tasks. Hawaii: Beckwith, 1940, 262, 264.

F610. Remarkably strong man. Hawaii: Fornander, 1916, IV, 32ff., 226; V, 208f.; Tonga: Brown, 1916, 426ff.; Samoa: Fraser, 1896, 177; N.Z.: Grace, 1907, 178; Rennell: Elbert-Monberg, 1964, No. 92.

F610.2. Dwarf-hero of superhuman strength. Hawaii: Fornander, 1918, V, 498ff.

F611.3.2. Hero's precocious strength. Has full strength when very young. Marquesas: Handy, 1930, 105; Samoa: Krämer, 1902, I, 108; Fijis: Beckwith, 1940, 483.

*F611.3.4. Small boy kills all but one of four companies of forty-eight men in fight. Hawaii: Fornander, 1918, V, 278.

*F611.3.5. Young chief becomes an accomplished surfboard rider at his first try. Hawaii: Westervelt, 1915, 227.

F614.2. Strong man uproots tree and uses it as weapon. Tuamotus: Henry, 1928, 524.

*F614.4.2. Strong man gives mighty stroke with paddle that sends canoe from Fiji (?) to Pukapuka. Pukapuka: Beaglehole, 1938, 383.

*F614.4.3. Strong man gives such a furious stroke with paddle that loaded canoe tips over. Pukapuka: Beaglehole, 1938, 385.

*F614.4.4. Boy wins canoe race against eight paddlers in opposing canoe. Hawaii: Fornander, 1918, V, 126ff.; Rice, 1923, 85ff.

F614.8. Strong man fells tree with one blow of axe. Hawaii: Rice, 1923, 96.

*F614.9.2. Youth clears taro patch overnight, throws brush so far it cannot be seen. Tubuai: Aitken, 1930, 110.

F614.10. Strong hero fights whole army alone. Cooks: Te Ariki, 1921, 55f.; Hawaii: Rice, 1923, 60; Samoa: Fraser, 1900, 132f.; Chatham Is.: Shand, 1896, 135; Fijis: Fison, 1904, 53.

F621. Strong man: tree puller. Can uproot and carry off trees. Tuamotus: Audran, 1918, 92; Societies: Henry, 1928, 538; Hawaii: Dickey, 1917, 23; Dixon, 1916, 90; Emerson, 1921, 16; Emory, 1924, 13, 14; Fornander, 1916, IV, 486; 1918, V, 200; Green, 1926, 91; 1929, 87ff.; Luomala, 1951, 21; Westervelt, 1915, 22; 1915a, 185; Futuna: Burrows, 1936, 227; Funafuti: David, 1899, 108; Lau Is.: St. Johnston, 1918, 109; Tikopia: Firth, 1961, 99.

F621.2. Trees pulled up by giant. Tonga: Collocott, 1921, 55.

F624. Mighty lifter. Hawaii: Fornander, 1918, V, 220, 366; Thrum, 1923, 254; Tikopia: Firth, 1961, 99.

F624.2. Strong man lifts large stone. Hawaii: Remy, 1868, 35.

F624.2.0.1. Strong man (goddess) throws enormous stone. Hawaii: Green, 1923, 9.

F624.2.0.1.1. Strong man throws mountain. Fijis: Rochereau, 1915, 419.

F624.2.0.2. Strong man moves enormous rock. Marquesas: Handy, 1930, 105.

F624.6. Strong man lifts house. Mangareva: Hiroa, 1938, 326.

F624.7. Strong man carries boat (ship). Tuamotus: Audran, 1919, 235; Stimson, n.d., T-G. 3/403; Tonga: Gifford, 1924, 127.

*F624.7.1. Strong man lifts canoe with little finger. Tokelaus: Macgregor, 1937, 88.

F624.8. Strong man throws opponent into the air. Hawaii: Fornander, 1916, IV, 36; Tonga: Gifford, 1924, 122.

*F624.11. Warrior throws his club, which knocks down a forest, which falls upon and destroys a hostile army. Hawaii: Fornander, 1918, V, 372.

*F624.12. Person smashes a canoe fleet with coconut log. Kapingamarangi: Elbert, 1949, 241.

311

*F624.13. Person throws a canoe as if it were a spear.
Hawaii: Fornander, 1918, V, 206.

*F624.14. Chief makes noise like thunder and flashes
like lightning when he throws his spear. Hawaii:
Fornander, 1916, IV, 226.

*F624.15. Two strong brothers throw pebbles from one to
the other when standing at opposite ends of an islan
Lau Is.: St. Johnston, 1918, 109.

*F624.16. Strong man can carry more than eight times as
much as 40,400 men can carry. Hawaii: Luomala,
1951, 28.

F626. Strong man pulls down mountains. Cooks: Large,
1903, 134.

F626.1. Strong man flattens hill (lops off hilltop).
Societies: Henry, 1928, 589; Fijis: Rochereau,
1915, 419.

F626.2. Strong man kicks mountain down. Marquesas:
Handy, 1930, 105.

F627. Strong man pulls down building. Hawaii: Rice,
1923, 95.

F628. Strong man as mighty slayer. Tahiti: Henry,
1928, 588; Cooks: Beaglehole, 1938, 407;
Hawaii: Emerson, 1921, 16ff.; Fornander, 1918, V,
378; Kamakau, 1961, 18; Remy, 1868, 43f.;
Tonga: Caillot, 1914, 292ff.

F628.1.4.2. Strong hero kills sharks with own hands.
Tuamotus: Stimson, n.d., Z-G. 3/1323; Cooks:
Gill, 1876, 226; Hawaii: Beckwith, 1940, 421;
Fornander, 1918, V, 200, 202; Tonga: Collocott,
1921, 52.

*F628.1.4.4. Strong man kills ferocious eel. Chatham Is.
Shand, 1896, 203.

F628.2.1. Strong man kills many men at once. Tubuai:
Aitken, 1930, 111; Cooks: Beckwith, 1940, 253;
Hawaii: Beckwith, 1940, 417; Westervelt, 1915a,
188; N.Z.: White, 1887-90, V, 31f.

*F628.2.1.1. Hero defeats an army. Australs: Aitken,
1923, 277, 282, 298; Hawaii: Dickey, 1917, 22;
Fornander, 1916, IV, 412, 446, 500, 516; V, 152,
316, 374, 378, 460, 472, 720; Thrum, 1907, 95ff.,

102, 159f., 209; Westervelt, 1915, 22; N.Z.: White, 1887-90, III, 10; Ellice Is.: Roberts, 1958, 406; Rennell: Elbert-Monberg, 1964, No. 222.

F628.2.5. Strong man kills men with his own hands. Mangareva: Caillot, 1914, 182; Tuamotus: Caillot, 1914, 37; Hawaii: Fornander, 1918, V, 138, 394; Thrum, 1923, 83, 153f.; Samoa: Stuebel, 1896, 144.

*F628.2.5.1. Hero's strength such that his slight shove kills a man. Hawaii: Beckwith, 1919, 384; Fornander, 1918, V, 406.

*F628.5.2. Hero's strength such that when he strikes opponents' chests, his fist comes out latters' backs. Hawaii: Beckwith, 1919, 334, 388; Fornander, 1918, V, 410.

*F628.5.2. Hero's strength such that his club-blow cleaves his opponent's body in two pieces. Hawaii: Fornander, 1918, V, 392; Green, 1929, 85.

*F631.7. Miscellaneous acts of strong man: pierces hole in bottom of lake. Bellona: Elbert-Monberg, 1964, No. 73.

F632. Mighty eater. Eats whole ox at time, or the like. Tuamotus: Stimson, n.d., T-G. 3/620, Z-G. 3/1241; Societies: Williams, 1895, 271; Cooks: Large, 1903, 134; Marquesas: Handy, 1930, 42; Hawaii: Beckwith, 1940, 419; Fornander, 1916, IV, 526; 1918, V, 2, 10, 20, 26; Tonga: Beckwith, 1940, 271; Gifford, 1924, 172f.; Samoa: Sierich, 1902, 181; N.Z.: White, 1887-90, II, 168; Rotuma: Hames, 1960, 33.

*F632.1. Prodigious eater: consumes both food and serving utensils. Tuamotus: Stimson, 1937, 93ff.; Tonga: Collocott, 1928, 14, 15; Reiter, 1934, 506, 512; Samoa: Krämer, 1902, I, 140; Powell-Pratt, 1891-93, 279.

*F632.2. Omnivorous eater: devours all kinds of inedible substances. N.Z.: White, 1887-90, II, 136; Rennell: Elbert-Monberg, 1964, No. 214.

*F632.3. Devil drinks immense amount of kava, eats the bowl in which it is served and the implements with which it is prepared. Tonga: Reiter, 1934, 504.

F633. Mighty drinker. Drinks up whole pools of water, or the like. Societies: Williams, 1895, 267, 271; Cooks: Large, 1903, 134; Tonga: Gifford, 1924, 159.

*F633.1. Mighty drinker empties ocean. Hawaii: Fornander, 1916, IV, 528; 1918, V, 366.

F636. Remarkable thrower. Hawaii: Beckwith, 1940, 421; Thrum, 1923, 234; Tonga: Reiter, 1919-20, 136; Samoa: Beckwith, 1940, 254.

F636.4. Remarkable stone-thrower. Tubuai: Aitken, 1930, 112; Marquesas: Steinen, 1934-35, 194; Tuamotus: Stimson, n.d., Z-G. 13/39; Cooks: Gill, 1876, 121; Hawaii: Beckwith, 1940, 242.

F639.1. Mighty digger. Cooks: Beckwith, 1940, 270.

*F639.1.3. Hero smashes an opening in a reef. Tuamotus: Stimson, 1937, 139; Hawaii: Forbes, 1882, 39.

F639.2. Mighty diver. Can stay extraordinary time under water. Mangareva: Hiroa, 1938, 329; Tuamotus: Caillot, 1914, 46; Societies: Henry, 1928, 541; Hawaii: Fornander, 1916, IV, 160, 162; 1918, V, 494; Thrum, 1906, 135, 167, 173, 218f.; Tonga: Reiter,1934, 509; Samoa: Fraser, 1900, 130, 132; N.Z.: Cowan, 1930, 125; White, 1887-90, V, 15.

*F639.11.1. Demigod smashes giant rock with his club. Hawaii: Smith, 1966, 10.

*F639.13. Person so strong that assailant who hits him breaks his own arms. Hawaii: Fornander, 1916, IV, 36.

*F639.14. Marvelous strength: person kicks over trees during walk. Hawaii: Thrum, 1907, 66.

*F639.15. Strong man holds river in its course. Hawaii: Forbes, 1882, 37; Thrum, 1907, 66.

F641. Person of remarkable hearing. Mangareva: Laval, 1938, 68; Hawaii: Fornander, 1918, V, 26, 278; Westervelt, 1915, 76; Tonga: Reiter, 1934, 500f.

F642. Person of remarkable sight. Cooks: Beaglehole, 1938, 384; Hawaii: Pukui-Curtis, n.d., 76ff.; Westervelt, 1915a, 76; Tonga: Reiter, 1934, 499.

*F645.3. Man can read character and appearance of person or beast. Hawaii: Fornander, 1918, V, 494.

F652. Marvelous sense of smell. Tonga: Reiter, 1934, 499f.; N.Z.: White, 1887-90, II, 129, 133, 138, 145; III, 124, 140; Wohlers, 1875, 28; Tikopia: Firth, 1930-31, 133.

F661. Skillful marksman. Hawaii: Fornander, 1916, IV, 226ff.; 1918, V, 216, 218, 222, 386, 452; Green, 1926, 69; Kamakau, 1961, 40, 88, 91; Pukui-Curtis, n.d., 89ff., 104; Rice, 1923, 61; Westervelt, 1915a, 79f.; Tonga: Collocott, 1921, 51; Rennell: Elbert-Monberg, 1964, No. 67; Bellona: ibid., No. 66.

*F661.13. Skillful marksman can pierce with arrow the whisker of a distant rat. Hawaii: Fornander, 1916, IV, 454; Pukui-Curtis, n.d., 80; Westervelt, 1915a, 158ff., 164.

*F661.14. Skillful spear-thrower hits target miles away. Hawaii: Fornander, 1916, IV, 506; 1918, V, 224, 564, 702; Thrum, 1907, 84; N.Z.: Cowan, 1930a, 68f.

F668.0.1. Skillful physician. Hawaii: Westervelt, 1915, 95ff.

F671. Skillful shipbuilder (canoe maker). N.Z.: White, 1887-90, I, 117f.

F675. Ingenious carpenter. Hawaii: Thrum, 1907, 87.

F676. Skillful thief. Hawaii: Fornander, 1918, V, 286ff.; Westervelt, 1915a, 150ff.

*F679.7.1. Mysterious card player always wins. N.Z.: Grace, 1907, 108ff.

*F679.10. Hero can prepare and cook a meal in less than a minute. Hawaii: Kamakau, 1961, 12f.

*F679.11. Marvelous thrower of stones makes them rebound from the sky or go enormous distance. Australs: Aitken, 1923, 289; Hawaii: Forbes, 1882, 37; Thrum, 1907, 65; Tonga: Collocott, 1921, 51.

*F679.12. Marvelous drum player can reveal his thoughts in his drumming. Hawaii: Westervelt, 1915, 50.

F681. Marvelous runner. Tuamotus: Stimson, n.d., T-G. 3/928; Marquesas: Lavondes, 1966, 52; Hawaii: *Beckwith, 1940, 151, 337f.; Fornander, 1916, IV, 310, 482; V, 164, 384, 434, 490ff., 496; Kamakau, 1961, 16, 56; Luomala, 1951, 15; Thrum, 1907, 104, 147ff.; Westervelt, 1915a, 75ff., 79ff.; N.Z.: Beattie, 1920, 193.

*F681.0.1. Marvelous runner: carries fish from one side of large island to other before it dies. Hawaii: McAllister, 1933, 190.

*F681.0.2. Marvelous runner can run up precipices. Hawaii: Westervelt, 1915, 197ff.

*F681.0.3. Champion strider takes steps of up to fifty miles in length. N.Z.: Best, 1925, 990.

*F681.0.4. Person travels so fast as to be invisible. Hawaii: Fornander, 1918, V, 150.

*F681.10.1. Extraordinary worker clears entire taro patch during one night. Australs: Aitken, 1923, 276; Tubuai: ibid., 281; Hawaii: Kamakau, 1961, 23f.; Thrum, 1907, 87.

*F681.14. Men run so fast that skin on backs of their legs is scorched. Niue: Loeb, 1926, 153.

F684. Marvelous jumper. Mangareva: Laval, 1938, 77, 81; Marquesas: Lavondes, 1964, 18; Hawaii: Dickey, 1917, 34; Kamakau, 1961, 17; Thrum, 1907, 83; Westervelt, 1915a, 105; N.Z.: White, 1887-90, V, 23.

*F684.0.1. Woman leaps to moon. Hawaii: Thrum, 1923, 71.

*F684.0.2. Marvelous jumper can leap up precipices. Hawaii: Dickey, 1917, 20.

*F684.1.1. Persons scale cliff as if they were flies. Hawaii: Emerson, 1915, 138.

F686. Body with marvelous heat. See F593. Reef Is.: *Elbert-Kirtley, 1966, 354f.

*F686.3. Seas within reef dry up in person's presence.
(Cf. F593.1.). Hawaii: Fornander, 1916, IV, 388.

F688.3. Voice heard over whole land. Hawaii: Fornander,
1918, V, 16.

F696. Marvelous swimmer. Hawaii: Beckwith, 1940, 509;
Thrum, 1923, 225f.; Samoa: Krämer, 1902, 107, 131f.,
133; Powell-Pratt, 1892, 98; Stuebel, 1896, 148;
N.Z.: Cowan, 1930, I, 220f.; White, 1887-90, II,
56.

F639.2. Mighty diver.

*F696.1. Couple swim from Hawaii to Tahiti. Hawaii:
Fornander, 1916, IV, 156.

*F696.2. Hero remains so long in sea that moss grows
on his body. Marquesas: Steinen, 1934-35, 207.

*F696.3. Man covered with shells after long undersea
voyage. N.Z.: Locke, 1921, 41.

*F696.4. Hero swims so long that he bears a sodden
odor afterwards. Societies: Henry, 1928, 543.

*F699.2. Man whose shadow causes vegetation to wither.
N.Z.: White, 1887-90, V, 58f.

*F699.3. Extraordinary fisherman: catches fish in
his hair. Rennell: Bradley, 1956, 335.

*F699.4. Person with marvelous ability to dodge spears
thrown at him. Hawaii: Fornander, 1916, IV, 268;
V, 18, 452, 698; Green, 1929, 37; Thrum, 1923, 158;
Westervelt, 1915a, 182f.; Bellona: Elbert-Monberg,
1964, No. 14.

*F699.5. Man twirls club so fast that his enemies'
missiles fail to strike him. Hawaii: Fornander,
1916, IV, 252.

*F699.6. Remarkable paddler: sends canoe several miles
with each stroke. See *F614.4.2. Hawaii:
Fornander, 1918, V, 8, 286, 700; Thrum, 1907, 85,
155; Westervelt, 1815, 144, 176; 1915a, 180;
N.Z.: Cowan, 1930, I, 24f.

*F699.7. Person so holy that sea water turns fresh at
his back. Hawaii: Fornander, 1916, IV, 388.

*F699.8. Great warrior causes flood every time he urinates. Hawaii: Fornander, 1918, V, 138.

F700--F899. EXTRAORDINARY PLACES AND THINGS

F701. Land of plenty. Hawaii: Fornander, 1916, IV, 498.

*F708.4. Country without women. Tonga: Collocott, 1924, 279.

F711.2.3. Sea of pumice. Tonga: Gifford, 1924, 149; Beckwith, 1940, 287.

F711.2.4. Sea of slime. Tonga: Gifford, 1924, 149.

*F711.2.6. Sea so thick that boat can move neither forward nor backward in it. Nukumanu: Sarfert, 1931, 452 n. 3, 453.

*F715.11. River which sends ripples to its source if anyone steps in it anywhere. Hawaii: Rice, 1923, 47.

F718.12. Origin of springs from broken coconut shell. Tonga: Gifford, 1924, 101.

*F718.13. Water in well mysteriously turns red. Tonga: Collocott, 1928, 11.

F721. Subterranean world. Hawaii: Fornander, 1918, VI, 336.

F721.1. Underground passages. Journey made through natural subways. Tokelaus: Macgregor, 1937, 85.

F721.4. Underground treasure chambers. Hawaii: Beckwith, 1940, 339.

F725. Submarine world. Australs: Aitken, 1923, 246, 258, 282; Mangareva: Hiroa, 1938, 316; Laval, 1938, 300; Tuamotus: Caillot, 1914, 57, 100; Stimson, n.d., Z-G. 13/249, Z-G. 13/441; 1937, 68ff., 75ff., 98ff.; Marquesas: Lavondes, 1966, 128; Hawaii: Fornander, 1918, V, 266, 288; Samoa: Stuebel, 1896, 144; N.Z.: Clark, 1896, 111; Lau Is.: St. Johnston, 1918, 42ff.

F725.3. Submarine castle (palace). Nukumanu: Sarfert, 1931, 334.

F725.3.3. Undersea house. Mangareva: Hiroa, 1938, 343.

F725.5. People live under sea. Australs: Aitken, 1923, 283; Rotuma: Russell, 1942, 243.

F737. Wandering island. Moves about at will and sometimes appears and disappears from sea. Mangareva: Laval, 1938, 306; Cooks: Beaglehole, 1938, 376; Hutchin, 1904, 174; Te Ariki, 1899, 171f.; 1920, 1f.; Hawaii: Beckwith, 1932, 189; 1940, 71f.; Emerson, 1915, IX; Fornander, 1916, IV, 436; Luomala, 1951, 9, 23, 26, 29; McAllister, 1933, 155; Rice, 1923, 20, 127; Thrum, 1921, 103; 1923, 199; Samoa: Krämer, 1902, I, 451; Fijis: Fison, 1904, 14, 16; Hocart, 1929, 195, 208.

*F737.1. Light seen where island sank. Samoa: Fraser, 1897, 70.

*F737.3. Woman breaks off point of land, uses it for raft. Tokelaus: Macgregor, 1937, 80.

F738. Flying island. Floats in sky. Tuamotus: Beckwith, 1940, 75; Hawaii: Luomala, 1951, 33; Niue: Loeb, 1926, 214; Rotuma: Russell, 1942, 247.

F742. Magic invisibility of otherworld island. Hawaii: Beckwith, 1932, 189; Dickey, 1917, 28; Fornander, 1918, V, 678; *Green, 1929, 5, n. d; Thrum, 1921, 107.

F748. Battle of islands. Easter I.: Métraux, 1940, 389.

*F749. Other extraordinary islands.

*F749.1. Island of pumice. Bellona: Elbert-Monberg, 1964, No. 52a.

*F749.2. Island of social wasps. Bellona: Elbert-Monberg, 1964, No. 52a.

*F749.3. Dancing reefs. Tikopia: Firth, 1961, 33.

*F754.1. A hill which attracts whales into stranding
themselves ashore. N.Z.: Best, 1925, 774.

F755. Living mountain. Cf. A964ff. and F1006ff.
Hawaii: Beckwith, 1940, 465f.; N.Z.: Best, 1905,
209; 1925, 980ff.

F755.5. Mountain has wife and children. N.Z.: Cowan,
1925, 20, 104; 1930, I, 255.

F755.6. Moving mountain. N.Z.: *Best, 1899, 118f.

*F755.6.1. Mountains travel at night: those caught
by light unable to move again. N.Z.: Best, 1899,
118.

*F755.6.2. Mountains quarrel: one moves location.
Marquesas: Steinen, 1933-34, 6-9; N.Z.: *Best,
1899, 118f.; Taylor White in "Notes and Queries,"
JPS VI (1897), 94.

*F755.6.2.1. Battle of volcanoes. Cf. *F755.8. Hawaii:
Thrum, 1923, 106f.

*F755.7. Fight between a magically rising mountain and
an elastic man. Hawaii: Forbes, 1882, 40.

*F755.8. Demons in form of volcanoes. N.Z.: Best, 1925,
977.

F756.2.2. Fertile valleys created by deity's stamping
down mountains. Tonga: Gifford, 1924, 18.

*F757.3. Bottomless pit. N.Z.: Cowan, 1930, I, 235.

F759.4. Perfumed mountain. Easter I.: Métraux, 1940,
369.

*F759.9. High mountain submerged in deluge; one less tal
not covered. Tahiti: Orsmond, 1933a, 84f.

*F759.10. Marvelous cliff -- can be raised upward.
Hawaii: Thrum, 1907, 72.

*F759.11. Stones thrown from volcano reenter the volcano
and are again thrown out - a continuing process.
Reef Is.: O'Ferrall, 1904, 228.

F770. Extraordinary buildings and furnishings. Tonga:
Collocott, 1921b, 163; N.Z.: Tregear, 1901, 185.

F771. Extraordinary castle (house). Fijis: Hocart, 1929, 196.

F771.1.9. House of skulls (bones). Hawaii: McAllister, 1933, 95f.; Samoa: Krämer,1902, I, 134; Tokelaus: Burrows, 1923, 161.

*F771.1.12. House made of beautiful feathers. Hawaii: Beckwith, 1919, 334, 366, 400; Dickey, 1917, 26; Fornander, 1916, IV, 170; Pukui-Curtis, n.d., 54f.; Westervelt, 1915, 47, 124, 184f.; Samoa: Sierich, 1902, 183.

*F771.1.13. House built of froth of waves. Tuamotus: Stimson, 1937, 77.

*F771.1.14. House made out of sand. Mangareva: Hiroa, 1938, 367f.

*F771.1.15. House built of women (men). Tonga: Collocott, 1928, 16, 17; Tokelaus: Burrows, 1923, 157.

F771.2.6. Revolving castle (house). Hawaii: Westervelt, 1915, 127; Tokelaus: Burrows, 1923, 169.

*F771.2.8. Fortress on turtles, which raise and lower it. Hawaii: Rice, 1923, 101.

*F789.4. A fence made of human bones. Hawaii: Fornander, 1916, IV, 574.

*F799. Extraordinary sky and weather phenomena -- miscellaneous.

*F799.1. Extraordinarily protracted rain falls so long upon two people that it sharpens their heads. Hawaii: McAllister, 1933, 90.

*F799.2. Red rain (mist). Hawaii: Fornander, 1916, IV, 78; Westervelt, 1915, 38, 145.

*F800.0.1. Living rock. Hawaii: Beckwith, 1940, 465f.

F802. Growing rocks. N.Z.: Cowan, 1930, I, 189.

*F802.2. Flat stones (female) and pointed stones(male) produce stone-children. Hawaii: Beckwith, 1940, 13.

*F804.1. Swimming stone. Hawaii: McAllister, 1933, 151.

F807.1. Crimson rock. N.Z.: Gudgeon, 1906, 34ff.

*F809.3.1. Stone contains lightning. N.Z.: Gudgeon, 1906, 30.

*F809.3.2. Rain-producing stone. N.Z.: Best. 1925, 973.

*F809.3.3. Sacred stone produces good catches of fish. Tikopia: Firth, 1961, 141.

F809.5. Traveling stone. (Cf. D1431.). Tonga: Collocott, 1928, 27.

*F809.5.1. Stone repeatedly found in nets cast in sea. Hawaii: McAllister, 1933,146; Thrum, 1907, 252.

*F809.5.2. Marvelous stone comes out of hut for a bath whenever it rains. Tokelaus: Burrows, 1923, 151.

*F809.5.3. Stone can only be retained as long as one's eyes are fixed on it. A wink and it returns to river bed. N.Z.: Gudgeon, 1906, 33.

*F809.5.3. Stone which, if moved, always returns to its original location. N.Z.: Best, 1925, 972f.

*F809.10. Pigs placed as offerings before sacred stone drop dead. Hawaii: McAllister, 1933, 147.

F811. Extraordinary tree. Societies: Henry, 1928, 421; Hawaii: Fornander, 1918, V, 596; Westervelt, 1915a, 23ff.; Tonga: Collocott, 1928, 12.

*F811.2.4. Trees, the leaves of which behave like humans. Hawaii: Westervelt, 1915, 39ff.

F811.4.1. Tree in midocean. Hawaii: Fornander, 1918, V, 656.

*F811.4.2.1. Banyan tree fished up from sea. Marquesas: *Steinen, 1934-35, 194, 199.

*F811.4.4. A pandanus tree stands at the edge of the world. Samoa: Brown, 1917, 94.

F811.5.3. Fish-producing tree. Hawaii: Beckwith, 1940, 520; Futuna: Burrows, 1936, 104.

*F811.10.2. Tree in which crowd of maidens sit. Marquesas: Steinen, 1933-34, 34.

F811.11. Trees disappear at sunset. Cooks: Te Ariki, 1920, 173.

F811.14. Giant tree: nuts fall miles away, etc. Marquesas: Handy, 1930, 70; Tonga: Reiter, 1934, 510f.

F811.20. Bleeding tree. Blood drops when tree is cut. Cf. *F815.8., *F816.3. Hawaii: Fornander, 1918, V, 578; Westervelt, 1915a, 28.

*F811.25. Traveling trees. Hawaii: Beckwith, 1932, 34; Tonga: Collocott, 1928, 17; N.Z.: Cowan, 1930, I, 248; Grey, 1855, 165; White, 1887-90, III, 215.

*F811.26. Marvelous tree attracts fish. Hawaii: Westervelt, 1915, 122f.

*F813.5.2. Great calabash: when filled with water, waves so great raised in it as to be felt on the open sea. Fijis: Rochereau, 1915, 407.

*F813.6.2. Battle of plantains and bananas. Samoa: Brown, 1915, 180.

F815.6.1. Taro planted in sacred spot inexhaustably prolific. Hawaii: Beckwith, 1940, 288.

F815.7.2. Gigantic vine. Samoa: Stuebel, 1896, 69.

*F815.7.4. Plants are girl's servants. Hawaii: Westervelt, 1915, 40f.

*F815.8. Ferocious kava plant. Samoa: Powell-Pratt, 1892, 98, 107.

*F815.9. Taro plants which move of their own volition. Hawaii: Westervelt, 1915, 27.

*F815.10. Plants bleed when gashed. Cf. F811.20., *F816.3. Rotuma: Russell, 1942, 245.

F816.2. Enormous kava plant. Tonga: Gifford, 1924, 123, 158.

*F816.2.1. Kava plant travels independently. Rotuma:
Churchward, 1937-38, 115.

*F816.3. Yam root breaks and blood pours out. Samoa:
Krämer, 1902, I, 265.

*F821.12. Cloak of snow. Hawaii: Beckwith, 1919,
486, 490.

*F827.4.1. Leis of sea-foam. Hawaii: Rice, 1923, 11.

*F827.4.2. Necklace of fingernails. Mangareva: Hiroa,
1938, 370.

F829.1. Rainbow as loin cloth. Hawaii: Beckwith, 1940,
508.

F829.2. Girdle made of a climbing-vine. Tuamotus:
Stimson, n.d., Z-G. 3/1174.

F834. Extraordinary spear. Hawaii: Fornander, 1918,
V, 150.

F834.4. All-conquering spear. Hawaii: Beckwith, 1940,
395.

F834.5. Remarkable spear used to dam stream. Hawaii:
Beckwith, 1940, 418.

F834.6. Remarkable spear used as windbreak. Hawaii:
Beckwith, 1940, 418.

F834.7. Warrior seeks combat when his spear consents.
Tuamotus: Stimson, n.d., Z-G. 13/48.

*F834.8. Remarkable spear ten fathoms long. Hawaii:
Rice, 1923, 64.

*F834.9. Remarkable spear made from whole tree. Hawaii:
Rice, 1923, 64.

*F834.11. Hero's spear can be lifted by none but himself.
Societies: Henry, 1928, 558.

F835. Extraordinary club. Hawaii: Beckwith, 1940,
204; Funafuti: David, 1899, 110; Tikopia:
Firth, 1961, 117ff.

F835.2. Remarkably large club. (Requires large number of ordinary men to lift). Cf. F. 621. Australs: Aitken, 1923, 287; Hawaii: Fornander, 1918, V, 52, 138, 220, 346; Green, 1929, 103; Tonga: Collocott, 1921, 55f.; Samoa: Stuebel, 1896, 155f.

F835.2.2. Club takes 4,000 men to carry it. Hawaii: Beckwith, 1940, 419.

*F835.2.3. Eighty people required to lift hero's club. Tubuai: Aitken, 1930, 112.

F836.0.1. Remarkable bowstring. Tuamotus: Stimson, n.d., Z-G. 13/127.

F837. Extraordinary battle-axe. Tuamotus: Stimson, 1937, 121; Hawaii: Fornander, 1916, IV, 418ff.

F837.1. Extraordinary keen stone axe. Hawaii: Beckwith, 1940, 395.

F839.7. Wooden lizard used to kill evil spirits. Easter I.: Métraux, 1940, 370.

*F839.8. Remarkable dart. N.Z.: Hongi, 1896, 234, 236; Tokelaus: Macgregor, 1937, 82.

F841. Extraordinary boat (ship). Hawaii: Emerson, 1915, 216; Fornander, 1918, V, 234; Westervelt, 1915, 142f., 176ff.; Samoa: Powell-Pratt, 1892, 105; N.Z.: Best, 1925, 923; White, 1887-90, I, 171; Fijis: Hocart, 1929, 218.

F841.1.1. Stone boat (ship). Nukumanu: Sarfert, 1931, 439.

F841.1.4.1. Canoe made from coconut. Marquesas: Handy, 1930, 46, 91; Beckwith, 1940, 484; Tahiaoteaa, 1933, 494; Hawaii: Westervelt, 1915, 173, 192, 211.

F841.1.12. Boat from gourd (calabash). Societies: Caillot, 1914, 112.

*F841.1.15. Boat made from shell. Hawaii: Emerson, 1915, 237; Westervelt, 1915, 43ff., 144, 148.

*F841.1.16. Canoe made of rotten, hollow fruit. Santa Cruz: Riesenfeld, 1950, 126.

*F841.1.17. Canoe made of white chicken feathers. Hawaii: Rice, 1923, 105.

*F841.1.18. Invisible canoe. N.Z.: Best, 1893, 216.

*F841.1.19. Canoe made of sand. Tuamotus: Seurat, 1905, 482; Marquesas: Tahiaoteaa, 1933, 494.

*F841.1.19.1. Boat made of earth. Tuamotus: Stimson, 1937, 117ff.

*F841.1.20. Cloud-boats. Hawaii: Westervelt, 1915, 145.

F841.2.7. Marvelous paddle sends canoe enormous distance with each stroke. Hawaii: Beckwith, 1940, 447.

*F841.2.7.1. Paddle which only hero can wield. Societies Henry, 1928, 558.

*F841.2.8. Snake used as halyard on ship. Fijis: Hocart, 1929, 223.

*F841.2.9. Octopus used as halyard on ship. Fijis: Hocart, 1929, 196.

F841.3.3. Enormous canoe. Easter I.: Métraux, 1940, 62; Marquesas: Lavondes, 1966, 82, 138; Hawaii: Beckwith, 1940, 420; Uvea: Burrows, 1937, 163; Rennell: Elbert-Monberg, 1964, No. 57b.

*F841.3.5. Extraordinary boat: a house which a man turned upside down. Mangareva: Hiroa, 1938, 326.

*F841.3.6. Toy boat made of earth sails faster than boats made of bamboo. Tuamotus: Stimson, 1937, 117f.

*F841.3.7. Extraordinary raft. Mangareva: Hiroa, 1938, 22; Laval, 1938, 5.

*F842.1.6. Bridge made of hair. Marquesas: Steinen, 1933-34, 369.

*F842.1.7. Bridge of spittle. Marquesas: Steinen, 1933-34, 369.

*F842.1.8. Moon stretches itself, makes bridge. Marquesas: Steinen, 1934-35, 232.

F843.1. Rope made of person's hair. Marquesas: Lagarde, 1933, 261.

*F843.2. Rope made of intestines. Hawaii: Beckwith, 1940, 449.

*F843.3. Stream of urine used as rope. Marquesas: Lagarde, 1933, 261.

*F847.1. Net made of rain drops. Samoa: Stair, 1895, 48.

*F855.5. Images of great power. Hawaii: Smith, 1955, 53.

*F865.2. A path paved with whale's teeth. Samoa: Sierich, 1902, 184.

*F887.2. Marvelous digging spade. Hawaii: Beckwith, 1919, 554.

*F887.3. Marvelous adze. N.Z.: Best, 1925, 689.

*F899.4. Marvelous fishhook. Tuamotus: Young, 1898, 109; Societies: Henry, 1928, 558; Cooks: Te Ariki, 1899, 72; Hawaii: Fornander, 1916, IV, 204, 488ff., 554ff.; V, 284; McAllister, 1933, 71; Thrum, 1923, 249, 252; Smith, 1966, 20; Tonga: Caillot, 1914, 254ff.; Samoa: Krämer, 1902, I, 393, 413, n. 5; Powell-Pratt, 1892, 242, 246; Stuebel, 1896, 148; Tokelaus: Burrows, 1923, 169; N.Z.: Best, 1929, 11f, 15 n., 16 n.; Grace, 1907, 37ff., 147ff.; White, 1887-90, I, 170; II, 69f, 75f., 84, 88, 99f., 111, 116; III, 53; Ontong Java: Sarfert, 1931, 440f.

*F899.4.1. Marvelous fishhook made from human bone. N.Z.: Best, 1925, 939ff., 963; Grace, 1907, 129; White, 1887-90, II, 69, 75, 80, 82, 84, 88, 99, 111, 113, 115; III, 53, 139f., 233; IV, 183f.; Wohlers, 1875, 13, 16.

*F899.4.2. After fish learn that a marvelous fishhook is properly bound, they bite incessantly. Samoa: Krämer, 1902, I, 415.

*F899.5. Marvelous shell. Hawaii: Westervelt, 1915, 106ff.

*F899.6. Remarkable red feathers. Mangareva: Laval, 1938, 54.

*F899.7. Marvelous kite. Hawaii: Smith, 1966, 17ff.; N.Z.: Best, 1925, 924, 930, n. 5.

F900--F1099.   EXTRAORDINARY OCCURRENCES

*F911.1.2. Woman swallows her children whole. N.Z.:
White, 1887-90, II, 169.

*F911.1.3. Gods in turn swallow and spit each other out.
Cooks: *Te Ariki, 1920, 63f.

F911.3. Animal swallows man (not fatally). Marquesas:
Steinen, 1934-35, 194; Societies: Henry, 1928,
562f.; Tonga: Caillot, 1914, 301f.; Collocott,
1921, 52.

F911.4. Jonah. Fish (or water monster) swallows a
man. Marquesas: Handy, 1930, 137; *Steinen,
1933-34, 347, 360; 1934-35, 194, 219; Tuamotus:
Beckwith, 1940, 503; Seurat, 1905, 433, 484;
Stimson, n.d., Z-G. 3/1100; Tahiti: Orsmond,
1933b, 171; Cooks: Dixon, 1916, 69; Gill, 1876,
147; Hawaii: Beckwith, 1940, 69, 132, 437, 443;
Fornander, 1916, IV,; 1918, V, 660;; Rice, 1923,
126; Tonga: Collocott, 1922, 163; N.Z.: Grace,
1907, 97; Gudgeon, 1905, 182; White, 1887-90, II,
170, 171; Niue: Smith, 1903, 102; Fijis: Hocart
1928, 212; Rennell: Elbert-Monberg, 1964, Nos. 33
34b; Bellona: ibid., No. 34a.

F911.4.1. Fish swallows ship. N.Z.: White, 1887-90,
III, 4.

F911.4.1.1. Party in canoe swallowed by great clam.
Tuamotus: Seurat, 1905, 484; Societies: Beckwith
1940, 260; Henry, 1928, 474.

F911.6. All-swallowing monster. N.Z.: Best, 1925,
968; Cowan, 1925, 168f.; White, 1887-90, III, 189

    F531.3.4.2. Giant drinks up a river.

*F911.8. Men and canoes sucked in and swallowed by
sea-monsters. N.Z.: Best, 1924, 196; Kauika, 190
95; Smith, 1905, 203.

F912. Victim kills swallower from within. Hawaii:
Fornander, 1918, V, 332; Rennell: Elbert-Monberg,
1964, No. 33; Bellona: ibid., No. 34a.

328

F912.1. Victim kills swallower from within by burning.
Cooks: Dixon, 1916, 69; Hawaii: Beckwith, 1940,
443.

F912.2. Victim kills swallower from within by cutting.
Marquesas: Beckwith, 1940, 502; Steinen, 1933-34,
347, 360; Tuamotus: Beckwith, 1940, 503f.; Caillot,
1914, 69f.; Seurat, 1905, 433; Cooks: Beckwith,
1940, 503; Savage, 1910, 151; Niue: Smith,
1903, 102; N.Z.: Best, 1924, 193; Fijis: Hocart,
1929, 212.

F912.3. Swallowed person eats on swallower's liver
(heart) until disgorged. Tuamotus: Stimson, n.d.,
Z-G. 3/1100; Hawaii: Beckwith, 1940, 140.

F913. Victims rescued from swallower's belly.
Mangareva: Hiroa, 1938, 335; Marquesas: *Steinen,
1934-35, 194f.; Tuamotus: Beckwith, 1940, 289;
Societies: Beckwith, 1940, 252; Cooks: Dixon,
1916, 69, 296; Kunike, 1928, 32.

*F916.3. Girl jumps down dog's throat. Hawaii:
Beckwith, 1940, 500.

F921. Swallowed person becomes bald. Tuamotus:
*Beckwith, 1940, 503; Seurat, 1905, 433; Marquesas:
Steinen, 1933-34, 347; Tahiti: Orsmond, 1933b, 171;
Hawaii: Beckwith, 1940, 132, 437; Fornander, 1916,
IV, 528; 1918, V, 298, 368.

F930.8. Chewed nut spread on waters clarifies them.
Hawaii: Beckwith, 1940, 436.

*F930.9. Person pours oil on ocean and is able to see
within its depths. N.Z.: Best, 1925, 989.

F931.4. Extraordinary behavior of waves. Tuamotus:
Henry, 1928, 523.

*F931.13. Sea, during deluge, covers highest peak,
leaves lower one uncovered. Societies: Henry,
1928, 445f.

F942. Man sinks into earth. Futuna: Burrows, 1930, 225,
227.

F942.1.1. Ground opens to hide fugitive. Societies:
Henry, 1928, 556; Hawaii: Beckwith, 1940, 212.

F943. Sinking into mud in duel. Cooks: Te Ariki, 1921, 60.

F944.3. Island sinks into sea. Tonga: Gifford, 1924, 185.

*F949.3. At moment body is lowered into grave, huge rock from hillside rolls down and crushes corpse and coffin. Chatham Is.: Travers, 1877, 24.

F950.8. Princess cured by seeing her lost lover dance. Tuamotus: Stimson, n.d., Z-G. 13/10.

F952. Blindness miraculously cured. Hawaii: Beckwith, 1940, 25.

      D2161.3.1. Blindness magically cured.

F952.3.1. Blindness cured by striking eyes. Tuamotus: Stimson, n.d., T-G. 3/931.

F953.1. Hunchback cured by having hump severely beaten. Hawaii: Beckwith, 1940, 233; Thrum, 1923, 254.

*F953.2. Persons' stolen bones replaced with the stems of plants. Hawaii: Emerson, 1915, 51.

*F959.3.6. Centipede falling on a wound or bruise effects cure. Tahiti: Henry, 1928, 391.

F960.1.1. Extraordinary nature phenomena at birth of royalty. Hawaii: Beckwith, 1919, 334, 348; Dickey, 1917, 21; Fornander, 1918, V, 192; Kamakau, 1961, 68; Thrum, 1907, 93; 1923, 150, 171, 179, 181f., 183; Westervelt, 1915, 21, 37, 117 170f.; 1915a, 73, 211, 244.

F960.1.1.3. Storm signs betray newly born child's chiefly rank. Hawaii: Beckwith, 1940, 428.

*F960.11. Extraordinary natural phenomena resulting from activities of royalty -- miscellaneous.

*F960.11.1. Rainbow hovers over royal personage. Marquesas: Lavondes, 1966, 10; Hawaii: Beckwith, 1919, 334, 348, 398, 494, 540ff.; 570, 578; Dickey, 1917, 21; Fornander, 1916, IV, 134, 168, 188, 218, 238, 244, 532, 546; Green, 1926, 75, 77; 1929, 15; Kamakau, 1961, 11, 24; Thrum, 1907,

74, 134; 1920, 71; 1923, 33, 168f., 217;
Westervelt, 1915, 22, 86, 145, 178, 207;
1915a, 174, 224f.

*F960.11.2. Rainbow serves chief as garland. Hawaii:
Westervelt, 1915, 133.

*F960.11.3. Natural disturbances (thunder, lightning,
eclipses, etc.) accompany travel and arrival of
royalty. Hawaii: Beckwith, 1919, 394, 550;
Green, 1929, 9; Westervelt, 1915, 188f., 211;
Samoa: Nelson, 1925, 138.

*F960.11.3.1. Mist shrouds princess from profane eyes.
Hawaii: Beckwith, 1919, 370, 532.

*F960.11.4. Natural disturbances at royal marriage.
Hawaii: Fornander, 1916, IV, 538.

*F960.11.5. A particular kind of cloud hovering on the
horizon as a sign of (royal) visitors. Tuamotus:
Clifford Gessler, Road My Body Goes (New York,
1937), 186; Hawaii: Beckwith, 1919, 394, 514;
Fornander, 1918, V, 166.

*F960.11.6. Star burns particularly brightly on night
a wicked king's people are massacred. Mangareva:
Caillot, 1914, 188.

*F960.12. At ogre's arrival the sky clouds over and a
spring of water jets upward. Marquesas: Lavondes,
1964, 8.

F961.2.5. Speaking star. Tuamotus: Stimson, n.d.,
T-G. 3/191.

*F961.3.4. Moon laughs. Marquesas: Steinen, 1934-35,
232.

*F961.3.5. Moon descends, becomes a bridge by which man
ascends cliff. Marquesas: Steinen, 1934-35, 232.

*F962.2.3.1. Fire which cannot be extinguished. Tuamotus:
Audran, 1918, 34.

*F963.5. Wind and surf still during time of sacred quiet.
Societies: Henry, 1928, 438.

F964. Extraordinary behavior of fire. Societies:
Henry, 1928, 144.

F966. Voices from heaven (or from the air). Hawaii: Westervelt, 1915, 111.

F971.1. Dry rod blossoms. Fijis: Fison, 1904, 51.

F979.21. Tree which has two singing blossoms. Hawaii: Beckwith, 1940, 284.

F979.22. Tree acts as master of ceremonies while gods drink. Tonga: Beckwith, 1940, 74.

*F983.0.2. Fish's (eel's) remarkably fast growth. Samoa: Stuebel, 1896, 67f.; Tokelaus: Burrows, 1923, 158.

*F985.6.1. Eyes of pigs living near temple turn red at approach of sacred nights of moon. Hawaii: Thrum, 1923, 119.

F986.5. Shores flooded with sea-fish. Hawaii: Fornander, 1918, V, 162.

*F988.4. Fish with small tree growing from back of head. N.Z.: Gudgeon, 1906, 28.

F989.12. Sea animal (whale) found inland. Niue: Loeb, 1926, 170; Tikopia: Firth, 1961, 113; Rennell: Bradley, 1956, 334.

*F989.25. Swordfish bores hole in canoe. Cooks: Beaglehole, 1938, 409.

*F989.26. Water monster has extraordinarily acute sense of smell. N.Z.: Smith, 1905, 202.

*F989.27. Swine hears master's voice at extremely great distance. Marquesas: Steinen, 1933-34, 28.

*F989.28. Pig prostrates itself at the feet of a chief. Hawaii: Kamakau, 1961, 11.

*F989.29. Eel which eats flowers. Marquesas: Steinen, 1933-34, 1.

*F989.31. Monster dog jumps from island to island. Hawaii: Rice, 1923, 31.

*F989.32. Oysters hold boat back from moving. N.Z.: White, 1887-90, V, 12.

*F989.33. Fish buried with chief are celebrating his funeral when uncovered. Mangareva: Laval, 1938, 53.

*F1006.4. Three mountains go fishing. Societies: Ropiteau, 1933, 127.

*F1009.5. Race between two rivers. N.Z.: Best, 1925, 987f.

*F1009.6. Battle between trees and stones. Samoa: Krämer, 1902, I, 361ff.

*F1009.7. Objects as humans. Tuamotus: Stimson, 1937, 50ff., 82ff. (stars); 144-145 (skeleton); Mangareva: Hiroa, 1938, 317 (Milky Way); Hawaii: Thrum, 1923, 171 (wind); Westervelt, 1915, 39ff. (shells); 46 (flowers), 124ff. (trees), 128ff. (clouds), 133f. (snow); N.Z.: Best, 1925, 841ff. (greenstone).

F1021. Extraordinary flights through air. N.Z.: Best, 1925, 989f.; White, 1887-90, II, 60.

*F1021.3.1. Person throws his club, clings to it, and thus flies. Hawaii: Fornander, 1918, V, 142, 146.

F1034.4. Person's armpit as hiding place. Hawaii: Beckwith, 1940, 169f.

F1034.5. Other parts of person's body as hiding place. Tuamotus: Stimson, n.d., Z-G. 1/96; Marquesas: Handy, 1930, 38; Lagarde, 1933, 260; *Steinen, 1933-34, 366, 368f.

*F1041.7.1. Man goes bald from terror. N.Z.: Grace, 1907, 207.

*F1041.17.2. Person, in fear, crunches flaming brand between his teeth. Lau Is.: St. Johnston, 1918, 121.

F1071. Prodigious jump. To fourth story (or the like). Tuamotus: Stimson, n.d., 13/499; Marquesas: Handy, 1930, 114; Hawaii: Beckwith, 1940, 242; Chatham Is.: Shand, 1896, 197; Ontong Java, Nukumanu: Sarfert, 1931, 436.

*F1084.0.5. Battle lasts seven days. Cooks: Te Ariki, 1921, 60.

*F1096.4. Man, from pride, remains standing after dying. Samoa: Krämer, 1902, I, 452.

*F1099.9. An adz is sharpened upon an old woman's back. Mangareva: Hiroa, 1938, 326; Tuamotus: Beckwith, 1940, 267; Seurat, 1905, 482;; N.Z.: Beckwith, 1940, 265; White, 1887-90, I, 69, 73; V, 9.

*F1099.10. Man shot in anus and arrow sticks out his mouth. Tonga: Collocott, 1928, 9.

G. OGRES

G0. Ogres. Easter I.: Knoche, 1920, 66; Chatham Is.:
Shand, 1896, 195, 201f.

G10--G399. KINDS OF OGRES

G10--G99. Cannibals and Canniablism

G10--G49. Regular cannibalism

G10. Cannibalism. Oceania: *Dixon, 1916, 61, 63, 69,
86, 130ff.; Easter I.: Englert, 1939, 76; Métraux,
1940, 76ff., 83f., 371, 377, 385; Mangareva:
Caillot, 1914, 168, 171, 179, 228, 230; Hiroa,
1938, 31, 33, 42, 47, 52, 54, 55, 58f., 62, 66,
68, 77, 84, 90, 94, 323, 357, 381f.; Laval, 1938,
30, 31, 68, 85, 88f., 91, 100, 107, 112, 114, 118,
123, 129, 134ff., 141, 147, 157, 177, 178, 179,
187, 198; Tuamotus: Audran, 1918, 30, 37, 57,
232, 236; Caillot, 1914, 43; Stimson, n.d.,
T-G. 3/515, Z-G. 3/1386, Z-G. 13/167; 1934, 13, 63;
1937, 69, 81; Marquesas: Handy, 1930, 126;
*Beckwith, 1940, 339f.; Lavondes, 1966, 20, 70;
Steinen, 1934-35, 230; Cooks: Browne, 1897, 6;
Low, 1935, 28, 78; Megen, 1928, 1054; Hawaii:
Beckwith, 1940, 21, 341f.; Emerson, 1915, 32;
1921, 16; Fornander, 1916, IV, 564ff.; V, 132,
312, 370, 516, 692; VI, 280; McAllister, 1933,
121f., 132, 137ff.; Pukui, 1933, 182; Westervelt,
1915a, 141ff., 189ff.; Tonga: Caillot, 1914,
259 n. 2; 1921, 56; 1928, 11, 12, 14, 34, 38,
59, 61; Gifford, 1924, 123; Lesson, 1876, 597;
Reiter, 1919-20, 137; 1933, 359; Samoa: Krämer,
1902, I, 135, 143, 210, 218, 270, 349, 431, 443,
454; Powell-Pratt, 1892, 128f.; Stuebel, 1896,
65f., 72f.; Niue: Loeb, 1926, 175; Tokelaus:
Burrows, 1923, 162f.; Lister, 1892, 60f.; N.Z.:
Beckwith, 1940, 266; Best, 1925, 933, 1060ff.;
Clark, 1896, 100, 159; Cowan, 1930, I, 33, 64f.,
70, 116, 152, 196, 205, 210, 234, 238, 246, 254;
1930a, 131, 147, 168ff.; Grace, 1907, 3, 99;
Grey, 1855, passim; White, 1887-90, I, 36f., 43,
79, 87, 93, 108, 127; II, 61, 134; III, 3f., 9,
14, 16, 21, 22, 23 119, 123, 130, 131, 150, 151, 168,

189ff., 227, 229, 230, 236, 242, 248, 249, 250,
261, 263, 272, 277, 298, 299; IV, 193; V, 15f.,
44, 120, 126, 187, 191, 213; Wohlers, 1875, 23;
Ellice Is.: Roberts, 1958, 372, 406; Rotuma:
Churchward, 1938-39, 329; Russell, 1942, 246ff.;
Fijis: Fison, 1904, xxvf., 164f.; Lau Is.: Hames,
1960, 19; Tikopia: Firth, 1961, 117, 124, 132;
Reef Is.: O'Ferrall, 1904, 232; Nukumanu:
Sarfert, 1931, 451; Rennell: Elbert-Monberg, 1964,
Nos. 20, 60, 116, 117, 228b, 229; Bellona: ibid.,
1964, No. 61; Kapingamarangi: Elbert, 1949, 241.

G11.0.1.   Cannibalistic god.   Samoa: Stuebel, 1896,
81; Tikopia: Firth, 1961, 87; Rennell: Elbert-
Monberg, 1964, No. 67; Bellona: ibid., No. 14.

G11.0.1.2.   Father of goddess as cannibal.   Hawaii:
Beckwith, 1940, 141.

G11.1.   Cannibal dwarfs.   Tuamotus: Henry, 1928, 503;
N.Z.: Grace, 1907, 55.

G11.2.   Cannibal giant.   See G100.   Giant ogre.   Easter I
Métraux, 1940, 377; Ra'iatea: Williams, 1895, 263,
275, 277; N.Z.: Grace, 1907, 53ff.; Fijis:
Fison, 1904, 121; Ellice Is.: Kennedy, 1931, 159.

G11.6.   Man-eating woman.   Easter I.:   Métraux, 1940, 370
Australs: Aitken, 1930, 109; Mangareva: Hiroa,
1938, 378ff.; Tuamotus: Leverd, 1911, 173;
Stimson, n.d., Z-G. 13/249, Z-G. 13/110, Z-G. 3/1276
1937, 82ff.; Marquesas: Handy, 1930, 77f.;
Societies: Baessler, 1905, 922; Beckwith, 1940,
197; Henry, 1928, 552, 554; Hawaii: Beckwith,
1940, 194; Samoa: Krämer, 1902, I, 123; Stuebel,
1896, 62f.; N.Z.: Clark, 1896, 39; White,
1887-90, I, 122; II, 60, 98f., 169f.; Wohlers,
1875, 15, 17f., 19; Kapingamarangi: Elbert, 1949,
244.

G11.8.1.   Stars as cannibals.   Tuamotus: Stimson, n.d.,
T-G. 3/931; Marquesas: Steinen, 1933-34, 372f.;
N.Z.: Best, 1925, 848, 852; Reef Is.: O'Ferrall,
1904, 231.

G11.10.   Cannibalistic spirits.   Australs: Aitken, 1923,
272; Hawaii: Emory, 1924, 13, 14; Fornander, 1916
IV, 476ff., 486; 1918, V, 214, 368, 428ff.; Samoa:
Krämer, 1902, I, 447; Sierich, 1901, 18, 20ff.;

Stuebel, 1896, 81f., 146; N.Z.: Wohlers, 1876, 112; Rotuma: Churchward, 1938-39, 120; Russell, 1942, 249ff.; Tokelaus: Macgregor, 1937, 87; Ontong Java: Sarfert, 1931, 325; Bellona: Elbert-Monberg, 1964, Nos. 1c, 2, 16, 50a; Rennell: ibid., 50c; Kapingamarangi: Elbert, 1948, 84, 108.

G11.10.1. Cannibalistic spirits in upper world. Cooks: Gill, 1876, 234; Hawaii: Rice, 1923, 23.

*G11.10.1.1. Cannibal woman from sky. N.Z.: *Lessa, 1961, 131ff.

*G11.10.2. Inhabitants of netherworld eat only human flesh. Marquesas: Steinen, 1934-35, 212 n. 4; N.Z.: Grey, 1855, 109.

*G11.11.0.1. Albinos as ogres. Nukumanu: Sarfert, 1931, 331.

G11.11.1. Albino twins with cannibal appetite. Tonga: Gifford, 1924, 192.

G11.11.2. Hairless cannibal. Hawaii: Beckwith, 1940, 344.

*G11.11.3. Cannibalistic dog-man. Hawaii: Westervelt, 1915, 85ff., 93ff.

G11.15. Cannibal demon. Tuamotus: Stimson, n.d., Z-G. 13/249.

G11.18.1. Cannibal people driven from land. Hawaii: Beckwith, 1940, 341.

*G11.19. Robber cannibal. Hawaii: Fornander, 1918, V, 210ff.

G12. Transformation in order to eat own kind. Man transforms self to animal and eats men. Hawaii: *Beckwith, 1940, 130,153; Rice, 1923, 111.

G13.1. Ritual cannibalism. Mangareva: Laval, 1938, 76; Tuamotus: Audran, 1919, 52; N.Z.: White, 1887-90, I, 42; Ellice Is.: Hedley, 1896, 51; Tikopia: Firth, 1961, 112, 149.

*G13.2. Enemy's eyeballs are drunk in a cup of kava. Hawaii: Thrum, 1923, 259.

*G13.3.   Two sisters eat the slayer of their brother.
Tuamotus: Caillot, 1914, 91f.

*G13.4.   Person eats his enemy's still-beating heart.
Rennell: Elbert-Monberg, 1964, No. 93.

G15.   Human being devoured daily. Rotuma: Churchward,
1938-39, 465.

G20.   Ghouls. Persons eat corpses. Ellice Is.:
Kennedy, 1931, 204.

G25.   Abandoned infant lives by eating corpse of murdered
father. Easter I.:   Métraux, 1940, 84, 385.

*G28.   Sharks come from sea at night and carry off bodies
of the newly dead. Hawaii: McAllister, 1933, 173.

G30.   Person becomes cannibal. Tahiti: Beckwith, 1940,
197;   Leverd, 1920, 1; Cooks: Beckwith, 1940, 340;
Niue: Loeb, 1926, 176;   Chatham Is.:   Shand, 1896,
202;   N.Z.:   Beckwith, 1940, 340;   Clark, 1896,
152.

*G38.   Woman becomes cannibal when her tooth is pulled
and a shark's tooth is substituted. Marquesas:
Tahiaoteaa,1933, 497.

*G39.   Spirits of dead wer-sharks possess bodies of
ordinary sharks, which then become man eaters.
Hawaii: Thrum, 1907, 266.

G50--G79.   Occasional cannibalism

G51.   Person eats own flesh. Nukumanu: Sarfert, 1931,
455.

*G51.2.   Demon eats his own liver. Samoa: Krämer, 1902,
I, 447.

G60.   Human flesh eaten unwittingly. Kapingamarangi:
Elbert, 1948, 106.

G61.   Relative's flesh eaten unwittingly. Hawaii:
Beckwith, 1940, 264;   Pukui, 1933, 173;   N.Z.:
Dixon, 1916, 195;   Grey, 1855, 204;   White,
1887-90, II, 23f.;   Ellice Is.:   Kennedy, 1931, 203.

*G65. Faithful retainer carries out dying king's command
to hide his bones where no mortal can find them.
Servant grinds them into powder and mixes them in
poi served at funeral feast. Hawaii: Fornander,
1916, IV, 434.

G70.1. Hungry seamen eat human flesh. N.Z.: White,
1887-90, III, 62, 72.

G72. Unnatural parents eat children. Hawaii: Beckwith,
1940, 199; Samoa: Krämer, 1902, I, 122; N.Z.:
Dixon, 1916, 85; White, 1887-90,II, 169; Rennell:
Elbert-Monberg, 1964, No. 205.

*G72.4. Cruel uncle kills and eats his nephews. Hawaii:
Thrum, 1907, 143.

G73.2. Brother eats brother. Tonga: Gifford, 1924, 28;
Samoa: Stuebel, 1896, 151, 153; Rennell: Elbert-
Monberg, 1964, No. 209.

*G73.3. Sister eats sister. Samoa: Stuebel, 1896, 62f.

G76. Aged person eaten. Easter I.: Métraux, 1940, 383.

G77. Husband eats wife. Rennell: Elbert-Monberg, 1964,
No. 199 .

G78.1. Cannibalism in time of famine. Samoa: Stuebel,
1896, 145; Fijis: Fison, 1904, 41.

*G79.2.1. Woman kills slave, cuts out his heart for a
cannibal gift. N.Z.: White, 1887-90, I, 95.

*G79.3. Cannibal grandmother. Tuamotus: Stimson, n.d.,
T-G. 3/931; Tahiti: Gill, 1876, 252f.; Hawaii:
Beckwith, 1940, 491; Rice, 1923, 23; Tonga:
Gifford, 1924, 192.

*G79.4. Man murders and eats three companions who escape
from slavery with him. N.Z.: R. E. M. Campbell,
"The Captives' Escape," JPS III (1894), 140-143.

G81. Unwitting marriage to cannibal. Tuamotus: Stimson,
n.d., Z-G. 13/249; Marquesas: Handy, 1930, 25;
N.Z.: Whetu, 1897, 97.

*G81.2. Ogress marries man by force. Polynesia: *Beckwith,
1940, 194ff.; Chatham Is.: Shand, 1896, 196;
N.Z.: Shand, 1896, 197.

*G82.1.2. Children fattened in loft by ogre deceive
him as to their corpulence. When he asks to feel
their feet, the child with deformed feet offers
his. Tonga: Collocott, 1928, 60.

G84. Fee-fi-fo-fum. Cannibal returning home smells
human flesh and makes exclamation. Tuamotus:
Stimson, n.d., T-G. 3/391, Z-G. 3/1276; 1934,
67; 1937, 82; Marquesas: Lavondes, 1964, 6;
Steinen, 1933-34,371ff.; 1934-35, 217; Hawaii:
Rice, 1923, 23; Thrum, 1907, 189; 1923, 295,
299; Westervelt, 1915, 54; Tonga: Collocott,
1928, 15; Gifford, 1924, 168; Reiter, 1934,
498; Samoa: Krämer,1902, I, 135; N.Z.: Clark,
1896, 39, 100; White, 1887-90, I, 79; Ontong
Java, Nukumanu: Sarfert, 1931, 424, 438; Reef Is.:
O'Ferrall, 1904, 231; Kapingamarangi: Elbert,
1948, 76, 84; Emory, 1949, 237.

*G86.2. Person's ears torn off and eaten before him.
N.Z.: White, 1887-90, II, 134.

G94.1. Ogress takes travelers out of cave and devours
them one by one. Hawaii: Beckwith, 1940, 264.

G100--G199. Giant ogres

G100. Giant ogre. (For motifs concerning giants who are
not malevolent, but merely large, see F531.)
Easter I.: Métraux, 1940, 377; Tuamotus: Audran,
1918, 92; Marquesas: Lavondes, 1964, 8; Samoa:
Krämer, 1902, I, 112; N.Z.: Grace, 1907, 55, 56;
White, 1887-90, III, 124f., 189, 190; Rotuma:
Hames, 1960, 23, 48; Fijis: Fison, 1904, 125.

*G113. White vampire-bat is messenger of giant ogre.
Fijis: Fison, 1904, 125.

*G127. Giant ogre covered with scales. N.Z.: White,
1887-90, III, 124, 190.

*G128. Giant ogre whose teeth are flaming coals. Rotuma:
Hames, 1960, 48.

*G162.1. Man-eating giant lives in a cave. Rotuma: Hame
1960, 48.

G200. Witch. Tuamotus: Stimson, n.d., Z-G. 3/1340,
Z-G. 13/499; 1937, 62ff., 81, 201; Tahiti:
Henry, 1928, 580; Hawaii: Emerson, 1915, 134, 136;
McAllister, 1933, 181; N.Z.: Best, 1924, 82;
White, 1887-90, II, 55ff.; Wohlers, 1876, 118ff;
Ellice Is.: Roberts, 1958, 369.

G211.3.1. Witch in form of hen. Hawaii: Fornander,
1918, V, 266.

*G225.9. Fish as witch's familiar. Tuamotus:
Stimson, n.d., Z-G. 13/499.

*G263.5.1. Witch steals corpse. Hawaii: Emerson, 1915,
134, 136.

*G271.2.7. Witches killed by incantations. Hawaii:
Emerson, 1915, 136.

G300--G399. Other ogres

G302. Demons. Tokelaus: Burrows, 1923, 165.

*G302.4.5.2. Demon with cloven feet. N.Z.: Grace, 1907,
196.

G303.4.5.3.1. Devil detected by his hoofs. N.Z.:
Grace, 1907, 108ff.

G303.9.5. The devil (demon) as an abductor. N.Z.:
Grace, 1907, 112.

G308.2. Water-monster. N.Z.: Best, 1925, 959; Cowan,
1930, I, 235f.; Grace, 1907, 94ff.; Grace, 1907,
96f., 173, 190.

*G308.2.1. Thousands of people overwhelmed by
water-monsters. N.Z.: Best, 1893, 217.

*G308.2.2. Water-monster as shape-changer. N.Z.:
Grace, 1907, 173.

G308.5. Shark-man ogre, eater of children swimming.
Tuamotus: Stimson, n.d., Z-G. 13/346; Hawaii:
Beckwith, 1940,191.

G308.8. Monsters of the sea: two whales of human
parentage. Tuamotus: Stimson, n.d., T-G. 3/912.

G308.9. Demon octopus. Tuamotus: Beckwith, 1940,
289; Marquesas: Handy, 1930, 76.

*G308.10. Supernatural plant-being spreads tentacles
across bay. Marquesas: Handy, 1930, 75.

*G308.11. Water-monster overturns canoes, eats
occupants. N.Z.: Grace, 1907, 174, 190.

G312. Cannibal ogre. Tuamotus: Caillot, 1914, 47;
Stimson, 1934, 63; 1937, 69, 81; Societies:
Best, 1924, 191; Cooks: Low, 1935, 28, 78;
Hawaii: Beckwith, 1940, 491; Emerson, 1921, 16;
Fornander, 1918, V, 370; Thrum, 1923, 165ff.;
Tonga: Collocott, 1928, 12, 14, 59f.; Samoa:
Krämer, 1902, I, 135, 143, 210, 218, 270, 349,
431, 443, 454; Sierich, 1901, 20ff.; Stuebel,
1896, 65f., 72f.; Tokelau: Burrows, 1923, 162f.;
Lister, 1892, 60f.; N.Z.: Best, 1924, 212;
Cowan, 1930, I, 64f.; 1930a, 131, 147, 168ff.;
White, 1887-90, I, 79, 87, 93, 127; II, 98f., 169f.
III, 3f.; Ellice Is.: Kennedy, 1931, 206; Rotuma:
Hames, 1960, 48; Russell, 1942, 246ff.; Lau Is.:
Hames, 1960, 19; Reef Is.: O'Ferrall,1904, 232;
Bellona: Elbert-Monberg, 1964, Nos. 60, 61.

*G312.3.1. Cannibal ogre crouches on limb over a lonely
river to drop upon any passerby. N.Z.: Cowan,
1930, I, 66f.

G321.2. Ogress (ogre) at a spot along the road takes
toll of lives. Hawaii: McAllister, 1933, 95f.

G322. Piercer-of-souls: fishes men. Tuamotus:
Leverd, 1911, 176f.; Stimson, 1937, 81; Societies:
Gill, 1876, 252; Henry, 1928, 560; Cooks: Gill,
1876, 110, 234; Te Ariki, 1921, 207.

G332. Sucking monster. Giant (sometimes a giant hall or cave) sucks in victims. Tuamotus: Henry, 1928, 503; Seurat, 1905, 484; Tahiti: Henry, 1928, 475; Cooks: Savage, 1910, 150f.; N.Z.: Best, 1924, 196; 1925, 968; Clark, 1896, 180.

*G337. Whirling monster. Societies: Williams, 1895, 285, 287.

*G338. Cannibalistic ogre carries victims in the hollow of his tongue. Hawaii: Rice, 1923, 23.

*G338.1. Ogress (mo'o) makes false bridge of her tongue with which to destroy travelers. Hawaii: Beckwith, 1940, 175.

*G343. Demon kills victims with hammer and chisel. Cooks: Gill, 1876, 235.

G346. Devastating monster. Lays waste to the land. Tubuai: Aitken, 1930, 112; Tuamotus: Leverd, 1911, 173; Stimson, 1937, 97; Hawaii: Beckwith, 1940, 491; N.Z.: Best, 1925, 919f.; Ellice Is.: Roberts, 1958, 365; Fijis (Lau): Hames, 1960, 19; Hocart, 1929, 218; Fison, 1904, 121; Reef Is.: O'Ferrall, 1904, 232; Santa Cruz: *Riesenfeld, 1950, 127; Bellona: Elbert-Monberg, 1964, No. 60.

*G349. Ogres' methods -- miscellaneous.

*G349.1. Strangling ogre (kills babies and maidens). Hawaii: Thrum, 1906, 126.

*G349.2. Ogress kills victims with her fingernails. Oceania: **Lessa, 1961; Australs: Aitkin, 1923, 263.

> F552.1.3. Extraordinary fingernails (used as weapons).

G351.1. Dog as ogre. Hawaii: Kamakau, 1961, 93 n.; Tonga: Beckwith, 1940, 342, 348; Gifford, 1924, 121; Reiter, 1919-20, 128; N.Z.: Cowan, 1930, I, 108, 109f.

*G351.3.1. Man-eating hog or pig. Hawaii: Westervelt, 1915, 252ff., 258ff.

G352.2. Wild boar as ogre. Cooks: Beckwith, 1940, 471;

Societies: Henry, 1928, 538.

*G352.3. Man-eating rat. Tonga: Reiter, 1917-18,
1042f.

*G352.4. Bat-like creature as ogre. N.Z.: Grace,1907,
73ff., 210ff.

G353. Bird as ogre. Tuamotus: Beckwith, 1940, 261;
Stimson, n.d., Z-G. 3/1229; Hawaii: Beckwith, 1940
493; Emory, 1924, 12; Westervelt, 1915, 68ff.,
96f.; Tonga: Reiter, 1917-18, 1044ff.; Samoa:
Stuebel, 1896, 145; Tokelaus: Burrows, 1923, 163f.
167; N.Z.: Grace, 1907, 81; N.Z.: White, 1887-90
II, 33; III, 194; Wohlers, 1876, 109f.; Rennell:
Bradley, 1956, 335.

G353.3. Duck as ogre. Tonga: Gifford, 1924, 104.

G354. Reptile as ogre. N.Z.: Best, 1925, 965; White,
1887-90, V, 56f.

G354.3. Lizard as ogre. Hawaii: Westervelt, 1915,
165ff.; 1915a, 180; Tonga: Reiter, 1917-18,
1044; Samoa: Beckwith, 1940, 128; N.Z.: Cowan,
1930, I, 188.

*G355. Fish (eel) as ogre. Marquesas: Lavondes, 1964,
4; Hawaii: Green, 1926, 102ff.; Pukui, 1933, 155;
Westervelt, 1915, 60ff.; Tonga: Collocott, 1921,
52; Samoa: Stuebel, 1896, 151, 153; Tokelaus:
Burrows, 1923, 156.

G360. Ogres with monstrous features. Funafuti: David,
1899, 107.

G361.2. Giant head as ogre. Head detached from body
pursues or flies about doing damage. Hawaii:
Thrum, 1923, 246f.; Fijis: Hocart, 1929, 192, 198,
215.

*G361.4. Giant bald-headed monster. Societies: Agostini,
1900, 88.

*G363.1.1. Ogre with flaming teeth. Rotuma: Hames, 1960,
48.

*G363.4. Ogress with teeth like obsidian, a mouth like a
barracuda, her hair like kelp. N.Z.: White, 1887-9C
II, 106f.

344

*G363.5. Monster with double-pointed tongue. Hawaii:
Thrum, 1923, 174.

*G363.6. Ogress' tongue trails behind her like a snake.
Lau: St. Johnston, 1918, 116.

*G363.7. Ogre with extremely long tongue. Hawaii:
Rice, 1923, 24.

*G363.8. Ogre with wooden teeth. Marquesas: Steinen,
1934-35, 205.

*G364. Ogre monstrous as to eyes.

*G364.1. Demon with many eyes. Samoa: Krämer, 1902, I,
1939.

*G366.2. Ogress' breasts strike ground as she runs and
sound like hoofbeats. Lau: St. Johnston, 1918,
116.

*G366.3. Ogress' stomach drags ground after cannibalistic
excesses. Samoa: Krämer, 1902, I, 136.

*G369.8. Ogre in form of plant. Samoa: Powell-Pratt,
1892, 98, 107.

*G381. Ogre carries a cluster of victims on his back.
Marquesas: Lavondes, 1964, 8.

*G382. Ogress with skirt of her victim's intestines.
Lau: Hames, 1960, 19.

*G383. Ogress takes shape of tree stump. Hawaii:
Emerson, 1915, 30.

*G384. Man-eating plant (tree). Tonga: Caillot, 1914,
292; Collocott, 1921, 50.

*G390. Rain, thunder, lightning, and earthquakes
accompany ogre's appearance. Tuamotus: Stimson,
1937, 97; Samoa: Krämer, 1902, I, 135.

G400--G499. Falling into ogre's power

G400. Person falls into ogre's power. Easter I.:
Métraux, 1940, 368; Tuamotus: Stimson, n.d.,
Z-G. 3/1276, Z-G. 13/301.

G401. Children wander into ogre's house. Chatham Is.: Beckwith, 1940, 474.

*G415. Ogress offers intended victims a cigar, and if they smoke it, they become bound to her. Lau: St. Johnston, 1918, 114.

*G416. A demon uses its tongue to simulate a bridge and this attracts victims. Hawaii: Emerson, 1915, 85.

G421. Ogre traps victim. Tuamotus: Stimson, 1934, 63; Cooks: Gill, 1876, 132; Hawaii: Beckwith, 1940, 194; Samoa: *Krämer, 1902, I, 218, 349, 349 n. 5; N.Z.: Wohlers, 1875,15; Futuna: Burrows, 1936, 105.

G422. Ogre imprisons victim. Cooks, N.Z., Rotuma: Dixon, 1916, 62; Hawaii: *Beckwith, 1940, 194, 195, 195 n. 12; N.Z.: Shand, 1896, 197.

*G441.1. Ogre abducts victim in bowl. Futuna: Burrows, 1936, 227.

*G441.2. Ogress carries away a man wrapped in his sleeping mat. Lau Is.: St. Johnston, 115.

*G441.3. Giant lifts canoe full of sleeping warriors and places it on the tops of trees. Cooks: Savage, 1910, 154, 155, n.

*G441.4. Bat-like cannibal monster flies carrying human on his back. N.Z.: Grace, 1907, 78, 210.

G442. Child-stealing demon. Australs: Aitken, 1930, 11(

*G442.3. Ogress kills new born children. Australs: Aitken, 1923, 268.

G455. Falling into ogre's power through fascination with his daughter. Tuamotus: Stimson, n.d., Z-G. 13/152; Hawaii: Beckwith, 1940, 264.

G466. Lousing as task set by ogre. Marquesas: Steinen, 1934-35, 217; Tuamotus: Stimson, n.d., T-G. 3/931; 1937, 66; Societies: Henry, 1928, 555; Samoa: Krämer, 1902, I, 143; Rotuma: Churchward, 1938-39, 219; Ontong Java: Sarfert, 1931, 456.

346

*G479. Girl mischievously strikes a great drum, and
an old hag appears and breaks her leg. Lau:
St. Johnston, 1918, 114.

G500--G599. Ogre defeated

G500. Ogre defeated. Hawaii: Thrum, 1923, 176f.;
Westervelt, 1915, 71ff., 167ff.

G501. Stupid ogre. Hawaii: Emory, 1924, 15; Rotuma:
Churchward, 1938-39, 224; Rennell: Elbert-Monberg,
1964, No. 2a.

G510. Ogre killed, maimed, or captured. Tahiti: Gill,
1876, 253; Tonga: Reiter, 1917-18, 1044ff.;
Chatham Is.: Shand, 1896, 202.

G510.4. Hero overcomes devastating animal. Societies:
Williams, 1895, 277.

*G510.6. Ogress forced to vomit up eaten victims.
Samoa: Krämer,1902, I, 136.

*G510.7. Ogre defeated: hit in the mouth with a tapa-
beater, he becomes an ordinary old man. Marquesas:
Lavondes, 1964, 6.

*G510.8. Man subdues and marries ogress. Tuamotus:
Stimson, 1937, 98.

*G510.9. Monster tamed: becomes a servant to men. N.Z.:
Grace, 1907, 179.

G511. Ogre blinded. Rennell: Elbert-Monberg, 1964,
No. 20.

G512. Ogre killed. Tuamotus: Stimson, n.d., Z-G. 13/174,
Z-G. 13/249; 1934, 32ff.; Hawaii: Fornander, 1916,
IV, 64ff.; Rice, 1923, 65; Thrum, 1907, 218f.;
Westervelt, 1915, 175, 212f.; 1915a, 219; Tonga:
Brown, 1916, 430; Caillot, 1914, 289ff., 291, 297ff.;
Collocott, 1914, 292; 1921, 50; Reiter, 1917-18,
1042f.; Samoa: Krämer, 1902, I, 139; Stuebel,
1896, 65; Niue: Smith, 1903, 112; Tokelau:
Burrows, 1923, 164, 175; N.Z.: Best, 1925, 922;
White, 1887-90, II, 33; Wohlers, 1875, 22; 1876,
110; Rotuma: Hames, 1960, 49f.; Russell, 1942,
244; Reef Is.: O'Ferrall, 1904, 232f.

G512.1. Ogre killed with knife (sword). Hawaii: Westervelt, 1915, 65, 70f.; Tokelaus: Burrows, 1923, 172.

G512.1.2. Ogre decapitated. N.Z.: White, 1887-90, I, 80.

G512.3. Ogre burned to death. Mangareva: Hiroa, 1938, 380; Tuamotus: Stimson, 1934, 67f.; Cooks: Kunike, 1928; Manihiki: *Beckwith, 1940, 196, 196 n. 18; Editors, JPS VI (1897), 97, n.; Tahiti: Beckwith, 1940, 251; Hawaii: Beckwith, 1940, 141, 195, 445; Emerson, 1921, 18; Emory, 1924, 15; Fornander, 1916, V, 482; 1918, V434; Grace, 1907, 41; Smith, 1966, 11; Thrum, 1923, 246f.; Tonga: Collocott, 1928, 27; Chatham Is.: Shand, 1896, 197; N.Z.: Beattie, 1920, 138; Beckwith, 1940, 196, 196 n. 18; Best, 1893, 219; Grace, 1907, 19f.; White, 1887-90, II, 29; III, 125, 190f.; Wohlers, 1876, 117; Ellice Is.: Roberts, 1958, 367, 400; Rennell: Elbert-Monberg, 1964, Nos. 2a, 2b; Kapingamarangi: Elbert, 1948, 89; Emory, 1949, 239.

G512.3.1. Ogre killed by throwing hot stones (metal) into his throat. Oceania: *Dixon, 1916, 61, 63, 69, 86, 133 n. 6; Tuamotus: Stimson, n.d., Z-G. 13/249; Societies: Baessler, 1905, 923; Beckwith, 1940, 197 n. 21, Ch. XIII passim; Henry, 1912, 2; N.Z.: *Beckwith, 1940,196; White, 1887-90, I, 92f.; II, 56f., 172; III, 4; Wohlers, 1876, 120; Bellona: Elbert-Monberg, 1964, Nos. 41a, 41b.

G512.3.2. Ogre burned in his own oven. Samoa: Krämer, 1902, I, 144-145; Ellice Is.: Kennedy, 1931, 179; Bellona: Elbert-Monberg, 1964, No. 52a; Rennell: ibid., 52b.

G512.4. Ogre persuaded to go into hole: buried alive. Marquesas: Steinen, 1933-34, 372.

G512.8. Ogre killed by striking. Australs: Aitken, 1923, 269, 275; Niue: Smith, 1903, 10, 112; Rennell: Elbert-Monberg, 1964, Nos. 175, 176.

G512.8.1. Ogre killed by striking with club Hawaii: Thrum, 1923, 160; N.Z.: White, 1887-90, V, 57.

G512.8.2. Ogre killed by striking with stones. Tuamotus: Audran, 1919, 37, 52; Societies: Beckwith, 1940, 340; Hawaii: Dickey, 1917, 33.

*G512.8.5. Woman smashes heads of ogres together, kills them. Kapingamarangi: Elbert, 1948, 82.

G512.9.1. Ogre killed by helpful dogs. Fijis: Hocart, 1929, 218.

G512.11. Ogre drowned. Tuamotus: Stimson, n.d., Z-G. 3/1110, Z-G. 13/249; Cooks: Low, 1935, 31f.; Hawaii: Beckwith, 1940, 174; Emerson,1921, 17ff.; 1924, 15; Emory, 1924, 15; Fornander, 1918, V, 300; Tokelaus: Burrows, 1923, 163, 172; Ontong Java: Sarfert, 1931, 456; Bellona: Elbert-Monberg, 1964, No. 63.

*G512.11.1. Village of cannibals is inundated, destroyed. Hawaii: Westervelt, 1915, 144.

*G512.12. Ogre killed when external (detachable) soul destroyed. Tuamotus: Stimson, n.d., Z-G. 13/174; N.Z.: Pakauwera, 1894, 103.

G514.3. Ogre caught in noose and killed. Australs: Aitken, 1923, 265, 272; 1930, 110; Tuamotus: Stimson, n.d., Z-G. 13/221; 1937, 89; Hawaii: Beckwith, 1940, 174; Dickey, 1917, 23; Fornander, 1916, IV, 530; V, 368; Green, 1929, 91; N.Z.: *Beckwith, 1940, 174, 265, 265 notes; Best, 1925, 965; Clark, 1896, 100; Cowan, 1930, I, 109, 236; Dixon, 1916, 61; Grace, 1907, 82f., 173ff.; Gudgeon, 1905, 183ff.; Hongi, 1894, 156; White, 1887-90, I, 72, 75, 76, 80, 93f.; II, 153; III, 4, 194f.; Wohlers, 1875, 22; Rennell: Elbert-Monberg, 1964, Nos. 2a, 2b, 2c, 50c; Bellona: ibid., No. 50a.

G514.5. Ogre tied to rock. Tuamotus: Beckwith, 1940, 268.

G514.6. Ogresses caught in flood of lava. Hawaii: Beckwith, 1940, 174.

G519.1.4. Ogress tricked into falling into boiling spring. N.Z.: Beckwith, 1940, 196; Cowan, 1930a, 124f.

*G519.6. Person tricks ogresses into killing a sister ogress; he leaves marks of turmeric on victim so that others will know she has slept with him. Marquesas: Lavondes, 1964, 24.

*G519.7. Ogre poisoned. Mangareva: Hiroa, 1938, 421; Tuamotus: Audran, 1918, 91; Marquesas: Lavondes, 1964, 6; Samoa: Andersen, 1925, 143.

*G519.8. Ogre frozen by magic rain. Bellona: Elbert-Monberg, 1964, No. 58.

*G519.9. Ogre caused to fall to death. Marquesas: Lavondes, 1964, 8; Rotuma: Russell, 1942, 247; Bellona: Elbert-Monberg, 1964, Nos. 60, 63.

*G529.1. Ogre duped into killing self: lured into house, killed. Hawaii: Fornander, 1916, IV, 482; Grace,1907, 41; N.Z.: Wohlers, 1876, 117; Kapingamarangi: Elbert, 1949, 245.

*G529.2. Stupid ogre wishes to be tattooed: women rub his body with red hot stones. Rotuma: Churchward, 1938-39, 224.

*G529.3. Man repeatedly lies to man-eating spirits when they ask where he will sleep. They begin dying from exhaustion following their fruitless searches. Hawaii: Emory, 1924, 13f., 14f.; Fornander, 1916, IV, 488.

*G529.4. Ogress killed trying to cross bridge of hair. Marquesas: Steinen, 1933-34, 369.

*G529.5. Ogre swallows inimical object, dies. Kapingamarangi: Elbert, 1948, 108.

G530. Ogre's relative aids hero. N.Z.: White, 1887-90, II, 162.

G530.1. Help from ogre's wife. Rennell: Elbert-Monberg, 1964, No. 20.

G530.2. Help from ogre's daughter. Tuamotus: Stimson, n.d., 3/1276, Z-G. 13/152.

G530.3. Help from ogre's mother. Tuamotus: Stimson, n.d., T-G. 3/931.

G530.4. Help from ogre's grandmother. Tuamotus: Stimson, 1937, 82ff.

*G538. Doorkeeper in house of ogre befriends hero. N.Z.: Best, 1925, 915.

G550. Rescue from ogre. Hawaii: *Beckwith, 1940, 194, 195 n. 12; Westervelt, 1915, 53; Samoa: Krämer, 1902, I, 135.

*G551.6. Rescue from ogre by sons. Cooks, Chatham Is., N.Z.: *Beckwith, 1940, 196, 196 n. 18.

G555. Rescue from ogre by means of singing. Samoa: Hambruch, 1914-15, 284f.

G570. Ogre overawed. Hawaii: Beckwith, 1940, 443.

*G586. Ogre frightened away by noise. Rotuma: Churchward, 1938-39, 122.

*G587. An ogre can be evaded only when the rays of the declining sun blind him. N.Z.: Best, 1925, 920.

G600--G699. Other ogre motifs

*G612.1. Ogresses's removable eyes stolen. Hawaii: *Beckwith, 1940, 199f.

G637. Ogres live in trees. Cooks: Gill, 1876, 84.

*G640. Lizard monsters are servants of ogre. Hawaii: Emerson, 1915, 35f.

*G641. Ogres live in cave(s). Australs: Aitken, 1923, 263; 1930, 109; Samoa: Krämer, 1902, I, 454; Niue: Smith, 1903, 10, 112; N.Z.: Cowan, 1930, I, 80f.

*G642. Ogres eat raw flesh. Chatham Is.: Shand, 1896, 195; N.Z.: Whetu, 1897, 98.

*G643. Birds are spies of ogre. Hawaii: Emerson, 1915, 36.

G691. Bodies of victims in front of ogre's house. N.Z.: White, 1887-90, II, 33.

*G691.5. Ogre's cave full of bodies, skulls, and bones. Marquesas: Lavondes, 1964, 8-10; Cooks: Low, 1935, 31.

*G691.6. Ogre's cave smells of rotten flesh. Niue:

Smith, 1903, 10, 112.

*G691.7. Bones of eaten humans stick out of ogre's body like spines of porcupine fish. N.Z.: Best, 1924, 212.

*G691.8. Fence of human bones around house of cannibal chief. Hawaii: Beckwith, 1940, 460; Fornander, 1916, IV, 574ff.; 1918, 396ff.

H. TESTS

H0--H199. Identity tests: recognition

H0. Identity tests. Ellice Is.: Roberts, 1958, 367.

H10. Recognition through common knowledge. Tuamotus:
Stimson, 1937, 17f.; Hawaii: Thrum, 1923, 65;
Tonga: Collocott, 1928, 27, 32; N.Z.: White,
1887-90, IV, 44, 198, 208.

*H11.1.5. Father recognizes his son from latter's
description of his mother's courtship. Tuamotus:
Stimson, 1934, 16; N.Z.: Best, 1925, 715.

H12. Recognition by song (chant, music). Marquesas:
Lavondes,1964, 72; Hawaii: Beckwith, 1940, 153,
530, 539; N.Z.: Best, 1925, 818; Dixon, 1916,
83; White, 1887-90, V, 19.

H41.10. Chief in disguise carries bundle so large
that rank is recognized. Hawaii: Beckwith, 1940,
388.

H45. Recognition (test) of deity (spirit). Hawaii:
Fornander, 1918, V, 312, 552; Thrum, 1907, 129;
Westervelt, 1915, 89ff.; Tonga: Collocott, 1928,
22, 28, 36; Gifford, 1924, 56; Samoa: Sierich,
1902, 175, 190, 236; N.Z.: White, 1887-90, II,
60; Rennell: Elbert-Monberg, 1964, Nos. 50b, 50c.

H45.5. Girl sleeping naked awakened. If mortal, she
will cover herself; if a goddess, will not. Tonga:
Gifford, 1924, 191.

H51.1. Recognition by birthmark. Marquesas: Lavondes,
1964, 98.

H55.3. Recognition by tattoo. Easter I.: Métraux,
1940, 370; Tuamotus: Audran, 1918, 30.

H56. Recognition by wound. Cooks: Te Ariki, 1920, 46;
Hawaii: Beckwith, 1940, 417; Fornander, 1916, IV,
470; Rice, 1923, 53; Tonga: Collocott, 1928, 23.

*H56.3. Recognition by club feet. Mangareva: Laval,
1938, 169.

H57.1. Recognition by broken tooth. Mangareva: Hiroa,
1938, 21; N.Z.: Beckwith, 1940, 505; Best, 1925,
773, 921; *Best, 1928, 261f., 264, 266; Cowan,
1930, I, 70; Dixon, 1916, 84; White, 1887-90,
II, 129f., 133, 138f., 146; Wohlers, 1875, 29.

*K722.∤ Messengers seeking person with
gapped teeth make people laugh with wild
dance.

H58. Tell-tale hand-mark. Marquesas: Steinen,
1934-35, 233; Hawaii: Rice, 1923, 110.

H58.2. Clandestine lover identified by scratches left
on face by lady. Marquesas: Steinen, 1933-34,
30, 32; N.Z.: Best, 1927, 269.

*H58.2.1. Person discovers wife's paramour from latter's
fingernails, which match marks on wife's face.
Kapingamarangi: Elbert, 1949, 245.

*H64.5. Man, transformed to fish killed, but recognized
by his tattoo marks. Rotuma: Churchward, 1937-38,
496.

H71.10. Marvel as sign of royalty. Societies: Henry,
1928, 611; Hawaii: Beckwith, 1940, 484.

*H71.12. Cord stretched across door of royalty drops of
itself when peers approach. Hawaii: Beckwith,
1940, 376.

H75. Identification by (lock of) hair. Tokelaus:
Burrows, 1923, 167f.

H75.7. Recognition of murderers by their short hair.
Tonga: Gifford, 1924, 34.

*H79.9. Recognition by tooth marks left in fruit. Tonga:
Caillot, 1914, 269; Collocott, 1921, 46; Reiter,
1917-18, 1031; Gifford, 1924, 69f.; Ellice Is.:
Kennedy, 1931, 175, 185; Rotuma: Russell, 1942,
244; Kapingamarangi: Emory, 1949, 235.

*H79.10. Recognition by fingernail marks on seed. Cooks:
Te Ariki, 1920,174; Kapingamarangi: Elbert, 1948,
113.

*H79.12. Blind father recognizes daughter by her crooked
toe. Rarotonga: Te Ariki, 1920, 46.

*H79.13. Spirits taste skins of sleepers for salt water
to see if they are refugees who swam from hostile
village. Samoa: Stuebel, 1896, 146.

H80--H149. Identification by tokens

H80. Identification by tokens. Hawaii: *Beckwith,
1940, 479f.; Fornander, 1916, IV, 184; Green,
1923, 53; Kamakau, 1961, 7; Remy, 1868, 20;
Thrum, 1921, 112; 1923, 96, 211; N.Z.: White,
1887-90, II, 129, 175.

H81.1. Hero lies by sleeping girl and leaves identification token with her. Hawaii: Beckwith, 1940, 86,
389.

H92. Identification by necklace. Hawaii: Beckwith,
1940, 514.

H111. Identification by garment. Hawaii: Beckwith,
1940, 480.

H111.2. Identification by feather cloak. Hawaii:
Beckwith, 1940, 420, 479.

H125.2. Identification by spear. Hawaii: Beckwith,
1940, 416, 480.

H125.3. Identification by war-club. Hawaii: Beckwith,
1940, 508.

H125.4. Recognition by dart (arrow). Hawaii: Fornander,
1916, IV, 36ff.; N.Z.: Beckwith, 1940, 482.

H151.9. Abandoned child joins parents in game:
recognition follows. N.Z.: Dixon, 1916, 42 n. 10.

*H151.10.1. Combat of father and son(s) brings about
recognition. Tuamotus: Stimson, n.d., Z-G. 13/127;
Niue: Smith, 1903, 94.

*H151.16. Child reveals kinship with parent by act of
audacity or impudence. Samoa: Sierich, 1901, 19;
Niue: Smith, 1903, 94; N.Z.: Best, 1925, 914;
White, 1887-90, II, 143f.; IV, 177ff., 198;
Wohlers, 1875, 10.

H161. Recognition of transformed person among identical companions. Hawaii: Beckwith, 1940, 541; Emerson, 1915, 228; Green, 1926, 116.

H165. Father recognizes son after having thrown him in oven. Marquesas: Beckwith, 1940, 482.

*H172.2. Black pig magically indicates royalty. Hawaii: Beckwith, 1940, 300; Fornander, IV, 178ff., 244ff.; 1918, V, 176ff., 378ff.

H175. Recognition by "force of nature." Unknown member of family immediately and magically recognize Ontong Java: Sarfert, 1931, 423; Bellona: Elbert-Monberg, 1964, No. 52a; Kapingamarangi: Emory, 1949, 230.

H200--H299. TESTS OF TRUTH

H210--H239. Tests of guilt or innocence

H220. Ordeals. Guilt or innocence thus established. Hawaii: Fornander, 1918, V, 270.

*H237. Ordeal: jumping from high tree. Fijis: Hocart, 1929, 209.

*H251.3.15. Fly will light upon upstretched finger of thief. Niue: Loeb, 1926, 193.

*H251.3.16. Thief discovered out of group which is lined up before a stick supposed to fall down before the guilty. The person going before it is the thief. N.Z.: Cowan, 1930, I, 85f.

*H251.3.17. Test of truth: a net is waved over a man's head and if he is guilty of lying, his soul will be caught. Lau: St. Johnston, 1918, 62.

*H265. Test of ownership: man falsely claiming canoe is unable to say charm that rightful owner can pronounce. Reef Is.: O'Ferrall, 1904, 227.

H300--H499. MARRIAGE TESTS

H310--H359. Suitor tests

H310. Suitor tests. Hawaii: Smith, 1955, 49f.; N.Z.: Grace, 1907, 163ff.

H311. Inspection test for suitors for princess's hand must present themselves for public inspection. Societies: Henry, 1928, 231; Kapingamarangi: Elbert, 1948, 108.

*H312.4.2. Male beauty contest to find princess's consort. Tonga: Collocott, 1928, 47, 50.

H322. Suitor test: finding princess. Tuamotus: Stimson, n.d., MB-DD-33, Z-G. 3/1241; Hawaii: Thrum, 1923, 142; Niue: Loeb, 1926, 195.

H324. Suitor test: choosing princess from others identically clad. Hawaii: Rice, 1923, 29.

H331. Suitor contests: bride offered as prize. Tuamotus: Stimson, n.d., T-G. 3/45, Z-G. 13/174, Z-G. 13/346; Societies: Henry, 1928, 561; Societies, Cooks, N.Z.: Dixon, 1916, 61, 64; Tokelaus: Burrows, 1923, 157; Macgregor, 1937, 83.

H331.5. Suitor contest: race. Hawaii: Westervelt, 1915, 30f.

H331.6. Suitor contest: wrestling. Hawaii: Thrum, 1906, 125ff.; 1907, 161.

H331.7. Suitor contest: aiming with missile. Hawaii: Pukui-Curtis, n.d., 96.

H335. Tasks assigned suitors. Bride as prize for accomplishment. Easter I.: Métraux, 1940, 57; Tuamotus: Stimson, n.d., T-G. 3/45, T-G. 3/49, Z-G. 3/174, Z-G. 3/1241, Z-G. 13/4, Z-G. 13/174, Z-G. 13/10, Z-G. 13/203, Z-G. 13/276, Z-G. 13/317, Z-G. 13/441, Z-G. 13/499, Z-G. 13/730, Z-G. 13/243, Z-G. 13/1241.

H335.3.7. Suitor task: to kill other monsters. Tuamotus: Stimson, n.d., T-G. 13/317.

H335.6. Suitor task: making weather calm. Tonga: Gifford, 1924, 176.

H335.6.1. Suitor task: controlling violent tide.
Tuamotus: Stimson, n.d., T-G. 3/720.

H360. Bride test. Hawaii: Beckwith, 1919, 546-548.

H400--H459. Chastity tests

H400. Chastity test. Various means are employed to
test a woman's (or man's) chastity. Hawaii:
Beckwith, 1940, 516, 535; Fornander, 1916, IV,
544; Samoa: Beckwith, 1940, 535.

H466.1. Feigned absence to test wife's faithfulness.
Tuamotus: Stimson, 1934, 44; Samoa: Krämer,
1902, I, 443f.; N.Z.: White, 1887-90, II, 23.

H480. Father tests. Test as to who is unknown father
of child. Hawaii: Rice, 1923, 75.

H500--H899. TESTS OF CLEVERNESS

*H509.6. Fish-naming contest. Ellice Is.: Roberts,
1958, 397.

H510. Tests in guessing. Hawaii: Westervelt, 1915a,
78.

H521. Test: guessing unknown propounder's name.
Ellice Is.: David, 1899, 105; Kennedy, 1931, 192.

H530--H899. Riddles

H541.1. Riddle propounded on pain of death. Hawaii:
*Beckwith, 1940, Ch. XXXII passim; Luomala, 1949,
77.

H548. Riddle contests. Hawaii: Beckwith, 1940, 427,
455 ff.; Fornander, 1918, V, 400, 418; Luomala,
1949, 77; McAllister, 1933, 91f.; Westervelt,
1915a, 75, 77f.

H551.2. Woman gives herself to solver of riddles.
Tuamotus: Stimson, n.d., Z-G. 13/203.

H611.3. Chief asks another for cutting of yams to complete his yam patch (daughter in marriage). Reply that seed yams for the year are shriveled and old and it is too early for seedlings (his daughters are too young or too old). Tonga: Gifford, 1924, 43.

H900--H1199. TESTS OF PROWESS: TASKS

H900--H999. Assignment and performance of tasks

H900-H949. Assignment of tasks

H900. Tasks imposed. Tonga: Gifford, 1924, 178.

H911. Tasks assigned at suggestion of jealous rivals. Rotuma: Churchward, 1938-39, 467.

H924. Tasks assigned prisoner so that he may escape punishment. Hawaii: Rice, 1923, 45.

H927.1. Tasks as trial of prowess of mortal by gods. Tuamotus: Stimson, n.d., Z-G. 13/441.

H931. Tasks assigned to get ride of hero. Tonga: Gifford, 1924, 104f.; Rotuma: Churchward, 1938-39, 467.

H950--H999. Performance of tasks

H970. Help in performing tasks. Samoa: Stuebel, 1896, 143.

H971. Task performed with help of old person. Tonga: Gifford, 1924, 159f.

H973. Tasks performed by helpful forest spirits. N.Z.: Dixon, 1916, 61.

H975. Tasks performed by deity. Hawaii: Westervelt, 1915, 31.

H982. Animals help man perform task. Rotuma: Churchward, 1938-39, 467.

*H999. Task accomplished with help of captive. Hawaii: Thrum, 1923, 147f.

H1010--H1049. Impossible or absurd tasks

*H1021.12. Task: to fill gourd with its neck held
downward. Hawaii: Thrum, 1907, 97ff.

*H1023.26. Task: to lift sky. Societies: Henry,
1928, 410f.

H1049.3. Task: setting back sun. Samoa: Beckwith,
1940, 439.

H1049.4. Task: stopping the rain. Samoa: Beckwith,
1940, 439 ; Stuebel, 1896, 143.

*H1049.5. Task: breathing under water. Samoa:
Stuebel, 1896, 143.

*H1103.4. Task: to gather huge quantities of fruit.
Tonga: Collocott, 1928, 14.

*H1109.5. Task: to catch fruit of shaken tree before
it hits the ground. Tonga: Collocott, 1928, 15f.

H1115.3. Task: cutting down a giant tree. Marquesas:
Beckwith, 1940, 470.

*H1118.4. Task: counting hairs on human head. Cooks:
Luomala, 1949, 78.

*H1118.5. Task: counting grains of sand on island.
Nuguria Is.: Luomala, 1949, 78.

*H1118.6. Task: counting coral. Cooks: Luomala, 1949,
78.

*H1118.7. Task: counting the stars. Cooks: Luomala,
1949, 78.

*H1121.1. Task: picking fruit of giant tree. Tonga:
Reiter, 1934, 510f.

H1132. Task: recovering lost objects. Societies:
Ropiteau, 1933, 128; Cooks: Gill, 1876, 291.

H1141. Task: eating enormous amount. Tonga:
Collocott, 1928, 14, 15; Reiter, 1934, 505f.

H1142. Task: to drink enormous amount. Tonga:
Reiter, 1934, 502f.

H1144.2. Task: counting the waves. Cooks: *Luomala,
1949, 78.

*H1149.11. Task: to control the sun during its daily
course. Samoa: Stuebel,1896, 143.

H1151. Theft as task. Hawaii: Westervelt, 1915a,
106ff., 153, 155ff.

H1151.5.1. Task: stealing girdle of goddess. Tuamotus:
Stimson, n.d., Z-G. 13/243.

*H1151.27. Task: stealing bananas guarded by great
bird. Rotuma: Churchward, 1937-38, 490.

*H1151.28. Task: stealing kava plant guarded by
gigantic bull-ants. Rotuma: Churchward, 1937-38,
491.

*H1154.4.1. Task: to catch extremely wild fish. Samoa:
Krämer, 1902, I, 257.

H1161. Task: killing ferocious beast. N.Z.: Best,
1927, 264; Tokelaus: Macgregor, 1937, 85.

*H1161.7. Task: killing fish of great size. Tokelaus:
Macgregor, 1937, 85.

*H1163.1. Task: to dig up magic kava. Samoa: Krämer,
1902, I, 257.

H1194. Task: making person laugh. Ellice Is.:
Roberts, 1958, 407.

*H1199.19. Task: to fetch pieces of enchanted oakum.
Tuamotus: Stimson, 1937, 128.

*H1199.20. Task: to remove huge stone. Samoa: Krämer,
1902, I, 258-259; Stuebel, 1896, 87.

H1200--H1249. Attendant circumstances of quests

H1228.2. Son goes out to avenge father's death.
Tuamotus: Stimson, 1934, 53ff.

H1233.6. Animals help hero on quest. Rotuma:
Churchward, 1938-39, 468.

H1239.5. Seductive women attempt to divert quester.
Tuamotus: Stimson, n.d., Z-G. 3/1174, Z-G. 3/1386,
Z-G. 13/221, Z-G. 13/1241.

H1241. Series of quests. One quest can be accomplished
when a second is finished, etc. Tuamotus: Henry,
1928, 522.

H1250--H1399. NATURE OF QUESTS

H1250--H1299. Quests to the other world

H1250. Quests to the other world. Cooks: Beaglehole,
1938, 326; Chatham Is.: Shand, 1898, 73; N.Z.:
Best ,925, 844; Locke, 1921, 42.

H1252. Quest to other world for relative. N.Z.:
Tregear, 1901, 185; Reef Is.: Elbert-Kirtley,
1966, 351.

H1252.1. Quest to other world for ancestor. Mangareva:
Hiroa, 1938, 321; Societies: Henry, 1928, 559,
561; N.Z.: Best, 1925, 911, 937; *Potae, 1928,
360, 366.

H1260. Quest to the upper world. Mangareva: Hiroa,
1938, 375; Hawaii: Beckwith, 1919, 554ff.; 1940,
532; Tonga: Collocott, 1928, 42.

*H1264.1. Quest to upper world to find sun and return
it to earth. Hawaii: Rice, 1923, 104.

H1267. Pregnant woman craving fish sends husband to
heaven after lucky fishhook. Samoa: Beckwith,
1940, 25.

H1270. Quest to lower world. Tuamotus: Stimson, n.d., Z-G. 13/276.

*H1284.2. Quest to land of sunrise for princess. Tuamotus: Stimson, n.d., T-G. 3/109.

*H1284.3. Quest after sun. Tonga: Collocott, 1922, 162.

*H1284.4. Quest after land in which there is daylight. Cooks: Guppy, 1890, 47.

H1301. Quest for the most beautiful of women. Tuamotus: Stimson, n.d., T-G. 3/109, T-G. 3/404; Hawaii: Rice, 1923, 94.

H1301.1. Quest for the most beautiful bride. Societies: Beckwith, 1940, 38.

H1301.1.3. Hero visits all islands to see if he can find woman to rival wife's beauty. Hawaii: Beckwith, 1940, 539.

*H1305.3. Quest to find certain kind of bananas. Rotuma: Russell, 1942, 244.

H1320. Quest for marvelous objects or animals. Hawaii: Fornander, 1916, IV, 560; Tonga: Caillot, 1914, 254f.; N.Z.: Tama-Rau, 1899, 51ff.

H1321.1. Quest for Water of Life (water which will resuscitate). Hawaii: Beckwith, 1940, 72, 257; Fornander, 1916, IV, 82ff.; Westervelt, 1915a, 40ff.

H1331. Quest for remarkable animal. Tuamotus: Stimson, 1937, 46; Hawaii: Pukui-Curtis, n.d., 94ff.; N.Z.: Best, 1925, 911, 917f.

H1331.1.2.1. Quest for remarkable bird feathers. Societies: Williams, 1895, 271; Marquesas: Handy, 1930, 130; *Steinen, 1933-34, 9ff.; Tuamotus: Stimson, n.d., Z-G. 3/1353, 13/276; N.Z.: Beckwith, 1940, 260; Clark, 1896, 265.

H1333.1. Quest for marvelous tree. Marquesas: Lavondes, 1966, 70ff.

H1371.1. Quest for the world's end. Ellice Is.:
Kennedy, 1931, 165.

H1381.2.2. Child seeks unknown parent. Tuamotus:
Seurat, 1905, 482; Cooks: Savage, 1910, 149ff.;
N.Z.: Best, 1925, 936.

H1381.2.2.1. Son seeks unknown father. Mangareva:
Hiroa, 1938, 379; Tuamotus: Stimson, n.d.,
Z-G. 13/127; 1934, 12; 1937, 17, 75ff.;
Marquesas: Lavondes, 1964, 66ff.; Steinen, 1933-34,
349, 363; Handy, 1930, 61, 131; Cooks:
Te Ariki, 1920, 119f.; Editors, JPS VI (1897),
97 n., 100; Hawaii: Beckwith, 1940, 86, 479, 514;
Fornander, 1916, IV, 182, 596ff.; Pukui, 1933, 179f.
Remy,1868, 20; Rice, 1923, 27; Thrum, 1896, 115;
1921, 112; 1923, 78, 210f.; Westervelt, 1915, 172ff
204ff.; Tonga: Brown, 1916, 428f.; Caillot, 1914,
259, n.2; Collocott, 1924, 280; 1928, 27f.;
Gifford, 1924, 112; Reiter, 1933, 357f.; Samoa:
Powell-Pratt, 1892, 243; Sierich, 1901, 18;
1902, 171f.; Tokelaus: Burrows, 1923, 168f.;
Macgregor, 1937, 84; N.Z.: Beattie, 1920, 137;
Best, 1925, 715; Shand, 1896, 198; White,
1887-90, II, 173ff.; III, 200; IV, 41, 175, 196,
197f., 205ff.; V, 18ff.; Ellice Is.: Kennedy,
1931, 157; Fijis: Fison, 1904, 35, 51; Ontong
Java, Nukumanu: Sarfert, 1931, 424; Bellona:
Elbert-Monberg, 1964, 52a; Rennell: ibid., 52b.

H1381.2.2.1.1. Boy twitted with illegitimacy seeks
unknown father. Hawaii: Beckwith, 1940, 263.

H1381.2.2.2. Child seeks unknown mother. Tuamotus:
Stimson, 1937, 98; N.Z.: Beckwith, 1940, 481;
White, 1887-90, II, 142ff.

H1381.3. Quest for unknown woman. Societies: Caillot,
1914, 117f.

H1381.3.1. Quest for bride. Hawaii: Beckwith, 1919,
378ff.; Fornander, 1918, V, 384; Thrum, 1923,
220ff.; Westervelt, 1915, 176ff.; Tonga:
Collocott, 1928, 42; Chatham Is.: Shand, 1895,
161.

H1381.3.1.2. Quest for bride for oneself. See
H1381.3.1. Tuamotus: Stimson, n.d., T-G. 3/900.

*H1381.7.1. Quest for husband. Mangareva: Hiroa,
1938, 375; Hawaii: Beckwith, 1919, 554ff.;
Emerson, 1915, 15ff.; Westervelt, 1915, 40ff.;
Tonga: Collocott, 1928, 18; Samoa: Krämer,
1902, I, 131-132, 133.

*H1382.4. Quest to ancestral land for sweet potato.
N.Z.: *White, 1887-90, IV, 3ff.

*H1384. Quest for unknown places.

*H1384.1. Quest for unknown island. Hawaii:
Emerson, 1915, Xff.; Fornander, 1916, IV, 46ff.,
116; Lau: St. Johnston, 1918, 30.

H1385.2. Quest for vanished daughter. Marquesas:
Steinen, 1934-35, 215f.; N.Z.: White, 1887-90,
I, 116ff.

H1385.3. Quest for vanished wife (mistress). Polynesia
(N.Z., Mangaia, Niue, Chatham Is., Hawaii):
*Dixon, 1916, 70 ff.; Hawaii: Green, 1926, 116;
Thrum, 1907, 169ff., 171ff.; Tokelaus: Burrows,
1923, 167; N.Z.: Smith, 1897, 22; White, 1887-90,
II, 136f.; IV, 223f.; Wohlers, 1875, 26f.;
Kapingamarangi: Elbert, 1949, 242.

*H1385.3.2. A father seeks his vanished son. Tuamotus:
Stimson, 1937, 101ff.

H1385.4. Quest for vanished husband. Oceanic:
*Beckwith, 1940, 169ff.

H1385.6. Quest for lost sister. Marquesas: Steinen,
1933-34, 371; Tokelaus: Burrows, 1923, 162f.;
Lister, 1892, 61; N.Z.: Best, 1925, 702;
Kapingamarangi: Elbert, 1948, 71.

H1385.8. Quest for lost brother. Hawaii: Fornander,
1916, IV, 122ff.; Thrum, 1923, 23ff.

H1386. Quest for lost object. Kapingamarangi:
Elbert, 1949, 243.

*H1386.5. Quest for lost pet fish (shark). Tonga:
Collocott, 1922, 160.

H1400--H1599. OTHER TESTS

H1400--H1449. Tests of fear

H1400. Fear test. Niue: Smith, 1903, 10, 112; Rennell: Elbert-Monberg, 1964, No. 115.

H1401.2. Ogress assumes frightful guises to frighten messengers. Hawaii: Beckwith, 1940, 174, 194.

*H1409. Fear test--miscellaneous.

*H1409.1. Two gods have a contest to determine who can frighten the other. Rennell: Elbert-Monberg, 1964, No. 18.

H1450--H1499. Tests of vigilance

H1450.1. Waking contest. Tuamotus: Stimson, n.d., Z-G. 3/1142; Kapingamarangi: Elbert, 1948, 82.

H1500--H1549. Tests of endurance and power of survival

H1511. Heat test. Attempt to kill hero by burning him in fire. Niue: Loeb, 1926, 120.

H1522. Killing trees threaten hero. Societies: Dixon, 1916, 64.

H1522.1. Bent tree test. Oceanic: Dixon, 1916, 321, n. 71.

H1535. Precipice test: jumping from cliff, survivor is winner. Hawaii: Thrum, 1923, 46f., 49.

*H1539. Miscellaneous tests.

*H1539.1. Task: to climb high tree in a wind storm. Mangareva: Hiroa, 1938, 367.

*H1539.2. Warriors tested for fitness by being placed in a dry river bed while a dam is broken. Those who survive are judged fit for projected raid. N.Z.: Grace, 1907, 17 ff.

366

H1543. Contest in remaining under water. Hawaii:
Beckwith, 1940, 354; Tonga: Gifford, 1924, 161;
Niue: Loeb, 1926, 118.

H1550--H1569. Tests of character

H1550. Tests of character. Tonga: Collocott, 1928,
22f., 29f.

*H1557.7. Test of obedience: person performs disgusting
task (such as eating lice) to signify obedience.
Tahiti: Beckwith, 1940, 246; Cooks: Beckwith,
1940, 247; Te Ariki, 1921, 2.

H1561.2. Single combat to prove valor. Tuamotus:
Stimson, n.d., T-G. 3/79, T-G. 3/191, T-G. 3/615;
Z-G. 3/1272; Marquesas: Steinen, 1933-34, 33;
Hawaii: Beckwith, 1940, 39.

H1561.3. Test of valor: not flinching under a blow.
Cooks: Beaglehole, 1938, 382.

H1561.6. Test of valor: fight with giant. Niue:
Loeb, 1926, 149.

*H1561.11. Test of valor: fighting ferocious animal.
Tuamotus: Stimson, n.d., Z-G. 13/499; Societies:
Henry, 1928, 562; Hawaii: Beckwith, 1940, 436;
Tonga: Gifford, 1924, 176f.; Ellice Is.: Beckwith,
1940, 270.

*H1561.12. Test of valor: going into ogre's cave. Niue:
Smith, 1903, 10,112.

*H1561.13. Test of valor: to ascend mountain against
hostile people who are rolling stones down
mountainside. Niue: Smith, 1903, 10, 112; Loeb,
1926, 149.

H1562. Test of strength. Cooks: Gill, 1876, 54f.;
Tonga: Gifford, 1924, 125.

H1562.2. Test of strength: lifting stone (log).
Cooks: Beaglehole, 1938, 408.

H1562.2.1. Test of strength: lifting sword (spear).
Niue: Loeb, 1926, 154.

H1562.4. Test of strength: prodigious jump. Niue: Loeb, 1926, 149; Smith, 1903, 10; Chatham Is.: Beckwith, 1940, 474.

*H1562.5.1. Contest: slinging stones. Australs: Aitken, 1930, 112; Tuamotus: Caillot, 1914, 87; Tonga: Gifford, 1924, 130.

*H1562.5.2. Contest to determine who can throw (toss) opponent highest. Tuamotus: Stimson, n.d., Z-G. 3/1260; Cooks: Hiroa, 1938, 215; Hawaii: Beckwith, 1940, 95, 436; Rotuma: Churchward, 1937-38, 491.

H1562.9. Test of strength: wrestling. Mangareva: Laval, 1938, 120; Cooks: Low, 1934, 258f.; Hawaii: Beckwith, 1940, 37; Fornander, 1918, V, 6; Thrum, 1907, 161; Westervelt, 1915a, 122, 201f.; Tonga: Brown, 1916, 429f.; Collocott, 1921, 47; Reiter, 1917-18, 1034f.; Samoa: Stuebel, 1896, 65; N.Z.: Grace, 1907, 168ff.; Ellice Is.: Kennedy, 1931, 157, 160; Tikopia: Firth, 1961, 118.

*H1562.9.1. Test of strength: boxing contest. Hawaii: Beckwith, 1919, 334, 386ff.; Fornander, 1918, V, 398ff., 408ff.; Thrum, 1907, 83; 1923, 153f.; Westervelt, 1915a, 122, 178.

*H1562.9.2. Test of strength: arm-twisting contest. Samoa: Stuebel, 1896, 144.

*H1562.15. Contest of pulling between two men. Samoa: Bülow, 1895, 141.

H1570--H1599. Miscellaneous tests

H1576. Tests of possession of magic powers. Tuamotus: Stimson, n.d., Z-G. 1/96; Cooks: Te Ariki, 1920, 108; N.Z.: Best, 1924, 82.

*H1576.3. Stretching contest. Tahiti: Beckwith, 1940, 468; Hawaii: Beckwith, 1940, 466; Thrum, 1907, 72; Fijis: Beckwith, 1940, 468; Hocart, 1929, 193.

H1591. Shooting contest. Hawaii: Beckwith, 1940, 425; Fornander, 1916, IV, 454ff., 462; 1918, V, 280; Pukui-Curtis, n.d., 77ff.; Westervelt, 1915a, 160ff.

H1591.1. Contest: spear-casting. Hawaii: Beckwith, 1940, 392; Fornander, 1918, V, 564; Green, 1929, 25ff.; Thrum, 1907, 84; Sierich, 1902, 182; N.Z.: White, 1887-90, II, 65, 80, 81, 142, 164; III, 245f.; IV, 174, 196.

*H1591.1.1. Spear-dodging contest. Hawaii: Green, 1929, 37.

H1594. Foot-racing contest. Tonga: Gifford, 1924, 97.

*H1594.3. Canoe (paddling) contest. Hawaii: Dickey, 1917, 24; Fornander, IV, 1916, 298ff.; V, 126ff.; Thrum, 1923, 59-61.

*H1594.4. Surf-riding contest. Hawaii: Fornander, 1916, IV, 212f.; Pukui, 1933, 181; Tonga: Gifford,1924, 161; Reiter, 1934, 507f.

H1596. Beauty contest. Mangareva: Hiroa, 1938, 342f.; Hawaii: Fornander, 1916, IV, 552; Pukui, 1933, 161; Tonga: Gifford, 1924, 186.

*H1601. Diving contest. N.Z.: Cowan, 1930, I, 146.

*H1601.1. Underwater diving contest. Tonga: Reiter, 1934, 508f.

*H1602. Contest in which contestants hit first their knees against those of opponents, then their chests, finally their heads. Marquesas: Lavondes, 1966, 90ff., 158ff., 170ff.

*H1603. Dancing contest. Samoa: Stuebel, 1896, 83f.

*H1604. Kite-flying contest. Hawaii: Thrum, 1923, 151f.; Westervelt, 1915a, 176.

*H1605. Contest in which opponents eat the other's liver. Tonga: Collocott, 1928, 24.

*H1606. Contest in fast-cooking. Hawaii: Fornander, 1918, V, 420; N.Z.: White, 1887-90, IV, 183.

*H1607. Top-spinning contest. N.Z.: White, 1887-90, IV, 174, 196; V, 18.

*H1608. Toy sailboat race. Tuamotus: Seurat, 1905, 482; Hawaii: Fornander, 1916, IV, 118ff., 160; Kamakau, 1961, 9; Thrum, 1923, 22f.

*H1610. Stealing contest. Hawaii: Fornander, 1918, V, 292.

*H1611. Chanting (singing) contest. Hawaii: Emerson, 1915, 170ff.; Fornander, 1916, IV, 280f.; Rennell: Elbert-Monberg, 1964, No. 111.

*H1612. Digging (usually for yam planting) contest. Tikopia: Firth, 1961,100.

*H1614. Contest between champions to determine whose girdle is larger. Tuamotus: Stimson, 1937, 127f., 129, 142.

*H1615. Club-fighting contest. Marquesas: Lavondes, 1964, 54ff.; Samoa: Powell-Pratt, 1891-93, 276, 279; Sierich, 1900, 230ff.

*H1617. Creek-damming contest. Cooks: Low, 1934, 183.

*H1618. Canoe-building contest. Hawaii: Luomala, 1951, 48.

*H1619. Floating contest. Samoa: Powell-Pratt, 1891-93, 280.

*H1620. Contest at leaping down cliff. Hawaii: Thrum, 1923 , 46f.

*H1621. Crab-catching contest. Tonga: Collocott, 1928, 16.

J. THE WISE AND THE FOOLISH

J0--J199. Acquisition and possession of
wisdom (knowledge).

J157. Wisdom (knowledge) from dream. Oceania:
**Lessa, 1961, 380ff.

J200--J499. CHOICES

J230--J299. Real and apparent values

*J268. Choice between two trees offered mortals:
Tree of Life and Tree of Women. They choose Tree
of Women and lose immortality. Ellice Is.:
Grimble, 1952, 65.

J600--J799. FORETHOUGHT

*J678. Hero immobilizes magic obstacles to his flight
by foresighted bribery. Marquesas: Lavondes,
1964, 12ff.

J711.1. Ant and lazy cricket (grasshopper). N.Z.:
Best, 1925, 990f.

J1100--J1699. CLEVERNESS

*J1144.3. Food theft discovered by examination of
suspects' stools. Tonga: Collocott, 1928, 59.

*J1149.13. Priest prohesies that certain birds can not
be found in mountains, only on shore. Priest's
enemies catch birds on shore but tell him they
came from mountains. Priest cuts open the birds
and extracts fish. Hawaii: Remy, 1868, 35f.

J1191. Reductio ad absurdum of judgment. Oceanic:
*Dixon, 1916, 199 n. 37.

*J1661.11. From muddy stream by ocean, man knows an army is in the mountains. Hawaii: Fornander, 1916, IV, 224; Kamakau, 1961, 17; Thrum, 1923, 101.

J1700--J2799. FOOLS(AND OTHER UNWISE PERSONS)

J1730--J1749. Absurd ignorance

*J1732.4. People who do not know of cooked food. Tuamotus: Caillot, 1914, 59.

*J1732.5. People eat tasteless berries and seaweed and regard tasty food as poisonous. Hawaii: Green, 1926, 118.

*J1732.6. Monstrous shark eats his friend because he fails to recognize him. Societies: Caillot, 1914, 141.

J1745. Absurd ignorance of sex. Mangareva: Hiroa, 1938, 341f.

*J1745.3. Ignorance of natural childbirth. Mangareva: Caillot, 1914, 149; Laval, 1938, 299; Tuamotus: Caillot, 1914, 58; Marquesas: Lavondes, 1964, 60; Niue: Smith, 1903, 5f., 102; N.Z.: White, 1887-90, II, 9f., 12f.; Wohlers, 1876, 123.

        A1351. Origin of childbirth.
        T584.3. Caesarian childbirth a custom.

*J1749.4. Fools fish in the woods. Fijis: Hocart, 1929, 211.

*J1794.5. Two people in canoe: each is paddling in opposite direction. Tokelau: Burrows, 1923, 158; Fijis: Hocart, 1929, 216; Bellona: Elbert-Monberg, 1964, No. 134.

*J1749.6. Man who can not paddle canoe: smashes the bow against rocks on one side of bay and stern against rocks on other side of bay. Hawaii: Fornander, 1918, V, 434.

*J1749.7. Blind men think ditch is dry and attempt to cross it; torrent sweeps them away. Hawaii: Pukui, 1933, 145.

*J1749.8. Blind men jump in ditch which they think has
water. It has an inch only; they break their legs.
Hawaii: Pukui, 1933, 145.

*J1749.9. Wild people do not know of fire or of
clothing. N.Z.: Best, 1925, 985.

*J1749.10. Ignoramuses take gunpowder for wild cabbage
and sow it. N.Z.: White, 1887-90, V, 152f.

J1750--J1849. ABSURD MISUNDERSTANDINGS

J1750--J1809. One thing mistaken for another

*J1759.6. Fishes jump to eat small fishes (who trans-
form themselves to sea foam), but tear each other
apart. Societies: Caillot, 1914, 139.

*J1769.4. Warriors attacking island dismayed when they
believe they see hero waiting in tree. In reality
he has fallen upon it and is impaled. Tonga:
Collocott, 1928, 7.

J1771.5. Island thought to be large dog. Hawaii:
Beckwith, 1940, 448.

J1772.5. Man puts food bowl on head thinking it is a
helmet. Hawaii: Beckwith, 1940, 413.

*J1772.15. Girl who does not know fire from a hibiscus
blossom. Samoa: Sierich, 1901, 16.

*J1772.16. People see dew in distance and, thinking it
is salt, throw away their supply of salt. Hawaii:
Emory, 1924, 20.

*J1782.6.1. White people believed to be ghosts. Reef Is.:
O'Ferrall, 1904, 225.

*J1789.3. European mistaken for a god. Hawaii: Kamakau,
1961, 92ff.

J1791.5. Diving for reflected enemy. See G512.11.
Hawaii: Beckwith, 1940, 441; Emerson, 1921, 19;
Emory, 1924, 15; Rennell: Bradley, 1956, 336;
Elbert-Monberg, 1964, No. 13.

J1791.6. Diving for reflection of beautiful woman.
Marquesas: Lavondes, 1966, 12.

J1791.6.0.1. Diving for reflected face (of man, people
in a coconut tree). Marquesas: Handy, 1930, 46;
Steinen, 1934-35, 222; Tikopia: Firth, 1961, 47.

*J1791.6.0.2. Maiden, thinking she sees the face of her
dead lover in the pool below her, jumps over
waterfall. Hawaii: Dickey, 1917, 34.

J1791.7. Man does not recognize his own reflection
in the water. Hawaii: Beckwith, 1940, 441.

*J1791.13. Evil spirits dive into pool for reflected
flowers. Rennell: Elbert-Monberg, 1964, No. 2a.

*J1797. Man thinks he will cause deaths to cease by
killing a rat which appears as a death-omen.
Lau: St. Johnston, 1918, 118.

*J1812.4.2. Three gourds popping in burning house
thought to be bodies of inmates. Hawaii: Beckwith,
1940, 21.

*J1812.6. Person curses his echo. Cooks: Gill,
1876, 115.

J1819.3. Fool wakes up with sleeping mat over head and
thinks it is still night. Marquesas: Handy,
1930, 25.

*J1819.4. People persuaded to pray all night for fifty
nights for a dying tree (it is shedding its leaves).
Societies: Agostini, 1900, 75f.

J1821.1. Trying to swim in the mist. Mistaken for sea.
Tonga: Gifford, 1924, 98.

*J1832.1. Fools see water foaming at bottom of cliff,
believe it is dye. One jumps, lands on back and dies.
His teeth show: people think he is laughing and
mistake his blood for dye. They jump also.
Fijis: Hocart, 1924, 211.

*J1849.5. Ignoramuses make axes from sheet lead, temper them in fire. N.Z.: White, 1887-90, V, 153.

J1850--J1999. ABSURD DISREGARD OF FACTS

J1850--J1899. Animals or objects treated as if human

J1896.1. Stones thought to reproduce. Hawaii: Beckwith, 1940, 88.

*J1919.10. Stupid persons starve to death because they are too busy devouring inedible trash to take real food. Rennell: Elbert-Monberg, 1964, No. 83.

J1932.7. Stones watered to make them grow. Hawaii: Beckwith, 1940, 88.

*J1937.3. Man, as a signal, is to whoop once if dead, twice if alive. Tikopia: Firth, 1961, 125, 125 n. 1.

*J1968.2. Man throws spear at gods during thunder storm. Niue: Loeb, 1926, 178.

*J1978. People dig huge oven to cook very small bird. Fijis: Hocart, 1929, 195.

*J1981. Blind man goes fishing, catches a dog. N.Z.: Grace, 1907, 233ff.

*J1982. Person at sea loads his boat until it sinks. Bellona: Elbert-Monberg, 1964, Nos. 57a, 57a n.

J2000-J2049. ABSURD ABSENT-MINDEDNESS

J2031.3. Culture hero throws coconuts to various islands, but forgets the one he stands on: hence none now on that island. Cooks: Beckwith, 1940, 104.

J2048./ Men sent to carry message forget it before they arrive. Hawaii: Green, 1929, 53.

J2048./ Lobster forgets to hide its antennae in game of hide-and-seek. Kapingamarangi: Elbert, 1949, 245.

*J2053. In war with birds, the fishes, after an initial victory, become giddy and suffer ultimate defeat. Samoa: Brown, 1915, 174.

*J2081.5. Deceptive bargain: smaller portion of a pig exchanged for the larger. Reef Is.: Elbert-Kirtley 1966, 361.

*J2099.2. A spirit exchanges his good hard wood club with a man for one of banana wood. The man then kills him. Hawaii: Emory, 1924, 15.

*J2119.10. Ignorant people, believing they are effectir a cure, burn diseased persons to death. Societies: Agostini, 1900, 76.

J2133.12. Woman tries to climb rope of excrement and urine. Marquesas: Handy, 1930, 40.

J2164.1. Rowers pull in opposite directions. See *J1794.5. Fijis: Hocart, 1929, 216.

J2171.1.3.1. Attempts to make canoe of sand. Marquesas: Handy, 1930, 45, 91; Cooks: Te Ariki, 1920, 119.

J2171.1.3.2. Building boat of clay. Tuamotus: Beckwith, 1940, 267.

*J2199.5. Two boys kills their father because they belie he killed their mother. When they find their mother is alive, they kill her as cause of father's death. Niue: Loeb, 1926, 77.

*J2199.6. Foolish spy reports that island has no men (they are all working in the fields or fishing at sea). Hawaii: Fornander, 1918, V, 448.

J2260--J2299. ABSURD SCIENTIFIC THEORIES

*J2271.4.2. Dwarf boasts he can catch moon by horn. Hawaii: Rice, 1923, 39.

J2300--J2349. GULLIBLE FOOLS

*J2349.5. A grandmother and grandchild hide from an ogre in a calabash (or bowl), and out of fear they continually break wind. When the ogre asks about this, the trickster hero says his vessels are customarily flatulent. Ogre accepts statement. Rennell: Elbert-Monberg, 1964, Nos. 41a, 41b.

*J2349.6. Woman told that to catch a fish she must weave a basket and place it on ocean's bottom does so, and she continually dives to inspect until her eyes and nose are inflamed. Hawaii: Thrum, 1923, 193f.

J2350--J2369. TALKATIVE FOOLS

*J2368. Fugitive told to speak up if near; does so and reveals his presence. Tikopia: Firth, 1961, 112.

J2400--J2449. FOOLISH IMITATION

J2401. Fatal imitation. Hawaii: Beckwith, 1940, 372; Tikopia: Firth, 1961, 101.

J2411.6.1. Sister of goddess trics to imitate her feat of being cooked without harm and dies in the attempt. Hawaii: Beckwith, 1940, 96; Green, 1926, 59; Pukui-Curtis, n.d., 48ff.; Smith, 1966, 25ff.; Westervelt, 1943, 14ff.

*J2443. Dupes imitate trickster, who lashes his boat with pandanus leaves. Their crafts come apart at sea. Reef Is.: *Elbert-Kirtley, 1966, 359f.; Bellona: Elbert-Monberg, 1964, Nos. 57a, 57a n; Rennell: ibid., 57c; Elbert-Kirtley, 1966, 364.

J2450--J2499. LITERAL FOOLS

*J2495.1. People told of heaven enter house, lash selves to beams, and wait to be transported. Rennell: Elbert-Monberg, 1964, Nos. 235a, 235b.

K. DECEPTIONS

K0--K99. Contests won by deception

K11. Race won by deception. Hawaii: Thrum, 1923, 59ff.

K11.1. Race won by deception: relative helpers. Rennell: Bradley, 1956, 334.

K17. Jumping contest won by deception. Cooks: Te Ariki, 1921, 209; Tikopia: Firth, 1961, 31.

*K32.1. Crab-catching contest won by deception: loser charms opponent to sleep and steals his crabs. Tonga: Collocott, 1928, 16; Cooks: Beckwith, 1940, 270.

K44. Deceptive contest in chopping. Niue: Loeb, 1926, 149.

K48./. Yam-staking contest won by hero who plants his stakes by throwing them as darts. Tikopia: Firth, 1961, 100.

K51. Waking contest won by deception. Kapingamarangi: Elbert, 1948, 82.

K51.1. Man bested in waking contest when given soporific. Tuamotus: Stimson, n.d., Z-G. 3/1142.

*K81.2.1. Deceptive eating contest: man pretends to eat but passes food to those behind him. Cooks: Beaglehole, 1938, 404.

K82.1.2. Deceptive drinking contest: attempted intoxication avoided by boring hole in bottom of cup Marquesas: Handy, 1930, 119.

*K96. Cooking contest won by deception. Hawaii: Fornander, 1918, V, 420.

*K97.3. Combat won when person in club fight has help of magic snare. Hawaii: Green, 1929, 91.

K98.1. Beauty contest won by deception: other
contestants covered with leaves. Tonga: Gifford,
1924, 186.

K98.1./ Cock fight won by deception. Tonga: Collocott,
1928, 45.

K100--K299. DECEPTIVE BARGAINS

K100. Deceptive bargains. Hawaii: Fornander, 1918,
V, 426.

K110--K149. Sale of worthless articles

*K139.2. Mosquitoes sold as musicians. Fiji: Fison,
1904, 91ff.

K148. Cheaters sell each other valueless articles.
Tonga: Collocott, 1928, 61.

*K149.2. Person pays for canoe with worthless shell
instead of shell-trumpet. Samoa: Stuebel,
1896, 148.

*K149.3. Deceptive bargain: trickster trades conch
shell which will not blow for one which will
resound. Reef Is.: Elbert-Kirtley, 1966, 360.

*K171.6.1. Stupid brother agrees that all fish caught
with two eyes belong to his brother. Hawaii:
Rice, 1923, 50.

*K171.6.2. When two brothers go hunting, wise one says
all birds with two holes in beak belong to him;
all others, to his brother. Hawaii: Fornander,
1918, V, 422; Rice, 1923, 49.

K200--K249. Deception in payment of debt

K231.2. Reward for accomplishment of task deceptively
withheld. Tuamotus: Stimson, n.d., Z-G. 13/420.

K300--K499. THEFTS AND CHEATS

K300. Thefts and cheats -- general. Hawaii: Dickey,
1917, 34; Fornander, 1916, IV, 140; V, 292;
Westervelt, 1915a, 106ff.; Samoa: Krämer, 1902,
I, 414f.; Powell-Pratt, 1892, 124; Tokelau:
Burrows, 1923, 169; N.Z.: White, 1887-90, IV,
80, 194, 205.

K306. Thieves steal from each other. Hawaii:
*Beckwith, 1940, 446; Fornander, 1918, V, 284ff.;
Westervelt, 1915a, 155f.

*K309. Trickster steals fish as fast as a victim catches
them. Reef Is.: O'Ferrall, 1904, 231.

K310--K349. Thefts

*K311.3.1. Cannibal woman imitates voice of man's
sweetheart, gains access to his cave, and eats
him. Tuamotus: Leverd, 1911, 174.

*K326. Thief steals food by tunneling from beneath.
Hawaii: Green, 1926, 67; Pukui-Curtis, n.d.,
73; Reef Is.: Elbert-Kirtley, 1966, 360f.

*K327. Boy is lowered with rope from cliff so that he
may steal food. Samoa: Sierich, 1901, 22f.

*K328. Person repeatedly puts out borrowed fire so
that he can have a chance to steal the principle of
fire. Tuamotus: Stimson, 1934, 19; Marquesas:
Lavondes, 1964, 50ff.; Tonga: Caillot, 1914,
273f.; Collocott, 1921, 47; Reiter, 1917-18,
1033f.; Samoa: Powell-Pratt, 1892, 81; N.Z.:
Best, 1925, 795; Clark, 1896, 42; Cowan, 1930,
I, 16; White,1887-90, II, 68, 74, 104, 108f., 109,
112f.; Wohlers, 1875, 12; Niue: Smith, 1903, 98;
Bellona: Elbert-Monberg, 1964, No. 47a.

*K329. Miscellaneous thefts.

*K329.1. Trickster dives beneath water, steals sinker
of demon, which is made of gold. N.Z.: Grace,
1907, 110f.

K331. Goods stolen while owner (guards) sleeps. Hawaii:
Beckwith, 1940, 350.

*K331.0.1. While his companions sleep, trickster eats
two fowl. Next day he says he dreamed of a feast.
N.Z.: Grace, 1907, 48ff.

K331.2. Owner put to sleep (with drugs) and goods
stolen. Tuamotus: Stimson, n.d., Z-G. 3/1142;
Cooks: Large, 1903, 134.

K333. Theft from blind person (hero's ancestress in
otherworld). Oceanic: **Dixon, 1916, 46, 59, 65;
Tuamotus: Stimson, n.d., T-G. 3/931; 1934, 63;
Leverd, 1911, 176; Marquesas: Steinen, 1933-34,
372; Societies: Gill, 1876, 252; Henry, 1928,
560; Cooks: Te Ariki, 1921, 207; Hawaii:
Beckwith, 1940, 230; Fornander, 1916, IV, 90ff.,
162, 598; Niue: Smith, 1903, 92; N.Z.: Best,
1925, 912; Clark, 1896, 160; *Potae, 1928, 361,
366; White, 1887-90, I, 57, 89, 100f., 116, 121f.,
128; Rotuma: Churchward, 1938-39, 330; Bellona:
Elbert-Monberg, 1964, Nos. 1a, 1b; Rennell:
ibid., 1c; Ontong Java, Nukumanu: Sarfert, 1931,
424.

        *F171.10. In otherworld hero meets blind
        ancesstress who ceaselessly counts items of
        food.

*K333.6. Man steals his wife's removable eyes. Hawaii:
McAllister, 1933, 94f.

*K335.0.14. Trickster delays supernaturals until dawn.
They flee light and leave behind their net. Niue:
Smith, 1903, 96; N.Z.: Tregear, 1901, 185.

        K1886.3.3. Mock sunrise causes supernaturals
        (thieves) to drop burdens and flee.

K341.16. Stone thrown to attract attention of shark
guardians. Man then slips in cave, steals lobsters.
Hawaii: Beckwith, 1940, 443; Fornander, 1918, V,
294.

*K341.17.2. Trickster persudes dupe to enter hopping contest; steals his food. Tikopia: Firth, 1961, 31.

*K341.30. Person makes image and puts it in canoe so that it will appear that he has departed. He is subsequently able to steal. Hawaii: Smith, 1966, 15.

*K341.31. Trickster throws lice in dupe's eyes so that he can steal from him. Rennell: Elbert-Monberg, 1964, No. 40.

*K342.1. Discoverers of island lose it when their guards deceive them. Cooks: Te Ariki, 1920, 3.

K351. Trickster permitted to try on clothes. Goes away with them. Cooks: Beckwith, 1940, 445; Gill, 1876, 89.

K351.3. Trickster permitted to try on ornaments. Goes off with them. Cooks: Beckwith, 1940, 445.

*K361.1.2. Grandparents sent with food to girl eat it themselves. Cooks: Gill, 1911, 212, 213.

K366.2. Thieving bird (steals yams for man). Easter I. Métraux, 1940, 374; Kapingamarangi: Elbert, 1948, 66.

K366.6. Thieving turtle. Easter I.: Metraux, 1940, 373.

K366.7. Thieving butterflies. Cooks: Clark, 1896, 146; Gill, 1876, 292.

K366.8. Thieving octopus. Easter I.: Métraux, 1940, 374.

K374. Trickster pretends to teach dance: flees with valuables. Hawaii: Beckwith, 1940, 445.

K401. Blame for theft fastened on dupe. Samoa: Sierich, 1902, 181; N.Z.: Grey, 1855, 183, 184; White, 1887-90, II, 168.

*K406.4. Theft by trick: stolen chestnuts partially cooked. Thief shows owner that they look different from those on latter's tree. Reef Is.: Elbert-Kirtley, 1966, 360.

K419.10. Blame for theft fastened on fairies.
N.Z.: Beckwith, 1940, 196; Clark, 1896, 196.

*K449. Other cheats -- miscellaneous.

*K449.1. A limited number of besieged villagers allowed
to get a drink. They soak their garments to take
back water to thirsty compatriots. N.Z.: White,
1887-90, III, 131f.

*K476.9. Chicken that will crow stolen and one that
will not crow put in its place. Reef Is.:
Elbert-Kirtley, 1966, 361.

*K499.11. A brother tricks reigning brother into laying
down tokens of royal authority and he then seizes
them for himself. Samoa: Powell-Pratt, 1891-93,
298f.

*K499.12. Trick used to prove group's claim to prior
occupancy of land. Rotuma: Russell, 1942,
232, 239; Tikopia: Firth, 1961, 34f.

*K499.13. Youngest child gets born first (establishing
his priority rights) by leaving mother's body
through head. Tikopia: Firth, 1961, 31.

K500--K699. ESCAPE BY DECEPTION

K500. Escape from death or danger by deception.
Rennell: Elbert-Monberg, 1964, No. 20.

K514. Disguise as girl to avoid execution. N.Z.:
White, 1887-90, V, 22f.

K515.1. Children hidden to avoid their execution.
Hawaii: Beckwith, 1919, 334, 348.

K522. Escape by shamming death. Hawaii: *Beckwith,
1930, 407ff.; Fornander, 1918, V, 2ff., 694ff.;
Tokelau: Burrows, 1923, 164.

K522.1. Escape by shamming death: blood and brains.
See also K959.6. Marquesas: Lavondes, 1964, 14.

*K522.9. Persons in burning hut cause gourds to explode;
enemies believe it to be human bodies. Hawaii:

Fornander, 1918, VI, 172.

K523. Escape by shamming illness. N.Z.: Clark, 1896, 167.

K525. Escape by use of substitued object. Tuamotus: Stimson, 1937, 40.

K525.1. Substituted object left in bed while intended victim escapes. Tuamotus: Stimson, n.d., T-G. 3/15; Societies: Dixon, 1916, 63; Henry, 1928, 554; Hawaii: Beckwith, 1940, 444; Rice, 1923, 68; N.Z.: Best, 1924, 190.

*K525.2.1. Boy lets his shadow fall on rock,which stupid ogress, thinking it him, gnaws. He cries out, as though in pain. Samoa: Stuebel, 1896.

K525.10. Escape by leaving behind false images made of spittle. Hawaii: Beckwith, 1919, 550; Beckwith, 1940, 176.

*K525.11. Blind ogress tries to catch hero upon fishhook. He puts hook in banana stalk. Cooks: Gill, 1876, 110.

*K525.12. Hero puts lizard on hook intended to catch himself. Marquesas: Steinen, 1933-34, 372.

K527. Escape by substituting another person in place of the intended victim. Tuamotus: Stimson, n.d., Z-G. 3/1314.

K527.1. Poisoned food (drink) fed to animal instead of to intended victim. Easter I.: Métraux, 1940, 365.

*K527.1.1. Coconut substituted for deadly drink. Man, given bowl of centipedes to eat, secretly lets them loose and consumes coconut concealed previously on his body. Cooks: Gill, 1876, 173.

*K527.6. Man imitates wife's voice while she flees from blind captors. Cooks: Gill, 1876, 224.

*K538.1. Captive at end of rope ties rope to object. Samoa: Sierich, 1902, 168; Tokelaus: Lister, 1892, 61f.; Burrows, 1923, 162f.; Smith, 1911, 13; N.Z.: Best, 1893, 217ff.; Cowan, 1925, 169; Grey, 1855, 139; Smith, 1911, 12; White, 1887-90, III, 124, 190.

*K539. People place their brush houses in a river, hide under them, and float past their enemies. N.Z.: White, 1887-90, V, 25.

K541. Escape by reporting oneself invulnerable. Easter I.: Métraux, 1940, 365.

K547. Escape by frightening would-be captors. Tonga: Collocott, 1928, 49.

K551.28. Captors give captive respite in order to witness alleged marvel. Hawaii: Beckwith, 1940, 511.

K553.1. "Let me catch you better game." Samoa: Sierich, 1901, 23.

*K557.1. Man lies about position of his sleeping place in order to deceive malignant spirits wishing to murder him in his sleep. Samoa (Savai'i): Krämer, 1902, I, 115.

K571. Escape by pretending to dance so as to be untied. (Captive released to exhibit dance, flees.) Polynesia: *Beckwith, 1940, 445, 446, n. 445, n. 446; N.Z.: Grey, 1855, 127.

*K581.1.1. Plea to be executed at sea. Hero says deceptively that if he is killed on land, he will arise; if dropped into sea, he will die. He knows his shark ancestors will save him. Tahiti: Henry, 1928, 630.

*K581.7. Man on stilts tells captors that if they cut them so he falls on land instead of sea, he will die. They cut stilts so he falls on ground; he runs away. N.Z.: Grey, 1855, 126.

*K585. Escape by pretending weakness. Man lingers behind, escapes in canoe. N.Z.: Clark, 1896, 167.

K601.2. "Don't eat your nephews." Giant thus dissuaded. Tuamotus: Stimson, n.d., Z-G. 3/1323.

K605. Cannibal sent for water with vessel full of holes; victim escapes. Societies: Baessler, 1905, 922f.; *Beckwith, 1940, 197, n. 21,

Ch. XIII passim; Dixon, 1916, 63; Leverd, 1912, 2; Hawaii: Beckwith, 1940, 194; Thrum, 1923, 190f.; Westervelt, 1915, 154ff.

K605.1. Cannibal sent for water which magically recedes from him: victim escapes. N.Z.: *Beckwith, 195ff., 196 n. 19; Dixon, 1916, 85; White, 1887-90, II, 159, 170; III, 3f.; Wohlers, 1876, 119.

K615. Boy in hole escapes descending log by digging hole. Oceania: **Lessa, 1961; Tikopia: Firth, 1961, 101.

*K625.0.1. Captive puts guards into magic sleep and escapes. N.Z.: Beattie, 1920, 133 f.

K625.2. Escape by making the watchmen drunk. Hawaii: Dickey, 1917, 26; Thrum, 1923, 146f.

*K629.2.3. Person escapes cannibal's oven by pretending to show a dance. N.Z.: White, 1887-90, II, 60.

K635. Sleeping enemies' hair tied to an object prevents pursuit. Tonga: Gifford, 1924, 50, 53; Niue: Loeb, 1926, 220.

K635.1. Hair of sleeping maiden tied to tree so that she is not able to rise. Tonga: Gifford, 1924, 50.

K636. Holes bored in enemies' boats prevent pursuit. Rennell: Elbert-Monberg, 1964, Nos. 228a, 228b.

*K636.2. People fleeing by canoe cut the lashings on the boats of their possible pursuers. N.Z.: White, 1887-90, IV, 130ff.

*K639. Escape by making pursuit difficult -- miscellaneou

*K639.1. Fugitives escape fast runner by magically laming him. Hawaii: Thrum, 1923, 81.

*K639.2. Pursuer chilled to point of helplessness by cold magic rain. Tokelau: Burrows, 1923, 163.

*K639.3. Hero escapes pursuers by smashing a hole in the earth into which they fall. Hawaii: Westervelt, 1915, 218.

K649.1. Confederate hides fugitive. Hawaii: Thrum, 1921, 105.

K649.1.3. Confederate sits on hero and saves him. Hawaii: Beckwith, 1940, 231.

K649.9. Confederate causes confusion so that prisoner may escape. Mangareva: Laval, 1938, 300.

*K649.13. Vision of woman shown to captors by a god; captors pursue vision, prisoner escapes. Hawaii: Beckwith, 1940, 205.

*K649.14. Person stowed away in canoe and thus escapes. Mangareva: Hiroa, 1938, 421; Laval, 1938, 301; N.Z.: Wohlers, 1876, 116f.

*K649.15. To hide identity of a king he is protecting, a commoner touches his head, considered sacred. Mangareva: Laval, 1938, 145.

*K673. Captive leaves limb of body in pursuer's hands; escapes. Hawaii: Beckwith, 1940, 242.

K676. Trickster persuades pursuers to ride in his basket. Leaves basket on limb of tree and escapes (dupes, feeling motion and seeing passing clouds, believe they are still being carried). Tonga: Gifford, 1924, 45, 198.

K678. Cutting rope to kill ogre who is climbing the rope to reach his victim. Marquesas: Handy, 1930, 41; Lagarde, 1933, 261.

*K688. Chief, in order to save his unpopular wife, induces people to promise not to injure her until after she bears her child. Tuamotus: Stimson, n.d., T-G. 3/600.

*K691. Man pursued by irate goddess in fire-form escapes by going to sea in canoe. Hawaii: *Beckwith, 1940, 191, 191 n. 7.

*K692. Woman saves baby son from hostile warriors by pretending infant is female. N.Z.: Tu-Whawhakia, 1896, 159 ff.

*K693. Fish caught in trap burrows into sand; escapes when door of trap is left open after removal of other fish. Tuamotus: Stimson, n.d., Z-G. 3/1151.

*K694. Night magically prolonged so that prisoner
may escape. Hawaii: Thrum, 1921, 105, 201.

*K695. Imprisonment avoided: attempt to close cave
entrance and trap hero fails when hero sticks
whale's tooth across entrance. Marquesas:
Handy, 1930, 104.

K700--K799. CAPTURE BY DECEPTION

K713.1. Deception into allowing oneself to be tied.
Tonga: Collocott, 1928, 22, 26; Tikopia: Firth,
1961, 51.

*K714.4.3. Hero gets goddesses in baskets upon poles;
he carries them a distance and leaves them
hanging in tree. Tonga: Brown, 1916, 431.

K714.8. Fish enticed into trap (promised new skins).
Tuamotus: Stimson, n.d., 3/1951.

*K723. Messengers seeking person with gapped teeth
make people laugh. Person sought is revealed.
N.Z.: Beckwith, 1940, 505; Best, 1925, 774,
922; Cowan, 1930, I, 70; Wohlers, 1875, 29.

H57.1. Recognition by broken tooth.

K726. Dupe persuaded to ride on trickster's back:
captured (eaten). Mangareva: Caillot, 1914,
195f.

K730. Victim trapped (netted). Hawaii: Rice, 1923,
91; Samoa: Krämer, 1902, I, 409; Stuebel,
1896, 84; N.Z.: Best, 1925, 834; Cowan, 1925,
86f., 138ff.; 1930, I, 108; Grey, 1855, 259.

*K730.2.1. Spider tricks moth into his web. Niue:
Loeb, 1926, 196.

K735. Capture in pitfall. Australs: Aitken, 1930,
111; Tuamotus: Stimson, n.d., Z-G. 1/89,
Z-G. 3/1323.

K735.1. Mats over holes as pitfall. N.Z.: Dixon,
1916, 61.

*K741.2. Capture by causing to stick to feelers of sea-slugs. Tuamotus: Stimson, 1937, 71.

*K741.3. Dupes adhere to wooden dummy. Spirits try to eat dummy, but their teeth stick fast in the wood; they are then killed. Hawaii: Rice, 1923, 68.

K743. Victim captured in a noose. Cooks: Low, 1934, 174; N.Z.: Beckwith, 1940, 250; Best, 1925, 989; Clark, 1896, 100; Kapingamarangi: Elbert, 1948, 131.

*K746. Eel tricks another eel into entering narrow passage in which it is caught and later killed. Marquesas: *Steinen, 1933-34, 1f.

K751. Capture by feigning death. Hawaii: Thrum, 1923, 159, 162.

K754.3. Capture by hiding in artificial bird. Hawaii: Beckwith, 1940, 431.

*K754.4. Hero hides in imitation fish in order to tempt person to take it. Kapingamarangi: Emory, 1949, 234.

K755. Capture by masking as another. Hawaii: Beckwith, 1940, 215f., 541.

*K768. Capture with aid of dummy; spirits captured by this trick. Mangareva: Massainoff, 1933, 55-56; Tonga: Collocott, 1928, 12.

*K773.1. Monster fish (land personified) caught by trick: told to open mouth to settle argument about number of his teeth. Hook then secured. Hawaii: Beckwith, 1940, 233; Thrum, 1923, 250f.

K775.1. Capture by taking aboard ship to inspect wares (shanghaied). N.Z.: Grey, 1855, 137.

K776. Capture by intoxication (or narcotic). Hawaii: Green, 1926, 102 n. 2.

*K788.2. Sound of laughter lures women into hills; they become lost. Hawaii: McAllister, 1933, 151.

*K788.3. Bird flutters just in front of boys; lures them into bush. N.Z.: Grace, 1907, 228.

*K788.4. Person tricked onto floating island and carried off as it is caused to drift away. Hawaii: Thrum, 1921, 103.

*K788.5. By promises of food and women, spirits lure canoes of men to haunted isle, where they eat them. Hawaii: Fornander, 1916, IV, 478.

*K788.6. House chinked up so that person will not know day has come; he oversleeps and is thus captured. See K839.6. Mangareva: Hiroa, 1938, 319; N.Z.: Cowan, 1925, 25f.

*K788.7. People of island plant coconut trees around strangers' canoes to prevent their leaving. Cooks: Beaglehole, 1938, 404.

K800--K999. KILLING OR MAIMING BY

DECEPTION

K800. Killing or maiming by deception. Mangareva: Laval, 1938, 29f., 31, 114, 116, 118, 131; Cooks: Low, 1935, 27; N.Z.: Te Whetu, 1894,18.

K811.1. Enemies invited to banquet and killed. Mangareva: Caillot, 1914, 179ff.; Tuamotus: Stimson, n.d., Z-G. 13/555; Tahiti: Henry, 1928, 246; Samoa: Hambruch, 1925, 104f.; Niue: Loeb, 1926, 140; N.Z.: White, 1887-90, III, 167f., 171f., 247f.; IV, 46, 102, 199, 209ff.; Lau: St. Johnston, 1918, 92.

*K811.6. Men attend festivity with concealed weapons, surprise and kill their enemies. Samoa: Stuebel, 1896, 84f., 85f., 87; N.Z.: White, 1887-90, V, 44.

*K815.20. Chief invites rival to reign for a while in his realm. The latter accepts and is murdered upon arrival. Hawaii: Fornander, 1916, IV, 350.

*K815.21. Person imitates the call of a fish's owner, summons the fish and kills him. Samoa: Sierich, 1902, 169; Tokelau: Burrows, 1923, 158.

*K815.22. Decoys entice robbers to attack: robbers then killed. Hawaii: Pukui, 1933, 133ff.

*K818.4.1. Indignant subjects pretend to bring their
king food, but instead they bring wrapped stones
with which they kill him. Hawaii: *Beckwith,
1940, 390ff.; Fornander, 1916, IV, 200ff.;
Remy, 1868, 33f.

K824. Sham doctor kills his patients. Tikopia:
Firth, 1961, 113f.

K831. Victim killed by being bathed. Cooks:
Te Ariki, 1921, 3f.

*K832.3.1. Woman dances nude to distract hostile war
party; while it watches, warriors of her village
assemble. N.Z.: White, 1887-90, V, 24.

K833. Man lured into aiding trickster,who has
feigned an accident or needs help. Tuamotus:
Stimson, n.d., T-G. 3/59.

K839.6. Supernaturals tricked into (fatal) exposure
to daylight. Marquesas: Beckwith, 1940, 257;
N.Z.: Best, 1924, 157; 1925, 776f., 867, 870,
915, 937; 1928, 257; Clark, 1896, 112;
Cowan, 1921, 99; Hongi, 1898, 41; Smith, 1910,
86f.; White, 1887-90, I, 56f., 101f.; II,
163.

*K839.6.1. Night magically prolonged so that dupe will
fall asleep and be easily killed. Hawaii: Thrum,
1923, 257.

*K839.7. Person induced to swallow object and is
caught as is a fish with a gorge. N.Z.: Best,
1925, 990.

*K839.8. While victim swallows proferred drink, his
throat is slit. Marquesas: Lavondes, 1966, 130ff.,
166.

*K839.9. War canoe is disguised as a peaceful raft, so
that warriors can get among their enemies.
Mangareva: Hiroa, 1938, 42.

*K839.10. Gods pretend to teach song to people in boat;
they press downward on mast until boat sinks and
and people drown. Fijis: Fison, 1904, 16-17.

*K839.11. Man asks wife to help him lash his canoe;
he binds her fingers in the cords then murders her.
Tuamotus: Stimson, n.d., T-G. 3/59.

*K839.12. To entice foes from fort, man pretends to be a seal or large fish washing back and forth in the surf. N.Z.: White, 1887-90, III, 243, 296f.

*K839.13. Victim lured ashore by false winter: god comes ashore only during winter. Hero releases cold mist from gourd; kills god when he approaches shore. Tuamotus: Henry, 1928, 528.

K851. Deceptive game: burning each other. Niue: Loeb, 1926, 120; Ontong Java, Nukumanu: Sarfert, 1931, 433f.

K855. Fatal swinging game. Hawaii: Fornander, 1916, IV, 530.

K856. Fatal game: dying and reviving. Tuamotus: Stimson, n.d., Z-G. 13/116.

K869.4. Fatal swimming race: to trick spirits, hero proposes swimming race. As each spirit arrives, hero drowns it. Hawaii: Beckwith, 1940, 441.

*K869.5. Fatal game: throwing heads into air. Man throws his head in air; it lands again on his body. Rival imitates him; man throws rival's body into sea while the head is still in air. Ontong Java: Sarfert, 1931, 385.

*K869.6. Fatal game: jumping from tree. Lizard jumps from tree, plays dead. Rat jumps, really dies. Nukumanu: Sarfert, 1931, 458.

*K869.7. Fatal flying contest: trickster (Maui) fatally tricks grandfather. Older man tries to fly; Maui flies under him, pulls his girdle and causes him to fall. Cooks: Gill, 1876, 68.

*K869.8. Dancing upon water: boy ties pumice stones on legs and dances upon sea. Giant lets boy tie real stones to legs; when he tries to dance, he sinks. Rotuma: Churchward, 1938-39, 220.

*K869.9. Dupe persuaded to ride on trickster's back: thrown into fire. Samoa: Stair, 1896, 52f.

*K869.10. Spirit tricked into eating own liver. Tonga: Collocott, 1928, 24; Samoa: Krämer, 1902, I, 447.

*K869.11. In game of entering completely the opponent's body, dupe is torn apart from within. Tuamotus: Stimson, 1934, 33.

*K869.12. Tossing game: trickster kills his opponent. Tuamotus: Stimson, 1934, 20ff.

K871. Fatal intoxication (with kava). Mangareva: Laval, 1938, 301; Hawaii: Beckwith, 1940, 441.

K891. Dupe tricked into jumping to his death. Ellice Is.: Kennedy, 1931, 215.

K891.5.3. Dupes deceived into falling over precipice. Easter I.: Métraux, 1940, 368; Tonga: Gifford, 1924, 101.

*K891.5.4.1. Dupe falls over disguised edge of precipice: to kill paramour's parents, man disguises edge of cliff, which they fall over. Tonga: Gifford, 1924, 101.

*K891.5.5. Wife shoves husband over precipice by ruse: she brings coconut shell with very little water in it; as he leans far over to drink, she shoves him over edge. Tonga: Gifford, 1924, 101.

*K891.5.6. Person falls and is killed when using a cliffside latrine with improperly made supports. N.Z.: Best, 1925, 818.

*K891.5.7. Person given a conch-horn of solid rock falls from tree and breaks neck when he tries to blow it. Samoa: Elbert-Kirtley, 1966, 361.

*K895.1. Dupe persuaded to climb on weakened limb; falls and dies. Rotuma: Russell, 1942, 247; Bellona: Elbert-Monberg, 1964, No. 63.

*K897.4. Person puts gift of fish by receiver's threshold so that latter steps on it, slips, and is injured. Samoa: Powell-Pratt, 1891-93, 274.

*K897.5. Lecherous eel enticed onto skidway, killed. N.Z.: Best, 1925, 834.

*K899. Dupe tricked into killing himself -miscellaneous.

*K899.1. Man puts sharpened stake in bed of adulterous wife; lover is killed by it. Rennell: Elbert-Monberg, 1964, No. 197.

*K899.2. Hero invites his enemies to throw a coconut
trunk at him. Trunk hits fence hero has
secretly built, bounces backward, kills hero's
assailants. Bellona: Elbert-Monberg, 1964,
No. 66.

K910. Murder by strategy. Tuamotus: Stimson, 1937,
142f.; Tokelau: Burrows, 1923, 171; N.Z.:
Grace, 1907, 169.

K911. Feigning death to kill enemy. Hawaii: *Beckwith,
1940, 405ff.; N.Z.: Grace, 1907, 129f.; Ontong
Java: Parkinson, 1898, 206.

*K912.4. Invaders enticed one by one into a dark hut,
where they are individually killed. Tokelau:
Burrows, 1923, 159; Tikopia: Firth, 1961, 115;
Reef Is.: O'Ferrall, 1904, 228.

*K912.5. Chiefs of island summoned individually to
king's abode and killed one by one. Hawaii:
Fornander, 1918, V, 264.

*K912.6. Man kills foes one by one as they descend
in single file down a cliffside. Hawaii:
Beckwith, 1940, 331; Fornander, 1916, IV, 224.

K922. Artificial whale made as a strategem. N.Z.:
White, 1887-90, II, 147.

*K929.7.1. Boy causes sharks to kill members of their
own band by accusing them of collaborating with
him. Hawaii: Beckwith, 1940, 443f.; Fornander,
1918, V, 294ff.

K929.9. Murder by pushing off cliff. Hawaii:
Beckwith, 1940, 331; McAllister, 1933, 176.

*K929.14. People caused to fight magic club in the dark.
Samoa: Powell-Pratt, 1891, 205.

*K929.15. Person deliberately misdirected to ogres'
house. Samoa: Krämer, 1902, 134.

*K929.16. Person throws valuable mat to his enemies.
While they quarrel about its possession, he attacks
them. N.Z.: White, 1887-90, V, 32.

*K929.17. Person distorts another's message to a king
so that the victim will be put to death. Hawaii:
Thrum, 1907, 221; 1921, 106.

*K929.18. Uncle dresses his nephew as cannibal to cause
his death. Mangareva: Laval, 1938, 39.

*K929.19. Man, in order to kill nephews, pretends
illness which can be cured only by eating meat
of dangerous animals. They try to get this
food for him. Tokelau: Burrows, 1923, 171.

*K929.20. Devil climbs tree where boys are hidden;
they wet trunk so that devil slips back and
breaks leg. Rennell: Bradley, 1956, 336.

*K929.21. Reptile monster tricked into chasing dog
past people, who topple trees on him. N.Z.:
Te Aro, 1894, 167.

*K929.22. Lizard monster killed by strategem: lured
from cave amid trees which are partly cut through.
The lashing of his tail knocks over trees which
crush him. N.Z.: Smith, 1905, 203ff.

*K929.23. Person marooned at sea by strategy: king's
fishermen take him to sea in canoe and pretend
to lose paddles. King swims after them;
fishermen take hidden paddles and leave king to
drown. Hawaii: Rice, 1923, 19ff.

*K929.24. Son of chief insulted by father. As
vengeance, he makes canoe with hole in bottom;
he invites elder sons of all chiefs of his
father's tribe for a sail. Once at sea he
removes his foot from hole; all drown but one.
N.Z.: Gudgeon, 1905, 186ff.

*K929.25. Hero kills rooster which wakens his enemy
at morning. Latter is then killed in his sleep.
Tuamotus: Beckwith, 1940, 268.

*K929.26. Raiding party stays far at sea during day,
attacks stealthily each night. Easter I.: Métraux,
1940, 382; Ellice Is.: Kennedy, 1931, 209.

*K929.27. Fish puts tail on beach; onlookers, thinking
fish dead, grab it and are pulled into ocean and
drowned. Marquesas: Handy,1930, 62.

K940.1. Man betrayed into eating his own children.
Mangareva: Laval, 1938, 118.

K940.2. Man betrayed into killing his wife. Rennell:
Elbert-Monberg, 1964, No. 20.

*K949. Deception into killing own family or animals -- miscellaneous.

*K949.1. Cannibal tricked into killing own daughter, who exchanges sleeping places with friend, and whom he clubs in the dark. Tonga: Collocott, 1928, 62.

*K951.4.1. Women put piece of wood in mat; ghost dives upon mat, swallows wood, and dies. Kapingamarangi: Emory, 1949, 238.

K952. Animal (monster) killed from within. Tuamotus: Stimson, 1934, 33; Societies: Orsmond, 1933, 172ff.; Cooks: Beckwith, 1940, 267; Savage, 1910, 151; Hawaii: Fornander, 1818, V, 296ff.; Thrum, 1923, 299; Tonga: Gifford, 1924, 79, 83; N.Z.: Grace, 1907, 192f.; Gudgeon, 1905, 182; Kauika, 1904, 96ff.; Santa Cruz: Riesenfeld, 1950, 126.

K952.1.2. Ungrateful rat defecates upon head of (or kills) octopus that rescues him from sea. Oceania: **Lessa, 1961, 69f., 245ff.; Cooks: Gill, 1876, 92; Tonga: Gifford, 1924, 206; Samoa: *Hambruch, 1914-15, 286f.; Krämer, 1902, I, 359; Rose, 1959, 149f.; Sierich, 1902, 186; Niue: Loeb, 1926, 194; Uvea: Burrows, 1937, 168f.; Ellice Is.: David, 1899, 100; Kennedy, 1931, 162.

R245. Whale boat.

K958. Murder by drowning. See *K929.24. Tonga: Brown, 1916, 431f.; N.Z.: White, 1887-90, III, 10, 24, 29, 30, 36f., 38f., 48f., 51, 52, 54.

*K958.1. Giant bird entices enemies to get on its back for flight; it then shakes them off into ocean to drown. Australs: Aitken, 1923, 242; Tuamotus: Seurat, 1905, 434.

*K958.2. Ghosts tricked into entering sea, where they are drowned. Hawaii: Beckwith, 1940, 443ff.; Fornander, 1918, V, 294ff.

*K958.3. Dupe persuaded to dive for allegedly stuck anchor. Left to drown. N.Z.: White, 1887-90, IV, 58.

*K958.4. Giant pig-man dams stream with own body. He
then releases water and drowns his enemies. Hawaii:
Westervelt, 1915, 254ff.

*K958.5. Man persuades another to allow stone to be
tied to him. Latter is thrown into sea and
drowns. Kapingamarangi: Emory, 1949, 235.

K959.6. Post-hole murder: people invite boy to enter
post-hole and then try to crush him with log.
Oceania: **Lessa, 1961, 393ff.; Tikopia: Firth,
1961, 101; Ellice Is.: David, 1899, 107; Ontong
Java, Nukumanu: Sarfert, 1931, 429.

*K959.7. People tricked into a position so that they
can be crushed by a heavy, deliberately-dropped
object. Mangareva: Hiroa, 1938, 31; Hawaii:
Fornander, 1918, V, 202ff.; Green, 1926, 91;
McAllister, 1933, 181; Remy, 1868, 32f.; N.Z.:
White, 1887-90, IV, 88.

*K959.8. Person killed when removable head hidden.
Rennell: Elbert-Monberg, 1964, Nc. 65.

*K959.9. Person killed when tricked into stepping
upon a pitfall. Australs: Aitken, 1923, 278, 282.

*K959.10. Murder by smashing victims' heads
together. Kapingamarangi: Elbert, 1948, 32.

K963. Rope cut and victim dropped. Niue: Loeb,
1926, 220; N.Z.: Kararehe, 1898, 60; Bellona:
Elbert-Monberg, 1964, No. 60.

K975.1.1. Hero tells enemies how he may be killed.
Marquesas: Handy, 1930, 105.

K982. Dupe induced to stand under falling tree.
Tonga: Collocott, 1928, 31.

K991.+ Persons tipped off precarious bridge if they
do not pay ordered fee. Hawaii: Emerson, 1915,
56f.

K991.+ Fishes invited aboard canoe. As they sit,
trickster puts knife under them and kills them.
Santa Cruz: Riesenfeld, 1950, 126.

K991.+ Man deceived into letting hair hang loose during
battle; enemies seize him by hair in ambush.
Niue: Loeb, 1926, 49.

*K991.+ Cave caused to crush man. Thief is killed by
mouth of his cave, which opens and shuts at
command, when a pursuer fathoms cave's secret.
Hawaii: Beckwith, 1940, 339.

K1000--K1199. DECEPTION INTO SELF INJURY

K1013. False beauty-doctor. Rennell: Elbert-Monberg,
1964, No. 37; Bellona: ibid., No. 38.

*K1013.2.3. Dupes, believing they are curing leprosy,
burn sick persons. Societies: Agostini, 1900,
76.

K1021.1. Tail buried (hair tied). N.Z.: Best, 1924,
190.

K1022.1. Wolf overeats in the cellar. Cannot escape
through entrance hole. Hawaii: Beckwith, 1940,
21.

*K1025.3. Demon tricked into eating own arms and legs.
Nukumanu: Sarfert, 1931, 455.

*K1035.1. Dupe persuaded to open giant shell-fish's
valves: he is firmly clasped and usually dies.
Australs: Aitken, 1923, 275; Niue: Morris, 1919,
226; Bellona: Elbert-Monberg, 1964, No. 63.

*K1035.2. Lobsters, which thief is tricked into hiding
in his back, kill him. Man steals fish and puts
them in his back, which he can open at will. His
sons leave live crabs, lobsters, etc., to tempt
him; when he places these in back, he is killed.
Marquesas: Handy, 1930, 38f.; Lagarde, 1933,
260; *Steinen, 1933-34, 366, 368ff.

*K1035.3. Hero tricks ogre into swallowing tree instead
of himself. Ellice Is.: Kennedy, 1931, 207.

K1044. Dupe induced to eat filth (dung). Marquesas:
Handy, 1930, 110; Steinen, 1933-34, 28; Hawaii:
Beckwith, 1940, 442; Fornander, 1918, V, 422;
Samoa: Stuebel, 1896, 66; Ontong Java, Nukumanu:
Sarfert, 1931, 430ff.

398

*K1078.+ People in fort given dried crawfish by attackers
and soon surrender because of thirst. N.Z.: White,
1887-90, III, 131f., 149.

K1113. Abandonment on stretching tree. Marquesas:
Lavondes, 1966, 78, 150.

K1172. Falling beam in cave kills travelers lured within.
Hawaii: Beckwith, 1940, 344.

*K1184. Demons guarding otherworld gate tricked into
catching themselves. Tuamotus: Stimson, n.d.,
Z-G. 13/221.

*K1185. Deception to cause shipwreck: trickster
pretends to lash his canoe with only pandanus leaves.
Dupes imitate him and their canoes come apart.
Reef Is.: *Elbert-Kirtley, 1966, 359f.; O'Ferral,
1904, 227; Rennel: Elbert-Monberg, 1964, No. 57c;
Bellona: ibid., Nos. 57a, 57a, n.

K1200--K1299. DECEPTION INTO HUMILIATING

POSITION

K1200. Deception into humiliating position. Tuamotus:
Stimson, n.d., T-G. 3/59.

*K1293. Man buries his feces and tricks ghosts into
thrusting their hands into the substance. Hawaii:
Fornander, 1918, V, 424.

*K1294. Girl's enemies invent game called "showing of
mothers" in order to cause her to reveal her fish
parentage. Tokelau: Burrows, 1923, 165f.

K1300--K1399. SEDUCTION OR DECEPTIVE MARRIAGE

K1310. Seduction by disguise or substitution. Hawaii:
Beckwith, 1919, 504ff.

K1311. Seduction by masking as woman's husband.
Mangareva: Hiroa, 1938, 307; Laval, 1938,
66f., 299; N.Z.: Best, 1925, 907.

K1315. Seduction by impostor. Tonga: Beckwith, 1940, 536.

K1315.1. Seduction by posing as a god. Oceania: *Lessa, 1961, 215ff.; Reef Is.: *Elbert-Kirtley, 1966, 365f.

*K1315.1.0.1. God bids goddess go mate with another god. He then changes himself into that form and sleeps with her. Societies: Beckwith, 1940, 224.

*K1315.1.0.2. Brothers seduce sister by deception: pretend they are so ordered by spirits. Oceania: **Lessa, 1961, 51ff., 215ff.; **Elbert-Kirtley, 1966, 365f.

K1315.2.1. Girl persuaded to sit on certain plant: seduced. Marquesas: Steinen, 1934-35, 233.

*K1315.2.5. Father poses as another man to seduce daughter. Man tells daughter she will meet another man with his appearance; he himself meets her. Marquesas: Steinen, 1934-35, 232.

K1317. Lover's place in bed usurped by another. Samoa: Sierich, 1902, 185.

K1340.+ Ugly man comes to women only at night. Samoa: Abercromby, 1891, 458; N.Z.: Cowan, 1930, I, 173ff.

K1344.1. Girl seduced from beneath grouna. Tuamotus: Stimson, 1937, 7f.

K1371. Bride-stealing. N.Z.: Grace, 1907, 3, 22.

K1371.5. Man gets bridegroom drunk and enjoys the bride. Hawaii: Beckwith, 1940, 424; Fornander, 1918, V, 388.

K1371.6. While chief is performing suitor task, rival steals the bride. Easter I.: Métraux, 1940, 57.

K1377.+ Twin sister of bride given to groom (instead of supposed). Hawaii: Beckwith, 1919, 336.

K1377.+ Woman seduced by magic. Tuamotus: Stimson, 1937, 112.

K1399.4. Woman secures man's spear (arrow), lures him with it into her hut. Hawaii: Beckwith, 1940, 47f.; N.Z.: Clark, 1896, 4.

K1399.5.+ Man, hoping to take woman from her lover, tells her distant sound of cheering is an audience responding to her lover's defamations of her character. Hawaii: Fornander, 1916, IV, 112.

K1399.5.+ In order to marry girl whose father wants a good fisherman to be her husband, man rubs self with fish oil and intestines to appear a thorough going fisherman. Hawaii: Green, 1926, 100.

K1399.5.+ Deserted woman pretends to have new husband and her man returns. Hawaii: Fornander, 1916, IV, 552ff.

K1399.5.+ Seduction by trick: man pretends to lose his foreskin. Woman is shown what he means. Reef Is.: Elbert-Kirtley, 1966, 364f.

K1399.5.+ Lovers trick unwelcome person into leaving in order to have intercourse. Easter I.: Métraux, 1940, 57.

K1399.5.+ Woman keeps man hidden and to herself on Island of Women. Marquesas: Handy, 1930, 57; Steinen, 1933-34, 348, 358.

K1399.5.+ Brother lures sister to top of platform by pretending he sees a distant ship: seduces her. Tonga: Gifford, 1924, 29, 46.

K1400--K1499. DUPE'S PROPERTY DESTROYED

K1400. Dupe's property destroyed. Rennell: Elbert-Monberg, 1964, No. 74; Bellona: ibid., No. 75.

*K1457. Clever magician persuades god of fish to send all of a species of edible fish to his island, presumably to hold a wake, but actually magician wants to net them. N.Z.: Grace, 1907, 156ff.

K1500. Deception connected with adultery. Societies: Caillot, 1914, 119f.; Hawaii: Fornander, 1916, IV, 100; Samoa: Krämer, 1902, 128f.

*K1514.19. Wife frightens husband away so that she may elope with paramour. Rennell: Elbert-Monberg, 1964, No. 196.

*K1564.1. Adultress marked with turmeric so that her transgression becomes known. Marquesas: Lavondes, 1964, 24.

*K1564.2. Chief makes his wife paint herself with yellow coloring. If pattern is disturbed, he knows she has been unfaithful. Samoa: Stuebel, 1896, 85f.

K1600--K1699. DECEIVER FALLS INTO

OWN TRAP

K1601. Deceiver falls into his own trap (literally). Marquesas: Steinen, 1933-34, 372; Fijis: Fison, 1904, 110f.

K1628.+ Servant sent to kill trickster and get his blood. Instead, trickster kills servant, gets blood; people drinking it become ill, die. Kapingamarangi: Elbert, 1948, 106; 1949, 243.

*K1697. Person who leaves clandestinely at night followed by trick: loincloth or girdle hidden. Easter I.: Métraux, 1940, 389; Tuamotus: Stimson, 1934, 17f.; Cooks: Banapa, 1920, 89f.; Gill, 1876, 101; Tonga: Caillot, 1914, 264ff.; Collocott, 1921, 45f.; Reiter, 1917-18, 1028ff.; Samoa: Bülow, 1895, 141; Krämer, 1902, I, 400f., 402; Lesson, 1876, 595; Stuebel, 1896, 65, 143; Niue: Loeb, 1926, 212f.; Thomson, 1902, 86; N.Z.: Best, 1929, 6, n. 15, n. 16; Luomala, 1949, 55; White, 1887-90, II, 66f., 72f., 94f.; Wohlers, 1875, 11; Ellice Is.: Kennedy, 1931, 164;

402

Rotuma: Churchward, 1937-38, 490; Russell, 1942, 243; Rennell: Elbert-Monberg, 1964, Nos. 31a, 31b, 33.

K1700--K2099. DECEPTION THROUGH SHAMS

K1700--K1799. Deception through bluffing

K1715.4. Enemies frightened away by making them think they will be eaten. Samoa: Stuebel, 1896, 81.

*K1715.4.0.1. People paint their teeth red in order to seem to be maneaters. Niue: Smith, 1903, 90.

K1715.4.1. Spirits frightened away by making them think they will be eaten. Hawaii: Beckwith, 1940, 443.

K1756.+ Enemies frightened by loud sound. Hawaii: Fornander, 1918, V, 424; Tikopia: Firth, 1961, 112.

K1800--K1899. Deception by disguise or illusion

K1811. Gods in disguise visit mortals. Hawaii: Beckwith, 1940, 69.

K1812. King in disguise. Hawaii: Beckwith, 1940, 95; Fornander, 1916, IV, 428.

K1815. Humble disguise. N.Z.: White, 1887-90, II, 41ff., 57f., 143, 148; IV, 228ff.; Wohlers, 1875, 23; 1876, 113.

K1816.0.3. Menial disguise of princess's lover. Tuamotus: Stimson, n.d., Z-G. 13/10, Z-G. 13/221, Z-G. 13/243.

K1817.1. Disguise as beggar. Cooks: Te Ariki, 1921, 204; Hawaii: Beckwith, 1940, 393.

*K1817.1.0.1. Hero in disguise as stinking and ugly old man. Marquesas: Steinen, 1933-34, 29, 31.

K1818.1. Disguise as leper. Tonga: Gifford, 1924, 193.

K1821.2. Disguise by painting body. Hawaii: Beckwith, 1940, 443; Fornander, 1916, IV, 92; 1918, V, 424.

403

K1821.8. Disguise as old man. Marquesas: Handy, 1930, 127; N.Z.: Beckwith, 1940, 250; Clark, 1896, 166; Wohlers, 1876, 120.

*K1821.11. Disguise by swallowing stones and posing as pregnant woman. Tonga: Collocott, 1928, 26.

K1823.6. Disguise as crab. Kapingamarangi: Elbert, 1949, 244.

K1825.5.+ Anonymous hero: person wins king's battles then flees without revealing his identity. Hawaii: Fornander, 1916, IV, 468; Thrum, 1907, 95ff., 98f., 100f.

K1836. Disguise of man in woman's dress. Niue: Loeb, 1926, 142.

K1839.15.+ Person puts calabash on his head so as to appear bald from a distance. Hawaii: Fornander, 1918, V, 50.

K1839.15.+ Man, to escape attentions of a female, smears his body with stinking shark oil. N.Z.: Cowan, 1925, 38.

K1853.2.1. Hero substitutes for princess as gift to monster. Kills him. Tonga: Beckwith, 1940, 345.

*K1858.3. Salt water is substituted by older brothers for their youngest brother's water-of-life. Hawaii: Westervelt, 1915, 45.

*K1859. Deception by substitution--miscellaneous.

*K1859.1. Corpse of murdered commoner for body of a king (which must be buried in secret location). Hawaii: *Beckwith, 1940, 391ff.; Fornander, 1916, IV, 234; Remy, 1868, 28.

*K1859.2. Brothers kill stranger and show his hands as evidence that their youngest brother was eaten by a shark. Hawaii: Fornander, 1916, IV, 132.

K1860. Deception by feigned death (sleep). N.Z.: Grey, 1855, 172ff.

*K1860.0.1. Hero abrades skin all over body in order to appear deceased. Marquesas: Handy, 1930, 92.

K1866. Death feigned in order to enter land of dead.
Hawaii: Beckwith, 1940, 147; Fornander, 1918, V,
186; Thrum, 1907, 45; Westervelt, 1915, 234;
Samoa: Krämer, 1902, I, 447.

K1872.1. Army appears like forest. Cooks: Te Ariki,
1920, 5.

K1875. Deception by sham blood. Tikopia: Firth, 1961,
100f.

K1875.+ Person catches thrown spear between elbow and
body and pretends to be wounded. Hawaii:
Fornander, 1918, V, 392.

K1881. Absent person seems to be present. Bellona:
Elbert-Monberg, 1964, No. 58.

K1883.8. Images set up to resemble watchmen. Hawaii:
Beckwith, 1940, 388, 409; Dickey, 1917, 22;
Fornander, 1916, IV, 248ff.; V, 1918, 180, 376ff.,
692; Kamakau, 1961, 30; Thrum, 1907, 34.

*K1883.8.1. People leave images in hut. Ghosts,
thinking they are humans, eat them. Hawaii:
Fornander, 1918, V, 432f.

K1883.9. Hero wears so many different costumes that he
is believed to represent a host. N.Z.: Beckwith,
1940, 398.

*K1883.10. Clumps of grass dressed to look like
warriors (enemy frightened by large number). N.Z.:
Beckwith, 1940, 398; Grey, 1855, 197.

K1886.3.1. Mock sunrise: person causes cock to crow
(or simulates cock crow). Tuamotus: Stimson,
n.d., T-G. 1/78, Z-G. 3/1146; 1937, 87, 142f.;
Marquesas: Handy, 1930, 32, 109; Steinen,
1933-34, 38; Societies: Henry, 1928, 589;
Ropiteau, 1933, 127; Tefaafana, 1917, 31;
Hawaii: Beckwith, 1940, 516; Fornander, 1916,
IV, 540ff.; Tonga: Gifford, 1924, 90, 144;
Samoa: Krämer, 1902, I, 448; Uvea: Burrows,
1937, 162; Fijis: Hocart, 1929, 213; Rotuma:
Beckwith, 1940, 197; Nukumanu: Sarfert, 1931,
454.

K1886.3.2. Mock sunrise: dupe made to believe that
flaunted bare buttocks are the rising sun.
Tonga: Collocott, 1928, 61; Gifford, 1924, 87ff.;

Samoa: Powell-Pratt, 1891, 204; Uvea: Burrows, 1937, 162.

K1886.3.3. Mock sunrise causes supernaturals (thieves) to drop burdens and flee. (Cf. F420.3.4.2.) Societies: Henry, 1928, 589; Ropiteau, 1933, 127; Tonga: Gifford, 1924, 88ff.; Uvea: Burrows, 1937, 162; Fijis: Hocart, 1929, 213; Nukumanu: Sarfert, 1931, 454.

K1887.2. Deceptive nocturnal noise. Tikopia: Firth, 1961, 60.

*K1889.7. Person places shells over his eyes to that in the dark he appears to be awake. Hawaii: Rice, 1923, 68; Niue: Loeb, 1926, 25; Smith, 1903, 6; N.Z.: Best, 1928, 262; Clark, 1896, 161; Grey, 1855, 95; White, 1887-90, I, 122f.; Wohlers, 1875, 18.

*K1889.8. Amazed awakening of transported sleeper. N.Z.: *Best, 1925, 774, 922; 1928, 261ff., 267; Rotuma: Churchward, 1938-39, 230.

K1894.+ Captive told roar of sea is sound of bushes waving. Niue: Loeb, 1926, 77.

K1894.+ Shell-fish, sea-shells put in coffin; children believe that their father is dead. Marquesas: Handy, 1930, 88; Tahiaoteaa, 1933, 493.

K1894.+ Women, to get rid of unwelcome visitors to their island, go out in canoes at night, appear off island at daylight, and appear to be hostile fleet to strangers. Tokelau: Burrows, 1923, 148f.

K1894.+ Trickster, to prevent rival tribe from fishing in river, makes artificial water monster. N.Z.: Grace, 1907, 23ff.

K1894.+ Man paints self with turmeric so that his rival will believe it came from sleeping with a woman. Samoa: Krämer, 1902, I, 446.

K1894.+ Ugly man takes handsome man's place by window, so that in the dark a young woman mistakenly marks his face with a scratch, which shows him to be her chosen suitor. N.Z.: Best, 1925, 729.

K1911. The false bride (substituted bride). Australs:
Aitken, 1923, 272; Marquesas: Lavondes, 1964,
26ff.; Cooks: Smith, 1897, notes; Ellice Is.:
Roberts, 1957, 365; Kapingamarangi: Elbert,
1948, 88; Bellona: Elbert-Monberg, 1964, No. 52a;
Rennell: ibid., 52b.

K1911.2.1. True bride transformed by false. Cooks:
Smith, 1897, 97, note.

K1915. The false bridegroom (substituted bridegroom).
Tuamotus: Stimson, 1937, 130; Tonga: Collocott,
1928, 48; Rennell: Bradley, 1956, 334f.

*K1919.2. Princess's servant pretends to be princess.
Societies: Henry, 1928, 608.

K1923.3. Barren woman pretends to bear child.
Substitutes another woman's child. Easter I.:
Métraux, 1940, 101.

*K1923.7. Woman pretends to give birth to a god's
child. Mangareva: Laval, 1938, 193.

K1931.1.1. Impostor tries to push foster brother
into water and then cuts rope so that he drifts alone
on sea in boat without oars. Tonga: Gifford, 1924,
128.

K1951. Sham warrior. Hawaii: Beckwith, 1940, 390ff.

*K1969.5. Sham traveler. Pretends to have made trip
to Rarotonga and is given charge of canoe fleet,
which he uses for his own purposes. Marquesas:
Handy, 1930, 119.

K1971. Man behind statue (tree) speaks and pretends
to be God (spirit). Hawaii: Beckwith, 1940, 437;
Fijis: Fison, 1904, 62.

*K1971.15. Ventriloquist pretends that a god is speaking.
Mangareva: Laval, 1938, 191f.

*K1971.16. Trickster makes spirits think he is helped

by god: an image and concealed man in basket give
directions. Hawaii: Beckwith, 1940, 431.

K1994.+ Ogress eats fish she catches: returns home
and complains of ill luck. Hawaii: Beckwith,
1940, 199.

K1994.+ Underseas party: trickster pretends to have
gotten garland at party being held beneath sea.
Tonga: Gifford, 1924, 199.

K2000--K2099. HYPOCRITES

K2098.+ Heron fighting serpent begs hero for help,
but snake says the two are having friendly
contest. Hero believes latter. Cooks: Gill,
1876, 143.

K2098.+ King tells daughter rescuer went to another
land; in reality father has forbidden hero's
seeing her. Tuamotus: Stimson, n.d., Z-G. 13/420.

K2098.+ Hypocritical excuse. Hero tells ogress that
fake cooking fires are a greeting to her.
Marquesas: Handy, 1930, 25.

K2100--K2199. FALSE ACCUSATIONS

K2112. Woman slandered as adulteress. Hawaii:
Beckwith, 1940, 152.

K2116.4. Murderer (thief) makes outcry so that
innocent person is accused. Hawaii: Fornander,
1918, V, 294ff.

K2121.2. King's faithful servant falsely accused of
familiarity with queen. Hawaii: Beckwith, 1940,
393.

K2124. Woman slandered as ogress. Tonga: Collocott,
1928, 36, 43; Samoa: Krämer, 1902, I, 140.

K2129.4. Family is accused of stinginess by recipients
of their hospitality. Tuamotus: Stimson, n.d.,
T-G. 3/515.

K2142.+ Two brothers create trouble between chiefs.
At the point of battle, they make peace and are
richly rewarded by weaker chief, who considers
them saviors. Hawaii: Beckwith, 1940, 310.

K2142.+ Men from country district are taught English
by trickster. They are beaten by sailors when
they use profane phrases. Hawaii: Fornander,
1918, V, 428.

K2142.+ Hero goes to brothers for breadfruit, and
after they give it to him, he breaks it open.
He tells his father his brothers gave it to him
in this state. Marquesas: Handy, 1930, 86.

K2142.+ Hero strikes own skin with thorny bush and
tells father his brother-in-law injured him.
Marquesas: Handy, 1930, 87.

K2142.+ Two boys gash heads and say it was caused
by the shark of god. Marquesas: Handy, 1930, 110.

K2142.+ Person breaks wind in woman's house, an act
causing husband to quarrel with his wife about a
smelly house. N.Z.: White, 1887-90, III, 83, 89.

K2153. Trickster wounds self and accuses others.
Marquesas: Handy, 1930, 87, 110.

*K2176. True prophet made to appear false. Prophet says
certain birds can be caught only on sea. Chief's
man brings birds caught only on sea, but says
they were found on mountain. Hawaii: Beckwith,
1940, 382.

            K2200--K2299. VILLAINS AND TRAITORS

K2211. Treacherous brother. Tuamotus: Stimson, n.d.,
T-G. 3/615; Marquesas: Handy, 1930, 86; Niue:
Loeb, 1926, 49.

K2213. Treacherous wife. Easter I.: Métraux, 1940, 381.

*K2219. Treacherous father. Kapingamarangi: Emory,
1949, 233.

K2221. Treacherous rival lover. Tuamotus: Stimson, n.d., Z-G. 13/10.

*K2221.2. Person overturns his canoe so that his jealous rival sails on. He then returns to island from which he started, his rival being gone. Cooks: Low, 1934, 82, 185.

K2246.1. Treacherous king. Tuamotus: Stimson, n.d., 13/420.

K2252. Treacherous maid-servant. Tuamotus: Stimson, n.d., Z-G. 3/1241.

K2300--K2399. OTHER DECEPTIONS

K2346. Wooden image frightens away invaders. Hawaii: Beckwith, 1940, 388.

K2357. Disguise to enter enemy's camp. Niue: Loeb, 1926, 142; Chatham Is.: Shand, 1895, 165.

K2357.3. Disguise as old man to enter hostile village. N.Z.: Beckwith, 1940, 250.

K2357.5. Weapons disguised as tribute; permit entry into enemies' camp. Hawaii: Beckwith, 1940, 390.

K2363. Spies' false report of enemies' weakness brings on premature attack. Hawaii: Beckwith, 1940, 394; Fornander, 1916, IV, 334ff.

*K2365.4. People are besieged and without water. To deceive enemy a chief stands upon platform and pretends to dry his washed hair. Samoa: Krämer, 1902, I, 449.

*K2368.5. Warriors each carry four torches to deceive enemy about their number. Hawaii: Fornander, 1916, IV, 324.

*K2385.1. Eels in woman's body tempted to come out by
fish bait: they are then killed. Marquesas:
Steinen, 1934-35, 226.

K2388.+ Person visits enemy at night and leaves a
token showing that he could have killed the latter.
N.Z.: Cowan, 1930, I, 126f.; White, 1887-90,
IV, 189.

K2388.+ Watercourse of river altered by trick. Cooks:
Manuiri,"The Story of the Visit of Longaiti to
Rarotonga," JPS V (1896), 142ff.

K2388.+ Parents secretly get food from other world;
do not let children know. Cooks: Banapa, 1920,
89.

K2388.+ Small trickster rewarded. Told he can have all
the food he can carry away, he takes the whole crop.
Hawaii: Beckwith, 1940, 436.

K2388.+ Father of hero eats cooked food (does not
disclose that it is cooked), gives his son raw
food. Niue: Loeb, 1926, 212.

K2388.+ Hero (Maui) gets fire from fire-god and
repeatedly puts it out on way back to world.
N.Z.: Clark, 1896, 42.

L. REVERSAL OF FORTUNE

L0--L99. Victorious Youngest Child

L10. Victorious youngest son. Polynesia: Dixon, 1916, 41; Easter I.: Métraux, 1940, 383; Tuamotus: Stimson, 1937, 28ff., 83; Societies: Henry, 1928, 614; Hawaii: Beckwith, 1940, 491; Dickey, 1917, 24; Fornander, 1916, IV, 32ff., 120, 160; 1918, V, 6; Rice, 1923, 93; Thrum, 1923, 22; Westervelt, 1915, 42ff.; Tokelau: Burrows, 1923, 162ff.; N.Z.: *Best, 1929, 3, 15 n., 16 n.; White, 1887-90, II, 27f., 66, 72, 80; Tikopia: Firth, 1961, 102; Rennell: Bradley, 1956, 336.

L10.2.+ Abused youngest son (by his elder brothers). Tuamotus: Stimson, n.d., T-G. 3/403, T-G. 3/615.

L11. Fortunate youngest son. Always has good luck. Nukumanu: Sarfert, 1931, 386.

L13. Compassionate youngest son. Kind to people or animals: rewarded. Societies: Henry, 1928, 555; Tokelau: Burrows, 1923, 162, 164.

L31. Youngest brother helps elder. Hawaii: Fornander, 1916, IV, 98.

L50. Victorious younger daughter. Mangareva: Hiroa, 1938, 344; Hawaii: Pukui-Curtis, n.d., 58ff.

L52. Abused youngest daughter. Tuamotus: Stimson, n.d., Z-G. 13/346; Hawaii: *Beckwith, 1940, 170, 170 n. 5.

L54. Compassionate youngest daughter. Hawaii: Emerson, 1915, 15.

L61. Clever youngest sister (of five). Hawaii: Beckwith 1919, 432.

L100--L199. Unpromising Hero (Heroine)

L101. Unpromising hero (male Cinderella). Usually, but not always, the unpromising hero is also the

youngest son. Hawaii: Beckwith, 1940, 408;
N.Z.: White, 1887-90, III, 236.

L102. Unpromising heroine. Usually, but not always,
the youngest daughter. Tuamotus: Stimson, n.d.,
Z-G. 13/346.

L111. Hero (heroine) of unpromising origin. Hawaii:
Fornander, 1916, IV, 134; N.Z.: White, 1887-90,
IV, 236ff.

L111.2. Foundling hero. Tonga: Gifford, 1924, 130;
Ontong Java: Sarfert, 1931, 442.

L111.2.2. Future hero found on shore. Tonga:
Gifford, 1924, 122.

L111.4. Orphan hero. Tuamotus: Stimson, n.d.,
T-G. 3/818; Marquesas: Lavondes, 1966, 58ff.,
98ff., 146ff., 178; N.Z.: White, 1887-90, IV,
174, 196; V, 18; Tikopia: Firth, 1961, 44.

L112. Hero (heroine) of unpromising appearance.
Tuamotus: Stimson, n.d., Z-G. 13/346.

L112.2. Very small hero. Cooks: Kunike, 1928, 32;
Samoa: Nelson, 1925, 135; Powell-Pratt, 1892,
245; Rennell: Bradley, 1956, 336.

L112.7.1. Leper hero. Tuamotus: Stimson, n.d.,
T-G. 3/45; Ellice Is.: Kennedy, 1931, 174.

L112.11. Heroine born with pigeon's head. Tonga:
Gifford, 1924, 31, 61, 65.

L113.1.+ Abused half-brother as hero. Tokelau:
Macgregor, 1937, 84.

*L113.11. Humble boy becomes king's steward. Hawaii:
Rice, 1923, 75.

L114.1. Lazy hero. Hawaii: Beckwith, 1940, 416;
Fornander, 1916, IV, 236; 1918, V, 156, 598ff.;
Luomala, 1951, 21; Tonga: Brown, 1916, 426.

L131. Hearth abode of unpromising hero. Marquesas:
Lavondes, 1966, 2.

L131.+ Cave abode of hero. Tuamotus: Henry,
1928, 520.

L140.+ Hero catches more fish with crude hook (tackle) than rivals do with splendid equipment. Marquesas: Steinen, 1933-34, 39.

L142.+ Child defeats men in riddling contest. Hawaii: Beckwith, 1940, 459.

L142.+ Child who is first inept later bests all other children at all games. Tuamotus: Stimson, n.d., Z-G. 3/1122.

L142.+ Four sons of great warrior have turtles taken away by villagers; when grown into powerful fighters, sons catch turtles and force villagers to try previous theft. Tuamotus: Stimson, n.d., T-G. 3/818.

L145. Ugly preferred to pretty sister. Ellice Is.: David, 1899, 97.

L151.+ Boy outsails brothers in canoe made of coconut sheath. Marquesas: Beckwith, 1940, 484.

L151.+ Long-ear people dig pit, build oven to kill and cook short-ear people. Latter discover plan and turn the tables. Easter I.: Métraux, 1940, 70.

L156.1.+ Dog destined to be eaten instead eats its masters. Hawaii: Pukui, 1933, 178.

L161. Lowly hero marries princess. Societies: Henry, 1928, 614; Hawaii: Thrum, 1923, 184.

L161.2.+ Youngest of brothers wins famed beauty. N.Z.: White, 1887-90, II, 27; Wohlers, 1876, 116.

L162. Lowly heroine marries prince (hero). Tuamotus: Stimson, n.d., Z-G. 13/346; Rarotonga: Te Ariki, 1921, 208.

L162.+ Brother and sister refugees marry children of king. Tonga: Gifford, 1924, 186.

L165. Lowly boy becomes king (chief). Tuamotus: Stimson, n.d., T-G. 3/45; Samoa: Sierich, 1900, 233.

L176. Despised boy wins race. Hawaii: Fornander, 1918, V, 126ff.

L200--L299. Modesty Brings Reward

L212. Choice among several gifts. Hero refuses to
take bright new fishhooks, takes old one. Tonga:
Caillot, 1914, 255f.; Samoa: Fraser, 1897, 71;
Krämer, 1902, I, 413 n. 5; Powell-Pratt, 1892, 243.

L215.+ Unpromising magic object chosen. Twins, told to
select bright fishhook, pick dull one, which is
magical. Tonga: Beckwith, 1940, 25; Gifford,
1924, 20.

L300--L399. Triumph of the Weak

L311. Weak (small) hero overcomes large fighter.
Tuamotus: Beckwith, 1940, 476; Cooks: Gill,
1876, 54ff., 67ff.; Hawaii: Beckwith, 1940,
465; Fornander, 1916, IV, 166ff.; Rice, 1923,
93; Westervelt, 1915a, 178; Samoa: Brown, 1915,
174f.; Tikopia: Firth, 1961, 115.

L351.+ Contest between fire and water. N.Z.: Hare
Hongi, 1894, 155ff.

L400--L499. Pride Brought Low

L410.6. Ruler enslaved. Hawaii: Fornander, 1916,
IV, 134.

L419.+ Dancing of leper judged better than dancing of
king. Tuamotus: Stimson, n.d., T-G. 3/45.

L431.+ Girls refuse two ugly boys. Boys are magically
beautified; they reject girls, who then throw
themselves off cliff. Chatham Is.: Shand,
1896, 134.

L432.4.+ In famine couple must beg from son-in-law
they drove away. Hawaii: Green, 1923, 39ff.

L435.+ Wife restored to rightful place after usurping
ogress burned. Ellice Is.: Roberts, 1957, 367.

M. ORDAINING THE FUTURE

M0--M99. Judgments and Decrees

M11. Irrevocable judgment causes judge to suffer
first. Societies: Henry, 1901, 52.

M100--M199. Vows and Oaths

M149.7.+ Chief vows to marry no one from his own
island. Hawaii: Beckwith, 1919, 374.

M150.+ Voyager vows to trample on breasts of gods.
Hawaii: Beckwith, 1940, 448.

M150.+ Vow to effect vengeance. Tuamotus:
Stimson, n.d., Z-G. 13/420.

M184.1. Vow that no daughter born to chief's wife
will be allowed to live until she bears a son.
Hawaii: Beckwith, 1919, 334, 344; 1940, 526.

M200--M299. Bargains and Promises

M203.3.+ Before battle, chief calls his warriors
brothers. A warrior later claims literal kinship,
and the king ackowledges him. Hawaii: Green,
1923, 32ff.

M205.1.1. Turtle carrying man through water upsets him
because of broken promise. Tuamotus: Stimson,
n.d., T-G. 3/600; Societies: Beckwith, 1940, 252;
Gill, 1876, 254; Cooks: Gill, 1876, 92; Tonga:
Collocott, 1928, 22; Tokelau: Burrows, 1923, 156;
Uvea: Burrows, 1937, 169; Kapingamarangi: Elbert,
1948, 76; 1949, 243.

> R245. Whale-boat. W154.9. Man rescued
> from drowning kills rescuer.

M205.1.1.1. Fish (whale) carrying man through water
shakes him off when man strikes him with coconut.
Tuamotus: Stimson, n.d., T-G. 3/600; Societies:

Beckwith, 1940, 252.

>K952.1. Ungrateful river passenger.
>R245. Whale-boat.

M218.+ Ruler of underworld teaches mortals. Her pupils rush from her house, and she takes the last two as payment. N.Z.: Kararehe, 1898, 60.

M221.+ Life spared in bargain: person at another's mercy is allowed to live as part of bargain. Tuamotus: Stimson, n.d., Z-G. 3/1314, Z-G. 3/1353, Z-G. 13/152, Z-G. 13/221, T-G. 3/13; Ellice Is.: Kennedy, 1931, 202, 207; Lau Is.: Hocart, 1929, 208.

M292.+ In return for passage on canoe, man promises to overcome all obstacles met on journey. Cooks: Beckwith, 1940, 268f., 450; Tokelau: Macgregor, 1937, 86.

M292.+ Fish releases boat from back in return for woman. Nukumanu: Sarfert, 1931, 452.

M292.+ Sun gives man fishhooks in return for release. Nukumanu: Sarfert,1931, 439.

M292.+ Man lets woman plant taro on his land in exchange for sexual favors. Ontong Java: Sarfert, 1931, 296.

M292.+ Wise god bargains for shell fish of another island: gives mosquitoes in exchange. Fijis: Fison, 1904, 94.

M296. Two men in love promise to have nothing to do with the girl without the other's consent. Hawaii: Beckwith, 1940, 153.

>M300--M399. Prophecies

M300. Prophecies. Societies: Seurat, 1905, 437; Hawaii: Fornander, 1916, IV, 62, 88, 182, 448; Kamakau, 1961, 39; Thrum, 1923, 63, 207ff.; Tokelau: Burrows, 1923, 168; N.Z.: White, 1887-90, I, 96, 121, 127; II, 143.

M311. Prophecy: future greatness of unborn child.
N.Z.: Luomala, 1949, 58.

M312.+ Prophecy: the coming of a canoe without an
outrigger. Societies: Luomala, 1949, 147.

M341. Death prophesied. Hawaii: Beckwith, 1940,
141; Tonga: Gifford, 1924, 50.

M353.+ Brother prophesies that his pregnant sister
will give birth to fish which he will eat.
Marquesas: Steinen, 1934-35, 234.

M399.+ Dying mother tells murderer that her son will
someday bite his hand. Easter I.: Métraux,
1940, 385.

M399.+ Warrior leaving on voyage warns people not
to leave land vacant lest it be occupied by
demons. Tuamotus: Stimson, n.d., T-G. 3/711.

N. CHANCE AND FATE

N0--N99. Wagers and gambling

N0. Wagers and gambling. Hawaii: Fornander, 1918, V, 420.

N2.2. Lives wagered. Hawaii: Beckwith, 1919, 382; 1940, 111, 459; Dickey, 1917, 2, 18f., 20f., 35; Fornander, 1916, IV, 256, 280ff., 292, 512ff., 576ff.; 1918, V, 128ff., 160, 224, 280, 400; Rice, 1923, 86; Thrum, 1907, 83, 106ff.; Westervelt, 1915, 88, 111f., 235; 1915a, 155f., 229ff.; Tonga: Collocott, 1928, 45; Samoa: Fraser, 1897, 112.

N2.5. Whole kingdom (all property) as wager. Hawaii: Beckwith, 1940, 429; Fornander, 1916, IV, 298ff., 310; 1918, V, 564; Westervelt, 1915a, 230ff.

N2.5.2. Half kingdom as wager. Hawaii: Fornander, 1916, IV, 296.

N2.6. Wife as wager. Hawaii: Fornander, 1916, IV, 312.

N2.6.2. Daughter as wager. Hawaii: Fornander, 1916, IV, 300ff.

N15.2.+ Wager: two chiefs bet their land upon whether one of them can successfully woo a princess. Hawaii: Beckwith, 1919, 446.

N78.+ Chiefs lay wager about the kind of fish which is caught on line. Hawaii: Fornander, 1916, IV, 296ff.

N78.+ Wager upon whether or not food is cooked. Hawaii: Fornander, 1918, V, 420.

N100--N299. The ways of luck and fate

N170.+ Party of fishermen dream they are swept away at whirlpool. Lurking enemy hears relation of dream, kills them, and throws them into whirlpool. Cooks: Gill, 1876, 165.

N300--N399. Unlucky accidents

N325.+ Man kills his uncle by mistake. Marquesas: Handy, 1930, 138.

N339.17.+ Man from bravado jumps in an earth oven, and a hot stone explodes and kills him. Niue: Smith, 1903, 114.

N349.3.+ Father has unrecognized son thrown into sea (killed). Hawaii: Beckwith, 1940, 480; Fornander, 1916, IV, 548.

N349.3.+ Trickster unknowingly fights and kills his own grandfather. Tonga: Caillot, 1914, 275.

N365.2. Unwitting father-daughter incest. Tuamotus: Stimson, n.d., Z-G. 13/116; Tonga: Reiter, 1907, 752.

N365.3. Unwitting brother-sister incest. Tuamotus: Stimson, n.d., T-G. 3/59; Cooks: Large, 1903, 138; Hawaii: Beckwith, 1940, 516; Tonga: Reiter, 1907, 751ff.

N400--N699. LUCKY ACCIDENTS

N440--N499. Valuable secrets learned

N455.3. Secret formula for opening treasure mountain overheard from robbers. (Open Sesame). Hawaii: Beckwith, 1940, 339.

N455.9. Location of sought object learned from overheard conversation of children. Tonga: Gifford, 1924, 54.

N600--N699. Other lucky accidents

N659.2.+ Man spared from sacrifice because of sound of mudhen. Hawaii: Fornander, 1916, IV, 140.

N688.+ Three boys make wishes overheard by king's spy. The king grants the wishes. Hawaii: Beckwith, 1940, 417.

N700--N799. Accidental encounters

N731.2. Father-son combat. Neither knows who the other is. Hawaii: Beckwith, 1940, 508.

N733.1. Brothers unwittingly fight each other. Tuamotus: Stimson, n.d., Z-G. 13/317; Ellice Is.: David, 1899, 109.

N774. Adventures from pursuing enchanted animal (bird). Tonga: Beckwith, 1940, 90.

N781. Hero (heroine) embarks in rudderless boat. Ellice Is.: Roberts, 1957, 365.

N792.+ Following thrown spear leads to adventure. Samoa: Sierich, 1902, 182ff.

N800--N899. Helpers

N812. Giant or ogre as helper. Tuamotus: Stimson, n.d., Z-G. 3/1122.

N812.7. Chief with three supernatural ogre helpers. Marquesas: Handy, 1930, 76.

N813. Helpful genie (spirit). Easter I.: Métraux, 1940, 319, 369, 375; Tuamotus: Beckwith, 1940, 450; Henry, 1928, 520f.; Stimson, n.d., T-G. 3/1007, Z-G. 13/174, Z-G. 13/221; Marquesas: Handy, 1930, 113; Lavondes, 1964, 36; Pukapuka: Beaglhole, 1938, 409; Hawaii: Fornander, 1918, V, 298ff.; Tonga: Collocott, 1928, 15; Samoa: Beckwith, 1940, 438, 442; Fijis: Fison, 1904, 107.

N813.+ Ghost of dead as helper. Hawaii: Westervelt, 1915, 87ff., 101ff.

N813.+ Ancestral spirit as helper. Hawaii: Fornander, 1916, IV, 40; Rotuma: Russell, 1942, 246.

N815. Fairy as helper. Hawaii: Westervelt, 1915, 141f., 145.

N817. Deity as helper. Marquesas: Steinen, 1933-34, 39; Rarotonga: Te Ariki, 1920, 177f.; Hawaii: Beckwith, 1940, 22, 111, 174; Rice, 1923, 58; Westervelt, 1915, 55f., 111ff.

N818.1. Sun as helper. Tokelau: Burrows, 1923, 169.

N825.2. Old man helper. Tuamotus: Stimson, n.d., Z-G. 13/174; Hawaii: Beckwith, 1940, 461; Fornander, 1916, IV, 88; Thrum, 1923, 254ff.

N825.3. Old woman helper. Polynesia: Beckwith, 1940, Ch. XVII passim; Tuamotus: Leverd, 1911, 117; Stimson, n.d., Z-G. 13/174; Marquesas: Lavondes, 1966, 94, 100ff., 146ff., 176ff.; Societies: Beckwith, 1940, 251; Henry, 1928, 559; Hawaii: Beckwith, 1940, 257, 264, 461, 476, 491; Fornander, 1916, IV, 448; Rice, 1923, 18, 97; Tonga: Gifford, 1924, 156; Samoa: Sierich, 1902, 178f.; Tokelau: Burrows, 1923, 168; N.Z.: Best, 1925, 912; Dixon, 1916, 59; Kapingamarangi: Elbert, 1948, 67.

N825.3.3. Help from grandmother. Hawaii: Fornander, 1916, IV, 90, 164, 448, 518, 532, 598; 1918, V, 412; Thrum, 1907, 72f.; Westervelt, 1915, 166; Tokelau: Burrows, 1923, 168; N.Z.: Cowan, 1930, I, 22; White, 1887-90, I, 58, 90, 111, 116, 123, 128f.; Wohlers, 1875, 18; Bellona: Elbert-Monberg, 1965, No. 52a.

N831. Girl (sister) as helper. Hawaii: Beckwith, 1919, 502ff., 524ff.; Westervelt, 1915, 104f.

N831.1. Mysterious housekeeper. Ellice Is.: David, 1899, 103.

N845. Magician as helper. Tuamotus: Stimson, n.d., Z-G. 13/203, Z-G. 13/317, Z-G. 3/1386.

N846.2. Priest as helper. Tuamotus: Stimson, n.d., Z-G. 3/1174.

P. SOCIETY

P0--P99. Royalty and nobility

P0.+ Name chant for royalty. Hawaii: Beckwith, 1940,
376.

P3. Issue of marriage of brother and sister of highest
chiefly rank is a god. Hawaii: Beckwith, 1940,
521.

P10.+ College of chiefs. Hawaii: Beckwith, 1940,
377.

P10.1. Special place where occur births of royalty.
Hawaii: Beckwith, 1940, 376; Dickey, 1917, 15;
Thrum, 1923, 87ff.; Westervelt, 1915a, 203.

P16.3. King killed when old. Hawaii: Beckwith, 1940,
409f.; Tonga: Gifford, 1924, 31.

P16.3.+ Kings killed for neglect of duty. Niue:
Loeb, 1926, 175.

P16.3.+ Person who hides king's corpse killed lest
he disclose burial location. Hawaii: Fornander,
1916, IV, 234; Kamakau, 1961, 33, 48.

P17.+ At coronation, head of king is anointed with oil.
Niue: Loeb, 1926, 169.

P17.+ At coronation, king stands on special stone.
Niue: Loeb, 1926, 169.

P17.+ Heir to kingship has wooden dummy crowned in
place of himself. Tonga: Gifford, 1924, 30.

P19.5.+ Shadow of highest chief renders ground tapu.
Hawaii: Beckwith, 1940, 378.

P19.5.+ Knowledge of calendar belongs to kings only.
Cooks: Gill, 1876, 317.

P19.5.+ Garments of king sacred. Hawaii: Fornander,
1918, V, 112.

P28.1. Chieftainess of such rank that none of her
countrymen can woo her. N.Z.: Clark, 1896, 2.

P32.1. All children born in realm on same day as chief's
son are brought to palace to be his companions.
Hawaii: Beckwith, 1940, 441.

P37. Birth rites confer royalty on infant prince. Easter I.: Métraux, 1940, 59.

P38.+ Prince and his mistress unable to go ashore together. Tuamotus: Stimson, n.d., Z-G. 13/4.

P40.+ Princess of a mountain. Tuamotus: Stimson, n.d., MB-FF/206.

P90.+ Both chiefs and priests are royal. Hawaii: Beckwith, 1940, 376.

P92. Bathing pool reserved for royalty. Tahiti: Henry, 1928 , 608.

P93. Certain foods, ornaments, feathers, etc., reserved for royalty. Hawaii: Beckwith, 1940, 376.

P94. Garment must be removed in presence of certain high chiefs. Hawaii: Beckwith, 1940, 376.

P100--P199. Other social orders

P170. Slaves. Easter I.: Métraux, 1940, 120.

P174. Children of slave and free person become slaves. Hawaii: Beckwith, 1940, 300.

P200--P299. The family

P200. The family. Pukapuka: Beaglehole, 1938, 405.

P210.+ Couple lives in husband's land after marriage. Tuamotus: Stimson, n.d., T-G. 3/109.

P210.+ Girl returns to home of parents when pregnant, leaving her husband temporarily. Tuamotus: Stimson, n.d., Z-G. 3/1340.

P230. Parents and children. N.Z.: Best, 1906,
5f., 25.

P231. Mother and son. Tuamotus: Stimson, n.d.,
Z-G. 13/127, Z-G. 13/317.

P250.1.+ Eldest sister sleeps in door facing west as
soon as sun sets; sleeps in door facing east as
soon as sun rises. Rotuma: Churchward, 1937-38,
112.

P294. Aunt. *Rivers, "The Father's Sister in Oceania,"
FL XXI 42.

P300--P399. Other social relationships

P312. Blood-brotherhood. Tuamotus: Stimson, n.d.,
Z-G. 13/203.

P360.+ Skilled runners used by chiefs to bring fish
from different ponds. Hawaii: Beckwith, 1940,
337.

P400--P499. Trades and professions

P475.+ Trained thieves used by chiefs to steal from
enemy. Hawaii: Beckwith, 1940, 337.

P475.+ Bone-breaking art (lua) practised by highwayman.
Hawaii: Beckwith, 1940, 340.

P500--P599. Government

P552.5. Haircut as preparation for war. N.Z.:
Beckwith, 1940, 250.

P555.+ Head of slain foe cut off and saved. Tuamotus:
Stimson, n.d., T-G. 1/18, Z-G. 13/276.

P555.2.1.2. Jawbone cut from slain opponent. Hawaii:
Beckwith, 1940, 422.

P600--P699. Customs

P682.2. Voyagers have right to ask landsman first questi
Marquesas: Handy, 1930, 56, 72.

P682.+ People go to bathe at third crowing of cock.
Marquesas: Handy, 1930, 30.

P682.+ Voyage begun at night. Tuamotus: Stimson, n.d.,
T-G. 3/403.

P682.+ Kava-drinking ceremony. Niue: Loeb, 1926, 28.

P682.+ Names exchanged. Marquesas: Steinen, 1933-34,
34; Tahiti: Henry, 1928, 233.

Q. REWARDS AND PUNISHMENTS

Q2. Kind and unkind (obedient and disobedient). Churlish person disregards requests of old person (animal) and is punished. Courteous person (often youngest brother or sister) complies and is rewarded. Tuamotus: Stimson, n.d., Z-G. 13/167; Marquesas: Lagarde, 1936, 261; Societies: Henry, 1928, 555f.; Cooks: Te Ariki, 1921, 2; Hawaii: Beckwith, 1940, 390; Fornander, 1916, IV, 178ff., 244ff.; 1918, V, 176ff., 378ff.; Pukui, 1933, 167; Pukui-Curtis, n.d., 42ff.; Westervelt, 1915, 40ff.; Kapingamarangi: Elbert, 1948, 67; 1949, 243.

Q5. Laziness punished; industry rewarded. Hawaii: Pukui, 1933, 169.

Q10--Q99. Deeds rewarded

Q20. Piety rewarded. Hawaii: Beckwith, 1940, 70.

Q42. Generosity rewarded. Societies: Beckwith, 1940, 38.

Q65. Filial duty rewarded. Cooks: Beckwith, 1940, 247; Tonga: Gifford, 1924, 34.

Q65.+ Mercy rewarded. Tonga: Gifford, 1924, 34.

Q72.+ Obedience rewarded. Samoa: Krämer,1902, I, 266.

Q100--Q199. Nature of rewards

Q111. Riches as reward. Hawaii: Thrum, 1907, 254; Tokelau: Burrows, 1923, 162; Kapingamarangi: Elbert, 1949, 243.

Q111.8. Large quantity of land as reward. Hawaii: Fornander, 1916, IV, 208ff.; 1918, V, 216; Rennell: Elbert-Monberg, 1964, No. 122.

Q112.0.1. Kingdom as reward. Samoa: Krämer, 1902, I, 266.

Q113.0.1. High honors as reward. Samoa: Sierich, 1900, 231.

Q115.+ Reward: person made chief (ruler). Tuamotus: Stimson, n.d., Z-G. 13/174, Z-G. 13/420, Z-G. 3/1142.

Q135.+ Marriage as reward. Samoa: Stuebel, 1896, 69.

Q135.+ Reward: chief's daughter. Hawaii: Fornander, 1916, IV, 462; 1918, V, 144.

Q147.+ Man rewarded for piety by being brought to earthly paradise. Hawaii: Rice, 1923, 127.

Q151. Life spared as reward. Tuamotus: Stimson, n.d., Z-G. 3/1260.

Q151.3. Hospitable person saved from death. Hawaii: Pukui-Curtis, n.d., 42ff.

Q151.13. Women rewarded with their lives for excellent dancing. Tuamotus: Stimson, n.d., Z-G. 3/1260.

Q152. City saved from disaster as reward. Hawaii: Beckwith, 1940, 63, 70.

Q172. Reward: admission to heaven. Futuna: Burrows, 1936, 105.

Q172.9. Reward: deification. Tahiti: Beckwith, 1940, 38.

Q200--Q399. Deeds punished

Q211. Murder punished. Tuamotus: Stimson, n.d., T-G. 3/818, Z-G. 3/1353, Z-G. 13/127; Societies: Caillot, 1914, 133f.; Hawaii: Fornander, 1918, V, 516; Remy, 1868, 38; Thrum, 1907, 224ff., 228f.; Westervelt, 1915, 57; Tonga: Reiter, 1933, 372; N.Z.: White, 1887-90, II, 148f., 150; Tikopia: Firth, 1961, 135; Bellona: Elbert-Monberg, 1964, No. 59.

Q211.0.3.+ Murder by sorcery punished. Rennell: Elbert-Monberg, 1964, No. 110.

Q211.4. Murder of children punished. Tuamotus:
Stimson, n.d., T-G. 3/15.

Q211.6. Killing an animal revenged. Hawaii:
Thrum, 1907, 274.

Q211.6.2. Punishment for killing sacred (pet) whale
(fish, turtle). Polynesia: *Beckwith, 1940,
504f.; Tuamotus: Beckwith, 1940, 505; Caillot,
1914, 87; Seurat, 1905, 436; Marquesas: Handy,
1930, 62; Cooks: Te Ariki, 1899, 174f.; Tonga:
Gifford, 1924, 143; Samoa: Beckwith, 1940, 505;
Brown, 1917, 96; Krämer, 1902, I, 130; Sierich,
1902, 170; Tokelau: Burrows, 1923, 158f.;
N.Z.: Beckwith, 1940, 505; White, 1887-90,
II, 130, 140, 146.

Q211.7.+ Punishment for cannibalism. N.Z.: Grey,
1855, 131.

Q211.12. Punishment for murder of parents (relatives).
Easter I.: Métraux, 1940, 385; Tuamotus:
Stimson, n.d., T-G. 3/818; Marquesas: Steinen,
1933-34, 39, 332; Tonga: Gifford, 1924, 53;
Chatham I.: Beckwith, 1940, 474.

Q211.13.+ Wizard's familiar punishes tribe of
sorcerer who killed its master. N.Z.: Grace,
1907, 190.

Q212. Theft punished. Easter I.: Métraux, 1940,
378; Hawaii: Beckwith, 1940, 122; Westervelt,
1915, 160f.; Samoa: Krämer, 1902, I, 129;
Tokelau: Burrows, 1923, 169f.; N.Z.: Grace,
1907, 38; Kapingamarangi: Emory, 1949, 233.

Q215. Cannibalism punished. Marquesas: Lavondes,
1964, 72.

Q217.+ Arson punished. N.Z.: Grace, 1907, 151.

Q220. Impiety punished. Hawaii: Beckwith, 1940,
18; Rice, 1923, 123.

Q220.1.+ Man violating tabu is killed. Mangareva:
Hiroa, 1938, 49, 422; Hawaii: Thrum, 1923, 49.

Q221. Personal offences against gods punished.
Marquesas: Handy, 1930, 133; Hawaii: *Beckwith,
1940, 132, 190 nn. 1-2, 233; Fornander, 1916, IV,
230.

Q221.1. Discourtesy to god punished. Easter I.:
Métraux, 1940, 141; Societies: Henry, 1928,
382; Niue: Loeb, 1926, 190; Hawaii: Thrum,
1907, 40; Samoa: Stuebel, 1896, 67, 147;
N.Z.: White, 1887-90, III, 279.

Q221.3. Blasphemy punished. (Blasphemer of Christian
God blinded by lightning.) Niue: Loeb, 1926,
37.

Q221.8.+ Man who mocks sacred animal has stomach swell,
dies. Niue: Loeb, 1926, 170.

Q221.8.+ Men boast they are gods: afterwards, nothing
prospers for them. Fijis: Fison, 1904, 71f.

Q221.8.+ As punishment for broken vow to goddess of
cold, a man's bride is made numb with cold on their
wedding night. Hawaii: Beckwith, 1919, 484ff.

Q221.8.+ Girl who compares her beauty with that of
goddess is killed. Hawaii: Fornander, 1918,
VI, 343.

Q221.8.+ Theft from gods punished. Hawaii: Thrum,
1923, 260.

Q222. Punishment for desecration of holy places
(images, etc.). Hawaii: Beckwith, 1940, 361;
Green, 1926, 120f.; Thrum, 1907, 187; N.Z.:
Beckwith, 1940, 260.

Q222.6.+ Two boys put to death for playing sacred
drum. Hawaii: Westervelt, 1915, 51.

Q222.6.+ Any person touched by temple smoke is
sacrificed. Hawaii: Green, 1926, 123.

Q222.6.+ People caught abroad during time of sacred
assembly are killed. Samoa: Krämer, 1902, I,
257.

Q223. Punishment for neglect of services to gods (God).
Easter I.: Métraux, 1940, 329; Marquesas: Handy,
1930, 81; Pukapuka: Hutchin, 1904, 174.

Q223.14. Punishment for failure to give customary
offering to gods. Marquesas: Handy, 1930, 81;
Easter I.: Métraux, 1940, 329.

Q227.3.+ Death as punishment for those disbelieving
prophet. Hawaii: Beckwith, 1919, 582.

430

Q235.1.+ Woman who cursed the moon translated there as punishment. N.Z.: White, 1887-90, II, 21, 26.

Q237.+ Incessant invocation of gods punished. Hawaii: Green, 1926, 61ff.

Q241. Adultery punished. Easter I.: Métraux, 1940, 114; Tuamotus: Luomala, 1949, 81; Stimson, 1937, 38; Marquesas: Handy, 1930, 113, 118; Lavondes, 1964, 106; Cooks: Large, 1903, 136; Hawaii: Beckwith, 1919, 612; 1940, 170, 500; Emerson, 1915, 193ff.; Fornander, 1918, V, 310; Green, 1926, 93; Thrum, 1907, 123; Tonga: Gifford, 1924, 76, 119; Reiter, 1933, 380; Samoa: Krämer, 1902, I, 257; Niue: Loeb, 1926, 170; N.Z.: Beattie, 1920, 193; Rennell: Elbert-Monberg, 1964, Nos. 196, 198.

Q244. Punishment for ravisher. Tuamotus: Stimson, 1934, 36; Samoa: Stuebel, 1896, 68.

Q244.1. Punishment for attempted rape. N.Z.: White, 1887-90, II, 76, 80, 84, 115f.

Q246.1. Goddess killed for infidelity with mortal. Hawaii: Beckwith, 1940, 37.

Q252.1. Wife-stealing punished with death. Marquesas: Handy, 1930, 103.

Q253.1. Bestiality punished. Marquesas: Handy, 1930, 121; Samoa: Beckwith, 1940, 103.

Q257.+ Men lying about seducing girl punished by death. Hawaii: Thrum, 1907, 130.

Q261. Treachery punished. Tuamotus: Stimson, n.d., T-G. 3/711; Hawaii: Beckwith, 1940, 153; Green, 129, 109; Rotuma: Russell, 1942, 248ff.

Q261.2. Treacherous wife punished. Tonga: Collocott, 1928, 43; Samoa: Krämer, 1902, I, 142.

Q262. Imposter punished. Samoa: Stuebel, 1896, 148.

Q263. Lying (perjury) punished. Tuamotus: Stimson, n.d., T-G. 3/711; Hawaii: Beckwith, 1940, 153; Thrum, 1923, 41.

Q266. Punishment for breaking promise. Hawaii: Beckwith, 1919, 486.

Q268.+ Woman stowaway upon canoe punished. Tonga:
Brown, 1916, 426.

Q272. Greed (gluttony) punished. Tuamotus: Beckwith,
1940, 504; Cooks: Gill, 1876, 221f.; Tonga:
Gifford, 1924, 207; N.Z.: Beckwith, 1940, 374.

Q274. Swindler punished. Easter I.: Métraux, 1940,
87f.

Q276. Stinginess punished. Hawaii: Beckwith, 1940,
390; Bellona: Elbert-Monberg, 1964, No. 66;
Rennell: ibid., Nos. 67, 81.

Q280. Unkindness punished. Kapingamarangi: Elbert,
1949, 243.

Q281. Ingratitude punished. Tonga: Beckwith, 1940,
504; Samoa: Beckwith, 1940, 505; N.Z.:
Beckwith, 1940, 505; Ellice Is.: David, 1899,
100; Kennedy, 1931, 162; Kapingamarangi:
Emory, 1949, 236.

Q285. Cruelty punished. Australs: Aitken, 1930, 109;
Mangareva: Hiroa, 1938, 377; Hawaii: Thrum,
1907, 130.

Q285.1. Cruelty to animals punished. Hawaii: Pukui,
1933, 175.

Q286. Uncharitableness punished. Futuna: Burrows,
1936, 225.

Q286.1. Uncharitableness to holy person punished.
Hawaii: Beckwith, 1940, 192.

Q292. Inhospitality punished. Hawaii: Beckwith, 1940,
174.

Q292.1. Inhospitality to saint (god) punished. Hawaii:
Emerson, 1915, 187.

Q312. Fault-finding punished. Tuamotus: Stimson, n.d.,
T-G. 3/59.

Q322. Dirtiness punished. Marquesas: Steinen,
1933-34, 28.

Q322.+ Person killed for urinating in water hole.
Bellona: Elbert-Monberg, 1964, No. 139.

Q325. Disobedience punished. Hawaii: McAllister, 1933, 155; Fijis: Fison, 1904, 83f.; Hocart, 1929, 204.

Q325.+ Sacred image which refuses to board a canoe is smashed. Hawaii: Green, 1929, 59.

Q326. Impudence punished. N.Z.: Grace, 1907, 85f.; 159; Tikopia: Firth, 1961, 135.

Q341. Curiosity punished. Hawaii: Beckwith, 1940, 135.

Q380.+ Weakness punished. Hawaii: Beckwith, 1940, 100.

Q395. Disrespect punished. Mangareva: Laval, 1938, 135f.; Societies: Beckwith, 1940, 244; Hawaii: Beckwith, 1940, 411; Fornander, 1918, V, 158; Samoa: Krämer, 1902, I, 416; Ellice Is.: Roberts, 1958, 401.

Q395.+ Mischievous youngster is killed for urinating upon sleepers. Ellice Is.: Roberts, 1958, 398f.

Q400--Q599. Kinds of punishment

Q411. Death as punishment. Tuamotus: Stimson, 1934, 36; Hawaii: Fornander, 1916, IV, 26; 1918, V, 158; Green, 1923, 44f.; Thrum, 1923, 260; Westervelt, 1915, 160f.; 183; Tonga: Collocott, 1928, 43; Samoa: Krämer, 1902, I, 130, 142, 416; Stuebel, 1896, 147; N.Z.: Grace, 1907, 151; White, 1887-90, II, 76, 80, 84, 115f.; Rotuma: Russell, 1942, 248f.; Rennell: Elbert-Monberg, 1964, No. 110.

Q411.0.1. Husband kills returning adulteress. Hawaii: Fornander, 1918, V, 188ff.; Kamakau, 1961, 48; Thrum, 1923, 112; N.Z.: White, Dixon, 1916, 80; White, 1887-90, II, 36, 45; III, 14.

Q411.0.1.1. Adulterer killed. Samoa: Krämer, 1902, I, 383; N.Z.: White, 1887-90, III, 14.

Q411.15.+ Priest making an error in ceremony is killed. N.Z.: White, 1887-90, III, 112.

Q413. Punishment: hanging. Marquesas: Handy, 1930, 63.

Q414. Punishment: burning alive. Ellice Is.: Kennedy, 1931, 199; N.Z.: White, 1887-90, II, 148f., 150.

Q415.9. Punishment: being eaten by fish. Tuamotus: Stimson, n.d., Z-G. 3/1301; Hawaii: Beckwith, 1940, 504; Niue: Loeb, 1926, 176; Rotuma: Churchward, 1938-39, 230.

Q418. Punishment by poisoning. Samoa: Krämer, 1902, I, 416; Stuebel, 1896, 68.

Q421. Punishment: beheading. N.Z.: White, 1887-90, II, 36, 45.

Q424. Punishment: strangling. Marquesas: Handy, 1930, 113, 129; Hawaii: Thrum, 1923, 196.

Q428. Punishment: drowning. Marquesas: Lavondes, 1964, 106; N.Z.: Grace, 1907, 159.

Q429.4.+ Punishment: disembowlment. Tonga: Brown, 1916, 426; Reiter, 1933, 372.

Q431. Punishment: banishment (exile). Societies: Henry, 1928, 543; Hawaii: Beckwith, 1940, 205, 214; Samoa: Krämer, 1902, I, 140.

Q431.19.+ Women taken to the moon as a punishment for insulting this orb. N.Z.: *Best, 1899, 100; Best, 1925, 803.

Q433. Punishment: imprisonment. Hawaii: Thrum, 1923, 41.

Q433.2.+ Demon condemned to live in sea (for eating human flesh). Tuamotus: Stimson, n.d., Z-G. 13/301.

Q433.2.+ Rebel god punished by being sent to lower world. Beckwith, 1940, 60.

Q451. Mutilation as punishment. Marquesas: Handy, 1930, 78, 121.

Q451.10. Punishment: genitalia cut off. Bellona: Elbert-Monberg, 1964, No. 59.

Q451.11. Piecemeal mutilation as punishment. Marquesas:
Handy, 1930, 78; Tonga: Gifford, 1924, 67;
Mangareva: Laval, 1938, 135f.; N.Z.: Grace,
1907, 38.

Q467.5. Marooning as punishment. Hawaii: Beckwith,
1940, 499f.; Tuamotus: Stimson, n.d.,
Z-G. 13/346.

Q478.1. The Eaten Heart. Adulteress is caused
unwittingly to eat her lover's heart. (Sometimes
other parts of his body.) Marquesas: Handy,
1930, 104; Hawaii: Beckwith, 1940, 136; Chatham
I.: Shand,1894, 193; Niue: Loeb, 1926, 170.

Q478.1.4.+ Man feeds his adulterous wife's heart to
their son. N.Z.: White, 1887-90, III, 14.

Q478.5.+ Punishment: eating foods tabu to eater.
Mangareva: Hiroa, 1938, 377.

Q482. Punishment: noble person must do menial service.
Stimson, n.d., Z-G. 13/48, Z-G. 3/1386.

Q495.+ Woman paraded nude as punishment. Ellice Is.:
Roberts, 1958, 401.

Q499.8.+ Man avenges insult to wife by feeding oily
fish to offenders,who disgrace themselves with
incontinent bowel movements. N.Z.: White,
1887-90, III, 43, 59.

Q499.8.+ Warrior urinates upon head of defeated enemy.
N.Z.: White, 1887-90, IV, 80, 90; V, 118.

Q499.8.+ Captive must serve as latrine attendant.
Mangareva: Hiroa, 1938, 328.

Q499.8.+ Person's body used as receptacle for filth.
Tuamotus: Stimson, 1934, 50.

Q503.1.+ Origin of first ghost: punishment for
adultery. Hawaii: Beckwith, 1919, 612.

Q551.3. Punishment: transformation. Tuamotus:
Stimson, 1937, 48.

Q551.6. Magic sickness as punishment. Tikopia: Firth,
1961, 135.

Q552.1. Death by thunderbolt as punishment. Hawaii:
McAllister, 1933, 155; Samoa: Stuebel, 1896, 67.

Q552.2. Sinking of earth as punishment. Tuamotus:
Henry, 1928, 511.

Q552.2.0.1. Quaking of earth as punishment. Hawaii:
Thrum, 1907, 40.

Q552.2.3.2.3.+ Island turned over as punishment.
Marquesas: Handy, 1930, 99.

Q552.3.1. Famine as punishment. Hawaii: Remy, 1868,
38; Ontong Java: Sarfert, 1931, 407.

Q552.3.1.1.+ Sterility of land as punishment.
Ellice Is.: Roberts, 1958, 406.

Q552.3.3. Drought as punishment. Hawaii: Beckwith,
1940, 431; Fornander, 1918, V, 516.

Q552.12 Punishment: shipwreck. Samoa: Stuebel, 1896,
148; Tokelau: Burrows, 1923, 169f.

Q552.14. Storm as punishment. Mangareva: Laval, 1938,
300; Hawaii: Fornander, 1918, V, 14; N.Z.: Grace,
1907, 85f.; Tikopia: Firth, 1961, 135.

Q552.19. Miraculous drowning as punishment. Tuamotus:
Stimson, n.d., Z-G. 13/167; Samoa: Stuebel,
1896, 148; Ellice Is.: Kennedy, 1931, 213.

Q552.19.6. Flood as punishment for murder. Hawaii:
Thrum, 1907, 191, 243; Westervelt, 1915, 57.

Q552.24. Punishment: lava flow. Hawaii: Beckwith,
1940, 500; Rice, 1923, 16; Thrum, 1907, 40.

Q555. Madness as punishment. Niue: Loeb, 1926, 36.

Q557. Miraculous punishment through animals. Hawaii:
Beckwith, 1940, 467.

Q557.8.+ Miraculous punishment through fish. Tuamotus:
Stimson, n.d., Z-G. 13/203, Z-G. 3/1301; Beckwith,
1940, 504; Marquesas: Handy, 1930, 127; Fijis:
Hocart, 1929, 212; Ontong Java, Nukumanu: Sarfert,
1931, 427.

Q559.11.+ Rock used as latrine punishes people by
leaving island, thus depriving them of good
harbor. Futuna: Burrows, 1936, 225f.

436

Q581.3.+ Boy who kills his grandfather is in turn slain by his father. Tonga: Collocott, 1921, 47.

Q581.3.+ Man who kills caterpillars is in turn killed by them. Hawaii: Green, 1923, 44f.

Q581.3.+ Children sent to feed a dragon eat its food. Dragon eats them. N.Z.: Cowan, 1925, 80ff.

Q581.3.+ Wizard evokes spell to kill first woman coming up path. Victim proves to be his sweetheart. N.Z.: Grace, 1907, 188.

Q581.3.+ Hero slays warrior who defeated his father. Tonga: Brown, 1916, 429f.

Q581.3.+ A killed squid comes alive; its killer acquires an unappeasible appetite for squid. Hawaii: Pukui, 1933, 175.

Q582.9.+ People practicing sorcery are themselves killed by magic. Hawaii: Pukui, 1933, 156f.

Q582.9.+ Greedy chief who always takes his subjects' fish is given so many fish that his boat sinks and he drowns. Hawaii: Green, 1926, 87ff.

Q582.9.+ Person who persecutes fisherman chokes to death on a fish. Hawaii: Thrum, 1907, 228f.; 1921, 106; 1923, 202.

Q582.9.+ Man eats fish which ate his son. N.Z.: Grace, 1907, 60.

Q582.9.+ Treacherous tribesmen who intend to massacre a group of guests are themselves murdered. N.Z.: White, 1887-90, V, 92f.

Q585.4.+ People wasteful of fish punished when all fish leave their district. Hawaii: Thrum, 1907, 224f., 240.

Q589.3.+ Fisherman who eats rare fish without giving chief his share is made to eat meal of fishes' scales. Samoa: Krämer, 1902, I, 458.

Q599.+ An affronted god betrays his worshipper to enemies. N.Z.: White, 1887-90, III, 279.

Q599.+ Girl disinherited for marrying person not chosen by her family. Hawaii: Beckwith, 1919, 512.

Q599.+ Person magically made hot as punishment. Hawaii: Beckwith, 1919, 486.

R. CAPTIVES AND FUGITIVES

R0--R99. Captivity

R10. Abduction. Rotuma: Russell, 1942, 248.

R10.1. Princess (maiden) abducted. Mangareva:
Hiroa, 1938, 377; Laval, 1938, 300; Tuamotus:
Audran, 1919, n. 35, 50f.; Stimson, n.d.,
Z-G. 13/4, T-G. 3/900; 1934, 35ff.; Marquesas:
Lavondes, 1964, 4, 52; Hawaii: Fornander,
1918, V, 236; Tonga: Collocott, 1928, 14, 17;
Niue: Smith, 1903, 5; N.Z.: White, 1887-90,
II, 38, 132; III, 137; IV, 49ff., 200ff.;
Rennell: Elbert-Monberg, 1964, No. 179;
Bellona: ibid., No. 180.

R10.3. Child(ren) abducted. Australs: Aitken,
1923, 276; Hawaii: Kamakau, 1961, 67; Samoa:
Krämer, 1902, I, 198.

R11. Abduction by monster (ogre). Marquesas:
Lavondes, 1964, 4; N.Z.: Best, 1925, 715, 919;
Bellona: Elbert-Monberg, 1964, No. 58.

R11.1. Princess (maiden) abducted by monster (ogre).
Tuamotus: Stimson, n.d., Z-G. 3/1386, Z-G.
13/174; N.Z.: Best, 1925, 188.

R11.2.2. Abduction by demon. Tuamotus: Stimson, n.d.,
Z-G. 3/1386; 1934, 50; 1937, 72; Hawaii:
Fornander, 1916, IV, 522; N.Z.: Grace, 1907, 64,
112, 210; Rennell: Bradley, 1956, 336.

R13.3. Person carried off by bird. Tuamotus:
Beckwith, 1940, 261; Henry, 1928, 496; Stimson,
n.d., Z-G. 3/1260; 1937, 100; Societies: Orsmond,
1933a, 172; Hawaii: Beckwith, 1940, 233; Westervelt, 1915, 68f.; N.Z.: Smith, 1897, 22: White,
1887-90, II, 132.

R13.3.2.+ Person abducted by bat. Tuamotus: Stimson,
1937, 44ff.; Hawaii: Thrum, 1923, 252ff.

R13.4.1. Abduction by snake. N.Z.: Best, 1893, 217.

R13.4.1.+ Sea-creature abduction of persons. Tuamotus:
Beckwith, 1940, 289; Stimson, n.d., Z-G. 3/1117.

R13.4.1.+ Abduction by a fish (eel). Mangareva: Laval, 1938, 306f.; Tuamotus: Seurat, 1905, 481.

R14. Deity (demigod) abducts person. Mangareva: Hiroa, 1938, 316; Hawaii: Fornander, 1918, V, 364.

R22.1.+ Abduction during sleep (often person's bed or part of house carried along). Easter I.: Métraux, 1940, 365; Knoche, 1920, 66; Marquesas: Handy, 1930, 24; Cooks: Te Ariki, 1899, 173; Samoa: Brown, 1917, 96.

R32. Abduction by stealing clothes of bathers. Oceania: **Lessa, 1961, 38f., 120ff.; Mangareva: Hiroa, 1938, 20f.; Samoa: Powell-Pratt, 1892, 98; Niue: Smith, 1903, 104; N.Z.: Best, 1925, 870.

> D361.1. Swan-maiden. K1335. Seduction (or wooing) by stealing clothes of bathing girl.

R39.1. Abduction by magician. Hawaii: Beckwith, 1919, 504ff.

R39.2.+ Man made captive by reptile-woman. N.Z.: Beckwith, 1940, 195.

R39.2.+ Abduction by mermaid. Hawaii: Green, 1926, 113.

R39.2.+ Abduction by moon. N.Z.: *Best, 1899, 100f.; Clark, 1896, 181 n.

R39.2.+ Girl borne away in a mist. Hawaii: Beckwith, 1940, 515.

R41.6. Captivity in a pillar (housepost). N.Z.: White, 1887-90, II, 162.

R41.7.+ Man keeps wife prisoner in hut surrounded by nets. Australs: Aitken, 1923, 241; Rennell: Elbert-Monberg, 1964, Nos. 228a, 228b.

R43. Captivity on island. Mangareva: Hiroa, 1938, 379ff.; N.Z.: White, 1887-90, V, 43.

R43.+ Captivity on floating island. Hawaii: Fornander, 1916, IV, 436ff.

R45.1. Man confined under roots of tree. Marquesas: Handy, 1930, 109.

R45.3. Captivity in cave (pit). (Cf. S146.). Hawaii:
    Fornander, 1916, IV, 64; Thrum, 1906, 131; 1907,
    22; Westervelt, 1915, 153; Samoa: Krämer, 1902,
    I, 258; Sierich, 1902, 167; Stuebel, 1896, 66;
    N.Z.: Best, 1893, 217; Smith, 1911, 13; Union
    Group: Smith, 1911, 13.

R46. Captivity under water. Mangareva: Laval, 1938,
    300; Tuamotus: Caillot, 1914, 57ff.; Hawaii:
    Fornander, 1916, IV, 44; Green, 1926, 113;
    Samoa: Stuebel, 1896, 144; N.Z.: White,
    1887-90, II, 162.

R47. Captivity in lower world. Mangareva: Hiroa,
    1938, 374; Tonga: Collocott, 1928, 14, 17.

R49.1. Captivity in tree. Tuamotus: Stimson, n.d.,
    T-G. 3/59; Marquesas: Lavondes, 1966, 78, 150.

R49.3.+ Captivity in the sky. Marquesas: Lavondes,
    1964, 52; Hawaii: Fornander, 1916, IV, 522;
    Samoa: Stuebel, 1896, 144.

R49.3.+ Captivity on inaccessible cliff (mountainside).
    Easter I.: Knoche, 1920, 66; Marquesas:
    Lavondes, 1964, 4; Societies: Henry, 1928, 223;
    Cooks: Te Ariki, 1920, 124; N.Z.: Cowan, 1930,
    121f.

R49.3.+ Captivity beneath stone. Ellice Is.: Kennedy,
    1931, 192.

R49.3.+ Captivity in a basket. Tonga: Brown, 1916,
    431; Rennell: Elbert-Monberg, 1964, No. 20.

R49.3.+ Prisoner kept immersed in latrine. Tuamotus:
    Leverd, 1911, 176; Stimson, n.d., T-G. 2/5,
    Z-G. 3/1146; Societies: Beckwith, 1940, 246;
    Henry, 1928, 561.

R51.1. Prisoners starved. Kapingamarangi: Elbert,
    1949, 243.

R51.4.+ Captive's body used as basket or holder.
    Tuamotus: Beckwith, 1940, 261, 267; Henry,
    1928, 509; Stimson, n.d., T-G. 1/18; Societies:
    Henry, 1928, 496.

R111. Rescue of captive maiden. Hawaii: Fornander,
    1918, V, 186; Kapingamarangi: Elbert, 1949, 243.

R111.1.5.+ Rescue of princess from giant snake.
Tonga: Gifford, 1924, 177.

R111.2.1. Princess (woman) rescued from lower world.
Marquesas: Lavondes, 1964, 82; Hawaii: Thrum,
1923, 81.

R111.3.1. Girl rescued by traveling through air.
Kapingamarangi: Elbert, 1949, 243.

R121.2. Rescuer impersonates captive and deceives
blind guardian while captive escapes. Cook Is.:
Dixon, 1916, 75.

R131.8. Other workmen rescue abandoned child. N.Z.:
Gudgeon, 1906, 48.

R135.1.1.+ Person breaks branches to mark his path,
but adversary magically restores the plants.
Rennell: Elbert-Monberg, 1964, No. 88.

R151. Husband rescues wife. Hawaii: Beckwith, 1940,
227.

R152. Wife rescues husband. Hawaii: Beckwith, 1940,
539; Bellona: Elbert-Monberg, 1964, Nos. 1a, 1b.

R153.3. Father rescues son(s). Marquesas: Handy,
1930, 63.

R153.3.1. Father rescues captured son. Tuamotus:
Stimson, n.d., Z-G. 3/1260.

R154. Children (child) rescues parents. Mangareva:
Hiroa, 1938, 328.

R154.1. Son rescues mother. Tuamotus: Beckwith, 1940,
268; Hawaii: Beckwith, 1940, 227.

R154.2. Son rescues father. Tuamotus: Stimson, n.d.,
Z-G. 3/1146; Manihiki, Chatham I., N.Z.:
*Beckwith, 1940, 196, 196 n. 18.

R154.2.2. Son recovers father's bones. Hawaii:
Beckwith, 1940, 259, 263, 346f.: Tahiti: ibid.,
266; Maori: ibid., *249.

R156. Brother rescues sister(s). Kapingamarangi:
Elbert, 1948, 78.

R157. Sisters rescue sisters. Hawaii: Beckwith, 1940, 213.

R161.1. Lover rescues his lady from abductor. Tuamotus: Stimson, n.d., Z-G. 13/174.

R169.16.+ Woman on porpoise saves shipwrecked mariner. Marquesas: Tahiaoteaa, 1933, 492.

R169.16.+ Sea-monster as rescuer. N.Z.: White, 1887-90, V, 43.

R200--R299. Escapes and pursuits

R211. Escape from prison. Rennell: Elbert-Monberg, 1964, Nos. 228a, 228b.

R211.3. Escape (from beleagured fortress) through underground passage. N.Z.: Cowan, 1930, I, 130f.; White, 1887-90, IV, 190.

R215. Escape from execution. Tonga: Collocott, 1928, 27, 32, 33.

R215.1.+ Escape from pyre by praying for rain. Tuamotus: Beckwith, 1940, 503.

R219.2.+ Escape from house through smoke hole. N.Z.: Beckwith, 1940, 250; Cowan, 1921, 145; Cook Is.: Te Ariki, 1920, 123; Ellice Is.: Kennedy, 1931, 194.

R219.2.+ Escape (from island or raft at sea) by clutching legs or wings of great bird. Hawaii: Thrum, 1923, 184; Tonga: Gifford, 1924, 139; Beckwith, 1940, 504; Samoa: Brown, 1917, 95; Fijis: Fison, 1904, 4; Hocart, 1929, 205; Ellice Is.: Kennedy, 1931, 168; Rennell: Elbert-Monberg, 1964, No. 13.

R253. Escape from nest of giant bird by seizing two young birds and jumping.

R228.+ Girl punished (for allowing bark cloth to get wet) runs away from home. Mangareva: Hiroa, 1938, 313; Tokelau: Burrows, 1923, 155ff.

R231. Obstacle flight -- Atalanta type. Oceania:

**Lessa, 1961, 403ff.; Hawaii: Beckwith, 1940, 431; Tokelau: Burrows, 1923, 156; N.Z.: Cowan, 1930, I, 108.

R231.2.1.+ Atalanta pursuit reversed: pursuing ogre magically causes food to appear before fugitives; they linger to eat it. Tonga: Collocott, 1928, 60.

R236.1. Fugitive aided by magic mist. N.Z.: White, 1887-90, III, 258.

R236.4.+ Persons descend from cliff cave by means of a rainbow. Hawaii: Fornander, 1916, IV, 66.

R242. Flight carrying friend (girl, child) on back. N.Z.: Cowan, 1930, I, 220f.

R245. Whale-boat. Tuamotus: Beckwith, 1940, 505; Caillot, 1914, 78; Seurat, 1905, 435; Stimson, n.d., T-G. 3/912; Marquesas: Lavondes, 1964, 66; Hawaii: Thrum, 1923, 305; Tonga: Gifford, 1924, 142; Tonga, Samoa, N.Z.: *Beckwith, 1940, 504f.; Samoa: Brown, 1917, 95; Krämer, 1902, I, 130; N.Z.: Best, 1925, 773; White, 1887-90, II, 129, 133, 136f., 145; Ellice Is.: Kennedy, 1931, 178.

> B541.1. Escape from sea on fish's back. K952.1.2. Ungrateful rat defecates upon head of (or kills) octopus that rescues him from sea. M205.1.1. Turtle carrying man through water upsets him because of broken promise. W154.9. Man rescued from drowning kills rescuer.

R245.2.+ Defeated warriors escape their foes while riding upon shark's back. Lau Is.: St. Johnston, 1918, 129.

R261.1. Pursuit by rolling head. Hawaii: Beckwith, 1940, 198; Fornander, 1918, V, 528; Thrum, 1923, 243f.

R261.1.+ Pursuit by headless body. Marquesas: Steinen, 1934-35, 227; Hawaii: Beckwith, 1940, 93.

R262. Magic (extraordinary) eel (fish) pursues person over land. (Cf. Kirtley, 1967.) Tuamotus: Caillot, 1914, 105; Tahiti: Beckwith, 1940, 103; Tonga:

Gifford, 1924, 98; Samoa: Andersen, 1925, 143;
Krämer, 1902, I, 439; Nelson, 1925, 132;
Powell-Pratt, 1892, 254ff.; Stuebel, 1896, 68.

R272.+ Ogress swims in relentless pursuit of ship.
Societies: Leverd, 1912, 2; Chatham Is.: Shand,
1896, 195; N.Z.: White, 1887-90, II, 56.

R272.+ Pursuit into sky. Samoa: Rose, 1959, 174.

R272.+ Pursuit upon a sea-dragon. Hawaii: Emerson,
1915, XIV, f.

R300--R399. Refuges and Recapture

R311. Tree refuge. Tuamotus: Audran, 1918, 29ff.;
Marquesas: Lavondes, 1964, 88ff.; N.Z.: Best,
1925, 768; Grace, 1907, 242ff.; Ellice Is.:
Kennedy, 1931, 206; Rennell: Elbert-Monberg,
1964, No. 13.

R311.1.+ Tree magically opens and hides fugitive.
Hawaii: Westervelt, 1915a, 31.

R315. Cave as refuge. Easter I.: Métraux, 1940,
368, 381; Mangareva: Laval, 1938, 144; Hawaii:
Dickey, 1917, 29; Fornander, 1918, V, 430;
Tonga: Collocott, 1921, 51f.; Reiter, 1919-20,
125; Samoa: Nelson, 1925, 140; Reef Is.:
O'Ferrall, 1904, 232.

R315.2.+ Refuge in a stone. N.Z.: Cowan, 1925, 123f.

R327. Earth opens to rescue fugitive. Oceania: **Lessa
1961; Hawaii: Pukui-Curtis, n.d., 39; Westervelt,
1915, 260.

R336.+ Goddess takes refuge in her giant brother's
loin-cloth. Hawaii: Emerson, 1915, IX.

R345. Cities of refuge. Hawaii: Dickey, 1917, 15;
Thrum, 1906, 133.

R345.+ Mountain refuge. Marquesas: Handy, 1930, 110.

R345.+ Refuge within friendly animal. Hawaii: Beckwith
1940, 500; Rice, 1923, 31.

R355.+ Harbor entrance closed against escaping canoe's
egress by a wizard. N.Z.: White, 1887-90, V, 12.

444

S. UNNATURAL CRUELTY

S0--S99. Cruel relatives

S10. Cruel parents. Marquesas: Lavondes, 1966, 2;
Hawaii: Rice 1923, 91.

S11. Cruel father. Tuamotus: Stimson, n.d., Z-G.
13/346; Societies: Beckwith, 1940, 471; Hawaii:
Thrum, 1906, 129ff.; Cooks: Large, 1903, 135;
Tonga: Gifford, 1924, 24; Niue: Loeb, 1926,
156; N.Z.: Gudgeon, 1906, 48; White, 1887-90,
III, 14.

S11.1. Father mutilates children. Rennell: Elbert-
Monberg, 1964, No. 31a, No. 33

S11.1.+ Father cuts open son's stomach to see if boy
had eaten stolen fruit. Hawaii: Thrum, 1923, 49.

S11.3. Father kills child. Hawaii: Beckwith, 1919,
344; Tonga: Collocott, 1921, 47; N.Z.: Best,
1925, 977.

S11.3.3. Father kills son (with spade). Tonga:
Caillot, 1914, 277.

S11.3.3.2. Father murders his two sons for whining.
Tonga: Gifford, 1924, 24.

S11.3.8. Father eats own children. Tonga: Collocott,
1928, 38; Rennell: Elbert-Monberg, 1964, No. 205.

S12. Cruel mother. Marquesas: Handy, 1930, 38;
Cooks: Clark, 1896, 77; Hawaii: Beckwith, 1940,
506, 508.

S12.2. Cruel mother kills child. Hawaii: Thrum, 1923,
227; Samoa: Krämer, 1902, I, 270; N.Z.: White,
1887-90, II, 169.

S20.2. Child hides food from starving parents.
Marquesas: Handy, 1930, 114.

S21. Cruel son. Marquesas: Handy, 1930, 114;
Hawaii: Beckwith, 1940, 508; Cooks: Te Ariki,
1921, 2; Niue: Loeb, 1926, 77; Tonga: Gifford,
1924, 189; N.Z.: White, 1887-90, IV, 241ff.

S21.1.+ Infant born without head, arms or legs, bores way into woman, kills her. Marquesas: Steinen, 1934-35, 227.

S22. Parricide. Marquesas: Lavondes, 1966, 128, 162; Tonga: Gifford, 1924, 189.

S31. Cruel stepmother. Mangareva: Hiroa, 1938, 376f.; Hawaii: *Dixon, 1916, 88, nn. 97ff.; Thrum, 1907, 133ff.; N.Z.: Grace, 1907, 224ff.; Chatham I.: Shand, 1896, 196.

S36. Cruel foster father. Hawaii: Beckwith, 1940, 480.

S54. Cruel daughter-in-law. Marquesas: Handy, 1930, 111.

S56. Cruel son-in-law. Marquesas: Handy, 1930, 126.

S56.+ Cruel brother-in-law. Chatham I.: Shand, 1894, 193.

S62. Cruel husband. Marquesas: Handy, 1930, 99; Tuamotus: Stimson, n.d., T-G. 3/59; Societies: Henry, 1928, 544, 589f.; Cooks: Te Ariki, 1920, 125; Hawaii: Beckwith, 1940, 152; Rennell: Elbert-Monberg, 1964, No. 195a.

S63.+ Cruel wife. Easter I.: Métraux, 1940, 385; Niue: Loeb, 1926, 78.

S71. Cruel uncle. Mangareva: Caillot, 1914, 167; Hiroa, 1938, 32f., 382; Laval, 1938, 39; Marquesas: Steinen, 1934-35, 219; Samoa: Beckwith, 1940, 473; Krämer, 1902, I, 270; Hawaii: Beckwith, 1940, 422; Thrum, 1907, 143; N.Z.: White, 1887-90, IV, 185; V, 25.

S72. Cruel aunt. Easter I.: Métraux, 1940, 383.

S73. Cruel (elder) brother(s). Tuamotus: Stimson, n.d., T-G. 3/615; Cooks: Browne, 1897, 6; Te Ariki, 1920, 116; Hawaii: Beckwith, 1940, 436; Fornander, 1916, IV, 23f., 32ff., 132, 186, 522; Kamakau, 1961, 10; Thrum, 1923, 32, 79ff.; Tonga: Gifford, 1924, 27, 83; Beckwith, 1940, 483; Samoa: Krämer, 1902, 125; Chatham I.: Shand, 1896, 202; N.Z.: Clark, 1896, 157; White, 1887-

90, I, 57, 97, 11f.;   III, 133f.;   Wohlers,
1876, 115;   Rennell: Elbert-Monberg, 1964, No. 209;
Nukumanu, Ontong Java: Sarfert, 1931, 411.

S73.1.   Fratricide. Mangareva: Hiroa, 1938, 22, 316;
Laval, 1938, 300;   Marquesas: Handy, 1930, 53;
Tuamotus: Stimson, n.d., T-G. 3/615;   Tonga:
Gifford, 1924, 83;   Caillot, 1914, 259 n. 2;
Collocott, 1928, 51;   Reiter, 1933, 359;   N.Z.:
White, 1887-90, I, 57;   Beckwith, 1940, 157;
Clark, 1896, 157;   Rennell: Elbert-Monberg, 1964,
No. 209;   Nukumanu: Sarfert, 1931, 446.

S73.1.2.   Brother kills and eats brother. Tonga:
Gifford, 1924, 27;   Collocott, 1924, 281.

S73.1.3.   Elder brother threatens to kill younger as
soon as he is born. Hawaii: Beckwith, 1940, 436.

S73.1.4.+   Fratricide among sons of first man. Hawaii:
Fornander, 1918, VI, 276.

*S75.1.Sororicide. Mangareva: Hiroa, 1938, 382;
Marquesas: Lavondes, 1964, 34;   Cooks: Megen, 1928,
1054;   Tonga: Collocott, 1928, 38;   Samoa: Sierich,
1900, 235;   Stuebel, 1896, 62f.

*S75.1.+   Cruel grandchild. Marquesas: Lavondes, 1964,
52;   Tonga: Collocott, 1921, 47;   Reiter, 1917-18,
1035;   N.Z.:   White, 1887-90, II, 98f.

*S75.1.+   Cruel (treacherous) brother-in-law. Tonga:
Collocott, 1928, 31, 37;   N.Z.:   White, 1887-90,
V, 21 ff., 42, 162f.

S100--S199.   Revolting murders or mutilations

*S101. Suicide. (Cf. T81.2.1.)   Mangareva: Hiroa,
1938, 49, 52, 75, 87;   Laval, 1938, 92, 172ff.;
Marquesas: Handy, 1930, 34;   Tuamotus: Beckwith,
1940, 246;   Societies: Caillot, 1914, 120f.;
Hawaii: Rice, 1923, 17;   Emory, 1924, 16, 18;
Fornander, 1918, V, 122, 184;   Green, 1926, 100;
Thrum, 1906, 139, 185;   Westervelt, 1915, 231;
Samoa: Krämer, 1902, I, 266, 303;   N.Z.:   Beattie,
1915, 198;   Cowan, 1930, I, 75ff., 94;   White,
1887-90, I; 131,   II; 22;   III; 142f.;   Niue:
*Loeb, 1926, 49, 85;   Tikopia: Firth, 1961, 138f.;
Rennell: Elbert-Monberg,1964, Nos. 200, 202a;

Bellona: ibid., No. 202b.

S110. Murders. Mangareva: Hiroa, 1938, 36, 39, 43, 48f., 53, 55, 68, 77, 84, 371, 373, 381f., 382; Easter I.: Métraux, 1940, 380, 387f.; Marquesas: Handy, 1930, 45; Lavondes, 1964, 19, 24, 50, 166, 174, 176; Tuamotus: Stimson, n.d., T-G. 3/49, Z-G. 3/1117, T-G. 3/818, Z-G. 3/1122, Z-G. 13/346, T-G. 3/1290; Pukapuka: Beagleholes, 1938, 380; Hawaii: Beckwith, 1940, 39, 123; Fornander, 1916, IV, 204, 214, 234; Kamakau, 1961, 48; Pukui, 1933, 163; Remy, 1868, 38; Thrum, 1907, 123ff.; 1923, 94f.; Westervelt, 1915a, 129f.; Tonga: Collocott, 1928, 31, 37; Reiter, 1936, 366; Samoa: Krämer, 1902, I, 129; Chatham I.: Beckwith, 1940, 375; N.Z.: Clark, 1896, 43; Potai, 1928, 360; Best, 1925, 860; Cowan, 1930, I, 81, 202, 209, 257; White, 1887-90, II, 135; III, 15, 35, 119, 196, 203, 232f., 251f., 259, 261, 267, 296; IV, 55, 181, 185, 210; V, 29, 40, 44, 69, 74, 75, 80, 96, 97, 99, 115f., 145, 161, 164, 167, 179f., 183ff., 224, 237, 251; Wohlers, 1875, 10, 23; Niue: Loeb, 1926, 49; Bellona: Elbert-Monberg, 1964, Nos. 59, 66, 137; Rennell: ibid., Nos. 67, 93, 101, 121, 123, 123 n., 233, 235a, 235b; Kapingamarangi: Emory, 1949, 239.

S110.1.1.+ Hero (Maui) starves grandfather to death. N.Z.: Luomala, 1949, 56.

S110.5.+ Regicide. Hawaii: Beckwith, 1940, 409f.; Tonga: Gifford, 1924, 31.

S110.5.+ Repeated murder: person, resuscitated after first death, is beaten to death a second time. Hawaii: Beckwith, 1940, 152f.

S110.5.+ Person burying bones of dead chief kills confederate who shares knowledge of interment site. Hawaii: Kamakau, 1961, 33, 48.

S110.5.+ Animal relative slain. Marquesas: Handy, 1930, 120; Tuamotus: Beckwith, 1940, 103; Hawaii: Beckwith, 1940, 136; N.Z.: Best, 1924, 189; Tonga: Gifford, 1924, 53; Kapingamarangi: Elbert, 1948, 97.

S111. Murder by poisoning. Ellice Is.: Kennedy, 1931, 197.

S111.9.+ Person is forced to eat tabu food, which kills him. Tuamotus: Caillot, 1914, 48.

S112.   Burning to death. Easter I.: Métraux, 1940,
84, 386; Marquesas: Handy, 1930, 132; Hawaii:
Rice, 1923, 48; Beckwith, 1940, 514; Samoa:
Stuebel, 1896, 80; Tonga: Gifford, 1924, 190;
Niue: Loeb, 1926, 134, 150, 176; Smith, 1903,
114; Ellice Is.: Kennedy, 1931, 172.

S112.0.2.   House burned with all inside. Easter I.:
Métraux, 1940, 386; Marquesas: Handy, 1930, 132;
Hawaii: Beckwith, 1940, 514; Thrum, 1907, 223;
N.Z.: Grace, 1907, 30; White, 1887-90, II, 148,
152f.; Wohlers, 1875, 24.

S112.6.   Murder by roasting alive in oven. Mangareva:
Laval, 1938, 177ff.; Hawaii: Fornander, 1918, V,
404; Tonga: Gifford, 1924, 190; N.Z.: Cowan,
1930, I, 124; Tikopia: Firth, 1961, 132;
Rennell: Elbert-Monberg, 1964, No. 189.

S113.   Murder by strangling. Hawaii: Beckwith, 1940,
205; N.Z.: White, 1887-90, II, 7f., 16;
Bellona: Elbert-Monberg, 1964, No. 132.

S113.1.   Murder by hanging. Tuamotus: Stimson, n.d.,
Z-G. 3/1353.

S113.2.   Murder by suffocation. Easter I.: Métraux,
1940, 386; Societies: Henry, 1928, 557.

S114.   Murder by flaying. Mangareva: Hiroa, 1938,
320f.

S115.   Murder by stabbing. Tuamotus: Stimson, 1934,
51.

S116.   Murder by crushing. Oceania: **Lessa, 1961, 17,
393ff.; Hawaii: Pukui, 1933, 133; Tonga:
Gifford, 1924, 184; Bellona: Elbert-Monberg, 1964,
No. 50a; Rennell: ibid., No. 50b.

>   K959.6. Post-hole murder: people invite
>   boy to enter post-hole and then try to
>   crush him with log.

S116.5.   Murder by crushing beneath falling tree. Tonga:
Gifford, 1924, 184.

S116.6.+   Murder by clubbing. Tikopia: Firth, 1961,
144, 145, 147.

S116.6.+   Murder by jumping down from height upon victim.
Rennell: Elbert-Monberg, 1964, No. 231.

449

S116.6.+ Humans used as skids for launching canoe. Marquesas: Lavondes, 1966, 38.

S118.1. Murder by cutting adversary in two. Hawaii: Dickey, 1917, 24.

S118.2.+ Pregnant woman ripped open and baby removed. Mangareva: Laval, 1938, 85.

S122. Flogging to death. Hawaii: Beckwith, 1940, 152.

S123. Burial alive. Societies: Henry, 1928, 557; Ellice Is.: Roberts, 1958, 399.

S127. Murder by throwing from height. Hawaii: Remy, 1868, 51; Fornander, 1918, V, 344; Tonga: Collocott, 1928, 7.

S131. Murder by drowning. Marquesas: Handy, 1930, 53; N.Z.: Beckwith, 1940, 318; White, 1887-90, III, 10, 24, 29, 30, 36f., 38f., 48f., 51, 52, 54; IV, 59.

S131.1.+ Murder by drowning in urine. Hawaii: Fornander, 1916, IV, 166.

S131.1.+ Men tie cord around woman's neck and tow her behind canoe until she dies. Tokelau: Burrows, 1923, 148f.

S133. Murder by beheading. Marquesas: Lavondes, 1966, 142.

S139.1. Murder by twisting out intestines. Easter I.: Métraux, 1940, 66, 384; Niue: Loeb, 1926, 154.

S139.2.1.1. Head of murdered man taken along as trophy. Easter I.: Englert, 1939, 58; Marquesas: Lavondes, 1966, 50; Hawaii: Kamakau, 1961, 31; Samoa: Brown, 1915, 176; N.Z.: Cowan, 1930, I, 202; White, 1887-90, I, 43.

S139.2.1.1.+ Scalps of murdered persons taken as trophies. N.Z.: White, 1887-90, IV, 178.

S139.2.2. Other indignities to corpse. N.Z.: White, 1887-90, I, 95.

S139.7. Murder by slicing person into small pieces. Mangareva: Laval, 1938, 135; Tuamotus: Stimson, n.d., T-G. 3/912; Stimson, 1937, 40f.; Marquesas: Lavondes, 1966, 50, 142ff., 172ff.; Hawaii: Beckwith, 1940, 154; Samoa: Krämer, 1902, I, 412.

S162.5.+ Chief has handsomely tattooed legs and arms
of subjects cut off and brought to him. Hawaii:
Fornander, 1918, V, 660.

S163. Mutilation: cutting (tearing) out tongue.
Tuamotus: Stimson, n.d., T-G. 3/600; Cooks:
Gill, 1876, 90.

S163.+ Mutilation: slitting tongue. Tuamotus:
Stimson, n.d., T-G. 3/600.

S163.+ Mutilation: lower jaw cut off. Hawaii:
Fornander, 1918, V, 210.

S165. Mutilation: putting (or plucking) out eyes.
Mangareva: Hiroa, 1938, 322; Tuamotus: Stimson,
n.d., Z-G. 3/1301; Stimson, 1934, 50; Societies:
Henry, 1928, 561; Beckwith, 1940, 251; Hawaii:
Beckwith, 1940, 245, 248; Fornander, 1916, IV,
324; Niue: Loeb, 1926, 78.

S165.5. Necklace made of torn out human eyes. Tuamotus:
Stimson, 1934, 50.

S165.6. Human eyes used as fishbait. Hawaii: Beckwith,
1940, 245; Dickey, 1917, 25; Fornander, 1918, V,
212; Thrum, 1923, 71f.

S166.+ Mutilation: implements (usually fishhooks) made
of bones of dead. Hawaii: Dickey, 1917, 25; N.Z.:
Beattie, 1915, 190; Clark, 1896, 50, 152; Luomala,
1949, 56; Cowan, 1930, I, 230; Grace, 1907, 127,
130, 131; White, 1887-90, II, 88; III, 260, 290;
V, 44, 77, 81; Lau Is.: St. Johnston, 1918, 34ff.;
Funafuti: David, 1899, 101.

S166.+ Mutilation: dead bodies defiled. Niue: Loeb,
1926, 144, 156.

S168. Mutilation: tearing off ears. N.Z.: White,
1887-90, II, 134; Rennell: Elbert-Monberg, 1964,
No. 114.

S176. Mutilation: sex organs cut off. Tuamotus:
Stimson, n.d., T-G. 3/109; Ontong Java: Sarfert,
1931, 443.

S176.1.+ Mutilation: breasts of all women to be cut off
by proclamation of chief. Hawaii: Fornander, 1918,
V, 660.

S176.1.+ Leg and arm bones are torn out as mutilation.
Hawaii: Emerson, 1915, 50f.

S139.7.+ Persons impaled. Tuamotus: Audran, 1918, 33.

S141. Exposure in boat. A person (usually woman or child) set adrift in a boat (chest, basket, cask). Tuamotus: Stimson, n.d., T-G. 3/45; Marquesas: *Beckwith, 1940, 502 n. 4; Tonga: Gifford, 1924, 128, 134, 154.

S141.3.+ Exposure at sea in wooden bowl. Marquesas: Lavondes, 1964, 60.

S142. Person thrown into the water and abandoned. Australs: Aitken, 1923, 299; Tuamotus: Stimson, n.d., T-G. 3/45, T-G. 3/403, Z-G. 3/117; Marquesas: *Beckwith, 1940, 502, 502 nn.4, 5; Lavondes, 1966, 28; Societies: Handy, 1930, 408; Williams, 1895, 273; Tonga: Gifford, 1924, 122; Samoa: Abercromby, 1891, 459; N.Z.: Beattie, 1915, 137f.; Whetu, 1897, 98; Shand, 1896, 197; Cooks: *Editors, 1897, 97 n.; Kapingamarangi: Elbert, 1948, 112; Emory, 1949, 239.

S144.1. Abandonment alone on foreign coast. Hawaii: Beckwith, 1919, 422.

S145. Abandonment on an island. Hawaii: Beckwith, 1940, 358; Emory, 1924, 13, 14; Fornander, 1916, IV, 132; Thrum, 1923, 32; N.Z.: Cowan, 1925, 95ff.

S145.+ Person marooned by enemy on rock so that he will drown at high tide. N.Z.: White, 1887-90, V, 162f.

S146. Abandonment in pit. Polynesia: *Dixon, 1916,243 n. 4 Hawaii: Beckwith, 1940, 491: Fornander, 1916,IV, 38.

S146.2. Abandonment in cave. Tuamotus: Beckwith, 1940, 471.

S153.+ Woman abandoned when people flee ravaging ogre. Oceania: **Lessa, 1961, 57f., 220; Ellice Is.: David, 1899, 107ff.; Reef Is.: O'Ferrall, 1904, 232.

S160.1. Self-mutilation. Cooks: Beckwith, 1940, 247, 253.

S162. Mutilation: cutting off legs (feet). Mangareva: Laval, 1938, 31; Hawaii: Beckwith, 1940, 242.

S182.+ Children impaled and dragged in wake of ship.
Tuamotus: Stimson, n.d., T-G. 3/515.

S183.2.+ Murderers have teeth pulled then must chew
dry kava. Tonga: Gifford, 1924, 34.

S186. Torturing by beating. Samoa: Krämer, 1902, I,
143.

S191.+ Old man tossed about as ball in a game. Tikopia:
Firth, 1961, 111f.

S191.+ Person's entire body-- including inside of
eyelids-- tattooed as torture. Hawaii: Kamakau,
1961, 58.

S191.+ Victims strung upon line like fish. Tuamotus:
Audran, 1917, 61.

S191.+ Person tickled to death. Bellona: Elbert-
Monberg, 1964, No. 139.

S191.+ Woman's throat pierced so that when she trys
to drink water pours out the wound. Mangareva:
Caillot, 1914, 178; Hiroa, 1938, 47.

S191.+ Captor urinates in eyes of captives. Hawaii:
Kamakau, 1961, 91.

S191.+ Person suspended by hook under his chin. N.Z.:
White, 1887-90, III, 285.

S200--S299. Cruel sacrifices

S260.1. Human sacrifice. Mangareva: Caillot, 1914, 183;
Hiroa, 1938, 74; Laval, 1938, 147, 149, 179;
Marquesas: Handy, 1930, 73; Beckwith, 1940, 269;
Steinen, 1933-34, 39, 342; Hawaii: Beckwith, 1919,
550; Dickey, 1917, 20; Fornander, 1916, IV, 126,
218; V, 168, 212, 540, 712; Green, 1929, 77, 119,
Kamakau, 1961, 14; Luomala, 1951, 23; Smith, 1966,
12, 27f.; Westervelt, 1915, 8, 32, 34; 1915a,
30ff., 142, 190ff.; 1943, 10ff.; Samoa: Krämer,
1902, I, 258, 431; Powell-Pratt, 1892, 123;
Stuebel, 1896, 155f.; N.Z.: Best, 1925, 706, 850,
1058ff.; Cowan, 1925, 16; White, 1887-90, I,
105ff.; III, 224f.; Wohlers, 1876, 122; Reef Is.:
O'Ferrall, 1904, 226; Ontong Java: Sarfert, 1931,
409.

S261. Foundation sacrifice. A human being buried alive at base of the foundation of a building or bridge. N.Z.: *S. Percy Smith, "An Ancient South American, Maori, and Indian Custom," JPS, 20: 15f.; Gudgeon, 1906, 48.

S263.4.1.+ Daily sacrifice to sun. Samoa: Stair, 1895a, 48.

S300--S399. Abandoned or murdered children

S300. Abandoned or murdered children. Chatham Is.: Travers, 1876, 25.

S301. Children abandoned (exposed). Easter I.: Métraux, 1940, 369, 385; Tuamotus: Stimson, n.d., Z-G. 3/1122; Beckwith, 1940, 471; Caillot, 1914, 43; Marquesas: Steinen, 1933-34, 29, 31; Handy, 1930, 114; Lavondes, 1966, 28; Societies: Williams, 1895, 263; Beckwith, 1940, 471; Cooks: Te Ariki, 1899, 69; 1920, 172; Pukapuka: Beaglehole,1938, 382; Hawaii: Rice, 1923, 93; Beckwith, 1940, 416, 523; Green, 1926, 71; Thrum, 1923, 226; Westervelt, 1915, 195; Tonga: Gifford, 1924, 31, 63, 122; Reiter, 1907, 752; Collocott, 1928, 59f.; Samoa: Fraser, 1900, 132; Krämer, 1902, I, 108; Powell-Pratt, 1892, 125; Niue: Loeb, 1926, 84f.; Smith, 1903, 92; N.Z.: Gudgeon, 1906, 48; White, 1887-90, II, 88; Fijis: Fison, 1904, xxvi; Nukumanu: Sarfert, 1931, 451; Tikopia: Firth, 1961, 132; Rennell: Elbert-Monberg, 1964, No. 206.

S302. Children murdered. Mangareva: Laval, 1938, 177f.; Cooks: Megen, 1928, 1054; Hawaii: Fornander, 1916, IV, 556; Thrum, 1907, 187; Westervelt, 1915, 200; Tonga: Brown,1916, 426; Samoa: Abercromby, 1891, 459; N.Z.: White, 1887-90, V, 9.

S314. Twins exposed. Marquesas: Steinen, 1934-35, 236.

S314.+ First born of twins slain. N.Z.: Best, 1907, 2.

S325.0.1. Monstrous (deformed) child exposed.
Marquesas: Handy, 1930, 114; Hawaii: Fornander,
1916, IV, 532; 1918, V, 136, 364; Tonga:
Gifford, 1924, 31, 60; N.Z.: White, 1887-90,
II, 92f.

S331. Exposure of child in boat. Hawaii: Westervelt,
1915, 195; Tonga: Brown, 1916, 427.

S353. Abandoned child reared by supernatural beings.
N.Z.: Dixon, 1916, 42.

S400--S499. Cruel persecutions

S432. Cast-off wife thrown into water. Cooks:
*Editors, JPS, 5: note; N.Z.: Beattie, 1915,
137f.; Shand, 1896, 197; Whetu, 1897, 98;
Kapingamarangi: Emory, 1949, 239.

S481.+ Cousin of two sisters relentlessly drives them
from places where they try to settle. Hawaii:
Fornander, 1916, IV, 104ff.

S481.+ Elder sister, jealous of younger sisters'
relations with her husband, drives them off and
persecutes them wherever they settle. Hawaii:
Thrum, 1923, 105ff.

S481.+ Man's body used as a latrine by demon captors.
Tuamotus: Stimson, 1937, 72, 107.

S481.+ Person's head stuck in ground and feet used as
rack for baskets. Tuamotus: Stimson, 1937, 117.

S481.+ Strangers arriving during time of sacred
ceremony seized for sacrifice. Hawaii: Thrum,
1923, 221.

S481.+ Cannibal monster placated with human bride.
N.Z.: Grace, 1907, 77f.

T. SEX

T0--T99. Love

T10. Falling in love. Hawaii: Westervelt, 1915, 27f.

T11.1. Love from mere mention or description. Tuamotus:
Stimson, n.d., T-G. 3/45, T-G. 3/109, Z-G. 13/317;
Hawaii: Thrum, 1907, 120.

T11.3. Love through dream. Hawaii: Beckwith, 1919,
374; 1940, 231, 508; Dickey, 1917, 16;
Fornander, 1916, IV, 536; 1918, V, 228;
Westervelt, 1915, 40, 175f., 220f.

T11.3.1. Lovers meet in their dreams. Hawaii:
*Beckwith, 1940, 177, Ch. XI passim, 517;
Fornander, 1918, V, 578.

*T11.3.1.1. God dreams of woman, succeeds in clutching
her in his sleep and marries her. Cooks: Gill,
1876, 7.

T11.5. Falling in love with reflection in water.
Marquesas: Lavondes, 1966, 12.

T11.5.+ Princess falls in love with chief whose sleep-
talking is carried to her upon a stream.
Rarotonga: Te Ariki, 1920, 173.

*T11.9. Person falls in love with unseen musician.
Marquesas: Lavondes, 1964, 98ff.; Hawaii:
Beckwith, 1919, 432; Dickey, 1917, 26; Green,
1923, 51ff.; Rice, 1923, 107; Thrum, 1923, 128ff.

*T11.10. Falling in love upon hearing person's name.
N.Z.: Clark, 1896, 148.

*T11.11. Woman falls in love with a man because of his
odor. Tuamotus: Stimson,1937, 84.

T15. Love at first sight. Marquesas: Lavondes, 1964,
8; Samoa: Abercromby, 1891, 456.

T16. Man falls in love with woman he sees bathing.
Hawaii: Fornander, 1918, V, 218.

*T16.3. Women fall in love with a man because of his
beautiful dancing. Hawaii: Fornander, 1918, V,
694; Remy, 1868, 40.

456

T22. Predestined lovers. Hawaii: Thrum, 1923, 206f.

T24.2. Swooning for love. Hawaii: Rice, 1923, 9.

*T29.2. Enemies fall in love: girl plots death of warrior until she sees him and falls in love. Tuamotus: Stimson, n.d., Z-G. 13/499.

T30.+ Village virgin. Tonga: Gifford, 1924, 58.

T35.1.+ Lovers' meeting at bathing pool. Societies: Beckwith, 1940, 38; Hawaii: Beckwith, 1940, 330, 389, 479.

T35.1.+ Lake as lovers' rendezvous. Man plays trumpet at night so his lover can swim lake to him using sound as guide. N.Z.: Clark, 1896, 62.

T51.1.+ Goddess sent by sister to fetch latter's lover from distant land falls in love with him herself. Hawaii: *Beckwith, 1940, 176, 177, 177 n. 12.

*T56.5. Person attracted by other's tattooing. Marquesas: Handy, 1930, 118.

*T61.5.4. Infant betrothal. Easter I.: Métraux, 1940, 199.

*T69.6. Bride captured. Samoa: Krämer, 1902, I, 409.

T72. Woman won and then scorned. Hawaii: Beckwith, 1940, 524.

T75. Man scorned by his beloved. N.Z.: Best, 1925, 938.

T75.1. Scorn of unloved suitor punished. Hawaii: Beckwith, 1940,147; Samoa: Beckwith, 1940, 254.

T80. Tragic love. N.Z.: Cowan, 1930, I, 159.

T81. Death from love. Polynesia: *Beckwith, 1940, Ch. X passim; Easter I.: Métraux, 1940, 112; Mangareva: Hiroa, 1938, 364f.; Marquesas: Beckwith, 1940, 149; Handy, 1930, 34, 49, 117, 120; Cooks: Gill, 1876, 228; Hawaii: Beckwith, 1940, 147f., 175; Fornander, 1918, V, 230, 242; Thrum, 1907, 45; N.Z.: Clark, 1896, 5.

T81.2.1. Scorned lover kills self. Societies: Caillot, 1914, 120f.; Hawaii: Fornander, 1918, VI, 343; Emerson, 1915, 8,; N.Z.: Best, 1925, 939; Cowan, 1930, I, 148f.; Westervelt, 1915, 243; White, 1887-90, II, 165.

*S101. Suicide.

T81.6. Girl kills herself after lover's death. N.Z.: Grace, 1907, 248.

*T81.7.1. Man dies of grief for dead wife. Hawaii: Thrum, 1907, 179.

T91.1. Giant's daughter loves hero. Tuamotus: Stimson, n.d., Z-G. 3/1276.

T91.6.4. Princess falls in love with lowly boy. Tuamotus: Stimson, n.d., T-G. 3/49.

*T99.3. Woman leaves husband when his skin, after long exposure to sea-water, turns black. Cooks: Gill, 1896, 226.

*T99.4. Two gods desire girl. They stop her breath and take her to land of the dead. Marquesas: Handy, 1930, 82.

T100--T199. Marriage

T111. Marriage of mortal and supernatural being. Societies: Henry, 1928, 220; Rennell: Elbert-Monberg, 1964, No. 183; Ellice Is.: Kennedy, 1931, 171; Kapingamarangi: Elbert, 1948, 108.

T111.1. Marriage of a mortal and a god. N.Z.: Dixon, 1916, 57.

*T111.2.1.0.1. Hero wins the dawn star for a wife. Tuamotus: *Beckwith, 1940, 256.

T111.2.3. Sun has a woman for his wife. Tonga: Collocott, 1922, 162.

*T111.2.4. Girl marries sun-man. Hawaii: Beckwith, 1940, 528.

*T117.5.2. Pandanus-root husbands. Marquesas: Handy, 1930, 56; Steinen, 1933-34, 348, 360.

T118. Girl (man) married to (enamored of) a monster. Societies: Agostini, 1900, 88; N.Z.: Grace, 1907, 77f., 210.

*T126.4. Hermaphrodite married to hero. Hawaii: Beckwith, 1940, 406.

*T126.5. Two sisters live with severed head of god. Marquesas: Handy, 1930, 106.

*T126.6. Two rocks marry each other. Hawaii: Green, 1926, 65.

T131.+ Half-brothers and sisters destined to marry. Hawaii: Beckwith, 1940, 147.

T132.1. Girl fattened before wedding. Ellice Is.: Kennedy,1931, 171.

T145. Polygamous marriage. Mangareva: Laval, 1938, 159; Tonga: Gifford, 1924, 36, 94; Reiter, 1933, 374f.; Niue: *Loeb, 1926, 79; N.Z.: Grace, 1907, 114; White, 1887-90, IV, 183; Fijis: Fison, 1904, 99; Reef Is.: O'Ferrall, 1904, 230.

T145.0.1. Polygamy. Mangareva: Caillot, 1914, 194; Hiroa, 1938, 89; Tuamotus: Audran, 1919, 235; Hawaii: Beckwith, 1919, 548; Fornander, 1916, IV, 118, 186; Pukui, 1933, 163; Thrum, 1923, 21; Tonga: Collocott, 1928, 39; Samoa: Sierich, 1902, 197; Stuebel, 1896, 69; N.Z.: Cowan, 1930, I, 143.

T146. Polyandry. Marquesas: Handy, 1930, 104, 138; Steinen, 1934-35, 226; Societies: Williams, 1895, 277; Hawaii: Fornander, 1916, IV, 98; 1918, V, 516.

T200--T299. Married Life

*T299.3. Wife leaves husband because he refuses to let her bear child in house. Chatham Is.: Shand, 1898, 74.

*T303. Tribal virgin. N.Z.: Cowan, 1930, 24; White, 1887-90, II, 163.

*T312.2. Girl, ignorant of sex, shown. Commits suicide in horror. Tonga: Gifford, 1924, 203.

T373. Heavy chastity belt imposed on wife. Hawaii: Fornander, 1916, IV, 112, 166.

T381. Imprisoned virgin to prevent knowledge of men. Easter I.: Métraux, 1940, 374; Tuamotus: Stimson, n.d., Z-G. 13/243; Tonga: Gifford, 1924, 60, 174; Samoa: Beckwith, 1940, 535; Chatham Is.: Shand, 1896, 135; N.Z.: Cowan, 1921, 98; Fijis: Fison, 1904, 32.

T381.0.2. Wife imprisoned in tower (house) to preserve chastity. Hawaii: Pukui, 1933, 151.

*T387. Goddess binds thighs against approach of lovers after a quarrel with man. Hawaii: Beckwith, 1940, 357, 361.

T400--T499. ILLICIT SEXUAL RELATIONS

T411. Father-daughter incest. Easter I.: Métraux, 1940, 315; Mangareva: Hiroa, 1938, 307; Laval, 1938, 299; Tuamotus: Stimson, n.d., Z-G. 13/116; 1937, 8; Marquesas: Handy, 1930, 26; Steinen, 1934-35, 232; Hawaii: Ii, 1959, 160; Tonga: Reiter, 1907, 752; N.Z.: Best, 1925, 766; Cowan, 1930, I, 8; Dixon, 1916, 164, n. 46; Grace, 1907, 211; White, 1887-90, I, 131,134, 145, 147; Wohlers, 1875, 8.

T411.1. Lecherous father. Tuamotus: Stimson, n.d., Z-G. 13/116; Hawaii: Beckwith, 1940, 235.

T412. Mother-son incest. Oceanic: *Dixon, 1916, 164, nn. 33-44; Rennell: Elbert-Monberg, 1964, Nos. 109, 235b.

*T412.5. Woman has raised child so that it may become her husband. Hawaii: Beckwith, 1940, 23.

T415. Brother-sister incest. Tuamotus: Stimson, n.d., T-G. 3/59; Marquesas: Lavondes, 1964, 82ff.; Steinen, 1933-34, 351; 1934-35, 233; Cooks: Large, 1903, 138; Hawaii: Fornander, 1916, IV, 540, 602ff.; Tonga: Gifford, 1924, 29; Reiter, 1907, 751; 1933, 377; Reef Is.: *Elbert-Kirtley, 1966, 365ff.; Rennell: Elbert-Monberg, 1964, Nos. 64, 235b.

T415.1. Lecherous brother. Hawaii: Beckwith, 1940, 480; Reef Is.: Elbert-Kirtley, 1966, 365ff.

*T415.1.1. A brother copulates with his sister while she sleeps. Samoa: Sierich, 1902, 174.

T415.5. Brother-sister marriage. Hawaii: Beckwith, 1940, 300, 520; Fornander, 1918, V, 192, 266; Pukui, 1933, 184; Thrum, 1921, 108; 1923, 206; Westervelt, 1915, 132ff., 228f.; Tonga: Caillot, 1914, 242ff.; Gifford, 1924, 19, 29; Samoa: Stuebel, 1896, 69; Niue: Loeb, 1926, 24; Tikopia: Firth, 1961, 75, 78; Reef Is.: Elbert-Kirtley, 1966, 365ff.; Bellona: Elbert-Monberg, 1964, No. 140.

*T421.1. Aunt attempts to seduce her nephew. Mangareva: Hiroa, 1938, 357.

*T421.2. Incest between cousins. Easter I.: Métraux, 1940, 109.

*T426. Grandfather-granddaughter incest. N.Z.: Best, 1925, 767.

T450. Prostitution and concubinage. Tonga: Reiter, 1933, 374ff.

T455. Woman sells favors for particular purpose. Mangareva: Hiroa, 1938, 358.

*T455.3.2. Princess offers to sleep with man in return for plumage of beautiful bird. Tuamotus: Stimson, n.d., Z-G. 13/276.

T458.+ Man coming to Island of Women is killed by their persistent attentions. Cooks: Beaglehole, 1938, 401.

T461.3. Tree as wife. N.Z.: White, 1887-90, I, 158.

*T461.4. Copulation with figure made of sand or clay.
Easter I.: Englert, 1939, 18; Tuamotus: Stimson,
n.d., Z-G. 13/116; 1937, 4.

*T461.5. Pandanus root as husband. See *T117.5.2.
Tuamotus: Caillot, 1914, 70; Marquesas: Lavondes,
1964, 60.

*T461.6. A god has sexual relations with water.
Easter I.: Englert, 1939, 17f.

*T461.7. A god has sexual relations with stones.
Easter I.: Englert, 1939, 17f.

T463. Homosexual love (male). Marquesas:
Tahiaoteaa, 1933, 494.

*T465.6. Sexual relations between woman and eel.
Cf. *T471.7. Eel rapes girl. Oceania: **Kirtley,
1967, 89f.; N.Z.: White, 1887-90, II, 83.

T467. The amorous bite. Hawaii: Fornander, 1916,
IV, 102, 544; 1918, V, 306; Thrum, 1923, 105;
Rennell: Elbert-Monberg, 1964, Nos. 21, 183.

T467.+ Young men masturbate with stones. Easter I.:
Métraux, 1940, 369.

T467.+ Woman preserves member of murdered paramour.
Easter I.: Métraux, 1940, 114.

T471. Rape. Mangareva: Caillot, 1914, 178; Hiroa,
1938, 37; Tuamotus: Stimson, n.d., Z-G. 3/1340;
1937, 8, 14, 61; Tonga: Caillot, 1914, 254;
Samoa: Krämer, 1902, I, 409; Stuebel, 1896, 140;
Niue: Smith, 1903, 98.

*T471.4. Hero rapes cannibal chief's concubines.
Tonga: Gifford, 1924, 135.

*T471.5. Man rapes his cousin, causes war. Easter I.:
Métraux, 1940, 109.

*T471.6. Woman (women) rapes man. Easter I.: Métraux,
1940, 368.

*T471.7. Eel rapes girl. Cf.*T465.6. Oceania:
**Kirtley, 1967, 89f.; Mangareva: Hiroa, 1938,
315; Samoa: Krämer, 1902, I, 393, 438f.;
Stuebel, 1896, 68.

*T475.3. Unknown paramour: comes at night, leaves
    before dawn. Easter I.: Métraux, 1940, 389;
    Mangareva: Hiroa, 1938, 319, 334; Societies:
    Agostini, 1900, 88; Hawaii: Rice, 1923, 110;
    N.Z.: Best, 1927, 269; Clark, 1896, 162.

T481. Adultery. Tuamotus: Caillot, 1914, 107;
    Stimson, 1934, 7f., 38, 42; Cooks: Large, 1903,
    133; Hawaii: Beckwith, 1919, 584ff., 602ff.;
    Fornander, 1916, IV, 270; V, 246, 534; Remy,
    1868, 18f.; Tonga: Collocott, 1924, 278;
    Samoa: Krämer, 1902, I, 267; N.Z.: Best, 1925,
    736; Cowan, 1930, I, 139ff.; White, 1887-90,
    I, 22f.; II, 7, 141; III, 14; IV, 192.

T481.2. Queen's illicit passion for diseased man.
    Tuamotus: Stimson, n.d., T-G. 3/45.

T481.2.1. Queen commits adultery with low-born man.
    N.Z.: Cowan, 1930, I, 44.

T494.+ Princess in Land of Women keeps male castaway
    all to herself. Marquesas: Lavondes, 1964, 60ff.

T494.+ Bird sleeps with woman when her husband is away.
    Marquesas: Handy, 1930, 121.

        T500--T599. CONCEPTION AND BIRTH

*T511.3.3. Conception from eating yam. Tonga:
    Gifford, 1924, 169.

T511.5.1. Conception from eating fish. Tonga: Gifford,
    1924, 152; Ellice Is.: Beckwith, 1940, 270.

T511.5.3. Conception from eating louse. Tuamotus:
    Stimson, 1937, 66; Tikopia: Firth, 1961, 44.

T511.5.4. Conception from eating bird. Tonga: Beckwith,
    1940, 429; Gifford, 1924, 60ff.

*T511.5.5. Woman becomes pregnant when two lizards jump
    down her throat. Reef Is.: O'Ferrall, 1904, 232.

T511.8.1. Conception from swallowing stone. Tonga:
    Collocott, 1928, 26.

*T511.8.7. Conception from eating coconut husks used to
    clean man's body. Tonga: Gifford, 1924, 103.

T515. Impregnation through glance. Kapingamarangi:
Elbert, 1948, 97; 1949, 244.

*T517.4. Conception from impregnation by bodiless head.
Marquesas: Handy, 1930, 106, 108.

T521. Coneption from sunlight. Tonga: Gifford,
1924, 114; Samoa: Beckwith, 1940, 512; *Dixon,
1916, 165, nn. 49f.; Krämer, 1902, I, 392, 404,
412; Sierich, 1902, 170; Tokelau: Burrows,
1923, 168; Fijis: Fison, 1904, 32; Reef Is.:
Elbert-Kirtley, 1966, 354f.; Nukumanu: Sarfert,
1931, 439f.

T524. Conception from wind. Tonga: Collocott, 1928,
21; Gifford, 1924, 48, 53.

T531. Conception from casual contact with man. Hawaii:
Beckwith, 1940, 229; Tonga: Gifford, 1924, 19f.

*T539.6. Woman impregnated from going near the dried
bones of culture hero. Tonga: Caillot, 1914,
305 n. 1; Collocott,1921, 54; 1922, 163;
Reiter, 1919-20, 132.

*T539.7. Clam impregnated by backwash of canoe paddle.
Tokelau: Burrows, 1923, 165.

T541.1.1. Birth from blood-clot. Oceania: *Gudman
Hatt, Asiatic Influences in American Folklore
(Copenhagen, 1949), 80ff.; *Dixon, 1916, 109,
251 n. 25; Mangareva: Hiroa, 1938, 359, 367f.,
421; Hawaii: Emerson, 1915, X; Fornander, 1918,
V, 546; Samoa: Abercromby, 1891, 460; *Krämer,
1902, I, 107, 202, 428, 428 n. 12; Stuebel, 1896,
146, 151, 154f.; N.Z.: Best, 1905, 212; Rotuma:
Churchward, 1937-38, 489.

T572.2.3. Hero an abortion thrown into bushes.

*T541.1.1.1. Hero born from a blood-defiled apron thrown
away. N.Z.: White, 1887-90, II, 65, 72, 79.

T541.2. Birth from wound or abcess. Oceania: Dixon,
1916, 113, 234 n. 44; 251, nn. 18-22.

T541.4. Birth from person's head. Oceania: **Lessa,
1961, 412ff.; Hawaii: Beckwith, 1940, 171, 278,
521; Emerson, 1915, X; McAllister, 1933, 89;
Ellice Is.: Kennedy, 1931, 190; Tikopia: Firth,
1961, 29, 31.

T541.4.1. Birth from mouth. Hawaii: Beckwith, 1940, 171.

*T541.6.1. Birth from armpit. N.Z.: Best, 1905, 209; 1925, 953; Tama-Rau, 1899, 55.

T541.7. Birth from an eye. Hawaii: *Beckwith, 1940, 171; Westervelt, 1915a, 35 n.

T541.8.1. Birth from excrement. Rennell: Elbert-Monberg, 1964, Nos. 31a, 31b; Bellona: ibid., No. 32.

T541.14. Birth through the ear. Mangareva: Hiroa, 1938, 425; Laval, 1938, 303.

T541.16. Birth from knee. Hawaii: Luomala, 1951, 40.

*T541.17. Birth of two daughters from breasts of goddess. Hawaii: Beckwith, 1940, 171.

*T541.18. Birth from hair (head or beard). Tikopia: Firth, 1961, 71, 73, 81, 84.

T542. Birth of human being from an egg. Tuamotus: Beckwith, 1940, 428f.; Marquesas: Beckwith, 1940, 470; Handy, 1930, 104, 125; Hawaii: Beckwith, 1940, 171, 423; Fornander, 1918, V, 384; Thrum, 1921, 107.

T565. Woman lays an egg.

*T543.7.1. Birth from masticated yam. Bellona: Elbert-Monberg, 1964, No. 5.

T544.1. Birth from rock (coral). Tonga: Gifford, 1924, 191; Samoa: Stuebel, 1896, 146.

T549.3.1. Fish when slit open gives up child. Marquesas: Handy, 1930, 135; Steinen, 1934-35, 238.

*T549.3.2. Clam gives birth to human child. Tonga: Collocott, 1928, 33, 43; Tokelau: Burrows, 1923, 165.

T549.4. Child born from miscarried fetus. Marquesas: Lavondes, 1966, 176; Hawaii: Fornander, 1918, V, 546; Samoa: Nelson, 1925, 134; N.Z.: Best, 1925, 935; White, 1887-90, II, 63, 71, 92f.; Rotuma: Russell, 1942, 243; Kapingamarangi: Elbert, 1949, 245.

T549.4.1. Child born from placenta. Tikopia: Firth, 1961, 29.

*T549.5. Girl found in intestines of pig. Marquesas: Handy, 1930, 135.

T550. Monstrous births. N.Z.: Grace, 1907, 220.

*T550.3.1. Siamese twins born from brother-sister incest. Tonga: Reiter, 1907, 751.

*T550.4.1. Monstrous birth during storm. Hawaii: Beckwith, 1940, 411.

*T550.8. Child born which is only bones and sinews. Tonga: Collocott, 1921, 54; Reiter, 1919-20, 133.

T551.1. Child born without limbs. Hawaii: Beckwith, 1940, 298.

T551.1.1. Child born as formless lump of flesh. N.Z.: Wohlers, 1875, 10.

*T551.2.1. Children born which are only heads. Societies: Henry, 1928, 421.

T551.3. Child born with animal head. Tonga: Gifford, 1924, 31, 62f.

*T551.16. Children of hero and amazon have wings. Tuamotus: Beckwith, 1940, 503.

*T554.0.2. Woman gives birth to mammal. Samoa: Fraser, 1897, 70; Fijis: Fison, 1904, 46.

T554.5. Woman bears tortoise (turtle). Samoa: Krämer, 1902, I, 130.

T554.7. Woman gives birth to a snake. Rennell: Elbert-Monberg, 1964, Nos. 51a, 51b.

*T554.7.1. Woman gives birth to reptile (lizard). Societies: Henry, 1928, 622; Hawaii: Fornander, 1918, V, 164; Tonga: Beckwith, 1940, 398; Gifford, 1924, 194.

T554.10. Woman gives birth to a bird (birds). Tuamotus: Stimson, n.d., T-G. 2/44, Z-G. 13/24; Hawaii: Beckwith, 1940, 231; Fornander, 1918, V, 538; Thrum, 1921, 104; 1923, 201, 211; Samoa: Krämer,

1902, I, 139; N.Z.: White, 1887-90, I, 84.

*T554.12. Woman gives birth to fish. Mangareva: Hiroa, 1938, 423; Marquesas: Handy, 1930, 111; Hawaii: Beckwith, 1940, 138; Green, 1926, 105; Thrum, 1923, 293; Tonga: Collocott, 1928, 32; Gifford, 1924, 152; Samoa: Brown, 1917, 95.

*T554.13. Woman gives birth to eel. Marquesas: Handy, 1930, 78; Steinen, 1933-34, 29, 31; Tonga: Gifford, 1924, 181; Samoa: Krämer, 1902, I, 121; Stuebel, 1896, 153; Niue: Loeb, 1926, 202.

*T554.14. Woman gives birth to whale. Tuamotus: Caillot, 1914, 74; Seurat, 1905, 435.

*T554.15. Woman gives birth to rat. Hawaii: Fornander, 1916, IV, 122,162; Thrum, 1923, 24; Westervelt, 1915a, 157ff., 175ff.

*T554.16. Woman gives birth to a hog. Hawaii: Thrum, 1921, 109; 1923, 207.

*T554.17. Woman gives birth to insect. Societies: Lagarde, 1933, 697.

T555. Woman gives birth to a plant. Hawaii: Beckwith, 1940, 297, 515; Fornander, 1916, IV, 532; Tonga: Gifford, 1924, 169.

*T556.1. Mixed birth: woman gives birth to fowl, pigs, and turtles at one delivery. Societies: Henry, 1928, 380.

*T558. Woman gives birth to a stone (coral). Marquesas: Lavondes, 1964, 30; Tonga: Gifford, 1924, 190.

*T561.5. Child born concealed in large clod. Tuamotus: Beckwith, 1940, 470.

*T563.5. Child born as piece of rope. Hawaii: *Beckwith, 1940, 414, 436, 464ff.; Fornander, 1916, IV, 436, 522; 1918, V, 136, 364; Rice, 1923, 93; Thrum, 1921, 110; 1923, 208f.

*T563.6. Child born in form of image. Hawaii: Beckwith, 1940, 516; Fornander, 1916, IV, 538.

T565. Woman lays an egg. Tuamotus: Stimson, n.d.,
Z-G. 13/24; Marquesas: Handy, 1930, 125;
Hawaii: Beckwith, 1940, 227, 423; Fornander,
1916, IV, 498; Westervelt, 1915a, 205ff.

T571. Unreasonable demands of pregnant women.
Polynesia: *Dixon, 1916, 233 n. 42; Mangareva:
Hiroa, 1938, 378; Marquesas: Handy, 1930, 104;
Lavondes, 1964, 78; Steinen, 1934-35, 224;
Societies: Henry, 1928, 580; Cooks: Beckwith,
1940, 104, 262; Savage, 1910, 145; Hawaii:
Beckwith, 1919, 348; 1940, 24, 405, 506; Green,
1929, 21; Tonga: Collocott, 1928, 25; Gifford,
1924, 62; Samoa: Beckwith, 1940, 25; Fraser,
1900, 131; Sierich, 1902, 188; Niue: *Loeb,
1926, 176; Tokelau: Macgregor, 1937, 80; N.Z.:
Beckwith, 1940, 260; Dixon, 1916, 60; White,
1887-90, I, 68; II, 173; IV, 113; Wohlers,
1875, 20; Ellice Is.: Roberts, 1958, 420.

T572.2.3. Hero an abortion thrown into the bushes.
N.Z.: Dixon, 1916, 42.

T541.1. Birth from blood-clot.

T573. Short pregnancy. Hawaii: Beckwith, 1940, 518;
Fornander, 1916, IV, 566; Westervelt, 1915a,
164f.; Rotuma: Churchward, 1937-38, 113; N.Z.:
Grace, 1907, 137; Fijis: Beckwith, 1940, 210.

*T573.2. Short pregnancy: woman gives birth to twelve
children in seven lunar months. Marquesas:
Steinen, 1933-34, 33.

T574. Long pregnancy. Marquesas: Lavondes, 1964, 30;
Hawaii: Fornander, 1916, IV, 522; Samoa: Sierich,
1902, 187; Rotuma: Churchward, 1937-38, 113.

*T574.3. Son born three years afer the absence of its
actual father. Hawaii: Rice, 1923, 27.

T575.1. Child speaks in mother's womb. Hawaii:
Beckwith, 1940, 231; Emory, 1924, 17; Fornander,
1916, IV, 522; V, 556; Samoa: Sierich, 1902,
187; Tokelau: Macgregor, 1937, 87; N.Z.:
White, 1887-90, II, 172.

*T575.5. Unborn child leaves mother's womb, plays pranks,
then returns. Hawaii: Beckwith, 1940, 230f.;
Emory, 1924, 17; Fornander, 1918, V, 286, 536, 558;
Thrum, 1923, 200f.

*T576.1. Man eats a red louse and later his child is born with ruddy skin. Mangareva: Hiroa, 1938, 319.

T578. Pregnant man. Tikopia: Firth, 1961, 73.

T581.2. Child born of woman abandoned in pit. Polynesia: Dixon, 1916, 234 n. 43.

T581.3. Child born in tree. Polynesia: Dixon, 234 n. 43; Ellice Is.: David, 1899, 107.

*T581.12. Child born in seaweed. Tuamotus: Stimson, n.d., Z-G. 3/1146.

*T581.13. Women give birth while floating in the sea. Samoa: Abercromby, 1891, 459.

*T582.5. Pregnant woman isolated in hut wrapped with a net. Australs: Aitken, 1930, 108.

*T583.1.2. Child trembles after birth owing to cold and fear its father experienced during its prenatal existence. Hawaii: Beckwith, 1940, 479.

T584. Parturition. Samoa: Powell-Pratt, 1891, 201ff.

*T584.0.7. At childbirth, women of island are cut open, die. Marquesas: Handy, 1930, 56; Steinen, 1934-35, 348, 360; Cooks: Gill, 1876, 266.

T584.2. Child removed from body of dead mother. Oceania: *Dixon, 1916, 132,n. 4; Marquesas: Lavondes, 1966, 54, 144; Steinen, 1934-35, 346; Tonga: Gifford, 1924, 124.

T584.3. Caesarean operation upon a woman at childbirth as a custom. (Cf. A1351. and J1745.3.) Oceania: **Gudman Hatt, Asiatic Influences in American Folklore (Copenhagen, 1949), 83f.; Tuamotus: Caillot, 1914, 58; Mangareva: Caillot, 1914, 149; Tonga: Brown, 1916, 426; N.Z.: White, 1887-90, II, 9f., 12f.; Kapingamarangi: Elbert, 1949, 244.

*T584.9. Afterbirth, cord, and navel string deposited in sacred spot. Hawaii: Beckwith, 1940, 377.

*T584.10. Child born by a sneeze. Samoa: Sierich, 1902, 187.

*T585.1.2. Infant born a giant. Societies: Beckwith, 1940, 469.

T585.2. Child speaks at birth. Hawaii: Dickey, 1917, 16.

T585.5. Child born with all his teeth. Hawaii: Fornander, 1916, IV, 522.

T585.5.1. Child born with hairy mane. Hawaii: Fornander, 1916, IV, 522.

*T585.9.+ Infant hurls axe five miles. Hawaii: Beckwith, 1940, 480.

*T585.9.+ Precocious infant pulls up all potato vines planted by supposed father. Hawaii: Beckwith, 1940, 480.

*T585.9.+ Precocious infant sets mother up as ruler. Hawaii: Beckwith, 1940, 481.

*T585.9.+ Infant kills men sent against it. Hawaii: Beckwith, 1940, 481.

*T587.4. Woman bears twins; a night later, bears another child. Societies: Henry, 1928, 447.

*T589.1.1. Woman in three successive births bears a stomach, sides, and a thigh. Marquesas: Handy, 1930, 114.

T596.2. Children named by numbers (1, 2, 3, etc.). Samoa: Elbert-Kirtley, 1966, 363.

T597.+ Relation between conception of children and the phases of the moon. Hawaii: Beckwith, 1940, 220.

T597.+ Mother who gives birth unaware when event happens. Marquesas: Handy, 1930, 180.

T600--T699. CARE OF CHILDREN

T605.+ Child raised in lower world. Mangareva: Hiroa, 1938, 365f.

T611.11.+ Child raised by spirits. Tuamotus: Caillot, 1914, 43; Hawaii: Fornander, 1918, V, 136; Tonga: Collocott, 1928, 60.

T611.11.+ Child lives upon stones, which he swallows
and rejects. Tuamotus: Beckwith, 1940, 471.

T611.11.+ Child nourished on air. Marquesas: Beckwith,
1940, 470.

T611.11.+ Children raised solely upon kava. Hawaii:
Westervelt, 1915, 165.

T611.11.+ Children raised solely on bananas. Hawaii:
Fornander, 1918, V, 136; Thrum, 1921, 110.

T612. Child born of slain mother cares for itself
during infancy. Oceania: Dixon, 1916, 132, 137.

*T612.1. Boy grows up alone and untended. Samoa:
Elbert-Kirtley, 1966, 361; Nelson, 1925, 134;
Ellice Is.: *Elbert-Kirtley, 1966, 358; Reef Is.:
ibid., 358.

*T612.2. Abandoned child raised by coral reef.
Marquesas: Lavondes, 1966, 28; Niue: Smith,
1903, 92.

*T614.1. Child rushes to kill its brothers the instant
it is born. N.Z.: White, 1887-90, II, 172.

T615. Supernatural growth. Oceania: **Lessa, 1961,
414ff.; Societies: Henry, 1928, 537; Hawaii:
Fornander, 1918, V, 274ff.; Westervelt, 1915a,
212; Samoa: Krämer, 1902, I, 108; N.Z.:
Grace, 1907, 138; Tikopia: Firth, 1961, 44.

*T615.6. Child born, walks, marries, becomes a father
and a grandfather, and dies upon the same day.
Hawaii: Westervelt, 1915a, 105.

T617. Boy reared in ignorance of the world. Mangareva:
Hiroa, 1938, 336, 381; Tuamotus: Stimson, n.d.,
Z-G. 1/84; Cooks: Beaglehole, 1938, 406; Hawaii:
Beckwith, 1919, 348; Fornander, 1918, V, 228;
Green, 1929, 23; Thrum, 1923, 95.

*T617.3. Child raised in secret (concealment). Tuamotus:
Stimson, n.d., Z-G. 13/24; Hawaii: Beckwith, 1940,
5ff.,523, 526.

*T617.4. Child raised in tabu temple. Hawaii: Fornander,
1918, V, 136; Westervelt, 1915, 165.

*T617.5. Children raised in a cave. Mangareva: Laval,
1938, 144; Hawaii: Dickey, 1917, 29; Samoa:
Krämer, 1902, I, 453.

*T618. Infant raised under a wooden bowl. Reef Is.:
*Elbert-Kirtley, 1966, 358.

*T622. Child raised in the earthly paradise (Paliuli).
Hawaii: Fornander, 1918, V, 386.

T645. Paramour leaves token with girl to give their
son. Tuamotus: Stimson, 1934, 8; Marquesas:
Lavondes, 1964, 62; Hawaii: Beckwith, 1940,
86, 330, 478f.; Fornander, 1916, IV, 180, 496,
548, 596; 1918, V, 170; Kamakau, 1961,3;
Pukui, 1933, 179; Pukui-Curtis, n.d., 26; Remy,
1868, 19; Thrum, 1921, 111; 1923, 55, 210;
Westervelt, 1915, 170; Samoa: Krämer, 1902, I,
404, 441f.; Powell-Pratt, 1892, 255; Sierich,
1901, 17, 170; N.Z.: Best, 1925, 907; White,
1887-90, IV, 40, 195, 205.

T646. Illegitimate child taunted by playmates.
Oceania: *Dixon, 1916, 67f., 82, 113.

T688.+ Mother instructs her son upon how to be
recognized by his father. Tuamotus: Stimson,
1934, 13.

V. Religion. See entries under "Religion" in
C. R. H. Taylor's A Pacific Bibliography
(London, 1965).

V0--V99. Religious services

V1.3. Worship of ancestors. Tuamotus: Stimson, n.d.,
T-G. 3/619; Societies: Henry, 1928, 561; Hawaii:
Beckwith, 1940, 160; Niue: Loeb, 1926, 165;
Tokelaus: Macgregor, 1937, 62; Nukumanu:
Sarfert, 1931, 334.

V1.4.2. Worship of the sun. Hawaii: Beckwith, 1940,
12.

V1.4.4.+ Worship of the Pleiades. Pukapuka: Gill,
1876, 317.

V1.5.6.1. Worship of rainbow. Ellice Is.: Hedley,
1896, 51.

V1.6.1.1. Worship of mountains and hills. N.Z.:
Cowan, 1930, I, 226.

V1.6.1.1.+ Sacred valley. Hawaii: Green, 1923, 50ff.

V1.6.1.1.+ Sacred isle. Cooks: Gill, 1876, 221.

V1.6.3.1. Sacred fire. N.Z.: Best, 1924, 267ff.;
Cowan, 1930, I, 264ff.

V1.6.4.1. Sacred stones. Societies: Henry, 1928,
382; Cooks: Gill, 1876, 33; Hawaii: Beckwith,
1940, 88ff.; McAllister, 1933, 100, 142, 143, 146;
Samoa: Stair, 1896, 34, 36; Tokelaus:
Macgregor, 1937, 59; N.Z.: Best, 1924, 298.

V1.6.4.2. Sacred shells. Societies: Henry, 1928, 391;
Tonga: Gifford, 1924, 52; Fijis: Fison, 1904, 26.

V1.7. Worship of trees and plants. Niue: Loeb, 1926,
171; N.Z.: Best, 1924, 297; Cowan, 1930, I, 187;
Reef Is.: O'Ferrall, 1904, 228f.

V1.8. Worship of animals (totemism). Easter I.:
Métraux, 1940, 312ff.; Marquesas: Handy, 1930,

104; Hawaii: Beckwith, 1940, 129; Tonga: Beckwith, 1940, 178; Tokelaus: Macgregor, 1937, 63; Niue: Loeb, 1926, 171, 174.

V1.8.7. Bird worship. Easter I.: Métraux, 1940, 313f.

V1.8.11. Fish worship. Marquesas: Handy, 1930, 104; Societies: Henry, 1928, 561; Hawaii: Beckwith, 1940, 129.

V1.9.3. Worship of hammer (axe). Societies: Henry, 1928, 147.

V1.10. Worship of fetish. Societies: Henry, 1928, 147, 392; Tonga: Gifford, 1924, 52; Samoa: Stair, 1896, 41; Niue: Loeb, 1926, 167f.; Futuna: Burrows, 1936, 110.

V1.10.3. Sacred feather. Tuamotus: Beckwith, 1940, 289; Stimson, 1937, 62.

V1.11.3. Worship of wooden idol. Hawaii: Beckwith, 1940, 16.

V5.+ Mistake in ceremony produces fatal results. N.Z.: Best, 1924, 265; Luomala, 1949, 62; Tama-Rau, 1899, 53.

V10. Religious sacrifices. Tuamotus: Stimson, n.d., MB-DD-38; Hawaii: Beckwith, 1940, 16, 70, 123; Samoa: Beckwith, 1940, 19; Stair, 1896, 48; Niue: Loeb, 1926, 174; N.Z.: Hare Hongi, 1896, 234.

V10.+ Human sacrifice. Easter I.: Métraux, 1940, 329; Marquesas: Handy, 1930, 70, 134; Cooks: Te Ariki, 1920, 6; Gill, 1876, 14, 289f.; Societies: Henry, 1928, 129; Hawaii: *Beckwith, 1940, 29, 130, 497; N.Z.: Hare Hongi, 1898, 38.

V11.9.1. Sacrifice to unknown god. Hawaii: Beckwith, 1940, 70.

V12.4.3.1. Hog as sacrifice. Hawaii: Beckwith, 1940, 123.

V12.4.10. Fish as sacrifice. Societies: Henry, 1928, 241; Hawaii: Beckwith, 1940, 420; Thrum, 1907, 83f., 216, 227, 270; 1921, 105; 1923, 27ff., 162, 263; Niue: Loeb, 1926, 174.

V12.7. Eyes (human or animal) as sacrifice.
Marquesas: Handy, 1930, 134; Hawaii: Beckwith,
1940, 130, 497.

V12.8. Flowers as sacrifice. Hawaii: Beckwith,
1940, 16.

V19.+ First fruits of harvest presented to god.
Cooks: Gill, 1876, 19; Niue: Loeb, 1926, 174;
N.Z.: Hare Hongi, 1920, 26.

V19.+ Heart of first slain enemy sacrificed to war
god. N.Z.: Best, 1924, 279.

V20. Confession of sins. Tahiti: Henry, 1928, 143.

V30.1. The eaten god. Niue: Loeb, 1926, 125.

V50. Prayer. Societies: Henry, 1928, 143; N.Z.:
Clark, 1896, 32.

V52.8. Prayer brings death to enemy. Hawaii:
Beckwith, 1940, 105, 345.

V53.1. Prayer unfastens boy's fetters. Hawaii:
Beckwith, 1940, 345.

V57.1. Prayer for good harvest. N.Z.: Clark, 1896,
32.

V58.1. Prayers at sunrise and sunset. Societies:
Henry, 1928, 143.

V60. Funeral rites. Cooks: Gill, 1876, 156.

V61.1. Dead placed on boat (canoe, raft). Mangareva:
Laval, 1938, 45; Niue: Loeb, 1926, 87.

V61.3.0.3.+ Dead buried with feet toward sun. Cooks:
Gill, 1876, 156.

V61.8.1. Chiefs buried in hidden caves. Societies:
Henry, 1928, 224; Hawaii: Beckwith, 1940, 160;
Rice, 1923, 132.

V61.11.+ Dead buried with bundles of leaves beneath
their arms. Ontong Java: Sarfert, 1931, 329.

V62.2.+ Body not buried until an insect comes to it.
Niue: Loeb, 1926, 89.

V63.+ Bones painted red. N.Z.: Clark, 1896, 101.

V67.5.+ Mourning rites. Niue: Loeb, 1926, 152.

V81.5. Sea bath as purificatory rite. Societies:
Henry, 1928, 144; Hawaii: Beckwith, 1940,
152, 176; Chatham I.: Shand, 1896, 131; N.Z.:
Clark, 1896, 152, 185.

V82. Circumcision. Niue: *Loeb, 1926, 175ff.

V100--V199. Religious edifices

and objects

V110. Religious buildings. Hawaii: Beckwith, 1940,
112; Rice, 1923, 35; Samoa: Fraser, 1897, 45.

V112. Temples. Rennell: Elbert-Monberg, 1964, No. 4.

V112.1. Spirit huts. Hawaii: Beckwith, 1940, 112.

V127. Image of deity in wood (stone). Marquesas:
Handy, 1930, 122; Societies: Henry, 1928, 344;
Cooks: Beckwith, 1940, 131; Hawaii: Beckwith,
1940, 111; N.Z.: *Hare Hongi, 1920, 26.

V134.4.+ Sacred pools. N.Z.: Best, 1924, 267.

V140. Sacred relics. Tuamotus: Audran, 1918, 134;
Ellice Is.: Hedley, 1896, 51.

V151.1.+ Sacred red garments. N.Z.: White, 1887-90,
II, 57.

V200--V299. Sacred persons

V202. Sacred spirits. Hawaii: *Beckwith, 1940, 104,
107f., 180, 382, 407, 447, 512; Samoa: *Stair,
1896, 37; Ellice Is.: Kennedy, 1931, 165.

V202.+ Town god. Fijis: Fison, 1904, 55.

V205.1. Third son of king possesses sacred power. Easter I.: Métraux, 1940, 130.

V205.1.+ Dead chiefs deified. Cooks: Te Ariki, 1920, 64; Hawaii: Rice, 1923, 41; Samoa: Stair, 1896, 33f.

V205.1.+ Sacred albino. Hawaii: Fornander, 1916, IV, 4.

V235.3.+ Gods visit pious man. Hawaii: Rice, 1923, 118.

*V295. Shamanism. Easter I.: Métraux, 1940, 380; Tuamotus: *Stimson, n.d., MB-DD-33; Hawaii: Beckwith, 1940, 180, 382; Niue: Loeb, 1926, 166; N.Z.: Beckwith, 1940, 447; *Luomala, 1949, 118; Fijis: *Fison, 1904, 166f.

V300--V399. Religious beliefs

V331. Conversion to Christianity. Societies: Henry, 1928, 178.

V347.+ Blasphemer of Christian God blinded by lightning. Niue: Loeb,1926, 37.

V500-V599. Religious motifs --
miscellaneous

V512.2.+ Word of God (Christian) comes down in lightning flashes. Niue: Loeb, 1926, 37.

V540.+ Mana. Personal spiritual power (possessed in eminent degree by priests and chiefs). Polynesia: *Luomala, 1949, 114ff.; Easter I.: Métraux, 1940, 130; Niue: *Loeb, 1926, 153, 184f.; N.Z.: *Described by Ngai-tahu to H. Beattie, "Mana," JPS XXX (1921), 16-18.

W. TRAITS OF CHARACTER

W0--W99. Favorable traits of character

W11.4.+ Person kills own child to feed guest. Easter I.: Métraux, 1940, 75; Tonga: Gifford, 1924, 71, 73.

W11.4.+ Hero feeds brother with own blood. Hawaii: Rice, 1923, 105.

W11.4.+ God transforms self into breadfruit tree out of pity for starving family. Societies: Beckwith, 1940, 101.

W11.5.1.1.+ Hero feeds starving brothers who tried to murder him. Hawaii: Fornander, 1916, IV, 50.

W11.5.1.1.+ Warrior enters hut of his sleeping enemy, but only leaves a token that he was there and had spared him. N.Z.: White, 1887-90, III, 219, 255.

W28.4.+ Youngest brother saves his elder brothers from being sacrificed by offering his own life. Hawaii: Fornander, 1916, IV, 152; Thrum, 1923, 45.

W28.4.+ Son starves self during famine to feed his father. Cooks: Gill, 1876, 136.

W28.4.+ Girl wishes to be eaten by cannibal in place of her lover. Tuamotus: Stimson, n.d., Z-G. 13/152.

W28.4.+ Faithful retainer of chief gives his body to chief for manufacture of fishing gear: his thigh bone is used as hook, his intestines as line, his head as sinker, and his flesh as bait. Hawaii: Fornander, 1916, IV, 292ff.

W28.4.+ A mother offers to take son's place as human sacrifice. Hawaii: Fornander, 1916, IV, 146.

W28.4.+ Girl dies rather than tell hiding place of brother. Easter I.: Métraux, 1940, 371.

W28.4.+ Man sacrifices life that others may kill foe. Rotuma: Churchward, 1937-38, 354.

W28.4.+ Whale, from compassion, tries to die alongside his brother. Tuamotus: Stimson, n.d., T-G. 3/912.

W34.4.+ The youngest sister jumps in a swamp into which another sister was pushed in order to die with her. Samoa: Sierich, 1900, 235.

W34.4.+ A son dies from sorrow at his father's death. Tonga: Reiter, 1919-20, 129f.

W34.4.+ Brother spurned by others retrieves lost battle for them. Hawaii: Beckwith, 1940, 398.

W100--W199. Unfavorable Traits of Character

W111.5.+ Suitor obliged to perform task secretly breaks tools and blames failure on their weakness. Tuamotus: Stimson, n.d., MB-FF/206.

W121.8.+ Man falls from cliff and is impaled on a tree. War party thinks he is alive and defiant: immediately retreats. Tonga: Gifford, 1924, 101.

W121.8.+ Warrior declines to fight for his mistress. Tuamotus: Stimson,n.d., Z-G. 13/4.

W121.8.+ People see ogress pursuing children. They flee, leaving children to their fate. Marquesas: Handy, 1930, 40.

W121.8.+ Men chosen as victims of cannibal meals on long sea voyage give their children as alternate victims. N.Z.: White, 1887-90, III, 72.

W121.8.+ Man flees and leaves his wife and children to be killed by his enemies. N.Z.: White, 1887-90, V, 83.

W133.+ Hero wins princess after many tests; then, offended by these, he rejects her. Societies: Henry, 1928, 563.

W133.+ Prince no longer desires girl after her magic clothes disappear. Tuamotus: Stimson, n.d., Z-G. 13/346.

W154. Ingratitude. Cooks: Low, 1934, 179f.

W154.5.1.1. Man kills whale (porpoise) which carried him home across sea. Marquesas: Lavondes, 1964, 66; Tonga: Gifford, 1924, 142; N.Z.: Cowan,

1940, I, 69; White, 1887-90, II, 127, 129, 133,
136f., 145; Wohlers, 1875, 28.

R245. Whale-boat.

W154.5.1.3.+ Ungrateful man causes bird who has transported him on long voyage to get killed. N.Z.:
Best, 1925, 920f.

W154.9. Man rescued from drowning kills rescuer.
Oceania: *Dixon, 1916, 193 nn. 20-25; Polynesia:
*Beckwith, 1940, 502ff.; Tuamotus: Stimson,
n.d., T-G. 3/912; Cooks: Te Ariki, 1899, 173ff.;
Tonga: Gifford, 1924, 142; Samoa: *Steinen,
1933-34, 256ff.; Niue: Loeb, 1926, 194; N.Z.:
*Best, 1928b, 261, 264; Rotuma: Churchward,
1938-39, 229; Ellice Is.: Kennedy, 1931, 162;
Fijis: Fison, 1904, 22.

> M205.1.1. Turtle carrying man through water
> upsets him because of broken promise. R245.
> Whale-boat.

W154.9.1. Whales rescue drowning king who planned
to kill them. Polynesia: Beckwith, 1940, 502ff.;
Tuamotus: Stimson, n.d., T-G. 3/912.

W154.28.+ Person kills the sons of the man who has
saved his life and raised him to maturity.
Mangareva: Laval, 1938, 157.

W154.28.+ Girl, given knife by strangers, slits their
tongues. Tuamotus: Stimson, n.d., T-G. 3/600.

W200--W299. Traits of character--miscellaneous

W226.+ Child cries at night if not in the moonlight.
Ellice Is.: Roberts, 1957, 368.

Z. MISCELLANEOUS GROUPS OF MOTIFS

Z0--Z99. Formulas

Z71.1. Formulistic number: three. Australs: Aitken,
1930, 109; Hawaii: Rice, 1923, 124f.; Westervelt,
1915, 106; Tonga: Collocott, 1928, 15; Niue:
Loeb, 1926, 169; Chatham I.: Shand, 1896, 201;
Rennell: Bradley, 1956, 336.

Z71.2. Formulistic number: four. Cooks: Gill,
1876, 53f., 67, 113, 140f.

Z71.3. Formulistic number: five. Mangareva: Caillot,
1914, 166.

Z71.5. Formulistic number: seven. Marquesas: Lavondes,
1966, 174; Steinen, 1934-35, 219; Tonga: Collocott,
1919, 237; 1924, 277; Ellice Is.: Hedley, 1896,
47.

Z71.6. Formulistic number: nine. Hawaii: Dickey,
1917, 17; Samoa: Powell-Pratt, 1891, 200 n. 10;
N.Z.: White, 1887-90, I, 23.

Z71.8. Formulistic number: twelve. N.Z.: Best,
1924, 104.

Z71.12. Formulistic number: forty. Marquesas:
Lavondes, 1966, 174; Hawaii: Beckwith, 1919,
394, 478; Fornander, 1916, IV, 500; 1918, V,
138, 200, 202, 212, 690; Green, 1926, 73; Rice,
1923, 15, 94; Westervelt, 1915a, 158.

Z71.16. Formulistic numbers--miscellaneous. Mangareva:
Laval, 1938, 25, 27, 28; Cooks: Te Ariki, 1921,
55f., 59; N.Z.: Grey, 1855, 114, 148, 170, 172ff.,
181, 257ff.; White, 1887-90, IV, 168, 182, 195,
221, 224; V, 19, 28, 30, 32, 36, 37, 65, 100.

Z71.16.1. Formulistic number: eight. Central and
Western Polynesia: *Beckwith, 1940, 209, 210,
nn. 18-35; Easter I.: Métraux, 1940, 80, 376;
Mangareva: Hiroa, 1938, 422; Luomala, 1949, 155,
158, 160; Marquesas: Steinen, 1934-35, 227;
Societies: Beckwith, 1940, 209; Cooks: Gill,
1876, 223, 226, 235; Te Ariki, 1899, 71; Hawaii:
Beckwith, 1919, 468; 1940, 233; Fornander, 1918,
VI, 335; Rice, 1923, 15; Thrum, 1907, 189;
Tonga: Collocott, 1928, 24, 27, 37; Samoa:
Powell-Pratt, 1892, 278, n.; Niue: Beckwith,

481

1940, 256; Tokelau: Beckwith, 1940, 256; Fijis: Fison, 1904, 46; Tikopia: Firth, 1961, 50.

Z71.16.2. Formulistic number: ten. Oceania: **Lessa, 1961, 434ff.; Marquesas: Steinen, 1934-35, 206f.; Societies: Henry, 1928, 430; Cooks: Gill, 1876, 109; Hawaii: Fornander, 1916, IV, 500; 1918, V, 156, 270; Westervelt, 1915a, 158; Tonga: Collocott, 1928, 16, 59f.; Samoa: Elbert-Kirtley, 1966, 363; Sierich, 1900, 233f.; Stuebel, 1896, 143; Tokelau: Burrows, 1923, 162f.; N.Z.: Best, 1925, 744; Cowan, 1930, I, 22; White, 1887-90, I, 57, 83, 100f., 123, 135; IV, 239; Wohlers, 1875, 8; Rotuma: Russell, 1942, 246ff.; Tikopia: Firth, 1961, 22, 46, 47, 48; Reef Is.: O'Ferrall, 1904, 232; Bellona: Elbert-Kirtley, 1964, Nos. 57a, 57a, n. 58.

Z71.16.16.+ Formulistic number: seventy. N.Z.: Best, 1925, 861; Cowan, 1930, I, 151; White, 1887-90, III, 20, 24, 54, 98, 163, 200, 201; IV, 3, 58, 85, 97, 121, 182, 189, 200, 210f., 224, 227, 242; V, 30.

Z71.16.16.+ Formulistic number: one hundred and forty. N.Z.: Best, 1925, 861; Cowan, 1930, I, 207, 256; Grey, 1855, 114, 148, 170, 172ff., 181, 257ff.; White, 1887-90, I, 108; III, 8, 10, 29, 36, 52, 80, 95, 99; IV, 56, 85, 97, 182, 189, 200, 210f., 224, 227, 242; V, 10, 18, 29, 64, 86, 90, 147.

Z100--Z199. Symbolism

Z100.+ Coconuts as phallic symbols. Hawaii: Beckwith, 1940, 487.

Z100.+ Phallic symbolism of god in aspect of spearthruster (Kane). Hawaii: Beckwith, 1940, 66.

Z100.+ Gourd symbol of fructifying powers. Hawaii: Beckwith, 1940, 32.

Z100.+ Spring of water symbol of female reproductivity. Hawaii: Beckwith, 1940, 66.

Z100.+ Priests purify with salt water: symbol of god's making ocean salt. Hawaii: Beckwith, 1940, 43.

Z111. Death personified. N.Z.: Best, 1925, 948.

Z112. Sickness personified. N.Z.: Best, 1924, 66.

Z115. Wind personified. Cooks: Te Ariki, 1899, 71; N.Z.: Best, 1925, 777; Ontong Java: Sarfert, 1931, 413.

Z118. Sea personified. N.Z.: Best, 1925, 772ff.

Z122.4.+ Summer personified. N.Z.: Best, 1925, 788.

Z132. War personified. N.Z.: Best, 1925, 770.

Z139.8.+ Light personified. N.Z.: Best, 1924, 96, 108.

Z139.8.+ Night and day personified. Samoa: Powell-pratt, 1892, 271.

Z139.8.+ Rain personified. Samoa: Stuebel, 1896, 144; N.Z.: Best, 1924, 155.

Z139.8.+ Thunder personified. Tokelau: Burrows, 1923, 163; N.Z.: Best, 1925, 877; White, 1887-90, I, 87, 127.

Z139.8.+ Lightning personified. Samoa: Stuebel, 1896, 67; Tokelau: Burrows, 1923, 163; N.Z.: Best, 1925, 872.

Z139.8.+ Knowledge personified. N.Z.: Best, 1924, 66.

Z139.8.+ Evil (Whiro) personified. N.Z.: Best, 1924, 66.

Z139.8.+ Procreative power personified. N.Z.: Best, 1924, 113; 1925, 763ff.

Z139.8.+ Volcanoes personified. Hawaii: Fornander, 1918, V, 576ff.

Z139.8.+ Earthquakes personified. Tonga: Collocott, 1928, 42.

Z139.8.+ Floods personified. N.Z.: Best, 1925, 882.

Z139.8.+ Clouds personified. Tikopia: Firth, 1961, 49.

Z139.8.+ Fire personified. N.Z.: Best, 1925, 792.

Z139.8.+ Hurricanes personified. Tonga: Collocott, 1928, 42.

*Z141.4. Red feathers as symbol of rank. N.Z.:
Clark, 1896, 167.

Z146.1. Brown hair sign child descended from goddess
(Pele). Hawaii: Beckwith, 1940, 285.

Z147. Symbolic color: purple. Societies: Henry,
1928, 384.

Z184. Symbols of divinity. Marquesas: Handy, 1930,
106; Societies: Henry, 1928, 413; Hawaii:
Beckwith,1940, 43,65; Samoa: Henry, 1928, 346;
Fijis: Fison, 1904, 42.

Z200--Z299. Heroes

Z210.1.+ Twins as heroes. Mangareva: Hiroa, 1938, 379;
Marquesas: Steinen, 1934-35, 235f.; Societies:
Lagarde, 1933, 699; Hawaii: Beckwith, 1919, 334,
348; Thrum, 1907, 133ff.; Tonga: Collocott,
1928, 26; N.Z.: Beattie, 1920, 137; Ellice Is.:
Roberts, 1957, 366; Rotuma: Churchward, 1937-38,
113; Reef Is.: O'Ferrall, 1904, 232; Nukumanu:
Sarfert, 1931, 456; Bellona: Elbert-Monberg, 1964,
No. 52a; Rennell: ibid., 52b; Santa Cruz:
*Riesenfeld, 1950, 127.

A515.1.1. Twin culture heroes.

Z211. Dreadnaught. Oceanic: Dixon, 1916, 131, 132 n. 2,
133; Tuamotus: Stimson, n.d., T-G. 3/818, Z-G.
3/1122, Z-G. 13/221; Marquesas: Handy, 1930, 105;
Cooks: Te Ariki, 1921, 5.

Z221.+ Hero with ruddy skin. Mangareva: Hiroa, 1938,
319ff.; Tuamotus: Audran, 1919, 35.

Z221.+ Albinos as heroes. Rotuma: Churchward,
1937-38, 353.

Z221.+ Insane hero. Easter I.: Métraux, 1940, 364.

Z221.+ Diminutive hero. Hawaii: Rice, 1923, 95; N.Z.:
Cowan, 1930, I, 33f.

Z221.+ One-eyed hero (Muni). Tonga: Gifford, 1924, 122.

Z221.+ Hero with flattened head. Tuamotus: Stimson,
1937, 38.

Z221.+ Hero with club foot. Tonga: Collocott, 1928, 59ff.

Z221.+ Inactive hero. (Cf. L114.1.) Hawaii: Beckwith, 1940, 24, 412; Tonga: Gifford, 1924, 133.

Z300--Z399. Unique exceptions

Z311. Achilles heel. Fijis: Fison, 1904, 125f.

Z311.+ Eel that can be killed only by being pounded on head. Ellice Is.: Kennedy, 1931, 213.

Z312. Unique deadly weapon. Hawaii: Rice, 1923, 66.

Z312.3. Unique source of weakness. Cooks: Gill, 1876, 284; Hawaii: Beckwith, 1940,204, 465; N.Z.: Best, 1929, 15 n., 16 n.; Clark, 1896, 38, 55.

Z312.4. Unique bait for fish. Hawaii: Beckwith, 1940, 216.

Z312.4.+ Unique vulnerability: person who can be killed only with hurled stones. Hawaii: Green, 1929, 95ff.

Z313.1. Only one person can overtake hero. N.Z.: Beckwith, 1940, 231.

Z316.+ Two persons with extraordinarily hard heads can be killed only when their heads are smashed together. Lau Is.: St. Johnston, 1918, 110.

Z356. Unique survivor. Easter I.: Englert, 1939, 76; Métraux, 1940, 71; Mangareva: Laval, 1938, 88, 102, 126; Tuamotus: Audran, 1917, 57, 61; Stimson, n.d., Z-G. 13/203; Marquesas: Handy, 1930, 77; Societies: Henry, 1928, 246; Hawaii: Beckwith, 1940, 135, 449; Fornander, 1916, IV, 520; V, 278, 316, 318, 320, 378, 472; Green, 1929, 67; Thrum, 1907, 191; Samoa: Krämer, 1902, I, 454; Niue: Loeb, 1926, 146; N.Z.: Grace, 1907, 172; Gudgeon, 1905, 186f.; White, 1887-90, I, 77, 78, 102; III, 5, 16, 35, 124, 153, 190; Ellice Is.: Roberts, 1958, 400; Bellona: Elbert-Monberg, 1964, No. 140.

Z357.+   Warrior is master of all weapons except one.
          Hawaii: Dickey, 1917, 24.

Z357.+   Wife teaches husband all her arts but one:
          that of stone-throwing.   Hawaii: Beckwith,
          1940, 406.